MODERN ADVANCED ACCOUNTING IN CANADA

EDITION 5

MURRAY W. HILTON

DARRELL HERAUF

McGraw-Hill Ryerson

Toronto Montréal Boston Burr Ridge, IL Dubuque, IA Madison, WI
New York San Francisco St. Louis Bangkok Bogotá Caracas Kuala Lumpur
Lisbon London Madrid Mexico City Milan New Delhi Santiago Seoul
Singapore Sydney Taipei

The McGraw·Hill Companies

Modern Advanced Accounting in Canada
Fifth Edition

ISBN-13: 978-0-07-097111-0
ISBN-10: 0-07-097111-0

1 2 3 4 5 6 7 8 9 10 TCP 0 9 8

Printed and bound in Canada

Extract from Financial Accounting: Consolidations & Advanced issues [FA4] examinations published by the Certified General Accountants Association of Canada, © 2002–2007 CGA-Canada, reproduced with permission. The contents of these examinations may be out of date; therefore the currency of the contents is the sole responsibility of the user.

Care has been taken to trace ownership of copyright material contained in this text; however, the publisher will welcome any information that enables them to rectify any reference or credit for subsequent editions.

Editorial Director: Joanna Cotton
Senior Sponsoring Editor: Rhondda McNabb
Senior Marketing Manager: Joy Armitage Taylor
Developmental Editor: Marcia Luke
Senior Developmental Editor: Suzanne Simpson
Supervising Editor: Graeme Powell
Copy Editor: Shirley Corriveau
Senior Production Coordinator: Madeleine Harrington
Cover Design: Michelle Losier
Cover Image: ©Larry Fisher/Masterfile
Interior Design: Michelle Losier
Page Layout: Bill Renaud
Printer: Transcontinental Gagne

Library and Archives Canada Cataloguing in Publication

Hilton, Murray W.
    Modern advanced accounting in Canada / Murray W. Hilton, Darrell Herauf. — 5th ed.

Includes bibliographical references and index.
ISBN 978-0-07-097111-0

    1. Accounting—Canada—Textbooks. I. Herauf, Darrell II. Title.

HF5635.H486 2008   657'.046   C2007-905804-3

Murray W. Hilton, FCA

Murray Hilton holds the rank of Senior Scholar at the University of Manitoba where he has continued to teach in the MBA programs since his retirement in 2002. For thirty-five years he was Professor of Accounting at the university's Asper School of Business, teaching graduate and undergraduate courses in financial accounting. A Chartered Accountant with business degrees from the University of Saskatchewan and Oregon State University, he has published five advanced accounting books. In addition, he has been active in university and faculty administration, having previously served as Head of the Department of Accounting and Finance and as Director of the Master of Accountancy Program. He is currently the Director of the Centre for Accounting Research and Education. Murray has also been very involved in the accounting profession, teaching CA and CMA courses for many years, and serving on numerous national and provincial committees of both accounting bodies. He has on two separate occasions been a member of the National Examination Board of the Society of Management Accountants of Canada. In 1991, he received the FCA designation from the Institute of Chartered Accountants of Manitoba, and in 1994 he was made an honorary member of the Society of Management Accountants of Manitoba. For relaxation, he enjoys reading, golfing, and fishing.

Darrell Herauf, CA, CGA

Darrell Herauf teaches graduate and undergraduate courses in financial and managerial accounting at the Eric Sprott School of Business, Carleton University. A Chartered Accountant and a Certified General Accountant with a business degree from the University of Saskatchewan, this new co-author of *Modern Advanced Accounting in Canada* is also the author of testbanks for several financial accounting textbooks. He is the recipient of numerous teaching awards, and participates on many committees at the university. Darrell has been involved in professional accounting education at the Institute of Chartered Accountants of Ontario for over 20 years in a variety of roles, including teaching, developing case/program material, and serving as a member of the Examinations subcommittee. For more than 15 years, he has been involved with the Certified General Accountants Association of Canada as national examiner, course author, and consultant. For relaxation, he enjoys cycling and skating.

Contents

iv

Preface

Welcome to the Fifth Edition of *Modern Advanced Accounting in Canada*. This book's well-deserved reputation for being the most current, concise, and technically accurate advanced accounting text on the market has not only been maintained but has been improved upon in this new edition. Currently, Canadian accounting standards are in the process of being converged with International Accounting Standards as part of an effort to harmonize the many different standards that have previously existed worldwide. Although international standards are not slated to be effective in Canada until January 1, 2011, we have made every effort to illustrate and explain the requirements of the current standards at the time of publication, anticipating how these might change, what the effects of the changes are, and what this means to the industry, professionals, and students.

We have also continued the presentation of advanced accounting topics that has been so well received by such a large number of instructors and students. Emphasis on the direct approach of preparing consolidated financial statements along with the "building block" development of the basics of consolidations has been maintained and strengthened. The working paper approach is provided in appendices at the end of the chapter where applicable.

Finally, as requested by instructors on behalf of their students, the following enhancements to problem material have been made in this edition:

- A new discussion question has been added for each chapter to encourage critical thinking and classroom analysis.

- One new case and two new problems have been included in each chapter.

- One new self-study problem has been added to four chapters.

- The questions and/or solutions have been revised for approximately 40 percent of the end-of-chapter material.

- Finally, even more problems and questions can be found online for additional study.

New Features

- All exposure drafts outstanding as of November 30, 2007, have been incorporated into the text in varying degrees. The text and end-of-chapter material have been revised to incorporate the exposure drafts on "Business Combinations" and "Intangible Assets" on the assumption that these exposures drafts will be approved and become effective in 2009. The main changes being proposed in the exposure drafts on "Joint Arrangements" and "Not-for-profit Organizations" have been outlined in Chapters 10 and 13, respectively.

- An International Perspective box has been added to each chapter to provide a context for the International Standards shift to the extent relevant to the chapter material.

- An introduction has been added for each chapter to highlight topics to be discussed in the chapter and to describe some real-life application of these topics.

- More charts and exhibits have been added to this edition with cross-referencing and bolding of key numbers to enhance the readability and clarity of the material

- New notes in the margin of the text help to reinforce concepts and provide clarification for in-text content.

- Major reorganization and rewriting has been done for the materials in Chapters 4, 5, 9, and 11.

- Material on control was moved from Chapter 4 to Chapter 3 and revised to eliminate repetition and provide additional guidance.

- New tables on the current status and effective usage dates for different methods and theories of accounting for business combinations has been included in Chapters 3 and 4.

- Parent company extension theory was added in Chapter 4 and included in the end-of-chapter material for Chapters 4 through 9.

- An expanded discussion of cost and equity methods was done for Chapter 5.

- New material on the effective interest method of bond amortization has been added to Chapters 5 and 8.

- The effect on Canadian companies of the requirement to consolidate variable interest entities has been outlined and discussed in Chapter 10.

- The net method of recording forward contracts has been added to Chapter 11.

Organization

Chapter 1 is a survey of international accounting practices and has been updated to include the latest shifts to International Financial Reporting Standards that have occurred throughout the world, as well as Canada's proposed convergence with IFRS to take place January 1, 2011. To illustrate some of the differences between Canadian GAAP and IFRS, the financial statements of a Canadian public company that uses both sets of standards has been reproduced in an appendix.

Chapter 2 commences with an overview of the CICA pronouncements that make up the "big picture." Readers are encouraged to revisit this "big picture" many times as consolidation topics are developed in later chapters so that they do not lose sight of the forest as they examine the myriad of details that make up the trees. Differential reporting is introduced and revisited in succeeding chapters in discussions of areas where it is allowed. The chapter continues with a comprehensive examination of held-for-trading, available-for-sale, and significant influence investments and concludes with a self-study problem. Coverage of the topics in this chapter could be postponed until after Chapter 7 without breaking continuity or could be omitted altogether if it is felt that adequate coverage has occurred in previous intermediate accounting courses.

Chapter 3 discusses two forms of business combinations and four methods that have been proposed or used to account for business combinations in past years. The acquisition of assets and the acquisition of voting shares are used to illustrate the acquisition method of accounting for a business combination. The concept of control is discussed and used as the criterion for preparation of consolidated financial statements.

Chapter 4 examines the preparation of consolidated financial statements as at the date a parent obtains control over a subsidiary. The direct and working-paper methods are both illustrated for 100-percent owned subsidiaries as well as for those that are less than 100- percent owned. Consolidation theory is introduced and the concept of push-down accounting is illustrated. Reverse takeovers are covered in an appendix.

Chapter 5 and 6 cover what is essentially one topic: the preparation of consolidated financial statements subsequent to the date of acquisition. Chapter 5 illustrates the procedures followed when the parent has used the equity method. A full discussion of the asset impairment tests is provided. Chapter 6 uses the same examples but assumes that the parent has used the cost method in its own accounting records. Each chapter concludes with a self-study problem and a solution prepared using the direct approach. Ten basic steps in the preparation of consolidated statements are introduced, which form the foundation for the consolidation topics in the chapters that follow.

Chapter 7 deals with the elimination of intercompany revenues and expenses as well as intercompany unrealized profits in inventory and land. The income tax matching associated with the holdback and realization of intercompany profits form an integral part of the discussions and illustrations. There is a short discussion on transfer pricing as a vehicle to minimize income taxes. The chapter concludes with a comprehensive self-study problem using the direct approach.

Chapter 8 discusses the elimination of intercompany profits in depreciable assets, the recognition of gains or losses resulting from the elimination of intercompany bond-holdings, and the related income tax adjustments that are required. Two self-study problems are presented with solutions using the direct approach.

Chapter 9 discusses the preparation of the consolidated cash flow statement and such ownership issues as subsidiaries with preferred shares, step purchases, reduction of parent's interest, and indirect holdings. In all situations, the direct approach is used.

Chapter 10 examines other consolidation reporting issues, including variable interest entities, the proportionate consolidation of joint ventures, future income taxes and business combinations, and segment disclosures.

Chapter 11 introduces the topic of foreign currency. Foreign currency transactions are discussed, as is the concept of hedging and hedge accounting. The handling of foreign currency gains and losses is illustrated as are the accounting for fair value and cash flow hedges. The appendix describes how discounting can be applied when determining the fair value of a forward contract.

Chapter 12 concludes the foreign currency portion of the text by examining and illustrating the translation and subsequent consolidation of integrated and self-sustaining foreign operations. The reporting of exchange gains and losses from the translation of self-sustaining subsidiaries in other comprehensive income is also illustrated.

Chapter 13 discusses in depth the seven not-for-profit sections in the *CICA Handbook*. The chapter concludes with a comprehensive illustration of the required journal entries and the preparation of financial statements, using both the deferred contribution method and the restricted fund method. Appendix 13A provides a real-life example of the deferred contribution method by reproducing the financial statements of the Winnipeg Foundation. Appendix 13B provides a comprehensive outline of the PSAB reporting requirements for federal, provincial, and local governments.

Note: Additional chapters online (www.mcgrawhill.ca/olc/hilton) include "Partnerships," and "Comprehensive Revaluation of Assets and Liabilities/Bankruptcy and Receivership."

For the Student

Online Learning Centre (www.mcgrawhill.ca/olc/hilton)

The Student Centre of this website contains an interactive student component with multiple-choice questions, true/false questions, a *Globe and Mail* news feed, and Internet exercises, as well as two additional chapters and appendices.

Instructor Resources

The Instructor's CD-ROM includes the following instructor supplements:

- Solutions Manual containing thorough, up-to-date solutions to the book's end-of-chapter material.
- Test Bank (Word document) containing approximately 750 multiple-choice and 150 problems.
- PowerPoint® slides to support and organize lectures.

Online Learning Centre (www.mcgrawhill.ca/olc/hilton)

This text-specific website provides vital support for learning and teaching. The Instructor Centre includes additional chapters, bonus cases and solutions, and downloadable supplements such as the Solutions Manual and PowerPoint® slides.

Services

*i*Learning Sales Specialist

Your Integrated Learning Sales Specialist is a McGraw-Hill Ryerson representative who has the experience, product knowledge, training, and support to help you assess and integrate any of the following products, technology, and services into your course for optimum teaching and learning performance. Whether it's using our test bank software, helping your students improve their grades, or putting your entire course online, your iLearning Sales Specialist is there to help you do it. Contact your local iLearning Sales Specialist today to learn how to maximize all of McGraw-Hill Ryerson's resources!

*i*Learning Services Program

McGraw-Hill Ryerson offers a unique iLearning Services package designed for Canadian faculty. Our mission is to equip providers of higher education with superior tools and resources required for excellence in teaching. For additional information visit http://www.mcgrawhill.ca/highereducation/iservices.

PageOut

Visit www.mhhe.com/pageout to create a web page for your course using our resources. PageOut is the McGraw-Hill Ryerson website development centre. This web page-generation software is free to adopters and is designed to help faculty create an online course complete with assignments, quizzes, links to relevant websites, and more—all in a matter of minutes.

Course Management

Content cartridges are available for the course management systems such as WebCT and Blackboard. These platforms provide you with user-friendly, flexible teaching tools. Please contact your local McGraw-Hill Ryerson iLearning Sales Specialist for details.

Primis Online

Primis Online gives you access to our resources in the best medium for your students: printed textbooks or electronic e-books. There are over 350,000 pages of content available from which you can create customized learning tools from our online database at www.mhhe.com/primis.

Acknowledgements

The accuracy of the text is due in large part to the efforts of technical checkers Ross Meacher and Richard Michalski. We extend our appreciation for their time and efforts. Also, extensive feedback from numerous reviews and the valuable suggestions provided by that process helped us develop and enhance this fifth edition. Thank you to the following colleagues for their invaluable advice:

Bill Dawson, University of Western Ontario
Robert Ducharme, University of Waterloo
David Hiscock, McMaster University
Bibi John, Seneca College
Stuart H. Jones, University of Calgary
Don Lockwood, University of British Columbia
Christine Maher, Conestoga College
James Myers, University of Toronto
Joe Nemi, University of Guelph Humber
Sandra Scott, York University
Deirdre Taylor, Ryerson University
John Western, Kwantlen University College

Thanks also to the Canadian Institute of Chartered Accountants for granting permission to reproduce material from the *CICA Handbook* as well as questions from UFE examinations and to the Certified General Accountants of Canada and the Certified Management Accountants for their permission to reproduce questions adapted from past examinations. Thank you to Peter Secord of St. Mary's University for all of his fine case contributions for this and previous editions.

We are very grateful to the staff at McGraw-Hill Ryerson, Sponsoring Editors Colleen Henderson and Rhondda McNabb and Developmental Editor Marcia Luke who applied pressure in a gentle but persistent manner when we strayed from the project's schedule, and to Graeme Powell, Supervising Editor, and Shirley Corriveau, Copyeditor, whose technical expertise was necessary to carry the project to its end.

And finally, we are grateful to our families for all of their support and encouragement.

Murray Hilton
Asper School of Business
University of Manitoba

Darrell Herauf
Eric Sprott School of Business
Carleton University

Prologue

Welcome to Advanced Accounting. We wish you a prosperous learning experience. We will study three major accounting topics: consolidations, foreign currency transactions and operations, and not-for-profit and government organizations. You may have had some exposure to these topics in your previous accounting courses. We will build on this prior knowledge and the conceptual framework studied in Intermediate Accounting while we develop a thorough understanding of these selected topics. Before embarking on the study of these topics, we should review the role of accountants and the objectives of reporting.

Objectives of Reporting

Professional accountants provide a variety of services ranging from accounting to tax planning to assurance to business consulting. In this course, we will focus on financial accounting, i.e. providing financial information to external users such as investors and creditors. These users usually have limited financial resources to invest in an entity. They wish to invest where they can earn the highest return with the lowest amount of risk. The general-purpose set of financial statements (balance sheet, income statement, cash flow statements, and notes to the financial statements) will be used by the external users to help them make their resource allocation decisions and to assess the stewardship of management. The general-purpose reports are not the only source of information but are a good starting point.

In most cases, users want to receive the general-purpose financial statements prepared in accordance with generally accepted accounting principles (GAAP) because by following these principles the information is understandable, comparable, and reliable. However, there are times when users may want or require financial information that does not follow GAAP. For example, entities may need to prepare non-GAAP-based statements for legislative or regulatory purposes, or for contract compliance. Or, a prospective lender may want to receive a balance sheet with assets reported at fair value rather than historical cost. As accountants, we should be able to provide financial information in a variety of formats or using a variety of accounting policies because we have the skills and abilities to produce this information. If we do provide fair-value-based financial statements, we would not be able to say that the statements were prepared in accordance with GAAP. We would simply state that the statements were prepared in accordance with the policies described in the notes to the financial statements.

In some cases, the users of the financial statements have access to information about the entity in addition to that provided in the financial statements. For example, the owner of a private company may also be the manager of the company and would have intimate knowledge of the company. In such cases, the owner may place less reliance on the financial statements than investors in public companies do. In other situations, the owner may not understand the financial reporting for complex transactions such as business combinations. In both of these situations, the owners may feel that the costs of complying with some of the complex sections of the

Handbook are not worth the benefit. They may prefer to issue more simplified statements. The CICA recognized this difference in users' needs and, in 2002, issued a new *Handbook* section on differential reporting. With the introduction of this section, qualifying enterprises can choose to apply differential reporting options and still be in compliance with GAAP.

Generally accepted accounting principles encompass broad principles and conventions of general application as well as rules and procedures that determine accepted accounting practices at a particular time.[1] The process of developing GAAP is a political process. Both preparers and users of financial statements have an opportunity to comment on a proposal for a new accounting standard before it becomes generally accepted. If a new rule is preferred by the preparers but not accepted by users, it is unlikely to become part of GAAP. Therefore, as we study existing accounting practices and proposed changes, we need to continually evaluate whether information provided by a reporting entity will satisfy users' needs.

The primary sources of GAAP in descending order of authority are Sections 1400 to 4460 of the *CICA Handbook*, accounting guidelines issued by the CICA, and abstracts of issues discussed by the Emerging Issues Committee (EIC Abstracts)[2]. The *CICA Handbook* is the most authoritative since many legal statutes require its use. For example, companies incorporated under the Canada Business Corporations Act and certain provincial Corporations Acts are required to prepare financial statements in accordance with the *CICA Handbook*. Publicly traded companies are required to submit financial statements that comply with GAAP to the securities commissions under which they are registered.

The primary sources of GAAP provide the financial statement accounting and reporting requirements as well as explanations and guidance for most transactions and events encountered by an entity. When an entity encounters transactions or events that are not explicitly addressed by the primary sources of GAAP, the entity should adopt accounting practices that are consistent with the spirit of the primary sources of GAAP and consistent with the financial statement concepts described in Section 1000 of the *Handbook*.

Financial Statement Concepts

Section 1000 of the *CICA Handbook* describes the concepts underlying the accounting principles used in general purpose financial statements. It is the most important section of the *Handbook* because it provides the conceptual framework for the development and issuance of other financial accounting standards. The main items included in this section are as follows:

- Objectives of reporting;
- Definitions of assets, liabilities, equity, revenues and expenses, gains and losses;
- Cost versus benefit and materiality constraints;
- Qualitative characteristics such as understandability, relevance, reliability, and comparability;
- Recognition criteria, the basis of measurement, and disclosure principles.

---

[1] *CICA Handbook*, Paragraph 1100.02

[2] The EIC was established by the CICA in 1988 to provide a forum for timely review of emerging accounting issues that are likely to receive divergent or unsatisfactory treatment in practice in the absence of some guidance.

You will probably recognize most of the concepts and remember studying them in your intermediate accounting courses. If you can explain the accounting practices learned there in terms of these basic concepts, you should have no trouble applying these concepts in the new situations we will encounter in this course. If you do not understand or cannot explain accounting rules in terms of these basic concepts, it is never too late to start. As you study the accounting rules in this course, try to understand them in terms of the basic concepts and principles that the *Handbook* describes.

By gaining a broad understanding of the logic and basic principles behind the accounting rules, you will develop confidence in being able to apply these basic principles in a wide variety of situations. Rather than simply accepting accounting practices or memorizing specific rules in the *Handbook*, you will begin to understand the logic of the rules and evaluate whether the rules are consistent with the basic financial statement concepts. You will soon realize that most of the rules in accounting can be understood, developed, and derived from these basic principles and concepts. Then, in turn, you will be able to use professional judgment to apply these basis principles to whatever situation you may encounter.

Professional Judgment

Judgment is the ability to make a decision in situations where the answer is not clear-cut. Professional judgment is the ability to make decisions for issues encountered by professionals in carrying out their day-to-day responsibilities. Judgment is a skill developed over many years of study and learning from one's experiences. Professional judgment is derived from knowledge and experience in the profession. It is not something that is learned from rote or memorization of rules or answers to certain problems. It often involves making choices between meaningful alternatives and the ability to understand the consequences of one's actions.

The professional accountant is continuously required to use judgment in making choices between meaningful alternatives. In the preparation of financial statements, there are three main areas where choices must be made. First, accounting policies such as when to recognize revenue, how to report an interest in a joint venture, and whether or not to consolidate a variable-interest entity involve making a choice between various methods. The method adopted for a particular company must be appropriate for that company based on its existing situation. For example, if Company A is selling to customers with poor credit history and without obtaining any security for the receivables from these customers, it would be appropriate to recognize revenue when cash is received even though most of its competitors may be recognizing revenue when the goods are delivered. If the competitors are selling to customers with very high credit ratings, it would be appropriate for them to recognize revenue on delivery. The professional judgment of an accountant will take in these factors and recognize that although one method is appropriate for the competitors, another may be more appropriate for Company A.

Secondly, judgment is involved in making accounting estimates of many kinds. What is the estimated useful life of capital assets? What is the fair value of goodwill? Will a forward contract be effective as a hedge of expected sales for the next three years? The answers to these questions are not clear-cut. In the classroom, we are usually provided with this information. In the real world, we must gather data and make our own assessment. Whether we feel that the decline in market value of the shares is temporary or permanent could have a material difference on the valuation of goodwill and the bottom line on the income statement.

Thirdly, judgment is involved in deciding what to disclose and how to disclose it in the notes to the financial statements. For example, in disclosing a contingent liability resulting from a lawsuit, the company could simply say that it has been sued but no provision is made in the financial statements because it feels that the lawsuit has no merit. Or, it could provide details of the lawsuit and give some probabilities of different outcomes.

Is there too much latitude in accounting? Do the financial statements ever portray the complete facts? One could argue that there is no latitude because accountants are not free to randomly select any reporting method. They must represent faithfully what really happened and what really exists using the generally accepted conceptual framework. If the revenue has been earned, then recognize the revenue. If the cost will provide a future benefit, then capitalize the cost as an asset. Latitude is necessary so that the accountant can choose the methods to reflect the real situation. If the rules are written too rigidly, companies may be forced to use methods that do not reflect their own situation.

If accountants take their jobs seriously and have high ethical standards, they will present the financial statements as reliably as possible using appropriate accounting policies, by making the best estimates possible, and by making honest and forthright statements in the notes to the financial statements. They will use judgment to fairly present the financial position and results of operations. Otherwise, the individual accountants and the entire accounting profession will lose credibility.

In this course, we will have an opportunity to develop our judgment skills and to exercise judgment through the use of cases. The cases provide realistic scenarios where conflicts exist and choices must be made. The answers are not usually clear-cut. In fact, different answers can be defended. For these cases, it is how you support your recommendation that is important as opposed to what your final recommendation is. You will need to apply basic principles and use judgment to come up with an answer that "tells it how it is" as accurately as possible. In so doing, you will be developing the skills required of a professional accountant.

Chapter 1 A Survey of International Accounting

LEARNING OBJECTIVES

After studying this chapter, you should be able to do the following:

- Identify factors that can influence a country's accounting standards.
- Describe areas where Canada's accounting standards differ from those used in other countries.
- Identify the role the IASB intends to play in the establishment of uniform worldwide accounting standards.
- Identify the direction that the CICA intends to follow.

INTRODUCTION

Canadian companies are now able to raise capital resources on the world's marketplace.

This book covers a number of topics that are often presented in the final course of the financial accounting sequence. The topics are presented and illustrated in accordance with the generally accepted accounting principles (GAAP) that exist today in Canada. Prior to the 1990s, the study of accounting principles as set out in the *CICA Handbook* was all that was necessary as preparation for students intending to pursue professional accounting as a career in Canada. But since then rapid changes have taken place throughout the world, and even more drastic changes are coming. Canadian companies now view the entire world as their marketplace; not only are they exporting their products to more countries than ever before, but they are also establishing factories and offices in foreign locations. Companies that used to raise capital resources strictly in their home countries are now finding that capital markets are available to them around the world. Because their shares trade on stock exchanges, they are often required to prepare financial reports using accounting principles other than Canadian. Many accounting firms have offices throughout the world, and there are abundant opportunities for their Canadian staff members to transfer to these offices. With all these changes taking place, an accounting education that takes a narrow, parochial view is clearly inadequate. Canadian students of accounting need to be fully aware of what is happening in the rapid movement toward worldwide accounting standards, and it is imperative that the textbooks of today address this topic.

A large portion of this book covers the preparation of consolidated financial statements and other directly related topics. Before we begin considering this very broad topic, we first survey the accounting principles and practices used in a sample of other countries. It is hoped that this exposure to international accounting will inspire readers to continue studying this exciting and fast-growing area.

A Survey of International Accounting

In past years the variety of different accounting principles being used throughout the world was large.

Generally accepted accounting principles have varied in the past from country to country around the world. If a detailed study had been made of the accounting practices used by every country in the world, it would probably have concluded that very few countries used exactly the same standards for external financial reporting purposes. Some comparisons would have yielded minor differences; others would have shown substantial ones. Differences existed in terminology and style of presentation, as well as in methods of measurement and disclosure.

Differences in measurement ranged from departures from historical cost to varying standards within the historical cost model. A variety of methods existed worldwide for measuring and reporting inventories, research and development costs, fixed assets, leases, computer software, and deferred income taxes. Income-smoothing devices varied from country to country. In Canada and the U.S., GAAP allowed little opportunity to smooth income, while in other countries income-smoothing devices were allowed under GAAP or were encouraged by government regulation. This was often accomplished by setting up reserves, which are special equity accounts, and using them to transfer amounts to and from the income statement as needed. Inadequate disclosures often masked the real effect on yearly income measurements.

Asset revaluations have been a common practice in many countries.

Asset revaluations have been acceptable in many countries. These circumstances range from price-level-adjusted historical costs, used to counteract distortions resulting from very high inflation rates, to the regular or periodic adjustment of asset measurements to current replacement costs. Even under historical costs, great variations have existed in yearly measurements. The accounting for the asset of goodwill, which arises as a result of one company buying another, is a prime example. Practices included the immediate write-off of purchased goodwill to equity; capitalization with amortization over greatly varying periods; capitalization without amortization (thus leaving it on the balance sheet forever); and capitalization and write-off to income only when there is evidence of impairment. Canada

Many countries have different descriptions and presentations of financial statement elements than those used in Canada.

Not only were there differences in measurement, but there were often also differences in the presentation and description of elements in financial statements. For example, in many countries, long-term assets were and continue to be presented before current assets on the balance sheet and shareholders' equity appears before liabilities.

Examples of areas where disclosure differences still exist are segment reporting, reporting financial forecasts, shareholder and environmental disclosures, and value-added reporting. While many foreign multinational companies disclose the lines of business they are in and the geographic area in which they operate, there is still inconsistency in the level of detail provided. While the provision of financial forecasts is not common in North America, some companies in Europe do provide this information. Foreign companies often provide voluminous disclosures about their shares, shareholders' rights, and changes in shareholders' equity. Finally, while not required by accounting standards, multinational companies are increasingly providing information about environmental safety and protection issues, and the ways in which they have added value to society by their distributions to owners, creditors, employees, and governments.

Information disclosed is often more voluminous in other countries than that required in Canada.

Differences in accounting standards have always existed, but they have been receiving greater attention in recent years because of the many changes taking place

[handwritten margin note: Global marketplace has increased demand for International GAAP.]

[handwritten note: Globalization]

in the world economy. For example, the dismantling of the former Soviet empire has been accompanied by a shift from controlled to market-driven economies, and most of the countries in Europe have joined together to form the European Union (E.U.). The North American Free Trade Agreement allows the free flow of goods and services among Canada, the United States, and Mexico, and this agreement may soon be expanded to include some countries in South America.

In the midst of all this, there have been major advances in computer and communication technology that are dramatically improving the global flow of information and changing how business activities are conducted. As a result, foreign currencies now trade 24 hours a day in the world's financial centres. Accompanying this shift toward a global marketplace has been substantial growth in the size and number of multinational corporations. This growth has been achieved to a great extent by takeovers and mergers, often financed through the capital markets of *many* countries. Not only has there been a shift to a global marketplace for goods and services, but there has also been a shift toward a global capital market. Many of the world's stock exchanges now list foreign companies.

With such a global capital market comes the need to provide the suppliers of capital with useful accounting information. Fragmented accounting principles seriously compromise comparability, which is one of the key concepts associated with information usefulness. To counter this, securities regulators in foreign countries often require foreign companies listed on their stock exchanges either to prepare financial statements in accordance with their domestic accounting standards, or to prepare reconciliations from foreign to domestic standards. For example, Canadian companies listed on U.S stock exchanges are required by the Securities and Exchange Commission (SEC) to prepare reconciliations of net income measured in accordance with Canadian GAAP to net income in accordance with U.S. GAAP. These requirements substantially increase a company's costs of preparing financial statements. Investment analysts and other users then incur further additional costs when interpreting financial statements prepared under different standards. Because of these problems, the world's securities regulators have been increasing their demands for some sort of accounting harmonization. It is not yet clear exactly when this will take place; but as we shall see later, a great deal of effort has been made to change the situation. However, in order to fully understand the issues and how changes may occur in the future, we must first examine the major causes of differences in GAAP.

The SEC requires Canadian companies to reconcile their earnings to U.S. GAAP.

Factors That Can Influence a Country's Accounting Standards

Many factors can influence a country's accounting standards. Usually none of them is dominant. The following five factors can affect standards.

The Role of Taxation   In some countries, income tax has a minimal effect on how net income is measured for financial reporting. Example: In Canada and the United States, companies often report net incomes on their operating statements that are substantially different from the taxable incomes they report on their tax returns. This has led to the GAAP concept of interperiod tax allocation, although in some countries where such differences exist, differences between net income and taxable income have not always resulted in full tax allocation being used.

In other countries, taxation has a profound effect on how accounting income is measured. Accounting income will not differ much from taxable income if a

Accounting income and taxable income are virtually the same in some countries.

country's tax statutes state that expenses must be recorded on the income statement if they are to be allowed as a deduction on the tax return. In countries where this is the case, the result is often the use of extreme conservatism in accounting measurements on the part of companies trying to keep their incomes as low as possible within the law. Germany and Japan are examples of countries whose tax laws have strongly influenced GAAP. In the United States, while taxable income and accounting income are different numbers, one area where consistency is required is the costing of inventory. If LIFO is to be used for tax purposes, it also must be used for financial reporting.

The Level of Development of Capital Markets In countries where publicly traded debt and equity securities play a substantial role in the financing of business activities, accounting and disclosure standards tend to be much more extensive than in countries where this is not the case. This is because highly developed public capital markets tend to have fairly sophisticated investors who demand current and useful information from those who have received their capital. Canada, the United Kingdom, and the United States all have highly developed capital markets and strong accounting and disclosure standards. In countries where business financing tends to be private rather than public, there is less reliance on extensive accounting standards, because the private suppliers of capital can demand and receive the information they need directly from the "consumers" of such capital. Japan is a prime example; there, corporate capital needs have been supplied by very large private suppliers such as banks. However, it should be noted that when Japan's economy took a severe dive in the 1990s, many of Japan's major banks incurred massive loan losses that nearly bankrupted them; this was cited as a major contributor to the Japanese recession. Germany and Switzerland also have very large banks that satisfy much of the capital needs of business. Historically, a large number of businesses in Mexico were state owned, but in the 1990s a change to private ownership resulted in a shift to financing through private and public capital markets.

> Highly developed capital markets often result in the development of quality accounting standards.

Differing Legal Systems Two different kinds of legal system are in existence today: code law systems and common law systems. Code law systems, which originated with the Roman Empire, contain very detailed statutes that govern a wide range of human activities. In general they specify what individuals and corporations *can* do. Common law systems have less detailed statutes, and rely on the court system to interpret statutes and thus establish precedents through case law. In general, they specify what individuals and corporations *cannot* do (that is, what is illegal).

> Code systems specify what individuals and corporations can do, while common law systems specify what cannot be done.

In many common law countries, governments tend to take a hands-off approach to the setting of accounting standards. While there may be statutes requiring that companies make information available to the providers of capital, the *type* of information required is left to the private sector. In the United States the SEC, which administers securities legislation, has given the right to develop accounting standards to a private group, the Financial Accounting Standards Board (FASB). In Canada, the *CICA Handbook* pronouncements constitute the accounting standards required by the provincial and federal Companies Acts and the Ontario Securities Commission. The United Kingdom also uses a private standard-setting body.

In code law countries such as Germany, France, and Japan, the private sector is involved only in an advisory capacity, and accounting standards are reflected in legal statutes, often as protection for creditors and other capital suppliers. It should not be

> In Germany, France, and Japan, accounting standards are set by legal statutes.

surprising to note that tax law also heavily influences accounting standards in these countries.

Ties Between Countries   Political and economic ties between countries have historically had some effect on accounting standards. Example: The accounting standards and professional accounting organizations of countries that were once colonies are often patterned after those of the "home" country. There have been strong similarities between the standards of India, South Africa, Australia, New Zealand, and Malaysia and those of Great Britain. During their early development, Canadian accounting standards were influenced by Great Britain's, but in later years this influence shifted away from Britain to the United States due to the very strong economic ties that developed between those two countries. The formation of the European Union has certainly had an effect on the accounting standards used by its member countries. We will see more of this later.

> **Canadian standards have been influenced by those of the United States.**

Inflation Levels   The historical cost model, which implicitly assumes a relatively stable unit of measure, is used by many countries. However, the model is not useful when inflation rates are very high. Countries that have experienced high inflation rates often make financial reporting adjustments to counteract the effects of inflation. These adjustments involve price-level-adjusted statements, or a shift from historical costs to current-value accounting, or both. Many countries in South America that have experienced inflation rates of 1,000 percent or more per annum have adopted inflation-based accounting.[1] Mexico uses price level accounting because of previous high inflation rates. Canada, the United States, and the United Kingdom all experimented with the supplemental reporting of price level and current value information in the 1970s when the inflation rate approached 20 percent. The experiment was not successful because of the high cost of providing such information and the general lack of comprehension on the part of financial statement users. All three countries abandoned the experiment when inflation declined.

> **High inflation rates often result in departures from historical cost measurements.**

Countries that have not had problems with inflation have usually stayed with the historical cost model, but there have been some exceptions. In the Netherlands, companies have been allowed to use current values instead of historical costs. This is not because of high inflation but rather because accounting education in that country has a strong economic component. Some major Dutch companies have shown current values in their financial statements.

Towards Accounting Harmonization and Convergence

A truly global economy will require some sort of harmonized accounting standards if it is to function properly. Two organizations that have been working towards accomplishing this objective are the European Union and the International Accounting Standards Board. The role of these two organizations is discussed next.

> **The European Union and the International Accounting Standards Board have both been working towards accounting harmonization.**

The European Union   In 1957, six European countries signed the Treaty of Rome, thereby establishing a common market for goods and services and common institutions for economic development. Originally called the European Economic

---

[1]   For example, Brazil's inflation rate was more than 2,000 percent in 1993.

Community, the agreement is now called the European Union (E.U.) and had 27 members at the end of 2006.[2] A major goal of the E.U. is the promotion of the free flow of goods, labour, and capital amongst member countries. In 1998, in order to establish a common economic policy for the area, a European central bank was established which subsequently issued a common currency called the euro.

The use of the euro as a common currency in the European Union has not been a resounding success.

The intent was that the currencies of the member nations would be gradually phased out with full adoption of this common currency. By the end of 2006, only 13 members had complied.[3] Both Sweden and Denmark held referendums in which their citizens voted to reject the adoption of the euro. The government of the United Kingdom, sensing that a referendum would be defeated, decided to wait until such time that the public mood had changed. A major reason for rejection by these three countries was the fact that they did not wish to individually relinquish their ability to determine economic policy. It was also observed that each country's economy had performed much better than many of the other E.U. member countries that had switched their currencies such as Germany, Italy, and France.

The E.U. has attempted to harmonize accounting standards used by its member countries.

The E.U. has also attempted to harmonize the accounting principles used by its member countries by issuing "directives." In order to minimize conflict with the legal reporting requirements of certain of its member nations, these directives often allowed many alternative reporting practices. This is particularly true with respect to the first accounting directive. The second directive, issued in 1983, requiring the presentation of consolidated financial statements, has had a major impact on the accounting of many countries where consolidation was not previously a common practice. While flexibility appears to be contrary to the concept of harmonization, the adoption of the directives has nevertheless caused major changes to the accounting practices of some of its members. In addition, former Soviet Bloc countries, including Hungary and Poland, established new accounting principles based on the E.U. directives, in anticipation of some day being admitted to the union. (They were admitted in 2004.)

The International Accounting Standards Board (IASB)   This board became operational in 2001 as a result of a major restructuring of its former organization, which was called the International Accounting Standards Committee (IASC). This committee, based in London, was formed in 1973 by an agreement between the professional accounting bodies of 10 countries with the purpose of establishing worldwide accounting principles. The founding members came from Australia, Canada, France, Germany, Japan, Mexico, the Netherlands, the United Kingdom, Ireland, and the United States. Over the years the membership grew so that it represented more than 140 accounting organizations from over 100 countries. It should be pointed out, however, that membership in the organization did not translate into the adoption of its standards, and the number of countries actually using IASC standards was a much lower number. The IASC's operating costs of approximately £2 million a year were

---

[2] Austria, Belgium, Bulgaria, the Czech Republic, Cyprus, Denmark, Estonia, Finland, France, Germany, Greece, Hungary, Ireland, Italy, Latvia, Lithuania, Luxemburg, Malta, the Netherlands, Poland, Romania, Slovenia, the Slovak Republic, Spain, Sweden, Portugal, and the United Kingdom.

[3] The countries that have maintained their own currencies are: Bulgaria, the Czech Republic, Cyprus, Denmark, Estonia, Hungary, Latvia, Lithuania, Malta, Poland, Romania, the Slovak Republic, Sweden, and the United Kingdom.

met by contributions from professional accounting bodies, accounting firms, and other organizations, and by the sale of IASC publications. It was governed by a board made up of representatives from 13 countries and 4 organizations. The committee met two or three times a year to release exposures of proposed standards, to examine public comments that resulted from them, and to issue International Accounting Standards. Initially, many of the standards issued by the IASC were characterized by the number of acceptable alternatives that were permitted; but in the early 1990s efforts were made to eliminate many of these alternatives. This initiative was partially successful, but it left a number of standards still allowing alternative treatments. Given that some of the board members came from countries whose accounting standards are reflected in legal statutes, it is understandable that the removal of alternatives can be a tricky political process requiring compromise. Notwithstanding this difficulty, achieving worldwide accounting uniformity will depend greatly on eliminating alternative accounting practices. To date, 49 standards have been issued and 38 are still in force. Exhibit 1.1 on page 8 provides a listing of the standards that were in force in July 2007. Where a standard has been superseded by a subsequent standard it is not included in the list.

Note that standards issued by the original International Accounting Standards Committee were issued in numerical order with the prefix IAS, while subsequent standards issued by the IASB were also issued numerically with the prefix IFRS. In future we will refer to the current collection of international financial reporting standards as IFRS.

In March 2001 a major restructuring of the IASB was completed and the board adopted the following major objectives:

- to develop a single set of high-quality, global accounting standards that require transparent and comparable information in general purpose financial statements.

- to cooperate with various national accounting standard-setters in order to achieve convergence in accounting standards around the world.

A dictionary meaning of the term converge is "to approach" or "to tend to meet." The hope of the board is that the appropriate national bodies will adjust their individual standards in such a way that the essence of the IASB standard is achieved even though the exact wording is not adopted.

The International Accounting Standards Board is now located in London, England, and has 14 members, 12 of whom are full time and 2 of whom are part time. The members are chosen more for their expertise than for geographical representation. However, seven of the members are expected to have formal liaison responsibilities with major national standard-setting bodies, but must not be actual members of such national bodies. These seven standard-setting bodies are located in Germany, France, the United States, Canada, Great Britain, Japan, and Australia–New Zealand. Presumably such a liaison will be instrumental in harmonizing the national standards of a very important group of countries with those of the IASB.

Shortly after being restructured, the IASB announced that previous standards issued by the IASC would continue in force (see Exhibit 1.1), and that it intended to issue new international financial reporting standards (IFRS) in areas where no international standards existed. It also announced an improvement project the purpose of which was to raise the quality and consistency of existing IASs. This project was completed in December 2003 when 13 standards were revised and one was withdrawn.

Exhibit 1.1

LIST OF CURRENT IASB STANDARDS
IN FORCE IN JULY 2007

IFRS 1	First-time Adoption of International Financial Reporting Standards
IFRS 2	Share-based Payment
IFRS 3	Business Combinations
IFRS 4	Insurance Contracts
IFRS 5	Non-current Assets Held for Sale and Discontinued Operations
IFRS 6	Exploration for and Evaluation of Mineral Assets
IFRS 7	Financial Instrument Disclosures
IFRS 8	Operating Segments
IAS 1	Presentation of Financial Statements
IAS 2	Inventories
IAS 7	Cash Flow Statements
IAS 8	Accounting Policies, Changes in Accounting Estimates and Errors
IAS 10	Events After the Balance Sheet Date
IAS 11	Construction Contracts
IAS 12	Income Taxes
IAS 14	Segment Reporting
IAS 16	Property, Plant and Equipment
IAS 17	Leases
IAS 18	Revenue
IAS 19	Employee Benefits
IAS 20	Accounting for Government Grants and Disclosure of Government Assistance
IAS 21	The Effects of Changes in Foreign Exchange Rates
IAS 23	Borrowing Costs
IAS 24	Related Party Disclosures
IAS 26	Accounting and Reporting by Retirement Benefit Plans
IAS 27	Consolidated and Separate Financial Statements
IAS 28	Investments in Associates
IAS 29	Financial Reporting in Hyperinflationary Economies
IAS 31	Interests in Joint Ventures
IAS 32	Financial Instruments: Presentation
IAS 33	Earnings per Share
IAS 34	Interim Financial Reporting
IAS 36	Impairment of Assets
IAS 37	Provisions, Contingent Liabilities and Contingent Assets
IAS 38	Intangible Assets
IAS 39	Financial Instruments: Recognition and Measurement
IAS 40	Investment Property
IAS 41	Agriculture

Source: Deloitte Touche Tohmatsu, www.iasplus.com

The number of countries adopting international standards has rapidly increased in recent years. Some of the increase has come from the adoption by those countries that previously had no standards, but because of a shift to a market economy, required new forms of financial reporting. China is an example of such a country. Most of the increase has come from initiatives of the European Union and the standard-setters from Australia and New Zealand. (These initiatives are fully discussed in the next section.) The result is that, as of June 2007, 79 countries required IFRS for all publicly traded domestic companies, 3 countries required IFRS for some companies, 24 countries permitted but did not require its use, and 30 countries did not permit the use of IFRS.[4] (Notable among the countries not allowing international standards were Japan, Canada, and the United States. More discussion about what these countries are doing appears later).

Companies in over 100 countries are now using IFRS.

Recent Initiatives from the European Union and Australia and New Zealand

A major development towards the convergence/harmonization of accounting standards throughout the world occurred in 2002 when the European Union issued a directive stating that, effective January 1, 2005, all European companies whose shares trade on stock exchanges would be required to prepare their consolidated financial statements in accordance with IFRS. Two other important developments occurred when Australia switched over to IFRS in 2005, and New Zealand switched in 2007. It should be noted that while these developments brought 29 countries into the international standards arena, the methods used to do so were different.

Public companies in the E.U. as well as in Australia and New Zealand are required to use IFRS.

The standards boards of both Australia and New Zealand issued new domestic standards which were "equivalent to" IFRS. In Australia's case, it was announced in 2002 that the Australian Accounting Standards Board intended to issue new standards that would essentially be the same as IFRS effective for all Australian business entities (public or private and incorporated or unincorporated). The issue of new standards was essential because Australian corporate law requires financial reports to comply with Australian accounting standards. The standards issued were not identical to IFRS. In some instances the new Australian standards restricted the use of the optional provisions allowed in some international standards, and in other cases required additional disclosures when international disclosure requirements did not match existing Australian ones. The standards board also indicated that it intends to issue additional standards to cover areas that are purely domestic and not covered by IFRS.

In the European Union situation, the directive did not require each of the 27 member countries to change their domestic accounting standards, but rather required all publicly traded companies located in union countries to prepare their financial statements in accordance with IFRS. Each of the member states was not required to issue new standards in such a short period of time but are expected to do so later. Keep in mind that the accounting standards of France and Germany are set by legislation and changes to legislation are not done quickly.

The European Union changeover affected more than 8,000 companies.

The European Union directive resulted in more than 8,000 listed companies implementing international standards in their 2005 financial reports. Ernst and Young has published "an overview of how some large multinationals reported their 2005 results using IFRS." (This document can be downloaded from the website www.ey.com and the company will also provide a hard copy upon request.) In general, the study concluded that the changeover was successful even though many companies found that they had to make significant changes in their measurement and disclosure practices.

Because IFRS do not require uniform presentation of the financial statement elements and descriptions, many companies were able to maintain previous presentations that were unique to their particular country. While this helps comparability from a domestic point of view, consistency and comparability are compromised from an international view when terminology differences are not understood.

---

[4] Deloitte, www.iasplus.com.

Significant changes to
corporate reporting were the
result of the switch to IFRS.

In many cases it was noted the IFRS statements were far more complex than those based on national standards. Overall the 2005 statements were 20 percent to 30 percent greater in length than the prior year's statements and contained far more notes than in prior years. The study questioned whether the overall usefulness of the financial information had been compromised as a result.

The study concluded that because IFRS are broad based, extensive judgment is required in their application, and if judgement is not performed on a consistent basis by the preparers of the financial statements in each of the union's countries, comparability could be, and probably is, severely compromised.

The Situation in the United States and Japan

The United States   Accounting principles in the United States are set by a private organization called the Financial Accounting Standards Board (FASB). FASB's pronouncements are rule-based and are far more detailed than both those of the *CICA Handbook* and IFRS which are often described as principle-based standards requiring greater application of professional judgment by the preparers and auditors of financial statements. (U.S. public accounting firms have often indicated their support for the rule-based FASBs over principle-based standards).

FASB's statements are
considered to be rule-based,
while IFRS are principle-
based.

Canada's standards are closer to those of the United States than to those of any other country, but even so, the differences that do exist are so great that Canadian companies whose shares trade on U.S. stock exchanges are required to prepare reconciliations to U.S. GAAP. These reconciliations often show substantial differences in reported earnings. For example, the December 31, 2005, annual report of Inco showed Canadian GAAP net earnings of $836 million and U.S. GAAP net earnings of $628 million. Both amounts are in U.S. dollars because Inco reports using the US. dollar as its measuring unit. The reconciliation showed differences in nine items of which the major ones were in the expenses of post-retirement benefits, currency translation losses, and research and development costs.

Canadian/U.S. GAAP
reconciliations often show
substantial differences in
reported earnings.

While FASB has often indicated its support for a single set of global accounting standards it has also stated its belief that its standards are the best in the world and therefore should be used as a benchmark by the IASB. This argument somewhat lost its thrust with the accounting scandals associated with companies such as Enron and WorldCom. Despite this setback, FASB still carries a lot of clout and its cooperation with the IASB is imperative if the goal of common worldwide standards is to be met. To achieve this cooperation, FASB and IASB announced a convergence project that was to have been completed by 2007.

FASB and the IASB have
undertaken a project to
converge their standards.

The first stage was to focus on the elimination of differences that appeared capable of quick resolution and were not part of major projects of either of the boards. Once completed, the two groups pledged to work together on much larger and contentious issues so that any standards released by each board would have similar outcomes.

The involvement of the
United States is necessary
for the achievement of global
accounting standards.

The overall goal is to have IFRS acceptable for use by all non-U.S. companies required to report under the rules of the SEC in the United States. The SEC used to require non-U.S. companies reporting using IFRS to prepare reconciliations that show what would have been achieved if U.S. GAAP had been used instead. For years ending after November 15, 2007 the SEC no longer requires this reconciliation to U.S. GAAP. This will save the companies millions of dollars every year. The success of this convergence project has yet to be determined. At the same time, if we are to achieve truly global standards and all the benefits that they will bring, accounting convergence must necessarily involve the United States, which accounts for nearly half of the world's total market capitalization.

Japan's accounting standards are set by statutes, which results in accounting income and taxable income being closely related.

Japan This is an example of a country whose accounting standards are greatly influenced by statutes. Two government bodies are very involved with the setting of standards, and Japan's tax laws require that expenses deducted for tax purposes also appear as deductions on the income statement. This leads to very conservative income measurements and efforts to smooth income are acceptable.

Under tax law, deductions for items such as bad debts, sales returns, and warranty costs do not have to bear any relationship with historical data or economic conditions. Depreciation rates reflect relatively short asset lives and provisions can be made for expected future maintenance costs. Both lessees and lessors report using the operating lease method, and because of the strong relationship between accounting and taxable income there is little call for any form of future (deferred) income tax accounting. Any future tax assets and liabilities that do appear on the consolidated statements often come from foreign subsidiaries.

Japanese companies typically have very high debt ratios.

Japanese companies tend to finance more with debt than equity resulting in very high debt/equity ratios even though some liabilities such as those from leases do not appear. Japan's accounting standards require only the presentation of a balance sheet and income statement; a cash flow statement is not required. From this discussion it is clear that Japan's standards would not measure up to IFRS (or to Canadian or U.S. standards, for that matter).

In 2004, the Accounting Standards Board of Japan and the IASB announced an agreement to launch a joint project which would examine and identify differences between the standards of both bodies, and in 2005 announced a further project to attempt to reduce differences between Japanese and international accounting standards. With two convergence projects occurring simultaneously, one is left to speculate which one will receive the highest priority by the IASB.

The statements of Fuji Heavy Industries Ltd. provide a good example of Japanese accounting practices.

An interesting example of Japanese financial reporting can be seen by downloading the 2006 consolidated financial statements of Fuji Heavy Industries Ltd. (www.fhi.co.jp/english).

The company has three major divisions: Automobiles, Industrial Products, and Aerospace. Note disclosure indicates that these consolidated statements have been prepared "in accordance with the provisions set forth in the Japanese Securities and Exchange Law and its related accounting regulations, and in conformity with accounting principles generally accepted in Japan," while the records of the 68 subsidiaries in the consolidated group have been prepared in accordance with the accounting principles in their respective country of domicile. As will be discussed in later chapters, Canadian practice would not allow the consolidation of companies using different principles.

In Canada all consolidated foreign subsidiaries must report using Canadian GAAP.

Large Japanese companies (as do many European companies) often provide English versions of their annual reports, and often translate the amounts into U.S. dollars as a mater of convenience for foreign readers. The rates used are the spot rates on the date of the financial statements, and because all elements are translated at the same rate, no foreign currency gains and losses result from such translation. As we will see in Chapter 12 this would not be the case if the statements were translated in accordance with GAAP in Canada.

While these statements look similar to those used in Canada, an examination of the notes to the statements will highlight some differences, and a full comprehension can only be achieved if the reader has some understanding of Japanese accounting principles and differences in culture and business practices between the two countries.

Where Is Canada Going?

At one time Canada intended to harmonize its standards with those of the United States.

At first glance, Canada seemed to be moving towards American accounting standards when in 1998 the CICA announced that it would work with FASB to harmonize the accounting standards of the United States and Canada while at the same time encouraging the IASB in its efforts to develop global accounting standards.

The concept of harmonization would probably have proven to be a fairly difficult one due to the fact that Canadian accounting standards tend to be broad based while American standards tend to be based on detailed rules. This problem was alleviated when the CICA's position changed in 2006 with the announcement of the adoption of a strategic plan that would see the harmonization of the *CICA Handbook* with IFRS.

Canada will now harmonize the *CICA Handbook* with IFRS effective January 1, 2011.

Harmonization was chosen instead of the simple adoption of the international standards because security regulations and federal and provincial Companies Acts require financial reporting to be in accordance with Canadian GAAP. Because of this requirement, after the usual public exposure, new *Handbook* sections will be issued that will result in Canadian standards being the same as IFRS. All publicly accountable enterprises (essentially those trading on stock exchanges) will have to use the new standards effective January 1, 2011.

During the transitional period between 2006 and 2011, any converged standards issued by FASB and IASB as a result of their agreement to attempt to eliminate differences between U.S. GAAP and IFRS will be adopted by the CICA. This should reduce the number of differences between Canadian GAAP and IFRS on the changeover date. In the meantime it is imperative that Canadian public companies begin to plan for this major change in financial reporting. Education and training will have to start early if the transition is to be a smooth one, and the CICA has indicated that it will not prepare training materials. Such materials were prepared by Australia and countries in the European Union when IFRS were adopted in 2005 and it is anticipated that various Canadian organizations involved in education and training will avail themselves of them. As an aid to users preparing for this transition the CICA has published a document which compares the *CICA Handbook* sections with the relevant IFRS.[5]

The CICA has published a document comparing current Canadian standards with IFRS.

While the document states that, in general, the international standards are quite similar to Canadian standards because they are based on similar conceptual frameworks and reach similar conclusions, there are very few section by section comparisons where no differences are noted. Often the document states that "*Handbook* Section X and IFRS Y are converged except for," and in many cases the list of exceptions is fairly lengthy. IFRS often allow for optional treatments and in some instances allow or require the use of fair values in financial statement measurements, whereas Canadian standards do not often allow optional treatments and tend to require more historical cost measurements.

IFRS allow the use of fair values and optional treatments to a greater degree than the *CICA Handbook* does.

---

[5] www.acsbcanada.org.

Canadian companies have a lot of work to do prior to January 1, 2011.

While the changeover date is expected to be January 1, 2011, Canadian companies will have to plan for the implementation of the change in years prior to this date. In both their 2008 and 2009 financial statements they will be required to disclose management's estimate of the effect that the subsequent changeover will have on their future financial statements.

In 2010 they will have to keep dual records in both Canadian GAAP and in IFRS, because their 2011 statements will be presented under the new standards with comparative amounts required to be shown for 2010.

There is still the issue of what standards to use for private companies and not-for-profits.

Private Companies and NFPOs   The current *CICA Handbook* has a number of sections that apply only to not-for-profit organizations (see Chapter 13). Many of the other sections, which apply mainly to business organizations, have paragraphs which allow private companies and unincorporated businesses to use differential reporting. (This concept which essentially allows relief from some of the more complex and onerous provisions contained in certain *Handbook* sections is discussed in Chapter 2.)

When the changeover takes place and the new sections of the *Handbook* become operative they will apply only to publicly accountable enterprises. Two questions arise. What about non-publicly accountable enterprises and NFPOs? What standards should they use? The CICA has not yet determined what to do here but is considering a number of options such as:

1. The new *Handbook* sections (which will be the same as international standards) should apply to all profit organizations.

2. The new *Handbook* sections should contain sections that allow for some sort of differential reporting.

3. There should be a new *Handbook* which contains a made-in-Canada set of accounting principles for private companies and unincorporated businesses.

4. If any of the above are adopted, some sort of accommodation will have to be considered for not-for-profit organizations. Perhaps the existing NFPO sections will be maintained.

The CICA has indicated that it intends to announce the direction it will take some time in 2008.

A Unique Example That Presents a Comparison Between Canadian GAAP and IFRS

Homburg uses both Canadian standards and IFRS.

Homburg Invest Inc. is a real estate investment and development company with its head office located in Halifax, Nova Scotia. The company owns office, retail, industrial, and residential apartment and townhouse properties in Canada, the Netherlands, Germany, and the United States. The company's real estate portfolio has grown rapidly from approximately $89 million in the year 2000 to approximately $2.0 billion in 2007 at which time it derived 81 percent of its net operating income from Europe, 17 percent from Canada, and 2 percent from the United States. Its shares are listed on both the TSX in Canada and the Euronext in Amsterdam, Holland. What makes this company particularly unique is that it presents its shareholders with two sets of annual financial statements; one prepared under Canadian GAAP, and the other in accordance with International Financial Reporting Standards.

Appendix 1A, at the end of this chapter, contains the Canadian GAAP consolidated balance sheet, statement of earnings, statement of retained earnings, and statement of cash flows for the year ended December 31, 2006. Appendix 1B contains the 2006 IFRS consolidated balance sheet, statement of earnings, statement of changes in equity, and statement of cash flows. (Notes to the statements have not been reproduced nor have the two auditors reports. If interested, readers can view these reports and notes on the company's Sedar web site: www.sedar.com.)

A cursory examination of the two sets of financial statements shows a few minor descriptive differences. It also shows that the form of the two sets of statements is basically the same (the retained earnings and changes in equity statements are quite different because of the greater disclosures required by the international standards).

The differences between reported earnings are very large.

It is when we examine the numbers presented in the statements, that we can see some very large differences. Net earnings are $94.7 million under IFRS while they are $22.9 million when measured under Canadian GAAP, a difference of over 400 percent.

A comparison of the two balance sheets indicates the cause of the major differences. Under IAS 40, companies have the option of reporting investment and development properties at either their historical cost (after taking appropriate depreciation), or at fair value (with no depreciation taken). Homburg has chosen the second option. The unrealized gains have been taken into income, and because they do not attract income tax, an appropriate deferred income tax liability has been created. While it was indicated earlier that the differences between the two sets of standards are not great, a comparison of the results presented by Homburg will allow readers to form their own conclusions.

SUMMARY

The diversity among the accounting principles in use throughout the world has long been viewed as a major stumbling block toward achieving the desired goal of a truly global capital market. The IASB has attempted to narrow this diversity by issuing a set of international standards, with the intent that they will be adopted worldwide. While a great deal of progress has been made, the goal of global harmonization and/or convergence has not yet fully been reached. Over 100 countries have adopted these standards, but Japan and the United States are still not on board. In the latter situation there is a potential clash that must be resolved between those who want detailed rule-based standards and those who would prefer standards that are less detailed and more based on broad principles. Even if this problem is solved, the concept of absolute comparability of financial information on a worldwide basis is still going to be difficult to achieve. There is a problem of consistency in the interpretation of the standards by preparers of financial statements because these standards are broad based, and require professional judgment. An additional problem is created by the fact that some countries are not adopting IFRS, but rather are modifying their own standards so that they are essentially but not completely the same. Other countries are adding additional "home-grown" standards where it is felt that the international standards are inadequate. Readers of the financial statements of companies from countries such as have just been described will have to understand where the differences lie if they wish to make realistic comparisons with companies in other countries.

The CICA has announced that Canadian public companies will report using IFRS in 2011. Some sort of GAAP for non-public companies and not-for-profit organizations will also have to be in place at that time. A great deal of preparation will be needed by Canadian business organizations and public accounting firms in the interim years.

APPENDIX 1A

Exhibit 1A.1

HOMBURG INVEST INC.
CONSOLIDATED BALANCE SHEET

(CAD $ thousands except per share amounts)	December 31 2006	December 31 2005
Assets		
Investment properties (Notes 3 & 5)*	**$1,696,295**	$682,476
Development properties (Notes 3 & 6)	**257,134**	134,557
Cash and cash equivalents (Note 3)	**66,743**	34,185
Long-term investments (Note 10)	**48,190**	18,886
Intangible assets (Notes 3 & 8)	**46,976**	9,910
Receivables and other (Note 9)	**40,613**	12,797
Deferred financing and leasing costs, net of accumulated amortization of $3,065 (2005 — $1,173)	**17,186**	11,812
Restricted cash (Note 7)	**20,892**	41,874
Currency guarantee receivable (Note 11)	**3,483**	
	$2,197,512	$946,497
Liabilities		
Long-term debt (Note 11)	**$1,599,780**	$678,951
Accounts payable and other liabilities (Note 13)	**135,576**	42,634
Construction financing (Note 12)	**91,201**	32,115
Future income taxes (Note 15)	**53,095**	37,991
Derivative instrument liability (Notes 3 & 16)	**2,180**	3,583
Intangible liabilities (Notes 3 & 8)	**732**	829
	1,882,564	796,103
Shareholders' Equity (Note 14)	**314,948**	150,394
	$2,197,512	$946,497

Commitments (Note 19)
Contingent liability (Note 24)
Indemnities (Note 25)
Subsequent events (Note 26)

Approved by the Board, February 8, 2007

"Signed"   "Signed"

Richard Homburg, Phzn, D. Comm.   Edward P. Ovsenny
Director   Director

See accompanying notes to these consolidated financial statements prepared under Canadian GAAP. Financial statements prepared under International Financial Reporting Standards are also available.

Source: www.sedar.com. Homburg Invest Inc., Audited Annual Financial Statements, March 19, 2007.

Exhibit 1A.2

HOMBURG INVEST INC.
CONSOLIDATED STATEMENT OF EARNINGS
Year Ended December 31

(CAD $ thousands except per share amounts)	2006	2005
Property revenue	$116,742	$56,401
Sale of properties developed for resale	45,968	
Gain on sale of assets	8,775	14,334
Other income	2,392	119
Gain on derivative instrument	1,680	653
Dividend income	1,312	40
	176,869	71,547
Interest on long-term debt	58,460	22,846
Cost of sale of properties developed for resale	44,591	
Depreciation and amortization	22,584	10,345
Property operating expenses	13,629	13,521
General and administrative	6,438	4,244
Stock-based compensation (Note 3i)*		1,143
	145,702	52,099
Earnings before income taxes	31,167	19,448
Income taxes (Note 15)	8,205	4,870
Net earnings	$ 22,962	$14,578

Earnings per share (Note 18)

Basic

Class A Subordinate voting	$0.22	$0.19
Class B Multiple voting	$0.22	$0.19

Diluted

Class A Subordinate voting	$0.21	$0.19
Class B Multiple voting	$0.21	$0.19

* See accompanying notes to these consolidated financial statements prepared under Canadian GAAP. Financial statements prepared under International Financial Reporting Standards are also available.

Source: www.sedar.com, Homburg Invest Inc., Audited Annual Financial Statements, March 19, 2007.

Exhibit 1A.3

HOMBURG INVEST INC.
CONSOLIDATED STATEMENT OF (DEFICIT) RETAINED EARNINGS
Year Ended December 31

(CAD $ thousands except per share amounts)	2006	2005
Retained earnings, beginning of year*	$ 4,989	$ 5,327
Net earnings	22,962	14,578
Dividends	(31,256)	(14,916)
(Deficit) Retained earnings, end of year	$ (3,305)	$ 4,989

* See accompanying notes to these consolidated financial statements prepared under Canadian GAAP.
Financial statements prepared under International Financial Reporting Standards are also available.

Source: www.sedar.com, Homburg Invest Inc., Audited Annual Financial Statements, March 19, 2007.

Exhibit 1A.4

HOMBURG INVEST INC.
CONSOLIDATED STATEMENT OF CASH FLOWS
Year Ended December 31

(CAD $ thousands except per share amounts)	2006	2005
Cash obtained from (used for)		
Operating activities		
Net earnings	$ 22,962	$ 14,578
Items not affecting cash:		
Gain on sale of assets	(8,775)	(14,334)
Gain on derivative instrument	(1,680)	(653)
Depreciation and amortization	22,584	10,345
Deferred rental income	(8,680)	(1,046)
Future and capital income taxes	3,120	2,174
Stock-based compensation		1,143
Foreign exchange (gain) loss	(654)	271
	28,877	12,478
Change in non-cash working capital (Note 20)*	(8,927)	2,890
Net cash from operating activities	19,950	15,368
Investing activities		
Investment in investment properties	(49,298)	(57,132)
Proceeds on sale of investment properties	2,566	75,707
Decrease (increase) in restricted cash	20,982	(31,410)
Proceeds on sale of investments	183	3,331
Purchase of long-term investments	(8,717)	(21,061)
Increase in intangibles	(951)	
Proceeds on sale of development properties	89,119	
Investment in development properties	(210,748)	(126,789)
Net cash used in investing activities	(156,864)	(157,354)
Financing activities		
(Decrease) increase in demand loans	(143,532)	13,969
Decrease in mortgages payable	(68,385)	(16,617)
Increase in mortgages payable	58,602	28,784
Proceeds from bonds	148,165	91,066
Decrease (increase) in related party receivable	166	(2,868)
Issue of common shares	68,912	13,380
Dividends paid	(11,165)	(14,916)
Increase in construction financing	59,086	32,115
Proceeds from subordinated notes	57,623	
Net cash from financing activities	169,472	144,913
Increase in cash and cash equivalents	32,558	2,927
Cash and cash equivalents, beginning of year	34,185	31,258
Cash and cash equivalents, end of year	$ 66,743	$ 34,185

* Supplemental cash flow information (Note 20). See accompanying notes to these consolidated financial statements prepared under Canadian GAAP. Financial statements prepared under International Financial Reporting Standards are also available.

Source: www.sedar.com, Homburg Invest Inc., Audited Annual Financial Statements, March 19, 2007.

APPENDIX 1B

Exhibit 1B.1

HOMBURG INVEST INC.
CONSOLIDATED BALANCE SHEET

(CAD $ thousands except per share amounts)	December 31 2006	December 31 2005 (As restated Note 4)
Assets		
Cash and cash equivalents	$ 66,743	$ 34,185
Receivables and other (Note 9)*	33,026	12,797
Long-term investments (Note 10)	42,255	18,677
Restricted cash (Note 8)	20,892	41,874
Deferred financing costs, net of accumulated amortization of $689 (2005 — $153)	11,257	2,255
Development properties (Notes 3 & 7)	301,757	183,485
Investment properties (Notes 3 & 6)	1,957,808	786,387
Currency guarantee receivable (Note 11)	3,483	
	$2,437,221	$1,079,660
Liabilities		
Accounts payable and other liabilities (Note 13)	$ 135,576	$ 42,632
Derivative instrument liability (Notes 3 & 16)	2,180	3,583
Construction financing (Note 12)	91,201	32,115
Long-term debt (Note 11)	1,599,780	678,951
Deferred income taxes (Note 15)	104,480	62,911
	1,933,217	820,192
Shareholders' Equity (Note 14)	504,004	259,468
	$2,437,221	$1,079,660

Commitments (Note 19)
Contingent liability (Note 20)
Indemnities (Note 21)
Subsequent events (Note 22)

Approved by the Board, February 8, 2007

"Signed"   "Signed"

Richard Homburg, Phzn, D. Comm.   Edward P. Ovsenny
Director   Director

* See accompanying notes to these consolidated financial statements prepared under International Financial Reporting Standards.

Source: www.sedar.com, Homburg Invest Inc., Audited Annual Financial Statements, March 19, 2007.

Exhibit 1B.2

HOMBURG INVEST INC.
CONSOLIDATED STATEMENT OF EARNINGS
Year Ended December 31

(CAD $ thousands except per share amounts)	**2006**	2005 (As restated Note 4)
Property revenue	**$116,742**	$ 56,743
Unrealized valuation changes	**76,225**	50,387
Sale of properties developed for resale	**45,968**	
Realized valuation changes	**8,775**	4,693
Other income	**2,392**	430
Gain on derivative instrument	**1,680**	653
Dividend Income	**1,312**	
	253,094	112,906
Interest on long-term debt	**58,270**	23,347
Cost of sale of properties developed for resale	**44,591**	
Property operating expenses	**13,629**	14,230
General and administrative	**6,438**	4,244
Amortization	**728**	340
Stock-based compensation (Note 3h)*		1,143
Foreign exchange loss		271
	123,656	43,575
Earnings before income taxes	**129,438**	69,331
Income taxes (Note 15)	**34,672**	14,468
Net earnings	**$ 94,766**	$ 54,863

Earnings per share (Note 18)
Basic

Class A Subordinate Voting	**$0.92**	$0.73
Class B Multiple Voting	**$0.92**	$0.73

Diluted

Class A Subordinate Voting	**$0.86**	$0.72
Class B Multiple Voting	**$0.86**	$0.72

See accompanying notes to these consolidated financial statements prepared under International Financial Reporting Standards.

Source: www.sedar.com, Homburg Invest Inc., Audited Annual Financial Statements, March 19, 2007.

Exhibit 1B.3

HOMBURG INVEST INC.
CONSOLIDATED STATEMENT OF CHANGES IN EQUITY
Year Ended December 31

(CAD $ thousands except per share amounts)

	Revaluation Surplus	Share Capital	Contributed Surplus	Cumulative Foreign Currency Translation Account	Retained Earnings (As Restated Note 4)	Total (As Restated Note 4)
Balance, December 31, 2004						
As previously reported	$	$ 63,035	$	$ (1,893)	$ 42,341	$ 103,483
Change in accounting policy (Note 4)*					176	176
As restated		63,035		(1,893)	42,517	103,659
Net earnings for the year					54,863	54,863
Exercise of options		1,256				1,256
Issue costs		(415)				(415)
Private placements		12,539				12,539
Acquisitions		72,482				72,482
Dividend reinvestment plan		12,773				12,773
Stock-based compensation			1,143			1,143
Dividends ($0.20 per share)					(14,916)	(14,916)
Revaluation surplus	39,953					39,953
Deferred taxes	(6,959)					(6,959)
Current period foreign currency reserve for foreign self-sustained operations				(16,910)		(16,910)
Balance, December 31, 2005	32,994	161,670	1,143	(18,803)	82,464	259,468
Net earnings for the period					94,766	94,766
Exercise of options		1,200				1,200
Dividends ($0.30 per share)					(31,256)	(31,256)
Acquisitions		40,798				40,798
Repayment of acquisitions-related debt		19,395				19,395
Dividend reinvestment plan		20,091				20,091
Issue costs		(466)				(466)
Public share issue		68,406				68,406
Acquisition of investment		66				66
Applied to stock options exercised			(227)			(227)
Current period foreign currency reserve for foreign self-sustained operations				31,763		31,763
Balance, December 31, 2006	**$32,994**	**$311,160**	**$ 916**	**$12,960**	**$145,974**	**$504,004**

* See accompanying notes to these consolidated financial statements prepared under International *Financial Reporting Standards.*

Source: www.sedar.com, Homburg Invest Inc., Audited Annual Financial Statements, March 19, 2007.

Exhibit 1B.4

HOMBURG INVEST INC.
CONSOLIDATED STATEMENT OF CASH FLOWS
Year Ended December 31

(CAD $ thousands except per share amounts)	2006	2005 (As restated Note 4)
Operating activities		
Net earnings	**$94,766**	$54,863
Adjustments for:		
Realized valuation changes	**(8,775)**	(4,693)
Deferred rental income	**(8,680)**	(1,046)
Unrealized valuation changes	**(76,225)**	(50,387)
Deferred and capital income taxes	**29,397**	12,640
Stock-based compensation		1,143
Amortization	**728**	340
Gain on derivative instrument	**(1,680)**	(653)
Foreign exchange (gain) loss	**(654)**	271
	28,877	12,478
Change in non-cash working capital (Note 23)*	**(7,089)**	9,581
Net cash from operating activities	**21,788**	22,059
Investing activities		
Investment in investment properties	**(52,087)**	(55,319)
Proceeds on sale of investment properties	**2,566**	75,707
Decrease (increase) in restricted cash	**20,982**	(31,410)
Proceeds on sale of investments	**183**	3,331
Proceeds on sale of development properties	**89,119**	
Purchase of long-term investments	**(8,717)**	(21,061)
Investment in development properties	**(210,748)**	(135,293)
Net cash used in investing activities	**(158,702)**	(164,045)
Financing activities		
(Decrease) increase in demand loans	**(143,532)**	13,969
Decrease in mortgages payable	**(68,385)**	(16,617)
Increase in mortgages payable for new debt	**58,602**	28,784
Proceeds from bonds	**148,165**	91,066
Decrease (increase) in related party receivable	**166**	(2,868)
Issue of common shares	**68,912**	13,380
Dividends paid	**(11,165)**	(14,916)
Increase in construction financing	**59,086**	32,115
Proceeds from subordinated notes	**57,623**	
Net cash from financing activities	**169,472**	144,913
Increase in cash and cash equivalents	**32,558**	2,927
Cash and cash equivalents, beginning of year	**34,185**	31,258
Cash and cash equivalents, end of year	**$ 66,743**	$ 34,185

Supplemental cash flow information (Note 23). See accompanying notes to these consolidated financial statements prepared under International Financial Reporting Standards.

Source: www.sedar.com, Homburg Invest Inc., Audited Annual Financial Statements, March 19, 2007

REVIEW QUESTIONS

1. Why is it important to supplement studies of Canadian accounting principles with studies of the accounting practices used in other countries?
2. In what manner has there been a shift toward a global capital market in recent years?
3. List the factors that have influenced the accounting standards used in a particular country.
4. The accounting standards of some countries have tended to minimize the use of interperiod income tax allocation. Explain why.
5. What role does the stage of development of a country's capital markets have on the direction taken by the country's accounting standards?
6. In what way has the level of inflation influenced the accounting standards of a particular country?
7. In which two countries mentioned in the chapter have accounting standards been set by statute?
8. Accounting standards determined by legislated authority often result in an income measurement of a certain type. Explain.
9. In what manner does the balance sheet format used by companies in other countries differ from the format used by Canadian companies?
10. Canadian companies whose shares trade on U.S. stock exchanges are required to reconcile Canadian GAAP income to U.S. GAAP income. What are some of the causes of differences?
11. What countries make up the European Union, and what is the E.U.'s purpose?
12. What is the goal of the IASB?
13. What does the FASB/IASB convergence project expect to achieve? How will it be carried out?
14. What evidence is there that IASB pronouncements are becoming acceptable throughout the world?
15. What direction does Canada propose to take with regard to the harmonization or convergence of accounting standards?
16. Explain why complete comparability on a worldwide basis is going to be difficult to achieve despite a switch-over to IFRS.

MULTIPLE-CHOICE QUESTIONS

1. Which of the following is not a reason for establishing international accounting standards?
   a. Some countries do not have the resources to develop accounting standards on their own.
   b. Comparability is needed between companies operating in different areas of the world.
   c. Some of the accounting principles allowed in various countries report markedly different results for similar transactions.
   d. Demand in Canada is heavy for an alternative to the principles found in the *CICA Handbook*.

2. A key factor necessary for the future realization of worldwide use of common accounting standards is the convergence of IASB standards with those of
   a. Canada.
   b. The European Union.
   c. China.
   d. The U.S.A.

3. The IASB–FASB convergence project has as its goal
   a. Having IASB standards acceptable for reporting under SEC regulations.
   b. Focusing on the elimination of minor differences that currently exist between the standards of the two bodies.
   c. Working together on the issuance of future standards in areas where serious differences exist.
   d. All of the above.

4. According to critics, what is the major problem with the original standards produced by the IASB?
   a. Too many popular methods have been eliminated.
   b. Too many optional methods have remained.
   c. The IASB has failed to examine and report on key accounting issues.
   d. The pronouncements have tended to be too similar to Canadian GAAP.

5. Accounting and other types of technology are imported and exported, and countries have similar accounting for this reason. Which one of the following reasons has been most significant in increasing the influence that the United States has had on accounting in Canada?
   a. Canadian companies routinely sell shares of stock or borrow money in the United States.
   b. The countries have similar political systems.
   c. Both countries are involved in the European Community.
   d. The countries are close geographically.

6. By which of the following means has the IASB made efforts to improve its standards?
   a. By ensuring member countries reflect IASB standards in legal statutes.
   b. By reducing the number of acceptable alternatives permitted.
   c. By requiring all member countries to comply with IASB standards.
   d. By adopting U.S. accounting standards.

7. Which of the following is *not* a fundamental focus of the IASB?
   a. To achieve harmonization with Canadian GAAP.
   b. To achieve convergence with FASB.
   c. To work with the FASB to agree on much-needed improvements to existing standards.
   d. To provide uniform accounting standards for multinational corporations.

8. How would you describe accounting principles in Japan?
   a. They are issued by a professional accounting body.
   b. They are the same as IASB standards.
   c. They are determined by government.
   d. They are quite liberal in nature.

9. Great strides have been made towards achieving international accounting harmonization over the last few years. Which of the following has helped to facilitate international accounting harmonization?

   a.   Harmonization of the tax systems of many countries.

   b.   The US Securities Exchange Commission.

   c.   Adoption in 2003 of an enforcement mechanism to ensure correct application of IASB standards.

   d.   A requirement that European companies report their results using IASB standards.

(CGA-Canada adapted)

Use the following information to answer Questions 10 and 11.

Lawland Co. owns 100 percent of the common shares of Minerva Co., a British company with a manufacturing plant in Oxford, England. Using IFRS, British companies are allowed to revalue their fixed assets to current values with the revaluation adjustment recorded in a reserve account in shareholders' equity. Amortization expense is based on the current values of any revalued assets. The revaluation adjustment is transferred from the reserve account directly to retained earnings over the life of the revalued asset. At the end of 2007, an appraisal of Minerva's manufacturing plant indicated that the current value was 500,000 pounds greater than its net book value and indicated an estimated remaining life of 10 years.

10.   If Minerva revalues its manufacturing plant, what impact will this revaluation have on its debt-to-equity ratio on the date of the revaluation?

   a.   It will not change.

   b.   It will decrease.

   c.   It will increase.

   d.   It cannot be determined.

11.   If Minerva revalues its manufacturing plant, what impact will this revaluation have on Minerva's income in the first year after the revaluation?

   a.   It will not change.

   b.   It will increase.

   c.   It will decrease.

   d.   It cannot be determined.

(CGA-Canada adapted)

12.   Which of the following best describes a difference in the application of Canadian and U.S. generally accepted accounting principles (GAAP)?

   a.   Income under Canadian GAAP is typically lower than income under U.S. GAAP.

   b.   American pronouncements tend to be more detailed than Canadian pronouncements.

   c.   Both countries adopt accounting standards based on income tax laws.

   d.   The level of inflation is a big factor in determining accounting standards in the United States but is not a big factor in Canada.

(CGA-Canada adapted)

13.   What changes will the CICA have to implement by 2011?

   a.   A new handbook will have to be issued in accordance with IFRS.

   b.   A decision will have to be made about accounting for not-for-profit organizations.

   c.   It will have to decide what to do about the financial reporting of private entities.

   d.   All of the above.

14. The European Union's directive of 2002 required
    a. All companies in Union countries to prepare their financial statements in accordance with IFRS in 2005.
    b. All member countries to change their accounting standards by 2005.
    c. All member countries to change their accounting standards by 2008.
    d. All publicly traded companies in Europe to report using IFRS in 2005.

CASES

CASE 1   You are examining the consolidated financial statements of a European company that have been prepared in accordance with IFRS. You determine that property, plant, and equipment is revalued each year to its current replacement cost; income and equity are adjusted; and the notes to the financial statements include the following items as a part of the summary of significant accounting policies.

- Tangible fixed assets are valued at replacement cost, less accumulated depreciation. The replacement cost is based on valuations made by internal and external experts, taking technical and economic developments into account and supported by the experience gained in the construction of plant assets throughout the world.
- Valuation differences resulting from revaluation are credited or debited to equity, where it is applicable, after deduction of an amount for deferred tax liabilities.
- Depreciation based on replacement cost is applied on a straight-line basis in accordance with the estimated useful life of each asset.

The provisions of IFRS permit the use of alternatives to historical cost in the valuation of assets. IAS 16 specifically notes that, as an allowed alternative treatment to historical cost:

Subsequent to initial recognition as an asset, an item of property, plant and equipment should be carried at a revalued amount, being its fair value at the date of the revaluation less any subsequent accumulated depreciation and subsequent accumulated impairment losses. Revaluations should be made with sufficient regularity such that the carrying amount does not differ materially from that which would be determined using fair value at the balance sheet date.

The auditor of the company has expressed his opinion on the financial statements, and concluded that they present a "true and fair view."

The use of replacement cost accounting is a departure from the historical cost principle, and represents a fundamental difference in the approach to financial reporting in this country as compared to Canada. The debate as to the relative importance of relevance and reliability is one that surfaces often in the study of international accounting issues. Many countries are very strict as to the use of historical cost for all valuations and in the computation of income, and often allow reductions from historical cost, but not increases (such as with the application of the lower of cost or market rule); others are very flexible in the choice of permissible approaches; still others are very strict in that particular alternatives to historical cost (such as replacement cost or general price level adjusted amounts) must be used.

Required:

(a) Can any alternative to historical cost provide for fair presentation in financial reports or are the risks too great? Discuss.

(b) Discuss the relative merits of historical cost accounting and replacement cost accounting. Consider the question of the achievement of a balance between relevance and reliability and the provision of a "true and fair view" or "fair presentation" in financial reporting.

CASE 2   John McCurdy has recently joined a consultant group that provides investment advice to the managers of a special investment fund. This investment fund was created by a group of non-profit organizations, all of which have endowment funds, and rather than investing their resources individually, they have instead chosen a pooled approach whereby a single fund invests their moneys and distributes the earnings back to them on an annual basis. The board of directors of the investment fund, made up of members from each of the non-profit organizations, meets periodically to review performance and to make investment decisions.

John has been following the fortunes of Ajax Communications Corporation for a number of years. Ajax is a Canadian company listed on the Toronto Stock Exchange. During the past year it made a major acquisition that has changed the basic parameters of the firm. It also obtained a listing on the New York Stock Exchange, and as result, it has presented two sets of year-end financial statements, one based on Canadian GAAP, and the other prepared in accordance with U.S. GAAP. John has been asked to prepare a report on Ajax that he will present to the board of the investment fund. He knows that the board will be interested in knowing why the two sets of financial statements show markedly different results. As a starting point John listed the following items taken from the year-end statements (in millions of dollars except for earnings per share):

	U.S. GAAP U.S. dollars	Canadian GAAP Canadian dollars
Extracts from the income statement		
Total revenue	$3,388.9	$2,611.9
Operating income	89.1	329.1
Income before extraordinary items	14.9	199.4
Net income	14.9	(66.2)
Earnings per share	$ 0.04	$(0.50)
Extracts from the balance sheet		
Total current assets	$ 862.1	$1,360.7
Investments	233.1	59.2
Property, plant, and equipment, net	889.9	1,866.5
Deferred income taxes	50.3	47.6
Intangibles, net	1,016.4	5,473.0
Total assets	$3,142.6	$9,072.1

Working with this list, John's next step will be to determine why there is such a difference in the numbers.

Required:

(a) As John McCurdy, outline the initial approach that you will take in order to determine the reasons for the differences in the numbers.
(b) List some of the obvious items that need resolution and indicate some of the possible causes of the discrepancies.

(Case developed by Peter Secord, St. Mary's University)

CASE 3 A shareholder of Homburg Invest Inc. has approached you with a copy of the company's 2006 financial statements prepared under both IFRS and Canadian GAAP (see Appendix 1A and 1B). This person indicates that they would gain a better picture as to where the differences in net earnings come from if they could see a reconciliation of net earnings under IFRS to net earnings under Canadian GAAP.

Required:

(a) Prepare such a reconciliation.

(b) Download the notes to the financial statements and using them write a brief note outlining why the differences shown in your reconciliation exist.

PROBLEMS

Problem 1 Listed below are some financial ratios used by analysts:
- Liquidity — current ratio; operating cash flow to current liabilities.
- Solvency — debt to equity; debt to assets.
- Profitability — return on assets; return on equity.

Assume that you are comparing the financial ratios of Fuji Heavy Industries with those of Canadian companies (see www.fhi.co.jp/english).

Required:

Using these ratios, do a comparative analysis of Fuji Industries, and comment on how the results would compare with a similar Canadian company.

Problem 2 The following websites contain financial statements for companies located in other countries:
- www.heinekeninternational.com
- www.volkswagen.com
- www.world honda.com
- www.cadburyschweppes.com
- www.gibsa.com
- www.novartis.com
- www.rolls-royce.com
- www.renault.com
- www.sony.net

Required:

Download any three companies' financial statements. For each, identify five major differences in the company's financial statements, compared with those of a typical Canadian corporation.

Problem 3 The following reconciliation was included in the notes to the 2002 financial statements of Cadbury Schweppes.

Required:

(a) Which country's accounting principles appear to be the most conservative? Why?

(b) Explain why you think the following adjustments were made:
  (i)   Goodwill and trademarks.
  (ii) Interest capitalization.
  (iii) Disposal gain.

(c) Download the current financial statements from the company's website (www. cadburyschweppes.com) and see if you can determine the differences between the GAAP used and Canadian GAAP. Outline any differences that you find.

Effect on profit of differences between U.K. and U.S. generally accepted accounting principles (in millions of pounds)

Profit for the Financial Year from continuing operations, net of tax (per U.K. GAAP)	548
U.S. GAAP adjustments	
Amortization of goodwill and trademarks	53
Restructuring costs	(1)
Depreciation of capitalized interest	4
Pension costs	10
Exceptional item/disposal gain adjustment	7
Derivatives	(8)
SAYE/LTIP	4
Taxation on above adjustments	(4)
Deferred taxation	(48)
Profit for the Financial Year from continuing operations, net of tax (per U.S. GAAP)	565

Problem 4 IAS 16, "Property, Plant, and Equipment" requires assets to be initially measured at cost. Subsequently, assets may be carried at cost less accumulated amortization or they can be revalued upward to current value and carried at the revalued amount less accumulated amortization. If revalued, the adjustment is recorded as a component of shareholders' equity. Subsequent amortization is based on the revalued amount. Canadian GAAP does not allow assets to be revalued at an amount exceeding historical cost less accumulated amortization.

ABC Ltd. lists its shares on an exchange that allows it to report either in accordance with Canadian GAAP or by using IFRS. On January 1, Year 1, it acquired an asset at a cost of $10 million, which will be amortized on a straight-line basis over an estimated useful life of 20 years. On January 1, Year 3, the company hired an appraiser who determined the fair value of the asset (net of accumulated amortization) to be $12 million.

Required:

(a) Determine the amortization expense recognized in Year 2, Year 3, and Year 4 under:
   1. the revaluation treatment allowed under IAS 16, and
   2. Canadian GAAP.

(b) Determine the book value of the asset under the two different sets of accounting rules at January 2, Year 3; December 31, Year 3; and December 31, Year 4.

(c) Summarize the difference in net income and in shareholders' equity over the 20-year life of the asset using the two different sets of accounting rules.

Chapter 2 Investments in Equity Securities

LEARNING OBJECTIVES

After studying this chapter, you should be able to do the following:

- Describe the broad relationship between all the relevant sections of the *CICA Handbook* that comprise the "big picture."
- Distinguish between held-for-trading, available-for-sale, and significant influence investments.
- Apply the basic concepts behind the cost and equity methods.
- Prepare equity method entries to amortize the purchase discrepancy.
- Prepare equity method journal entries to reflect unrealized profits on asset transfers.
- Explain the concepts involved with differential reporting.

INTRODUCTION

Emera Inc. is an energy and services company with 570,000 customers and $4.0 billion in assets. Emera operates two wholly owned regulated utility subsidiaries, Nova Scotia Power Inc. and Bangor Hydro-Electric Company. Nova Scotia Power supplies over 95 percent of the electric generation, transmission, and distribution in Nova Scotia. Bangor Hydro provides electricity transmission and distribution service to 110,000 customers in eastern Maine. In addition to its electric utilities, Emera owns a 12.5 percent interest in the Maritimes & Northeast Pipeline that transports Sable natural gas to markets in Maritime Canada and the northeastern United States.

Such information is hardly uncommon in the business world; corporate as well as individual investors frequently acquire ownership shares of both domestic and foreign businesses. These investments can range from a few shares to the acquisition of 100 percent control. There are many different methods of reporting these investments ranging from fair value approaches to cost-based approaches. Unrealized gains can be recognized in regular income or in a new category of income called other comprehensive income.

Over the next nine chapters we will examine various methods for reporting investments in equity securities. The focus is on investments where one firm possesses either significant influence or control over another through ownership of voting shares. Transactions between these non-arm's-length entities require special scrutiny and special accounting procedures. We will begin our journey by reviewing the recently enacted rules for financial instruments and then spend considerable time in preparing consolidated financial statements under increasingly more complicated situations.

31

Equity Investments — The Big Picture

Equity investments are investments in shares of another company.

This is the first of nine chapters that make up a single accounting topic. This topic can be described by the following question: How should a Canadian company report, in its financial statements, an investment in the shares of another company?

There are five different types of share investments:

- Significant influence.
- Control.
- Joint control.
- Held-for-trading.
- Available-for-sale.

The first three types of investments are called strategic investments because the investor intends to establish or maintain a long-term operating relationship with the entity in which the investment is made. The last two types are nonstrategic investments. The method of reporting these investments is summarized in Exhibit 2.1. We will discuss and illustrate the accounting for these different types of investments later in this chapter and throughout the text.

Exhibit 2.1

REPORTING METHODS FOR INVESTMENTS IN EQUITY SECURITIES

Type of Investment	Reporting Method	Reporting of Unrealized Gains
Significant influence	Equity method	Not applicable
Control	Full consolidation	Not applicable
Joint control	Proportionate consolidation	Not applicable
Held-for-trading	Fair value method	In net income
Available-for-sale		
—Market value available	Fair value method	In other comprehensive income
—Market value not available	Cost method	Not applicable

A major subset of this large topic is the preparation of consolidated financial statements, which in itself is fraught with complexity. There is always a danger that, in attempting to absorb a large amount of new material, you will concentrate on the details to the point of losing sight of the big picture. It is very important that you don't lose sight of the forest when you study the trees.

Always try to understand the forest before looking at the trees.

Before proceeding with our examination of the "trees," it would be useful to look at this "forest." The question posed above provides a path into the forest. The accounting principles involved with this question are contained in numerous sections of the *CICA Handbook* and in the statements issued by the Emerging Issues Committee (EIC) of the CICA.

We will use a summarized balance sheet to illustrate the question, and then outline the possible answers that are contained in the *Handbook* sections.

Shown on the next page is the balance sheet of J Company Ltd.

J COMPANY LTD.
BALANCE SHEET

Miscellaneous assets	$ XXX	Liabilities	$ XXX
Investment in shares		Shareholders' equity	
of K Corporation	**XXX**	Capital stock	XXX
	....	Retained earnings	XXX
	$ XXX		$ XXX

Dollar amounts have been omitted from the statement because our focus is on the amount that should be shown for "Investment in shares of K Corporation."

Four *Handbook* sections are directly related to providing an answer to this question; a further eleven sections, one accounting guideline and numerous Emerging Issues Abstracts must also be considered. A brief summary of the provisions contained in these sections is presented next.

A Cautionary Note At the time of writing this fifth edition, there was an exposure draft outstanding on topics relevant to this course. The exposure draft on proposed *Handbook* Section 1582, "Business Combinations," attempts to harmonize Canadian standards with International Financial Reporting Standards and standards issued by the U.S. Financial Accounting Standards Board (FASB). This exposure draft received lots of opposition especially as it relates to the valuation of goodwill and noncontrolling interest when preparing consolidated financial statements for a nonwholly owned subsidiary. As a result, the IASB is contemplating making revisions to the proposed standards but has not yet finalized their standards. This text is written on the basis that the CICA will adopt the revised standards being contemplated by IASB and that they will be effective as of January 1, 2011. We will use the Online Learning Centre (OLC) to keep you informed of any further revisions to the standards for Business Combinations.

Directly Related *Handbook* Sections

1. Section 1590: "Subsidiaries"

Consolidated financial statements are prepared when one company controls another company.

If J Company controls K Corporation, then J Company is called a parent company and K Corporation is called a subsidiary, and GAAP requires the preparation of consolidated financial statements by J Company. This involves removing the investment in K Corporation from J Company's balance sheet and replacing it with the assets and liabilities from the balance sheet of K Corporation. This process is illustrated at the end of Chapter 3 and in the chapters that follow it.

Control is the ability to determine the key policies without the cooperation of others.

Control exists if J Company has the continuing power to determine the strategic operating, investing, and financing policies of K Corporation without the cooperation of others.[1] Control would generally be presumed if J Company's investment consists of a majority of the voting shares of K Corporation; but as we will see in later discussions,[2] control can exist with smaller holdings and does not necessarily exist with majority holdings.

If the investment is not one that produces control, then *CICA Handbook* Sections 3051, 3055, and 3855 must be examined to determine the required financial reporting.

---

[1] *CICA Handbook*, paragraph 1590.03.
[2] The concept of control is discussed in greater detail in Chapter 3.

2. Section 3051: "Investments"

This section describes the financial reporting required for significant influence investments. Significant influence refers to an investment that does not convey control and is not an investment in a joint venture, but that does allow the investor to exercise significant influence over the strategic operating, investing, and financing policies of the investee. The *Handbook* indicates that an investment of 20 percent or more of the voting shares of K Corporation, without control being present, would be presumed to be a significant influence investment, unless there is evidence to the contrary. Such evidence is discussed later in this chapter.

If J Company's investment is one of significant influence, it must be reported by the equity method. Thus the investment is initially recorded at cost and then adjusted thereafter to include J Company's pro rata share of the earnings or losses of K Corporation adjusted for the purchase discrepancy[3] and the elimination and subsequent recognition of all unrealized intercompany profits that occur as a result of transactions between the two companies. Dividends received from K Corporation are recorded as a reduction of the investment.

The accounting for significant influence investments will be illustrated fully in later sections of this chapter.

The equity method is used when the investor has significant influence over the investee.

3. Section 3055: "Interests in Joint Ventures"

If the investment is not one of the two just described, it may possibly be a joint venture investment if the following general provisions of this section are satisfied.

For a joint venture to exist, the owners (the venturers) must have made a contractual arrangement that establishes joint control over the venture. Under such joint control, each venturer shares in some manner the power to determine strategic operating, financing, and investing policies, and no single venturer is able to unilaterally control the venture.

Under this section, J Company Ltd. (the "venturer") reports its investment in K Corporation Ltd. (the "venture") by consolidating K Corporation using the proportionate consolidation method. This method involves applying the proprietary theory of consolidation and is illustrated in Chapter 10.

Proportionate consolidation is required when the investor has joint control over a joint venture.

4. Section 3855: "Financial Instruments — Recognition and Measurement"

This relatively new section identifies two types of investments relevant to this course: investments held for trading and available-for-sale investments. These investments are initially recorded at cost and revalued at fair value at each subsequent reporting date, with one exception. Available-for-sale investments are reported at cost when a quoted market price for the shares in an active market is not available. Accounting for these investments under the cost method will be illustrated later in this chapter.

The cost method is used when market value is not available for available-for-sale investments.

Other Related *Handbook* Sections

The remaining eleven important *Handbook* sections and one accounting guideline are directly related to the four sections that were just outlined and are discussed briefly below.

---

[3] The concept of a purchase discrepancy is discussed later.

5. Section 1300: "Differential Reporting"

Under differential reporting, qualifying companies may opt for simpler methods of reporting.

While the objective of financial reporting is to provide useful information to users of financial statements, it is acknowledged that the costs of providing such information may exceed the benefits received in some situations. It is also acknowledged that the owners of certain private companies often are able to obtain financial information from management and may place less reliance on financial statements than do the owners of public companies. Under this section, privately held enterprises, may omit the requirements from certain *Handbook* sections, and by doing so still receive an unqualified audit opinion. The options that these enterprises may consider are discussed later in this and succeeding chapters.

6. Section 1530: "Comprehensive Income"

This relatively new section requires reporting enterprises to differentiate between net income as traditionally reported on the income statement and other comprehensive income. Other comprehensive income would include unrealized gains on available-for-sale investments (described later in this chapter) and exchange gains and losses related to certain hedges of foreign currency transactions and operations (illustrated in Chapters 11 and 12).

7. Section 1582: "Business Combinations"

A business combination is an economic event whereby one company acquires net assets that constitute a business or equity interests of another company and, as a result, obtains control over that company.

A business combination can occur indirectly by buying shares or directly by buying net assets of another company.

J Company Ltd. obtains *control* over the net assets of K Corporation by either:

(a) investing in the voting shares of K Corporation (a parent–subsidiary relationship), or

(b) purchasing the net assets of K Corporation (not a parent–subsidiary relationship).

Business combination accounting is explained in Chapter 3. It should be noted that the term "control" is also used in Section 1590. On the date that a parent–subsidiary relationship is established, a business combination has occurred.

8. Section 1600: "Consolidated Financial Statements"

This section details the accounting principles to be followed in preparing consolidated financial statements. The pronouncements of this section will receive extensive attention in the chapters that follow.

9. Section 1625: "Comprehensive Revaluation of Assets and Liabilities"

A comprehensive revaluation of the assets and liabilities of an enterprise can take place under the provisions of this section when:

(a) there has been a change in control because all or virtually all of the equity interests of the enterprise have been acquired by another enterprise, *or*

(b) the enterprise has been subject to a financial reorganization, and as a result the previous owners have lost control.

Under push-down accounting, a subsidiary may revalue its assets and liabilities.

A revaluation under the first condition is permitted but not required by a subsidiary when it is acquired by a parent, and is the application of "push-down" accounting. Under the second condition, which arises when the entity is in serious financial distress, a revaluation is mandatory. A full discussion and illustration of the concepts contained in Section 1625 can be found on the Online Learning Centre associated with this book (www.mcgrawhill.ca/college/hilton). The basics of push-down accounting are discussed in Chapter 4.

10. Section 1651: "Foreign Currency Translation"

This section deals with the translation of the financial statements of foreign investees, subsidiaries, and joint ventures, and with the translation of transactions denominated in foreign currencies.

Provisions of this section would apply if:

Foreign transactions and foreign financial statements must be translated to the currency of the reporting entity.

(a) K Corporation was located in a foreign country and/or prepared its financial statements in a foreign currency, or

(b) J Company Ltd. had borrowings or lendings and/or export/import activities denominated in foreign currencies.

Chapters 11 and 12 examine the accounting concepts involved here.

11. Section 1701: "Segment Disclosures"

Segment disclosures provide a breakdown of the aggregated information into various operating and geographical segments.

Consolidated financial statements often result in the aggregating of the statements of companies in diverse businesses located in countries throughout the world. Disaggregation into operating segments and disclosures about products, geographic areas, and major customers is required by this section in order to improve the information content of the consolidated statements. Segment disclosures are discussed in Chapter 10.

12. Section 3064: "Goodwill and Other Intangible Assets"

Section 1582 "Business Combinations" outlines the procedures for allocating the acquisition cost of a subsidiary company to identifiable net assets and goodwill. Section 3064 provides additional guidance regarding the allocation problem by detailing the various intangible assets that might have been acquired. In addition, this section establishes the standards for the impairment testing of both intangibles and goodwill. This topic is discussed in Chapter 5.

13. Section 3465: "Income Taxes"

The provisions of this section add some complications to the asset valuations associated with business combinations and consolidated financial statements. These provisions are discussed in Chapter 10.

14. Section 3475: "Disposal of Long-lived Assets and Discontinued Operations"

This section discusses the reporting requirements when a business segment, such as a subsidiary or joint venture, has been sold.

This topic is well covered in most intermediate accounting texts.

15. Section 3865: "Hedges"

Under hedge accounting, the hedging item offsets the gains and losses on the hedged item.

This relatively new section indicates when and how hedge accounting can be used to ensure that gains and losses on a hedged item are reported in income in the same period as the gains and losses on the hedging item. In Chapters 11 and 12, we will illustrate fair value hedges, cash flow hedges, and hedges of a net investment in a self-sustaining foreign operation.

16. Accounting Guideline 15: "Consolidation of Variable Interest Entities"

The collapse of Enron Corporation focused attention on the growing use of "special purpose entities" (SPEs) that allowed companies to employ "off-balance-sheet financing" by not consolidating certain entities in which they did not own shares but nevertheless were able to control by other means. This pronouncement, effective November 1, 2004, was aimed at stopping this practice. Variable interest entities are discussed in Chapter 10.

EIC Abstracts are primary sources of GAAP.

Related EIC Abstracts   In 1988, the CICA formed its Emerging Issues Committee (EIC) to recommend the appropriate accounting for emerging accounting issues. These are issues that either have not been covered by existing *Handbook* sections or for which additional guidance is required regarding the appropriate accounting method. While the pronouncements of this committee do not carry the same degree of authority as the *Handbook* sections, they are considered to be primary sources of generally accepted accounting principles in Canada.[4] A number of the abstracts issued by the EIC are related to the *Handbook* sections outlined in this introduction. A listing of these particular abstracts and the *Handbook* sections to which they relate can be found on the Online Learning Centre associated with this text.

The big picture, the details of which are contained in a number of later chapters in this book, has been outlined in this overview. You will find it useful to refer to this overview and the "forest" described as you study the material that follows. We will now begin our examination of the "trees."

This chapter examines situations where a share investment does not constitute control or joint control. We will segregate our discussion of these investments on the basis of whether the investments are or are not valued at fair value on each reporting date.

Investments Valued at Fair Value

Unrealized gains/losses are reported in regular income for held-for-trading investments.

Section 3855, "Financial Instruments — Recognition and Measurement," came into effect on October 1, 2006, for public companies and October 1, 2007, for private companies. It deals with investments valued at fair value. Investments held for trading are classified as current assets on the basis that these investments are actively traded and intended by management to be sold within one year. These investments are initially reported at cost and subsequently revalued at fair value at each reporting date. The unrealized gains and losses are reported in regular income along with dividends received or receivable.

Unrealized gains/losses are reported in other comprehensive income for available-for-sale investments.

Available-for-sale investments are classified as current or noncurrent assets depending on how long company managers intend to hold on to these shares. These investments are initially reported at cost and subsequently revalued at fair value at each reporting date, with one exception. If a quoted market price in an active market is not available, these investments will be accounted for using the cost method. When these shares are valued at fair value, the unrealized gains and losses are reported in other comprehensive income. When the investment is sold, the previously reported unrealized gains and losses will be removed from other comprehensive income and realized gains and losses will be reported in regular income. Dividends are recorded as income when they are declared.

---

[4] *CICA Handbook*, paragraph 1100.02.

Other comprehensive income is a new term in accounting and requires further explanation. Other comprehensive income comprises revenues, expenses, gains, and losses that are required by primary sources of GAAP to be included in comprehensive income, but excluded from net income[5] and includes such items as:

- gains and losses on available-for-sale securities;
- gains and losses on derivatives designated as cash flow hedges;
- unrealized gains and losses on translating financial statements of self-sustaining foreign operations.

Other comprehensive income can be reported in a number of ways. The entity could prepare a new financial statement called the Statement of Comprehensive Income. This statement will take the net income from the regular income statement and then present the components of other comprehensive income to arrive at total comprehensive income for the period. Alternatively, the components of other comprehensive income could be presented immediately below the total for regular net income in the income statement. In either case, the regular net income is added to retained earnings as in the past and other comprehensive income is added to cumulative other comprehensive income. Retained earnings and cumulative other comprehensive income must be reported as separate components of shareholders' equity. We will illustrate the presentation of other comprehensive income and cumulative other comprehensive income in Chapters 11 and 12.

> **Other comprehensive income is not included in retained earnings but is included in a separate component of shareholders' equity.**

Investments Not Valued at Fair Value

Sections 3855 and 3051 cover two types of investments which will not be valued at fair value at each reporting date and describe two methods of accounting for them. The two types are available-for-sale investments for which a quoted market price in an active market is not available and significant influence investments. The two distinct accounting methods are the cost method and the equity method.

Available-for-sale Investments With No Quoted Market Price

If a quoted market price in an active market is not available for available-for-sale investments, then these investments are reported using the cost method. Under this method the amount in the investment account remains at the original acquisition cost, and the investor's share of the dividends received is reported as income. There are only two exceptions to this:

> **A liquidating dividend is a dividend in excess of income earned to date.**

1. Any dividends received that are greater than the total of the net incomes earned since acquisition are treated by the investor as a reduction in the investment account. Dividends are a company's method of distributing earnings to its owners; it follows that a company cannot distribute as income more than it has earned. When it does so it is really returning to its owners a portion of the capital that they have contributed (a liquidating dividend).

> **The investment must be written down when there is a permanent impairment.**

2. If the value of the investment is permanently impaired, the investment must be written down to reflect this new value and the loss reflected in income. If the value of the investment subsequently recovers, a write-up is not permitted. The decline must be permanent for this treatment to be applicable.

---

[5] *CICA Handbook,* paragraph 1530.03b.

Illustration   On January 1, Year 1, Jenstar Corp. purchased 10 percent of the outstanding common shares of Safebuy Company at a cost of $95,000. Safebuy reported net incomes and paid dividends at the end of each year as follows:

	Net income	Dividends
December 31, Year 1	$100,000	$75,000
December 31, Year 2	65,000	75,000
December 31, Year 3	30,000	75,000

Utilizing the cost method to account for its investment, Jenstar would make the following journal entries:

Jan. 1, Year 1

Investment in Safebuy	95,000	
Cash		95,000
To record the acquisition of 10% of Safebuy's shares		

Under the cost method, income is recognized when dividends are received/receivable.

Dec. 31, Year 1

Cash	7,500	
Dividend income		7,500
Receipt of dividend from Safebuy		

Dec. 31, Year 2

Cash	7,500	
Dividend income		7,500
Receipt of dividend from Safebuy		

Dec. 31, Year 3

Cash	7,500	
Dividend income		4,500
Investment in Safebuy		3,000
Receipt of dividend from Safebuy		

The entries in Years 2 and 3 need further clarification. The dividends paid in Year 2 were greater than the net income for that year, and from Jenstar's perspective it is possible that a portion of the dividend received should be recorded as a reduction in the investment account. However, total net income earned since acquisition is greater than total dividends paid since that date, so the dividends received are considered revenue in both years. In Year 3 the dividends paid were greater than the net income earned, and so we again have to compare total net income earned with total dividends paid. Total income since acquisition date amounts to $195,000, while dividends in the same period are $225,000. Therefore, $30,000 of these dividends are really liquidating dividends from the point of view of Jenstar. Because no liquidating dividends have yet been recorded, $3,000 (10 percent × $30,000) is recorded as a reduction to the investment account in Year 3, and the remaining $4,500 is dividend income.

A liquidating dividend reduces the investment account and is not recognized as income.

Significant Influence Investments

A significant influence investment is an investment in the voting shares of a corporation that permits the investor to exercise significant influence over the strategic operating, financing, and investing policies of the investee; at the same time, however, it does not establish control or joint control over that investee. Note that the *Handbook*'s criteria for this type of investment require only the *ability* to exercise significant influence; there is no requirement to show that such influence is actually being exercised in a particular situation.

The following conditions are possible indicators that significant influence is present:

- The ability to elect members to the board of directors.
- The right to participate in the policy-making process.
- Significant intercompany transactions between the two companies.
- The size of ownership of the other shareholders of the investee.
- Exchanges of management and technology between the two companies.

A guideline (not a rigid rule) in determining whether there is significant influence is 20 to 50 percent.

Section 3051 suggests that a holding between 20 percent and 50 percent may indicate the presence of significant influence, but it also states that a holding of this size does not necessarily mean that such influence exists. The following scenarios will illustrate this.

Given that A Company owns 60 percent of the voting shares of C Company (probably a control investment), does B Company's holding of 30 percent of C Company's shares indicate that B Company has a significant influence investment? Not necessarily. If B Company is unable to obtain membership on the board of directors of C Company or participate in its strategic policymaking because of A Company's control, it would be difficult to justify calling B Company's holding a significant influence investment. In such a situation, B Company's holding would be considered an available-for-sale investment. Would this situation be different if B Company were allowed membership on C Company's board of directors? Section 3051 indicates that a substantial or majority ownership by another investor would not necessarily preclude an investor from exercising significant influence.

When one investor has control, other investors usually do not have significant influence.

In other words, another company's control investment in C Company does not mean that B Company's 30 percent investment in C Company can never be considered to be significant influence. Determination of significant influence depends on the particular circumstances.

On the other hand, is it possible to have significant influence with less than 20 percent? Normally, an investment of less than 20 percent would not allow the investor to elect any members to the board of directors of the investee corporation; because of this, it probably cannot exert any influence on the decision-making processes of that company. However, 20 percent is only a guideline, and an examination of the facts may suggest some other type of investment. For example, if the investee's shares are widely distributed, and all the other shareholders hold very small blocks of shares and display indifference as to the make-up of the board of directors, an investment of less than 20 percent may be considered a significant influence investment. This certainly could be the case if some of the remaining shareholders gave the investor proxies to vote their shares. From all these discussions and examples, it should be obvious that considerable professional judgment is required in determining whether an investor has significant influence. In later chapters, when we discuss the criteria used to determine whether a particular investment establishes control over an investee, we will also conclude that considerable professional judgment is required.

When an investor has less than 20 percent of the voting shares, it would not usually have significant influence.

The *CICA Handbook* requires that significant influence investments be reported by the equity method. The basic concept behind the equity method is that the investor records its proportionate share of the investee's income as its own income and reduces the investment account by its share of investee dividends declared.

Illustration of Equity Method Basics

We return to the example of the Jenstar and Safebuy companies. All the facts remain the same, including the 10 percent ownership, except that we assume this is a significant influence investment. Using the equity method, Jenstar's journal entries would be as follows:

Jan. 1, Year 1

Investment in Safebuy	95,000	
Cash		95,000
To record the acquisition of 10% of Safebuy's shares		

Dec. 31, Year 1

Investment in Safebuy	10,000	
Investment income		10,000
10% of Safebuy's Year 1 net income		
Cash	7,500	
Investment in Safebuy		7,500
Receipt of dividend from Safebuy		

Dec. 31, Year 2

Investment in Safebuy	6,500	
Investment income		6,500
10% of Safebuy's Year 2 net income		
Cash	7,500	
Investment in Safebuy		7,500
Receipt of dividend from Safebuy		

Dec. 31, Year 3

Investment in Safebuy	3,000	
Investment income		3,000
10% of Safebuy's Year 3 net income		
Cash	7,500	
Investment in Safebuy		7,500
Receipt of dividend from Safebuy		

Under the equity method, income is recognized based on the income reported by the investee.

Dividends are reported as a reduction of the investment account under the equity method.

The equity method picks up the investor's share of the changes in the investee's shareholder's equity.

Under the equity method, the investor's investment account changes in direct relation to the changes taking place in the investee's equity accounts. The accounting objective is to reflect in the investor's financial statements the financial results arising from the close relationship between the companies. The equity method is effective at achieving this. Because the investor is able to influence the investee's dividend policy, dividends could end up being paid in periods during which the investee was suffering considerable losses. The cost method of reporting would reflect investment income, whereas the equity method would report investment losses during these periods.

The equity method provides information on the potential for future cash flows.

The equity method reflects the accrual method of income measurement. As the investee earns income, the investor accrues its share of this income. The investee is not obligated to pay out this income as a dividend on an annual basis. The investor can expect to get the dividend at a later date or expect to sell its shares at a higher value if the income is not paid out as a dividend. Therefore, the equity method does provide useful information about the future cash flow potential from the investment and is required by Section 3051 as indicated by the following:

In those situations in which the investor has the ability to exercise significant influence, shareholders ought to be informed of the results of operations of the investee, and it is appropriate to include in the results of operations of the investor its share of the income or losses of the investee. The equity method of accounting for the investment provides this information.

DISCUSSION QUESTION

How Should We Account for This Change?

Hil Company purchased 10,000 common shares (10 percent) of Ton Inc. on January 1, Year 4, for $345,000 when Ton's shareholders' equity was $2,600,000 and classified the investment as an available-for-sale security. On January 1, Year 5, Hil acquired an additional 15,000 common shares (15 percent) of Ton for $525,000. On both dates, any difference between the purchase price and the book value of Ton's shareholder's equity is attributed to patents, which are expected to provide benefit until the end of Year 7. The market value of Ton's common shares was $35 per share on December 31, Year 4, and $37 per share on December 31, Year 5. Ton reported net income of $500,000 in Year 4 and $520,000 in Year 5 and paid dividends of $450,000 in both years.

The management of Hil is very excited about the increase in ownership interest in Ton because Ton has been very profitable. Hil pays a bonus to management based on its net income determined in accordance with GAAP. Net income is defined to include net income before extraordinary items.

The management of Hil is wondering how the increase in ownership will affect the reporting of the investment in Ton. Will Hil continue to classify the investment as available-for-sale? What factors will be considered in determining whether the equity method should now be used? If the equity method is now appropriate, will the change be made retroactively and will the other comprehensive income be brought into income from continuing operations? They would like to see a comparison of income for Years 4 and 5 and the balance in the investment account at the end of Year 5 under the two options for reporting this investment. Last but not least, they would like to get your opinion on which method should be used to evaluate management's performance for Year 5.

Additional Features Associated with the CICA Equity Method

The previous example illustrated the basic concepts of the equity method. Besides these fundamentals, three other major features referred to in the *Handbook* must be considered. These are:

- the accounting for non-operating income,
- acquisition costs greater than book value, and
- unrealized intercompany profits.

Investee Income from Non-operating Sources   The following extract from Section 3051 outlines the accounting treatment in this situation:

In accounting for an investment by the equity method, the investor's proportionate share of the investee's discontinued operations, extraordinary items, changes in accounting policy, corrections of errors relating to prior period financial statements and capital transactions should be presented and disclosed in the investor's financial statements according to their nature.

The investor's income statement should reflect its share of the investee's income according to the different categories of income.

Companies report certain items separately on their income statements so that financial statement users can distinguish between the portion of net income that comes from continuing operations and the portion that comes from other sources, such as discontinued operations and extraordinary items. Retroactive restatements of prior period results and capital transactions are shown as separate components of retained earnings, or are disclosed in the footnotes. What the above paragraph is telling us is that because the equity method reflects the investor's share of changes in equity of the investee, the reader of the investor's statements should be provided with information to distinguish changes that came from the investee's continuing operations, from all other changes that occurred.

Example   A Company owns 30 percent of B Company. The income statement of B Company for the current year is as follows:

B COMPANY
INCOME STATEMENT — CURRENT YEAR

Sales	$500,000
Operating expenses	200,000
Operating income before income tax	300,000
Income tax	120,000
Income from operations	180,000
Loss from discontinued operations (net of tax)	40,000
Income before extraordinary items	140,000
Extraordinary gain (net of tax)	10,000
Net income	$150,000

Upon receiving this income statement, A Company makes the following journal entry to apply the equity method:

The investor's share of income from continuing operations, discontinued operations, and extraordinary items are reported separately.

Investment in B Company (30% × 150,000)	45,000	
Investment loss, discontinued operations*	12,000	
Investment gain, extraordinary item**		3,000
Investment income (30% × 180,000)		54,000

  *   30% × 40,000
** 30% × 10,000

All three investment income items, which total $45,000, will appear on A Company's income statement. The investment loss from discontinued operations and the investment gain from extraordinary items require the same presentation as would be made if A Company had discontinued operations or extraordinary items of its own. Full footnote disclosure is required to indicate that these particular items arise from a significant influence investment accounted for by the equity method. Materiality has to be considered because these items do not require special treatment in A Company's income statement if they are not material from A Company's point of view, even though they *are* material from B Company's perspective.

Two other major features of equity method reporting as envisioned in the *CICA Handbook* are captured in the following paragraphs from Section 3051:

The equity method is sometimes referred to as the one-line consolidation.

Investment income as calculated by the equity method should be the amount necessary to increase or decrease the investor's income to that which would have been recognized if the results of the investee's operations had been consolidated with those of the investor.

The investor's total income under the equity method should be equal to consolidated net income.

Accounting for an investment under the equity method generally results in the net income of the investor being the same as what the consolidated net income would have been had the financial statements of the investee been consolidated with those of the investor. Depreciation and amortization of investee assets are based on the assigned costs of such assets at the date(s) of acquisition. The portion of the difference between the investor's cost and the amount of its underlying equity in the net assets of the investee that is similar to goodwill (equity method goodwill) is not amortized. No part of an impairment write-down of an investment accounted for by the equity method is presented in the income statement as a goodwill impairment loss (see Goodwill and Other Intangible Assets, Section 3064). Unrealized intercompany gain or loss, and any gain or loss that would arise in accounting for intercompany bond holdings, are eliminated.

Taken by themselves, these two paragraphs are difficult to interpret at this stage because of the reference made to the consolidation process. This material, which is covered in Section 1600, will be the main focus of the remaining chapters of this book. We next discuss two major features of the consolidation process mentioned above because these features are fully applicable to the equity method of accounting for significant influence investments. Readers should revisit the concepts discussed here after Chapters 4 to 8 have been covered.

Acquisition Costs Greater Than Book Values   In the previous examples we recorded Jenstar's investment at its cost, but we did not consider the implications of this cost with regard to Safebuy's book value at the time. We now add a new feature to equity method reporting by indeed paying attention to the book value of an investee's net assets.

The amount paid for shares is usually different than the net book value of the investee's shareholders' equity.

Companies' shares often trade at prices that are different from their book values. There are many reasons for this, such as current economic conditions, anticipation of future profits, and the perceived worth of the company as a whole. It is this last reason that we will now focus on. Because it uses historical costs, a balance sheet does not reflect the worth of a company's assets. The asset values that do appear are often less than current values, and some assets do not appear at all. Stock market prices often reflect some of these differences. When an investor purchases an equity position in an investee that results in significant influence (or control or joint control), the cost to the investor has to be reflected when the investor's returns from the investment are measured. The logic behind this process can be captured in the following scenario.

Buying 100 percent of the shares should produce similar results to buying 100 percent of the net assets of an investee company.

An investor corporation that acquires all the revenue-earning assets of an investee will allocate the total acquisition cost to the assets purchased. In order to measure the returns from these assets, it will amortize their cost against the revenues they generate as part of the matching process. Suppose that instead of buying all of the assets, the investor buys all the common shares of the investee. Logic should direct us to the conclusion that if the price is identical, the net return should be identical.[6] The investor's return is its share (100 percent in this scenario) of the investee's yearly reported income. However, the investee's earnings are based on historical cost amortizations and allocations, which do not reflect the investor's acquisition cost. To properly measure the return from its common share investment, the investor has to adjust its share of the investee's yearly net income to take this acquisition cost into

---

[6] This assumes that the income tax effects of either scenario would be identical.

Purchase discrepancy is the difference between purchase price and investor's share of investee's identifiable net assets.

account. When the investment is less than 100 percent, as in the case of significant influence, the reasoning is similar.

This process of properly measuring the investor's return from investment requires that we calculate, allocate, and amortize an item we call "the purchase discrepancy." This purchase discrepancy is calculated as the difference between the investor's cost and the investor's percentage of the book value of the investee's "identifiable" net assets.[7] The investor allocates this discrepancy to specific assets[8] of the investee, and then amortizes the allocated components to reduce its income from the investment. The allocation is based on the investor's share of the difference between current fair values and carrying values as at the date of acquisition. The amortization is based on the estimated remaining lives of the specific assets.

Goodwill must be written down if it is permanently impaired.

Prior to June 30, 2001, any goodwill resulting from the allocation of the purchase discrepancy had to be amortized over its estimated useful life, which could not exceed 40 years. As of June 30, 2001, goodwill that is implicit from an investment accounted for by the equity method is no longer amortized, but is assessed for impairment, which would be deemed to have happened if the market price of the shares had permanently declined below the investor's carrying value. The write-down of the investment would reduce the unamortized purchase discrepancy and would first be allocated to write down the goodwill until it was zero. After goodwill had been removed, any further write-down would be allocated to reduce the remaining unamortized purchase discrepancy.

Section 3051 states that impairment write-downs of significant influence investments are not presented separately on the income statement of the investor. Rather, they would be deducted to reduce the amount of the investment income from the investee that the investor company would otherwise report.

These new requirements should produce substantial differences in the amount of equity method income reported by an investor. While a significant influence investment allows an investor to have some say in the activities of the investee, it does not necessarily allow unlimited access to the investee's accounting records. Because the fair values of an investee's identifiable net assets are difficult for the investor to determine, a large portion of the purchase discrepancy is probably allocated to goodwill. Before the requirements were changed, the goodwill had to be amortized on a yearly basis, which reduced the amount reported by the investor as income from the investment. The new requirements do not require this yearly charge; thus, earnings from investment should be higher, and will only be affected in years when an impairment loss occurs.

The following example will illustrate the allocation and amortization of the purchase discrepancy.

Example Hartley Inc. paid $40,000 to acquire 30 percent of the outstanding voting shares of Ivan Company. Ivan's net assets had a book value of $90,000 at the time, and specific plant assets were undervalued by $22,000 relative to current fair values.

Net assets are the difference between assets and liabilities and are equal to shareholders' equity.

---

[7] Net assets are equal to total assets less total liabilities. Shareholders' equity also equals net assets. In making this type of calculation, it is often easier to use the amount for shareholders' equity rather than compute the amount for net assets.

[8] The purchase discrepancy can also be allocated to liabilities. This concept will be examined in a later chapter.

Hartley will determine the purchase discrepancy and its allocation by the following calculation:

The purchase discrepancy is allocated first to identifiable assets and liabilities and then to goodwill.

Cost of 30% investment		$40,000
Book value of Ivan's net assets	90,000	
Hartley's %	30%	27,000
Purchase discrepancy		13,000
Allocated:		
Undervalued plant assets 22,000 × 30%		6,600
Goodwill		$ 6,400

The amount of the purchase discrepancy that cannot be allocated to specific identifiable assets of the investee is considered to be the intangible asset goodwill. In some situations this amount can be negative, but we will leave all discussions of this to later chapters. Hartley's journal entry to record its 30 percent investment is:

Investment in Ivan Company	40,000	
Cash		40,000

The investee's income does not reflect any amortization of the purchase discrepancy.

One year later, when Ivan reports a net income of $20,000, Hartley will make the following journal entry to take up its share of this income:

Investment in Ivan Company	6,000	
Investment income		6,000

In measuring this investment income on the basis of its acquisition cost, Hartley determines that the specific undervalued plant assets of Ivan have a remaining useful life of six years and decides that there has been no permanent decline in the market value of Ivan's shares.

The amortization of the purchase discrepancy is accomplished by the following journal entry:

The investor's investment income must reflect the amortization/impairment of the purchase discrepancy.

Investment income	1,100	
Investment in Ivan Company		1,100
Amortization of the purchase discrepancy as follows:		
Plant assets 6,600 ÷ 6 years = $1,100		
Goodwill = 0		
Total amortization $1,100		

Hartley's investment income of $4,900 ($6,000 – $1,100) appears as a separate item on its income statement.

Consolidated statements should only reflect results of transactions with outsiders.

Unrealized Profits   As we will see in later chapters, consolidated financial statements result from combining the financial statement of a parent company with the financial statements of its subsidiaries. The end result is the financial reporting of a single economic entity, made up of a number of separate legal entities. One of the major tasks in this process is to eliminate all intercompany transactions—especially intercompany "profits"—so that the consolidated statements reflect only transactions with outsiders. The basic premise behind the elimination is that from the point of view of this single accounting entity, "you can't make a profit selling to yourself." Any such "unrealized profits" from intercompany transfers of inventory (or other assets) must be held back until the specific assets involved are sold to outside entities.

In the case of a significant influence investment, any transactions between the investor and investee (they are related parties) must be scrutinized so that incomes

Profits from intercompany transactions must be eliminated until the assets are sold to outsiders or consumed by the purchaser.

are not overstated through the back-and-forth transfer of assets. From an accounting perspective, any transfer is acceptable provided that both parties record the transfer at the value that it is being carried at in the records of the selling company. However, if the transfer involves a profit, that profit must be held back on an after-tax basis in the investor's equity method journal entries. When the asset in question is sold outside or consumed by the purchaser, the after-tax profit is realized through an equity method journal entry, again made by the investor. The amount of before-tax profit being held back is the difference between cost and selling price, which in the case of inventory is the gross profit. The selling company pays tax on the profit, which means that it is the after-tax gross profit that is considered unrealized until it is confirmed by a sale to an outside entity. The final dollar amount used in the journal entry depends on whether the sale was "downstream" or "upstream." The following diagram illustrates the two streams:

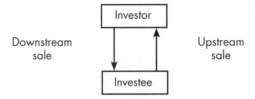

Downstream sale   Upstream sale

In the two examples that follow we will illustrate the differences in the handling of the two streams of sales.

Profit was recorded by the investor on the downstream transaction.

Example   Harrison Corp. owns 35 percent of Gunn Inc. and uses the equity method to account for this significant influence investment. During Year 1, Harrison sold inventory to Gunn and recorded a 60 percent gross profit on the transaction. At the end of Year 1, the inventory of Gunn contained items purchased from Harrison for $75,000. Harrison pays income tax at a rate of 40 percent. The items of inventory in question were sold by Gunn to outsiders in Year 2. Note that the total amount of inventory sales that Harrison made to Gunn in Year 1 is not mentioned. This amount is not an issue in this particular context, although there will have to be full disclosure about such sales in the notes to Harrison's financial statements.[9] What is an issue is the amount of profit that is unrealized because it has not been sold to outsiders. The calculations required are as follows:

Items in Gunn's inventory	$75,000
Gross profit percentage	60%
Unrealized before-tax profit	45,000
Income tax (40%)	18,000
Unrealized after-tax profit	$27,000

Harrison's equity method journal entry to hold back the unrealized profit from this downstream sale at the end of Year 1 is:

The unrealized profit must be eliminated from the investor's investment income.

Investment income	27,000	
Investment in Gunn Inc.		27,000
To hold back the after-tax unrealized profit on the sale of inventory to Gunn		

---

[9] *CICA Handbook*, paragraph 3840.46.

The investment income that is being reduced here is Harrison's share of Gunn's Year 1 net income. This deferral remains in force until the inventory is sold outside, at which time the entry is reversed. In this case the inventory was sold in Year 2, so the entry that Harrison will make at that time to realize the profit is:

> **The previously held-back profit should be recognized by the investor when the inventory is sold to outsiders.**

Investment in Gunn Inc.	27,000	
Investment income		27,000
To realize the after-tax profit that was held back in Year 1		

UPSTREAM

Another Example The previous example illustrated the handling of unrealized profits from downstream sales. In the present example, all of the facts (gross profit, tax rates, etc.) remain the same except that we assume an upstream sale in which Gunn sold the inventory to Harrison. The calculation changes slightly in this situation.

> **On an upstream transaction, the investor only holds back its percentage interest of the unrealized profit.**

Items in Harrison's inventory	$75,000
Gross profit percentage	60%
Unrealized before-tax profit	45,000
Income tax (40%)	18,000
Unrealized after-tax profit	27,000
Harrison's ownership of Gunn	35%
Amount held back	$ 9,450

The amount of unrealized profit held back on an upstream sale is the investor's share of the profit that was recorded during the year by the investee. The investor takes up its share of the investee's net income for the year as a normal application of equity accounting, and then accounts for the fact that not all of this income was realized, because of an upstream sale of inventory.

Harrison's journal entry to hold back this unrealized profit at the end of Year 1 would be:

Investment income	9,450	
Investment in Gunn Inc.		9,450
To hold back the after-tax unrealized profit on Gunn's sale of inventory to Harrison		

At the end of Year 2, Harrison would make the following entry to realize the profit:

Investment in Gunn Inc.	9,450	
Investment income		9,450
To realize the after-tax profit that was held back in Year 1		

In the above illustrations of the holdback and realization of intercompany profits, the asset involved was inventory. The same basic concepts apply when assets other than inventory are sold in a similar manner. This topic will be discussed thoroughly in the consolidation chapters that follow.

Miscellaneous Considerations

The equity method as described in Section 3051 involves the investor recording its proportionate share of investee earnings from continuing operations adjusted for both the amortization of the purchase discrepancy and the holdback and realization of intercompany after-tax profits. Earnings from sources other than continuing operations are recorded separately. The following are some additional items that must also be considered.

Changes to and from the Equity Method The classification of long-term investments will change as the particular facts change. An investment may initially be available for sale and subsequently change to one of significant influence. This could transpire if additional shares were acquired. Once significant influence has been achieved, a switch from the previous way of reporting is made on a prospective basis. If the available-for-sale investment was previously reported at fair value, the fair-value carrying value on this date becomes its new cost. Any previous gain or loss that had been recognized in other comprehensive income should remain in cumulative other comprehensive income until the investment is sold when it should be recognized in net income. If the available-for-sale investment was previously reported at cost (because the market value was not readily available), carrying value becomes its new cost for purpose of applying the equity method. If there was more than one acquisition of shares, and it was the last one that gave significant influence, the investment cost used at the commencement of the equity method is the sum of the costs of the individual acquisitions. If circumstances change, significant influence may also be achieved without additional shares being acquired, in which case the equity method would commence. For example, the holdings of a large block of investee shares by another company could prevent an investor from exercising significant influence. But if that other company sells its block on the market, the investor's previous available-for-sale investment may now amount to significant influence.

When an investment changes from significant influence to available for sale, the equity method ceases to be appropriate and either the fair value method or the cost method takes its place, also on a prospective basis. If the market value of the investment is readily available, the available-for-sale investment should be reported at fair value and the adjustment to fair value should be reported in other comprehensive income. If the market value of the investment is not readily available, the available-for-sale investment should be reported at cost and the investment's carrying value, which was arrived at through the appropriate use of the equity method, becomes the new cost basis. The *Handbook* is unclear as to what to do with previously unrealized profits that were held back because of the related party status of the investor and investee. Logic would suggest that because the investor and investee are no longer related parties,[10] the investment account should be increased by the amounts that were previously held back.

When an investment changes from significant influence to control, the preparation of consolidated statements commences, again on a prospective basis. The concepts relating to this particular situation will be discussed at length in later chapters.

Loss in Market Value of Investment As previously mentioned, the carrying amount of a significant influence investment is reduced to market value if the decline is considered to be permanent. Evidence to support such permanence might include a prolonged period during which market was below carrying value, continued losses of the investee, suspension of trading in the investee, and serious going-concern problems. Once an investment has been written down to reflect a loss in value, the write-down should not be reversed if there is a subsequent increase in value. The increase in value will only be recognized when the investment is sold.

Changes in reporting methods are accounted for prospectively if they are changed because of a change in circumstance.

The carrying value on the date of the change becomes the cost of the investment for future reporting.

The investment account is written down if there is a permanent impairment.

---

[10] *CICA Handbook*, paragraph 3840.03(g).

If an investor guarantees an investee's obligations, the investor could end up reporting its investment as a liability rather than an asset.

Losses Exceeding the Balance in the Investment Account   A question arises as to the appropriate accounting when an investor's share of investee losses exceeds the carrying amount of the investment. There are two possible ways to treat this. The investor could reduce the investment account to zero and commence the use of the equity method when its share of investee earnings exceeds its share of losses. Alternatively, the investor could continue to accrue losses even though they result in a negative balance in the investment account. Section 3051 is silent on this issue, but the Emerging Issues Committee saw fit to address it with EIC-8. Their conclusion was that if the investor considers itself finished with the investee, it should not record losses past a zero balance in the investment account. However, if the investor has guaranteed the investee's obligations, or is committed to providing additional financial support, it would be appropriate to continue recording losses such that the balance in the investment account becomes negative. No mention is made of where to present this credit balance in the investor's balance sheet, but logically it should be shown under liabilities, and there should be full disclosure of the investor's commitments to the investee.

Average cost should be used in determining any gain or loss when an investor sells part of its investment.

Gains and Losses on Sale of Investments   When all the shares that make up a long-term investment are sold, the gain (loss) is shown on the income statement and is calculated as the difference between the sale proceeds and the carrying value of the investment. When only some of the shares are sold, the gain is calculated using the average carrying value of the investment. Cost flows such as FIFO or LIFO or specific identification are not permitted. If a portion of a significant influence or a control investment is sold, a re-evaluation must be made to determine whether the previous classification is still valid.

Differential Reporting

Should the *CICA Handbook*'s sections on financial reporting apply to all Canadian companies, or should certain companies be allowed to use different standards? This question has been the topic of discussions in Canada off and on over the last twenty years of the twentieth century.

The cost-benefit constraint is used in determining whether differential reporting standards should be adopted by a particular organization.

During the 1980s considerable time and effort was spent by CICA on the concept of Big GAAP / Little GAAP. It was argued that accounting standards were becoming increasingly complex and that a small company's costs of preparing its financial statements in compliance with the standards were greater than the benefits received by the users of such statements. Hence, small companies should be granted some sort of relief from having to use complex and hard-to-understand standards. Counter-arguments suggested that the concept of fair presentation could not be achieved with different sets of standards and the dividing line between big and small would be too arbitrary to be useful. After much study and discussion the concept of Big GAAP / Little GAAP was abandoned.

In the meantime the issuance of new complex financial reporting standards continued and the last straw, so to speak, was the issuance of both the section on reporting and disclosure of financial instruments and the exposure draft on the related measurement issues. The issue of different standards was revisited again by a CICA task force but this time in relation to public / non-public companies. The task force considered two basic approaches:

- A non-GAAP approach whereby non-public companies could use accounting policies completely separate from GAAP. An example would be the use of cash-basis reporting instead of the required accrual basis. This approach was abandoned mainly because provincial and federal Companies Acts require companies to prepare financial statements in accordance with GAAP.

- A GAAP approach. This was looked at from two perspectives: full differentiation and partial differentiation. Full differentiation would encompass two distinct sets of GAAP somewhat similar to the accounting for non-profit organizations and governments (discussed in Chapter 13). Partial differentiation encompasses one set of accounting standards with different treatments. This latter approach was the one eventually adopted when Section 1300 was issued and certain sections of the *CICA Handbook* were amended to allow optional treatments.

Companies are following GAAP when they adopt differential reporting options.

Section 1300   This section on differential reporting was issued effective January 1, 2002, and allows a qualifying enterprise to select which reporting options it will apply when it prepares its financial statements. The differential reporting options allowed are contained in individual *Handbook* sections, and to date, only a few sections contain such options.

Section 1300 is a part of the *Handbook* and is considered a primary source of GAAP. When a company adopts one or more of the differential reporting options, it is still considered to be following GAAP.

An enterprise is a *qualifying enterprise* if:

Only non-public companies can apply differential reporting and only if there is unanimous consent of the owners.

- It is a non-public company (one whose shares or debt instruments do not trade in a public market), and

- Its owners unanimously consent to the differential reporting options that it adopts. This consent can either be obtained annually or the owners can pass a resolution that is good until rescinded.

A qualifying enterprise chooses which options it intends to use (there is no requirement to choose all options available), and then obtains the unanimous consent from its shareholders for the options that it adopts. A switch to a differential reporting option is viewed as an accounting change and thus the effect of the change must be dealt with retroactively in accordance with Section 1506 of the *Handbook* when first applied.

A company can adopt some or all of the differential reporting options and must disclose which options it has adopted.

A company must disclose that differential reporting has been adopted, which options it has adopted, and that unanimous consent has been obtained from all owners. Each option selected has its own additional disclosure requirements, many of which are extensive.

Differential reporting options are available for some of the topics discussed in this text. At the end of each chapter any such options will be briefly discussed.

Significant-influence Investments   Section 3051 is the first section that we have discussed which allows a differential reporting option. The following paragraphs from *CICA Handbook* Section 3051 outline the option available:

An enterprise that qualifies under Differential Reporting, Section 1300, may elect to use the cost method to account for its investments in companies subject to significant influence that would otherwise be accounted for by the equity method in accordance with Section 3051. All investments in companies subject to significant influence should be accounted for using the same method.

Investments in companies subject to significant influence accounted for using the cost method should be presented separately on the balance sheet. Income from those investments should be presented separately in the income statement.

An enterprise that has applied the alternative method should disclose the basis of accounting used to account for investments in companies subject to significant influence.

An International Perspective

The IASB requires that a significant-influence investment be reported under the equity method and uses the quantitative guideline of 20 percent to assess significant influence. Section 3051 of the *CICA Handbook* and the corresponding requirements in IAS 28 and IAS 36 are *converged, except* that IFRSs: (i) require an impairment to be recognized when the recoverable amount of an asset is less than the carrying amount, rather than when there is a significant or prolonged decline in value below the carrying amount; (ii) determine the impairment loss as being the excess of the carrying amount above the recoverable amount rather than the excess of the carrying amount above the undiscounted future cash flows of the asset; and (iii) require the reversal of an impairment loss when the recoverable amount changes. The CICA expects that it will take considerable time before the impairment requirement is fully converged.

Canadian standards are substantially the same as the IASB standards for significant-influence investments.

The IASB standards for held-for-trading and available for sale investments are basically the same as Canadian standards *except* that IAS 39: (i) restricts the circumstances in which the option to measure a financial instrument at fair value through profit or loss is available; (ii) requires all available-for-sale financial assets to be measured at fair value unless fair value is not reliably determinable, whereas Section 3855 requires non-quoted equity instruments classified as available for sale to be measured at cost; and (iii) requires reversal of impairment losses. In the long term, IASB, FASB and CICA are all considering improvements to their standards on financial instruments. However, the intention would be to converge with one another on any improvements.

Canadian standards are substantially the same as the IASB standards for held-for-trading and available-for-sale investments.

SUMMARY

Investments held for trading and most available-for-sale investments are reported at fair value. Dividends from these investments are reported in income when they are declared. Unrealized gains and losses are reported in regular income for held-for-trading investments and in other comprehensive income for available-for-sale investments. If a quoted market price in an active market is not available for the available-for-sale investments, these investments are reported using the cost method.

An investment where the investor is able to influence the operations of the investee is called a significant-influence investment and must be accounted for using the equity method, as described in Section 3051 of the *Handbook*. This requires the investor to record its share of all increases in the shareholders' equity of the investee, adjusted for the amortization of the purchase discrepancy and the holdback and realization of upstream and downstream profits from the sale of assets.

SELF-STUDY PROBLEM

Part A   On January 1, Year 5, High Inc. purchased 10% of the outstanding common shares of Lowe Corp. for $75,000. Lowe's shareholders' equity had a book value of $700,000 on this date. From High's perspective, Lowe was an available-for-sale investment without a quoted market price; however, it did not give High significant influence.

On January 1, Year 6, High purchased an additional 25% of Lowe's shares for $300,000. This second purchase allowed High to exert significant influence over Lowe. As of this date the plant and equipment of Lowe, which had an estimated remaining life of five years, were undervalued by $90,000, and its patents, which had an estimated remaining life of seven years, were undervalued by $30,000.

During the two years, Lowe reported the following:

	Net income	Dividends
Year 5	$200,000	$120,000
Year 6	270,000	130,000

Additional Information

- During Year 5, High transferred assets to Lowe and recorded a profit of $35,000 on the transaction.
- During Year 6, Lowe sold inventory to High at a gross profit rate of 40%. At the end of Year 6, High's inventory contained purchases made from Lowe amounting to $75,000. High sold this inventory to its unrelated customers in Year 7.
- Assume tax rates of 40% for both companies for all of the years involved in this question.

Required:

With respect to this investment, prepare High's journal entries for both Year 5 and Year 6.

Part B The following are summarized income statements for the two companies for Year 7:

	High Inc.	Lowe Corp.
Revenues	$900,000	$600,000
Expenses (including income tax)	450,000	400,000
Income before extraordinary items	450,000	200,000
Extraordinary loss (net of tax)	—	20,000
Net income	*$450,000	$180,000

* The net income of High does not include any investment income from its investment in Lowe Corp.

Lowe paid no dividends in Year 7. At the end of Year 7, an impairment test revealed that High's share of Lowe's goodwill was impaired by $6,000.

Required:

(a) Prepare the journal entries that High should make at the end of Year 7 with respect to its investment in Lowe.

(b) Prepare the income statement of High, taking into consideration the journal entries in part (a).

Solution to Self-study Problem

Part A The 10% purchase should be accounted for under the cost method. Because of this, the intercompany asset transfer that occurs in Year 5 is considered to be between unrelated parties, which means that there are no unrealized profits as a result of the transaction. High's journal entries during Year 5 are:

Investment in Lowe	75,000	
Cash		75,000
Purchase of 10% of shares of Lowe		

Cash	12,000	
Dividend revenue		12,000
10% × 120,000		

The 25% purchase in Year 6 changes the investment to one of significant influence, which is accounted for prospectively. The following calculation is made as of this date:

Cost of 10%		$ 75,000
Cost of 25%		300,000
Total cost of significant influence investment		375,000
Book value of Lowe:		
On Jan. 1, Year 5	700,000	
Net income Year 5	200,000	
Dividends Year 5	(120,000)	
	780,000	
	35%	273,000
Purchase discrepancy		102,000
Allocated:		
Plant and equipment — 90,000 × 35%	31,500	
Patents — 30,000 × 35%	10,500	42,000
Balance — goodwill		$ 60,000

The yearly purchase discrepancy amortization during the next five years will be:

Plant and equipment	31,500 ÷ 5 years =	$ 6,300
Patents	10,500 ÷ 7 years =	1,500
		$ 7,800

Because this is now a significant influence investment, Year 6 intercompany up-stream sales are between related parties, and any unrealized profits at the end of the year must be deferred. The calculation is as follows:

Items in High's inventory	$75,000
Gross profit percentage	40%
Unrealized before-tax profit	30,000
Income tax (40%)	12,000
Unrealized after-tax profit	18,000
High's ownership of Lowe	35%
Amount held back	$ 6,300

The journal entries that High makes in Year 6 are as follows:

Investment in Lowe	300,000	
Cash		300,000
Purchase of 25% of shares of Lowe		
Investment in Lowe	94,500	
Investment income		94,500
35% × 270,000 net income		
Cash	45,500	
Investment in Lowe		45,500
35% × 130,000 dividends		
Investment income	7,800	
Investment in Lowe		7,800
Amortization of purchase discrepancy		
Investment income	6,300	
Investment in Lowe		6,300
To hold back unrealized profit on upstream sale of inventory		

Part B   (a) Applying the CICA equity method, High makes the following journal entries in Year 7:

Investment in Lowe*	63,000	
Investment loss extraordinary**	7,000	
Investment income***		70,000

  *   35% × 180,000
 **   35% × 20,000
*** 35% × 200,000

Investment income	7,800	
Investment in Lowe		7,800
Amortization of purchase discrepancy		
Investment in Lowe	6,300	
Investment income		6,300
To realize profit on upstream sale of inventory held back in Year 6		
Investment income	6,000	
Investment in Lowe		6,000
To recognize a goodwill impairment loss		

(b) Investment income — Year 7

Share of ordinary net income	$70,000
Realization of profit on upstream sales	6,300
Purchase discrepancy amortization & goodwill impairment loss	(13,800)
	$62,500

HIGH INC.
INCOME STATEMENT
year ended December 31, Year 7

Operating revenue	$900,000
Expenses (including income tax)	450,000
Income from operations	450,000
Investment income*	62,500
Income before extraordinary items	512,500
Investment loss — extraordinary (net of tax)*	7,000
Net income	$505,500

* A footnote would disclose that these items came from a 35% investment in Lowe, accounted for using the equity method.

REVIEW QUESTIONS

1. How is the concept of a business combination related to the concept of a parent–subsidiary relationship?

2. What is the purpose of the Emerging Issues Committee? Are the abstracts issued by this committee considered to be GAAP in Canada?

3. Distinguish between the financial reporting for available-for-sale investments without a quoted market price and that for significant influence investments.

4. What is the difference between a "control" investment and a "joint control" investment?

5. What event is necessary before a Canadian company is permitted to revalue all its assets and liabilities?

6. What is the purpose of the *Handbook* section on segment disclosures?

7. What is the purpose of *Handbook* Section 1300, "Differential Reporting"?

8. What criteria would be used to determine whether the equity method should be used to account for a particular investment?

9. The equity method records dividends as a reduction in the investment account. Explain why.

10. What factors would be used as evidence that an investor had obtained significant influence over an investee?

11. The Ralston Company owns 35% of the outstanding voting shares of Purina Inc. Under what circumstances would Ralston determine that it is inappropriate to report this investment in its financial statements using the equity method?

12. Because of the acquisition of additional investee shares, an investor may need to change from the fair-value method for an available-for-sale investment to the equity method for a significant influence investment. What procedures are applied to effect this accounting change?

13. BOM Company owns 30% of the shares of BAR Ltd. and accounts for its investment using the equity method. During the current year, the market value of BAR's common shares dropped substantially and are now worth less than the carrying value of BOM's investment. The decline in market value is felt to be permanent. How should BOM account for the decline in market value?

14. An investor uses the equity method to report its investment in an investee. During the current year the investee reports an extraordinary gain on its

income statement. How should this item be reflected in the investor's financial statements?

15. Ashton Inc. acquired a 40% interest in Villa Corp. at a bargain price because Villa had suffered significant losses in past years. Ashton's cost was $200,000. In the first year after acquisition, Villa reported a loss of $700,000. Using the equity method, how should Ashton account for this loss?

16. Under the equity method, a portion of an investor's purchase price is assigned either to specific assets of the investee or to goodwill. How is this done? Why is it done?

17. Able Company holds a 40% interest in Baker Corp. During the year, Able sold a portion of this investment. How should this investment be reported after the sale?

18. What differentiates a downstream sale from an upstream sale? Are the equity method journal entries the same for each?

19. Explain what a "qualifying enterprise" is, and the context in which the term is used.

20. When a qualifying enterprise adopts the cost method to account for its significant influence investment is it complying with GAAP? Explain.

MULTIPLE-CHOICE QUESTIONS

1. Which one of the following accounting methods is recommended by *Handbook* Section 3855 for reporting held-for-trading investments?
   a. Cost method.
   b. Fair value method.
   c. Equity method.
   d. Consolidation.

2. Which one of the following would not be a factor to consider when determining whether an investment results in significant influence?
   a. Whether the investor held a position on the investee's board of directors.
   b. Whether the investor purchased a significant amount of the investee's production output.
   c. Whether the investor and the investee operated in the same country.
   d. Whether the investor and the investee exchanged technical expertise.

3. Perez Inc. owns 25% of Senior Ltd. During Year 5, Perez sold goods with a 40% gross profit to Senior. Senior sold all of these goods in Year 5. How should Perez report the effect of the intercompany sale on its Year 5 income statement?
   a. Sales and cost of goods sold should be reduced by the amount of the intercompany sales.
   b. Sales and cost of goods sold should be reduced by 25% of the amount of the intercompany sales.
   c. Investment income should be reduced by 25% of the gross profit on the intercompany sales.
   d. No adjustment is necessary.

4. On January 1, Year 5, PORT acquired 100,000 common shares of SUN (a 10% voting interest) for $1,000,000. PORT designates this investment as available for sale and shows it as a long-term investment. On December 31,

Year 5, the shares of SUN were trading at $9.50 per share. On March 15, Year 6, when PORT's financial statements were finalized, SUN's shares were trading at $11.00 per share. How should PORT report its investment in SUN on its balance sheet at December 31, Year 5?

a. At $1,000,000, with the market value of the shares disclosed as additional information.

b. At $1,100,000, with the cost of the purchase presented as additional information.

c. At $950,000, with the unrealized loss reported in other comprehensive income.

d. At $950,000, with the unrealized loss reported in net income.

(CGA-Canada adapted)

5. When an investor uses the equity method to account for investments in equity securities, how should the investor account for cash dividends received from the investee?

a. As a deduction from the investor's share of the investee's profits.

b. As dividend income.

c. As a deduction of dividends paid by the investor.

d. As a deduction from the investment account.

Use the following data for Questions 6 and 7.

AB Company purchased 25% of the shares of KC Corporation on July 1, Year 5, for $100,000, which allows it to exercise significant influence. Both companies had December 31, Year 5 year-ends. During Year 5, KC had a net income of $120,000 ($10,000/month) and paid dividends of $80,000 ($20,000 every 3 months, on the last day of each fiscal quarter).

6. As at December 31, Year 5, how much would AB's investment in KC be on AB's balance sheet?

a. $100,000

b. $105,000

c. $110,000

d. $120,000

7. Assuming that AB's 25% investment in KC did not allow it to exercise significant influence, how much income would AB report from its investment in KC for the year ended December 31, Year 5?

a. $10,000

b. $20,000

c. $30,000

d. $40,000

8. On January 1, Year 5, X Company acquired 20% of Y Company for $4,800,000. On the acquisition date, Y Company had common shares of $6,000,000 and retained earnings of $12,000,000. The only purchase price discrepancy adjustment is the annual amortization of the purchase discrepancy of $120,000 (X's portion). From January 1, Year 5, to December 31, Year 7, Y Company earned net income of $3,600,000 and paid dividends of $1,200,000. What would be the balance in the Investment in Y Company account in the accounting records of X Company on December 31, Year 7?

a. Assuming X Company uses the cost method, $4,920,000.

b. Assuming X Company uses the cost method, $5,160,000.

    c.   Assuming X Company uses the equity method, $4,920,000.

    d.   Assuming X Company uses the equity method, $5,280,000.

(CGA-Canada adapted)

9. How should an investment be accounted for where the investor exercises significant influence over the investee?

    a.   At cost plus the investor's share of the investee's change in retained earnings since the date of acquisition.

    b.   At cost plus the investor's share of the investee's net income, adjusted annually through retained earnings.

    c.   At market value with changes in market value adjusted through income.

    d.   At market value with changes in market value adjusted through retained earnings.

(CGA-Canada adapted)

10. RU Ltd. has invested in several domestic manufacturing corporations. Which of the following investments would most likely be accounted for under the equity method on the consolidated financial statements of RU?

    a.   A holding of 2,000 of the 50,000 outstanding common shares of SU.

    b.   A holding of 3,000 of the 10,000 outstanding preferred shares of TU.

    c.   A holding of 15,000 of the 60,000 outstanding common shares of XU.

    d.   A holding of 20,000 of the 25,000 outstanding common shares of VU.

(CGA-Canada adapted)

11. On January 1, Year 5, Top Company purchased a 10% interest in the common shares of Bottom Ltd. for $60,000. Bottom reported net incomes and paid dividends as follows:

    Year 5 — net income $72,000; dividends paid $96,000.

    Year 6 — net income $126,000; dividends paid $96,000.

    Assume that Top uses the cost method to account for its investment in Bottom. Which of the following is the amount that a balance sheet for Top would report as "Investment in Bottom" at December 31, Year 6?

    a. $57,600

    b. $59,400

    c. $60,000

    d. $60,600

12. Pipe Ltd. acquired a 30% interest in the common shares of Tobacco Ltd. on January 1, Year 5. The purchase difference of $10,000 was identified and allocated entirely to patents, which were estimated to have a 10-year useful life. During Year 5, Tobacco sold merchandise to Pipe at 50% gross profit. At December 31, Year 5, Pipe's inventory includes merchandise from Tobacco purchased by Pipe for $4,800. For Year 5, Tobacco reported net income of $70,000 and paid dividends of $20,000. Both companies are subject to 40% tax rates.

    If Pipe uses the equity method to account for its investment in Tobacco, how much investment income will it report in Year 5?

    a. $18,560

    b. $19,568

    c. $20,000

    d. $21,000

13. Pink Co. owns 10% of the common shares of Blue Ltd. On December 31, Year 5, the market value of this investment was less than the carrying value on Pink's books. In which of the following situations will the investment *not* be reported at market value?

a.   Pink plans to report the investment as a held-for-trading investment, and the decline in market value is believed to be temporary.

b.   Pink plans to report the investment as a held-for-trading investment, and the decline in market value is believed to be permanent.

c.   Pink plans to report the investment as a significant influence investment, and the decline in market value is believed to be temporary.

d.   Pink plans to report the investment as a significant influence investment, and the decline in market value is believed to be permanent.

(CGA-Canada adapted)

Use the following data for Questions 14 and 15.

On January 1, Year 5, Xanadu Co. purchased a 20% interest in Zap Inc. for $4,000,000. In Year 5, Zap reported net income from operations of $525,000 and an extraordinary gain of $83,000 (net of tax). Zap declared and paid dividends of $90,000 on December 31, Year 5.

14.   Assume the above is an available-for-sale investment without a quoted market price. Which of the following is the amount that would be reported on Xanadu's Year 5 income statement relating to Zap?

a.   Investment income of $116,600.

b.   Dividend income of $90,000.

c.   Investment income of $105,000 and investment gain extraordinary item of $16,600.

d.   Dividend income of $18,000.

15.   Assume the above is a significant influenced investment. Which of the following is the amount that would be reported on Xanadu's Year 5 income statement relating to Zap?

a.   Investment income of $121,600 and investment gain extraordinary item of $16,600.

b.   Investment income of $121,600.

c.   Investment income of $105,000 and investment gain extraordinary item of $16,600.

d.   Dividend income of $18,000.

16.   Price Co. has gradually been acquiring shares of Berry Co. and now owns 37% of the outstanding voting common shares. The remaining 63% of the shares are held by members of the family of the company founder. To date, the family has elected all members of the board of directors, and Price Co. has not been able to obtain a seat on the board. Price is hoping eventually to buy a block of shares from an elderly family member and thus one day own 60%. The shares of Berry Co. are not traded in an active market.

How should the investment in Berry Co. be reported in the financial statements of Price Co.?

a.   Consolidation.

b.   Cost method.

c.   Equity method.

d.   Fair value method.

(CGA-Canada adapted)

17.   PCI is a distributor of maintenance equipment. Early in Year 5, PCI acquired 165,000 voting shares of Duracom (a 25% voting interest) for a total consideration of $165,000. PCI is one of Duracom's major customers. PCI invested in Duracom to ensure a degree of stability in the price and

quality of its supplies and is able to exercise significant influence. In Year 5 and Year 6, Duracom earned a net income of $60,000 and $80,000 respectively, and declared annual dividends of $40,000 to holders of voting shares. On December 31, Year 6, the fair market value of Duracom's shares was $0.90 per share. On March 15, Year 7, when PCI's financial statements were finalized, Duracom shares were trading at $1.10.

How should PCI report its investment in Duracom in its balance sheet as at December 31, Year 6?

a. At $148,500, with the $165,000 cost of the purchase presented as additional information.

b. At $165,000, with the market value of the shares presented as additional information.

c. At $180,000, with no additional information presented about market value.

d. At $181,500, with the $165,000 cost of the purchase presented as additional information.

(CGA-Canada adapted)

18. Which is true for differential reporting?

a. It allows a company to use non-GAAP financial reporting.

b. It is applicable to all sections of the *CICA Handbook*.

c. It was introduced so that the cost of providing information to the users of financial statement information is not greater than the benefits provided.

d. It is available to all corporations in Canada.

19. A qualifying enterprise

a. is one that may not use differential reporting options.

b. is one that is non-public and has received the consent of the majority of its owners to use differential reporting options.

c. is one that is non-public and has received the consent of all of its owners to use differential reporting options.

d. is one that is public and has received the consent of all of its owners to use differential reporting options.

20. DER Ltd. has owned 10% of LAS Company for several years but did not have significant influence over LAS. DER recently purchased an additional 20% of LAS and now has significant influence. How will this change be reported by DER?

a. A cumulative effect of an accounting change is shown in the current income statement.

b. A cumulative effect of an accounting change is shown in the statement of retained earnings.

c. The equity method should be used starting from the date of the 20% acquisition.

d. DER can use either the cost method or equity method to account for the change in ownership.

CASES

Case 1   Floyd's Specialty Foods Inc. (FSFI) operates over 60 shops throughout Ontario. The company was founded by George Floyd when he opened a single shop in the city of Cornwall. This store sold prepared dinners and directed its products at customers who were too busy to prepare meals after a long day at work. The concept proved to be very successful and more stores were opened in Cornwall. Recently new stores were opened in five other Ontario cities. Up to the current year, the shares of FSFI have been owned entirely by Floyd. However during this year, the company suffered severe cash flow problems, due to too-rapid expansion exacerbated by a major decline in economic activity. Profitability suffered and creditors threatened to take legal action for long-overdue accounts. To avoid bankruptcy, Floyd sought additional financing from his old friend James Connelly, who is a majority shareholder of Cornwall Autobody Inc. (CAI). Subsequently, CAI paid $950,000 cash to FSFI to acquire enough newly issued shares of common stock for a one-third interest.

At the end of this year, CAI's accountants are discussing how they should properly report this investment in the company's financial statements.

One argues for maintaining the asset at original cost, saying, "What we have done is to advance money to bail out these stores. Floyd will continue to run the organization with little or no attention to us, so in effect we have loaned him money. After all, what does anyone in our company know about the specialty food business? My guess is that as soon as the stores become solvent, Floyd will want to buy back our shares."

Another accountant disagrees, stating that the equity method is appropriate. "I realize that our company is not capable of running a specialty food company. But the rules state that ownership of over 20 percent is evidence of significant influence."

A third accountant supports equity method reporting for a different reason. "If the investment gives us the ability to exert significant influence, that is all that is required. We don't have to actually exert it. One-third of the common shares certainly gives us that ability."

Required:

How should Cornwall Autobody Inc. report its investment? Your answer should include a discussion of all three accountants' positions.

Case 2   Magno Industries Ltd. is a major supplier to the automotive replacement parts market, selling parts to nearly every segment of the industry. Magno has a September 30 year-end.

During January Year 5, Magno acquired a 13 percent interest in the common stock of Grille-to-Bumper Automotive Stores and in June Year 5 it acquired an additional 15 percent. Grille-to-Bumper is a retail chain of company-owned automotive replacement part stores operating in most Canadian provinces. Its shares are not traded in an active market. Grille-to-Bumper has a December 31 year-end and, despite being profitable each year for the last 10 years, has never paid a dividend. While Magno occasionally makes sales to Grille-to-Bumper, it has never been one of its major suppliers.

After the second acquisition of Grille-to-Bumper's shares, Magno Industries contacted Grille-to-Bumper to obtain certain financial information and to discuss mutual timing problems with respect to financial reporting. In the initial contact, Magno found Grille-to-Bumper to be uncooperative. In addition, Grille-to-Bumper accused Magno of attempting to take it over. Magno replied that it had no intention of attempting to gain control, but rather was only interested in making a sound long-term investment. Grille-to-Bumper was not impressed with this explanation and refused to have any further discussions regarding future information exchanges and the problems created by a difference in year-ends.

At the year-end of September 30, Year 5, Magno's management expressed a desire to use the equity method to account for its investment. On that date, the value of its investment in Grille-to-Bumper common stock had declined by 8.5 percent over its acquisition cost.

Required:

a. What method of accounting would you recommend Magno Industries use for its investment in Grille-to-Bumper Automotive common stock? As part of your answer, discuss the alternatives available.

b. Why would the management of Magno want to use the equity method to account for the investment, as compared to other alternatives that you have discussed?

c. Are there any circumstances under which the method you have recommended might have to be changed? If so, how would Magno Industries account for such a change?

Case 3   On January 1, Year 6, Progress Technologies Inc. acquired 40 percent (10,000 shares) of the voting shares of the Calgana Corp. Toward the end of Year 6, it seemed likely that Progress would have earnings for the year of approximately $10,000 (exclusive of earnings attributed to its investment in Calgana) and that Calgana would have earnings of approximately $50,000. The CEO of Progress was disappointed in the forecast earnings of both companies. Prior to Year 6, Progress had increased its earnings by 10 percent each year, and Progress would have to report total earnings in Year 6 of $45,000 if the trend was to continue.

Required:

a. Suppose Progress Technologies Inc. reports its interest in Calgana Corp. using the equity method.
   (1) If Calgana is to declare its usual dividend of $.50 per share, what would be the total reported income of Progress?
   (2) The CEO of Progress suggested that Calgana be directed to declare a special dividend of $3 per share. What impact would the additional dividend have on the reported earnings of Progress?

b. Suppose that Progress Technologies Inc. reports its investment in Calgana Corp. using the cost method.
   (1) What would be the total reported earnings of Progress if Calgana declared its regular dividend of $.50 per share?
   (2) What impact would the additional dividend of $3 per share have on reported earnings of Progress?

c. Explain fully why the equity method (rather than the cost method) is appropriate for firms that can exert significant influence over other companies in which they have an interest.

Case 4   In the course of the audit of King Limited (King), CA, while reviewing the draft financial statements for the year ended August 31, Year 17, noticed that King's investment in Queen Limited (Queen) was valued on the cost basis. In Year 16, it had been valued on the equity basis. Representing a 22 percent interest in Queen, this investment had been made 10 years ago to infuse fresh equity, with a view to protecting King's source of supply for drugs.

King's controller informed CA that Queen had suffered a large loss in Year 17, as shown by the May interim financial statements. King's representative on Queen's board of directors had resigned because King's purchases from Queen now constitute less than 5 percent of its total purchases. In addition, Queen had been uncooperative in providing profit data in time to make the year-end equity adjustment. Consequently, King's controller had revised the method of accounting for the investment in Queen.

CA then found out that King's managers are planning a share issue in Year 18 and do not want their earnings impaired by Queen's poor performance. However, they are reluctant to divest themselves of Queen in case the rumoured development by Queen of a vaccine for a serious viral disease materializes.

When CA approached Queen's managers, they refused to disclose any information on Queen's operations. CA then learned from a stockbroker friend that Queen's poor results were due to its market being undercut by generic drug manufacturers. The loss had been increased when Queen's management wrote off most of Queen's intangible assets. CA summarized the relevant information on the treatment of the investment for his audit file (Exhibit I).

Required:

Discuss how King should report its investment in Queen and describe what should be disclosed in the notes to the Year 17 financial statements. Assume that King and Queen are public companies.

(CICA-adapted)

EXHIBIT I

CA'S NOTES ON KING'S INVESTMENT IN QUEEN'S SHARES

Extracts from King's draft financial statements for the year ended August 31, Year 17, in thousands of dollars, follow:

	Year 17	Year 16
Investment in Queen (Note 1)	$25,000	$27,400
Retained Earnings:		
Opening balance	$ 6,500	$ 2,350
plus: net earnings	4,500	7,300
	11,000	9,650
less: prior period adjustment (Note 2)	2,400	-
dividends	2,250	3,150
Closing balance	$ 6,350	$ 6,500

Note 1:
The investment in Queen originally cost $25 million. The carrying value under the equity method at the end of Year 16 was $27.4 million. The equity adjustment for Year 16 involved the elimination of King's share of the $5 million unrealized profit included in ending inventory, on sales from Queen to King.

Note 2:
In the nine months ended May 31, Year 17, Queen reported a net loss of $140 million after writing off development and patent costs as extraordinary items. At the end of Year 17, King changed its method of accounting for the investment from the equity method to the cost method and reduced the investment account from $27.4 million back to its original cost of $25 million. The unrealized profit in King's ending inventory for Year 17 amounts to $1 million. King has not made any adjustment for its share of this unrealized profit in the investment account.

Stock market trading in Queen's common shares has been heavy in the last year. Prices were as follows:

August 31, Year 16	$20.00
February 28, Year 17	5.00
August 31, Year 17	13.00

King owns 2,000,000 common shares of Queen. Queen did not pay any dividends in Year 16 or Year 17.

PROBLEMS

Problem 1   *PART A*

On January 1, Year 5, Anderson Corporation paid $650,000 for 20,000 (20%) of the outstanding shares of Carter Inc. The investment was considered to be one of significant influence. The balance sheet of Carter showed net assets of $3,000,000 on this date. Any purchase discrepancy was allocated to equipment with a remaining life of 10 years. In Year 5, Carter reported earnings of $95,000; in Year 6 its earnings were $105,000. Dividends paid were $50,000 in each of the two years.

Required:

(a) Calculate the balance in Anderson's investment account as at December 31, Year 6.

PART B

Now assume that on December 31, Year 6, Anderson lost its ability to significantly influence the operating, investing, and financing decisions for Carter when another party obtained sufficient shares in the open market to obtain control over Carter. Accordingly, the investment in Carter was reclassified to an available-for-sale investment. The fair value of the Carter shares was $35 per share on this date.

In Year 7, Carter reported earnings of $115,000 and paid dividends of $50,000. On December 31, Year 7, Anderson sold its investment in Carter for $37 per share.

Required:

(a) Prepare the journal entry at December 31, Year 6 to reclassify the investment from significant influence to available-for-sale.
(b) Prepare all journal entries for Year 7 related to Anderson's investment in Carter.

Problem 2   Baskin purchased 20,000 common shares (20%) of Robbin on January 1, Year 5, for $275,000 and classified the investment as available-for-sale. Robbin reported earnings of $85,000 in Year 5 and $90,000 in Year 6 and paid dividends of $40,000 in each year. Robbin's shares were trading at $15 per share on December 31, Year 5, and January 1, Year 6. On January 1, Year 6, Baskin obtained significant influence over the operating, investing, and financing decisions of Robbin when the controlling shareholder sold some shares in the open market and lost control over Carter. Accordingly, the investment in Carter was reclassified to a significant-influence investment. On January 1, Year 6, Robbin's shareholders' equity was $1,250,000 and Robbin owned a building which was undervalued by $80,000 and had a remaining useful life of 8 years. On December 31, Year 6, Baskin sold its investment in Robbin for $16 per share.

Required:

Prepare all journal entries for Years 5 and 6 related to Baskin's investment in Robbin.

Problem 3   Big Corp. owns 30% of Small Inc. On the last day of the current year, Small buys inventory at a cost of $90,000 and sells it to Big for $115,000 cash. Big is still holding this inventory. Assume a 40% tax rate and that the shares of Small are not traded in an active market.

Required:

Prepare the journal entry relating to this transaction that Big should make at the end of the current year, assuming that this is:
(a) an available-for-sale investment.

(b) a significant influence investment.

Problem 4   On January 1, Year 5, Blake Corporation purchased 30% of the outstanding common shares of Stergis Limited for $1,500,000. On that date the net assets of Stergis had a book value of $4,800,000, and all of the individual assets of Stergis had fair values that were equal to their book values except for:

	Fair value	Book value
Buildings (remaining life 10 years)	$1,068,000	$984,000

The following relates to Stergis since the acquisition date:

Year	Net income	Dividends paid
Year 5	$ 42,000	$60,000
Year 6	120,000	60,000

Required:

(a) Assume that the number of shares held by Blake is enough to give it significant influence over Stergis. Prepare all the journal entries that Blake should make regarding this investment in Year 5 and Year 6.

(b) Assume that Blake uses the cost method to account for its investment. Prepare all the journal entries that Blake should make regarding this investment in Year 5 and Year 6.

Problem 5   Poole Corp. owns 45% of Campbell Company, which enables it to exercise significant influence over that company. During the current year the companies sold merchandise to each other. At the end of the current year a portion of this merchandise remained in the inventory of both companies.

Required:

(a) How is the amount of unrealized profit calculated?

(b) What is the distinction between an upstream transfer and a downstream transfer?

(c) Does the direction (upstream or downstream) affect the amount of profit held back?

(d) Explain how Poole would calculate the amount of investment income to recognize this year.

(e) Explain how Poole would calculate the amount of investment income next year.

(f) Suppose that none of the merchandise transferred between the two companies remained in inventory at the end of the current year, but each company recorded a substantial profit in its sales to the other company. Would the fact that these transfers were made during the year affect how the equity method was applied?

(g) How would these intercompany transfers affect the financial reporting in the current year by Campbell?

Problem 6   On January 1, Year 6, Harley Company paid $55,000 for a 40% interest in Davis Inc. when Davis Inc. had total equity of $110,000. Davis reported earnings of $30,000 for Year 6 and declared dividends of $18,000 on December 31, Year 6.

Required:

Prepare the journal entries to record these facts on the books of Harley:

(1) assuming the cost method is used to account for the investment.

(2) assuming the equity method is used to account for the investment (any difference between investment cost and book value acquired is to be assigned to equipment and amortized over a 10-year life).

Problem 7 On January 1, Year 1, Crown Ltd. purchased 25% of the outstanding shares of Head Corp. The cost of the investment was $195,000, and the shareholders' equity of Head amounted to $510,000 on this date. Crown plans to treat any difference between the investment's cost and the proportionate share of the shareholders' equity of Head as equipment to be amortized on a straight-line basis over five years.

Head Corp. has a December 31 year-end. Its income statements for the next two years showed the following:

	Year 1	Year 2
Net income (loss) before extraordinary items	$310,000	$(70,000)
Extraordinary gain (net of tax)	55,000	—
Net income (loss)	$365,000	$(70,000)

On December 31 in each of Years 1 and 2, Head paid dividends of $80,000.

Required:

(a) Prepare Crown's journal entries in each of the two years, assuming that this is a significant influence investment.

(b) Prepare Crown's journal entries in each of the two years, assuming that it uses the cost method.

Problem 8 On January 1, Year 5, Donatello Inc. acquired 30% of the outstanding voting shares of Nestell Corp. for $400,000. The balance sheet of Nestell and the fair value of its assets and liabilities on this date were as follows:

	Book value	Fair value
Accounts receivable	$ 200,000	$200,000
Inventory	300,000	300,000
Plant assets (net)	800,000	860,000
	$1,300,000	
Liabilities	$ 100,000	100,000
Common shares	700,000	
Retained earnings	500,000	
	$1,300,000	

Nestell's plant assets had a remaining life of 10 years on this date.

The following are the income statements of the two companies for the year ended December 31, Year 5, prior to Donatello accounting for any income from its investment in Nestell:

	Donatello	Nestell
Sales	$900,000	$700,000
Operating expenses (including tax)	600,000	500,000
Net income from continuing operations	300,000	200,000
Extraordinary gain (loss)(net of tax)	25,000	(80,000)
Net income	$325,000	$120,000

On December 31, Year 5, Donatello received a dividend from Nestell amounting to $30,000. Because the company's accountant was not certain how to properly record it, an account called "suspense" was credited with $30,000.

Required:

PART A

Assume that this is a significant influence investment requiring the equity method of accounting.

(1) Prepare all the journal entries with regard to this investment that Donatello Inc. would be required to make in Year 5.

(2) Prepare a summarized income statement for Donatello, taking into account the journal entries in (1) above.

PART B

Assume that this is an available-for-sale investment requiring the cost method of accounting.

(1) Prepare all the journal entries with regard to this investment that Donatello would be required to make in Year 5.

(2) Prepare a summarized income statement for Donatello taking into account the journal entries in (1) above.

Problem 9 Crown Inc. owns 35% of the shares of Jewel Corp. and has the ability to significantly influence the operations and decision making of that company. On January 1, Year 5, the balance in the investment in Jewel account was $340,000. Amortization associated with the investment was $12,000 per year. On December 31, Year 5, Jewel reported earnings of $85,000 and declared dividends of $20,000. In Year 4, Jewel had sold inventory costing $24,000 to Crown for $40,000. This merchandise was still on hand in Crown's inventory at December 31, Year 4, and was finally sold to Crown's outside customers in Year 5. During Year 5, Crown sold inventory to Jewel and recorded a profit of $50,000 on the transaction. On December 31, Year 5, 30% of this inventory was still on hand. Assume a 40% tax rate.

The following summarized income statement was prepared by the accountant for Crown Inc. before any equity method journal entries were prepared with respect to the investment in Jewel.

CROWN INC.
INCOME STATEMENT — YEAR 5

Sales	$997,000
Operating expenses (including income tax)	625,000
Net income	$372,000

Required:

(a) Prepare a summarized income statement for Crown after the investment in Jewel has been accounted for in accordance with GAAP.

(b) What is the balance in the investment account at the end of Year 5?

Problem 10 Pender Corp. paid $234,000 for a 30% interest in Saltspring Limited on January 1, Year 6, when Saltspring's shareholders' equity consisted of $600,000 capital stock and $240,000 retained earnings. The price paid by Pender reflected the fact that Saltspring's inventory was overvalued by $60,000. The overvalued inventory items were sold in Year 6. During Year 6 Saltspring paid dividends of $100,000 and reported income as follows:

Income before extraordinary items	$290,000
Extraordinary loss (net of tax)	30,000
Net income	$260,000

Pender Corp.'s net income for Year 6 consisted of $900,000 sales, expenses of $600,000, and its investment income from Saltspring. The shares of Saltspring are not traded in an active market.

Required

PART A

Assume that Pender's investment is significant influence.

(1) Prepare all journal entries necessary to account for Pender's investment for Year 6.
(2) Determine the correct balance in Pender's investment account at December 31, Year 6.
(3) Prepare an income statement for Pender for Year 6.

PART B

Assume that Pender's investment would be considered available for sale.

(1) Prepare all journal entries necessary to account for Pender's investment for Year 6.
(2) Determine the correct balance in Pender's investment account at December 31, Year 6.
(3) Prepare an income statement for Pender for Year 6.

Problem 11　On January 1, Year 1, Parkade Company purchased, for $89,000, 35% of the outstanding voting shares of Summit Company. The following is Summit's balance sheet at that date:

	Book value
Cash	$ 20,000
Accounts receivable	30,000
Equipment (net)	80,000
	$130,000
Accounts payable	$ 10,000
Common stock	20,000
Retained earnings	100,000
	$130,000

Book values were equal to fair values except for equipment, which had a net fair value of $100,000. Summit is depreciating the equipment on a straight-line basis, and the remaining life is 7 years. Summit reported profits and paid dividends as follows:

	Profits	Dividends
Year 1	$10,000	$ 5,000
Year 2	15,000	15,000
Year 3	20,000	30,000

Required:

(a) Calculate the amount of goodwill at the date of acquisition of this investment.
(b) Calculate the balance in Parkade Company's investment account at the end of Year 3 if the equity method is used.
(c) Calculate the balance in this account at the end of Year 3 if the cost method is used.

(CGA-Canada, from 2002 to 2007)

Problem 12　Her Company purchased 20,000 common shares (20%) of Him Inc. on January 1, Year 4 for $340,000. On that date, the shareholders' equity of Him was $1,700,000. Additional information on Him for the 3 years ending December 31, Year 6, is as follows:

Year	Net Income	Dividends Paid	Market Value per Share at December 31
Year 4	$200,000	$150,000	$18
Year 5	225,000	160,000	20
Year 6	240,000	175,000	23

On December 31, Year 6, Her sold its investment in Him for $460,000.

Required:

(a) Compute the balance in the investment account at the end of Year 5 assuming that the investment is classified as:
   (i)   Available-for-sale (and market value is readily available).
   (ii) Available-for-sale (and market value is not readily available).
   (iii) Held-for-trading.
   (iv) Held for significant influence.

(b) Calculate how much income will be reported in net income and other comprehensive income in each of Years 4, 5, and 6, and in total for the three years assuming that the investment is classified as:
   (i)   Available-for-sale (and market value is readily available).
   (ii) Available-for-sale (and market value is not readily available).
   (iii) Held-for-trading.
   (iv) Held for significant influence.

(c) What are the similarities and differences in your answers for the four parts of (b)?

Problem 13   COX Limited is a multinational telecommunication company owned by a Canadian businesswoman. It has numerous long-term investments in a wide variety of equity instruments. Prior to the new *Handbook* section on Financial Instruments — Recognition and Measurement, equity investments were reported using either the cost method, equity method, or on a consolidated basis. For fiscal years commencing after October 1, 2007, COX will need to apply the following *Handbook* sections:

Section 3855   Financial Instruments — Recognition and Measurement
Section 1530   Comprehensive Income

Under these *Handbook* sections, some investments will have to be reported at fair value at each reporting date. In turn, the unrealized gains will either be reported in net income or other comprehensive income. Since COX has considerable external financing through a number of Canadian banks, it does not use differential reporting in its general-purpose financial statements.

The CFO of COX has heard about these new reporting standards but has had limited time to study them in detail. He would like you to prepare a presentation on the new reporting requirements. He wants to understand how equity investments should be reported. More specifically, he wants to know:

• Which investments must be reported at fair value and what is the main rationale for this change in reporting.

• How to determine whether the unrealized gains are to be reported in net income or other comprehensive income and what is the main rationale for the difference in reporting.

• Which investments, if any, will still be reported using the cost method, equity method, or on a consolidated basis.

Required:

Prepare the slides for the presentation. Limit your presentation to six slides. Ignore the new *Handbook* section on Hedging. Your presentation should cover the reporting of (1) held-for-trading, (2) available-for-sale, (3) held-for-significant influence and (4) held-for-control investments.

(CGA-Canada, from 2002 to 2007)

Chapter **3** **Business Combinations**

LEARNING OBJECTIVES

After studying this chapter, you should be able to do the following:

- Define a business combination, and describe the two basic forms for achieving a business combination.
- Describe the current acceptable method of accounting for a business combination.
- Compare and contrast the acquisition and new entity methods.
- Prepare a balance sheet immediately after a purchase-of-net assets business combination, using the acquisition method.
- Prepare a balance sheet immediately after a purchase-of-shares business combination, using the acquisition method.
- Compare the balance sheet of the acquirer after a purchase-of-net assets business combination and the consolidated balance sheet after a purchase-of-shares business combination.
- Identify all factors that will determine if control exists.

INTRODUCTION

The parent is the controlling company and the subsidiary is the controlled company.

In Chapter 2 we examined the accounting for two types of long-term intercorporate investments: available-for-sale and significant influence. The next seven chapters are largely devoted to the accounting for a third type — long-term investments that enable the investor to control the investee. When one company obtains control of another company, a business combination has occurred. In such cases, GAAP requires that we prepare consolidated financial statements to combine the financial position and results of operations of the controlling company (the parent) and the controlled company (the subsidiary). A business combination also occurs when one enterprise acquires the net assets (acquires all of the assets and assumes all of the liabilities) of another enterprise.

There are many types of business combinations. A *conglomerate business combination* involves economic units operating in widely different industries. A *horizontal business combination* involves economic units whose products are similar. A *vertical business combination* involves economic units where the output from one can be used as input for

72

another.[1] Other terms that are often used synonymously with the term business combination are *takeover*, *amalgamation*, *acquisition*, and *merger*.

For a business combination to exist, one economic unit must control substantially all of the net assets of another economic unit. The purchase of some but not all of an entity's assets is not considered a business combination. While the units involved are usually incorporated, this is not a requirement for a business combination. Also, the units involved cannot have been under common control immediately before the combination. The transfer of assets or the exchange of shares between two subsidiaries of the same parent, or between a parent and its subsidiary, would not be considered a business combination.[2]

Business combinations are frequent events in Canada and the United States and throughout the world. Hardly a week passes without some reference in the press to actual or proposed takeovers and mergers.

Many people think that the typical takeover involves an American multinational swallowing up a smaller Canadian firm. But that is not always the case. In fact, figures for Canadian M&A activity show that Canadian acquisitions of foreign companies outpaced foreign acquisitions of Canadian companies from 2002 to 2004. However, in recent years, the tide has turned and many big-name Canadian companies have fallen under foreign control as indicated by the following:

- Falconbridge of Sudbury, Ontario, was acquired by Swiss-based Xstrata for $18 billion.
- Houston-based Kinder Morgan Inc. bought Vancouver-based utility company Terasen Inc. for $6.9 billion.
- Hamilton steelmaker Dofasco was purchased for $4.7 billion by Luxembourg-based Arcelor SA.
- Graphics chip-maker ATI Technologies of Markham, Ontario, was sold to California-based Advanced Micro Devices Inc. for $5.34 billion U.S.
- The Fairmont Hotel chain (the Chateau Frontenac, the Banff Springs hotel among others) was bought for $3.24 billion by an investor group led by a Saudi prince.
- Intrawest, owner of B.C.'s famed Whistler resort, was sold to a New York firm for $1.8 billion US.
- Vincor, Canada's largest winemaker, was sold to N.Y.-based Constellation Brands for $1.1 billion.
- The Hudson's Bay Co., owner of the Bay and Zellers, was taken private by South Carolina investor Jerry Zucker for $860 million.
- Sleeman Breweries of Guelph, Ontario, was bought by Japan's Sapporo Breweries for $400 million.
- Nickel giant, Inco, of Sudbury, Ontario, was sold to a company from Brazil for more than $19 billion to form one of the largest mining companies in the world.

Business combinations can be described as either friendly or hostile. Often a merger is initiated by one company submitting a formal tender offer to the

---

In a business combination, one company unites with or obtains control over another company.

Many big-name Canadian companies have been taken over by foreign companies in recent years.

---

[1] *Terminology for Accountants*, 4th edition, Toronto: CICA, 1992, p. 35.
[2] *CICA Handbook*, paragraph 1582.03.

shareholders of another company. In a friendly combination, the top management and the board of directors of the companies involved negotiate the terms
of the combination and then submit the proposal to the shareholders of both
companies along with a recommendation for approval. An unfriendly combination occurs when the board of directors of the target company recommends that
its shareholders reject the tender offer. The management of the target company
will often employ defences to resist the takeover. They include:

There are many tactics to resist takeover.

- *Poison pill.* This occurs when a company issues rights to its existing shareholders, exercisable only in the event of a potential takeover, to purchase additional shares at prices below market. Chapters attempted to use such a plan
  to squash Trilogy's takeover, but on appeal by Trilogy, the Ontario Securities
  Commission disallowed the poison pill.

- *Pac-man defence.* This involves the target company making an unfriendly
  countervailing takeover offer to the shareholders of the company that is
  attempting to take it over.

- *White knight.* In this case, the target company searches out another company that will come to its rescue with a more appealing offer for its shares.
  Example: In February 2001, it was reported that Anadarko Petroleum Corp.
  had agreed to buy Berkley Petroleum Corp. for $1.7 billion in cash in a friend-
  ly deal that outbid a hostile bid made by Hunt Oil Corp. Hunt had made an
  offer in December 2000, and Berkley's management scrambled to find a white
  knight after rejecting the offer and refusing to take it to their shareholders for
  approval.

- *Selling the crown jewels.* This involves selling certain desirable assets to other
  companies so the would-be acquirer loses interest.

In the next section of this chapter we discuss the two basic forms of business
combinations. The discussion then proceeds to the accounting for business combinations and the acceptable methods that have been used. We will then focus
on current GAAP in Canada.

Forms of Business Combinations

Essentially, there are only two forms of business combinations. One company can
obtain control over the net assets of another company by (a) purchasing its net assets,
or (b) acquiring enough of its voting shares to control the use of its net assets. In examining these two forms of combination, one must also consider closely the method of
payment used. Payment can be cash, or promises to pay cash in the future, or the issuance of shares, or some combination of these. As we will see later, the method of payment has a direct bearing on the determination of which company is the acquirer.

When purchasing assets, the transaction is carried out with the selling company.

Purchase of Assets   An obvious way to obtain control over another company's assets
is to purchase them outright. The selling company is left only with the cash or other
consideration received as payment from the purchaser, and the liabilities present
before the sale. Often, the acquirer purchases all of the assets of the acquiree and
assumes all its liabilities and records these assets and liabilities in its accounting
records. The shareholders of the selling company have to approve the sale, as well as
decide whether their company should be wound up or should continue operations.

Purchase of Shares   An alternative to the purchase of assets is for the acquirer to purchase enough voting shares from the shareholders of the acquiree that it can determine the acquiree's strategic operating, investing, and financing policies without the cooperation of others. This is the most common form of combination, and it is often achieved through a tender offer made by the management of the acquirer to the shareholders of the acquiree. These shareholders are invited to exchange their shares for cash or for shares of the acquirer company.

> **When purchasing shares, the transaction is consummated with the shareholders of the selling company.**

The share purchase form of combination is usually the least costly to the acquirer because control can be achieved by purchasing less than 100 percent of the outstanding voting shares. In addition, in Canada there can be important tax advantages to the vendor if shares rather than assets are sold.

Because the transaction is between the acquirer and the acquiree's shareholders, the acquiree's accounting for its assets and liabilities is not affected,[3] and this company carries on as a subsidiary of the acquirer. The acquirer becomes a parent company and therefore must consolidate its subsidiary when it prepares its financial statements.

> **The acquired company makes no journal entries when the acquiring company purchases shares.**

Both forms of business combination result in the assets and liabilities of the acquiree being combined with those of the acquirer. If control is achieved by purchasing net assets, the combining takes place in the accounting records of the acquirer. If control is achieved by purchasing shares, the combining takes place when the consolidated financial statements are prepared.

Variations   One variation from the two basic forms of business combination occurs when the companies involved agree to create a new company, which either purchases the net assets of the combining companies, or purchases enough shares from the shareholders of the combining companies to achieve control of these companies. While this may appear to be a third form of combination, the substance of the transaction indicates otherwise.

Another variation that can occur is a *statutory amalgamation*, whereby under the provisions of federal or provincial law, two or more companies incorporated under the same companies act can combine and continue as a single entity. The shareholders of the combining companies become shareholders of the surviving company, and the nonsurviving companies are wound up. The substance of a statutory amalgamation indicates that it is simply a variation of one of the basic forms. If only one of the companies survives, it is essentially a purchase of assets, with the method of payment being shares of the surviving company.

Methods of Accounting for Business Combinations

There are four methods of accounting for business combinations that have either been used in practice or discussed in theory over the years:
- the purchase method;
- the acquisition method;
- the pooling-of-interests method; and
- the new entity method.

---

[3] An exception to this occurs when the acquiree applies "push-down accounting." This topic is discussed in Chapter 4.

The following table indicates the current status and effective usage dates for these four methods:

Method	Status
Purchase method	Required GAAP prior to adoption of Acquisition method, which must be adopted by January 1, 2011 but can be adopted earlier
Acquisition method	New method must be adopted by January 1, 2011 but can be adopted earlier
Pooling-of-interests method	Acceptable in limited situations prior to July 1, 2001, but no longer acceptable
New entity method	Never achieved status as an acceptable method but worthy of future consideration

We will now briefly discuss the merits of these four methods.

Net assets of the acquired company are reported at the amount paid by the acquiring company under the purchase method.

Prior to 2011 (or sooner if Section 1582 is adopted earlier), but can be adopted earlier if one of the combining companies could be identified as the acquirer, the *purchase method* was used to account for the combination. Under this method, the acquiring company reported the net assets of the acquired company at the price that it paid. This price included any cash payment, the fair market value of any shares issued, and the present value of any promises to pay cash in the future. Any excess of the price paid over the fair value of the acquired company's identifiable net assets was recorded as goodwill. The fair values of the identifiable net assets acquired were systematically charged against earnings in the normal manner of expense matching. In addition, any goodwill was regularly reviewed for impairment and any impairment loss was reflected as a charge against earnings. As a result, the price paid for the acquired company was reflected as a deduction from the revenues generated from that company over time. This method of accounting was consistent with the historical cost principle of accounting for any assets acquired by a company. Such assets were initially recorded at the price paid for them, and subsequently their cost was charged against earnings over their useful lives.

Identifiable net assets of the acquired company are reported at their fair value under the acquisition method.

After January 1, 2011 (or sooner if Section 1582 is adopted earlier), if one of the combining companies can be identified as the acquirer, Section 1582 of the *CICA Handbook* requires that the *acquisition method* be used to account for the combination. Under this method, the acquiring company reports the *identifiable* net assets being acquired at the fair value of these net assets regardless of the amount paid for these net assets. When the purchase price is greater than the fair value of identifiable net assets, the excess is reported as goodwill similar to the purchase method. When the purchase price is less than the fair value of identifiable net assets, the identifiable net assets are still reported at fair value and the deficiency in purchase price is reported as a gain on purchase. This practice is not consistent with the historical cost principle where assets are reported at the amount paid for the assets. However, it is consistent with the general trend in financial reporting to use fair value more and more often to report assets and liabilities. We will illustrate the acquisition method in detail later in this chapter. Unless otherwise noted, all of the illustrations throughout this text and in the end-of-chapter material will use the acquisition method.

Prior to July 1, 2001, *the pooling-of-interests method* was used to account for those business combinations where an acquirer could not be identified. Pooling of interests could only be used when there was an exchange of shares between the combining companies and the shares were distributed in such a manner that an acquirer could not be identified. The idea behind pooling came from the concept of "a merger of equals," whereby the shareholders of the companies involved agreed to combine their companies. Under pooling, there was no concept of an acquired company, and so the accounting for the combination involved simply adding together the book values of the combining companies. This was justified by the argument that because they were simply carrying on the business of two (or more) former entities as one company, with no major disruptions in operations or key personnel, there was no need to revalue the assets of any of the entities. A major problem with this concept was determining if companies involved really were "equals."

Despite the fact that the pooling of interests is no longer accepted as a method of accounting for business combinations occuring after July 1, 2001, its effects on the financial statements of many large corporations in the United States and Canada will be felt for many years to come. Assets acquired in a combination often have lives ranging up to 20 or 30 years. Differences in yearly reported earnings between the two methods will exist during these time periods because of the fair value amortizations that have to take place under the acquisition method. A large portion of the acquisition price of a purchase business combination is typically allocated to goodwill. Eventually, earnings will reflect goodwill write-offs if impairment occurs. Under pooling this does not take place. Even though pooling is no longer acceptable, financial statement analysts will need to understand its accounting and its affects on financial statements well into the future. For further discussion and illustration of the pooling-of-interests method, see the Online Learning Centre associated with this text.

The fourth method, the *new entity method*, has been proposed in the past as an alternative to the pooling of interests. It has been suggested that a new entity has been created when two companies combine by the joining together of two ownership groups. As a result, the assets and liabilities contributed by the two combining companies should be reported by this new entity at their fair values. This method has received virtually no support because of the additional revaluation difficulties and costs that would result. Furthermore, it has been argued that if the owners were simply combining their interests, there would be no new invested capital and therefore no new entity created.

Net assets of the acquired company are reported at their net book value under the pooling-of-interests method.

The pooling method is not acceptable in Canada or the United States for business combinations occurring after July 1, 2001.

Net assets of both the acquiring company and acquired company are reported at their fair value under the new entity method.

DISCUSSION QUESTION

How Far Should We Extend This Fair Value Accounting?

On December 30, Year 7, Pepper Company agreed to form a business combination with Salt Limited. Pepper issued 2,320 of its common shares for all (2,900) of the outstanding common shares of Salt. This transaction increased the number of outstanding Pepper shares from 3,800 to 6,120. The market value of the shares was $50 per share for Pepper and $40 for Salt. The balance sheets for the two companies on this date were as follows (in 000s):

	Pepper		Salt	
	Book Value	Fair Value	Book Value	Fair Value
Identifiable assets	$200	$250	$100	$130
Goodwill	0	100	0	70
	$200	$350	$100	$200
Liabilities	$150	$160	$ 80	$ 84
Shareholders' equity	50	190	20	116
	$200	$350	$100	$200

Consolidated financial statements will be prepared to combine the financial statements for the two companies. The management of Pepper is concerned about not exceeding a debt to equity ratio of 3:1 because of a covenant in a borrowing agreement with its bank. It wants to see how these consolidated statements would differ under two different methods of reporting: acquisition and new entity. Management also has the following questions when reporting this business combination:

- Why, under the acquisition method, is one set of assets and liabilities adjusted to fair value whereas the other set is left at book value?

- Given that under the acquisition method we can measure and report the net assets at fair values at the date of acquisition, why would we not report fair values at each subsequent reporting date?

- Which balance sheet best reflects the economic reality of the business combination?

Provisions of Section 1582

Section 1582 of the *Handbook* outlines the accounting requirements for business combinations:

The acquisition method is required for all business combinations in Canada after January 1, 2011.

- All business combinations should be accounted for by applying the acquisition method.

- An acquirer should be identified for all business combinations.

- The acquisition date is the date the acquirer obtains control of the acquiree.

- The acquirer should measure the fair value of the acquiree, as a whole, as of the acquisition date. Unless there is evidence to the contrary, the fair value of the consideration given would be used to determine the fair value of the acquired business. Other business valuation techniques would be used to measure the fair value of the business acquired if no consideration is transferred, or if the consideration transferred does not represent the fair value of the business acquired. Certain business valuation techniques are referred to in Section 1582 but are beyond the scope of this book.

- The acquirer should generally measure the identifiable assets acquired and the liabilities assumed at fair value and report them separately from goodwill.

Identifying the Acquirer   Section 1582 outlines the requirements for identifying the company that is the acquirer in the business combination. This is important because it is the net assets of the acquiree that are reported at fair values. Considerations in determining which company is the acquirer are as follows:

- If the means of payment is cash or a promise to pay cash in the future, the acquirer has been identified as the company making the payment.

An acquirer must be identified for all business combinations.

- If shares are issued as a means of payment, a key element would be the relative holdings of the voting shares of the combined company by shareholders as a group of the combining companies. In a combination involving two companies, if one shareholder group holds more than 50 percent of the voting shares of the combined company, that company is the acquirer. If more than two companies are involved, the shareholder group that holds the largest number of voting shares identifies the company that is the acquirer.

- When an acquirer cannot seem to be determined by examining voting rights because each group of shareholders owns the same percentage, then the makeup of the board of directors and senior management is examined to see which company is dominant.

- When there has been a share exchange, the acquirer is often (but not always) the company that issues shares.

- The acquirer is often (but not always) the larger company.

After an acquirer has been identified, the acquisition cost has to be determined and then allocated to the assets and liabilities acquired.

Acquisition Cost   The acquisition cost is made up of:

The acquisition cost is measured as the fair value of consideration given to acquire the business.

- any cash paid
- the fair value of assets transferred
- the present value of any promises to pay cash in the future
- the fair market value of any shares issued. The value of shares is based on the market price of the shares over a reasonable period of time before and after the date of the combination.
- Contingent consideration. Contingent consideration is illustrated in Chapter 4.

The acquisition cost does not include related costs such as professional fees or costs of issuing shares.

The acquisition cost does not include costs such as fees for consultants, accountants, and lawyers. These costs do not increase the fair value of the acquired company and therefore should not be included in the values assigned to net assets acquired in the business combination. These costs would either be recorded as a deferred charge and amortized over a period in which the business combination is expected to provide future benefits or be expensed in the period of acquisition.

Costs incurred in issuing shares are also not considered part of the acquisition cost. These costs should be deducted from the amount recorded for the proceeds received for the share issue, e.g., deducted from common shares.

Allocation of the Acquisition Cost   The acquisition cost is allocated to the acquirer's interest[4] in the fair value of the identifiable assets and liabilities of the acquired

---

[4] This reference to the acquirer's interest applies only to the consolidation of a subsidiary that is less than 100 percent owned.

Identifiable assets and liabilities should be recorded separate from goodwill.

company. An identifiable asset is not necessarily one that is presently recorded in the records of the acquiree company. For example, the acquiree company may have patent rights that have a definite market value but are not shown on the balance sheet because they have been developed internally. Or the acquiree's balance sheet may show a pension asset, though an up-to-date actuarial valuation may make it necessary to report a net pension obligation.

The *Handbook* directs the management of the acquirer to make a strong effort to recognize and measure unrecorded intangible assets of the acquired company with the following statement:

> An intangible asset is identifiable when
> (a) the asset arises from contractual or other legal rights (even if the asset is not transferable or separable from the acquiree or from other rights and obligations); or
> (b) is capable of being separated or divided from the acquiree and sold, transferred, licensed, rented, or exchanged, either individually or together with a related contract, asset, or liability (even if there is no intent to do so).

Paragraphs A27 to A61 of the appendix to *Handbook* Section 1582 provide additional guidance along with an extensive list of possible intangibles that would satisfy the recognition criteria.

It has been implied in the past that a large portion of the acquisition cost in a business combination ends up as goodwill. This is because the amount recorded as goodwill is often made up of a mixture of goodwill itself plus intangible assets that were not identified and measured. It will be interesting to see if this additional guidance results in a better measure of goodwill.

Not all assets and liabilities on the balance sheet of the acquired entity are considered identifiable. Future income tax assets and liabilities are not fair valued and carried forward. Instead, new amounts for future tax assets and liabilities become part of the allocation of the acquisition cost. Because of the added complexity that this brings, discussion and illustration of this topic is saved until a later chapter.

Goodwill is the excess of the purchase price over the fair value of identifiable assets and liabilities.

If the acquisition cost is greater than the acquirer's interest in the identifiable assets and liabilities acquired, the excess is recorded in the acquirer's financial statements as goodwill. In theory, goodwill represents the amount paid for excess earning power; in practice, it represents the premium paid to achieve control.

Negative goodwill could result in the reporting of a gain on purchase by the acquiring company.

If the acquisition cost is less than the fair value of the identifiable net assets acquired, we have what is sometimes described as a "negative goodwill" situation. This negative goodwill is accounted for by reducing the amount of the goodwill that otherwise would be recognized for the acquired company. If the goodwill related to that business combination is reduced to zero, any remaining excess is recognized as a gain attributable to the acquirer on the acquisition date. We will illustrate the accounting for negative goodwill in Chapter 4.

Financial Reporting After the Combination The net income generated by the net assets of the acquired company is reported in the financial statements of the acquirer commencing with the date of acquisition. The expenses used to arrive at this income must be based on the amortizations of the fair values used and any goodwill losses due to impairment. Prior years' comparative financial statements are not retroactively changed to reflect the combination.

Illustrations of Business Combination Accounting

To illustrate the accounting involved using the acquisition method, we will use the summarized balance sheets of two companies. Summarized statements are used here so that we can focus completely on the broad accounting concepts. In later examples, detailed statements will be used. Exhibit 3.1 presents the December 31, Year 1, balance sheets of the two companies that are party to a business combination.

Because the identification of an acquirer requires the analysis of shareholdings after the combination, Notes 1 and 2 are presented in the exhibit to identify the shareholders of each company as belonging to two distinct groups.

A Company Ltd. will initiate the takeover of B Corporation. The first two illustrations will involve the purchase of net assets with cash and the issuance of shares as the means of payment. Later illustrations will have A Company purchasing enough shares of B Corporation to obtain control over that company's net assets, and will introduce the preparation of consolidated statements.

Exhibit 3.1

Company A and Company B are separate legal entities.

A COMPANY LTD.
BALANCE SHEET
December 31, Year 1

Assets	$300,000
Liabilities	$120,000
Shareholders' equity	
Common stock (5,000 shares) (Note 1)	100,000
Retained earnings	80,000
	$300,000

Note 1
The shareholders of the 5,000 common shares issued and outstanding are identified as Group X.

B CORPORATION
BALANCE SHEET
December 31, Year 1

Assets	$ 88,000
Liabilities	$ 30,000
Shareholders' equity	
Common stock (——— shares) (Note 2)	25,000
Retained earnings	33,000
	$ 88,000

The fair values of B Corporation's identifiable assets and liabilities are as follows as at December 31, Year 1:

Fair value of assets	$109,000
Fair value of liabilities	29,000
Fair value of net assets	$ 80,000

Note 2
The shareholders of the common shares of B Corporation are identified as Group Y.
The actual number of shares issued and outstanding has been purposely omitted because this number would have no bearing on the analysis required later.

Purchase of Assets

In the following independent illustrations, A Company offers to buy all assets and to assume all liabilities of B Corporation. The management of B Corporation accepts the offer.

Illustration 1   Assume that on January 1, Year 2, A Company pays $95,000 in cash to B Corporation for all of the net assets of that company, and that no direct expenses are involved. Because cash is the means of payment, A Company is the acquirer. The acquisition cost is allocated in the following manner:

Purchase price	$95,000
Fair value of net assets acquired	80,000
Difference — goodwill	$15,000

A Company would make the following journal entry to record the acquisition of B Corporation's net assets:

The acquiring company records the assets purchased on its own books at fair value.

Assets (in detail)	109,000	
Goodwill	15,000	
Liabilities (in detail)		29,000
Cash		95,000

A Company's balance sheet after the business combination would be as shown at the bottom of this page.

Using the acquisition method to account for the business combination, the identifiable net assets acquired were recorded at fair values, with the purchase price difference recorded as goodwill. The balance sheet of A Company is not a consolidated balance sheet. But note that if A Company had paid $95,000 cash for 100 percent of the common shares of B Corporation, the consolidated balance prepared immediately after the business combination would be identical to the one shown below. (See Exhibit 3.2 on page 90.)

A COMPANY LTD.
BALANCE SHEET
January 1, Year 2

The acquiring company's own assets and liabilities are not revalued when it purchases the net assets of the acquired company.

Assets (300,000 – 95,000* + 109,000)	$314,000
Goodwill	15,000
	$329,000
Liabilities (120,000 + 29,000)	$149,000
Shareholders' equity	
Common stock	100,000
Retained earnings	80,000
	$329,000

* $95,000 cash paid by A Company to B Corporation

While this illustration focuses on the balance sheet of A Company immediately after the business combination, it is also useful to look at B Corporation in order to see the effect of this economic event on that company. The balance sheet of B Corporation immediately after the sale of all of its net assets follows.

The selling company records the sale of its net assets on its own books.

B CORPORATION LTD.
BALANCE SHEET
January 1, Year 2

Cash	$95,000

Shareholders' equity	
Common stock	$25,000
Retained earnings (33,000 + 37,000*)	70,000
	$95,000

The gain on sale of the net assets amounts to $37,000 ($95,000 − $58,000).

The management of B Corporation must now decide the future of their company. They could decide to invest the company's cash in productive assets and carry on in some other line of business. Alternatively, they could decide to wind up the company and distribute the sole asset (cash) to the shareholders.

Illustration 2   Assume that on January 1, Year 2, A Company issues 4,000 common shares, with a market value of $23.75 per share, to B Corporation as payment for the company's net assets. B Corporation will be wound up after the sale of its net assets. Because the method of payment is shares, the following analysis is made to determine which company is the acquirer.

	Shares of A Company
Group X now holds	5,000
Group Y will hold (when B Corporation is wound up)	4,000
	9,000

The acquirer is determined based on which shareholder group controls Company A after B Corporation is wound up.

Group X will hold 5/9 (56 percent) of the total shares of A Company after the combination, and Group Y will hold 4/9 (44 percent) of this total after the dissolution of B Corporation. Because one shareholder group holds more than 50 percent of the voting shares, an acquirer has been identified. The purchase price is allocated in the following manner:

Purchase price (4,000 shares @ $23.75)	$95,000
Fair value of net assets acquired	80,000
Difference — goodwill	$15,000

A Company would make the following journal entry to record the acquisition of B Corporation's net assets and the issuance of 4,000 common shares at fair value on January 1, Year 2:

Assets (in detail)	109,000	
Goodwill	15,000	
Liabilities (in detail)		29,000
Common stock		95,000

A Company's balance sheet after the business combination would be as follows:

A COMPANY LTD.
BALANCE SHEET
January 1, Year 2

The acquiring company's recently purchased assets are recorded at fair value and the old assets are retained at book value.

Assets (300,000 + 109,000)	$409,000
Goodwill	15,000
	$424,000
Liabilities (120,000 + 29,000)	$149,000
Shareholders' equity	
Common stock (100,000 + 95,000)	195,000
Retained earnings	80,000
	$424,000

This balance sheet was prepared by combining the book values of A Company's assets and liabilities with the fair values of those of B Corporation.

B Corporation's balance sheet immediately following the sale of its net assets is reproduced below:

B CORPORATION
BALANCE SHEET
January 1, Year 2

The selling company records the sale of its net assets in exchange for shares of the acquiring company.

Investment in shares of A Company	$95,000
Shareholders' equity	
Common stock	$25,000
Retained earnings (33,000 + 37,000)	70,000
	$95,000

B Corporation is wound up and distributes the investment, consisting of 4,000 shares of A Company, to its shareholders (Group Y). The reason for winding up B Corporation should be intuitively obvious. B Corporation's sole asset is 4,000 of the issued shares of A Company. This single block represents a voting threat to A Company's shareholders (Group X). A Company will insist that B Corporation be wound up and distribute these 4,000 shares to its shareholders (Group Y), who presumably will not get together to determine how to vote them.

Control and Consolidated Financial Statements

Distinguish between separate entity financial statements and consolidated financial statements.

When a parent–subsidiary relationship is the result of a business combination, the two (or more) companies involved continue as separate legal entities, with each maintaining separate accounting records and producing separate financial statements. GAAP ignores this separate-company legal status and views the substance of the relationship as one that has created a single economic entity that should report as such.

The requirement for, and rationale behind, the preparation of consolidated financial statements is stated in Section 1590 of the *CICA Handbook* as follows:

> An enterprise should consolidate all of its subsidiaries. [1590.16]

> Consolidated financial statements recognize that, even though the parent and its subsidiaries may be separate legal entities, together they constitute a

Consolidated financial statements combine the financial statements of the parent and its subsidiaries as if they were one entity.

single economic unit. Such financial statements provide the most appropriate basis for informing users of the parent's financial statements about the resources and results of operations of the parent and its subsidiaries as a group. This presentation, supplemented by segment information prepared in accordance with "Segment Disclosures," Section 1701, and any other information necessary for fair presentation in accordance with generally accepted accounting principles, is more informative to the shareholders than separate financial statements of the parent and each of its subsidiaries. [1590.17]

The following definitions have been adopted for purposes of Section 1590:

(a) A *subsidiary* is an enterprise controlled by another enterprise (the parent) that has the right and ability to obtain future economic benefits from the resources of the enterprise and is exposed to the related risks.

(b) *Control* of an enterprise is the continuing power to determine its strategic operating, investing and financing policies without the co-operation of others. [1590.03]

When a parent company has control over one or more subsidiaries, it has the right to benefit economically from the subsidiaries' resources and at the same time is exposed to the related risks involved. Consolidated financial statements reflect a group of economic resources that are under the common control of the parent company even though these resources are owned separately by the parent and the subsidiary companies. Notice that the key concept is *common control*. This concept is reinforced in Section 1000 of the *Handbook*, where the definition of an asset focuses on control rather than ownership.[5] When control over a subsidiary is present, the parent is required to consolidate its subsidiaries for external reporting purposes. In other words, the parent and subsidiary will each prepare their own financial statements (which we will refer to as separate-entity financial statements). The consolidated financial statements are additional financial statements, which combine the separate-entity financial statements of the parent and subsidiary under the hypothetical situation that these two legal entities were operating as one single entity. The consolidated financial statements are prepared by the parent company and are often referred to as the third set of financial statements.

All intercompany transactions are eliminated in the preparation of the consolidated statements. As a result, these statements reflect only transactions of this single entity with those outside the entity. (The process required to eliminate these intercompany transactions will be discussed thoroughly in later chapters.)

Consolidated financial statements are prepared primarily for the benefit of the shareholders and creditors of the parent company.

Consolidated statements are considered more useful to financial statement users than would be the separate financial statements of all of the companies that make up the group. Present and prospective shareholders of the parent company are interested in future profitability and cash flows. Creditors of the parent company have interests and information needs similar to those of the shareholders. The profitability and financial health of the parent is directly related to that of the companies it controls.

While consolidated statements are considered the best vehicle to satisfy user needs, they also have limitations. A poor performance by certain subsidiaries can be hidden as a result of the aggregation process. In addition, many parent companies

---

[5] *CICA Handbook*, paragraph 1000.29.

The minority shareholders and creditors of the subsidiary find the separate-entity statement of the subsidiary more useful than the consolidated statements.

Control is the ability to determine the key policies of the subsidiary without the cooperation of others.

Owning greater than 50 percent of the voting shares usually, but not always, indicates control.

have subsidiaries in different industries in various countries throughout the world, and this can be hidden in a single set of statements. Footnote disclosures that present details about the companies' operating segments help to alleviate this problem. Finally, the information needs of minority shareholders and creditors of the subsidiary companies are not served by consolidated statements. This sector relies on the separate statements to determine the operating results and financial position of these companies.

How Is Control Determined?   As we have seen from the *Handbook* definition, control is the continuing power of one company to determine the strategic operating, investing, and financing policies of another company without the cooperation of others. The ability to exercise this power is all that is required; it is not necessary to actually exercise it. Because the board of directors establishes the strategic policies of a corporation, the ability to elect a majority of the members of the board would generally be evidence of control. Therefore, control is presumed to exist if the parent owns directly or indirectly enough voting shares to elect the majority of the board of directors of a subsidiary. Indirect control would exist if, for example, B Company controls C Company and C Company controls D Company. B Company has direct control over C Company and indirectly controls D Company. Consolidation when control is achieved through indirect holdings is discussed in Chapter 7.

In most situations, more than 50 percent of the voting shares are required to elect the majority of the board, and so control is presumed to exist if the percentage owned is over 50 percent. However, we have to look at all factors and at the same time keep in mind the phrase "without the cooperation of others."

For example, if A Company owns 60 percent of the voting shares of B Company and C Company owns the other 40 percent, then we can presume that A Company controls B Company. But if C Company owns convertible bonds of B Company or options or warrants to purchase B Company shares, which if converted or exercised would give C Company 62 percent of the outstanding shares of B Company, then A Company needs the cooperation of C Company not to convert or exercise. A Company does not have the continuing power to control without the cooperation of others.

There is also a presumption that a holding of less than 50 percent of the voting shares does not constitute control. This presumption can be overcome if other factors clearly indicate control. For example, an irrevocable agreement with other shareholders to convey voting rights to the parent would constitute control, even when the parent owned less than 50 percent of the voting shares. A parent may also have control despite owning less than 50 percent of the voting shares if its holdings of rights, warrants, convertible debt, or convertible preferred shares would give it enough voting power to control the board of directors of the subsidiary. Exercise or conversion would not be necessary, only the right to exercise or convert.

It is also possible for a parent to have control without a majority share ownership if it also has agreements in writing the nature of which allow it to dictate subsidiary operating policies and which result in it receiving fees, royalties, and profits from intercompany sales.

> A parent's control over a subsidiary and its exposure to risks and rewards associated with the subsidiary's resources, though normally acquired through an equity interest in the subsidiary, may be acquired by other means. The form

in which a parent controls a subsidiary and receives economic benefits from it does not determine the substance of their relationship.[1590.06]

A parent could have control with less than 50 percent of the voting shares when contractual agreements give the parent control.

One parent could have control with less than 50 percent of the voting shares when contractual agreements give the parental control. In Chapter 10, we will discuss special purpose entities where control exists through operating agreement. For these situations, the primary beneficiary makes the key decisions, receives the majority of the benefits and absorbs most of the risk even though he/she may own very few, if any, of the shares in the controlled company.

In another example, X Company owns 40 percent of Y Company, which is the largest single block of shares of that company outstanding. The other 60 percent is very widely held and only a very small proportion of the holders appear at the annual meeting of Y Company. As a result, X Company has had no trouble electing the majority of the board of directors. While this appears to be control, it would not be considered so because the cooperation of the other 60 percent to not vote is needed by X Company.

If control is present, a parent must consolidate a subsidiary; if control ceases, consolidation is discontinued. The seizure of the company's assets by a trustee in a receivership or bankruptcy situation would be evidence that control has probably ceased, as would the imposition of governmental restrictions over a foreign subsidiary's ability to pay dividends to its parent. However, when a receiver seizes a specific asset in satisfaction of a default under a loan agreement but permits the subsidiary to continue in business under the direction of the parent, this is not a loss of control.

Normal business restrictions do not preclude control by the parent.

Normal business restrictions, whether placed on a parent directly or on the resources of a subsidiary, do not preclude control by the parent. Restrictions that are commonly encountered and do not normally prevent control include those contained in a debt covenant or set by a regulatory body. A parent may pledge to a creditor as collateral the voting shares that give it control of a subsidiary. In many circumstances, the parent is able to continue to exercise the right to vote the shares and thereby retain control. However, in the case of default by the parent, the creditor may exercise its right to take the voting shares and the parent may, consequently, lose control of the subsidiary. Regulation of the business activities of an enterprise, such as a pipeline or other public utility, does not normally prevent its directors from managing its business and, in the same way, does not normally prevent the holder of the majority of voting shares from controlling the enterprise. [1590.14]

While numerical guidelines are the starting point in determining whether or not control exists, professional judgment plays a major role because of all the relevant factors that must be taken into account.

Item of Interest The collapse of Enron Corporation has often been in the news since it occurred in 2001 and litigation against the company and criminal charges against management and auditors are still before the courts.

One of the many financial reporting problems involved with this debacle occurred because of the company's use of special-purpose entities. SPEs were well known in the business world because they often allowed companies to employ "off-balance-sheet financing" by obtaining the use of borrowed money without showing the liability on its balance sheet. For example, an organization might create a SPE to borrow funds (guaranteed by the organization) that are then used to purchase assets. These assets are fully pledged against the borrowed funds and are then leased back to the organization with terms that make it an operating lease. Often the SPE has a very small equity, and the organization that created it does not own any of its shares.

The accounting standards in existence at the time of the Enron collapse allowed the company to argue against the consolidation of its many SPEs and therefore leave billions of dollars of liabilities off its balance sheet. Its auditors, Arthur Andersen, accepted the argument. In the resulting investigation it appeared obvious that control was achieved even though no voting shares were held. In 2003, FASB strengthened its standards by issuing Interpretation no. 46, "Consolidation of Variable Interest Entities." Shortly after, the CICA issued an accounting guideline with the same title.

> The collapse of Enron caused the standard-setters to quickly introduce new standards for consolidation of variable interest entities.

Now that we have a better understanding of the concept of control, we will turn our attention to the most common form of combination, the purchase of shares. We will continue to use the financial statements of the two companies in Exhibit 3.1.

In the next two illustrations, A Company issues a tender offer to the shareholders of B Corporation (Group Y) for all of their shareholdings. Group Y accepts the offer.

Illustration 3   Assume that on January 1, Year 2, A Company pays $95,000 in cash to the shareholders of B Corporation for all of their shares, and that no expenses are involved. Because cash was the means of payment, A Company is the acquirer.

A Company's journal entry to record the acquisition of 100 percent of B Corporation's shares on January 1, Year 2, is as follows:

Investment in B Corporation	95,000	
Cash		95,000

> With a purchase of shares, the transaction is with the shareholders of the acquired company, not with the acquired company itself.

The financial statements of B Corporation have not been affected by this transaction because the shareholders of B Corporation, not B Corporation itself, sold their shares. A Company is now a parent company and must prepare consolidated financial statements for external reporting purposes. We will now illustrate the preparation of the consolidated balance sheet as at January 1, Year 2, using a working paper approach.

Before preparing the working paper, it is useful to calculate and allocate the purchase discrepancy. The purchase discrepancy is defined as "the difference between the amount paid by an acquiring company for shares and its proportionate interest in the net book value of the assets of the acquired limited company, at the date of acquisition."[6] This concept was introduced in Chapter 2.

The required calculation and allocation is shown in Schedule 3.1.

The $95,000 cost of the investment represents the total value of the subsidiary on the date of acquisition. The $95,000 value can be segregated into three components as indicated in the following bar chart:

---

[6] *Terminology for Accountants*, 4th edition, Toronto: CICA, 1992, p. 168.

Total Value of Subsidiary

The total value of the subsidiary can be segregated into three components.

Net book value of
identifiable assets and liabilities
$58,000

Excess of fair value over carrying value
of identifiable assets and liabilities
$22,000

Goodwill
$15,000

Since assets minus liabilities equals shareholders' equity, the top component of the bar chart could be described as either net book value of identifiable assets and liabilities or net book value of shareholders' equity. The net book value component is the amount reflected on the subsidiary's separate entity balance sheet. The other two components, which together equal the purchase discrepancy, will be reflected on the consolidated balance sheet at the date of acquisition.

Schedule 3.1

CALCULATION AND ALLOCATION
OF THE PURCHASE DISCREPANCY

The purchase discrepancy is comprised of two components — a fair value excess (or deficiency) and goodwill.

Cost of A Company's investment			$95,000
Net book value of B Corporation			
Common stock		25,000	
Retained earnings		33,000	
		58,000	
A Company's proportionate interest		100%	58,000
Purchase discrepancy			37,000

Allocated as follows:

	Fair value	–	Book value	×	Ownership percentage			
Assets	109,000	–	88,000	×	100%	=	21,000	
Liabilities	29,000	–	30,000	×	100%	=	1,000	22,000
Balance — goodwill								$15,000

Section 1600 of the *Handbook*, "Consolidated Financial Statements," does not mention an item called the purchase discrepancy; instead, it describes the calculation of goodwill with the following statement:

> Where the cost of an investment exceeds the parent's portion of the costs assigned to the subsidiary's identifiable assets acquired and liabilities assumed,

such an excess is a payment for an unidentifiable asset and should be accounted for in consolidated financial statements as goodwill. [1600.16]

The costs assigned to the subsidiary's net assets mentioned in this paragraph are fair values on the date of acquisition. If we calculate goodwill in accordance with the *Handbook*'s description, we get the same amount for goodwill, as the following demonstrates:

Goodwill is the difference between the acquisition cost and the fair value of identifiable net assets.

Cost of A Company's investment			$95,000
Fair value of B Corporation's identifiable net assets			
Assets		109,000	
Liabilities		29,000	
		80,000	
A Company's proportionate interest		100%	80,000
Balance — goodwill			$15,000

Because consolidated working papers use the financial statements of the parent and its subsidiary, which do not contain fair values, the calculation and allocation of the purchase discrepancy is necessary because it provides the amounts needed to make the working paper eliminations and adjustments.

The working paper for the preparation of the consolidated balance sheet on the date of acquisition is shown in Exhibit 3.2.

Exhibit 3.2

A COMPANY LTD.
CONSOLIDATED BALANCE SHEET WORKING PAPER
January 1, Year 2

The consolidated balance sheet produces the same financial position as when A Company purchased the net assets directly.

	A Company	B Corp.	Adjustments and Eliminations Dr.	Cr.	Consolidated balance sheet
Assets	$205,000	$88,000	(2) $ 21,000		$314,000
Investment in B Corporation	95,000			(1) $ 95,000	
Purchase discrepancy			(1) 37,000	(2) 37,000	
Goodwill			(2) 15,000		15,000
	$300,000	$88,000			$329,000
Liabilities	$120,000	$30,000	(2) 1,000		$149,000
Common stock	100,000				100,000
Retained earnings	80,000				80,000
Common stock		25,000	(1) 25,000		
Retained earnings		33,000	(1) 33,000		
	$300,000	$88,000	$132,000	$132,000	$329,000

The following points should be noted regarding the preparation of this working paper:

1. A Company's asset "Investment in B Corporation" and B Corporation's common shares and retained earnings do not appear on the consolidated balance sheet.

These items are eliminated by a working paper elimination entry because they are reciprocal in nature. The entry labelled (1) eliminates the parent's ownership percentage of the shareholders' equity of the subsidiary against the parent's investment account. These shareholders' equity accounts are separately shown in the working paper to facilitate this. The purchase discrepancy that results is the portion of the investment account not eliminated.

2. The purchase discrepancy does not appear on the consolidated balance sheet. With reference to the calculations of Schedule 3.1, the purchase discrepancy is allocated to revalue the net assets of B Corporation for consolidation purposes. This is accomplished by the entry labelled (2).

The consolidated balance sheet reflects the acquiring company's net assets at book value and the acquired company's net assets at fair value.

3. When we add the book value of the net assets of B Corporation to 100 percent of the difference between their fair value and book value, the resulting amount used for the consolidation is the fair value of each individual asset and liability of B Corporation.

4. The elimination entries are made on the working paper only. They are not entered in the accounting records of the parent or the subsidiary.

The consolidation entries are made on the consolidated working papers and not in the accounting records of the combining companies.

5. The consolidated balance sheet is prepared from the amounts shown in the last column of the working paper.

6. Under the acquisition method of accounting, consolidated shareholders' equity on acquisition date is that of the parent.

Illustration 4   Assume that on January 1, Year 2, A Company issues 4,000 common shares, with a market value of $23.75 per share, to the shareholders of B Corporation (Group Y) for all of their shares, and that there are no expenses involved. The analysis made in Illustration 2 indicates that A Company is the acquirer.

A Company's January 1, Year 2, journal entry to record the issuance of 4,000 shares at market value in payment for the acquisition of 100 percent of B Corporation's shares is:

Investment in B Corporation (4,000 × $23.75)	95,000	
Common stock		95,000

The calculation and allocation of the purchase discrepancy is identical to the one used in the last illustration (see Schedule 3.1). The working paper for the preparation of the consolidated balance sheet as at January 1, Year 2, is shown in Exhibit 3.3 on page 92.

The accounting for a business combination has been examined in four illustrations. The first two involved the acquisition of net assets, and the last two the acquisition of 100 percent of shareholdings. Because the amount paid was the same in each of these paired illustrations, the balance sheets prepared immediately after the combination are identical for each pair.

Financial Statement Disclosure

Section 1582 of the *CICA Handbook* sets forth detailed disclosure requirements with respect to business combinations completed during the year. It requires details of the assets and liabilities of an acquired entity to be presented in condensed form.

Exhibit 3.3

A COMPANY LTD.
CONSOLIDATED BALANCE SHEET WORKING PAPER
January 1, Year 2

	A Company	B Corp.	Adjustments and Eliminations Dr.	Cr.	Consolidated balance sheet
Assets	$300,000	$88,000	(2) $ 21,000		$409,000
Investment in					
B Corporation	95,000			(1) $ 95,000	
Purchase					
discrepancy			(1) 37,000	(2) 37,000	
Goodwill			(2) 15,000		15,000
	$395,000	$88,000			$424,000
Liabilities	$120,000	$30,000	(2) 1,000		$149,000
Common stock	195,000				195,000
Retained earnings	80,000				80,000
Common stock		25,000	(1) 25,000		
Retained earnings		33,000	(1) 33,000		
	$395,000	$88,000	$132,000	$132,000	$424,000

The allocation of the purchase discrepancy is made on the consolidated worksheet and is not recorded in the accounting records of the combining companies.

The consolidated financial statements are a third set of financial statements supported by a working paper which combines the separate entity financial statements of the parent and subsidiaries.

The following footnote from Bell Canada Enterprise Inc.'s 2006 financial statements[7] illustrates how this company complied with the *Handbook's* disclosure requirements:

We made various business acquisitions in 2006 for a total consideration of $82 million.

	TOTAL
Consideration received:	
Non-cash working capital	2
Capital assets	3
Other long-term assets	3
Indefinite-life intangible assets	19
Goodwill	49
Long-term debt	(2)
Other long-term liabilities	(4)
Non-controlling interest	3
	73
Cash and cash equivalents	9
Net assets acquired	82
Consideration given:	
Cash	76
Acquisition costs	4
Non-cash	2
	82

The footnote discloses the assets and liabilities acquired in the business combination and consideration given to carry out the business combination.

An International Perspective

It is fairly standard practice throughout the world to report investments in controlled companies by means of consolidated financial statements. Control is sometimes defined as greater than 50 percent of the voting shares, although many countries

---

7 www.sedar.com, Bell Canada International Inc., Audited Annual Financial Statements, April 4, 2007.

seem to follow Canada's method, which is to define control without mentioning a quantitative number.

Once Section 1582 on Business Combinations goes into effect (which is expected to be on January 1, 2011), the Canadian standards for business combinations will be converged with the IASB standards. Until then, the standards are much the same except for the following:

1. IFRS requires the acquisition date to be the date on which the acquirer obtains control over the acquired entity or business whereas the date that consideration is given may be used under Section 1581.

2. IFRS does not allow, but the CICA does allow, the use of the acquiree's share of the fair value of the net assets or equity instruments acquired, if that is more reliably measurable, in determining the cost of a business combination.

Canadian accounting practices for business combinations are basically the same as accounting practices recommended by the IASB.

IASB presently allows some subsidiaries to not be consolidated.

Section 1600 and IFRS 3 and IAS 27 are converged, except that IFRS allows subsidiaries to not be consolidated where control is temporary, or where there are long-term restrictions that impair the subsidiary's ability to transfer funds to its parent. The IASB describes control as the power to govern the financial and operating policies of an enterprise so as to benefit from its activities. Control is presumed to exist when the parent owns more than half of the voting rights of the enterprise, and even if more than half of the voting rights are not owned, there may be other evidence of the existence of control. Unlike the Canadian standard, there is no mention of the concept "without the cooperation of others."

IASB and FASB have commenced a project on consolidation, which intends to develop a comprehensive definition of control and to converge their standards on consolidations. The CICA intends to issue converged standards once the standards for consolidations are finalized by the IASB.

Purchased in-process research and development is another area that produces diversity in accounting practices, particularly between Canada and the United States. In-process research and development is often a valuable asset purchased in a takeover. The FASB requires that the amount of the acquisition price allocated to this asset be written off immediately, which is consistent with its requirements for internally generated research and development. Canada would allow the development component to be capitalized and amortized over its estimated useful life.

SUMMARY

A *business combination* takes place when one company gains control over the net assets of another company. Control can be achieved by the purchase of the net assets or by the purchase of enough voting shares to gain control over the use of the net assets. In the latter situation a parent–subsidiary relationship is created that requires the preparation of consolidated financial statements.

Prior to 2001, both the purchase method and the pooling-of-interests method were acceptable methods to account for a business combination. Pooling could be used only if there was a share exchange and even then only in exceptional circumstances. On July 1, 2001, pooling was disallowed in both Canada and the United States, leaving the purchase method as the only acceptable method to account for a business combination. Effective January 1, 2011, the *acquisition method* must be used to report a business combination and an acquirer must be identified.

Under the acquisition method, the identifiable assets and liabilities acquired are recorded at fair values, with the acquisition cost excess recorded as goodwill.

SELF-STUDY PROBLEM

On December 31, Year 1, P Company wants to take control over the net assets of S Company by buying the net assets directly or by purchasing 100 percent of the common shares of S Company. In either case, P Company will pay for the purchase by issuing common shares with a fair value of $44,000. In addition, P Company paid $1,000 for professional fees to facilitate the transaction. The following information has been assembled:

	P Company		S Company	
	Book Value	Fair Value	Book Value	Fair Value
Current assets	$ 50,000	$ 55,000	$15,000	$14,000
Plant assets	80,000	90,000	20,000	26,000
Goodwill	0	38,000	0	22,000
	$130,000	$183,000	$35,000	$62,000
Current liabilities	$ 30,000	$30,000	$10,000	$10,000
Long-term debt	25,000	29,000	7,000	8,000
Shareholders' equity	75,000		18,000	
	$130,000		$35,000	

Required:

(a) Prepare P Company's balance sheet immediately after the combination assuming that P acquires the net assets directly.

(b) Prepare a consolidated balance sheet for P Company immediately after the combination under the
   (i) the acquisition method.
   (ii) the new entity method.

(c) Describe the similarities in the balance sheet for the purchase of net assets in part (a) as compared to the consolidated balance under the acquisition method in part (b) (i).

Solution to Self-study Problem

P COMPANY
Balance Sheet
At December 31, Year 1
(See notes)

	(a)	(b) (i)	(b) (ii)
Current assets	$ 63,000	$ 63,000	$ 69,000
Plant assets	106,000	106,000	116,000
Goodwill	22,000	22,000	60,000
	$191,000	$191,000	$245,000
Current liabilities	$ 40,000	$ 40,000	$ 40,000
Long-term debt	33,000	33,000	37,000
Shareholders' equity	118,000	118,000	168,000
	$191,000	$191,000	$245,000

(c) The consolidated financial position for the parent and subsidiary in part (b) (i) is exactly the same as the separate entity balance sheet for P Company when P Company acquired the net assets directly.

Notes:

1. The balance sheet values for assets and liabilities are calculated as follows:
   (a) Book values for P and fair values for S.

(b) (i) Book values for P and fair values for S.

(b) (ii) Fair values for P and fair values for S.

2. The $1,000 paid for professional fees reduces cash (which is included in current assets) and increase expenses (which reduces shareholders' equity)

3. Shareholders' equity is the amount required to balance the balance sheet.

REVIEW QUESTIONS

1. What key element must be present in a business combination?

2. Can a statutory amalgamation be considered a form of business combination?

3. Explain how an acquirer is determined in a business combination.

4. Outline the accounting involved with the acquisition method.

5. Briefly describe the accounting involved with the new entity method.

6. If one company issued shares as payment for the net assets of another company, it would probably insist that the other company be wound up after the sale. Explain why this condition would be part of the asset purchase agreement.

7. What criteria must be met for a subsidiary to be consolidated? Explain.

8. What part do irrevocable agreements, convertible securities, and warrants play in determining whether control exists? Explain.

9. What is a purchase discrepancy, and where does it appear on the consolidated balance sheet?

10. What are some reasons for the purchase price being in excess of the carrying value of the acquiree's assets and liabilities? What does this say about the accuracy of the values used in the financial statements of the acquiree?

11. How is goodwill determined at the date of acquisition? Describe the nature of goodwill.

12. When must an intangible asset be shown separately from goodwill? What are the criteria for reporting these intangible assets separately from goodwill?

13. What is negative goodwill and how is it accounted for?

14. Does the historical cost principle or fair value reporting take precedence when preparing consolidated financial statements at the date of acquisition under the entity method? Explain.

MULTIPLE-CHOICE QUESTIONS

1. When a parent uses the acquisition method to consolidate a wholly owned subsidiary, what amount will appear as "common shares" in the equity section of the consolidated balance sheet?
   a. The book value of the parent's common shares plus the book value of the subsidiary's common shares.
   b. The book value of the parent's common shares plus the fair value of the subsidiary's common shares.
   c. The fair value of the parent's common shares on the date of the purchase of the subsidiary.
   d. The book value of the parent's common shares at the date of consolidation.

2. P Company acquires 100% of the common shares of S Company by issuing non-voting preferred shares. For both P Company and S Company, the fair value of all assets is greater than recorded book values. Which of the following approaches to consolidation will show the highest total asset value on the consolidated balance sheet on the date of acquisition?
    a. Acquisition.
    b. Purchase.
    c. New entity.
    d. Cannot be determined based on the information provided.

3. Which of the following characteristics is not associated with a business combination in Canada today?
    a. A clearly identified acquisition cost is evident for the transaction.
    b. Two subsidiaries of a single parent merge together as one.
    c. Cash or debt or shares can be used as payment for the acquired company.
    d. One company can always be identified as the acquirer.

The following data should be used for Questions 4 and 5.

Harper Corp. has only three assets:

	Book value	Fair value
Inventory	$ 165,000	$ 225,000
Land	1,050,000	900,000
Buildings	1,050,000	1,350,000

Kandon Inc. purchases Harper's assets by issuing 100,000 common shares with a market value of $30 per share.

4. At what amount will the inventory, land, and buildings respectively appear on Kandon's balance sheet?
    a. $165,000, $900,000, $1,350,000
    b. $165,000, $1,050,000, $1,050,000
    c. $225,000, $900,000, $1,350,000
    d. $225,000, $1,050,000, $1,350,000

5. What is the amount of goodwill from this business combination?
    a. $525,000
    b. Negative $525,000
    c. $735,000
    d. Nil

6. On January 1, Year 5, KL Corporation and XT Corporation entered into a business combination. On that date, the fair value of KL's net assets was greater than the book value. Similarly, the fair value of XT's net assets was greater than book value. Both companies have been profitable every year from Year 2 through Year 4. Which of the following is true regarding the earnings for the business combination on the Year 5 consolidated financial statements?
    a. The acquisition method would produce higher earnings than the new entity method.
    b. The new entity method would produce higher earnings than the acquisition method.
    c. Earnings would be the same under the acquisition and new entity method.
    d. The relative earnings of the two methods cannot be determined based on the information provided.

(CGA-Canada, from 2002 to 2007)

The following data should be used for Questions 7 and 8.

On January 1, Year 6, Green Company acquired 100% of the outstanding common shares of Blue Inc. by issuing 10,000 common shares. The book values and the fair values of both companies immediately before the acquisition were as follows:

	Green Company		Blue Inc.	
	Book values	Fair values	Book values	Fair values
Assets	$2,175,000	$2,400,000	$900,000	$1,042,500
Liabilities	$1,155,000	1,132,000	$375,000	405,000
Common shares*	450,000		97,500	
Retained earnings	570,000		427,500	
	$2,175,000		$900,000	

* *Immediately before the acquisition transaction, Green Company had 20,000 common shares outstanding and Blue Inc. had 6,500 common shares outstanding. Green's shares were actively trading at $75.00 on the date of the acquisition.*

7. What amount would Green Company report on its consolidated financial statements for assets immediately after the acquisition transaction?
   a. $3,075,000
   b. $3,217,500
   c. $3,330,000
   d. $3,442,500

8. What amount would Green Company report on its consolidated financial statements for common shares immediately after the acquisition transaction?
   a. $450,000
   b. $547,500
   c. $1,200,000
   d. $1,297,500

9. Which of the following is the best theoretical justification for consolidated financial statements?
   a. In form, the companies are one entity; in substance, they are separate.
   b. In form, the companies are separate; in substance, they are one entity.
   c. In form and substance, the companies are one entity.
   d. In form and substance, the companies are separate.

10. What is the appropriate accounting treatment for the value assigned to in-process research and development acquired in a business combination?
    a. Always expense upon acquisition.
    b. Always capitalize as an asset with future economic benefit.
    c. Expense if there is no alternative use for the assets used in the research and development and technological feasibility has yet to be reached.
    d. Expense until future economic benefits become certain and then capitalize as an asset.

11. An acquired entity has a long-term operating lease for an office building used for central management. The terms of the lease are very favourable relative to current market rates. However, the lease prohibits subleasing or any other transfer of rights. How should the acquiring firm report the value assigned to the lease contract in its financial statements?
    a. As an intangible asset under the contractual-legal criterion.
    b. As a part of goodwill.
    c. As an intangible asset under the separability criterion.
    d. As a building.

12. When one company controls another company, the *CICA Handbook* recommends that the parent report the subsidiary on a consolidated basis. Which of the following best describes the primary reason for this recommendation?
    a. To report the combined retained earnings of the two companies, allowing shareholders to better predict dividend payments.
    b. To allow for taxation of the combined entity.
    c. To report the total resources of the combined economic entity under the control of the parent's shareholders.
    d. To meet the requirements of the federal and provincial securities commissions.

13. Which of the following is not a necessary condition for consolidating another enterprise in a reporting enterprise's financial statements?
    a. The reporting enterprise has control over the other enterprise.
    b. The reporting enterprise has the right and ability to obtain future economic benefits from the resources of the other enterprise.
    c. The reporting enterprise is exposed to the risks associated with the other enterprise.
    d. The reporting enterprise owns, either directly or indirectly, more than 50% of the other enterprise's voting shares.

    (*CICA adapted*)

14. Which of the following is not an appropriate reason for leaving a subsidiary unconsolidated?
    a. The subsidiary is in bankruptcy.
    b. The subsidiary is in an industry that is significantly different from that of the parent.
    c. A foreign government threatens to take over the assets of the subsidiary.
    d. The subsidiary is to be sold in the near future.

15. In which of the following situations would PUR have the ability to control the strategic operating, investing, and financing activities of SUR?
    a. PUR owns 48% of the voting shares of SUR, and the remaining shares are widely held.
    b. PUR owns 40,000 of the 100,000 voting shares of SUR and 80% of the non-voting shares of SUR.
    c. PUR owns 60,000 of the 100,000 voting shares of SUR and 10,000 of the 50,000 convertible non-voting shares. Each of the non-voting shares is convertible into one voting share.
    d. PUR owns 40,000 of the 100,000 voting shares of SUR and 44,000 of the 50,000 convertible non-voting shares. Each of the non-voting shares is convertible into one voting share.

    (*CGA-Canada, from 2002 to 2007*)

CASES

Case 1   Z Ltd. is a public company with factories and distribution centres located throughout Canada. It has 100,000 common shares outstanding. In past years it has reported high earnings, but in Year 5 its earnings declined substantially due in part to a loss of markets as a result of the North American Free Trade Agreement. In Year 6 it closed a large number of its manufacturing and distribution facilities and reported a substantial loss for the year.

Prior to Year 6, 70,000 of Z Ltd.'s shares were held by C Ltd., with the remaining shares being widely distributed in the hands of individual investors in Canada and the United States. During Year 6, C Ltd. sold 40,000 of its shares in Z Ltd. to W Corporation.

W Corporation is a joint venture that was formed in Year 6 by A Ltd. and B Inc. Each company owns 50 percent of the common shares of W Corporation, and they have agreed in writing that all major decisions will be made jointly. W Corporation's sole asset is its holding of 40,000 shares of Z Ltd.

Required:

(a) How should C Ltd. report its investment in Z Ltd., both before the sale of 40,000 shares and after the sale?
(b) How should W Corporation report its investment in Z Ltd.?
(c) How should A Ltd. and B Inc. report their investments in W Corporation? Explain fully, and include in your answers a reference to Z Ltd.'s Year 6 loss.

Case 2   The directors of Atlas Inc. and Beta Corp. have reached an agreement in principle to merge the two companies and create a new company called AB Ltd. The basics of the agreement confirmed so far are outlined below.

The new company will purchase all of the assets and assume all of the liabilities of Atlas and Beta by issuing shares. After the sale the two companies will be wound up. Some but not all members of the top management of each company will be retained.

The number of AB shares that will be issued has not yet been determined.

The chair of the merger committee has asked you to provide him with advice as to the accounting implications that will result from this merger, even though many of the details have not yet been ironed out. He has requested that you submit to him a preliminary report.

Required:

Prepare an outline of your report.

Case 3   Manitoba Peat Moss (MPM) was the first Canadian company to provide a reliable supply of high-quality peat moss to be used for greenhouse operations. Owned by Paul Parker, the company's founder and president, MPM began operations approximately 30 years ago when demand for peat moss was high. It has shown consistently high profits and stable growth for over 20 years. Parker holds all of the 50,000 outstanding common shares in MPM.

Prairie Greenhouses (PG), a publicly traded company that purchases over 70 percent of MPM's output, provides tree seedlings to various government agencies and logging companies for reforestation projects. In Year 5, PG approached MPM with an offer to buy all of the company's outstanding shares in exchange for a part ownership in PG, with a view to vertically integrating. Parker was very interested in the offer, since he hoped to soon retire. PG currently has 100,000 shares outstanding and widely distributed. It would issue 100,000 new common shares in a two-for-one exchange for all of MPM's shares. PG's shares are currently trading on the TSX at $60 per share.

The board of directors of PG is uncertain as to the accounting implications of the proposed share exchange. They believe that since they are purchasing all of the outstanding common shares of MPM, it is similar to buying the company outright; as a result they want to report all of MPM's assets on PG's consolidated financial statements at fair value. This will be very advantageous to PG, because the land carried on MPM's books was purchased 30 years ago and has appreciated substantially in value over the years.

The board has asked you, as its accounting adviser, to prepare a report explaining how PG's purchase of shares should be reported. They are particularly interested in how the increase in the value of the land will be shown on the consolidated statements.

The condensed balance sheets of the two companies at the time of the offer are shown below:

	PG	MPM
Current assets	$ 870,000	$ 450,000
Capital assets	8,210,000	2,050,000
	$9,080,000	$2,500,000
Current liabilities	$ 525,000	$ 200,000
Long-term debt	2,325,000	1,300,000
Common stock	4,000,000	500,000
Retained earnings	2,230,000	500,000
	$9,080,000	$2,500,000

Note: Land held by MPM at a book value of $1,000,000 has a fair value of $6,000,000. All other assets of both companies have book values approximately equal to their fair values.

Required:

Prepare the report to the board of directors.

(Adapted from a case prepared by J.C. (Jan) Thatcher, Lakehead University and Margaret Forbes, University of Saskatchewan.)

Case 4   John Williams is the sole owner of Northern Flight Services, a small airline company with 12 float planes servicing remote communities in northern Manitoba and Ontario. He wants to expand, and approaches Billy Johnston, owner of Bearcat Airlines, which operates 15 planes providing freight and passenger services in the same area.

Scenario One   Williams suggests that they join together and form one company. "We can probably save money on maintenance and overhead, and we can benefit from the discounts that suppliers will give us when we issue larger orders. Instead of each of us owning a small company, we will be co-owners of a larger airline operating 27 planes in the same area. Our company will be more profitable if we combine. I currently own all of the 3,000 outstanding shares of Northern Flight Services, and I will issue shares to you in exchange for all of the shares of Bearcat Airlines."

Scenario Two   Williams approaches Johnston with a proposal, saying: "I will buy you out. I will pay cash for all of your assets or, if you prefer, for all of your shares. The amount will be based on our agreement as to the fair value of your company. You can continue to work for me or you can retire. I think it will be beneficial to have one company owning 27 planes."

Required:

What is the basic difference from an accounting point of view between Scenario One and Scenario Two? Explain how each scenario would be accounted for.

Case 5   The following are a number of scenarios that show variations in the nature of long-term intercorporate investments.

1. A Ltd. owns 45% of B Co. Typically, only about 70% of the outstanding shares are voted at the annual meetings of B Company. Because of this, A Ltd. always casts a majority of the votes on every ballot when it votes the shares it holds.

2. A Ltd. holds no shares of B Co.; however, it holds convertible bonds issued by B Co. which, if A Ltd. converted them, would result in the ownership of 51% of the outstanding shares of B Co.

3. A Ltd. owns 75% of B Co. Recently a receiver, acting on behalf of a bank, seized a portion of B Co.'s inventory when B Co. defaulted on a loan.

4. Last year B Co. was a wholly owned subsidiary of C Inc. At the beginning of this year, B Co. was put up for sale and A Ltd. purchased all of its 100,000 voting shares from C Inc. by making a cash payment of 40% of the purchase price and by issuing a promissory note for the balance owing, due in equal instalments over the next two years.

     B Co. has a bond issue outstanding that can be converted at the option of the holder into 150,000 voting common shares of that company. At the time of the sale, C Inc. held 80% of these bonds; and it has agreed to sell these bonds proportionately to A Ltd. as it receives the proceeds from the promissory note.

5. A Ltd. owns 100% of B Co., which is insolvent. All of its assets have been seized by a licensed trustee in bankruptcy.

6. B Co. is located in a foreign country. This country requires that a majority of the ownership of all businesses be held by its citizens. A Ltd. has the expertise and technical knowledge required to successfully operate B Co. In order to satisfy the country's foreign ownership requirements, B Co. has been structured as a partnership, with 50 partners each having a 2% equity interest. Forty-nine of the partners, who are all citizens of the foreign country, have signed an irrevocable agreement that establishes A Ltd. as the managing partner, with complete authority to determine the operating, financing, and investing policies of B Co.

Required:

For each scenario, discuss how A Ltd. should report its investment in B Co.

Case 6 Regina Communications Ltd. develops and manufactures equipment for technology and communications enterprises. Since its incorporation in Year 5, it has grown steadily through internal expansion. In mid Year 14, Arthur Lajord, the sole owner of Regina, met a couple of engineering students who were working on new technology to increase the efficiency of data transferred over cable lines. Arthur has provided moral support and some financial support to these students over the past few months. At a lunch with the students last Friday, the students told Arthur that they had been able to register a patent to protect their technology. Furthermore, they were interested in selling their business, Davin Technologies Inc., which owns the patent and some other assets used in the development of this technology. After a week of negotiation, Arthur and the students agreed to the following:

- Rather than buying the shares of Davin, Regina would buy the assets and assume the liabilities of Davin effective January 1, Year 15.

- The purchase price would be payable as follows:
  — $200,000 on January 1, Year 15
  — $100,000 a year for three years commencing January 1, Year 16

- The students would commit to work for Regina as consultants over the next three years and would be paid $40 per hour for their services.

- The students would get an additional $200,000 if the patent were sold by Regina for more than $1,000,000 or if Regina were to go public on or before January 1, Year 18.

The condensed balance sheet for Davin at January 1, Year 15 was as follows:

	Net book value	Fair value
Current assets	$ 50,000	$50,000
Computer equipment	30,000	35,000
Patent registration costs	25,000	?
	$105,000	
Liabilities	$ 10,000	$10,000
Shareholders' equity	95,000	?
	$105,000	

Arthur was pleased and excited about the acquisition. He felt that it was a fair deal for both parties given that the business had not yet earned any revenue. He was particularly pleased that the students agreed to be paid over three years becau?se he otherwise would have had to arrange a bank loan with an interest rate of 8%.

Arthur is now worried about the accounting for this acquisition because it is the first time that his company has purchased another business. Although Regina has always followed generally accepted accounting principles, he is wondering whether now is the time to opt for a simpler approach. In particular, he is wondering whether the entire purchase discrepancy can be allocated to goodwill. This would keep it simple and would also avoid a charge to income over the first few years since goodwill does not need to be amortized. If the purchase discrepancy is allocated to patent, then Arthur would like to write off the patent over the maximum period of 20 years.

Arthur has asked you, a CGA, to prepare a presentation on the accounting implications for the proposed acquisition. He wants to understand how to determine the purchase price, how the purchase price would be allocated to individual assets and liabilities, and how this allocation would affect net income in the first year after the date of acquisition.

Required:

Prepare the presentation slides and related speaker's notes for the presentation. Limit your presentation to five slides. Your presentation should provide recommendations related to the issues raised by Arthur. Use financial statement concepts to support your recommendations. Provide a detailed calculation to show the impact on net income for Year 15. State your assumptions.

(CGA-Canada, from 2002 to 2007)

PROBLEMS

Problem 1   G Company is considering the takeover of K Company, whereby it will issue 6,000 common shares for all of the outstanding shares of K Company. K Company will become a wholly owned subsidiary of G Company. The following information has been assembled:

	G Company		K Company	
	Book value	Fair value	Book value	Fair value
Current assets	$ 40,000	$47,500	$10,000	$ 9,200
Plant assets	60,000	70,000	20,000	25,000
	$100,000		$30,000	
Current liabilities	$ 20,000	20,000	$ 5,000	5,000
Long-term debt	15,000	19,000	2,500	3,200
Common stock	30,000		10,000	
Retained earnings	35,000		12,500	
	$100,000		$30,000	

Required:

Prepare G Company's consolidated balance sheet immediately after the combination using:

(a) the new entity method, and

(b) the acquisition method.

(Assume that G Company had 20,000 shares outstanding which were trading at $4.90 on the date of the takeover.)

Problem 2

Horizontal - b/c same industry

Three companies, A, L, and M, whose December 31, Year 5, balance sheets appear below, have agreed to combine as at January 1, Year 6.

Each of the companies has a very small proportion of an intensely competitive market dominated by four much larger companies. In order to survive, they have decided to merge into one company. The merger agreement states that Company A will buy the assets and liabilities of each of the other two companies by issuing 27,000 common shares to Company L and 25,000 common shares to Company M, after which the two companies will be wound up.

Company A's shares are currently trading at $5 per share.

Company A will incur the following costs:

Costs of issuing shares	$ 8,000
Professional fees	20,000
	$28,000

The following information has been assembled regarding the three companies:

COMPANY A

	Book value	Fair value
Current assets	$ 99,900	$102,000
Plant and equipment	147,600	160,000
	$247,500	
Liabilities	$ 80,000	$ 75,000
Common stock (50,000 shares)	75,000	
Retained earnings	92,500	
	$247,500	

COMPANY L

	Book value	Fair value
Current assets	$ 60,000	$ 65,000
Plant and equipment	93,000	98,000
	$153,000	
Liabilities	$ 35,000	$ 36,000
Common stock (24,000 shares)	48,000	
Retained earnings	70,000	
	$153,000	

COMPANY M

	Book value	Fair value
Current assets	$ 52,000	$ 68,000
Plant and equipment	115,000	120,000
	$167,000	
Liabilities	$ 72,000	$ 70,000
Common stock (33,000 shares)	60,000	
Retained earnings	35,000	
	$167,000	

Required:

Prepare the balance sheet of Company A on January 2, Year 6, after Company L and Company M have been wound up.

Problem 3   The balance sheet of Bagley Incorporated as at July 31, Year 4, is shown below:

BAGLEY INCORPORATED
BALANCE SHEET
July 31, Year 4

	Book value	Fair value
Current assets	$ 455,000	$507,000
Plant and equipment	910,000	1,053,000
Patents	—	78,000
	$1,365,000	
Current liabilities	$ 273,000	$273,000
Long-term debt	390,000	416,000
Common stock	182,000	
Retained earnings	520,000	
	$1,365,000	

On August 1, Year 4, the directors of Bagley were considering a takeover offer from Davis Inc. whereby the corporation would sell all of its assets and liabilities. Davis's costs of investigation and drawing up the merger agreement would amount to $19,500.

Required:

PART A

Assume that Davis made a $1,040,000 cash payment to Bagley for its net assets. Prepare the journal entries in the accounting records of Davis to record the business combination.

PART B

Assume that Davis issued 130,000 common shares, with market value of $8 per share, to Bagley for its net assets. Legal fees associated with issuing these shares amounted to $6,500 and were paid in cash. Davis had 150,000 shares outstanding prior to the takeover.

(a) Prepare the journal entries in the records of Davis to record the business combination.

(b) Prepare the balance sheet of Bagley immediately after the sale.

Problem 4   The shareholders of Prong Company and Horn Company agreed to a statutory amalgamation under which a share exchange took place. On September 1, Year 5, Prong Company issued 50,000 common shares for all of the common shares of Horn Company, after which Horn Company was dissolved. The common shares of Prong Company traded at $7.00 per share on this date.

After the amalgamation, Prong Company changed its name to Pronghorn Corporation.

The balance sheets of the two companies on August 31, Year 5, were as follows:

	Prong Company	Horn Company
Current assets	$135,000	$170,000
Plant and equipment (net)	430,000	300,000
Other assets	41,000	20,000
	$606,000	$490,000
Current liabilities	$ 96,000	$ 30,000
Long-term debt	180,000	160,000
Common stock (note 1)	70,000	100,000
Retained earnings	260,000	200,000
	$606,000	$490,000

Note 1

Common shares outstanding	70,000 sh.	25,000 sh.

The book values of the net assets of both companies were equal to fair values except for plant and equipment. The fair values of plant and equipment were:

Prong Company	$ 500,000
Horn Company	280,000

Required:

Prepare the balance sheet of Pronghorn Corporation immediately after the statutory amalgamation.

Problem 5 The balance sheet of Drake Enterprises as at December 31, Year 5, is as follows:

Assets

Cash	$ 99,000
Accounts receivable	143,000
Inventory	191,400
Land	132,000
Plant and equipment (net)	660,000
	$1,225,400

Liabilities and Equity

Current liabilities	$ 242,000
Bonds payable	352,000
Common stock (100,000 shares)	220,000
Retained earnings	411,400
	$1,225,400

Effective January 1, Year 6, Drake proposes to issue 82,500 common shares (currently trading at $20 per share) for all of the assets and liabilities of Hanson Industries. In determining the acquisition price, the management of Drake noted that Hanson Industries has unrecorded customer service contracts and directed their accounting staff to reflect this when recording the acquisition. An independent appraiser placed a value of $150,000 on this unrecorded intangible asset. Costs of the acquisition are expected to be:

Costs of issuing shares	$44,000
Professional fees	38,500
	$82,500

The balance sheet of Hanson Industries as at December 31, Year 5, is as follows:

	Book value	Fair value
Cash	$ 55,000	$ 55,000
Accounts receivable	275,000	280,500
Inventory	187,000	178,200
Land	99,000	126,500
Plant and equipment (net)	770,000	891,000
	$1,386,000	
Current liabilities	$ 137,500	$137,500
Liability for warranties	99,000	129,800
Common stock	660,000	
Retained earnings	489,500	
	$1,386,000	

Hanson Industries is to be wound up after the sale.

Required:

Assume that Drake's offer is accepted by the shareholders of Hanson on the proposed date. Prepare Drake's January 2, Year 6, balance sheet.

Problem 6 D Ltd. and H Corporation are both engaged in the manufacture of computers. On July 1, Year 5, they agree to a merger whereby D will issue 300,000 shares with current market value of $7.80 each for the net assets of H.

Summarized balance sheets of the two companies prior to the merger are presented below:

BALANCE SHEET
June 30, Year 5

	D Ltd. Book value	H Corporation Book value	Fair value
Current assets	$ 450,000	$ 500,000	$ 510,000
Fixed assets (net)	4,950,000	3,200,000	3,500,000
	$5,400,000	$3,700,000	
Current liabilities	$ 600,000	$ 800,000	$ 800,000
Long-term debt	1,100,000	900,000	920,000
Common stock	2,500,000	500,000	
Retained earnings	1,200,000	1,500,000	
	$5,400,000	$3,700,000	

Required:

Prepare the July 1, Year 5, balance sheet of D, after the merger.

Problem 7 The July 31, Year 3, balance sheets of two companies that are parties to a business combination are as follows:

	Red Corp. Book value	Sax Inc. Book value	Fair value
Current assets	$1,600,000	$ 420,000	$468,000
Plant and equipment	1,080,000	840,000	972,000
Patents	—	—	72,000
	$2,680,000	$1,260,000	
Current liabilities	$1,360,000	$ 252,000	$252,000
Long-term debt	480,000	360,000	384,000
Common stock	720,000	168,000	
Retained earnings	120,000	480,000	
	$2,680,000	$1,260,000	

Effective on August 1, Year 3, the shareholders of Sax accepted an offer from Red Corporation to purchase all of their common shares. Red's costs for investigating and drawing up the share purchase agreement amounted to $18,000.

Required:

PART A

Assume that Red made an $960,000 cash payment to the shareholders of Sax for 100% of their shares.

(a) Prepare the journal entry in the records of Red to record the share acquisition.

(b) Prepare the consolidated balance sheet of Red Corp. as at August 1, Year 3.

PART B

Assume that Red issued 120,000 common shares, with market value of $8 per share, to the shareholders of Sax for 100% of their shares. Legal fees associated with issuing these shares amounted to $6,000 and were paid in cash. Red is identified as the acquirer.
(a) Prepare the journal entries in the records of Red to record the share acquisition.
(b) Prepare the consolidated balance sheet of Red as at August 1, Year 3.

PART C

Would the assumption in Part A result in higher future earnings to Red than those resulting from the assumption in Part B? Explain.

Problem 8   The following are summarized balance sheets of three companies as at December 31, Year 3:

	Company X	Company Y	Company Z
Assets	$400,000	$300,000	$250,000
Liabilities	$232,500	$182,000	$155,000
Common stock (note 1)	75,000	48,000	60,000
Retained earnings	92,500	70,000	35,000
	$400,000	$300,000	$250,000
Note 1			
Shares outstanding	50,000 sh.	12,000 sh.	16,500 sh.

The fair values of the identifiable assets and liabilities of the three companies as at December 31, Year 3, were as follows:

	Company X	Company Y	Company Z
Assets	$420,000	$350,000	$265,000
Liabilities	233,000	180,000	162,000

On January 2, Year 4, Company X will purchase the assets and assume the liabilities of Company Y and Company Z. It has been agreed that Company X will issue common shares to each of the two companies as payment for their net assets as follows:

> to Company Y — 13,500 shares
> to Company Z — 12,000 shares

The shares of Company X traded at $14.00 on December 31, Year 3.
Company X will incur the following costs associated with this acquisition:

Costs of registering and issuing shares	$12,000
Other professional fees associated with the takeover	30,000
	$42,000

Company Y and Company Z will wind up after the sale.

Required:

(a) Prepare a summarized pro forma balance sheet of Company X as at January 2, Year 4, after the purchase of net assets from Company Y and Company Z.
(b) Prepare the pro forma balance sheets of Company Y and Company Z as at January 2, Year 4, after the sale of net assets to Company X and prior to being wound up.

Problem 9   Myers Company Ltd. was formed 10 years ago by the issuance of 22,000 common shares to three shareholders. Four years later the company went public and issued an additional 30,000 common shares.

The management of Myers is considering a takeover in which Myers would purchase all of the assets and assume all of the liabilities of Norris Inc. Other costs associated with the takeover would be as follows:

Legal, appraisal, and finders' fees	$ 5,000
Costs of issuing shares	7,000
	$12,000

Two alternative proposals are being considered:

PROPOSAL 1
Myers would offer to pay $300,000 cash for the Norris net assets, to be financed by a $300,000 bank loan due in five years.

PROPOSAL 2
Myers would issue 50,000 shares currently trading at $8.00 each for the Norris net assets. Norris shareholders would be offered five seats on the 10-member board of directors of Myers, and the management of Norris would be absorbed into the surviving company.

Balance sheet data for the two companies prior to the combination are as follows:

	Myers	*Norris*	
	Book value	*Book value*	*Fair value*
Cash	$ 140,000	$ 52,500	$ 52,500
Accounts receivable	167,200	61,450	56,200
Inventory	374,120	110,110	134,220
Land	425,000	75,000	210,000
Buildings (net)	250,505	21,020	24,020
Equipment (net)	78,945	17,705	15,945
	$1,435,770	$337,785	
Current liabilities	$ 133,335	$ 41,115	$ 41,115
Noncurrent liabilities	—	150,000	155,000
Common stock	500,000	100,000	
Retained earnings	802,435	46,670	
	$1,435,770	$337,785	

Required:

(a) Prepare the journal entries of Myers for each of the two proposals being considered.
(b) Prepare the balance sheet of Myers after the takeover for each of the proposals being considered.

Problem 10 Refer to Problem 9. All of the facts and data are the same except that in the proposed takeover, Myers Company will purchase all of the outstanding common shares of Norris Inc.

Required:

(a) Prepare the journal entries of Myers for each of the two proposals being considered.
(b) Prepare the balance sheet of Myers after the takeover for each of the proposals being considered.

Problem 11   Baker Corporation has the following account balances at December 31, Year 4:

Receivables	$ 80,000
Inventory	200,000
Land	600,000
Building	500,000
Liabilities	400,000
Common stock	200,000
Retained earnings, 1/1/Year 4	700,000
Revenues	300,000
Expenses	220,000

Several of Baker's accounts have fair values that differ from book value: land — $400,000; building — $600,000; inventory — $280,000; and liabilities — $330,000. Home Inc. purchases all of the outstanding shares of Baker by issuing 20,000 shares of common stock with a market value of $55 per share. Stock issuance costs amount to $10,000.

Required:

(a) What is the purchase price in this combination?
(b) What is the book value of Baker's net assets on the date of the takeover?
(c) How does the issuance of these shares affect the shareholders' equity accounts of Home, the parent?
(d) How are the stock issuance costs handled?
(e) What allocations are made of Home's purchase price to specific accounts and to goodwill for the consolidated financial statements?
(f) How do Baker's revenues and expenses affect consolidated totals? Why?
(g) How does Baker's common stock affect consolidated totals?
(h) If Home's stock had been worth only $40 per share rather than $55, how would the consolidation of Baker's assets and liabilities have been affected?

Problem 12   The financial statements for CAP Inc. and SAP Company for the year ended December 31, Year 5 follow:

	CAP	SAP
Revenues	$ 900,000	$ 300,000
Expenses	660,000	200,000
Net income	$ 240,000	$ 100,000
Retained earnings, 1/1/Year 5	$ 800,000	$ 200,000
Net income	240,000	100,000
Dividends paid	90,000	0
Retained earnings, 12/31/Year 5	$ 950,000	$ 300,000
Cash	$ 80,000	$ 110,000
Receivables and inventory	400,000	170,000
Patented technology (net)	900,000	300,000
Equipment (net)	700,000	600,000
Total assets	$2,080,000	$1,180,000
Liabilities	$ 600,000	$ 410,000
Common stock	530,000	470,000
Retained earnings	950,000	300,000
Total liabilities and equities	$2,080,000	$1,180,000

On December 31, Year 5, after the above figures were prepared, CAP issued $300,000 in debt and 15,000 new shares to the owners of SAP to purchase all of the outstanding shares of that company. CAP shares had a fair value of $40 per share.

CAP also paid $30,000 to a broker for arranging the transaction. In addition, CAP paid $40,000 in stock issuance costs. SAP's equipment was actually worth $710,000 but its patented technology was valued at only $270,000.

Required:

What are the consolidated balances at December 31, Year 5, for the following accounts?

(a) Net income
(b) Retained earnings, 12/31/Year 5
(c) Equipment
(d) Patented technology
(e) Goodwill
(f) Liabilities
(g) Common stock

Chapter **4** Consolidated Statements on Date of Acquisition

LEARNING OBJECTIVES

After studying this chapter, you should be able to do the following:

- Calculate and allocate the purchase discrepancy, including the allocation of negative goodwill.
- Prepare a consolidated balance sheet on acquisition date, using both the working paper and direct approaches when the parent owns 100 percent and less than 100 percent of the subsidiary.
- Apply the concept of push-down accounting.
- Explain the differences between the four consolidation theories, and apply these theories by preparing a consolidated balance sheet on acquisition date.
- Account for contingent consideration based on its classification as a liability or equity.
- Explain and illustrate the concepts behind a reverse takeover.

INTRODUCTION

Financial statements, published and distributed to owners, creditors, and other interested parties, appear to report the operations and financial position of a single company. In reality, these statements frequently represent a number of separate organizations tied together through common control (a *business combination*). Whenever financial statements represent more than one corporation, we refer to them as *consolidated financial statements*.

Consolidated financial statements are typical in today's business world. Most major organizations, and many smaller ones, hold control over an array of organizations. For example, between 2002 and 2006, Cisco Systems, Inc., reported 30 business acquisitions that now are consolidated in its financial reports. PepsiCo, Inc., as another example, annually consolidates data from a multitude of companies into a single set of financial statements. By gaining control over these companies which include among others Pepsi-Cola Company, Quaker Foods, and Frito-Lay, a single business combination and single reporting entity is formed by PepsiCo.

The consolidation of financial information as exemplified by Cisco Systems and PepsiCo is one of the most complex procedures in all of accounting. To comprehend this process completely, the theoretical logic that underlies the creation of a business combination must be understood. Furthermore, a variety of procedural steps must be mastered to ensure that proper accounting is achieved for this single reporting entity. In this chapter, we will begin our coverage of the consolidation process including the calculation and allocation of the purchase discrepancy.

111

Consolidation of Wholly Owned Subsidiaries

The Canadian accounting principles involved in the preparation of consolidated financial statements are found in Section 1600 of the *Handbook*. In the material that follows in this and later chapters, the preparation of consolidated statements will follow this section's requirements unless the contrary is indicated. Consolidated statements consist of a balance sheet, an income statement, a retained earnings statement, a cash flow statement, and the accompanying notes. In this chapter we will illustrate the preparation of the consolidated balance sheet on the date that control is obtained by the parent company. Consolidation of other financial statements will be illustrated in later chapters.

The acquisition method is required by GAAP and will be used throughout the rest of this book.

In Chapter 3, we introduced the preparation of a consolidated balance sheet immediately after a business combination, using the acquisition method. Summarized financial statements were used to focus on the basic concepts involved. In this chapter we elaborate on these concepts and use more detailed financial statements. The following example will form the basis of many of the illustrations that will be used in this chapter.

We will call the two companies to be consolidated P Ltd. and S Ltd. Both companies have a June 30 fiscal year-end. The balance sheets of the two companies on June 29, Year 1, are shown in Exhibit 4.1.

On June 30, Year 1, P Ltd. obtains control over S Ltd. by paying cash for a portion of that company's outstanding common shares from the shareholders of S Ltd. No additional transactions take place on this date. Immediately after the share acquisition, P Ltd. prepares a consolidated balance sheet.

Exhibit 4.1

BALANCE SHEET
June 29, Year 1

	P Ltd. Book value	S Ltd. Book value	S Ltd. Fair value
Cash	$100,000	$ 12,000	$12,000
Accounts receivable	90,000	7,000	7,000
Inventory	130,000	20,000	22,000
Plant	280,000	50,000	59,000
Patent	—	11,000	10,000
	$600,000	$100,000	
Current liabilities	$ 60,000	$ 8,000	$ 8,000
Long-term debt	180,000	22,000	25,000
Common stock	200,000	40,000	
Retained earnings	160,000	30,000	
	$600,000	$100,000	

These balance sheets present the financial position just prior to the business combination.

100 Percent Ownership

Illustration 1   Assume that on June 30, Year 1, P Ltd. purchases 100 percent of S Ltd. for a total cost of $81,000. Given that P Ltd. paid $81,000 for 100 percent of the shares of S Ltd., we will assume (and it is logical to assume) that the fair value of S Ltd. as a whole was $81,000 on the date of acquisition. P Ltd.'s journal entry to record the acquisition is as follows:

The investment is recorded in the separate-entity records of the parent.

Investment in S Ltd.	81,000	
Cash		81,000

P Ltd.'s year-end is June 30, and the only consolidated statement prepared at this time would be the balance sheet. The income statement, retained earnings statement, and cash flow statement present only the parent's income, retained earnings and cash flows since the two entities were not operating as a combined entity throughout the year.

The calculation and allocation of the purchase discrepancy is a useful first step in the preparation of the consolidated balance sheet. The information provided in this calculation forms the basis of the elimination and adjusting entries required. This calculation is shown in Exhibit 4.2.

Exhibit 4.2

CALCULATION AND ALLOCATION OF PURCHASE DISCREPANCY
(100 percent owned subsidiary)

The purchase price consists of two components — book value of subsidiary's shareholders' equity and purchase price discrepancy.

Cost of 100 percent of S Ltd.			$81,000
Shareholders' equity of S Ltd.			
Common stock		40,000	
Retained earnings		30,000	
		70,000	
P Ltd.'s ownership		100%	70,000
Purchase discrepancy			11,000
Allocated:	*(FV – BV) × 100%		
Inventory	+ 2,000		
Plant	+ 9,000		
Patent	– 1,000		
	10,000		
Long-term debt	+ 3,000		7,000
Balance — goodwill			$ 4,000

* FV fair value
BV book value

The preparation of the consolidated balance sheet using a working paper approach is illustrated in Exhibit 4.3 on the next page.

The consolidated balance sheet is the third balance sheet involving the two entities.

Note that the parent's cash has been reduced by the cost of the acquisition. Two elimination entries are used in the working paper. Entry #1 eliminates the parent's share of the shareholders' equity accounts of the subsidiary and the parent's investment account, with the difference established as the purchase discrepancy. Entry #2 allocates the purchase discrepancy to the identifiable assets and liabilities of the subsidiary, and establishes the goodwill resulting from the business combination. (It should be obvious that only one entry needs to be used if the purchase discrepancy is not established.) The amounts shown in the consolidated balance sheet column are used to prepare the consolidated balance sheet. The two working paper entries are summarized next:

These entries are made on the consolidated worksheet and not in the separate records of the two companies.

#1	Common stock — S Ltd.	40,000	
	Retained earnings — S Ltd.	30,000	
	Purchase discrepancy	11,000	
	Investment in S Ltd.		81,000

#2 Inventory — S Ltd.	2,000	
Plant — S Ltd.	9,000	
Goodwill	4,000	
Patent — S Ltd.		1,000
Long-term debt — S Ltd.		3,000
Purchase discrepancy		11,000

It must be emphasized that these entries[1] are made only in the working paper; they are *not* entered in the accounting records of either P Ltd. or S Ltd.

The Direct Approach An alternative approach to the preparation of consolidated financial statements is to prepare the statements directly without the use of a working paper. It should be obvious from examining the working paper that the investment account, the purchase discrepancy, and the shareholders' equity accounts of the subsidiary do *not* appear on the consolidated balance sheet. The calculation of the purchase discrepancy in a sense eliminates the investment and shareholders' equity accounts. The allocation of the purchase discrepancy provides the amounts used to revalue the net assets of the subsidiary. Having made the necessary calculations, the preparer ignores these accounts (i.e., eliminates them) and prepares the consolidated balance sheet. This is done by combining, on an item-by-item basis, the balance sheets of the parent and the subsidiary while at the same time revaluing for consolidation purposes the balance sheet items of the subsidiary. The basic process involved in the direct approach is as follows:

$$\begin{array}{ccccccc} \text{Book value} & + & \text{Book value} & +(-) & \text{Purchase} & = & \text{Consolidated} \\ \text{(parent)} & & \text{(subsidiary)} & & \text{discrepancy} & & \text{amounts} \end{array}$$

Exhibit 4.3

P LTD.
CONSOLIDATED BALANCE SHEET WORKING PAPER
June 30, Year 1

The investment account now appears on P's separate-entity records.

When consolidating, S's assets and liabilities replace the investment account.

	P Ltd.	S Ltd.	Adjustments and Eliminations Dr.	Adjustments and Eliminations Cr.	Consolidated balance sheet
Cash	$ 19,000	$ 12,000			$ 31,000
Accounts receivable	90,000	7,000			97,000
Inventory	130,000	20,000	(2) $ 2,000		152,000
Plant	280,000	50,000	(2) 9,000		339,000
Patent		11,000		(2) $ 1,000	10,000
Investment in S Ltd.	81,000			(1) 81,000	
Purchase discrepancy			(1) 11,000	(2) 11,000	
Goodwill			(2) 4,000		4,000
	$600,000	$100,000			$633,000
Current liabilities	$ 60,000	$ 8,000			$ 68,000
Long-term debt	180,000	22,000		(2) 3,000	205,000
Common stock	200,000				200,000
Retained earnings	160,000				160,000
Common stock		40,000	(1) 40,000		
Retained earnings		30,000	(1) 30,000		
	$600,000	$100,000	$96,000	$96,000	$633,000

---

[1] In later chapters, the working paper eliminations will be illustrated without the intermediate step of setting up the purchase discrepancy.

The preparation of the consolidated balance sheet using the direct approach is shown in Exhibit 4.4. The non-bolded amounts shown in brackets come from the balance sheets of P Ltd. and S Ltd. The bolded amounts in brackets are consolidation adjustments related to the allocation of the purchase discrepancy. It should be noted that under the acquisition method of accounting for a business combination, consolidated shareholders' equity on acquisition date is always that of the parent company.

Exhibit 4.4	Illustration of the Direct Approach

P LTD.
CONSOLIDATED BALANCE SHEET
June 30, Year 1

Cash (100,000 − 81,000* + 12,000)	$ 31,000
Accounts receivable (90,000 + 7,000)	97,000
Inventory (130,000 + 20,000 + **2,000**)	152,000
Plant (280,000 + 50,000 + **9,000**)	339,000
Patent (11,000 − **1,000**)	10,000
Goodwill (0 + 0 + **4,000**)	4,000
	$633,000

On the date of acquisition, consolidated shareholders' equity = parent's shareholders' equity.

Current liabilities (60,000 + 8,000)	$ 68,000
Long-term debt (180,000 + 22,000 + **3,000**)	205,000
Common stock	200,000 (Parent's)
Retained earnings	160,000
	$633,000

Cash paid by P Ltd. to acquire S Ltd.

Consolidated net income, retained earnings, and cash flows only include the subsidiary's income and cash flows subsequent to the date of acquisition.

Income Statement in Year of Acquisition When a business combination is accounted for using the acquisition method, only the net income earned by the subsidiary after the date of acquisition is included in consolidated net income. For example, if the acquisition occurred halfway through the fiscal year, consolidated net income would consist of the net income of the parent for the full year plus the half-year net income earned by the subsidiary after the acquisition date.[2] In the example used here, both P Ltd. and S Ltd. have a June 30 year-end. P Ltd.'s consolidated financial statements for the year ended June 30, Year 1, would consist of a consolidated balance sheet and P Ltd.'s separate entity statements of net income, retained earnings, and cash flows. This is consistent with what would be done if the parent had purchased the net assets directly from the subsidiary. When a company acquires assets, it records these assets on its own books; it does not record the profit earned by the assets when they belonged to the previous owner. The parent's income and retained earnings do not change on the date of acquisition. The consolidated statements will combine the results of the parent and subsidiary for transactions occurring on and subsequent to the date of acquisition. Notes to the consolidated financial statements in the year of acquisition should disclose revenues, net income, and earnings per share as though the acquisition had occurred at the beginning of the fiscal period.[3]

---

[2] The net income of the subsidiary earned after the acquisition date would be reduced by the amortization of the purchase discrepancy because the asset values in the accounting records of the subsidiary are not the values used for consolidation. This concept will be discussed in Chapter 5.

[3] *CICA Handbook*, paragraph 1581.80.

Under push-down accounting, the subsidiary revalues its assets and liabilities based on the price paid by the parent to acquire these net assets.

Push-down Accounting Under push-down accounting, on the date of acquisition the subsidiary revalues its assets and liabilities based on the parent's acquisition cost. The allocation of the purchase discrepancy is "pushed down" to the actual accounting records of the subsidiary. This practice became permissible under GAAP in 1992 with the issuance of Section 1625, "Comprehensive Revaluation of Assets and Liabilities."

Push-down accounting is another example where GAAP allows a departure from historical cost accounting and allows the use of current values in financial reporting. Even though the subsidiary was not involved in the transaction with the parent (the transaction involved the parent and the shareholders of the subsidiary), the subsidiary is allowed to revalue its assets and liabilities based on the value paid by the parent to acquire these net assets. Since the parent and subsidiary were not related prior to the acquisition, the amount paid by the parent is probably equal to or fairly close to the fair value of these net assets. So, why not use these values to provide more useful, yet very reliable, information to the users of the subsidiary's financial statements.

We will use data from Exhibits 4.1 and 4.2 to illustrate the application of push-down accounting. We assume that on June 30, Year 1, P Ltd. acquires 100 percent of S Ltd. for a total cost of $81,000. After calculating and allocating the purchase discrepancy as shown in Exhibit 4.2, P Ltd. directs the accountants of S. Ltd to revalue the company's assets and liabilities in accordance with the purchase discrepancy allocation.

S Ltd. prepares the following journal entry to record the comprehensive revaluation of all of its assets and liabilities:

By revaluing the assets and liabilities, the subsidiary's shareholders' equity is also revalued.

Inventory	2,000	
Plant	9,000	
Goodwill	4,000	
Long-term debt		3,000
Patent		1,000
Common stock	(plug)	11,000

Section 1625 requires that net increase or decrease resulting from the revaluation be recorded as capital stock or contributed surplus or some other component of shareholders' equity that is readily identified. The section also requires that any retained earnings on acquisition date be reclassified as share capital, contributed surplus, or a separately identified component of shareholders' equity. To satisfy this requirement, S Ltd. makes the following entry:

The subsidiary's common stock is now equal to the amount paid by the parent to acquire the shares of the subsidiary.

Retained earnings	30,000	
Common stock		30,000

Exhibit 4.5 shows the balance sheet of P Ltd, the balance sheet of S Ltd. after recording the push-down journal entries, and the consolidated balance sheet of P Ltd.

Preparing consolidated financial statements is easier if the subsidiary uses push-down accounting.

When push-down accounting has been used by a subsidiary, the preparation of a consolidated balance sheet is considerably simplified, requiring only the elimination of the investment account of the parent company against the shareholders' equity accounts of the subsidiary and the adding together of each of the assets and liabilities of the two companies. Consolidated shareholders' equity is that of the parent company.

Exhibit 4.5

BALANCE SHEET
June 29, Year 1

The carrying value of the subsidiary's assets and liabilities are now equal to the values paid by the parent to acquire these items.

	P Ltd.	S Ltd.	Consolidated
Cash	$ 19,000	$ 12,000	$ 31,000
Accounts receivable	90,000	7,000	97,000
Inventory	130,000	22,000	152,000
Plant	280,000	59,000	339,000
Investment in S Ltd.	81,000		
Patent	—	10,000	10,000
Goodwill	—	4,000	4,000
	$600,000	$114,000	$633,000
Current liabilities	$ 60,000	$ 8,000	$ 68,000
Long-term debt	180,000	25,000	205,000
Common stock	200,000	81,000	200,000
Retained earnings	160,000	—	160,000
	$600,000	$114,000	$633,000

ELIMINATION

Investment in S Ltd.	$81,000
Shareholders' equity — S Ltd.	
Common Stock	81,000
Difference	-0-

Section 1625 allows push-down accounting only when a subsidiary is at least 90 percent owned by a parent, and so theoretically a parent could require a 95 percent-owned subsidiary to use it. Practically, it probably would not, because when a non-controlling interest is present, the consolidation becomes very complex and the benefits from its use disappear. We will not illustrate the use of push-down accounting in years subsequent to the acquisition of a subsidiary; however, for those readers that wish to pursue this further, a full discussion and illustration of comprehensive revaluations can be found on the Online Learning Centre associated with this book (www.mcgrawhill.ca/college/hilton).

When the parent establishes a new company as a subsidiary, there should be no purchase discrepancy.

Subsidiary Formed by Parent In some situations a subsidiary is not acquired through a share purchase, but rather by the parent company forming the subsidiary company. The parent company purchases all of the initial share issue after the subsidiary is incorporated.[4] At this time, the book values and fair values of the subsidiary's net assets are obviously equal, and there is no goodwill. It should also be obvious that the subsidiary has no retained earnings at this time. The preparation of the consolidated balance sheet on the date of formation of the subsidiary is simplified, requiring only the elimination of the parent's investment account against the subsidiary's share capital.

---

[4] It is also possible for a parent to form a less than 100 percent owned subsidiary, or for a 100 percent owned subsidiary to later issue shares that are not purchased by the parent. In either case, the observations made in this paragraph are basically the same.

Illustration 2 — Negative Goodwill   Assume that on June 30, Year 1, P Ltd. purchased 100 percent of the outstanding shares of S Ltd. at a total cost of $75,000. P Ltd.'s journal entry to record the acquisition is as follows:

Investment in S Ltd.	75,000	
Cash		75,000

The calculation and allocation of the purchase discrepancy on this date is shown in Exhibit 4.6.

Exhibit 4.6

CALCULATION AND AMORTIZATION OF PURCHASE DISCREPANCY
(negative goodwill)

The purchase price ($75,000) is less than the fair value of identifiable net assets ($70,000 + $7,000).

Cost of investment in S Ltd.			$75,000
Shareholders' equity of S Ltd.			
Common stock		40,000	
Retained earnings		30,000	
		70,000	
P Ltd.'s ownership		100%	70,000
Purchase discrepancy			5,000
Allocated:	(FV – BV) × 100%		
Inventory	+ 2,000		
Plant	+ 9,000		
Patent	– 1,000		
	10,000		
Long-term debt	+ 3,000		7,000
Balance — "negative goodwill" (recognize as gain)			$–2,000

Negative goodwill arises when the purchase price is less than the fair value of identifiable net assets.

The calculations for the purchase discrepancy and for its initial allocation are similar to what is shown in Exhibit 4.2. However, in this situation the goodwill is negative because the acquisition cost is less than the fair value of identifiable net assets. A business combination that results in negative goodwill is often described as a "bargain purchase." This means that the parent gained control over the subsidiary's assets and liabilities at a price that was less than the fair values assigned to those assets and liabilities. This can occur when share prices are depressed or the subsidiary has a recent history of operating losses. Regardless of the cause, the *Handbook* requires that negative goodwill be allocated to reduce the value of the subsidiary's goodwill to zero and to record any remaining amount as a gain. To record a gain on a purchase of an investment may seem very strange but it is required according to Section 1582:

> If the fair value of the acquirer's interest in the acquiree exceeds the fair value of the consideration transferred for that interest, the acquirer accounts for that excess by reducing the amount of goodwill that otherwise would be recognized. If the goodwill related to that business combination is reduced to zero, any remaining excess is recognized as a gain attributable to the acquirer on the acquisition date.

This paragraph was changed effective January 1, 2011. Prior to this date, the purchase method of accounting was required, negative goodwill was assigned to certain nonmonetary assets and gains on purchases would have been very rare. Subsequent to this date, the acquisition method is required, the subsidiary is valued at fair value regardless of the purchase price, and gains are recognized when the purchase price is less than the fair value of identifiable net assets. This change is consistent with the general trend of revaluing assets and liabilities at fair value and recognizing unrealized gains in income.

The negative goodwill is recognized as a gain on the date of acquisition.

Since there is no goodwill on the subsidiary's books, none of the negative goodwill can be used to reduce goodwill to zero. Therefore, the entire $2,000 of negative goodwill is recorded as a gain on the consolidated income statement and ends up in consolidated retained earnings at the date of acquisition. The working paper to prepare the consolidated balance sheet is shown in Exhibit 4.7.

Entry #1 eliminates the parent's share of the subsidiary's shareholders' equity accounts and the parent's investment account, and establishes the difference as the purchase discrepancy. Entry #2 allocates the purchase discrepancy to revalue the net assets of the subsidiary, and to recognize the gain as shown in the summary at the bottom of Exhibit 4.6.

Exhibit 4.7

P LTD.
CONSOLIDATED BALANCE SHEET WORKING PAPER
June 30, Year 1

	P Ltd.	S Ltd.	Adjustments and Eliminations Dr.	Adjustments and Eliminations Cr.	Consolidated balance sheet
The subsidiary's assets and liabilities are valued at fair value on the consolidated balance sheet.					
Cash	$ 25,000	$ 12,000			$ 37,000
Accounts receivable	90,000	7,000			97,000
Inventory	130,000	20,000	(2) $ 2,000		152,000
Plant	280,000	50,000	(2) 9,000		339,000
Patent		11,000		(2) $ 1,000	10,000
Investment in S Ltd.	75,000			(1) 75,000	
Purchase discrepancy			(1) 5,000	(2) 5,000	
	$600,000	$100,000			$635,000
The gain from the bargain purchase is recorded in income and ends up in consolidated retained earnings on the date of acquisition.					
Current liabilities	$ 60,000	$ 8,000			$ 68,000
Long-term debt	180,000	22,000		(2) 3,000	205,000
Common stock	200,000				200,000
Retained earnings	160,000			2,000	162,000
Common stock		40,000	(1) 40,000		
Retained earnings		30,000	(1) 30,000		
	$600,000	$100,000	$86,000	$86,000	$635,000

The two working paper elimination entries are shown next:

#1	Common stock — S Ltd.	40,000	
	Retained earnings — S Ltd.	30,000	
	Purchase discrepancy	5,000	
	Investment in S Ltd.		75,000

#2	Inventory — S Ltd.	2,000	
	Plant — S Ltd.	9,000	
	Patent — S Ltd.		1,000
	Long-term debt — S Ltd.		3,000
	Purchase discrepancy		5,000
	Retained earnings — P Ltd. (gain on purchase)		2,000

It must be emphasized again that these worksheet entries are made only in the working paper; they are *not* entered in the accounting records of either P Ltd. or S Ltd. If the parent company uses the equity method to account for its investment in the subsidiary, the following entry should be made in the parent's separate-entity records to record the $2,000 gain resulting from the bargain purchase:

Investment in S Ltd.	2,000	
Gain on purchase of S Ltd.		2,000

The equity method makes the parent's separate-entity income equal to consolidated income.

This entry will result in the investment account being valued at the fair value of identifiable net assets of the subsidiary. Furthermore, the parent's separate-entity income under the equity method will now be equal to consolidated net income. As we learned in Chapter 2 and as we will study further in Chapter 5, the parent's income under the equity method should be equal to consolidated net income.

The Direct Approach   Exhibit 4.8 shows the preparation of the consolidated balance sheet on June 30, Year 1, using the direct approach. The summary of the allocation of the purchase discrepancy (Exhibit 4.6) provides all the information needed to avoid having to use a working paper.

Exhibit 4.8

Illustration of the Direct Approach
(negative goodwill)

P LTD.
CONSOLIDATED BALANCE SHEET
June 30, Year 1

Under the direct approach, we add the parent's book value + subsidiary's book value + purchase discrepancy for each asset and liability.

Cash (100,000 − 75,000* + 12,000)	$ 37,000
Accounts receivable (90,000 + 7,000)	97,000
Inventory (130,000 + 20,000 + **2,000**)	152,000
Plant (280,000 + 50,000 + **9,000**)	339,000
Patent (11,000 − **1,000**)	10,000
	$635,000
Current liabilities (60,000 + 8,000)	$ 68,000
Long-term debt (180,000 + 22,000 + **3,000**)	205,000
Common stock	200,000
Retained earnings (160,000 + 0 + **2,000**)	162,000
	$635,000

---

* *Cash paid by P Ltd. to acquire S Ltd.*

A negative purchase price discrepancy is not the same as negative goodwill.

Negative Purchase Discrepancy   It is possible for a purchase discrepancy to be negative. In this situation the parent's interest in the book values of the subsidiary's net assets exceeds the acquisition cost. A negative purchase discrepancy is not the same as negative goodwill, nor does it necessarily imply that there will be negative goodwill. If the fair values of the subsidiary's net assets are less than their book values, the amounts used to revalue the specific identifiable net assets of the subsidiary downward could be greater than the negative purchase discrepancy, resulting in positive goodwill.

Illustration 3 — Subsidiary with Goodwill   The goodwill appearing on the balance sheet of a subsidiary on the date of a business combination is not carried forward

The subsidiary's goodwill arose in a previous business combination.

when the consolidated balance sheet is prepared. At some date in the past the subsidiary was the acquirer in a business combination and recorded the goodwill as the difference between the acquisition cost and the fair value of the net identifiable assets acquired. Now this company has itself become an acquiree. From the perspective of its new parent, the goodwill is not considered to be an identifiable asset at the time of the business combination. The purchase discrepancy is calculated as if the goodwill had been written off by the subsidiary, even though in fact this is not the case. The purchase discrepancy is allocated first to the fair value excess for identifiable net assets and secondly, the remaining balance goes to goodwill. In effect, the old goodwill is ignored and the purchase price determines the value, if any, of new goodwill at the date of acquisition. The following illustration will examine the consolidation process when the subsidiary has existing goodwill.

Assume that on June 30, Year 1, P Ltd. purchased 100 percent of the outstanding shares of S Ltd. for a total cost of $75,000, paid in cash. Exhibit 4.9 shows the balance sheets of the two companies at this time.

Notice that the goodwill (highlighted in boldface), in the amount of $11,000, was called a patent in Exhibit 4.1. Notice also that the acquisition cost is the same as in Illustration 2, where the result turned out to be negative goodwill. When we calculate and allocate the purchase discrepancy in this illustration, the result is positive goodwill of $8,000, as shown in Exhibit 4.10.

The working papers for the preparation of the June 30, Year 1, consolidated balance sheet are presented in Exhibit 4.11.

Three working paper entries are required. Entry #1 writes off the previous goodwill (labelled "old" goodwill in the working paper) to S Ltd.'s retained earnings for purposes of consolidation. Entry #2 eliminates the parent's share of the subsidiary's common stock and adjusted retained earnings and the parent's investment account, and establishes the difference as the purchase discrepancy. Entry #3 allocates the purchase discrepancy to revalue the net assets of the subsidiary and establishes the new goodwill from the business combination

---

Exhibit 4.9

The goodwill on the subsidiary's books (its old goodwill) will be revalued on the date of acquisition.

BALANCE SHEET
June 29, Year 1

	P Ltd. Book value	S Ltd. Book value	S Ltd. Fair value
Cash	$100,000	$ 12,000	$12,000
Accounts receivable	90,000	7,000	7,000
Inventory	130,000	20,000	22,000
Plant	280,000	50,000	59,000
Goodwill	—	**11,000**	
	$600,000	$100,000	
Current liabilities	$ 60,000	$ 8,000	$ 8,000
Long-term debt	180,000	22,000	25,000
Common stock	200,000	40,000	
Retained earnings	160,000	30,000	
	$600,000	$100,000	

Exhibit 4.10

CALCULATION AND ALLOCATION OF PURCHASE DISCREPANCY
(subsidiary with goodwill)

The subsidiary's goodwill is currently worth $8,000 based on the price paid by the parent.

Cost of investment in S Ltd.			$75,000
Shareholders' equity of S Ltd.			
Common stock		40,000	
Retained earnings		30,000	
		70,000	
Deduct old goodwill of S Ltd.		11,000	
Adjusted shareholders' equity		59,000	
P Ltd.'s ownership		100%	59,000
Purchase discrepancy			16,000
Allocated:	(FV – BV) × 100%		
Inventory	+ 2,000		
Plant	+ 9,000		
	11,000		
Long-term debt	+ 3,000		8,000
Balance — goodwill			$ 8,000

Exhibit 4.11

P LTD.
CONSOLIDATED BALANCE SHEET WORKING PAPER
June 30, Year 1

The revalued goodwill appears on the consolidated balance sheet.

	P Ltd.	S Ltd.	Adjustments and Eliminations Dr.		Adjustments and Eliminations Cr.		Consolidated balance sheet
Cash	$ 25,000	$ 12,000					$ 37,000
Accounts receivable	90,000	7,000					97,000
Inventory	130,000	20,000	(3)	$ 2,000			152,000
Plant	280,000	50,000	(3)	9,000			339,000
Goodwill — old		11,000			(1)	$ 11,000	
Investment in S Ltd.	75,000				(2)	75,000	
Purchase discrepancy			(2)	16,000	(3)	16,000	
Goodwill			(3)	8,000			8,000
	$600,000	$100,000					$633,000
Current liabilities	$ 60,000	$ 8,000					$ 68,000
Long-term debt	180,000	22,000			(3)	3,000	205,000
Common stock	200,000						200,000
Retained earnings	160,000						160,000
Common stock		40,000	(2)	40,000			
Retained earnings		30,000	(1)	11,000			
			(2)	19,000			0000000,
	$600,000	$100,000		$105,000		$105,000	$633,000

The three working paper elimination entries are shown below:

#1	Retained earnings — S Ltd.	11,000	
	Goodwill — old — S Ltd.		11,000

These worksheet entries establish the appropriate account balances for the consolidated balance sheet.	#2 Common stock — S Ltd.	40,000	
	Retained earnings — S Ltd.	19,000	
	Purchase discrepancy	16,000	
	Investment in S Ltd.		75,000
	#3 Inventory — S Ltd.	2,000	
	Plant — S Ltd.	9,000	
	Goodwill	8,000	
	Long-term debt — S Ltd.		3,000
	Purchase discrepancy		16,000

Entry #1 was only a working paper entry and was not recorded in the records of S Ltd. If P Ltd. directs S Ltd. to actually write off its $11,000 goodwill as at June 30, Year 1, no further working paper entries will be required for this item in future years. However, if S Ltd. does not write off its recorded goodwill, the preparation of consolidated statements in Year 2 and all future years will require working paper entries, to write off any goodwill that still exists in S Ltd.'s records and to reverse any goodwill impairment that has been recorded.

The Direct Approach   Using the calculations shown in Exhibit 4.10, the consolidated balance sheet can easily be prepared without the use of a working paper, as Exhibit 4.12 shows.

Exhibit 4.12

Illustration of the Direct Approach
(subsidiary with goodwill)

P LTD.
CONSOLIDATED BALANCE SHEET
June 30, Year 1

The direct approach produces the same results as the working paper approach but appears to be easier to perform.	Cash (100,000 – 75,000* + 12,000)	$ 37,000
	Accounts receivable (90,000 + 7,000)	97,000
	Inventory (130,000 + 20,000 + **2,000**)	152,000
	Plant (280,000 + 50,000 + **9,000**)	339,000
	Goodwill (0 + 0 + **8,000**)	8,000
		$633,000
	Current liabilities (60,000 + 8,000)	$ 68,000
	Long-term debt (180,000 + 22,000 + **3,000**)	205,000
	Common stock	200,000
	Retained earnings	160,000
		$633,000

* Cash paid by P Ltd. to acquire S Ltd.

Consolidation of Non-Wholly Owned Subsidiaries

In the first three illustrations, the parent acquired 100 percent of the subsidiary. The subsidiary's assets and liabilities were brought onto the consolidated balance at fair value.[5] We will now consider situations where the parent acquires less than 100 percent of the shares. We will still prepare consolidated financial statements when the

---

[5] Book value + 100% × (FV – BV) = Fair value.

The part of the subsidiary not owned by the parent is called noncontrolling interest (NCI).

parent acquires sufficient shares to control the subsidiary. The shares not acquired by the parent are owned by other shareholders, which are referred to as the noncontrolling shareholders. The value of the shares attributed to the noncontrolling shareholders when presented on the consolidated financial statements is referred to as noncontrolling interest, which is abbreviated as NCI.

Three questions arise when preparing consolidated financial statements for less than 100 percent owned subsidiaries:

1. How should the portion of the subsidiary's assets and liabilities, which were not acquired by the parent, be valued on the consolidated financial statements?

2. How should NCI be valued on the consolidated financial statements?

3. How should NCI be presented on the consolidated financial statements?

The following theories have developed over time and have been proposed as solutions to preparing consolidated financial statements for non-wholly owned subsidiaries:

- proprietary theory
- parent company theory
- parent company extension theory
- entity theory

Each of the theories has been or is currently required by GAAP. The following table indicates the current status and effective usage dates for these four theories:

All four theories have been or will soon be required under Canadian GAAP under specified situations.

Method	Status
Proprietary theory	Present GAAP when consolidating joint ventures but may be discontinued within the next few years as Canadian GAAP converges with international accounting standards
Parent company theory	Is GAAP for consolidating subsidiaries January 1, 2011, (or sooner if Section 1582 is adopted earlier) but is not acceptable under GAAP after January 1, 2009
Parent company extension	An acceptable method of consolidating subsidiaries after January 1, 2011, (or sooner if Section 1582 is adopted earlier) when total value of the subsidiary's goodwill is not reasonably measurable on the date of acquisition
Entity theory	The preferred method for consolidating a subsidiary after January 1, 2011, (or sooner if Section 1582 is adopted earlier) when total value of the subsidiary's goodwill is reasonably measurable on the date of acquisition

The merits of these four theories are discussed in the following section.

Introduction to Consolidation Theories

These four theories differ in the valuation of the noncontrolling interest and how much of the subsidiary's value pertaining to the noncontrolling interest is brought into the consolidated financial statements. The following chart highlights the differences between the four theories. The left side for each theory shows the portion of the subsidiary owned by the parent while the right side shows the portion owned by the noncontrolling interest. The shaded area represents the values brought into the consolidated financial statements.

	Proprietary		Parent Company		Parent Company Extension		Entity	
	Parent	NCI	Parent	NCI	Parent	NCI	Parent	NCI
Book value of Sub's net assets								
Fair value excess								
Goodwill								

The parent's portion of the subsidiary's value is fully represented under all theories. The NCI's share varies under the four theories.

We will illustrate the preparation of consolidated financial statements under these four theories using the following example. Assume that on June 30, Year 1, P Ltd. purchased 80 percent of S Ltd. at a total cost of $64,800. P Ltd.'s journal entry to record this purchase is as follows:

| Investment in S Ltd. | 64,800 | |
| Cash | | 64,800 |

We will use the balance sheets of the two companies on June 29, Year 1 as shown in Exhibit 4.1. Note that the amount paid of $64,800 is 80 percent of $81,000 that was the amount paid in Illustration 1 when P Ltd. acquired 100 percent of S Ltd.

DISCUSSION QUESTION

How Can We Determine Goodwill?

On December 31, Year 7, Maple Company issued preferred shares with a fair value of $600,000 to acquire 12,000 (60 percent) of the common shares of Leafs Limited. The Leafs shares were trading in the market at around $40 per share just days prior to the purchase by Maple. Maple had to and was willing to pay a premium of $10 per share or $120,000 in total in order to gain control over Leafs. The balance sheets for the two companies just prior to acquisition were as follows (in 000s):

	Maple		Leafs	
	Book value	Fair value	Book value	Fair value
Identifiable assets	$2,000	$2,500	$1,000	$1,300
Goodwill	0	??	0	??
	$2,000		$1,000	
Liabilities	$1,500	$1,600	$ 800	$ 840
Shareholders' equity	500	??	200	??
	$2,000		$1,000	

Consolidated financial statements will be prepared to combine the financial statements for the two companies. The management of Maple is concerned about the valuation of goodwill on the consolidated financial statements. It was willing to pay a premium of $120,000 to gain control of Leafs. It maintains that it would have paid the same premium in total whether it acquired 60 percent or 100 percent of the shares of Leafs.

Given that the return on assets is a closely monitored ratio by the shareholders, the management of Maple would like to minimize the value assigned to goodwill on consolidation. Management wants to see how these consolidated statements would differ under four different theories of reporting: proprietary, parent company, parent company extension, and entity. Management also has the following questions when reporting this business combination:

- How are we going to determine the value of the goodwill for the subsidiary?
- How will this affect the valuation of noncontrolling interests?
- Will we have to revalue the subsidiary's assets and liabilities every year when we prepare the consolidated financial statements?
- Which consolidation theory best reflects the economic reality of the business combination?

Proprietary Theory

The proprietary theory focuses solely on the parent's percentage interest in the subsidiary.

Proprietary theory views the consolidated entity from the standpoint of the shareholders of the parent company. The consolidated statements do not acknowledge or show the equity of the noncontrolling shareholders. The consolidated balance sheet on the date of acquisition reflects only the parent's share of the assets and liabilities of the subsidiary, based on their fair values, and the resultant goodwill from the combination. The allocation of the purchase price is shown in Exhibit 4.13:

Exhibit 4.13

CALCULATION OF PURCHASE DISCREPANCY
(proprietary theory)

Cost of 80 percent investment in S Ltd.				$64,800
Shareholders' equity of S Ltd.				
Common stock			40,000	
Retained earnings			30,000	
			70,000	
P Ltd.'s ownership			80%	56,000
Purchase discrepancy				8,800
Allocated:	(FV − BV) × 80%			
Inventory	+ 2,000 × 80%	=	+ 1,600	
Plant	+ 9,000 × 80%	=	+ 7,200	
Patent	− 1,000 × 80%	=	− 800	
			8,000	
Long-term debt	+ 3,000 × 80%	=	+ 2,400	5,600
Balance — Goodwill				$ 3,200

The purchase discrepancy consists of 80 percent of the fair value excess plus the parent's share of the goodwill.

Only the parent's share of the fair values of the subsidiary is brought onto the consolidated balance sheet.

Using the direct approach, the consolidated balance sheet is prepared by combining, on an item-by-item basis, the book values of the parent with *the parent's share* of the fair values of the subsidiary which is derived by using the parent's share of the net book value of the subsidiary plus the purchase discrepancy. Goodwill is established based on the parent's acquisition cost. This process is shown in Exhibit 4.14.

Proprietary theory is not used in practice to consolidate a parent and its subsidiaries. However, its use is required by the *Handbook* as the means of reporting an investment in a joint venture, and the consolidation process is described as "proportionate consolidation." This topic will be fully covered in Chapter 10.

Exhibit 4.14

Illustration of the Direct Approach
(proprietary theory)

P LTD.
CONSOLIDATED BALANCE SHEET
June 30, Year 1

NCI is not recognized under the proprietary theory.

Cash (100,000 − 64,800* + 80% × 12,000)		$ 44,800
Accounts receivable (90,000 + 80% × 7,000)		95,600
Inventory (130,000 + 80% × 20,000 + **1,600**)		147,600
Plant (280,000 + 80% × 50,000 + **7,200**)		327,200
Patent (0 + 80% × 11,000 − **800**)		8,000
Goodwill (0 + 0 + **3,200**)		3,200
		$626,400
Current liabilities (60,000 + 80% × 8,000)		$ 66,400
Long-term debt (180,000 + 80% × 22,000 + **2,400**)		200,000
Total liabilities		266,400
Shareholders' equity		
Common stock	200,000	
Retained earnings	160,000	360,000
		$626,400

Cash paid by P Ltd. to acquire S Ltd.

Entity Theory

The entity theory gives equal attention to the controlling and noncontrolling shareholders.

The entity theory views the consolidated entity as having two distinct groups of shareholders — the controlling shareholders and the noncontrolling shareholders. This theory was described in an American Accounting Association publication, "The Entity Theory of Consolidated Statements," by Maurice Moonitz. Under this theory the consolidated balance sheet reflects the full fair values of the subsidiary's net assets and an amount for goodwill determined as if the parent had acquired 100 percent of the subsidiary's outstanding shares, instead of the less than 100 percent actually acquired. Noncontrolling interest is presented in consolidated shareholders' equity. The amount is based on the fair value of the subsidiary's net assets and the goodwill shown on the consolidated balance sheet. The calculation of the goodwill and the noncontrolling interest is shown in Exhibit 4.15.

Exhibit 4.15

The purchase discrepancy consists of 100 percent of the fair value excess plus the implied value of total goodwill.

CALCULATION OF PURCHASE DISCREPANCY
(entity theory)

Cost of 80 percent investment in S Ltd.			$64,800
Implied cost of 100 percent investment in S Ltd. (64,800 ÷ 80%)			$81,000
Shareholders' equity of S Ltd.			
Common stock		40,000	
Retained earnings		30,000	
			70,000
Implied purchase discrepancy			11,000
Allocated:	(FV – BV) × 100%		
Inventory	+ 2,000 × 100% =	+ 2,000	
Plant	+ 9,000 × 100% =	+ 9,000	
Patent	– 1,000 × 100% =	– 1,000	
		10,000	
Long-term debt	+ 3,000 × 100% =	+ 3,000	7,000
Balance — Goodwill			$ 4,000

CALCULATION OF NONCONTROLLING INTEREST

Implied value of 100 percent investment in S Ltd.	$81,000
Noncontrolling ownership	20%
	$16,200

The value for NCI is based on fair value of the subsidiary.

It should be noted that the entity theory requires an inference as to what the cost of 100 percent would be when the parent has acquired less than 100 percent of the subsidiary's shares. In this particular situation it might be valid to assume that if P Ltd. paid $64,800 for 80 percent of the shares of S Ltd., the cost of 100 percent would have been approximately $81,000. However, in situations where the parent's ownership percentage is much smaller — say, for example, 55 percent — this approach loses much of its validity. It also loses validity in situations where the parent's ownership percentage increases through a series of small purchases and control is eventually achieved after more than 50 percent of the subsidiary's shares have been acquired.

So, while it may, at first, appear to be a simple exercise to determine the implied cost of 100 percent of the subsidiary, this is usually not the case. Business valuation techniques may have to be applied to determine this value. Not only is a business valuation a very costly exercise, it also involves a lot of judgment. In some cases, the cost of determining the implied value of the subsidiary as a whole may not be worth the benefit of the information provided. If so, there would be lots of opposition to using the entity theory.

We should note that the value assigned to the subsidiary as a whole will have a big impact on the value allocated to goodwill. The fair values of identifiable assets and liabilities are usually readily available because these items are traded quite often in the marketplace. However, goodwill is not traded in the marketplace in and by itself. Therefore, determining a value for goodwill is quite subjective and is directly tied to the overall value of the firm. In the example in Exhibit 4.15, if the implied value of the subsidiary as a whole were $84,000 rather than $81,000, goodwill would be $7,000 rather than $4,000. In turn, noncontrolling interest would be

$16,800 rather than $16,200. Throughout this text, unless otherwise noted, the implied value of the subsidiary as a whole will be calculated by dividing the price paid for the shares purchased by the percentage acquired. We recognize that this is an oversimplication. However, the material in this text is complicated enough as is; by keeping it simple in some cases, we may be able to see the forest rather than the multitude of trees.

Using the direct approach, the consolidated balance sheet is prepared by combining on an item-by-item basis the book values of P Ltd. with the fair values[6] of S Ltd. The calculated goodwill is inserted on the asset side, and the calculated noncontrolling interest is shown in shareholders' equity. Exhibit 4.16 illustrates the preparation of the consolidated balance sheet.

Exhibit 4.16	

Illustration of the Direct Approach
(entity theory)

P LTD.
CONSOLIDATED BALANCE SHEET
June 30, Year 1

100 percent of the subsidiary's fair values are brought on to the consolidated balance sheet.

Cash (100,000 – 64,800* + 12,000)	$ 47,200
Accounts receivable (90,000 + 7,000)	97,000
Inventory (130,000 + 20,000 + **2,000**)	152,000
Plant (280,000 + 50,000 + **9,000**)	339,000
Patent (0 + 11,000 – **1,000**)	10,000
Goodwill (0 + 0 + **4,000**)	4,000
	$649,200
Current liabilities (60,000 + 8,000)	$ 68,000
Long-term debt (180,000 + 22,000 + **3,000**)	205,000
Total liabilities	273,000

Noncontrolling interest is presented as a separate component in shareholders' equity.

Shareholders' equity		
Controlling interest		
Capital stock	200,000	
Retained earnings	160,000	
	360,000	
Noncontrolling interest	16,200	376,200
		$649,200

Cash paid by P Ltd. to acquire S Ltd. — Cash paid to shareholders.

The working paper used to prepare the consolidated balance sheet is shown in Exhibit 4.17.

Three working paper entries are used. Entry #1 eliminates the parent's share of the subsidiary's shareholders' equity accounts and the parent's investment account, with the difference established as the purchase discrepancy. Entry #2 eliminates the noncontrolling interest's share of the subsidiary's shareholders' equity accounts and establishes the noncontrolling interest on the consolidated balance sheet with the difference going to purchase discrepancy. Entry #3 allocates the purchase discrepancy to revalue the net assets of the subsidiary and establishes the resulting goodwill.

---

[6] Book value + (FV – BV) × 100% = Fair value

The three working paper elimination entries are:

The first two entries record the purchase price discrepancy and NCI on the consolidated balance sheet.

#1	Common stock — S Ltd.	32,000	
	Retained earnings — S Ltd.	24,000	
	Purchase discrepancy	8,800	
	Investment in S Ltd.		64,800

#2	Purchase discrepancy	2,200	
	Common stock	8,000	
	Retained earnings — S Ltd.	6,000	
	Noncontrolling interest		16,200

The implied purchase discrepancy is allocated to identifiable assets and liabilities and goodwill.

#3	Inventory — S Ltd.	2,000	
	Plant — S Ltd.	9,000	
	Goodwill	4,000	
	Patent — S Ltd.		1,000
	Long-term debt — S Ltd.		3,000
	Purchase discrepancy		11,000

Exhibit 4.17

P LTD.
CONSOLIDATED BALANCE SHEET WORKING PAPER
(entity theory)

	P Ltd.	S Ltd.	Adjustments and Eliminations Dr.		Adjustments and Eliminations Cr.		Consolidated balance sheet
The subsidiary's assets and liabilities are brought onto the consolidated balance sheet at 100 percent of their fair values.							
Cash	$ 35,200	$ 12,000					$ 47,200
Accounts receivable	90,000	7,000					97,000
Inventory	130,000	20,000	(3)	$ 2,000			152,000
Plant	280,000	50,000	(3)	9,000			339,000
Patent		11,000			(3)	$ 1,000	10,000
Investment in S Ltd.	64,800				(1)	64,800	
Purchase discrepancy			(1)	8,800	(3)	11,000	
			(2)	2,200			
Goodwill			(3)	4,000			4,000
	$600,000	$100,000					$649,200
Current liabilities	$ 60,000	$ 8,000					$ 68,000
Long-term debt	180,000	22,000			(3)	3,000	205,000
Common stock	200,000						200,000
Retained earnings	160,000						160,000
NCI is presented as a component of shareholders' equity on the consolidated balance sheet. Common stock		40,000	(1)	32,000			
			(2)	8,000			
Retained earnings		30,000	(1)	24,000			
			(2)	6,000			
Noncontrolling interest					(2)	16,200	16,200
	$600,000	$100,000		$96,000		$96,000	$649,200

Unless otherwise noted, all of the illustrations throughout this text and in the end-of-chapter material will use the entity theory. It is the theory normally required by Canadian GAAP when the total value of goodwill of the subsidiary can be reasonably measured at the date of acquisition.

Parent Company Theory

Parent company theory focuses on the parent company but gives some recognition to NCI.

Parent company theory is similar to proprietary theory in that the focus of the consolidated statements is directed toward the shareholders of the parent company. However, noncontrolling interest is recognized and reflected as a liability in the consolidated balance sheet; its amount is based on the book values of the net assets of the subsidiary.

Noncontrolling interest is calculated as follows:

Shareholders' equity of S Ltd.	
Common stock	$40,000
Retained earnings	30,000
	70,000
Noncontrolling ownership percentage	20%
Noncontrolling interest	$14,000

The consolidated balance sheet is prepared by combining, on an item-by-item basis, the book value of the parent with 100 percent of the book value of the subsidiary *plus* the parent's share of the purchase discrepancy.

Under this theory, the parent's share of the subsidiary is valued at fair value whereas the NCI's share is valued at the subsidiary's book value on the consolidated balance sheet. This process is consistent with the historical cost principle because the parent's portion of the subsidiary's net asset is being acquired by the parent at the date of acquisition. Since the NCI's share of the subsidiary's net assets is not being purchased and is not changing hands, this portion is retained at book value. Exhibit 4.18 shows the preparation of the consolidated balance sheet under the parent company theory. This theory was required by GAAP prior to January 1, 2011.

Exhibit 4.18

Illustration of the Direct Approach
(parent company theory)

P LTD.
CONSOLIDATED BALANCE SHEET
June 30, Year 1

100 percent of the subsidiary's book values plus the parent's share of the fair value excess are brought onto the consolidated balance sheet.

Cash (100,000 – 64,800* + 12,000)	$ 47,200
Accounts receivable (90,000 + 7,000)	97,000
Inventory (130,000 + 20,000 + **1,600**)	151,600
Plant (280,000 + 50,000 + **7,200**)	337,200
Patent (11,000 – **800**)	10,200
Goodwill (0 + 0 + **3,200**)	3,200
	$646,400

Noncontrolling interest is presented as a liability.

Current liabilities (60,000 + 8,000)	$ 68,000
Long-term debt (180,000 + 22,000 + **2,400**)	204,400
Noncontrolling interest	14,000
Total liabilities	286,400

Shareholders' equity		
Capital stock	200,000	
Retained earnings	160,000	360,000
		$646,400

* Cash paid by P Ltd. to acquire S Ltd.

Parent Company Extension Theory

Parent company extension theory was invented to address the concerns about goodwill valuation under the entity theory. Given that many people feel that goodwill for the subsidiary, as a whole, is not a linear extrapolation of what the parent paid for its

All of the subsidiary's value except for the NCI's share of goodwill is brought onto the consolidated balance sheet.

share of goodwill, they did not support the use of the entity theory. However, there is much support for valuing the subsidiary's identifiable assets and liabilities at their full fair value on the consolidated statements. The parent company extension theory does just that — it values both the parent's share and the noncontrolling interest's share of identifiable net assets at fair value. Only the parent's share of the subsidiary's goodwill is brought onto the consolidated statements at the value paid by the parent. Since the total value of the subsidiary's goodwill is not reasonably measurable, the noncontrolling interest's portion of the subsidiary's goodwill is not valued and not brought onto the consolidated statements.

Under the parent company extension theory, noncontrolling interest is recognized and reflected between liabilities and shareholders' equity in the consolidated balance sheet. Its amount is based on the fair values of the identifiable net assets of the subsidiary; it excludes any value pertaining to the subsidiary's goodwill. Noncontrolling interest is calculated as follows:

NCI is based on the fair value of identifiable assets and liabilities.

Shareholders' equity of S Ltd.	
Common stock	$ 40,000
Retained earnings	30,000
	70,000
Excess of fair value over book value for identifiable net assets (see Exhibit 4.15)	7,000
Fair value of identifiable net assets	77,000
Noncontrolling ownership percentage	20%
Noncontrolling interest	$15,400

The consolidated balance sheet is prepared by combining, on an item-by-item basis, the book value of the parent with the fair value of the subsidiary's identifiable assets plus the parent's share of the subsidiary's goodwill. Exhibit 4.19 shows the preparation of the consolidated balance sheet under the parent company extension theory. This theory can be used under Canadian GAAP when the total value of the subsidiary's goodwill cannot be reasonably measured.

Exhibit 4.19

Illustration of the Direct Approach
(parent company extension theory)

P LTD.
CONSOLIDATED BALANCE SHEET
June 30, Year 1

100 percent of the subsidiary's fair values of identifiable assets and liabilities plus the parent's share of the subsidiary's goodwill are brought onto the consolidated balance sheet.

Cash (100,000 – 64,800* + 12,000)		$ 47,200
Accounts receivable (90,000 + 7,000)		97,000
Inventory (130,000 + 20,000 + **2,000**)		152,000
Plant (280,000 + 50,000 + **9,000**)		339,000
Patent (0 + 11,000 – **1,000**)		10,000
Goodwill (0 + 0 + **3,200**)(1 – .2)×4000		3,200
		$648,400

NCI is presented as a separate category between liabilities and shareholders' equity.

Current liabilities (60,000 + 8,000)		$ 68,000
Long-term debt (180,000 + 22,000 + **3,000**)		205,000
Total liabilities		273,000
Noncontrolling interest		15,400
Shareholders' equity		
Capital stock	200,000	
Retained earnings	160,000	360,000
		$648,400

Cash paid by P Ltd. to acquire S Ltd.

Contingent Consideration

The terms of a business combination may require an additional cash payment, or an additional share issue contingent on some specified future event. The accounting for contingent consideration is contained in Section 1582 of the *Handbook*; the material that follows illustrates the concepts involved.

Contingent consideration should be recorded at the date of acquisition when it is measurable and is likely to occur.

If the amount of contingent consideration can be reasonably estimated on the date of the business combination, and the outcome is considered reasonably certain to occur, it is recorded at fair value and is considered part of the purchase cost.

The contingent consideration will be classified either as a liability or equity depending on its nature. If the contingent consideration will be paid in the form of cash or another asset, it will be classified as a liability. If issuing additional shares will pay the contingent consideration, it will be classified as equity. After the initial recognition, the contingent consideration classified as equity will not be remeasured.

After the acquisition date, the fair value of contingent consideration classified as a liability may change due to changes in circumstances like meeting specified sales targets, fluctuations in share price, or subsequent events like receiving government approval on an in-process research and development project. Changes in the fair value of contingent consideration classified as a liability due to changes in circumstances since the acquisition date should be recognized in earnings. Changes in the fair value of contingent consideration due to gathering of new information about facts and circumstances that existed at the acquisition date, however, would be considered measurement period adjustments and reflected in the purchase price.

Given the uncertainty involved, the following should be disclosed regarding contingent consideration:

- The amount of contingent consideration recognized on the acquisition date.
- The range of potential payments (undiscounted).

The range of potential payment for contingent consideration should be disclosed.

- Changes in the amounts recognized for the contingent consideration, changes in the range of outcomes (undiscounted), and the reasons for the changes. That disclosure would be required each period until the contingent consideration is settled.
- The valuation techniques used to measure contingent consideration.

The following discussions illustrate the two types of contingent consideration discussed above.

Contingency Classified as a Liability

If the contingency is classified as a liability, any consideration issued at some future date is recorded at fair value and the change in fair value is recognized in net income. The following example will illustrate this situation.

Able Corporation issues 500,000 no-par-value common shares for all of the outstanding common shares of Baker Company on January 1, Year 1. The shares issued have a fair value of $10 at that time. Able's journal entry on January 1, Year 1, is:

Investment in Baker Company	5,000,000	
Common shares		5,000,000

The business combination agreement states that if the earnings of Baker Company exceed an average of $1.75 per share over the next two years, Able Corporation will make an additional cash payment of $600,000 to the former shareholders of Baker Company. The amount of the possible future payment is known, but because there is no assurance that it will have to be paid, no provision is made for this contingency on January 1, Year 1.

Because Able's fiscal year end falls on December 31, Year 1, the consolidated financial statements are prepared using the $5,000,000 purchase price. This amount is allocated to the identifiable net assets of Baker Company in the usual manner and may result in goodwill, or "negative goodwill." If at the end of the two-year period it is determined that Baker's earnings exceeded the average of $1.75 per share, the required cash payment will be recorded by Able on December 31, Year 2, as follows:

Changes in contingent consideration classified as a liability are reported in net income.

Loss from contingent consideration	$600,000	
Cash		$600,000

Item of Interest West Fraser Timber Co. Ltd. is one of North America's leading forest product companies. With more than 6,900 employees, it produces lumber, kraft paper, and newsprint at more than 30 facilities in British Columbia, Alberta, and the southern U.S.A. On December 31, 2004, the company acquired the only issued share of Weldwood of Canada Limited ("Weldwood"), an integrated forest products company, for net cash consideration of $1.1 billion. The terms of the transaction provided that the seller is entitled to the net after-tax value of any refunds of softwood lumber duties paid by Weldwood before December 31, 2004, and to further cash consideration, not to exceed $50 million in aggregate, if the average market price of NBSK pulp per tonne exceeds the greater of US$710 and Cdn $950 during any quarter ending on or before June 30, 2007.

Changes in contingent consideration classified as equity are reported as adjustments to equity.

Contingency Classified as Equity If the contingency is classified as equity, any consideration issued at some future date will be recorded at fair value but will not be considered an additional cost of the purchase. Instead, the consideration issued will be treated as a reduction in the amount recorded for the original share issue. The following example illustrates this.

Alpha Corporation issues 500,000 no-par-value common shares for all the outstanding common shares of Beta Company on July 1, Year 1. If the shares issued have a fair market value of $5.00, Alpha's journal entry is:

Investment in Beta Company	2,500,000	
Common shares		2,500,000

The combination agreement states that if the market price of Alpha's shares is below $5.00 one year from the date of the agreement, Alpha will issue additional shares to the former shareholders of Beta in an amount that will compensate them for their loss in value. On July 1, Year 2, the market price of Alpha's shares is $4.50. In accordance with the agreement, Alpha Corporation issues additional shares of 55,555.55 ($2,500,000 ÷ $4.50 − 500,000) and records the transaction as follows:

The additional consideration compensates for the loss in value for shares originally issued as consideration for the purchase.

Common shares — old shares (55,555.55 X 4.50)	250,000	
Common shares — new shares		250,000

Footnote disclosure in the Year 2 statements will be made for the amount of consideration, providing the reasons therefore and the accounting treatment used.

Financial Statement Disclosure

Most Canadian companies disclose their policies with regard to long-term investments in accordance with the requirements of Section 1505, "Disclosure of Accounting Policies." The following footnote is taken from the financial statements of Moore Corporation Limited and is fairly typical in content:

> **Principles of consolidation** The financial statements of entities which are controlled by the Corporation, referred to as subsidiaries, are consolidated; entities which are jointly controlled are proportionately consolidated; entities which are not controlled and which the Corporation has the ability to exercise significant influence over are accounted for using the equity method; and investments in other entities are accounted for using the cost method.

The following two paragraphs contain the major disclosure requirements of Section 1590:

An entity should disclose when it has the ability to control without owning a majority interest in the other company

> When a reporting enterprise does not own, directly or indirectly through subsidiaries, an equity interest carrying the right to elect the majority of the members of the board of directors of a subsidiary, the reporting enterprise should disclose (i) the basis for the determination that a parent–subsidiary relationship exists, (ii) the name of the subsidiary, and (iii) the percentage ownership (if any). [1590.22]

An entity should disclose when it does not have the ability to control even when it has a majority interest in the other company

> When a reporting enterprise owns, directly or indirectly through subsidiaries, an equity interest carrying the right to elect the majority of the members of the board of directors of an investee that is not a subsidiary, the reporting enterprise should disclose (i) the basis for the determination that a parent–subsidiary relationship does not exist, (ii) the name of the investee, (iii) the percentage ownership, and (iv) either separate financial statements of the investee, combined financial statements of similar investees or, provided all information significant to the consolidated financial statements is disclosed, condensed financial statements (including notes) of the investee. [1590.23]

Earlier in this chapter, we discussed the general presumptions regarding the factors that establish a control investment and noted that these presumptions could be overcome in certain situations. The above two disclosure paragraphs require a company to give full details when the normal quantitative guidelines of 50 percent ownership of voting shares are not used by an investor. Note that the last two words of paragraph 22 seem to indicate that it is possible for an investor to have a control investment without owning any shares of an investee.

Item of Interest On December 31, 2005, The Coca-Cola Company (the Company) owned approximately 36 percent of the voting shares of Coca-Cola Enterprises Inc. (CCE). Under agreements with the Company, CCE has exclusive rights to bottle and market the Company's products in specified territories throughout the world using containers authorized by the Company. The agreements also require CCE to use concentrates and syrups purchased from the Company in the products that it manufactures. The sale of Coca-Cola products makes up about 90 percent of CCE's revenues. On December 31, 2005, CCE showed the following in its financial statements:

Total assets	$25 billion
Total liabilities	$20 billion
Sales	$19 billion

The Coca-Cola Company reports its investment in CCE as a significant-influence investment using the equity method, because U.S. GAAP requires a majority ownership in order to consolidate an investee company. If U.S. GAAP defined control in the manner that Canadian GAAP does, the Coca-Cola Company would probably have to consolidate CCE and bring its assets and liabilities onto its consolidated balance sheet and its sales revenues onto its consolidated income statement. Consolidated net income would not change but many financial ratios used by analysts to assess performance and position could be quite different.

Differential Reporting

A qualifying enterprise could use the cost method or equity method to report its investment in subsidiaries instead of reporting on a consolidated basis.

As discussed in previous chapters, a qualifying enterprise is one that is a non-public company whose shareholders have unanimously agreed to apply differential reporting options. Under Section 1590, "Subsidiaries," a qualifying enterprise may elect to report all of its subsidiaries by using the equity method or the cost method. If there has been a permanent loss in value of an investment in a nonconsolidated subsidiary, the investment must be written down and the loss reflected in income.

An International Perspective

In some countries, control is defined as having greater than 50 percent of the voting shares.

Once Section 1582 on Business Combinations goes into effect (which is expected to be on January 1, 2011), the Canadian standards for business combination will be converged with the IASB standards. Until then, the standards are much the same except for the following:

1. IFRS requires that contingent consideration be recognized when it is probable that it will be paid and can be reliably measured whereas the CICA states that the contingency should not be recognized until the contingency is resolved and consideration is issued or issuable.

2. IFRS requires that any negative goodwill be recognized immediately in profit or loss whereas the CICA requires that the negative goodwill be first allocated to certain non-monetary assets and any residual recognized in income as an extraordinary item.

The IASB, FASB, and CICA should have converged standards for consolidations within a few years.

3. IFRS uses the parent company extension method whereas the CICA uses the parent company method.

SUMMARY

Consolidated financial statements present the financial position and operating results of a group of companies under common control as if they constitute a single entity. When one company gains control over another company, it becomes a parent company and GAAP requires it to present consolidated statements for external reporting purposes. The preparation involves eliminating the parent's investment account and the parent's share of the subsidiary's shareholders' equity accounts; revaluing the net assets of the subsidiary to fair value; and establishing the noncontrolling interest in the fair value of the subsidiary's net assets. If the subsidiary applies push-down accounting, the revaluations used to consolidate are recorded in the records of the subsidiary; this simplifies the consolidation process. A working paper can be used to prepare the consolidated statements, and is necessary if there are a large number of subsidiaries to consolidate. A computerized spreadsheet is particularly useful in this situation. When there are only one or two subsidiaries, the direct approach is by far the fastest way to arrive at the desired results.

SELF-STUDY PROBLEM

On December 31, Year 1, CAN Company takes control over the net assets of UKS Company by purchasing 80% of the common shares of UKS Company. CAN Company will pay for the purchase by issuing common shares with a fair market value of $35,200. The following information has been assembled:

	CAN Company	UKS Company	
	Book value	Book value	Fair value
Current assets	$ 50,000	$15,000	$14,000
Plant assets	80,000	20,000	26,000
Goodwill	0	0	22,000
	$130,000	$35,000	$62,000
Current liabilities	$ 30,000	$10,000	$10,000
Long-term debt	25,000	7,000	8,000
Shareholders' equity	75,000	18,000	
	$130,000	$35,000	

Required:

Prepare a consolidated balance sheet for CAN Company immediately after the combination under the:

(a) Proprietary theory.
(b) Parent company theory.
(c) Parent company extension theory.
(d) Entity theory.

Solution to Self-study Problem

CAN COMPANY
Balance Sheet
At December 31, Year 1
(See notes)

	(a)	(b)	(c)	(d)
Current assets	$ 61,200	$ 64,200	$ 64,000	$ 64,000
Plant assets	100,800	104,800	106,000	106,000
Goodwill	17,600	17,600	17,600	22,000
	$179,600	$186,600	$187,600	$192,000
Current liabilities	$ 38,000	$ 40,000	$ 40,000	$ 40,000
Long-term debt	31,400	32,800	33,000	33,000
Noncontrolling interest		3,600	4,400	
Shareholders' equity				
CAN	110,200	110,200	110,200	110,200
Noncontrolling interest				8,800
	$179,600	$186,600	$187,600	$192,000

Notes:
1. The assets and liabilities are calculated as follows:
    (a) Book values for CAN and 80% of fair values for UKS.
    (b) Book values for CAN and book values for UKS plus 80% of fair value excess for UKS's identifiable assets and liabilities plus 80% of the value of UKS's goodwill.
    (c) Book values for CAN and book values for UKS plus 100% of fair value excess for UKS's identifiable assets and liabilities plus 80% of the value of UKS's goodwill.
    (d) Book values for CAN and book values for UKS plus 100% of fair value excess for UKS's identifiable assets and liabilities plus 100% of the value of UKS's goodwill.
2. The noncontrolling interest is calculated as follows:
    (b) 20% × book value of UKS' shareholders' equity.
    (c) 20% × fair value of UKS' identifiable assets and liabilities.
    (d) 20% × fair value of UKS' identifiable assets, identifiable liabilities, and goodwill.

APPENDIX 4A

Reverse Takeovers

Section 1582 of the *Handbook* describes a reverse takeover in the following paragraph:

For accounting purposes, the acquirer is identified based on which shareholder group has control over the combined entity.

Occasionally, an enterprise obtains ownership of the shares of another enterprise but, as part of the transaction, issues enough voting shares as consideration that control of the combined enterprise passes to the shareholders of the acquired enterprise (commonly referred to as a "reverse takeover"). Although legally the enterprise that issues the shares is regarded as the parent or continuing enterprise, the enterprise whose former shareholders now control the combined enterprise is treated as the acquirer. As a result, the issuing enterprise is deemed to be a continuation of the acquirer and the acquirer is deemed to have acquired control of the assets and business of the issuing enterprise in consideration for the issue of capital.

While not a common event, this form of business combination is often used by active non-public companies as a means to obtain a stock exchange listing without having to go through the listing procedures established by the exchange. A takeover of a dormant company that has a stock exchange listing is arranged in such a way that the dormant company emerges as the legal parent.

While Section 1582 describes how a reverse takeover can occur, it does not adequately explain how to account for it. There must have been a need for guidance in this matter, because in 1990 the Emerging Issues Committee issued an abstract to deal with the accounting involved. The following example illustrates the required accounting as outlined in EIC-10, "Reverse Takeover Accounting."

Reverse Takeover Illustration   The balance sheets of Reverse Ltd. and Takeover Co. on the date of a reverse takeover business combination are shown in Exhibit 4A.1.

Reverse is a dormant company (not currently engaged in any business activity) with a listing on a major stock exchange. Takeover is an active company not listed on any exchange. A business combination is initiated by Takeover whereby Reverse issues 240 shares to the shareholders of Takeover for 100 percent of their shareholdings. By structuring the combination in this manner, Reverse becomes the legal parent and Takeover the legal subsidiary.

An examination of the shares held by the two shareholder groups in the following manner clearly indicates that Takeover is identified as the acquirer:

In a reverse takeover, the legal parent is deemed to be the subsidiary for accounting purposes and the legal subsidiary is deemed to be the parent.

	Shares of Reverse Ltd.	%
Shareholders of Reverse Ltd.	160	40%
Shareholders of Takeover Co.	240	60%
	400	100%

Exhibit 4A.1

BALANCE SHEETS

	Reverse Ltd. Book value	Reverse Ltd. Fair value	Takeover Co. Book value
Current assets	$ 560	$ 700	$1,560
Fixed assets	1,600	1,650	5,100
	$2,160		$6,660
Liabilities	$ 720	$ 720	$3,060
Common stock (160 shares)	500		
Retained earnings	940		
Common stock (96 shares)*			1,080
Retained earnings			2,520
	$2,160		$6,660

* The shares of Takeover Co. have a current market value of $30 per share.

Under the acquisition method of accounting for a business combination, the fair value of the net assets of the acquiree is combined with the book value of the net assets of the acquirer. Because Takeover is the acquirer, the acquisition cost is determined *as if* Takeover had issued shares to the shareholders of Reverse. A calculation has to be made to determine the number of shares that Takeover would have issued to achieve the same result (i.e., so that its shareholders would end up holding 60 percent of Takeover's outstanding shares). The number of shares can be determined as follows:

The acquisition cost for the deemed parent is determined based on a hypothetical situation that could have achieved the same percentage ownership in the combined entity.

1. Before the combination the shareholders of Takeover hold 96 shares in that company.
2. Takeover would have to issue X additional shares, such that the 96 shares will represent 60 percent of the total shares outstanding.
3. After the share issue, the total shares outstanding will be 96 + X shares.
4. 96 = 0.6 (96 + X). Therefore, X = 64 shares.

If Takeover had issued 64 shares, the holdings of the two groups of shareholders would have been as follows:

	Shares of Takeover Co.	%
Shareholders of Takeover	96	60%
Shareholders of Reverse	64	40%
	160	100%

The acquisition cost is the number of shares that Takeover would have issued valued at their fair market value, and is allocated in the following manner:

Goodwill of the deemed subsidiary is based on the hypothetical acquisition cost.

Acquisition cost — 64 shares @ $30	$1,920
Fair value of identifiable net assets of Reverse Co.	1,630
Goodwill	$ 290

The balance sheet of the combined company immediately after the business combination is prepared by combining the fair value of the net assets of Reverse, including the goodwill from the combination, with the book value of the net assets of Takeover. It should be noted that Takeover's shareholders' equity becomes the shareholders' equity of the combined company. The amount shown for common stock is determined by summing the common stock of Takeover before the combination and the deemed issue of 64 shares at market value. However, the number of shares shown as issued are the outstanding shares of the legal parent Reverse. The consolidated balance sheet of Reverse immediately after the reverse takeover takes place is shown in Exhibit 4A.2.

Shareholders' equity should reflect the shareholders' equity of the deemed parent.

The financial statements of Reverse would contain the following footnote to describe this event:

During the year Reverse Ltd. entered into a share exchange agreement with the shareholders of Takeover Co. Under this agreement Reverse exchanged 240 common shares for 100% of the issued and outstanding shares of Takeover. As a result of the share exchange, Reverse obtained control over Takeover.

Legally Reverse is the parent of Takeover, however, as a result of the share exchange, control of the combined companies passed to the shareholders of Takeover, which for accounting purposes is deemed to be the acquirer. For financial reporting purposes, this share exchange is considered to be a reverse takeover and Reverse is considered to be a continuation of Takeover. The net assets of Takeover are included in the balance sheet at book values, and the deemed acquisition of Reverse is accounted for by the acquisition method, with

Note disclosure is required to explain that the reporting follows the substance (rather than the legal form) of who has control.

Exhibit 4A.2

The legal parent/deemed subsidiary's assets are brought in at fair value while the legal subsidiary/deemed parent's assets are brought in at book value.

REVERSE LTD.
CONSOLIDATED BALANCE SHEET

Current assets (700 + 1,560)	$2,260
Fixed assets (1,650 + 5,100)	6,750
Goodwill	290
	$9,300
Liabilities (720 + 3,060)	$3,780
Common stock* (1,080 + 1,920)	3,000
Retained Earnings	2,520
	$9,300

* The number of shares issued and outstanding would be shown as 400 shares (160 + 240).

the net assets of Reverse recorded at fair values. The fair value of Reverse on the date of acquisition was as follows:

Current assets	$ 700
Fixed assets	1,650
Goodwill	290
Liabilities	(720)
	$1,920

In this example the acquisition cost was determined by multiplying the number of shares that the legal subsidiary would have had to issue by the market price of that company's shares. This market price is probably the most appropriate one to use, because if the legal parent is dormant, the market price of its shares may not be indicative of true value, or its shares may not be trading on the exchange. However, because the legal subsidiary is often a private company, the market value of its shares may have to be determined using business valuation concepts. If a market price cannot be determined for the shares of the legal subsidiary, the fair value of the net assets of the legal parent would be used to determine acquisition cost.

The comparative amounts are those of the legal subsidiary/ deemed parent.

Comparative amounts presented in the consolidated financial statements of the legal parent are those of the legal subsidiary. In the year of the reverse takeover, consolidated net income is made up of the income of the legal subsidiary *before* the takeover and the income of the combined company *after* the takeover.

Because the outstanding shares shown on the consolidated balance sheet are those of the legal parent, the calculation of earnings per share is based on these shares; so is the calculation of the weighted average shares outstanding in the year of the takeover.

In the example of Reverse, assuming the combination date was July 31, the weighted average shares outstanding for the fiscal year December 31 is 307 shares, calculated as follows:

- 240 shares deemed outstanding for 7 months, *and*
- 400 shares outstanding for 5 months

The consolidated financial statements use the name and shares outstanding of the legal parent.

This calculation is in contrast to the normal calculation of weighted average shares outstanding and requires further clarification. Remember that the consolidated statements of Reverse (the legal parent) are considered to be a continuation of those of Takeover (the legal subsidiary) and that the accounting assumes that the legal subsidiary acquired the legal parent. But the shares outstanding are those of the legal parent.

Consolidated net income for the year *does not* contain the income of Reverse prior to the takeover date because this income is considered to be preacquisition earnings. Reverse picked up the first seven months' income of Takeover with the issue of 240 shares. The last five months' income is that of Takeover and Reverse, during which time 400 shares (160 + 240) were outstanding.

The consolidated financial statements use values consistent with whom, in substance, is the parent and with whom, in substance, is the subsidiary.

The consolidated balance sheet of Reverse Ltd. (Exhibit 4A.2) was prepared using a non–working paper (or direct) approach. We will now illustrate the preparation of the consolidated balance sheet using a working paper (Exhibit 4A.3). On the date of the reverse takeover, Reverse (the legal parent) would make the following journal entry to record the acquisition of 100 percent of the outstanding shares of Takeover by the issuance of 240 common shares:

Investment in Takeover Co.	1,920	
Common shares (new)		1,920

These "new" shares are issued at the deemed acquisition cost and are shown separately on the working paper to simplify the consolidation process.

The calculation and allocation of the purchase discrepancy is as follows:

The purchase allocation uses the acquisition cost under the hypothetical situation.

	(FV – BV)		
Acquisition cost of Takeover Co.			$1,920
Book value of Reverse Ltd.			
Common stock		500	
Retained earnings		940	1,440
Purchase discrepancy			480
Allocated:			
Current assets	140		
Fixed assets	50		190
Goodwill			$ 290

Elimination entry #1 eliminates Reverse's investment in Takeover against *Reverse's precombination shareholders' equity*, with the purchase discrepancy the balancing amount.

Elimination #2 allocates the purchase discrepancy to revalue the net assets of Reverse.

The consolidated common stock is the common stock of Takeover (the legal subsidiary) before the takeover plus the new shares issued by Reverse, which are valued at Takeover's deemed acquisition cost of Reverse.

Exhibit 4A.3

REVERSE LTD.
CONSOLIDATED BALANCE SHEET WORKING PAPER
(immediately after the reverse takeover)

		Reverse Ltd.	Takeover Co.	Adjustments and Eliminations Dr.	Cr.	Consolidated balance sheet
The assets reflect the fair values of the deemed subsidiary and book values of the deemed parent.	Current assets	$ 560	$1,560	**(2)** $ 140		$2,260
	Fixed assets	1,600	5,100	**(2)** 50		6,750
	Investment in Takeover Co.	1,920			**(1)** $1,920	
	Purchase discrepancy			**(1)** 480	**(2)** 480	
	Goodwill			**(2)** 290		290
		$4,080	$6,660			$9,300
Retained earnings are the retained earnings of the deemed parent.	Liabilities	$ 720	$3,060			$3,780
	Common stock (old)	500		**(1)** 500		
	Retained earnings	940		**(1)** 940		
	Common stock		1,080			3,000
	Common stock (new)	1,920				
	Retained earnings		2,520			2,520
		$4,080	$6,660	$2,400	$2,400	$9,300

REVIEW QUESTIONS

Questions, cases, and problems that deal with the appendix material are denoted with an asterisk.

1. In the preparation of a consolidated balance sheet, the parent's share of the fair value–book value differences are used. Would these differences be used if the subsidiary applied push-down accounting? Explain.

2. What does push-down accounting mean and under what conditions is push-down accounting considered appropriate?

3. Is a negative purchase discrepancy the same as negative goodwill? Explain.

4. With respect to noncontrolling interest, what are the major differences between proprietary, parent, and entity theories?

5. How is the goodwill appearing on the balance sheet of a subsidiary prior to a business combination treated in the subsequent preparation of consolidated statements? Explain.

6. Under the entity theory, consolidated goodwill is determined by inference. Describe how this is achieved and comment on its shortcomings.

7. What is noncontrolling interest, and how is it reported in the consolidated balance sheet if Canadian GAAP is applied?

8. Explain how changes in the fair value of contingent consideration should be reported assuming that the contingent consideration will be paid in the form of cash.

9. What differential reporting options are available in Section 1590?

*10. What is a reverse takeover, and why is such a transaction entered into?

*11. Explain how the acquisition cost is determined for a reverse takeover.

MULTIPLE-CHOICE QUESTIONS

1. What is push-down accounting?
   a. The parent company revalues its shareholders' equity to reflect the market value of its shares on the date of acquisition of a wholly owned subsidiary.
   b. The parent company revalues its investment in a subsidiary at fair value at the date of acquisition and at each reporting date subsequent to the date of acquisition.
   c. The subsidiary company revalues its shareholders' equity at the date of acquisition based on the price paid by the parent to acquire the subsidiary.
   d. The subsidiary company revalues its shareholders' equity to fair value at each reporting date subsequent to the date of acquisition.

2. Which of the following does the proprietary theory require the parent to report when consolidating its subsidiary?
   a. The subsidiary's assets at 100% of book value plus the parent's share of fair value increments or decrements.
   b. The subsidiary's assets at the parent's share of fair values.
   c. The subsidiary's assets at the parent's share of book values.
   d. The subsidiary's assets at 100% of fair value.

The following data should be used for Questions 3 and 4.

On January 1, Year 5, Poor Co. acquired 80% of the outstanding common shares of Standard Inc. by paying cash of $275,000. The book values and fair values of both companies immediately before the acquisition were as follows:

	Poor Co.		Standard Inc.	
	Book values	Fair values	Book values	Fair values
Current assets	$ 470,000	$ 485,000	$100,000	$120,000
Fixed assets	2,879,000	3,200,000	175,000	250,000
Intangibles	45,000	50,000	50,000	75,000
	$3,394,000		$325,000	
Current liabilities	$ 367,000	$ 355,000	$125,000	$125,000
Long-term debt	1,462,000	1,460,000	50,000	40,000
Common stock	1,000,000		60,000	
Retained earnings	565,000		90,000	
	$3,394,000		$325,000	

3. Assume that intangibles do not include goodwill. What amount would Poor Co. report on its consolidated financial statements immediately after the acquisition transaction for goodwill?
   a. $25,000
   b. $51,000
   c. $63,750
   d. $87,750

4. What amount would Poor Co. report on its consolidated financial statements immediately after the acquisition transaction for fixed assets?
   a. $3,129,000
   b. $3,114,000
   c. $3,079,000
   d. $3,054,000

*5. At December 31, Year 5, Alpha Company has 20,000 common shares out-standing while Beta Inc. has 10,000 common shares outstanding. Alpha wishes to enter into a reverse takeover of Beta to gain its listing on the stock exchange. Which one of the following describes how many shares would have to be issued, and by which company, for this to occur?
   a. Alpha would have to issue more than 10,000 shares.
   b. Alpha would have to issue more than 20,000 shares.
   c. Beta would have to issue more than 10,000 shares.
   d. Beta would have to issue more than 20,000 shares.

*6. Refer to Question 5. Which company's name would appear on the financial statements of the combined company after the reverse takeover?
   a. Alpha Company.
   b. Beta Inc.
   c. Both names would appear on the statements, by law.
   d. A new name would have to be created to identify the new economic entity that has been created.

The following scenario applies to Questions 7 and 8, although each question should be considered independently.

A parent company acquires 80% of the shares of a subsidiary for $400,000. The carrying value of the subsidiary's net assets is $350,000. The market value of the identifiable net assets of the subsidiary is $380,000.

7. Which of the following represents the amount of goodwill that should be reported at the time of the acquisition?
   a. $16,000
   b. $20,000
   c. $96,000
   d. $120,000

(CICA adapted)

8. Which of the following represents the noncontrolling shareholder's interest that should be reported when the acquisition takes place?
   a. $70,000
   b. $76,000
   c. $80,000
   d. $100,000

(CICA adapted)

9. During Year 5, XYZ Ltd. purchased all of the 100,000 outstanding Class B shares of Sub Limited. Each share carries one vote. The previous owner, Mr. Bill, retained all 80,000 outstanding Class A shares of Sub, each also carry-ing one vote. In order to avoid sudden changes, Mr. Bill stipulated in the sale agreement that he was to retain the right to veto management appointments for Sub and to approve any significant transactions of Sub. How should XYZ report its investment in Sub assuming that the fair value of Sub's shares is not readily available?
   a. Full consolidation
   b. Proportionate consolidation
   c. Equity method
   d. Cost method

(CICA adapted)

10. XT follows generally accepted accounting principles for consolidation of companies involved in a business combination. It owns 80 percent of the shares of its subsidiary, YB. Which of the following combinations of YB's net book value (NBV) and fair value increments (FVI) would be included in its consolidated asset values?
    a. 80% of NBV and 80% of FVI
    b. 100% of NBV and 80% of FVI
    c. 100% of NBV and 100% of FVI
    d. 80% of NBV and 100% of FVI

    (CGA-Canada, from 2002-2007)

The following data should be used for questions 11 and 12.

On August 1, Year 5, Aluminum Company acquired 70 percent of the common shares of Copper Company for $700,000. On that date, the fair value of Copper's identifiable net assets was $600,000 and the book value of its shareholders' equity was $500,000.

11. Assume that the acquisition method, entity theory will be used to prepare consolidated financial statements. What amount of noncontrolling interest should be reported on the consolidated balance sheet on the date of acquisition?
    a. $0
    b. $150,000
    c. $180,000
    d. $300,000

12. Assume that the acquisition method, parent company theory will be used to prepare consolidated financial statements. What amount of noncontrolling interest should be reported on the consolidated balance sheet on the date of acquisition?
    a. $0
    b. $150,000
    c. $180,000
    d. $300,000

13. On January 1, Year 5, PEB acquired 100 percent of the common shares of SEB for $600,000. On that date, the fair value of SEB's identifiable net assets was $700,000. Which of the following is the appropriate treatment of the $100,000 purchase price discrepancy?
    a. It should be recognized as a gain on purchase.
    b. It should be allocated to identifiable non-monetary assets.
    c. It should be allocated to non-current assets with any remaining balance reported as an extraordinary item.
    d. A deferred credit should be set up and amortized over a maximum of 40 years.

    (CGA-Canada, from 2002-2007)

14. Under differential reporting, a qualifying enterprise may elect to:
    a. Consolidate only those subsidiaries that are homogeneous.
    b. Account for some subsidiaries by the cost method and some subsidiaries by the equity method.
    c. Consolidate all subsidiaries using the proportionate consolidation method.
    d. Account for all subsidiaries by either the cost method or by the equity method.

CASES

Case 1 Eternal Rest Limited (ERL) is a public company; its shares are traded on a stock exchange in Canada. ERL operates both funeral homes and cemeteries in Canada. Funeral services (casket, flowers, cemetery stone, prayer service) are sold on an "as needed" basis and also "in advance" (prepaid). ERL recognizes revenue only as the funeral services are performed.

Cemetery land is purchased years in advance, and carrying costs (e.g., interest and property taxes) are capitalized. The company sells burial plots or gravesites in advance, or on an "as needed" basis. Revenues from plots sold in advance are recognized upon signing a contract, regardless of the timing of receipt of cash. The cost of maintenance for 100 years is recognized as an expense of earning revenue. By law, funds for maintenance are sent to a trustee, for investment. Funds are allowed to be withdrawn annually for current maintenance costs. The cost of the cemetery land and land improvements (including trees, fencing, and pathways) is allocated to cost of sales.

As a result of acquisitions, ERL tripled its assets in fiscal Year 5. Effective September 1, Year 4, ERL acquired the assets and liabilities of Tranquil Cemeteries Limited (Tranquil) by issuing common shares and debt. ERL also acquired, effective November 1, Year 4, 70% of the voting common shares of Peaceful Cemeteries Limited (Peaceful), in exchange for $1 million cash (borrowed from ERL's banker) plus common shares of ERL. Peaceful was privately owned by a single shareholder before the purchase of its shares by ERL. The common shares of ERL that were issued with respect to the acquisitions have been escrowed, and may not be sold for one year from their issuance date.

You, CA, are a new manager with a CA firm. Your firm was appointed as the auditor of ERL in September Year 4, for the year ending June 30, Year 5. Your firm was also appointed as the auditor of Peaceful.

It is now September Year 5. Your firm has experienced severe staffing shortages. The partner has advised you that because of the recent departure of another manager, you have been assigned to the ERL and Peaceful engagements. The audit fieldwork has been completed, but the file review has not taken place. The partner has asked you to review the audit files and notes prepared by the senior in charge of the engagements and to prepare a memo that provides your analysis and disposition of the accounting issues.

The following information was assembled from your review of the working papers of ERL and Peaceful.

1. The acquisition of Tranquil's net assets resulted in the following additions to ERL's balance sheet as of September 1, Year 4 (in thousands of dollars):

Working capital	$ 850
Land	1,400
Buildings and equipment, net	3,700
Non-competition agreements	3,000
Goodwill	11,250
Total net assets of Tranquil	$20,200

The $20.2 million was paid as follows:	
5-year non-interest-bearing first mortgage bonds of ERL	$18,150
Common shares of ERL, escrowed for one year	2,050
	$20,200

The auditors read the purchase and sale agreement and noted that $820,000 of the working capital represented funds that were being held in trust for future maintenance of the cemetery lands. The new common shares issued by ERL were valued at the market price on the day prior to the signing of the agreement.

The $3 million paid for non-competition agreements represents a payment to the sellers of Tranquil in exchange for their commitment not to engage in the same type of business for five years. The $3 million represents the otherwise expected earnings of the sellers, discounted at the 9% market rate of interest that prevailed at the time. The $1.4 million and $3.7 million assigned to land and buildings and equipment represent management's estimates of the fair values of these assets and coincide with book values on Tranquil's books.

2. The shares of Peaceful were acquired primarily because the company had non-capital loss carry-forwards for income tax purposes. The purchase price for the acquisition was a $1 million cash payment by ERL plus the issuance of $24 million of ERL shares for the 70% ownership. The purchase price was allocated to assets and liabilities in a manner similar to the allocation for the Tranquil acquisition. The auditors did not request that the estimated value of the loss carry-forward be recorded. ERL attributed $4 million to non-competition agreements (to be amortized over five years) and $14 million to goodwill.

3. After the acquisition of Peaceful by ERL, sufficient business was directed to Peaceful to commence the process of utilizing the tax loss carry-forwards. During fiscal Year 5, the benefit realized from the utilization of the loss carry-forwards amounted to $2.36 million and was credited to extraordinary gain on the income statement.

4. Excess cemetery land (acquired in the purchase of Tranquil) was sold in December Year 4 at a gain of $1.2 million. The proceeds were reported as "other revenue."

5. One working paper entitled "Land" contains the following note: "Land recorded on the books at $2,305,600 and called 'Sunset Hill' is undeveloped and is not scheduled for use until Year 8 or Year 9. It is subject to a Year 5 government order requiring that ERL clear up environmental concerns on the site. I asked one employee what the cost would be and was told 'half a million dollars.' No amount was accrued, because of uncertainty."

6. A working paper entitled "Management Compensation" shows that senior management shares in what is called a "Bonus Pool." The bonus is 15% of income before income taxes.

Required:

Prepare the memo.

(CICA adapted)

Case 2   *PART A*

On its year-end date, Donna Ltd. purchased 80% of the outstanding shares of Gunn Ltd. Before the purchase, Gunn had a deferred charge of $10.5 million on its balance sheet. This item consisted of organization costs that were being amortized over a 20-year period in accordance with company policy.

Required:

What amount should be reported in Donna's consolidated statements, issued in accordance with GAAP, for Gunn's deferred charge? Provide support for your recommendation.

PART B

CE Ltd. purchased 100% of the outstanding common shares of May Ltd. by issuing shares of CE to the shareholders of May. The former shareholders of May now own 65% of the outstanding common shares of CE. Before the purchase date, May had organization costs of $10.5 million on its balance sheet.

Required:

What amount should be reported in CE's consolidated financial statements, issued in accordance with GAAP, for May's organization costs? Provide support for your recommendations.

(CICA adapted)

Case 3 Factory Optical Distributors (FOD) is a publicly held manufacturer and distributor of high-quality eyeglass lenses located in Burnaby, B.C. For the past 10 years, the company has sold its lenses on a wholesale basis to optical shops across Canada. Beginning in Year 3, the company began to offer franchise opportunities to opticians wanting to sell only FOD lenses.

The franchise agreements contain the following stipulations:

- Each franchise must be a corporation. FOD (Burnaby) will purchase 35% of the corporation's outstanding common shares and the franchisee will hold the remaining 65%. No other equity instruments can be issued.
- Franchises can be established in new locations or in existing locations under the name Factory Optical Distributors. If a new building is required, FOD (Burnaby) will guarantee the mortgage to ensure that the best interest rates can be obtained. If an existing location is used, it must be renovated to meet company specifications, and again FOD (Burnaby) will guarantee any required financing.
- To qualify as a franchisee, an individual must be a licensed optician, and must commit to 40 hours a week in the franchise location, managing the day-to-day activities.
- Franchisees are to be paid a salary that does not exceed 1.5 times the industry average for opticians with equivalent experience.
- The franchise agreement specifies that only FOD lenses can be sold in franchise locations. FOD lenses can be purchased by franchisees at 5% below normal selling price for the first $500,000 of purchases, and at 10% below cost if purchases exceed $500,000.
- The agreement also requires that frames sold by the franchisee be purchased from designated suppliers, to ensure the best quality and fit to FOD lenses.
- All franchise advertising must be approved by FOD (Burnaby). Franchisees must allocate 1% of revenue to advertising each month.
- The franchisee is required to participate in special promotions and seasonal sales as determined by FOD (Burnaby).
- A franchise fee of 2% of sales is payable monthly to FOD (Burnaby).
- Other products and services can be sold from the franchise location provided that they do not negatively impact the sale of FOD lenses.

During Year 5, eight franchise agreements were signed in locations across Canada. At December 31, Year 5, the company's year end, five of these locations were open for business.

It is now January Year 6. You are the senior auditor on the FOD (Burnaby) account. The company's comptroller has come to you with the franchise agreement to discuss how FOD must report its share ownership in the five operating franchises. She has heard that recent changes to the *CICA Handbook* have expanded the definition of control to include some situations where 50% share ownership does not exist.

Required:

Examine the details of the franchise agreement. Do you think FOD controls the franchise operations? Would consolidation be required? Explain.

(*Adapted from a case prepared by J.C. Thatcher, Lakehead University and Margaret Forbes, University of Saskatchewan*)

*Case 4 Uni-Invest Ltd. was traded on the Canadian Venture Exchange, under the symbol "UIL." The company holds commercial and residential real estate interests, located in Nova Scotia, New Brunswick, Prince Edward Island, Alberta, and British Columbia. On October 23, Year 10, Basic Realty Investment Corporation acquired 100% of the outstanding common shares of Uni-Invest Ltd. in exchange for 32,584,051 common shares of Basic.

At October 31, Year 9, Basic had 3,333,320 common shares, and 6,000,001 Class C preferred shares issued and outstanding. Prior to the acquisition, the 6,000,001 Class C preferred shares were converted to common shares on a share-for-share basis. Then, on October 23, Year 10, the 9,333,321 common shares were consolidated five for one to yield 1,866,664 common shares, with a book value of $746, and a fair value of $2,024,845. Values for Basic's shareholders' equity are summarized as follows:

Capital stock issued	Number of shares	Amount
Balance prior to investment in Uni-Invest	1,866,664	$ 746
Issued to effect investment on October 23, Year 10, net of costs of $84,177	32,584,051	33,236,248
Balance December 31, Year 10	34,450,715	$33,236,994

Details of the fair value excess for the assets acquired and liabilities assumed on the transaction are as follows:

Assets acquired
Property and equipment	$4,632,398
Other assets	271,436
	4,903,834

Liabilities assumed
Long-term debt	2,707,504
Other liabilities	143,000
	2,850,504
Fair value excess for net assets acquired	$2,053,330

Required:

Based on this information, how should this investment be reported? More specifically, which company is the parent? Which is the subsidiary? Why? What earnings, and for what period, are reported in the consolidated financial statements for the year ended December 31, Year 10? Why?

(*Adapted from a case prepared by Peter Secord, St. Mary's University*)

PROBLEMS

Problem 1 The balance sheets of Pork Co. and Barrel Ltd. on December 31, Year 2, are shown next:

	Pork Co.	Barrel Ltd.
Cash	$ 22,000	$ 60,000
Accounts receivable	80,000	48,000
Inventory	120,000	102,000
Plant and equipment (net)	400,000	270,000
Investment in Barrel Ltd.	294,000	—
	$916,000	$480,000
Current liabilities	$216,000	$ 72,000
Long-term debt	240,000	108,000
Common stock	260,000	120,000
Retained earnings	200,000	180,000
	$916,000	$480,000

Pork acquired 70% of the outstanding shares of Barrel on December 30, Year 2, for $294,000. Direct costs of the acquisition amounted to $12,000. The book values of the net assets of Barrel approximated fair values except for plant and equipment, which had a fair value of $320,000.

Required: — Balance sheet already reflects cash disbursements, ¿...on balance sheet?

(a) Prepare a consolidated balance sheet on December 31, Year 2, under the entity theory.

(b) Calculate goodwill and noncontrolling interest on the consolidated balance sheet on December 31, Year 2, under the parent company extension theory.

Problem 2 The balance sheets of Par Ltd. and Sub Ltd. on December 31, Year 1, are as follows:

	Par Ltd.	Sub Ltd.
Cash	$100,000	$ 2,000
Accounts receivable	25,000	7,000
Inventory	30,000	21,000
Plant	175,000	51,000
Trademarks	—	7,000
	$330,000	$88,000
Current liabilities	$ 50,000	$10,000
Long-term debt	80,000	20,000
Common stock	110,000	30,000
Retained earnings	90,000	28,000
	$330,000	$88,000

The fair values of the identifiable net assets of Sub on December 31, Year 1, are:

Cash		$ 2,000
Accounts receivable		7,000
Inventory		26,000
Plant		60,000
Trademarks		14,000
		109,000
Current liabilities	10,000	
Long-term debt	19,000	29,000
Net assets		$ 80,000

Assume that the following took place on January 1, Year 2. (Par acquired the shares with a cash payment to the shareholders of Sub.)

Case 1. Par paid $95,000 to acquire all of the common shares of Sub.

Case 2. Par paid $76,000 to acquire 80% of the common shares of Sub.

Case 3. Par paid $80,000 to acquire all of the common shares of Sub.

Case 4. Par paid $70,000 to acquire all of the common shares of Sub.

Case 5. Par paid $63,000 to acquire 90% of the common shares of Sub.

Required:

For each of the five cases, prepare a consolidated balance sheet as at January 1, Year 2.

Problem 3   The balance sheets of Petron Co. and Seeview Co. on June 29, Year 2 were as follows:

	Petron	Seeview
Cash and receivables	$ 80,000	$ 16,250
Inventory	47,500	7,500
Plant assets (net)	190,000	58,750
Intangible assets	20,000	5,000
	$337,500	$ 87,500
Current liabilities	$ 52,500	$ 25,000
Long-term debt	81,250	37,500
Common stock	127,500	38,750
Retained earnings (deficit)	76,250	(13,750)
	$337,500	$ 87,500

On June 30, Year 2, Petron Co. purchased 90% of the outstanding shares of Seeview Co. for $31,500 cash. Legal fees involved with the acquisition were an additional $1,000. The book value of Seeview's net assets were equal to fair value except for:

	Fair value
Inventory	8,750
Plant assets	67,500
Intangible assets	7,500
Long-term debt	32,500

Required:

Prepare the consolidated balance sheet of Petron Co. on June 30, Year 2. (Round all calculations to the nearest dollar.)

Problem 4   The balance sheets of Hill Corp. and McGraw Ltd. on December 31, Year 4, are shown on the next page.

On December 30, Year 4, Hill purchased all of the common shares of McGraw for $339,300. On this date the inventory of McGraw had a fair value of $214,500, its land had a fair value of $91,000, and its plant and equipment had a fair value of $364,000.

Required: _Balance sheet already reflects cash disb.

(a) Prepare a consolidated balance sheet as at December 31, Year 4.

(b) Prepare McGraw's journal entries if it applies push-down accounting.

	Hill Corp. book value	McGraw Ltd. book value FMV
Cash	$ 13,000	$ 6,500
Accounts receivable	130,000	45,500
Inventory	117,000	208,000
Land	91,000	52,000
Plant and equipment	468,000	377,000
Investment in McGraw Ltd.	339,300	—
Goodwill	117,000	39,000
	$1,275,300	$728,000
Current liabilities	$ 156,000	$104,000
Long-term debt	416,000	286,000
Common stock	520,000	390,000
Retained earnings	183,300	(52,000)
	$1,275,300	$728,000

Handwritten annotations: "214500", "91000", "36400" near Inventory, Land, Plant and equipment rows.

Problem 5

Following are the balance sheets of Blue Ltd. and Joy Corp. on December 31, Year 2.

	Blue Ltd. book value	Joy Corp. book value
Cash	$ 17,000	$ 5,000
Accounts receivable	78,000	35,000
Inventory	105,000	220,000
Plant and equipment	440,000	320,000
Investment in Joy Corp.	424,000	—
	$1,064,000	$580,000
Current liabilities	$ 168,000	$ 80,000
Long-term debt	250,000	240,000
Common stock	422,000	300,000
Retained earnings	224,000	(40,000)
	$1,064,000	$580,000

On December 30, Year 2, Blue purchased a percentage of the outstanding common shares of Joy. On this date all but two categories of Joy's identifiable assets and liabilities had fair values equal to book values.

Below is the consolidated balance sheet for Blue at December 31, Year 2.

BLUE LTD.
CONSOLIDATED BALANCE SHEET
(Year 2)

Cash	$ 22,000
Accounts receivable	113,000
Inventory	345,000
Plant and equipment	860,000
Goodwill	150,000
	$1,490,000
Current liabilities	$ 248,000
Long-term debt	490,000
Noncontrolling interest	106,000
Common stock	422,000
Retained earnings	224,000
	$1,490,000

Required:

(a) From the information provided, determine the percentage of Joy's common shares purchased by Blue on December 30, Year 2.

(b) Which of Joy's assets or liabilities had fair values that were not equal to their book values at acquisition? Calculate the fair value of each of these assets at December 30, Year 2.

Problem 6   The balance sheets of E Ltd. and J Ltd. on December 30, Year 6, were as follows:

	E Ltd.	J Ltd.
Cash and receivables	$ 96,000	$ 19,500
Inventory	57,000	9,000
Plant assets (net)	228,000	70,500
Intangible assets	24,000	6,000
	$405,000	$105,000
Current liabilities	$ 63,000	$ 30,000
Long-term debt	97,500	45,000
Common stock	153,000	46,500
Retained earnings (deficit)	91,500	(16,500)
	$405,000	$105,000

On December 31, Year 6, E issued 350 shares, with a fair value of $40 each, for 70% of the outstanding shares of J. Costs involved in the acquisition, paid in cash, were as follows:

Costs of arranging the acquisition	$2,500
Costs of issuing shares	1,600
	$4,100

The book values of J's net assets were equal to fair values on this date except for these:

	Fair value
Plant assets	$65,000
Long-term debt	40,000

E was identified as the acquirer in the combination.

Required:

Prepare the consolidated balance sheet of E Ltd. on December 31, Year 6, under each of the following:

(a) proprietary theory
(b) parent company theory
(c) parent company extension theory
(d) entity theory

Problem 7 On December 31, Year 1, P Company purchased 80% of the outstanding shares of S Company for $6,960 cash.

The balance sheets of the two companies immediately after the acquisition transaction appear below.

	P Company Book value	S Company Book value	Fair value
Cash	$ 1,500	$ 1,050	$1,050
Accounts receivable	3,150	1,800	1,800
Inventory	5,160	3,750	3,900
Plant and equipment (net)	8,100	6,900	6,000
Investment in S Company	6,960	—	
	$24,870	$13,500	
Accounts payable	$ 600	$ 700	$ 700
Other current liabilities	1,200	1,800	1,800
Long-term liabilities	4,200	2,000	2,000
Common stock	10,500	3,000	
Retained earnings	8,370	6,000	
	$24,870	$13,500	

Required:

Prepare a consolidated balance sheet at the date of acquisition under each of the following:

(a) proprietary theory
(b) parent company theory
(c) parent company extension theory
(d) entity theory

*Problem 8 The balance sheets of X Ltd. and Y Ltd. on December 30, Year 7, are as follows:

	X Ltd. Book value	Fair value	Y Ltd. Book value	Fair value
Current assets	$ 300	$ 300	$1,000	$1,000
Fixed assets	1,500	1,700	2,700	2,800
	$1,800		$3,700	
Current liabilities	$ 400	$ 400	$ 900	$ 900
Long-term debt	300	300	800	800
Common shares — issued 100 sh.	400			
Common shares — issued 60 sh.			600	
Retained earnings	700		1,400	
	$1,800		$3,700	

On December 31, Year 7, X issued 150 common shares for all 60 outstanding common shares of Y. The fair value of each of Y's common shares was $40 on this date.

Required:

(a) Explain why this share issue most likely occurred.
(b) Prepare the consolidated balance sheet of X Ltd. on December 31, Year 7.

(CICA adapted)

Problem 9   On January 1, Year 5, Black Corp. purchased 90% of the common shares of Whyte Inc. On this date the following differences were observed with regard to specific net assets of Whyte:

	Fair value–book value differences
Land	+50,000
Buildings (net)	+20,000
Equipment (net)	–10,000
Notes payable	+ 5,000

The unconsolidated and consolidated balance sheets of Black Corp. on January 1, Year 5, are presented below. Whyte's retained earnings were $140,000 on this date.

	Unconsolidated	Consolidated
Cash	$ 36,000	$ 52,000
Accounts receivable	116,000	168,000
Inventory	144,000	234,000
Investment in Whyte	292,500	—
Land	210,000	280,000
Buildings (net)	640,000	720,000
Equipment (net)	308,000	338,000
Goodwill	—	50,000
	$1,746,500	$1,842,000
Accounts payable	$ 88,000	$ 96,000
Notes payable	507,500	562,500
Noncontrolling interest	—	32,500
Common stock	380,000	380,000
Retained earnings	771,000	771,000
	$1,746,500	$1,842,000

Required:

Prepare the January 1, Year 5, balance sheet of Whyte Inc.

Problem 10   The balance sheets of Percy Corp. and Saltz Ltd on December 31, Year 10 are shown below:

	Percy	Saltz
Cash	$200,000	$ 4,000
Accounts receivable	50,000	14,000
Inventory	60,000	42,000
Plant	350,000	102,000
Trademarks	—	14,000
	$660,000	$176,000
Current liabilities	$100,000	$ 20,000
Long-term debt	160,000	40,000
Common stock	220,000	60,000
Retained earnings	180,000	56,000
	$660,000	$176,000

The fair values of the identifiable net assets of Saltz Ltd. on December 31, Year 10 are as follows:

Cash		$ 4,000
Accounts receivable		14,000
Inventory		52,000
Plant		120,000
Trademarks		28,000
		218,000
Current liabilities	20,000	
Long-term debt	38,000	58,000
Net assets		$160,000

On January 1, Year 11, Percy Corp paid $190,000 in cash to acquire all of the common shares of Saltz Ltd., and instructed the management of Saltz Ltd. to apply push-down accounting as an aid in the preparation of future consolidated financial statements.

Required:

(a) Prepare Saltz Ltd.'s push-down journal entries.
(b) Prepare the consolidated balance sheet on January 1, Year 1.

Problem 11   The balance sheets of Prima Ltd. and Donna Corp. on December 31, Year 5 are shown below:

	Prima	Donna
Cash	$ 320,000	$ 6,400
Accounts receivable	80,000	22,400
Inventory	96,000	67,200
Plant	560,000	163,200
Patents	100,000	22,400
	$1,156,000	$281,600
Current liabilities	$ 160,000	$ 32,000
Long-term debt	256,000	64,000
Common stock	352,000	96,000
Retained earnings	388,000	89,600
	$1,156,000	$281,600

The fair values of the identifiable net assets of Donna Corp. on this date are as follows:

Cash	$ 6,400
Accounts receivable	20,000
Inventory	85,000
Plant	192,000
Trademarks	30,000
Patents	50,000
Current liabilities	32,000
Long-term debt	70,000

On January 1, Year 6, Prima Ltd. paid $306,000 in cash to acquire 90 percent of the common shares of Donna Corp.

Required:

(a) Prepare the consolidated balance sheet on January 1, Year X under the entity theory.
(b) Calculate goodwill and noncontrolling interest on the consolidated balance sheet on January 1, Year 6, under the parent company extension theory.

Problem 12   On January 1, Year 5, FLA Company issued 6,300 common shares from treasury to purchase 9,000 common shares of MES Company. Prior to the acquisition, FLA had 180,000 and MES had 10,000 common shares outstanding, which were trading at $5.00 and $3 per share, respectively. The information presented on the next page has been assembled for these two companies at the date of acquisition:

Required:

(a) Prepare a consolidated balance for FLA Company and its non-wholly owned subsidiary at January 1, Year 5, under each of the following:
   (i) proprietary theory
   (ii) parent company theory

(iii) parent company extension theory
(iv) entity theory
(b) Which of the above theories does Canadian GAAP require?

| | FLA Company | | MES Company | |
	Book value	Fair value	Book value	Fair value
Current assets	$ 40,000	$47,500	$10,000	$11,200
Plant assets	60,000	70,000	20,000	25,000
	$100,000		$30,000	
Current liabilities	$ 20,000	$20,000	$ 5,000	$ 5,000
Long-term debt	15,000	19,000	2,500	3,200
Common stock	30,000		10,000	
Retained earnings	35,000		12,500	
	$100,000		$30,000	

Problem 13 The condensed financial statements for OIL Inc. and ERS Company for the year ended December 31, Year 5, follow:

	OIL	ERS
Revenues	$ 900,000	$ 300,000
Expenses	660,000	200,000
Net income	$ 240,000	$ 100,000
Retained earnings, 1/1/Year 5	$ 800,000	$ 200,000
Net income	240,000	100,000
Dividends paid	90,000	0
Retained earnings, 12/31/Year 5	$ 950,000	$ 300,000
Cash	$ 80,000	$ 110,000
Receivables and inventory	400,000	170,000
Patented technology (net)	900,000	300,000
Equipment (net)	700,000	600,000
Total assets	$2,080,000	$1,180,000
Liabilities	$ 600,000	$ 410,000
Common stock	530,000	470,000
Retained earnings	950,000	300,000
Total liabilities and equities	$2,080,000	$1,180,000

On December 31, Year 5, after the above figures were prepared, OIL issued $240,000 in debt and 12,000 new shares to the owners of ERS for 80% of the outstanding shares of that company. OIL shares had a fair value of $40 per share.

OIL also paid $30,000 to a broker for arranging the transaction. In addition, OIL paid $32,000 in stock issuance costs. ERS's equipment was actually worth $690,000 but its patented technology was appraised at only $280,000.

Required:

What are the consolidated balances at December 31, Year 5, for the following accounts?
(a) Net income
(b) Retained earnings, 1/1/Year 5
(c) Equipment
(d) Patented technology
(e) Goodwill
(f) Liabilities
(g) Common stock

Chapter 5

Consolidation Subsequent to Acquisition Date — Parent Uses Equity Method

LEARNING OBJECTIVES

After studying this chapter, you should be able to do the following:

- Explain the basic differences between the cost and equity methods of reporting investments.
- Describe the composition of and/or calculate consolidated net income.
- Explain how impairment tests are performed on long-lived assets, other intangibles, and goodwill.
- Calculate the amortization and/or impairment of purchase discrepancy on both an annual and cumulative basis.
- Explain how the matching principle is applied when amortizing or writing off the purchase discrepancy.
- Prepare journal entries under the equity method to report changes in the investment account during the year.
- Prepare consolidated financial statements in years subsequent to acquisition date when the parent has used the equity method to account for its investment.

INTRODUCTION

In Chapters 3 and 4, we discussed and illustrated the preparation of a consolidated balance sheet immediately after a parent company gained control over a subsidiary. We saw that the purchase price discrepancy was allocated to identifiable assets and liabilities when the fair values were different than book values and the excess was allocated to goodwill. In this chapter, we will see that the purchase price discrepancy must be amortized and tested for impairment when preparing financial statements subsequent to the date of acquisition. The impairment testing can result in huge impairment losses when business slows down as indicated in the following example for Nortel Networks Corporation, one of Canada's most famous hi-tech companies.

During the high-tech boom in the late 1990s, Nortel stock prices soared to over $120 a share and the company used these high prices to embark on an acquisitions binge. In one year alone it acquired eleven companies for a total cost of $20.4 billion, with payment being made by the issuance of new shares in nearly all cases. Allocated to goodwill was $18.5 billion, which represented over 90 percent of the total acquisition cost. Shortly after making these acquisitions, the tech bubble burst and the prolonged bear market that followed saw Nortel's share price drop to less than $1. With such a substantial decline in the fair value of the company, it came as no surprise when Nortel announced that it was going to write down its intangible assets (mostly goodwill) by $12.3 billion, and in addition, was going to take an $830 million restructuring charge as a result of closing plants and discontinuing operations. Many of these operations that were abandoned had just recently been purchased. All of this resulted in a second-quarter loss of $19.2 billion, the largest ever reported by a Canadian company.

In this chapter, we will prepare the consolidated income statement, retained earnings statement, and balance sheet at fiscal year ends after the date of acquisition. The consolidated cash flow statement will be discussed in a later chapter. We will start by looking at how the parent accounts for its investment on its separate entity books.

DISCUSSION QUESTION

How Does a Company Really Decide Which Investment Method to Apply?

During the early stages of Year 4, Carleton Inc. bought a controlling interest in Ravens Technology Ltd. Shortly after the acquisition, a meeting of Carleton's accounting department is convened to discuss the accounting method to be used in Carleton's general ledger. Each member of the staff has a definite opinion as to whether the equity method or cost method should be adopted. To resolve this issue, Carleton's chief financial officer outlines several of her concerns about the decision.

"I really understand how each method works. I know the general advantages and disadvantages of each method. I realize, for example, that the equity method provides more detailed information whereas the cost method is much easier to apply. What I need to know are the factors specific to our situation that should be considered in deciding which method to adopt. I must make a recommendation to the president on this matter, and he will want firm reasons for my favouring a particular approach. I don't want us to select a method and then find out in six months that the information is not adequate for our needs or that the cost of adapting our system to monitor Ravens outweighs the benefits derived from the data."

Required:

What are the factors that Carleton's officials should evaluate when making this decision?

Methods of Accounting for an Investment in a Subsidiary

The cost and equity methods are methods of accounting in the parent's own separate accounting records.

There are two methods available to a parent company to account for an investment in a subsidiary in its own separate accounting records in periods subsequent to the date of acquisition: the *cost method* and the *equity method*. The cost and equity methods of accounting were discussed in depth in Chapter 2 with regard to available-for-sale and significant-influence investments. While this chapter is concerned with control investments (requiring consolidation), the accounting concepts involved with the cost and equity methods are identical to those presented in Chapter 2. These concepts will be outlined again in this chapter and in the ones that follow. The key difference is that here they are discussed in relation to the preparation of consolidated financial statements, whereas before, the emphasis was on the presentation in an investor's unconsolidated financial statements.

The cost method records income when dividends are received or receivable.

The *Handbook* describes the *cost method* as

> a basis of accounting for investments whereby the investment is initially record-ed at cost; earnings from such investments are recognized only to the extent received or receivable.[1]

The cost method is the simplest of the two methods because the only entry made by the parent each year is to record, as revenue, its pro rata share of dividends declared by the subsidiary from net income earned subsequent to the acquisition date.

The *equity method* is described as

The equity method captures the investor's share of any changes to the investee's shareholders' equity.

> a basis of accounting for long-term investments whereby the investment is initial-ly recorded at cost and the carrying value, adjusted thereafter to include the inves-tor's pro rata share of post-acquisition earnings of the investee, computed by the consolidation method. The amount of the adjustment is included in the determi-nation of net income by the investor, and the investment account of the investor is also increased or decreased to reflect the investor's share of capital transactions (including amounts recognized in other comprehensive income) and changes in accounting policies and corrections of errors relating to prior period financial statements applicable to post acquisition periods. Profit distributions received or receivable from an investee reduce the carrying amount of the investment.[2]

The equity method captures the net effect of any adjustments that would be made on the consolidated financial statements.

By requiring that the equity method include the investor's pro-rata share of the investee's post-acquisition retained earnings as computed by the consolida-tion method, the equity method is designed to produce the same net income and retained earnings on the parent's separate entity financial statements as reported on the consolidated financial statements. As such, the equity method is often referred to as the "one-line consolidation." This means that the investment revenue is reduced by the yearly amortization and write-offs associated with the purchase discrepancy because, although the subsidiary's net assets are being consolidated using fair values, these fair values are not reflected in the subsidiary's records, and therefore the sub-sidiary's expenses are incorrect for consolidated purposes.[3] In addition, any unreal-ized intercompany profits are not reflected in consolidated net income until they are realized through a sale to outsiders. From a single-entity point of view, "you cannot record a profit selling to yourself." An equity method journal entry is required to adjust for the effect of such unrealized profits.[4]

It is very important that we differentiate between the financial statements of the separate entities and the consolidated financial statements. The parent and the sub-sidiary are separate legal entities. They each prepare their own individual financial statements, which are called separate entity financial statements. Since the parent

---

[1] *CICA Handbook*, Section 3051.03.

[2] Ibid.

[3] We are assuming in all cases that subsidiary companies do not use push-down accounting. Consolidation when the subsidiary has used push-down accounting is discussed in Chapter 4.

[4] The accounting for unrealized profits is discussed in Chapters 7 and 8.

controls the subsidiary, we prepare a third set of statements, the consolidated financial statements. The following diagram shows the interrelationships between the various statements:

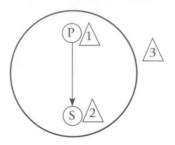

Each circle represents a different set of financial statements. The triangle indicates the number given to the set of financial statements — the parent's separate entity set is number 1, the subsidiary's set is number 2, and the consolidated set is number 3. In this chapter, the parent will be using the equity method on set number 1. In Chapter 6, the parent will be using the cost method on set number 1. The adjustments required to get from set 1 to set 3 in Chapter 5 will be different than the adjustments required to get from set 1 to set 3 in Chapter 6. But, the end result, the consolidated financial statements, will look exactly the same.

> **Consolidated net income will be the same regardless of whether the parent used the cost method or equity method for its separate-entity accounting records.**

The parent is free to choose which method it will use to account for its investment on set 1 because this set of statements will not be the primary statements used by external users. The consolidated statements will be the primary statements used by the shareholders and bankers of the parent. The income tax authorities will be the main user of the parent's separate entity financial statements, i.e., set 1. Since dividend income under the cost method and investment income under the equity method are not taxable, these items will have to be eliminated when preparing the income tax returns. Accordingly, the income tax authorities are indifferent as to whether the parent uses the cost method or equity method on its separate entity financial statements.

Consolidated Income and Retained Earnings Statements

> **The parent's separate entity net income accounted for under the equity method should always be equal to consolidated net income.**

Before examining the details for preparing consolidated income and retained earnings statements, it is useful to outline the overall consolidation process. Just as a consolidated balance sheet is prepared basically by combining, on an item-by-item basis, the assets and liabilities of the parent and the subsidiary, the consolidated income statement is prepared by combining, on an item-by-item basis, the revenues and expenses of the two companies. The parent's investment does not appear on the consolidated balance sheet, and some of the subsidiary's assets and liabilities are revalued to reflect the fair values used in the consolidation process. In a similar manner, the parent's investment revenue from its subsidiary does not appear on the consolidated income statement, and some of the expenses of the subsidiary are revalued to reflect the amortizations of the fair values being used in the consolidated balance sheet. But except for the eliminations and adjustments that are required, the whole consolidation process is basically one of combining the components of financial statements. No preparation is required for the consolidated retained earnings statement when the parent has used the equity method.[5]

We commence our discussion of the preparation of the consolidated income statement by describing the make-up of the bottom line: consolidated net income. Consolidated net income for any fiscal year is made up of the following:

	The net income of the parent from its own operations	
	(i.e., excluding any income resulting from its investment in the subsidiary)	$ XXX
plus:	**the parent's share of the net income of the subsidiary**	XXX
less:	**the amortization of the purchase discrepancy**	(XXX)
equals:	**consolidated net income**	$ XXX

The amortization of the purchase discrepancy is reflected on the consolidated financial statements — not on the subsidiary's financial statements.

Take, for example, a 100 percent owned subsidiary that was purchased at book value (i.e., no purchase discrepancy and no fair value–book value differences). Consolidated net income will be made up of the sum of the parent's and the subsidiary's net incomes. If the subsidiary was purchased at a price greater than book value, the subsidiary's net income will not be correct from a consolidated-single-entity point of view because the subsidiary's expenses have not been measured using amortizations of the fair values being used in the consolidated balance sheet. Therefore, the third component — the amortization of the purchase discrepancy — must be deducted in determining consolidated net income.

The purchase discrepancy is amortized or written off on consolidation as if the parent had purchased these net assets directly.

A purchase discrepancy is allocated to revalue the assets and liabilities of the subsidiary for consolidated purposes. It must be amortized or written off for consolidation purposes to reflect the use, impairment, or sale of the underlying net assets. The amount amortized or written off is calculated in the same way as if these items were owned directly by the parent. The purchase discrepancy related to long-term assets with definite useful lives (such as buildings, equipment, and patents) is amortized over the useful lives of these assets. Inventory is not amortized, but is reflected on the income statement as cost of goods sold expense when it is sold. The amount allocated to land is not amortized and its cost is only reflected as a charge on the income statement when it is sold. Goodwill and certain other intangible assets are also not amortized, but instead a loss is reflected on the income statement when a test indicates that they are impaired. Testing for impairment is explained in more detail in the following section.

All of these charges against consolidated income will collectively be referred to as "the amortization of the purchase discrepancy," even though technically some of them are not really amortizations. In the same manner the balances not yet written off for consolidation purposes will be referred to as the "unamortized purchase discrepancy."

The parent's separate entity retained earnings accounted for under the equity method should always be equal to consolidated retained earnings.

Consolidated retained earnings on the date of acquisition is the parent's retained earnings only. The changes in consolidated retained earnings subsequent to acquisition consist of the yearly consolidated net incomes, less the yearly dividends declared by the parent. Dividends paid or declared by a subsidiary company do not appear on the consolidated retained earnings statement. When dividends are paid by a 100 percent owned subsidiary, the subsidiary's cash decreases and the parent's cash increases, but the single entity's cash remains unchanged, as does the shareholders' equity of the entity.

---

[5] This statement is not correct when the parent has used the cost method.

Testing Goodwill and Other Intangibles for Impairment

Starting in 2001, goodwill and certain intangible assets were no longer amortized but tested for impairment on an annual basis.

Prior to July 1, 2001, any goodwill recognized as a result of a business combination had to be amortized over its estimated useful life, which could not exceed 40 years. This resulted in substantial reductions to reported earnings due to yearly goodwill amortization. On July 1, 2001, Section 1581, "Business Combinations," and Section 3062, "Goodwill and Other Intangible Assets," were introduced into the *Handbook*. In 2003 a related Section 3063, "Impairment of Long-lived Assets," was also introduced. These new sections provide more workable guidelines for the recognition and measurement of intangibles other than goodwill and, in addition, replace the annual amortization of goodwill with periodic reviews for impairment. In addition, extensive guidelines are provided for the impairment testing of all long-lived assets including intangibles. Sections 1581 and 3062 were replaced with Sections 1582 and 3065 in 2008.

Intangible assets should be amortized over their useful lives unless their lives are considered to be indefinite.

Intangible assets recognized in a business combination should be amortized over their useful lives unless their lives are considered to be indefinite. Intangible assets that are subject to amortization are periodically reviewed for impairment in accordance with *Handbook* Section 3063, "Impairment of Long-Lived Assets." The new requirements for this type of asset impairment testing are discussed next. We will then examine the impairment tests for other intangibles, and finally the goodwill impairment tests.

Testing Long-Lived Assets for Impairment, Section 3063

Section 3063 went into effect on April 1, 2003. It applies to long-lived, non-monetary assets and intangible assets with finite useful lives. It does not apply to goodwill nor to intangible assets with indefinite lives, although as our discussions proceed it will soon become clear that guidelines for impairment testing of indefinite life intangibles are very similar to those contained in this section.

Impairment testing requires the estimation of future net cash flows (cash inflows less cash outflows) associated with a long-lived asset. In many instances it is impossible to associate cash flows with a single asset, and so the section suggests that it should be accomplished with asset groups defined as "the lowest level (smallest combination) of assets and liabilities for which identifiable cash flows are largely independent of the cash flows of other assets or groups of assets and liabilities." [3063.03(a)]

The test has two steps as follows:

In step 1, an asset is not recoverable if the undiscounted future cash flows are less than carrying value.

1) A test is performed to see whether the carrying amount of an asset (or asset group) is recoverable. If the sum of the undiscounted cash flows associated with it exceeds its carrying amount, the carrying amount is recoverable and no further testing is required. It is not recoverable if the carrying amount exceeds the sum of the cash flows, in which case the second stage is applied.

In step 2, an asset is impaired if the fair value is less than carrying value.

2) The second step requires comparing the carrying value of the asset (or group) with its fair value, and if the fair value is the lower amount impairment loss is recognized for the difference. Fair value is defined as "the amount of the consideration that would be agreed upon in an arm's-length transaction between knowledgeable, willing parties who are under no compulsion to act." [3063.03(b)]

Fair values can be determined by using quoted market prices, if available, or by making comparisons with the prices of other similar assets. The section also indicates that valuation techniques such as the traditional present-value approach (discounting a best estimate of yearly cash flows), or the expected present value approach (using multiple cash flow scenarios that reflect a range of possible outcomes), would be acceptable methods of estimating fair value.

The asset group may contain current assets such as receivables and inventory, and also liabilities associated with it. These current assets would be evaluated in accordance with other *Handbook* sections before being included in the group. Any impairment loss associated with an asset group is used to reduce the carrying amounts of the long-lived assets only. It is not allocated to liabilities or to current assets. The loss would be allocated to the long-lived assets in the group on the basis of their relative carrying amounts. While this type of impairment testing would probably be carried out on a separate entity basis, it would also have to be considered on a consolidated basis as well. For example, a subsidiary that does not use push-down accounting could determine that there is no impairment of its assets because it is using the carrying values from its records as the comparison. If, instead, consolidation carrying values were used, the comparison might indicate that there has been impairment.

Testing Other Intangibles for Impairment, Section 3064

Intangible assets that are not subject to amortization because they have indefinite[6] lives fall under the provisions of Section 3064 for purposes of impairment testing. A test is performed annually by comparing the fair value of an intangible asset (other than goodwill) with its carrying amount, and any resultant loss is included in income. It is suggested that the guidelines from Section 1582, "Business Combinations" could be used to determine fair value.[7] The problems of associating cash flows with a single intangible asset are still present and so it would seem logical to use the group approach that we have just discussed. In addition to providing guidelines for the impairment testing of this particular type of intangible, Section 3064 also requires special guidelines and tests for goodwill impairment. This is discussed next.

Testing Goodwill for Impairment, Section 3064

Once recognized, goodwill is tested yearly for impairment, and if the fair value of the goodwill is less than its carrying amount, it is written down and a loss is reported in income. The process is carried out at the level of a reporting unit, which is described as "the level of reporting at which goodwill is tested for impairment and is either an operating segment (see "Segment Disclosures," Section 1701), or one level below (referred to as a component). A component of an operating segment is a reporting unit when the component constitutes a business for which discrete financial information is available and segment management regularly reviews the operating results of that component." [3064.08(d)]

On the date of a business combination, a comparison is made between the cost of acquiring a subsidiary company and the parent's share of the fair value of the subsidiary's identifiable net assets (including previously unrecognized intangibles). The excess of cost over fair value is recorded as goodwill. In order to be able to conduct

It is possible for an asset not to be impaired at the subsidiary level but to be impaired at the consolidated level.

An intangible asset that is not subject to amortization is tested for impairment (step 2 above).

Goodwill is tested for impairment at the reporting unit level.

---

[6] Indefinite does not necessarily mean an infinite life, but rather one that extends beyond the foreseeable future.

[7] That section also mentions the use of present value techniques as a method of arriving at a fair value.

future goodwill impairment testing, this goodwill is allocated to the reporting units of the subsidiary as of this date. The process is as follows:

- The total purchased price is allocated to each reporting unit.
- The fair value of the subsidiary's individual net assets is also allocated to each reporting unit. This will become carrying value (amortized) when impairment tests are performed later.
- For each reporting unit, the allocated purchase price is compared with the parent's share of the fair value of the unit's net assets.
- The difference is the goodwill of the reporting unit.
- The sum of each reporting unit's goodwill equals the total acquisition goodwill.

Each year thereafter this goodwill is tested for impairment. Before the testing process is started, the net assets (other than goodwill) are tested for impairment. If any of these assets are written down due to impairment, their resultant value becomes the fair value used. Next, the fair value of each reporting unit as a whole has to be determined. Basically this value is the amount that a willing purchaser would pay for the unit. In the same manner as was outlined previously when Section 3063 was discussed, various estimation and valuation techniques could be used, except here it is performed at the reporting unit level whereas in Section 3063 it is performed at the asset group level. Finally, fair values have to be assigned to the unit's individual net assets.

There are two steps involved in the goodwill-testing process:

1. The fair value of each reporting unit is compared with its carrying amount, including goodwill. If the fair value exceeds the carrying amount, goodwill is not impaired and step 2 is not performed.
2. If the carrying amount of the reporting unit exceeds its fair value, a possibility exists that goodwill impairment has occurred. The test involves comparing the carrying value of the goodwill with its fair value. Because goodwill is a residual, its market value cannot be observed and therefore an implied value has to be determined in the same fashion that the goodwill of a business combination is determined. This is accomplished by comparing the fair value of a reporting unit with the sum of the fair values of the unit's identifiable net assets. The difference becomes the implied fair value of the goodwill of that unit. The comparison is made, and if the carrying amount of a reporting unit's goodwill exceeds its fair value, the difference is reported on the income statement as an impairment loss, and the carrying amount of the entity's goodwill on the balance sheet is reduced by this amount.

> In step 1, the fair value of the reporting unit as a whole is compared to the carrying amount of net assets of the reporting unit.
>
> In step 2, the fair value of the implied goodwill of the reporting unit is compared to the carrying amount of goodwill of the reporting unit.

The goodwill impairment test is performed annually unless there are clear indicators that no impairment has occurred such as:

(a) very little change in the make-up of the assets and liabilities of the reporting unit since the most recent fair value determination, and

(b) the most recent fair value determination yielded an amount that substantially exceeded the carrying amount of the reporting unit, and

(c) based on analyzing events since the most recent fair value determination, it is unlikely that that a current fair value determination would be less than the carrying value of the reporting unit.

There may also be indicators that suggest that an impairment test should be performed more often than annually such as when circumstances or events have occurred which make it more likely than not that fair values of the reporting unit are less than carrying amounts.

The impairment tests are complex and often require considerable professional judgment.

The discontinuance of the amortization of goodwill, and the subsequent introduction of complex impairment testing rules for goodwill and all other tangible and intangible assets have added a new and complex valuation exercise to the consolidation process. The determination of fair values will be a costly one for many companies and their auditors, requiring the yearly services of business valuation specialists. The large auditing firms will no doubt have business valuators on board as part of their audit staff, but smaller audit firms will have to hire outside valuators if any of their clients prepare consolidated statements.

Now that we have seen how to test for impairment, we will illustrate the preparation of consolidated financial statements subsequent to the date of acquisition. The first illustrations assume that the subsidiary is 100 percent owned. Later illustrations will assume a less than 100 percent owned subsidiary.

Consolidation of a 100 Percent Owned Subsidiary

Company P purchased 100 percent of the outstanding common shares of Company S on January 1, Year 1, for $19,000. On that date Company S's common stock was $10,000 and its retained earnings balance was $6,000. The inventory of Company S had a fair market value that was $2,000 greater than book value, and the book values of all other assets and liabilities of Company S were equal to fair market values. Any goodwill will be tested yearly for impairment. Both companies have a December 31 year-end. The journal entry made by Company P to record the acquisition of 100 percent of Company S was as follows:

Investment in S	19,000	
Cash		19,000

There is no compelling reason for Company P to prepare a consolidated balance sheet on acquisition date; however, it is useful to illustrate its preparation as the starting point for the preparation of consolidated statements in subsequent years. The calculation and allocation of the purchase discrepancy is shown in Exhibit 5.1.

Exhibit 5.1

COMPANY P
CALCULATION OF PURCHASE DISCREPANCY
January 1, Year 1

The purchase price is comprised of the carrying value of the subsidiary's assets and liabilities plus the purchase discrepancy.

Cost of 100 percent of Company S		$19,000
Book value of Company S:		
Common stock	10,000	
Retained earnings	6,000	
	16,000	
Parent's ownership	100%	16,000
Purchase discrepancy		3,000
Allocated:	FV – BV × 100%	
Inventory	2,000 × 100%	2,000
Balance — goodwill		$ 1,000

Below are the individual balance sheets of Company P and Company S on January 1, Year 1, along with Company P's consolidated balance sheet prepared using the *direct approach*.

BALANCE SHEETS — January 1, Year 1

	Company P	Company S	Consolidated
Assets (miscellaneous)	$139,000	$17,000	$156,000
Inventory	22,000	10,000	34,000
Investment in S	19,000	—	—
Goodwill	—	—	1,000
	$180,000	$27,000	$191,000
Liabilities	$ 45,000	$11,000	$ 56,000
Common stock	50,000	10,000	50,000
Retained earnings	85,000	6,000	85,000
	$180,000	$27,000	$191,000

The investment account is replaced by the carrying value of the subsidiary's assets and liabilities plus the purchase discrepancy.

The consolidated balance sheet was prepared by eliminating the shareholders' equity of Company S ($16,000) against Company P's investment account ($19,000) and then allocating the resultant purchase discrepancy ($3,000) to the inventory of Company S ($2,000), with the unallocated balance recorded as goodwill ($1,000).

On December 31, Year 1, Company S reported a net income of $7,300 for the year and paid a cash dividend of $2,500. Company P's net income for the year was $18,300 at this time (not including income from its investment in Company S). Using the equity method to account for its investment, Company P will record the cash dividend received as a reduction to the investment account and increase the investment account with its share (100 percent) of Company S's net income. An additional entry is required to record the amortization of the purchase discrepancy. Company P prepares a purchase discrepancy amortization schedule to be used both for the equity method journal entries required and for the actual preparation of the consolidated financial statements. This amortization schedule is prepared as follows:

PURCHASE DISCREPANCY AMORTIZATION SCHEDULE

	Balance Jan. 1, Year 1	Amortization Year 1	Balance Dec. 31, Year 1
Inventory	$2,000	$2,000	$ —
Goodwill	1,000	50	950
	$3,000	$2,050	$950

The details of the Year 1 amortizations are explained as follows:

The purchase discrepancy related to inventory is expensed when the inventory is sold.

1. The inventory of Company S was revalued for consolidated purposes on January 1, Year 1, to reflect its fair value. It is safe to assume that this inventory was sold during Year 1. If we assume that Company S uses a FIFO cost flow,[8] it would be safe to assume that this inventory was sold. Since the cost of sales of Company S does not reflect the $2,000 additional cost, cost of sales on the Year 1 consolidated income statement will be increased by $2,000 to reflect all of this.

2. An impairment test on goodwill conducted on December 31, Year 1, indicated that a $50 loss had occurred.

---

[8] Since LIFO is no longer acceptable under Canadian GAAP, we will assume a FIFO cost flow in all examples.

3. The $1,000 goodwill is not reflected in the financial statements of Company S, nor is the impairment loss. The consolidated income statement will have to reflect this loss, and at December 31, Year 1, the consolidated balance sheet will have to show the balance not written off.

Because the amortizations affect consolidated net income, they must also be reflected in the parent's December 31, Year 1, equity method journal entries. These entries are shown below:

The net effect of any adjustments made on consolidation must be captured under the equity method.

Investment in S	7,300	
Investment income		7,300
100 percent of Company S Year 1 net income		
Cash	2,500	
Investment in S		2,500
Dividend received from Company S		
Investment income	2,050	
Investment in S		2,050
Purchase discrepancy amortization — Year 1		

After these journal entries are posted, the account for Investment in S and the investment income account in the records of P Company will show the following changes and balances:

Dividends from the subsidiary reduce the investment account and do not affect income under the equity method.

	Investment in S	Investment income
January 1, Year 1	$19,000	$ nil
December 31, Year 1:		
Income from S	7,300	7,300
Dividends from S	(2,500)	—
Purchase discrepancy amort.	(2,050)	(2,050)
Balance, December 31, Year 1	$21,750	$5,250

Company P adds the investment income ($5,250) to its earnings from its own operations ($18,300) and reports a final net income of $23,550.

Consolidated Statements, End of Year 1, Direct Approach

The financial statements of Company P and Company S prepared on December 31, Year 1, are presented in Exhibit 5.2.

These financial statements and the purchase discrepancy amortization schedule become the basis for the preparation of Company P's consolidated financial statements. We will prepare the consolidated financial statements using the direct approach. The working paper approach for this same example is illustrated in Appendix 5A.

Exhibit 5.2

YEAR 1 INCOME STATEMENTS

	Company P	Company S
Sales	$50,000	$30,000
Investment income	5,250	—
Total revenue	55,250	30,000
Cost of sales	26,500	14,700
Expenses (miscellaneous)	5,200	8,000
Total expenses	31,700	22,700
Net income	$23,550	$ 7,300

YEAR 1 RETAINED EARNINGS STATEMENTS

	Company P	Company S
Balance, January 1	$ 85,000	$ 6,000
Net income	23,550	7,300
	108,550	13,300
Dividends	6,000	2,500
Balance, December 31	$102,550	$10,800

BALANCE SHEETS — December 31, Year 1

	Company P	Company S
Assets (miscellaneous)	$147,800	$18,300
Inventory	30,000	14,000
Investment in S (equity method)	21,750	—
	$199,550	$32,300
Liabilities	$ 47,000	$11,500
Common stock	50,000	10,000
Retained earnings	102,550	10,800
	$199,550	$32,300

The investment account has been adjusted for the entries made on the previous page.

When the parent has used the equity method to account for its investment, the following relationships exist:

- Parent's net income equals consolidated net income.

- Parent's retained earnings equal consolidated retained earnings.

The preparation of the consolidated income statement will be discussed first. The revenue item of Company P "Investment income," which is determined using the equity method, does not appear in the consolidated income statement; it is replaced with the revenues and expenses from the income statement of Company S adjusted for the amortization of the purchase discrepancy. This replacement leaves the net income of Company P unchanged but equal to consolidated net income. The replacement that takes place is illustrated below:

Investment income is replaced by the subsidiary's revenues and expenses and the amortization of the purchase discrepancy.

Replace —

Investment income (from S)	$ 5,250

With —

	Company S statement	Amortization of purch. disc.	Total
Sales	$30,000		$30,000
Cost of sales	14,700	$2,000	16,700
Expenses (misc.)	8,000	—	8,000
Goodwill impairment loss	—	50	50
Total expenses	22,700	2,050	24,750
Revenues less adjusted expenses	$ 7,300	$2,050	$ 5,250

The reason why consolidated net income is equal to Company P's net income under the equity method is as follows:

- Company S's income of $7,300 is included on the consolidated income statement on a line-by-line basis and is included on one line, investment income, on Company P's income statement
- The amortization of the purchase discrepancy of $2,050 is included on the consolidated income statement on a line-by-line basis and is included on one line, investment income, on Company P's income statement

As long as the equity method accurately picks up Company P's share of the amounts reported on the consolidated net income related to the investment in Company S, consolidated net income will always be equal to Company P's income under the equity method.

No preparation is required for the consolidated retained earnings statement when the parent has used the equity method of accounting. The consolidated retained earnings statement is identical, on a line-by-line basis, with that of the parent.

The consolidated balance sheet is prepared in much the same way as the consolidated income statement. When the parent has used the equity method, consolidated shareholders' equity is identical to that of the parent company. Company P's asset "Investment in S" does not appear in the consolidated balance sheet; it is replaced with the individual assets and liabilities from the balance sheet of Company S, revalued by the unamortized purchase discrepancy. This replacement is illustrated as follows:

The investment account is replaced by the carrying value of the subsidiary's assets and liabilities plus the unamortized purchase discrepancy.	**Replace —**	
	Investment in S	$21,750

With —

	Company S statement	Unamortized purch. disc.	Total
Assets (miscellaneous)	$18,300	$ —	$18,300
Inventory	14,000	—	14,000
Goodwill	—	950	950
	32,300	950	33,250
Liabilities	11,500	—	11,500
Net assets	$20,800	$950	$21,750

The amortization/impairment of the various components of the purchase discrepancy are reflected on the consolidated financial statements.

The preparation of the Year 1 consolidated financial statements is shown in Exhibit 5.3. The consolidated amounts were determined by adding the amounts shown in brackets. These amounts came from the financial statements of Company P and Company S and from the purchase discrepancy amortization schedule.

Note the bracketed amounts shown for goodwill impairment loss and for the goodwill on the balance sheet. The two zero amounts indicate that these items do not appear in the financial statements of Company P and Company S.

Exhibit 5.3

Year 1 Consolidated Financial Statements
(direct approach)

COMPANY P
CONSOLIDATED INCOME STATEMENT
for the Year Ended December 31, Year 1

Consolidated net income is equal to the parent's separate-entity net income under the equity method.

Sales (50,000 + 30,000)	$80,000
Cost of sales (26,500 + 14,700 + **2,000**)	43,200
Goodwill impairment loss (0 + 0 + **50**)	50
Expenses (miscellaneous) (5,200 + 8,000)	13,200
	56,450
Net income	$23,550

COMPANY P
CONSOLIDATED STATEMENT OF RETAINED EARNINGS
for the Year Ended December 31, Year 1

Balance, January 1	$ 85,000
Net income	23,550
	108,550
Dividends	6,000
Balance, December 31	$102,550

COMPANY P
CONSOLIDATED BALANCE SHEET
December 31, Year 1

Assets (miscellaneous) (147,800 + 18,300)		$166,100
Inventory (30,000 + 14,000)		44,000
Goodwill (0 + 0 + **950**)		950
		$211,050

Consolidated retained earnings are equal to the parent's separate-entity retained earnings under the equity method.

Liabilities (47,000 + 11,500)		$ 58,500
Shareholders' equity		
Common stock	50,000	
Retained earnings	102,550	152,550
		$211,050

We will now continue our example by illustrating the preparation of Company P's Year 2 consolidated statements.

On December 31, Year 2, Company S reported earnings of $10,000 for the year and paid a cash dividend of $3,000. Company P's net income for the year was $19,000 at this time (excluding any income from its investment in Company S). An impairment test conducted on December 31, Year 2, indicated that the goodwill had a fair value of $870. As a result a loss of $80 has occurred. Company P prepared the following purchase discrepancy amortization schedule at the end of Year 2:

PURCHASE DISCREPANCY AMORTIZATION SCHEDULE

	Balance Dec. 31, Year 1	Amortization Year 2	Balance Dec. 31, Year 2
Inventory	$ —	$ —	$ —
Goodwill	950	80	870
	$950	$80	$870

On December 31, Year 2, Company P makes the following equity method journal entries:

These entries are made in the parent's separate-entity accounting records.

Investment in S	10,000	
Investment income		10,000
100 percent of Company S Year 2 net income		
Cash	3,000	
Investment in S		3,000
Dividend received from Company S		
Investment income	80	
Investment in S		80
Purchase discrepancy amortization — Year 2		

After these journal entries are posted, the investment in S account and the investment income account in the records of Company P show the following changes and balances:

Investment income includes the parent's share of the subsidiary's income less the amortization of the purchase discrepancy for Year 2.

	Investment in S	Investment income
Balance, December 31, Year 1	$21,750	$ nil
December 31, Year 2:		
Income from S	10,000	10,000
Dividends from S	(3,000)	—
Purchase discrepancy amort.	(80)	(80)
Balance, December 31, Year 2	$28,670	$ 9,920

Company P combines its Year 2 investment income ($9,920) with the earnings from its own operations ($19,000) and reports a final net income of $28,920.

The investment in S account includes all entries for Years 1 and 2, i.e., cumulative adjustments since the date of acquisition. The investment income account includes entries for Year 2 only. These two accounts are related in that some entries are the same for both accounts. However, they are very different; one is a balance sheet account at a point in time and one is an income statement account for a period of time.

The financial statements of Company P and Company S on December 31, Year 2, are shown in Exhibit 5.4.

Exhibit 5.4

YEAR 2 INCOME STATEMENTS

Investment income is the amount required to make the parent's separate entity income equal to consolidated net income.

	Company P	Company S
Sales	$ 60,000	$40,000
Investment income	9,920	—
Total revenue	69,920	40,000
Cost of sales	32,000	18,000
Expenses (miscellaneous)	9,000	12,000
Total expenses	41,000	30,000
Net income	$ 28,920	$10,000

YEAR 2 RETAINED EARNINGS STATEMENTS

	Company P	Company S
Balance, January 1	$102,550	$10,800
Net income	28,920	10,000
	131,470	20,800
Dividends	8,000	3,000
Balance December 31	$123,470	$17,800

BALANCE SHEETS — December 31, Year 2

	Company P	Company S
Assets (miscellaneous)	$131,800	$21,000
Inventory	35,000	16,000
Investment in S (equity method)	28,670	—
	$195,470	$37,000
Liabilities	$ 22,000	$ 9,200
Common stock	50,000	10,000
Retained earnings	123,470	17,800
	$195,470	$37,000

The investment account was updated for the entries made on the previous page.

Consolidated Statements, End of Year 2, Direct Approach

The two replacements that are made in the consolidation process when the parent has used the equity method are shown below:

Replace —

Investment income (from S) $ 9,920

With —

The subsidiary's revenues and expenses plus the amortization of the purchase discrepancy replace investment income.

	Company S statement	Amortization of purch. disc.	Total
Sales	$40,000		$40,000
Cost of sales	18,000		18,000
Expenses (misc.)	12,000		12,000
Goodwill impairment loss	—	$80	80
Total expenses	30,000	80	30,080
Revenues less adjusted expenses	$10,000	$80	$ 9,920

Replace —

Investment in S $28,670

With —

The investment account is replaced by the carrying value of the subsidiary's assets and liabilities plus the unamortized purchase discrepancy.

	Company S statement	Unamortized purch. disc.	Total
Assets (misc)	$21,000	$ —	$21,000
Inventory	16,000	—	16,000
Goodwill	—	870	870
	37,000	870	37,870
Liabilities	9,200	—	9,200
Net assets	$27,800	$870	$28,670

The consolidated financial statements for Year 2 are shown in Exhibit 5.5. The amounts shown in brackets came from the financial statements of the two companies and the purchase discrepancy amortization schedule. The consolidated retained earnings statement was prepared by reproducing, line by line, the retained earnings statement of Company P.

Exhibit 5.5

Year 2 Consolidated Financial Statements
(direct approach)

COMPANY P
CONSOLIDATED INCOME STATEMENT
for the Year Ended December 31, Year 2

Consolidated net income is equal to the parent's separate-entity net income under the equity method.

Sales (60,000 + 40,000)	$100,000
Cost of sales (32,000 + 18,000)	50,000
Goodwill impairment loss (0 + 0 + **80**)	80
Expenses (miscellaneous) (9,000 + 12,000)	21,000
	71,080
Net income	$ 28,920

CONSOLIDATED STATEMENT OF RETAINED EARNINGS
for the Year Ended December 31, Year 2

Balance, January 1	$102,550
Net income	28,920
	131,470
Dividends	8,000
Balance, December 31	$123,470

CONSOLIDATED BALANCE SHEET
December 31, Year 2

Assets (miscellaneous) (131,800 + 21,000)		$152,800
Inventory (35,000 + 16,000)		51,000
Goodwill (0 + 0 + **870**)		870
		$204,670

Consolidated retained earnings are equal to the parent's separate-entity retained earnings under the equity method.

Liabilities (22,000 + 9,200)		$ 31,200
Shareholders' equity		
Common stock	50,000	
Retained earnings	123,470	173,470
		$204,670

The consolidation of the 100 percent owned subsidiary for Year 2 financial statements using the working paper approach is illustrated in Appendix 5A.

Consolidation of an 80 Percent Owned Subsidiary

The first example was used to illustrate the consolidation of Company P and its 100 percent owned subsidiary Company S over a two-year period. The next example will examine the consolidation of a less than 100 percent owned subsidiary using the same financial statements of Company P and Company S.

Assume that on January 1, Year 1, instead of purchasing 100 percent of Company S for $19,000, Company P purchased 80 percent for $15,200. All other facts about the two companies remain the same as in the previous example. The journal entry of Company P on January 1, Year 1, is:

Investment in S	15,200	
Cash		15,200

The calculation and allocation of the purchase discrepancy and the calculation of the noncontrolling interest on January 1, Year 1, are shown in Exhibit 5.6.

Exhibit 5.6

COMPANY P
CALCULATION OF PURCHASE DISCREPANCY
January 1, Year 1

The imputed value of the subsidiary is derived by taking the purchase price and dividing by the ownership percentage acquired by the parent.

Cost of 80 percent of Company S		$15,200
Imputed value of 100 percent of company S		19,000
Book value of Company S, Jan. 1, Year 1:		
Common stock	10,000	
Retained earnings	6,000	
		16,000
Imputed purchase discrepancy		3,000
Allocated:	FV − BV × 100%	
Inventory	2,000 × 100%	2,000
Balance — goodwill		$ 1,000

CALCULATION OF NONCONTROLLING INTEREST — January 1, Year 1

NCI is based on the imputed fair value of the subsidiary as a whole.

Imputed shareholders' equity, Company S (above)	$19,000
Noncontrolling interest's ownership	20%
Noncontrolling interest	$ 3,800

The individual balance sheets of Company P and Company S, and Company P's consolidated balance sheet on January 1, Year 1, prepared using the direct approach, are shown below.

BALANCE SHEETS — January 1, Year 1

The subsidiary's assets and liabilities are brought onto the consolidated financial statements at 100 percent of their fair values.

	Company P	Company S	Consolidated
Assets (miscellaneous)	$142,800	$ 17,000	$159,800
Inventory	22,000	10,000	34,000
Investment in S	15,200	—	—
Goodwill	—	—	1,000
	$180,000	$ 27,000	$194,800
Liabilities	$ 45,000	$ 11,000	$ 56,000
Common stock	50,000	10,000	50,000
Retained earnings	85,000	6,000	85,000
Noncontrolling interest	—	—	3,800
	$180,000	$ 27,000	$194,800

The consolidated balance sheet was prepared by:

1. eliminating the investment account and Company S's shareholders' equity

2. adding the imputed purchase price discrepancy to Company S's assets and liabilities to use 100% of the fair values for Company S's assets and liabilities

3. reporting noncontrolling interest as a component of shareholders' equity at a value representing the noncontrolling interest's share of Company S's imputed value

On December 31, Year 1, Company S reported a net income of $7,300 for the year and paid a cash dividend of $2,500. Company P's net income for the year was $18,300 at this time (not including income from its investment in Company S). An impairment test on goodwill conducted on December 31, Year 1, indicated that a $50 loss had occurred. To assist in the preparation of the Year 1 consolidated financial statements, and the equity method journal entries that will be made, Company P prepares the following schedule:

PURCHASE DISCREPANCY AMORTIZATION SCHEDULE

	Balance Jan. 1, Year 1	Amortization Year 1	Balance Dec. 31, Year 1
Inventory	$2,000	$2,000	$ —
Goodwill	1,000	50	950
	$3,000	$2,050	$950
Company P's share (80%)	$2,400	$1,640	$760
Noncontrolling interest's share (20%)	600	410	190

The purchase price discrepancy is allocated between the parent and noncontrolling interest.

Company P makes the following journal entries using the equity method to account for its investment:

Investment in S	5,840	
Investment income		5,840
80% of Company S Year 1 net income		

The equity method captures the parent's share of the net effect of any adjustments made on consolidation.

Cash	2,000	
Investment in S		2,000
80% of the dividend paid by Company S		

Investment income	1,640	
Investment in S		1,640
Purchase discrepancy amortization — Year 1		

After these journal entries are posted, the two related accounts in the records of Company P will show the following changes and balances:

	Investment in S	Investment income
January 1, Year 1	$15,200	$ nil
December 31, Year 1		
Income from S	5,840	5,840
Dividends from S	(2,000)	—
Purchase discrepancy amort.	(1,640)	(1,640)
Balance, December 31, Year 1	$17,400	$4,200

The investment in S shows the balance at the end of the year whereas investment income shows the income for one year.

Company P increases its earnings from its own operations ($18,300) by the investment income ($4,200) and reports a final net income of $22,500 in Year 1.

The financial statements of Company P and Company S as at December 31, Year 1, are presented in Exhibit 5.7. These statements, along with the purchase discrepancy amortization schedule, are used to prepare the Year 1 consolidated statements.

Exhibit 5.7

These are the separate-entity financial statements of the two legal entities.

YEAR 1 INCOME STATEMENTS

	Company P	Company S
Sales	$ 50,000	$30,000
Investment income	4,200	—
Total revenue	54,200	30,000
Cost of sales	26,500	14,700
Expenses (miscellaneous)	5,200	8,000
Total expenses	31,700	22,700
Net income	$ 22,500	$ 7,300

YEAR 1 RETAINED EARNINGS STATEMENTS

	Company P	Company S
Balance, January 1	$ 85,000	$ 6,000
Net income	22,500	7,300
	107,500	13,300
Dividends	6,000	2,500
Balance, December 31	$101,500	$10,800

BALANCE SHEETS — December 31, Year 1

	Company P	Company S
Assets (miscellaneous)	$151,100	$18,300
Inventory	30,000	14,000
Investment in S (equity method)	17,400	—
	$198,500	$32,300
Liabilities	$ 47,000	$11,500
Common stock	50,000	10,000
Retained earnings	101,500	10,800
	$198,500	$32,300

Consolidated Statements, End of Year 1, Direct Approach

The approach used to prepare a consolidated income statement when the subsidiary is 80 percent owned is basically the same as the one used for 100 percent ownership. All of the revenues and expenses of Company S are used even though the consolidated net income contains only 80 percent of the net income of Company S. This introduces a new "expense" or deduction in the consolidated income statement that is described as noncontrolling interest. The amount is determined by multiplying the reported net income of Company S by the ownership percentage not owned by Company P and then deducting the noncontrolling interest's share of the amortization of the purchase discrepancy. In Year 1, the noncontrolling interest on the consolidated income statement amounts to $1,050 (20% × $7,300 − $410). The replacement that takes place in the preparation of the consolidated income statement is shown below:

Investment income is replaced by the subsidiary's revenues and expenses, the amortization of the purchase discrepancy, and noncontrolling interest.

Replace —

Investment income (from S)			$ 4,200

With —

	Company S statement	Amortization of purch. disc.	Total
Sales	$30,000		$30,000
Cost of sales	14,700	$2,000	16,700
Expenses (misc.)	8,000	—	8,000
Goodwill impairment loss	—	50	50
Total expenses	22,700	2,050	24,750
Revenues less adjusted expenses	7,300	2,050	5,250
Less noncontrolling interest	1,460	410	1,050
Company P's share (80%)	$ 5,840	$1,640	$ 4,200

The reason why consolidated net income is equal to Company P's net income under the equity method is as follows:

- Company S's income of $7,300 is included on the consolidated income statement on a line-by-line basis. Then, noncontrolling interest of $1,460 is deducted on the consolidated income statement. The difference between S's total income and the amount allocated to NCI is $5,840, which is Company P's share of Company S's income. This income is included on one line, investment income, on Company P's separate entity income statement.

- The amortization of the purchase discrepancy of $2,050 is included on the consolidated income statement on a line-by-line basis. The NCI is charged with $410, their share of this amortization. The remainder, $1,640, is Company P's share. This amount is included on one line, investment income, on Company P's separate entity income statement.

Under the entity theory, both the parent's share and the noncontrolling interest's share of the assets and liabilities of Company S and the unamortized purchase discrepancy must be shown in the consolidated balance sheet. The calculation of the amount shown for noncontrolling interest as at December 31, Year 1, is:

Common stock — Company S	$10,000
Retained earnings — Company S	10,800
	20,800
	20%
	4,160
Plus: unamortized purchase discrepancy	190
	$ 4,350

The following replacement takes place on the balance sheet:

The investment account is replaced by the carrying value of the subsidiary's assets and liabilities, the unamortized purchase discrepancy, and noncontrolling interest.

Replace —

Investment in S			$17,400

With —

	Company S statement	Unamortized purch. disc.	Total
Assets (misc.)	$18,300	$ —	$18,300
Inventory	14,000	—	14,000
Goodwill	—	950	950
	32,300	950	33,250
Liabilities	11,500	—	11,500
Net assets	20,800	950	21,750
Noncontrolling interest (20%)	4,160	190	4,350
Company P's share (80%)	$16,640	$760	$17,400

Exhibit 5.8 shows the Year 1 consolidated financial statements prepared using the direct approach.

Exhibit 5.8

Year 1 Consolidated Financial Statements
(direct approach)

COMPANY P
CONSOLIDATED INCOME STATEMENT
for the Year Ended December 31, Year 1

Consolidated net income and retained earnings are equal to the parent's separate-entity net income and retained earnings under the equity method.

Sales (50,000 + 30,000)	$80,000
Cost of sales (26,500 + 14,700 + **2,000**)	43,200
Goodwill impairment loss (0 + 0 + **50**)	50
Expenses (miscellaneous) (5,200 + 8,000)	13,200
	56,450
Net income — entity	23,550
Less noncontrolling interest	1,050
Net income	$22,500

COMPANY P
CONSOLIDATED STATEMENT OF RETAINED EARNINGS
for the Year Ended December 31, Year 1

The consolidated balance sheet includes 100 percent of the value of the subsidiary's assets and liabilities on a line-by-line basis even though the parent only owns 80 percent of the subsidiary.

Balance, January 1	$ 85,000
Net income	22,500
	107,500
Dividends	6,000
Balance, December 31	$101,500

COMPANY P
CONSOLIDATED BALANCE SHEET
December 31, Year 1

Assets (miscellaneous) (151,100 + 18,300)	$169,400
Inventory (30,000 + 14,000)	44,000
Goodwill (0 + 0 + **950**)	950
	$214,350

Liabilities (47,000 + 11,500)	$ 58,500
Common stock	50,000
Retained earnings	101,500
Noncontrolling interest	4,350
	$214,350

The amortization/impairment of the various components of the purchase discrepancy are reflected on the consolidated financial statements.

    The bracketed items come from the statements of Company P and Company S and the purchase discrepancy amortization schedule. A new item has been introduced in the consolidated income statement called "Net income — entity." This amount is the difference between consolidated revenues and expenses. There are two equities shown on a consolidated balance sheet: the equity of the controlling interest (the parent's shareholders' equity) and the noncontrolling interest's equity. The income earned by this single consolidated entity is allocated to the two equity interests. The allocation of the net income to the controlling interest is readily seen in the consolidated retained earnings statement. Consolidated financial statements do not show the changes that have taken place in the noncontrolling interest because the statements are directed to the shareholders of the parent company. The changes in noncontrolling interest *could* be presented, in a statement similar to the retained earnings statement, as follows:

CHANGES IN NONCONTROLLING INTEREST

Noncontrolling interest on the balance sheet increases when the subsidiary earns income and decreases when the subsidiary pays a dividend.

Balance, January 1	$3,800
Allocated income of entity	1,050
	4,850
Dividends to noncontrolling shareholders	500*
Balance, December 31	$4,350

* $2,500 × 20% = $500.

    While this statement is not part of consolidated financial statements, it is often useful to prepare this reconciliation when preparing a solution to consolidation problems, because it helps show where the allocated income of this single entity and the dividends of the subsidiary end up in the consolidated financial statements. The consolidated retained earnings statement does not contain the dividends of the subsidiary. In this example, Company S paid $2,500 in dividends. Eighty percent of this amount ($2,000) was paid to Company P and therefore did not leave the consolidated entity. The other 20 percent ($500) was paid to the noncontrolling shareholders and reduced the equity of that group, as shown in the statement.

    The consolidation of the 80 percent owned subsidiary for Year 1 financial statements using the working paper approach is illustrated in Appendix 5A.

Consolidated Statements, End of Year 2, Direct Approach

On December 31, Year 2, Company S reported earnings of $10,000 for the year and paid a cash dividend of $3,000. Company P's earnings for the year were $19,000 at this time (excluding any income from its investment in Company S). An impairment test conducted on December 31, Year 2, indicated that the goodwill had a fair value of $870, and therefore an $80 impairment loss had occurred. Company P prepared the following purchase discrepancy amortization schedule:

PURCHASE DISCREPANCY AMORTIZATION SCHEDULE

	Balance Jan. 1, Year 2	Amortization Year 2	Balance Dec. 31, Year 2
Inventory	$ —	$—	$ —
Goodwill	950	80	870
	$950	$80	$870
Company P's share (80%)	$760	$64	$696
Noncontrolling interest's share (20%)	190	16	174

On December 31, Year 2, Company P makes the following equity method journal entries:

These entries are made in the parent's separate-entity accounting records.

Investment in S	8,000	
Investment income		8,000
80% of Company S, Year 2, net income		

Cash	2,400	
Investment in S		2,400
Dividends received from Company S		

Investment income	64	
Investment in S		64
Purchase discrepancy amortization — Year 2		

After these journal entries are posted, the investment in S account and the investment income account in the records of P Company will show the following changes and balances:

Investment income includes the parent's share of the subsidiary's income less the amortization of the purchase discrepancy for Year 2.

	Investment in S	Investment income
December 31, Year 1	$17,400	$ nil
December 31, Year 2		
Income from S	8,000	8,000
Dividends from S	(2,400)	
Purchase discrepancy amort.	(64)	(64)
Balance, December 31, Year 2	$22,936	$7,936

Company P combines its Year 2 investment income ($7,936) with the earnings from its own operations ($19,000) and reports a final net income of $26,936.

The financial statements of Company P and Company S on December 31, Year 2, are shown in Exhibit 5.9.

Exhibit 5.9

YEAR 2 INCOME STATEMENTS

	Company P	Company S
Sales	$60,000	$40,000
Investment income	7,936	—
Total revenue	67,936	40,000
Cost of sales	32,000	18,000
Expenses (miscellaneous)	9,000	12,000
Total expenses	41,000	30,000
Net income	$26,936	$10,000

Investment income is the amount required to make the parent's separate entity income equal to consolidated net income.

YEAR 2 RETAINED EARNINGS STATEMENTS

	Company P	Company S
Balance, January 1	$101,500	$10,800
Net income	26,936	10,000
	128,436	20,800
Dividends	8,000	3,000
Balance, December 31	$120,436	$17,800

BALANCE SHEETS — December 31, Year 2

	Company P	Company S
Assets (miscellaneous)	$134,500	$21,000
Inventory	35,000	16,000
Investment in S (equity method)	22,936	—
	$192,436	$37,000
Liabilities	$ 22,000	$ 9,200
Common stock	50,000	10,000
Retained earnings	120,436	17,800
	$192,436	$37,000

The investment account was updated for the entries made on the previous page.

The two replacements that are made in the consolidation process when the parent has used the equity method are shown below:

Replace —

Investment income (from S)	$ 7,936

With —

	Company S statement	Amortization of purch. disc.	Total
Sales	$40,000	$ —	$40,000
Cost of sales	18,000		18,000
Expenses (misc.)	12,000		12,000
Goodwill impairment loss	—	80	80
Total expenses	30,000	80	30,080
Revenues less adjusted expenses	10,000	(80)	9,920
Less: noncontrolling interest (20%)	2,000	(16)	1,984
Company P's share (80%)	$ 8,000	$(64)	$ 7,936

Investment income is replaced by the subsidiary's revenues and expenses, the amortization of the purchase discrepancy, and noncontrolling interest.

The investment account is replaced by the carrying value of the subsidiary's assets and liabilities, the unamortized purchase discrepancy, and noncontrolling interest.

Replace —

Investment in S			$22,936

With —

	Company S statement	Unamortized purch. disc.	Total
Assets (misc.)	$21,000	$ —	$21,000
Inventory	16,000	—	16,000
Goodwill	—	870	870
	37,000	870	37,870
Liabilities	9,200	—	9,200
Net assets	27,800	870	28,670
Less: Noncontrolling interest (20%)	5,560	174	5,734
Company P's share (80%)	$22,240	$696	$22,936

The consolidated financial statements for Year 2 are shown in Exhibit 5.10. The amounts shown in brackets came from the financial statements of the two companies and the purchase discrepancy amortization schedule. The consolidated retained earnings statement was prepared by reproducing, line by line, the retained earnings statement of Company P.

Exhibit 5.10

Year 2 Consolidated Financial Statements
(direct approach)

COMPANY P
CONSOLIDATED INCOME STATEMENT
for the Year Ended December 31, Year 2

Consolidated net income is equal to the parent's separate-entity net income under the equity method.

Sales (60,000 + 40,000)	$100,000
Cost of sales (32,000 + 18,000)	50,000
Goodwill impairment loss (0 + 0 + **80**)	80
Expenses (misc.) (9,000 + 12,000)	21,000
	71,080
Net income — entity	28,920
Less noncontrolling interest	1,984
Net income	$ 26,936

COMPANY P
CONSOLIDATED STATEMENT OF RETAINED EARNINGS
for the Year Ended December 31, Year 2

Balance, January 1	$101,500
Net income	26,936
	128,436
Dividends	8,000
Balance, December 31	$120,436

COMPANY P
CONSOLIDATED BALANCE SHEET
December 31, Year 2

Assets (misc.) (134,500 + 21,000)	$155,500
Inventory (35,000 + 16,000)	51,000
Goodwill (0 + 0 + **870**)	870
	$207,370

Consolidated retained earnings are equal to the parent's separate-entity retained earnings under the equity method.	Liabilities (22,000 + 9,200)	$ 31,200
	Common stock	50,000
	Retained earnings	120,436
	Noncontrolling interest	5,734
		$207,370

The consolidation of the 80%-owned subsidiary for Year 2 financial statements using the working paper approach is illustrated in Appendix 5A.

The preceding illustrations have presented the basics for preparing consolidated financial statements when the parent has used the equity method to account for its investment subsequent to the date of acquisition. The parent's use of this method always produces the following results:

The equity method captures the parent's share of the net effect of any adjustments made on consolidation and is referred to as the one-line consolidation.

- Consolidated net income in any one year will always be equal to the parent's net income in that year.
- Consolidated retained earnings are always equal to the parent's retained earnings.

The equity method captures the parent's share of the net effect of any adjustments made on consolidation. The investment in S and investment income accounts are sometimes referred to as the one-line consolidation accounts.

Chapter 6 will examine the preparation of the consolidated statements in situations where the parent has used the cost method. The cost method is the one most widely used by Canadian parent companies, probably because of its simplicity. When this method has been used, consolidated net income and retained earnings *do not* equal the parent's net income and retained earnings. However, one of the consolidation procedures involved when the cost method has been used is to adjust the parent's accounts to the balances that would have resulted if the equity method had been used instead. Having done this, the remainder of the consolidation procedures are the same as were illustrated in this chapter. A thorough understanding of the equity method and the financial statement numbers that it produces is fundamental to the overall understanding of the consolidated statement preparation process.

Purchase Discrepancy Assigned to Liabilities

With the considerable swings in interest rates over the past decade, companies often find that liabilities assumed in a business combination have fair values different from their carrying values. As with assets acquired, liabilities assumed in a business combination must be valued at their fair values. The difference between fair value and carrying value for these liabilities is similar to a bond premium or discount that must be amortized over its remaining life.

The effective interest method should be used to account for financial assets and liabilities.

Prior to 2006, the *CICA Handbook* was silent on the amortization method to be used in amortizing any premium or discount on a bond payable or investment in bonds. Companies could use either the straight-line method or effective interest method. Most companies used the straight-line method because it is simpler to use. The new *Handbook* section on "Financial Instruments" (Section 3855) requires the use of the effective interest method. Some companies may continue to use the straight-line method where the difference between the two methods is not material. In this text, we will use both the straight-line and effective interest methods.

For situation A, assume that Pubco acquires 100 percent of the common shares of Subco on December 31, Year 2. On that date, Pubco had no bonds payable outstanding and Subco had bonds payable with a carrying value of $100,000 and a fair value of $105,154. These bonds were issued on January 1, Year 1, at their par value of $100,000 and mature on December 31, Year 5. The bonds pay interest on December 31 each year at a stated rate of 10 percent. The market rate of interest was 8 percent on December 31, Year 2. Given that the stated rate of interest was higher than the market rate, the bonds were trading at a premium. The fair value of the bonds can be determined by taking the present value of future cash flows using a discount rate of 8 percent as follows:

Principal $100,000 × (P/F, 8%, 3 years) (0.79383)	$ 79,383
Interest 10,000 × (P/A, 8%, 3 years) (2.57710)	25,771
	$105,154

The purchase discrepancy of $5,154 is considered a premium on the bonds from a consolidated viewpoint. On the date of acquisition, the entire $5,154 is assigned to the bonds payable and bonds payable will be reported at $105,154 on the consolidated balance sheet. The following schedule shows the amortization of this premium using the effective interest method as if Pubco had actually issued these bonds at $105,154:

Period	Interest paid	Interest expense	Amortization of bond premium	Unamortized bond premium	Bond carrying value
Year 2				$5,154	$105,154
Year 3	$10,000[1]	$8,412[2]	$1,588[3]	3,566[4]	103,566
Year 4	10,000	8,285	1,715	1,851	101,851
Year 5	10,000	8,149	1,851	0	100,000

[1] $100,000 × 10% = $10,000   [2] $105,154 × 8% = $8,412
[3] $10,000 − $8,412 = $1,588   [4] $5,154 − $1,588 = $3,566

In preparing consolidated financial statements subsequent to the date of acquisition, interest expense and bonds payable must be adjusted as follows to obtain the same results as if the parent had issued the bonds itself:

Period	Subco's interest expense	Adjustment on consolidation	Consolidated interest expense	Subco's bond payable	Adjustment on consolidation	Consolidated bond payable
Year 2				$100,000	$5,154	$105,154
Year 3	$10,000	$1,588	$8,412	100,000	3,566	103,566
Year 4	10,000	1,715	8,285	100,000	1,851	101,851
Year 5	10,000	1,851	8,149	100,000	0	100,000

Subco's interest expense is equal to the interest paid because the bonds were issued at par.

For situation B, assume that Subco had issued the bonds on January 1, Year 1, at $92,791 when the market rate of interest was 12 percent and everything else was the same as situation A. Given that the stated rate of interest was lower than the market rate, the bonds were issued at a discount. The following schedule shows how Subco would amortize this discount on its own financial statements:

The subsidiary amortizes the bond discount for its separate entity financial statements.

Period	Interest paid	Interest expense	Amortization of bond discount	Unamortized bond discount	Bond carrying value
Year 0				$7,209	$ 92,791
Year 1	$10,000[1]	$11,135[2]	$1,135[3]	6,074[4]	93,926
Year 2	10,000	11,271	1,271	4,803	95,197
Year 3	10,000	11,424	1,424	3,379	96,621
Year 4	10,000	11,594	1,594	1,785	98,215
Year 5	10,000	11,785	1,785	0	100,000

[1] $100,000 \times 10\% = \$10,000$ [2] $\$92,791 \times 12\% = \$11,135$
[3] $\$10,000 - \$11,135 = \$1,135$ [4] $\$7,209 - \$1,135 = \$6,074$

The purchase discrepancy on December 31, Year 2, the date of acquisition, would now be $9,957 ($105,154 – $95,197) and is considered a premium on the bonds from a consolidated viewpoint. The entire $9,957 is assigned to the bonds payable and bonds payable will be reported at $105,154 (same amount as Situation A) on the consolidated balance sheet. In preparing consolidated financial statements subsequent to the date of acquisition, interest expense and bonds payable must be adjusted as follows to obtain the same results as in Situation A:

Period	Subco's interest expense	Adjustment on consolidation	Consolidated interest expense	Subco's bond payable	Adjustment on consolidation	Consolidated bond payable
Year 2				$ 95,197	$9,957	$105,154
Year 3	$11,424	$3,012	$8,412	96,621	6,945	103,566
Year 4	11,594	3,309	8,285	98,215	3,636	101,851
Year 5	11,785	3,636	8,149	100,000	0	100,000

The straight-line and effective interest methods produce the same results in total over the life of the bond.

In both situations, the purchase discrepancy was amortized over the three-year term to maturity of the bonds. Under the effective interest method, the annual amortization changes over time. If the straight-line method were used, the annual amortization would be the same each year. The following schedule summarizes the amortization of the purchase discrepancy under the effective interest and straight-line methods:

	Purchase discrepancy at acquisition	Amortization of purchase discrepancy			
		Effective interest method			St-line per year
		Year 3	Year 4	Year 5	
A	$5,154	$1,588	$1,715	$1,851	$1,718
B	9,957	3,012	3,309	3,636	3,319

If Pubco acquired less than 100 percent of Subco, the noncontrolling interest would absorb their share of the purchase discrepancy and amortization of the purchase discrepancy.

Intercompany Receivables and Payables

Consolidated financial statements are designed to reflect the results of transactions between the consolidated single entity and those outside the entity. All transactions

The consolidated financial statements should only reflect the result of transactions with outsiders.

between the parent and its subsidiaries, or between the subsidiaries of a parent, must be eliminated in the consolidation process to reflect this single-entity concept. While many of these intercompany eliminations are discussed in later chapters, we will introduce the topic now by discussing the elimination of intercompany receivables and payables. If the parent's accounts receivable contain a receivable of $5,000 from its subsidiary, then the accounts payable of the subsidiary must contain a $5,000 payable to the parent. If these intercompany receivables and payables were not eliminated in the consolidation process, both the accounts receivable and the accounts payable on the consolidated balance sheet would be overstated from a single-entity point of view. The working paper entry to eliminate these intercompany balances would be:

Accounts payable — subsidiary	5,000	
Accounts receivable — parent		5,000

Because the net assets (assets less liabilities) are unchanged after this elimination, the equities of the noncontrolling and controlling interests are not affected.

When Control Ceases

When the parent ceases to control the subsidiary, consolidated financial statements will no longer be required.

After control has been obtained, GAAP requires the parent to prepare consolidated statements for purposes of external reporting. When control ceases, the former parent ceases consolidation and for external-reporting purposes would report on the following basis depending on the type of investment it now has:[9]

No.	Type of investment	Market value readily available?	Method of reporting
1	Significant influence	Not applicable	Equity method
2	Available-for-sale	No	Cost method
3	Available-for-sale	Yes	Fair value method

If a parent has decided to dispose of a subsidiary, it continues to consolidate until the date of disposal. During this interval, it applies the provisions of Section 3475, "Disposal of Long-lived Assets and Discontinued Operations," to segregate the operations of the subsidiary in the consolidated income statement.

---

[9] Prior to the loss of control, the former parent was using the equity method on its separate-entity records to account for its investment. In situation 1, the former parent will continue to use the equity method on its separate entity records but will now report under the equity method for external reporting purposes as well. In situation 2, the balance in the investment account at the time of loss in control will become the cost of the investment for purpose of applying the cost method. The former parent will report on the cost method for external reporting purposes from this point forward. In situation 3, the former parent will revalue the investment account to fair value at the time of loss in control and from this date forward. The fair value adjustment will be reported in other comprehensive income.

Impairment testing for a qualifying enterprise is not required annually but only when circumstances would indicate the carrying value might not be recoverable.

Differential Reporting

The differential reporting options available for topics in this chapter are not extensive. Whereas it is required that goodwill be tested for impairment on an annual basis, a qualifying enterprise may elect to test for impairment only when it is obvious that the fair value of the reporting unit may be less than its carrying amount because of events that have occurred during the year.

In a similar manner, whereas it is required that an intangible asset not subject to amortization be tested for impairment annually, a qualifying enterprise may elect to test for impairment "only when events or changes in circumstances indicate that its carrying amount may not be recoverable."

An International Perspective

The Canadian standards for goodwill are basically the same as IASB standards with two exceptions. First, IAS 36 might require goodwill impairment assessments to be made below the level of the reporting unit, i.e., at the cash-generating unit. Secondly, IAS 36 determines an impairment loss as the excess of the carrying amount above the recoverable amount of the cash-generating unit to which the goodwill is allocated, rather than the difference between carrying amount and fair value of the reporting unit's goodwill.

SUMMARY

While a parent company can account for its investment by either the equity method or the cost method, the consolidated statements are the same regardless of the method used. When the parent uses the equity method, the income and retained earnings reported by the parent on its separate-entity financial statements will be equal to consolidated net income and consolidated retained earnings, respectively. The method of presentation is quite different between the separate-entity financial statements and the consolidated financial statements. On the separate-entity financial statements, the parent's share of the subsidiary's income and net assets are shown in one line on the income statement (investment income) and one line on the balance sheet (investment in subsidiary). Accordingly, the equity method is sometimes referred to as the one-line consolidation. On the consolidated financial statements, the parent's share of the subsidiary's income and net assets are shown line by line.

This chapter has illustrated the preparation of consolidated financial statements covering a two-year period after the date of acquisition when the parent has used the equity method to account for its investment. The direct approach was used in the main body of the chapter and the working paper approach is used in Appendix 5A. The same examples will be used in Chapter 6, when the parent uses the cost method.

The basic steps in the consolidation process when the parent has used the equity method are outlined in Exhibit 5.11.

Exhibit 5.11

PREPARATION OF CONSOLIDATED FINANCIAL STATEMENTS
(basic steps)

1. Calculate and allocate the purchase discrepancy on the date of acquisition.
2. Prepare a purchase discrepancy amortization schedule (date of acquisition to present date).
3. Prepare the consolidated income statement.
4. Prepare the consolidated retained earnings statement.
5. Calculate noncontrolling interest at the end of the year (for the consolidated balance sheet).
6. Prepare a statement of changes in noncontrolling interest (optional).
7. Prepare a consolidated balance sheet.

SELF-STUDY PROBLEM

On January 1, Year 1, Allen Company acquired 70% of the outstanding common shares of Bell Company for $87,500 in cash. On that date Bell had common stock of $50,000 and retained earnings of $45,000. At acquisition, the identifiable assets and liabilities of Bell had fair values that were equal to book values except for plant assets, which had fair values $30,000 greater than book value; inventory, which had a fair value $8,000 less than book value; and bonds payable, which had fair values $12,420 greater than book value. The plant assets had a remaining useful life of 8 years on January 1, Year 1, and are amortized on a straight-line basis. The bonds payable mature on December 31, Year 8, and are amortized using the effective interest method. The market rate of interest for similar bonds was 6% on January 1, Year 1.

Financial statements for the Year 6 fiscal year are as follows:

	Allen	Bell
Income statements		
Sales	$ 400,000	$100,000
Rent revenue	15,000	—
Investment revenue	195	—
	415,195	100,000
Cost of sales	200,000	45,000
Depreciation	55,000	20,000
Interest expense	32,000	8,000
Other expenses	28,000	17,000
	315,000	90,000
Net income	$ 100,195	$ 10,000
Retained earnings statements		
Balance, January 1	$ 453,426	$135,000
Net income	100,195	10,000
	553,621	145,000
Dividends	30,000	5,000
Balance, December 31	$ 523,621	$140,000
	Allen	Bell
Balance sheets		
Cash	$ 12,500	$ 10,000
Accounts receivable	60,000	25,000
Inventory	200,000	40,000
Investment in Bell — equity method	137,621	—
Plant and equipment	1,200,000)	470,000
Accumulated depreciation	(300,000)	(220,000)
	$1,310,121	$325,000

Accounts payable	$ 86,500	$ 35,000
Bonds payable, 8%	400,000	100,000
Common stock	300,000	50,000
Retained earnings	523,621	140,000
	$1,310,121	$325,000

Additional Information

In Year 2, a goodwill impairment loss of $10,000 was recorded. Subsequent goodwill testing yielded no further evidence of impairment until Year 6, when a substantial decline in the fair value of Bell Company occurred and management decided to reflect an impairment loss of $7,650 in the year's consolidated statements.

On December 31, Year 6, Bell Company owes Allen Company $9,000.

Required:

1. Using the direct approach, prepare the following Year 6 consolidated financial statements:
   (a) Income statement.
   (b) Retained earnings statement.
   (c) Balance sheet.
2. Prepare a schedule of the Year 6 changes in noncontrolling interest.

Solution to Self-study Problem

Cost of 70% of Bell			$ 87,500
Imputed value of 100% of Bell			$125,000
Book value of Bell			
Common stock		50,000	
Retained earnings		45,000	
			95,000
Purchase discrepancy — January 1, Year 1			30,000
Allocated:	FV – BV		
Plant assets	30,000		
Inventory	–8,000		
	22,000		
Bonds payable	12,420		9,580
Goodwill			$20,420

BOND AMORTIZATION SCHEDULE

Date	Cash paid	Interest expense	Bond premium amortization	Carrying amount of bonds
Jan 1/ Year 1				$112,420
Dec 31/ Year 1	$ 8,000	$ 6,745	$ 1,255	111,165
Dec 31/ Year 2	8,000	6,670	1,330	109,835
Dec 31/ Year 3	8,000	6,590	1,410	108,425
Dec 31/ Year 4	8,000	6,506	1,494	106,931
Dec 31/ Year 5	8,000	6,416	1,584	105,347
	40,000	32,927	7,073	
Dec 31/ Year 6	8,000	6,321	1,679	103,668
Dec 31/ Year 7	8,000	6,220	1,780	101,888
Dec 31/ Year 8	8,000	6,112	1,888	100,000
	$64,000	$51,580	$12,420	

PURCHASE DISCREPANCY AMORTIZATION SCHEDULE

	Balance Jan. 1 Year 1	*Amortization* To end of Year 5	Year 6	Balance Dec. 31 Year 6
Plant assets	$30,000	$18,750	$ 3,750	$ 7,500
Inventory	–8,000	–8,000	—	—
Goodwill	20,420	10,000	7,650	2,770
	42,420	20,750	11,400	10,270
Bonds payable	12,420	7,073	1,679	3,668
	$30,000	$13,677	$ 9,721	$ 6,602

1. (a)

ALLEN COMPANY
CONSOLIDATED INCOME STATEMENT
for the Year Ended December 31, Year 6

Sales (400,000 + 100,000)	$500,000
Rent revenue	15,000
	515,000
Cost of sales (200,000 + 45,000)	245,000
Depreciation (55,000 + 20,000 + **3,750**)	78,750
Interest expense (32,000 + 8,000 – **1,679**)	38,321
Other expenses (28,000 + 17,000)	45,000
Goodwill impairment loss (0 + 0 + **7,650**)	7,650
	414,721
Net income — entity	100,279
Less: noncontrolling interest [(30% x (10,000 – 9,721))]	84
Net income	$100,195

(b)

ALLEN COMPANY
CONSOLIDATED RETAINED EARNINGS STATEMENT
for the Year Ended December 31, Year 6

Balance, January 1	$453,426
Net income	100,195
	553,621
Dividends	30,000
Balance, December 31	$523,621

CALCULATION OF NONCONTROLLING INTEREST — December 31, Year 6

Common stock — Bell	$ 50,000
Retained earnings — Bell	140,000
	190,000
Unamortized purchase discrepancy	6,602
	196,602
	30%
	$ 58,981

(c)
ALLEN COMPANY
CONSOLIDATED BALANCE SHEET
December 31, Year 6

Cash (12,500 + 10,000)	$ 22,500
Accounts receivable (60,000 + 25,000 – **9,000**)	76,000
Inventory (200,000 + 40,000)	240,000
Plant and equipment (1,200,000 + 470,000 + **30,000**)	1,700,000
Accumulated depreciation (300,000 + 220,000 + **18,750** + **3,750**)	(542,500)
Goodwill (0 + 0 + **2,770**)	2,770
	$1,498,770
Accounts payable (86,500 + 35,000 – **9,000**)	$ 112,500
Bonds payable (400,000 + 100,000 + **3,668**)	503,668
	616,168
Common stock	300,000
Retained earnings	523,621
Noncontrolling interest	58,981
	$1,498,770

2.
YEAR 6 CHANGES IN NONCONTROLLING INTEREST

Balance, January 1 (30% × 201,323*)		$60,397
Allocation of entity net income		84
		60,481
Dividends (30% × 5,000)		1,500
Balance, December 31		$58,981
* Common stock	$ 50,000	
Retained earnings, January 1	135,000	
	185,000	
Unamortized purchase discrepancy (30,000 – 13,677)	16,323	
	$201,323	

APPENDIX 5A

Preparing Consolidated Financial Statements Using the Working Paper Approach

In this chapter, we illustrated the direct approach for preparing consolidated financial statements when the parent used the equity method to account for its investment. In the examples used, we first examined the situation where the subsidiary was 100 percent owned, and then the situation where the parent's ownership was 80 percent. We will now illustrate the working paper approach using the same examples.

Consolidated Statements, End of Year 1, 100% Owned Subsidiary

These entries bring the consolidated account balances to the desired amounts.

Exhibit 5A.1 shows the preparation of Company P's consolidated financial statements using a working paper. To compare it to the direct approach, see Exhibit 5.3. In Chapters 3 and 4 the working paper entries were described as "adjustments and eliminations." Here we have shortened the description to "eliminations." Before we explain the three elimination entries used, a few comments about the overall format would be useful.[1]

Exhibit 5A.1

CONSOLIDATED FINANCIAL STATEMENT WORKING PAPER
December 31, Year 1 (equity method)

	P	S	Eliminations Dr.	Cr.	Consolidated
Sales	$ 50,000	$30,000			$ 80,000
Investment income	5,250	.	**(1)** $ 5,250		.
	55,250	30,000			80,000
Cost of sales	26,500	14,700	**(3)** 2,000		43,200
Goodwill impair. loss			**(3)** 50		50
Miscellaneous exp.	5,200	8,000			13,200
	31,700	22,700			56,450
Net income	$ 23,550	$ 7,300	$ 7,300		$ 23,550
Retained earnings, Jan. 1	$ 85,000	$ 6,000	**(2)** $ 6,000		$ 85,000
Net income	23,550	7,300	7,300		23,550
	108,550	13,300			108,550
Dividends	6,000	2,500		**(1)** $ 2,500	6,000
Retained earnings, Dec. 31	$102,550	$10,800	$13,300	$ 2,500	$102,550
Assets, misc.	$147,800	$18,300			$166,100
Inventory	30,000	14,000			44,000
Investment in S	21,750			**(1)** $ 2,750	
				(2) 19,000	
Purchase discrepancy			**(2)** $ 3,000	**(3)** 3,000	
Goodwill	.	.	**(3)** 950		950
	$199,550	$32,300			$211,050
Liabilities	$ 47,000	$11,500			$ 58,500
Common stock	50,000	10,000	**(2)** 10,000		50,000
Retained earnings	102,550	10,800	13,300	2,500	102,550
	$199,550	$32,300	$27,250	$27,250	$211,050

Investment income is replaced by the subsidiary's revenues and expenses plus the amortization of the purchase discrepancy.

The investment account is replaced by the carrying value of the subsidiary's assets and liabilities plus the unamortized purchase discrepancy.

1. In observing the effect of the elimination entries, the reader must take into account the debit and credit balances of the financial statement items. Revenues, net income, retained earnings, liabilities, and share capital accounts have credit balances, while expenses, dividends, and assets have debit balances. The debit and credit elimination entries are either increasing or decreasing these financial statement items depending on their nature.

2. Some elimination entries affect two or more of the financial statements, but the total debits and credits for each entry are equal.

---

[1] It should be emphasized again that the elimination entries shown in the working paper are not recorded in the accounting records of either the parent or the subsidiary.

3. The totals from the net income line from the income statement, including the totals of the elimination entries made there, are carried down to the net income line in the retained earnings statement. In a similar manner, the end-of-year retained earnings totals are carried down to the retained earnings on the balance sheet. Because the cumulative effect of the elimination entries from each statement has been carried down to the balance sheet, the total elimination debits and credits on that statement are equal.

The working paper elimination entries are reproduced below, with an explanation of each.

Investment income is eliminated since it will be replaced by the subsidiary's revenues and expenses plus the amortization of the purchase discrepancy.

#1	Investment income — Company P	5,250	
	Dividends — Company S		2,500
	Investment in S — Company P		2,750

The parent's equity method investment income does not appear in the consolidated income statement, and the subsidiary's dividends do not appear in the consolidated retained earnings statement. Therefore, these accounts need to be eliminated. Through an elimination of the investment income and the parent's share of the subsidiary's dividends against the investment account, this account has been adjusted to its start-of-year balance ($19,000).

The investment account is eliminated since it will be replaced by the carrying value of the subsidiary's assets and liabilities plus the unamortized purchase discrepancy.

#2	Retained earnings Jan. 1 — Company S	6,000	
	Common stock — Company S	10,000	
	Purchase discrepancy	3,000	
	Investment in S — Company P		19,000

This entry eliminates the parent's share of the start-of-year retained earnings and common stock of Company S, and the investment in S account of Company P, and establishes the purchase discrepancy at the beginning of the year. (In Year 1 this is the purchase discrepancy on acquisition date.)

#3	Cost of sales — Company S	2,000	
	Goodwill impairment loss (expense)	50	
	Goodwill	950	
	Purchase discrepancy		3,000

This entry eliminates the purchase discrepancy established by entry #2 and allocates it in accordance with the purchase discrepancy amortization schedule by (a) adjusting the expenses of Company S and (b) reflecting the unamortized balance at the end of the year on the consolidated balance sheet.

At this point it is useful to discuss a further relationship that results from the use of the equity method of accounting. The balance in the investment account at any point in time can be broken down into two components — the book value of the subsidiary's shareholders' equity and the unamortized purchase discrepancy. The following illustrates this point at December 31, Year 1:

At any point, the investment account under the equity method can be reconciled to the subsidiary's shareholders' equity plus the unamortized purchase discrepancy.

Shareholders' equity, Company S (Dec. 31, Year 1)		
Common stock	$10,000	
Retained earnings	10,800	
	20,800	
Parent's ownership	100%	
Book value component		$20,800
Unamortized purchase discrepancy		950
Balance in investment account, Dec. 31, Year 1		$21,750

Consolidated Statements, End of Year 2, 100 Percent Owned Subsidiary

Exhibit 5A.2 illustrates the preparation of Company P's consolidated statements on December 31, Year 2, using a working paper. To compare it to the direct approach, see Exhibit 5.5.

The working paper elimination entries are reproduced below, with an explanation of each.

#1	Investment income — Company P	9,920	
	Dividends — Company S		3,000
	Investment in S — Company P		6,920

This entry eliminates Company P's investment income account and the dividend account of Company S against the investment in S account of Company P. This leaves the investment account with a December 31, Year 1, balance of $21,750.

Exhibit 5A.2

CONSOLIDATED FINANCIAL STATEMENT WORKING PAPER
December 31, Year 2 (equity method)

	P	S	Eliminations Dr.	Eliminations Cr.	Consolidated
Sales	$ 60,000	$40,000			$100,000
Investment income	9,920	.	(1) $ 9,920		.
	69,920	40,000			100,000
Cost of sales	32,000	18,000			50,000
Goodwill impair. loss			(3) 80		80
Miscellaneous exp.	9,000	12,000			21,000
	41,000	30,000			71,080
Net income	$ 28,920	$10,000	$10,000		$ 28,920
Retained earnings, Jan. 1	$102,550	$10,800	(2) $10,800		$102,550
Net income	28,920	10,000	10,000		28,920
	131,470	20,800			131,470
Dividends	8,000	3,000		(1) $ 3,000	8,000
Retained earnings, Dec. 31	$123,470	$17,800	$20,800	$ 3,000	$123,470
Assets, misc.	$131,800	$21,000			$152,800
Inventory	35,000	16,000			51,000
Investment in S	28,670			(1) $ 6,920 (2) 21,750	
Purchase discrepancy			(2) $ 950	(3) 950	
Goodwill	.	.	(3) 870		870
	$195,470	$37,000			$204,670
Liabilities	$ 22,000	$ 9,200			$ 31,200
Common stock	50,000	10,000	(2) 10,000		50,000
Retained earnings	123,470	17,800	20,800	3,000	123,470
	$195,470	$37,000	$32,620	$32,620	$204,670

The entries on the income statement are adjustments for one period to bring the accounts to the desired balance for one period of time, i.e., for one year.

The entries on the balance sheet are cumulative adjustments to bring the accounts to the desired balance at the end of the period, i.e., at a point in time.

#2	Retained earnings Jan. 1 — Company S	10,800	
	Common stock — Company S	10,000	
	Purchase discrepancy	950	
	Investment in S		21,750

These entries bring the consolidated account balances to the desired amounts.

This entry eliminates the capital stock and retained earnings of Company S on December 31, Year 1, against the December 31, Year 1, balance of Company P's investment account; it also establishes the difference as the *unamortized* purchase discrepancy on that date. This relationship was illustrated on page 195.

#3	Goodwill impairment loss (expense)	80	
	Goodwill	870	
	Purchase discrepancy		950

This entry eliminates the unamortized purchase discrepancy at the end of Year 1 and allocates it in accordance with the Year 2 purchase discrepancy amortization schedule.

Consolidated Statements, End of Year 1, 80 Percent Owned Subsidiary

Exhibit 5A.3 illustrates the preparation of the consolidated financial statements as at December 31, Year 1, using the working paper approach. To compare it to the direct aproach, see Exhibit 5.8. The only new items here are the entries required to establish the noncontrolling interest. The working paper entries are produced and explained below.

Investment income is eliminated since it will be replaced by the subsidiary's revenues and expenses, amortization of the purchase discrepancy, and noncontrolling interest.

#1	Investment income — Company P	4,200	
	Dividends — Company S		2,000
	Investment in S — Company P		2,200

Exhibit 5A.3

CONSOLIDATED FINANCIAL STATEMENT WORKING PAPER
December 31, Year 1 (equity method)

The entries on the worksheet are recorded only on the worksheet and are not recorded in the separate-entity books of the parent or subsidiary.

	P	S	Eliminations Dr.	Eliminations Cr.	Consolidated
Sales	$ 50,000	$30,000			$ 80,000
Investment income	4,200	.	**(1)** $ 4,200		.
	54,200	30,000			80,000
Cost of sales	26,500	14,700	**(3)** 2,000		43,200
Goodwill impair. loss			**(3)** 50		50
Misc. expense	5,200	8,000			13,200
	31,700	22,700			56,450
Net income — entity					23,550
Noncontrolling interest	.	.	**(4)** 1,050		1,050
Net income	$ 22,500	$ 7,300	$ 7,300		$ 22,500
Retained earnings, Jan. 1	$ 85,000	$ 6,000	**(2)** $ 6,000		$ 85,000
Net income	22,500	7,300	7,300		22,500
	107,500	13,300			107,500
Dividends	6,000	2,500		**(1)** $2,000	6,000
				(5) 500	
Retained earnings, Dec. 31	.	.	.	.	.
	$101,500	$10,800	$13,300	$2,500	$101,500

	Company P	Company S	Dr	Cr	Consolidated
Assets, misc.	$151,100	$18,300			$169,400
Equipment (net)	30,000	14,000			44,000
Investment in S	17,400			(1) $ 2,200	
				(2) 15,200	
Purchase discrepancy			(2) $ 3,000	(3) 3,000	
Goodwill			(3) 950		950
	$198,500	$32,300			$214,350
Liabilities	$ 47,000	$11,500			$ 58,500
Common stock	50,000	10,000	(2) 10,000		50,000
Retained earnings	101,500	10,800	13,300	2,500	101,500
Noncontrolling interest				(2) 3,800	
			(5) 500	(4) 1,050	4,350
	$198,500	$32,300	$27,750	$27,750	$214,350

NCI appears both on the income statement (for a period of time) and on the balance sheet (at a point in time).

This entry eliminates the investment income and Company P's share of the dividends of Company S against the investment account. The investment account has now been adjusted to the balance at the beginning of the year ($15,200).

The investment account is eliminated since it will be replaced by the carrying value of the subsidiary's assets and liabilities, the unamortized purchase discrepancy, and noncontrolling interest.

#2	Retained earnings, Jan. 1 — Company S	6,000	
	Common stock — Company S	10,000	
	Purchase discrepancy	3,000	
	Investment in S — Company P		15,200
	Noncontrolling interest		3,800

This entry eliminates 100 percent of the start-of-year shareholders' equity of Company S and the investment account, and establishes the purchase discrepancy and the noncontrolling interest as at the beginning of the year.

#3	Cost of sales — Company S	2,000	
	Goodwill impairment loss	50	
	Goodwill	950	
	Purchase discrepancy		3,000

In accordance with the schedule, this entry reflects the purchase discrepancy amortization on the consolidated income statement and the unamortized balance of the purchase discrepancy on the consolidated balance sheet.

#4	Noncontrolling interest (income statement)	1,050	
	Noncontrolling interest (balance sheet)		1,050

This entry allocates the noncontrolling interest in the entity's income to the noncontrolling interest on the consolidated balance sheet.

#5	Noncontrolling interest (balance sheet)	500	
	Dividends — Company S		500

This final entry eliminates 20 percent of the dividends of Company S that were paid to the noncontrolling interest shareholders and reduces the equity of that group on the consolidated balance sheet.

As a final look at the consolidated process in Year 1, we again examine the relationship that exists when the equity method has been used.

	Total 100%	P's share 80%	NCI's share 20%
Shareholders' equity, Company S (Dec. 31, Year 1)			
Common stock	$10,000		
Retained earnings	10,800		
	20,800	$16,640	$4,160
Unamortized purchase discrepancy	950	760	190
	$21,750		
Balance in the investment account		$17,400	
Noncontrolling interest			$4,350

At any point, the investment account under the equity method and noncontrolling interest can be reconciled to the subsidiary's shareholders' equity plus the unamortized purchase discrepancy.

Consolidated Statements, End of Year 2, 80 Percent Owned Subsidiary

These entries bring the consolidated account balances to the desired amounts.

Exhibit 5A.4 illustrates the preparation of the Year 2 consolidated financial statements of Company P using a working paper. To compare it to the direct approach, see Exhibit 5.10. Each of the five elimination entries is reproduced and explained below.

#1	Investment income — Company P	7,936	
	Dividends — Company S		2,400
	Investment in S — Company P		5,536

This entry eliminates Company P's investment income account and 80 percent of the dividends of Company S against Company P's investment account. The investment account now has a December 31, Year 1, balance of $17,400. The remaining 20 percent of the dividends of Company S are eliminated in entry #5.

#2	Retained earnings, January 1 — Company S	10,800	
	Common stock — Company S	10,000	
	Purchase discrepancy	950	
	Investment in S — Company P		17,400
	Noncontrolling interest		4,350

This entry eliminates 100 percent of the start-of-year retained earnings and common stock accounts of Company S against the start-of-year balance in Company P's investment account, and establishes both the unamortized purchase discrepancy and the noncontrolling interest at the beginning of Year 2. The amount for noncontrolling interest ($4,350) is 20 percent of the start-of-year common stock and retained earnings accounts of Company S plus 20 percent of the unamortized purchase discrepancy.

#3	Goodwill impairment loss	80	
	Goodwill	870	
	Purchase discrepancy		950

Entry #3 allocates the unamortized purchase discrepancy in accordance with the Year 2 amortization schedule.

These journal entries appear only on the consolidated worksheet and are not posted to the separate-entity accounting records.

#4	Noncontrolling interest (income statement)	1,984	
	Noncontrolling interest (balance sheet)		1,984

Entry #4 allocates the net income of the entity for Year 2 to the equity of the noncontrolling interest on the balance sheet.

Exhibit 5A.4

CONSOLIDATED FINANCIAL STATEMENT WORKING PAPER
December 31, Year 2 (equity method)

		P	S	Eliminations Dr.	Cr.	Consolidated
Consolidated net income is the same regardless of whether the parent used the cost method or equity method on its separate-entity books.	Sales	$ 60,000	$40,000			$100,000
	Investment income	7,936		**(1)** $ 7,936		
		67,936	40,000			100,000
	Cost of sales	32,000	18,000			50,000
	Goodwill impair. loss			**(3)** 80		80
	Misc. expenses	9,000	12,000			21,000
		41,000	30,000			71,080
	Net income — entity					28,920
	Noncontrolling interest	.	.	**(4)** 1,984		1,984
	Net income	$ 26,936	$10,000	$10,000		$ 26,936
	Retained earnings, Jan. 1	$101,500	$10,800	**(2)** $10,800		$101,500
	Net income	26,936	10,000	10,000		26,936
		128,436	20,800			128,436
	Dividends	8,000	3,000		**(1)** $ 2,400	8,000
					(5) 600	
	Retained earnings, Dec. 31	$120,436	$17,800	$20,800	$ 3,000	$120,436
	Assets, misc.	$134,500	$21,000			$155,500
	Inventory	35,000	16,000			51,000
	Investment in S	22,936			**(1)** $ 5,536	
					(2) 17,400	
	Purchase discrepancy			**(2)** $ 950	**(3)** 950	
	Goodwill			**(3)** 870		870
		$192,436	$37,000			$207,370
Consolidated retained earnings are the same regardless of whether the parent used the cost method or equity method on its separate-entity books.	Liabilities	$ 22,000	$ 9,200			$ 31,200
	Common stock	50,000	10,000	**(2)** 10,000		50,000
	Retained earnings	120,436	17,800	20,800	3,000	120,436
	Noncontrolling interest			**(2)** 4,350		5,734
				(5) 600	**(4)** 1,984	.
		$192,436	$37,000	$33,220	$33,220	$207,370

#5	Noncontrolling interest (balance sheet)	600	
	Dividends — Company S		600

The final entry eliminates the remaining 20 percent of the dividends of Company S and reduces the equity of the noncontrolling interest on the balance sheet by this amount.

In this appendix, we have illustrated the working paper approach. This approach allows the reader to see where all of the eliminations end up. However, as we proceed with some of the more difficult aspects of consolidated statement preparation, the number of elimination entries used becomes overwhelming. Not only that, there is no set standard working-paper approach. This appendix presented elimination entries associated with a financial statement working paper. Other approaches could use a different set of entries and still arrive at the same consolidated amounts. If a trial balance working-paper approach had been used instead, the entries would have been different. In practice, a computerized spreadsheet or a specialized software program would probably be used in the majority of cases. The working paper entries required by these programs would no doubt be different from those illustrated here.

As you will see, working papers gradually disappear in the chapters that follow. The reason for this is that the major focus of this text is the direct approach, which stresses understanding of relationships rather than memorization of working-paper entries. If a thorough understanding of the consolidation process is present, it can then be applied to any computerized working paper program that may be seen in practice. When consolidation questions appear on professional accounting examinations in Canada, a direct approach is invariably expected to be used when formulating an answer.

REVIEW QUESTIONS

1. Briefly outline the process for determining if goodwill is impaired.
2. Is the impairment test for intangibles other than goodwill the same as the one used for goodwill? Briefly explain.
3. When the parent has used the equity method, the parent's net income equals consolidated net income, and the parent's retained earnings equal consolidated retained earnings. However, the parent's financial statements are not the same as consolidated statements. On consolidated statements, which assets and income are replaced from the parent's statements, and what are they replaced with?
4. A parent company's 75%-owned subsidiary declared and paid a dividend totalling $10,000. How would the parent company record this dividend under the equity method? And under the cost method?
5. By which method — cost or equity — does the *CICA Handbook* require a parent company to record its investment in a subsidiary? Why?
6. A consolidated retained earnings statement shows dividends declared during the year. Do these dividends consist of the parent's, or the subsidiary's, or both? Explain.
7. "A purchase discrepancy allocated to revalue the land of a subsidiary on acquisition date will always appear on subsequent consolidated balance sheets." Do you agree? Explain.
8. Describe the make-up of consolidated net income in any year subsequent to acquisition date.
9. How are dividends received in excess of the parent's share of post-acquisition earnings recorded by the parent company under the cost method?
10. "Under the equity method, the investment account is adjusted for the inves-

tor's share of post-acquisition earnings computed by the consolidation method." Explain this statement.

11. A 75%-owned subsidiary paid dividends of $50,000 during the year. How would these dividends be reflected in the consolidated balance sheet prepared at the end of the year?

12. At the end of the year, the parent's investment account had an equity method balance of $120,000. At this time its 75%-owned subsidiary had shareholders' equity totalling $125,000. How much was the unamortized purchase discrepancy at the end of the year?

13. On the consolidated balance sheet, what effect does the elimination of intercompany receivables and payables have on shareholders' equity and noncontrolling interest?

14. Explain how the parent reports its investment in the subsidiary after losing control of the subsidiary.

15. Explain how the matching principle is applied when amortizing the purchase discrepancy.

MULTIPLE-CHOICE QUESTIONS

1. When a company uses the equity method to record its investment in a subsidiary during the year, which of the following will be included in the journal entry to record the parent's share of the subsidiary's net income (assuming a positive net income)?
   a. Debit cash.
   b. Credit investment in subsidiary.
   c. Debit investment income.
   d. Credit investment income.

2. When should a goodwill impairment loss be recognized for a subsidiary?
   a. When (and if) both the market value of a reporting unit and the goodwill of this unit fall below their respective carrying values.
   b. Whenever the market value of the subsidiary declines.
   c. When (and if) the market value of the subsidiary declines below its original acquisition price.
   d. On a systematic and rational basis each year.

Use the following data for Questions 3 to 6.
   The following information appeared on the balance sheets and income statements of Plunge Inc. and Sink Co. on December 31, Year 6:

	Plunge	Sink
Common stock (1,200,000 shares)	$1,200,000	
Common stock (480,000 shares)		$480,000
Retained earnings at January 1, Year 6	720,000	120,000
Net income from operations	320,000	100,000
Dividends declared	120,000	40,000

Plunge acquired an 80% interest in Sink on January 1, Year 6, for $600,000. At the date of acquisition, it was determined that Sink's plant assets with a 10-year remaining useful life were undervalued by $50,000, and patents with a 5-year life were undervalued by $100,000.

3. What is goodwill on the consolidated balance sheet on January 1, Year 6?
   a. There is negative goodwill, which would be reported as a gain on purchase.
   b. $0
   c. $80,000
   d. $100,000

4. What is the amount that Plunge would report on the equity basis for "investment income" from Sink at December 31, Year 6? Assume there were no intercompany transactions during the year.
   a. $60,000
   b. $61,000
   c. $64,000
   d. $80,000

5. What is the amount that Plunge would report as "noncontrolling interest" relating to its investment in Sink on its consolidated balance sheet at December 31, Year 6?
   a. $120,000
   b. $132,000
   c. $150,000
   d. $157,000

*6. Under the working paper approach to consolidation, which of the following will be included in the elimination journal entry to remove dividends paid by subsidiary during Year 6?
   a. Debit nontrolling interest $8,000.
   b. Credit nontrolling interest $8,000.
   c. Debit dividends $32,000.
   d. Credit dividends $32,000.

7. On January 1, Year 3, CD Corp. acquired 70 percent of the common shares of XY Inc. for $980,000. In allocating the purchase price, $120,000 was assigned to goodwill. CD did not have any goodwill recorded on its separate-entity financial statements on January 1, Year 3. A goodwill impairment loss of $36,000 was recorded in Year 5, and on December 31, Year 6, the fair value of the goodwill was determined to be $70,000. What value would be reported for goodwill on the consolidated balance sheet at December 31, Year 6?
   a. $58,800
   b. $70,000
   c. $84,000
   d. $120,000

8. Parent Inc. purchased all of the outstanding shares of Sub Ltd. on January 1, Year 1, for $214,000. Amortization of the purchase discrepancy amounted to $16,000 in each of Years 1 and 2. Parent Inc. reported net income of $100,000 in Year 1 and $110,000 in Year 2, and paid $40,000 in dividends each year. Sub Ltd. reported net income of $33,000 in Year 1 and $39,000 in Year 2, and paid $8,000 in dividends each year. What is the Investment in Sub Ltd. balance on Parent's books as at December 31, Year 2, if the equity method has been used?
   a. $238,000
   b. $246,000

*Pertains to Appendix 5A.

c. $278,000
d. $286,000

9. Burns Ltd. purchased 100% of the outstanding shares of Simon Inc. on January 1, Year 1, at a price that was in excess of the subsidiary's book value. On that date, Burns' equipment (10-year life) had a book value of $300,000 and a fair value of $400,000. Simon had equipment with a book value of $200,000 and a fair value of $250,000. Burns uses the equity method to record its investment. On December 31, Year 3, Burns has equipment with a book value of $210,000 and a fair value of $330,000. Simon has equipment with a book value of $140,000 and a fair value of $220,000. What is the balance for equipment on the consolidated balance sheet on December 31, Year 3?
a. $385,000
b. $430,000
c. $455,000
d. $550,000

10. Noncontrolling interest on a consolidated balance sheet prepared in accordance with GAAP represents which of the following?
a. An equity interest in a subsidiary company that exists because the parent's interest in the subsidiary is less than 100%.
b. A liability of the parent company.
c. The net amount by which subsidiary assets and liabilities have been revalued following a business combination.
d. An equity interest in the subsidiary's income earned for the year.

11. Which of the following *best* describes accounting for intangible assets (other than goodwill) that have an indefinite useful life?
a. They should be amortized in a systematic and rational manner.
b. They should be tested annually for impairment, with any impairment amortized to expense in a systematic and rational manner.
c. They should be carried at fair value on the balance sheet.
d. They should be tested annually for impairment, with any impairment recorded as a loss.

(CGA-Canada, from 2002 to 2007)

12. OP Corporation acquired 60% of KD Corporation on March 31, Year 6. Because OP controls KD, it uses the consolidation method for *reporting* its investment. OP should use which of the following for *recording* its investment in KD?
a. The cost method must be used.
b. The equity method must be used.
c. The cost method or the equity method may be used.
d. The consolidation method must be used.

(CGA-Canada, from 2002 to 2007)

13. What would be the effect on the consolidated financial statements if an unconsolidated subsidiary is accounted for by the equity method but consolidated financial statements are prepared with other subsidiaries?
a. Dividend revenue from the unconsolidated subsidiary will be reflected in consolidated net income.
b. All of the unconsolidated subsidiary's accounts will be included individually in the consolidated financial statements.

    c. The consolidated retained earnings will not reflect the earnings of the unconsolidated subsidiary.

    d. The consolidated retained earnings will be the same as if the subsidiary had been included in the consolidation.

(CGA-Canada, from 2002 to 2007)

14. In accordance with the *CICA Handbook*, goodwill on the date of a business combination must be allocated to a subsidiary's reporting units in order to apply subsequent impairment tests. If the fair value of a reporting unit with goodwill allocated to it falls below its carrying amount, which of the following is true?

    a. A goodwill impairment loss is recognized for the difference between the reporting unit's fair value and its carrying amount.

    b. No goodwill impairment loss is recognized unless the fair value of the goodwill exceeds its carrying amount.

    c. The reporting unit reduces the amount of its long-term assets to reflect its fair value.

    d. No goodwill impairment loss is recognized unless the carrying amount for goodwill exceeds its fair value.

15. Albany Ltd. purchased all of the outstanding shares of Gerrard Inc. on January 1, Year 4, for $1,200,000. The price resulted in a $90,000 allocation to equipment and goodwill of $75,000. Because the subsidiary earned especially high profits, Albany was required to pay the previous owners of Gerrard an additional $200,000 on January 1, Year 6. How should this extra amount be reported?

    a. The $200,000 additional payment is reflected as a reduction in consolidated retained earnings.

    b. A retroactive adjustment is made to record the $200,000 as an additional expense for Year 4.

    c. Consolidated goodwill is increased by $200,000 as at January 1, Year 6.

    d. The $200,000 is recorded as an expense in Year 6.

16. Jonston Ltd. owns 75% of the outstanding shares of Saxon Corp. Saxon currently owes Jonston $400,000 for inventory acquired during the last month. In preparing consolidated financial statements, what amount of this debt should be eliminated?

    a. $0

    b. $100,000

    c. $300,000

    d. $400,000

CASES

Case 1 When Conoco Inc. of Houston, Texas, announced the CDN$7 billion acquisition of Gulf Canada Resources Limited of Calgary, Alberta, a large segment of the press release was devoted to outlining all of the expected benefits to be received from the assets acquired. The acquisition price represented a 35 percent premium over Gulf's closing stock price on the announcement date. Included in the assets of Gulf were the following:

- Proved reserves of over 1 billion barrels of oil;
- Probable reserves of approximately 1.2 billion barrels of oil;
- Proved reserves of 1.4 trillion cubic feet of natural gas;
- Probable reserves of 2.9 trillion cubic feet of natural gas;

- Four million acres of undeveloped land in Western Canada;
- A 72 percent interest in Gulf Indonesia Resources Limited; included in this company's assets were reserves of 180 million barrels of oil and 1.5 trillion cubic feet of gas;
- A 9 percent interest in joint venture, Syncrude Canada Ltd., which is developing the heavy oil tar sands in northern Alberta;
- Long-term contracts to deliver 3 trillion cubic feet of natural gas to Southeast Asia;
- Recent exploration successes in Sumatra and offshore Java.

Required:

Many of the assets acquired in this business combination present particular valuation challenges. Provide guidance to the financial staff of Conoco as to how the aggregate purchase price should be allocated among the various tangible and intangible assets and liabilities included in the portfolio of Gulf Canada Resources Limited. Explain your answer in terms of the provisions of the *CICA Handbook*.

(*Case prepared by Peter Secord, St. Mary's University.*)

Case 2   When Valero Energy Corp. acquired Ultramar Diamond Shamrock Corp. (UDS) for US$6 billion, it created the second-largest refiner of petroleum products in North America, with over 23,000 employees in the United States and Canada, total assets of $10 billion, and combined revenues of $32 billion. Combined, it had 13 refineries with a total throughput capacity of just under 2 million barrels per day (BPD); it also became one of the continent's largest retailers, with more than 5,000 retail outlets in the U.S. and Canada. The Canadian operations of UDS continued to operate under the Ultramar brand.

It was announced that the combination of Valero's complex refining system and an extensive UDS refining, logistics, and retail network created synergies and strategic benefits that would result in cost savings of approximately $200 million per year and the enhanced ability to compete effectively in a rapidly consolidating industry.

The retail assets included in the acquisition included the brands Ultramar, Diamond Shamrock, Beacon, and Total. UDS had more than 2,500 company-owned sites in the U.S. and Canada, and also supplied 2,500 dealer, truck-stop, and cardlock sites. The company-owned stores had extensive brand support programs such as proprietary consumer and fleet credit cards, radio and television brand support, and strong in-store marketing programs, to which Valero was able to add its 350-store retail network in California. In addition, UDS operated one of the largest home heating oil businesses in North America, selling heating oil to approximately 250,000 households.

The acquisition clearly included more than the physical assets of Ultramar Diamond Shamrock. A variety of unrecorded intangible assets were represented in the portfolio of assets held by UDS; and these are the matters that require your attention at this time.

Required:

With reference to Section 1582 of the *CICA Handbook*, prepare a memorandum to the chief financial officer of Valero. In this memo:

- discuss the valuation of the various intangible assets included in this acquisition;
- indicate which items should be included in the amount assigned to goodwill in the acquisition;
- indicate which items should be separately identified and valued as intangible assets;

- discuss how you would assign values to the various items identified and what amortization policy (if any) is appropriate.

(*Case prepared by Peter Secord, St. Mary's University.*)

Case 3   Good Quality Auto Parts Limited (GQ) is a medium-sized, privately owned producer of auto parts, which are sold to car manufacturers, repair shops, and retail outlets. In March Year 10, the union negotiated a new three-year contract with the company for the 200 shop-floor employees. At the time, GQ was in financial difficulty and management felt unable to meet the contract demands of the union. Management also believed that a strike of any length would force the company into bankruptcy.

The company proposed that, in exchange for wage concessions, the company would implement a profit-sharing plan whereby the shop floor employees would receive 10% of the company's annual after-tax profit as a bonus in each year of the contract. Although the union generally finds this type of contract undesirable, it believed that insisting on the prevailing industry settlement would jeopardize GQ's survival. As a result, the contract terms were accepted.

The contract specifies that no major changes in accounting policies may be made without the change being approved by GQ's auditor. Another clause in the contract allows the union to engage a chartered accountant to examine the books of the company and meet with GQ's management and auditor to discuss any issues. Under the terms of the contract, any controversial accounting issues are to be negotiated by the union and management to arrive at a mutual agreement. If the parties cannot agree, the positions of the parties are to be presented to an independent arbitrator for resolution.

GQ presented to the union its annual financial statements and the unqualified audit report, for the year ended February 28, Year 11, the first year during which the profit-sharing plan was in effect. The union engaged you, CA, to analyze these financial statements and determine whether there are any controversial accounting issues. As a result of your examination, you identified a number of issues that are of concern to you. You met with the controller of the company and obtained the following information:

1. GQ wrote off $250,000 of inventory manufactured between Year 4 and Year 7. There have been no sales from this inventory in over two years. The controller explained that up until this year she had some hope that the inventory could be sold as replacement parts. However, she now believes that the parts cannot be sold.

2. The contracts GQ has with the large auto manufacturers allow the purchaser to return items for any reason. The company has increased the allowance for returned items by 10% in the year just ended. The controller contends that, because of the weak economy and stiff competition faced by the auto manufacturers with whom GQ does business, there will likely be a significant increase in the parts returned.

3. In April Year 10, GQ purchased $500,000 of new manufacturing equipment. To reduce the financial strain of the acquisition, the company negotiated a six-year payment schedule. Management believed that the company would be at a serious competitive disadvantage if it did not emerge from the current downturn with updated equipment. GQ decided to use accelerated depreciation at a rate of 40% for the new equipment. The controller argued that because of the rapid technological changes occurring in the industry, equipment purchased now is more likely to become technologically, rather than operationally, obsolete. The straight-line depreciation method applied to the existing equipment has not been changed.

4. In Year 5, GQ purchased a small auto parts manufacturer and merged it into its own operation. At the time of acquisition, $35,000 of goodwill was recorded and was

being amortized over 35 years. The company has written off the goodwill in the year just ended. The controller explained that the poor performance of the auto parts industry, and of GQ in particular, has made the goodwill worthless.

5. In February Year 11, the president and the chairman of the board, who between them own 75% of the voting shares of the company, received bonuses of $250,000 each. GQ did not pay any dividends during the current year. In the prior year, dividends amounting to $650,000 were paid. The controller said that the board of directors justified the bonuses as a reward for keeping the company afloat despite extremely difficult economic times.

6. Until this year, GQ used the taxes-payable method for accounting purposes. In all previous years the company received a qualified audit opinion from the auditors due to this deviation from generally accepted accounting principles (GAAP). This year, the company has used the liability method of accounting for income taxes. The change has been made retroactively. The effect of the change has been to reduce net income for fiscal Year 11. The controller argued that, because the company is likely to need significant external financing from new sources in the upcoming year, a clean audit opinion would reduce any fears prospective lenders might have about the company. The controller also believed that, in light of the contract with the union, the financial statements should be prepared in accordance with GAAP.

The union has asked you to prepare a report on the position it should take on the issues identified when discussing them with management. The union also wants to know what additional information you require in order to support this position.

Required:

Prepare the report.

(CICA adapted)

PROBLEMS

Problem 1   Peach Ltd. acquired 70% of the common shares of Cherry Company on January 1, Year 4. On that date, Cherry had common stock of $600,000 and retained earnings of $300,000.

The following is a summary of the changes in Peach's investment account from January 1, Year 4, to December 31, Year 6:

INVESTMENT IN CHERRY

January 1, Year 4	Cost	$651,000
December 31, Year 4	Investment income	51,800
	Dividends	(28,000)
December 31, Year 5	Investment income	63,700
	Dividends	(35,000)
December 31, Year 6	Investment income	78,400
	Dividends	(42,000)
	Balance	$739,900

Other Information

- Dividends declared by Cherry each year were equal to 50% of Cherry's reported net income each year.
- On January 1, Year 4, the book values of the identifiable net assets of Cherry were equal to fair values.

Required:

Calculate the following:
(a) The amount of dividends declared by Cherry in Year 4.
(b) The reported net income of Cherry for Year 5.
(c) The amount for noncontrolling interest that would appear in the Year 6 consolidated income statement and balance sheet.
(d) The amount of goodwill that would appear on the December 31, Year 6, consolidated balance sheet.

Problem 2   Poplar Ltd. purchased 100% of Ash Company on January 1, Year 1, for $600,000, when the balance sheet of Ash showed common stock of $400,000 and retained earnings of $100,000. On that date, the inventory of Ash was undervalued by $40,000, and a patent with an estimated remaining life of 5 years was overvalued by $70,000.

Ash reported the following subsequent to January 1, Year 1:

	Net income	Dividends
Year 1	$ 80,000	$25,000
Year 2 (loss)	(35,000)	10,000
Year 3	100,000	40,000

A test for goodwill impairment by Poplar on December 31, Year 3, resulted in a loss of $19,300 being recorded.

Required:

PART A

Prepare the equity-method journal entries of Poplar each year.

PART B

Compute the following on December 31, Year 3:
(a) Investment in Ash.
(b) Consolidated goodwill.
(c) The unamortized purchase discrepancy using the account "Investment in Ash Company" from section (a).

Problem 3   On June 30, Year 6, the following financial statements were prepared. Peters Ltd. uses the equity method to account for its investment.

	Peters	Singer
INCOME STATEMENTS		
Sales	$ 90,000	$54,000
Investment income	10,728	—
Total revenue	100,728	54,000
Cost of sales	46,700	31,460
Expenses (miscellaneous)	10,360	9,400
Total expenses	57,060	40,860
Net income	$ 43,668	$13,140
RETAINED EARNINGS STATEMENTS		
Balance, July 1	$153,000	$10,800
Net income	43,668	13,140
	196,668	23,940
Dividends	10,800	4,500
Balance, June 30	$185,868	$19,440

BALANCE SHEETS — June 30, Year 6

Miscellaneous assets	$291,980	$42,940
Equipment (net)	34,000	15,200
Investment in Singer	34,488	—
	$360,468	$58,140
Liabilities	$ 84,600	$20,700
Common stock	90,000	18,000
Retained earnings	185,868	19,440
	$360,468	$58,140

Other Information

Peters purchased 80% of the common shares of Singer on July 1, Year 5, for $27,360. On that date the equipment of Singer had a fair value that was $7,200 less than book value, with an estimated remaining life of 8 years. All other assets and liabilities of Singer had book values equal to fair values. A goodwill impairment test on June 30, Year 6, indicated a loss of $630.

Required:

(a) Prepare the consolidated financial statements of Peters as at June 30, Year 6.
(b) Prepare a schedule showing the changes in noncontrolling interest during the year.

Problem 4 Foster Corporation acquired a 70% interest in Spencer Ltd. on December 31, Year 1, for $700,000. On that date Spencer had common stock of $350,000 and retained earnings of $300,000. The imputed purchase discrepancy was allocated $80,000 to inventory, with the balance to unrecorded patents being amortized over 10 years. Spencer reported a net income of $50,000 in Year 2 and $70,000 in Year 3. While no dividends were declared in Year 2, Spencer declared dividends amounting to $35,000 in Year 3.

Required:

(a) Prepare the equity-method journal entries of Foster for Years 2 and 3.
(b) Calculate consolidated patents on December 31, Year 3.
(c) Prepare a statement that shows the changes in the noncontrolling interest in Year 3.

Problem 5 On July 1, Year 4, Ash Ltd. purchased 80% of the voting shares of Lake Ltd. for $543,840. The balance sheet of Lake Ltd. on that date was as follows:

LAKE LTD.
BALANCE SHEET
as at July 1, Year 4

	Net book value	Fair value
Cash	$ 96,000	$ 96,000
Accounts receivable	120,000	144,004
Inventory	180,000	228,000
Fixed assets (net)	540,000	450,000
	$936,000	
Current liabilities	$107,200	$107,200
Bonds payable	200,000	186,534
Common shares	120,000	
Retained earnings	508,800	
	$936,000	

The accounts receivable of Lake Ltd. were collected in October Year 4, and the inventory was completely sold by May, Year 5. The fixed assets of Lake Ltd. had a remaining life of 15 years on July 1, Year 4, and the bonds payable mature on June 30, Year 8. The bonds were issued on June 30, Year 1. The stated rate of interest on the bonds is 6% payable semi-annually. The market rate of interest was 8% on July 1, Year 4. The annual tests for goodwill impairment indicated a loss of $8,329 in Year 5 and $5,553 in Year 6.

The financial statements for Ash Ltd. and Lake Ltd. at December 31, Year 6, are as follows:

BALANCE SHEETS

	Ash Ltd.	Lake Ltd.
Cash	$ 120,000	$ 84,000
Accounts receivable	180,000	114,000
Inventory	300,000	276,000
Fixed assets (net)	720,000	540,000
Investment in Lake Ltd. (equity method)	520,319	—
Other investments	250,666	—
	$2,090,985	$1,014,000
Current liabilities	$ 180,200	$ 135,800
Bonds payable	315,000	200,000
Common shares	300,600	120,000
Retained earnings	1,295,185	558,200
	$2,090,985	$1,014,000

INCOME STATEMENTS

	Ash Ltd.	Lake Ltd.
Sales	$1,261,000	$1,200,000
Investment income (equity method)	4,394	—
Income from other investments	25,000	—
	1,290,394	1,200,000
Cost of goods sold	840,000	1,020,000
Depreciation	60,000	54,000
Interest	37,000	26,400
Other	227,000	91,200
	1,164,000	1,191,600
Net income	$ 126,394	$ 8,400

Required:

(a) Prepare the consolidated financial statements for the year ended December 31, Year 6.
(b) Calculate goodwill impairment loss and noncontrolling interest on the consolidated income statement for the year ended December 31, Year 6, under the parent company extension theory.
(c) Calculate goodwill and noncontrolling interest on the consolidated balance sheet at December 31, Year 6, under the parent company extension theory.

Problem 6 On January 1, Year 2, Allen Corporation acquired 70% of the outstanding common shares of Bingham Company for a total cost of $87,500. On that date, Bingham had $35,000 of common shares outstanding and $25,000 of retained earnings. The book values of each of Bingham's identifiable assets and liabilities were equal to their fair values except for the following:

	Book Value	Fair Value
Inventory	$ 45,000	$ 55,000
Equipment	70,000	90,000

The equipment had an estimated useful life of 10 years as at January 1, Year 2, and the entire inventory was sold during Year 2. The following are the financial statements of Allen and Bingham as at December 31, Year 6:

BALANCE SHEETS

	Allen	Bingham
Assets		
Cash	$ 95,000	$ 10,000
Accounts receivable	115,000	75,000
Inventory	150,000	80,000
Investment in Bingham	86,100	—
Equipment, net	327,400	160,000
	$773,500	$325,000
Liabilities and shareholders' equity		
Accounts payable and accrued liabilities	$120,000	$180,000
Income taxes payable	84,900	60,000
Common shares	300,000	35,000
Retained earnings	268,600	50,000
	$773,500	$325,000

INCOME STATEMENTS

	Allen	Bingham
Sales	$ 750,000	$ 612,000
Cost of goods sold	(500,000)	(450,000)
Gross margin	250,000	162,000
Investment income	27,300	—
Amortization expense	(35,000)	(20,000)
Other expenses	(86,000)	(62,000)
Income tax expense	(60,000)	(32,000)
Net income	$ 96,300	$ 48,000

STATEMENTS OF RETAINED EARNINGS

	Allen	Bingham
Retained earnings, January 1, Year 6	$ 172,300	$ 32,000
Net income	96,300	48,000
Dividends	—	(30,000)
Retained earnings, December 31, Year 6	$ 268,600	$ 50,000

Additional Information

- Allen uses the equity method to account for its investment in Bingham.
- An independent valuator has estimated that the goodwill associated with Allen's acquisition of Bingham had a fair value of $28,000 as of December 31, Year 6. (Note: no impairment losses have been recognized in all years prior to Year 6.)

Required:

(a) Prepare the consolidated financial statements of Allen as at December 31, Year 6.

(b) If the independent appraisal of the fair value of goodwill as at December 31, Year 6, showed an amount of $8,000 instead of the $28,000 indicated above, determine the amounts for the following items in the year-end consolidated financial statements:

1. Consolidated net income
2. Consolidated retained earnings
3. Noncontrolling interest in net income

Problem 7 On January 1, Year 1, Parent Company acquired 90% of the common shares of Subsidiary Corporation at a total cost of $486,000. The following information was taken from the records of Subsidiary on January 1, Year 1:

	Carrying value	Fair value
Miscellaneous assets	$ 800,000	$ 800,000
Inventory (FIFO)	150,000	175,000
Land	110,000	140,000
Equipment	225,000	240,000
	1,285,000	1,355,000
Miscellaneous liabilities	835,000	835,000
Net assets	$ 450,000	$ 520,000

Subsidiary records depreciation on its equipment using the declining balance method at a 20% rate. A goodwill impairment loss of $2,400 occurred in Year 3. During the three-year period ending December 31, Year 3, Subsidiary's net income totalled $84,000 and dividends totalling $45,000 were declared and paid. Parent uses the equity method to account for its investment.

Required:

(a) Prepare a purchase discrepancy amortization schedule for the three-year period ending December 31, Year 3.

(b) Compute the balance in the account "Investment in Subsidiary Corporation common stock" on December 31, Year 3.

(c) Verify the total unamortized purchase discrepancy on December 31, Year 3, by using the amounts computed in part (b).

(d) Compute the noncontrolling interest at December 31, Year 3.

Problem 8 The financial statements on the next page were prepared by Peter Corp. on December 31, Year 6.

Other Information

Peter Corp. purchased 75% of the outstanding voting stock of Saint Company for $2,400,000 on July 1, Year 2, at which time Saint's common stock was $1,600,000 and its retained earnings were $400,000. The purchase discrepancy on this date was allocated as follows:

- 30% to undervalued inventory.
- 40% to equipment; remaining life 8 years.

- Balance to goodwill.

Saint owes Peter $75,000 on December 31, Year 6.

Saint's common share balance has remained constant, and its dividends for Year 6 were $200,000.

Goodwill impairment losses were recorded as follows:

- Year 4: $70,000.
- Year 6: $20,000.

BALANCE SHEET

	Nonconsolidated	Consolidated
Cash	$ 300,000	$ 400,000
Accounts receivable	200,000	125,000
Inventory	2,000,000	2,420,000
Plant and equipment	3,000,000	6,170,000
Accumulated depreciation	(750,000)	(1,330,000)
Goodwill	—	270,000
Investment in Saint Company — equity method	2,310,000	—
	$7,060,000	$8,055,000
Liabilities	$ 900,000	$1,125,000
Capital stock	2,850,000	2,850,000
Retained earnings	3,310,000	3,310,000
Noncontrolling interest	—	770,000
	$7,060,000	$8,055,000

INCOME STATEMENT

Sales	$4,000,000	$5,000,000
Investment income	240,000	
Total revenue	4,240,000	5,000,000
Cost of sales	2,500,000	2,900,000
Miscellaneous expenses	320,000	390,000
Depreciation expense	80,000	150,000
Goodwill impairment loss	—	20,000
Income tax expense	250,000	370,000
Noncontrolling interest	—	80,000
Total	3,150,000	3,910,000
Net income	$1,090,000	$1,090,000

RETAINED EARNINGS STATEMENT

Balance, January 1	$2,720,000	$2,720,000
Net income	1,090,000	1,090,000
	3,810,000	3,810,000
Dividends	500,000	500,000
Balance, December 31	$3,310,000	$3,310,000

Required:

(a) Prepare the financial statements for Peter's subsidiary, Saint Company, as at December 31, Year 6.

(b) Calculate goodwill impairment loss and noncontrolling interest on the consolidated income statement for the year ended December 31, Year 6 under the parent company extension theory.

(c) Calculate goodwill and noncontrolling interest on the consolidated balance sheet at December 31, Year 6, under the parent company extension theory.

Problem 9 On December 31, Year 2, Abbot Inc. purchased 80 percent of the outstanding common shares of Drexel Company for $310,000. At that date, Drexel had common shares of $200,000 and retained earnings of $60,000. In negotiating the purchase price, it was agreed that the assets on the balance sheet of Drexel were fairly valued except for capital assets, which had a $40,000 excess of fair value over net book value. It was also agreed that Drexel had unrecognized intangible assets consisting of customer lists that had an estimated value of $24,000. The capital assets had a remaining useful life of eight years at the acquisition date and the customer lists would be amortized over a 12-year period. Any goodwill arising from this business combination will be tested periodically for impairment. Abbot accounts for its investment using the equity method.

Financial statements for Abbot and Drexel for the year ended December 31, Year 6, were as follows:

BALANCE SHEET
December 31, Year 6

	Abbot	Drexel
Assets		
Cash	$ 20,000	$ 30,000
Accounts receivable	88,000	160,000
Notes receivable	—	10,000
Inventory	100,000	180,000
Capital assets — net	230,000	160,000
Other investments	82,000	22,000
Investment in Drexel Company	347,000	—
	$867,000	$562,000
Liabilities and Shareholders' Equity		
Accounts payable	$ 80,000	$ 62,000
Other current liabilities	10,000	50,000
Notes payable	130,000	100,000
Common shares	500,000	200,000
Retained earnings	147,000	150,000
	$867,000	$562,000

STATEMENTS OF INCOME AND RETAINED EARNINGS
Year ended December 31, Year 6

	Abbot	Drexel
Sales	$ 870,000	$ 515,000
Cost of goods sold	(638,000)	(360,000)
Gross profit	232,000	155,000
Amortization expense	(22,000)	(35,000)
Other expenses	(144,000)	(72,000)
Equity earnings from Drexel	21,800	
Interest and investment income	14,000	2,000
Net income	101,800	50,000
Retained earnings, beginning of year	81,200	120,000
Dividends declared	(36,000)	(20,000)
Retained earnings, end of year	$ 147,000	$ 150,000

Other Information

Impairment tests performed at the end of Year 6 indicated that the goodwill had a fair value of $50,000 and the customer lists had a fair value of $13,750. The impairment in these assets occurred entirely in Year 6.

Required:

Prepare consolidated financial statements.

Problem 10   Balance sheet and income statement data for two affiliated companies for the current year are given below:

BALANCE SHEET DATA
at December 31, Year 4

	Able	*Baker*
Cash	$ 40,000	$ 21,000
Receivables	92,000	84,000
Inventories	56,000	45,000
Land	20,000	60,000
Plant and equipment	200,000	700,000
Accumulated depreciation	(80,000)	(350,000)
Investment in Baker Company (equity)	344,240	—
Advances to Baker Company *cancels eachother out*	100,000	—
	$772,240	$560,000
Accounts payable	$130,000	$ 96,500
Advances payable	—	100,000
Common stock	400,000	200,000
Retained earnings	242,240	163,500
	$772,240	$560,000

INCOME STATEMENT DATA
Year Ended December 31, Year 4

Sales revenues	$600,000	$400,000
Interest income	6,700	—
Investment income	11,360	—
Total revenues	618,060	400,000
Cost of goods sold	334,000	225,000
Depreciation expense	20,000	70,000
Selling and administrative expense	207,000	74,000
Interest expense	1,700	6,000
Income taxes expense	20,700	7,500
Total expenses	583,400	382,500
Net income	$ 34,660	$ 17,500

Other Information

- Able acquired an 80% interest in Baker on January 1, Year 1, for $272,000. On that date the following information was noted about specific net assets of Baker:

	Book value	Fair value
Inventory	$20,000	$50,000
Land	25,000	45,000
Equipment (estimated life 15 years)	60,000	78,000
Misc. intangibles (estimated life 20 years)	—	42,000

- On January 1, Year 1, Baker had a retained earnings balance of $30,000.
- Able carries its investment at equity.

Required:

Prepare the following:
(a) Consolidated income statement.
(b) Consolidated balance sheet.

Problem 11   Romeo Corp. purchased 75% of the outstanding shares of Juliet Ltd. on January 1, Year 3, at a cost of $117,000. On January 1, Year 3, Juliet had common shares of $50,000 and retained earnings of $30,000, and fair values were equal to carrying values for all the net assets except the following:

	Carrying value	Fair value
Inventory	$30,000	$19,000
Equipment	45,000	69,000
Software	—	15,000

The equipment had an estimated remaining life of six years on January 1, Year 3, and the software was to be amortized over 10 years. Romeo uses the equity method to account for its investment. The testing for impairment as at December 31, Year 6, yielded the following fair values:

Software	$ 8,000
Goodwill	20,000

The impairment loss on these assets occurred entirely in Year 6.

The following are the financial statements of Romeo Corp. and its subsidiary Juliet Ltd. as at December 31, Year 6:

BALANCE SHEETS
December 31, Year 6

	Romeo Corp.	Juliet Ltd.
Cash	$ —	$ 10,000
Accounts receivable	40,000	30,000
Note receivable	—	40,000
Inventory	66,000	44,000
Equipment, net	220,000	76,000
Land	150,000	30,000
Investment in Juliet	154,500	—
	$630,500	$230,000
Bank indebtedness	$ 90,000	$ —
Accounts payable	70,000	60,000
Notes payable	40,000	—
Common shares	150,000	50,000
Retained earnings	280,500	120,000
	$630,500	$230,000

STATEMENTS OF RETAINED EARNINGS
Year ended December 31, Year 6

	Romeo Corp.	Juliet Ltd.
Retained earnings, January 1, Year 6	$195,375	$ 92,000
Net income	115,125	48,000
Dividends	(30,000)	(20,000)
Retained earnings, December 31, Year 6	$280,500	$120,000

INCOME STATEMENTS
Year ended December 31, Year 6

	Romeo Corp.	Juliet Ltd.
Sales	$821,000	$320,000
Investment income	10,125	3,600
	831,125	323,600
Cost of sales	480,000	200,000
Amortization	40,000	12,000
Miscellaneous expenses	116,000	31,600
Income taxes	80,000	32,000
	716,000	275,600
Net income	$115,125	$ 48,000

Other Information

The notes payable are intercompany.

Required:

(a) Prepare the Year 6 consolidated financial statements.
(b) Calculate goodwill impairment loss and noncontrolling interest on the consolidated income statement for the year ended December 31, Year 6, under the parent company extension theory.
(c) Calculate goodwill and noncontrolling interest on the consolidated balance sheet at December 31, Year 6, under the parent company extension theory.

Problem 12   On January 2, Year 1, Shy Ltd. purchased 80% of the outstanding shares of Meek Ltd. for $4,120,000. On that date Meek's balance sheet and the fair value of its identifiable assets and liabilities were as follows:

	Book value	Fair value
Cash	$ 500,000	$ 500,000
Accounts receivable	1,500,000	1,500,000
Inventory	2,000,000	2,200,000
Plant and equipment (net)	4,500,000	4,500,000
Patents (net)	1,000,000	1,500,000
	$9,500,000	
Accounts payable	$2,000,000	$2,000,000
10% bonds payable	3,000,000	3,300,000
Common stock	2,000,000	
Retained earnings	2,500,000	
	$9,500,000	

The patents had a remaining life of 10 years at the date of acquisition. The bonds were issued at par on January 1, Year 1, and mature on December 31, Year 10. Both companies use the straight-line method to account for premiums/discounts on bonds. Goodwill impairment losses were recorded as follows:

- Year 1: $25,000.
- Year 3: $12,500.

On December 31, Year 3, the financial statements of the two companies are as follows:

	Shy	Meek
BALANCE SHEETS		
Cash	$ 400,000	$ 600,000
Accounts receivable	1,000,000	1,300,000
Inventory	4,600,000	1,900,000
Plant and equipment (net)	8,000,000	5,000,000
Patents (net)	—	700,000
Investment in Meek (equity)	4,362,000	—
	$18,362,000	$9,500,000
Accounts payable	$ 3,000,000	$1,400,000
Bonds payable	4,000,000	3,000,000
Common stock	5,000,000	2,000,000
Retained earnings	6,362,000	3,100,000
	$18,362,000	$9,500,000

INCOME STATEMENTS		
Sales	$10,000,000	$5,000,000
Investment revenue	134,000	—
	10,134,000	5,000,000
Cost of goods sold	7,000,000	3,000,000
Depreciation expense	900,000	400,000
Patent amortization expense	—	100,000
Interest expense	480,000	300,000
Other expense	680,000	850,000
Income taxes	600,000	150,000
	9,660,000	4,800,000
Net income	$ 474,000	$ 200,000

Required:

Prepare consolidated financial statements as at December 31, Year 3.

Problem 13   The PET Company purchased 70% of the common stock of SET Company on January 1, Year 6, for $490,000 when the latter company's common stock and retained earnings were $500,000 and $40,000, respectively. On this date, an appraisal of the assets of SET disclosed the following differences:

	Carrying value	Fair value
Inventory	$120,000	$108,000
Land	150,000	200,000
Plant and equipment	700,000	770,000

The plant and equipment had an estimated life of 20 years on this date. A goodwill impairment test at the end of Year 6 indicated an impairment loss of $20,000.

PET accounts for its investment under the equity method but has not yet made the entry to record the amortization/impairment of the purchase price discrepancy for Year 6. Both companies pay income tax at the rate of 40%.

Selected account balances from the records of PET and SET for the year ended December 31, Year 6, were as follows:

	PET	SET
Inventory	$ 500,000	$ 130,000
Land	600,000	150,000
Plant and equipment — net	1,100,000	665,000
Retained earnings, end of year	2,400,000	1,100,000
Cost of sales	3,100,000	1,700,000
Depreciation expense	80,000	35,000
Income tax expense	80,000	50,000

Required:

(a) Determine the amount to report on the Year 6 consolidated financial statements for the above noted accounts.

(b) Indicate how noncontrolling interest on the Year 6 consolidated income statement and Year 6 consolidated balance sheet will be affected by the allocation and amortization of the purchase price discrepancy.

Problem 14   On January 1, Year 1, the PAR Company purchased 80% of the outstanding voting shares of the SART Company at a price $300,000 in excess of PAR's share of SART's shareholders' equity. The carrying value was equal to fair value for all of SART's identifiable net assets except for inventory, which was undervalued by $35,000 and plant, which was undervalued by $125,000. At the acquisition date, the plant had an estimated remaining useful life of 10 years with no net salvage value. The value of the goodwill declined by $50,000 in Year 1 and $70,000 in Year 2.

PAR uses the equity method to account for its investment in SART. After preparing the draft consolidated income statement for Years 1 and 2 as set out below, the accountant for PAR realized that something was wrong because the consolidated net income was not equal to PAR's income under the equity method. He then realized that he had forgotten to adjust for the amortization/impairment of the purchase price discrepancy on the consolidated income statements.

CONSOLIDATED INCOME STATEMENTS

	Year 1	Year 2
Revenues	$750,000	$825,000
Cost of sales	400,000	492,000
Gross margin	350,000	333,000
Depreciation expense	75,000	82,000
Noncontrolling interest	35,000	27,000
Net income	$240,000	$224,000

Required:

Prepare correct consolidated income statements for Years 1 and 2.

Chapter 6 Consolidation Subsequent to Acquisition Date — Parent Uses Cost Method

LEARNING OBJECTIVES

After studying this chapter, you should be able to do the following:

- Calculate yearly consolidated net income when the parent has used the cost method to account for its investment.
- Calculate consolidated retained earnings when the parent has used the cost method to account for its investment.
- Prepare consolidated financial statements in years subsequent to acquisition date when the parent has used the cost method to account for its investment.
- Explain how the approach required for the preparation of consolidated financial statements differs when the parent has used the equity method rather than the cost method to account for the investment in the subsidiary.
- Describe the preparation of consolidated statements when the subsidiary is acquired on a date other than the fiscal year-end.

INTRODUCTION

In the mid-1980s, General Electric Co. (GE) acquired the National Broadcasting Company (NBC) as part of its $6.4 billion cash purchase of RCA Corporation. Although this transaction involved well-known companies, it was not unique; mergers and acquisitions have long been common in the business world.

The current financial statements of GE indicate that NBC is still a component of this economic entity. NBC continues to be a separately incorporated concern long after its purchase. Thus, for more than 20 years, the financial data for GE and NBC have been brought together through consolidated financial statements.

In Chapter 5, we indicated that the parent could use either the cost method or equity method to account for its investment in the subsidiary. Many companies use the cost method for internal reporting purposes because it is simple and involves very few entries, which are usually straightforward and take little time to prepare. However, when it is time to prepare the consolidated financial statements, numerous schedules are usually prepared and many adjustments are usually required. These adjustments are not recorded on the separate entity records of the parent but are recorded on the working papers used to support the consolidated financial statements.

In Chapter 5, we illustrated the preparation of consolidated financial statements subsequent to the date of acquisition when the parent used the equity method. In this chapter we will use the same examples of Company P and

The cost and equity methods are methods of accounting in the parent's own accounting records.	Company S, but here we will assume that Company P uses the cost method. Following the major focus of this text with respect to consolidations, all illustrations will use the direct method of preparing consolidated financial statements. In the appendix at the end of the chapter, the working paper approach for the same examples will be illustrated.

Consolidation of a 100 Percent Owned Subsidiary — Direct Approach

Company P purchased 100 percent of the outstanding common shares of Company S on January 1, Year 1, for $19,000. On that date the common stock and retained earnings of Company S totalled $16,000, and its inventory had a fair value that was $2,000 greater than book value. The book values of all other assets and liabilities of Company S were equal to fair values, and any goodwill will be tested yearly for impairment. Both companies have a December 31 year-end. The journal entry made by Company P to record the acquisition of 100 percent of Company S was as follows:

The investment is recorded in Company P's accounting records at cost.

Investment in S	19,000	
Cash		19,000

The calculation and allocation of the purchase discrepancy is shown in Exhibit 6.1.

Exhibit 6.1

**COMPANY P
CALCULATION OF PURCHASE DISCREPANCY**
January 1, Year 1

Cost of 100 percent of Company S			$19,000
Book value of Company S			
Common stock		10,000	
Retained earnings		6,000	
		16,000	
Parent's ownership		100%	16,000
Purchase discrepancy			3,000
Allocated:		FV – BV	
Inventory		2,000	2,000 (a)
Balance — goodwill			$ 1,000 (b)

The purchase discrepancy will be recorded on the consolidated financial statements.

The following are the individual balance sheets of Company P and Company S on January 1, Year 1, and Company P's consolidated balance sheet prepared using the *direct* approach.

BALANCE SHEETS — January 1, Year 1

The investment account is replaced by the carrying value of the subsidiary's assets and liabilities plus the purchase discrepancy.

	Company P	Company S	Consolidated
Assets (misc.)	$139,000	$17,000	$156,000
Inventory	22,000	10,000	34,000
Investment in S	19,000	—	—
Goodwill	—	—	1,000
	$180,000	$27,000	$191,000

Liabilities	$ 45,000	$11,000	$ 56,000
Common stock	50,000	10,000	50,000
Retained earnings	85,000	6,000	85,000
	$180,000	$27,000	$191,000

The consolidated balance sheet was prepared by eliminating the shareholders' equity of Company S ($16,000) against Company P's investment account ($19,000) and allocating the resultant purchase discrepancy ($3,000) to the inventory of Company S ($2,000), with the unallocated balance recorded as goodwill ($1,000).

The consolidation process is becoming increasingly more complicated as we proceed from one chapter to the next. To make it easier to follow the consolidation adjustments, a referencing system will be adopted for subsequent illustrations in the book and starting with Exhibit 6.3 below. The references will be placed either after the account name or before the dollar figure to which they relate. The references will look something like this, (1b), which means that we are referring to item "b" in Exhibit 1 for this chapter.

Consolidated Statements, End of Year 1

On December 31, Year 1, Company S reported a net income of $7,300 for the year and paid a cash dividend of $2,500. Company P's net income for the year was $18,300 at this time (not including income from its investment in Company S). Using the cost method to account for its investment, Company P makes a single entry to record the dividend received from Company S on December 31, Year 1, as follows:

Cash	2,500	
Dividend income		2,500
Dividend received from Company S		

The cost method records income when dividends are received or receivable.

Company P adds the dividend income ($2,500) to its earnings from its own operations ($18,300) and reports a final net income for Year 1 of $20,800. An impairment test on goodwill conducted on December 31, Year 1, indicated that a $50 loss had occurred.

The financial statements of Company P and Company S as at December 31, Year 1, are presented in Exhibit 6.2 on page 224.

Before beginning to prepare the consolidated financial statements, Company P prepares Exhibit 6.3 (see page 224), which shows the amortization of the purchase discrepancy for Year 1. This schedule and the financial statements of the two companies shown in Exhibit 6.2 form the basis for the preparation of Company P's Year 1 consolidated statements.

In Chapter 5 it was shown that when the parent has used the equity method to account for its investment, the following relationship exists:

- Parent's net income equals consolidated net income, and
- Parent's retained earnings equal consolidated retained earnings.

Exhibit 6.2

YEAR 1 INCOME STATEMENT

The parent's income from its own operations is $20,800 − $2,500 = $18,300.

	Company P	Company S
Sales	$ 50,000	$ 30,000
Dividend income	2,500	—
Total revenue	52,500	30,000
Cost of sales	26,500	14,700
Expenses (miscellaneous)	5,200	8,000
Total expenses	31,700	22,700
Net income	$ 20,800	$ 7,300

YEAR 1 RETAINED EARNINGS STATEMENTS

	Company P	Company S
Balance, January 1	$85,000	$ 6,000
Net income	20,800	7,300
	105,800	13,300
Dividends	6,000	2,500
Balance, December 31	$99,800	$10,800

BALANCE SHEETS — December 31, Year 1

The investment account remains at the original cost in the parent's separate-entity balance sheet.

	Company P	Company S
Assets (misc.)	$147,800	$ 18,300
Inventory	30,000	14,000
Investment in S (cost method)	19,000	—
	$196,800	$ 32,300
Liabilities	$ 47,000	$ 11,500
Common stock	50,000	10,000
Retained earnings	99,800	10,800
	$196,800	$ 32,300

Exhibit 6.3

PURCHASE DISCREPANCY AMORTIZATION SCHEDULE

The amortization of the purchase discrepancy will be recorded on the consolidated financial statements.

	Balance Jan. 1, Year 1	Amortization Year 1	Balance Dec. 31, Year 1
Inventory **(1a)**	$2,000	$2,000	$ — **(a)**
Goodwill **(1b)**	1,000	50	950 **(b)**
	$3,000	$2,050	$950 **(c)**

When the parent has used the cost method, the equalities shown above do *not* exist and additional computations are required. Recall from Chapter 5 that the make-up of consolidated net income can be described as shown below:

The parent's income for its separate-entity accounting records under the cost method will be different than consolidated net income.

The net income of the parent from its own operations
(i.e., excluding any income resulting from its investment in the subsidiary) $XXX

Plus:	**the parent's share of the net income of the subsidiary**	XXX
Less:	**the amortization of the purchase discrepancy**	(XXX)
Equals:	**consolidated net income.**	$XXX

Using this approach, we make the following calculation:

CALCULATION OF CONSOLIDATED NET INCOME — Year 1

This calculation starts with income under the cost method and converts it to consolidated net income.

Company P net income — cost method		$20,800
Less dividend income from Company S		2,500
Company P net income, own operations		18,300
Company S net income	7,300	
Company P ownership	100%	
		7,300
Purchase discrepancy amortization	(2,050)	
Company P ownership	100%	
		(2,050)
Consolidated net income (which is equal to company P's net net income under the equity method)		$23,550

Consolidated net income is equal to the parent's income if the parent used the equity method.

The calculation of consolidated net income also restates Company P's reported net income (computed using the cost method) *to what it would have been* had Company P used the equity method. Note that dividend income from Company S is not included in consolidated net income. The consolidated income statement is prepared by excluding the dividend income and adding the revenues and expenses of the two companies, while adjusting the expenses of Company S with the purchase discrepancy amortization for the year (see Exhibit 6.4).

In Chapter 5 we indicated that no preparation is required for the consolidated retained earnings statement when the parent has used the equity method, because the parent's net income and retained earnings are always equal to consolidated net income and retained earnings. When the parent has used the cost method, this is not the case. If we are consolidating more than one year after acquisition, we have to calculate a number for consolidated retained earnings at the beginning of the year. If we are consolidating only one year after acquisition (as in this case), consolidated retained earnings and the parent's retained earnings on acquisition date are equal. The Year 1 consolidated retained earnings statement is prepared using the January 1 retained earnings of Company P, consolidated net income, and Company P's dividends (see Exhibit 6.4). Only the parent's dividends are included on the consolidated statement of retained earnings because only the parent's dividends were paid to shareholders outside of the consolidated entity. The subsidiary's dividends were received by the parent and were not paid to anyone outside of the consolidated entity and therefore are eliminated when preparing the consolidated financial statements.

The underlying assets and liabilities of the subsidiary plus the unamortized purchase price discrepancy replace the investment account.

The parent's investment account does not appear on the consolidated balance sheet. Consolidated shareholders' equity contains the capital stock accounts of the parent and retained earnings from the consolidated retained earnings statement. The net assets of the parent are combined with the net assets of the subsidiary revalued with the unamortized purchase discrepancy.

Exhibit 6.4 shows the preparation of Company P's Year 1 consolidated financial statements using the direct approach. The bracketed amounts are taken from the individual financial statements of the two companies and the purchase discrepancy amortization schedule.

Exhibit 6.4	**Year 1 Consolidated Financial Statements**

(direct approach)

COMPANY P
CONSOLIDATED INCOME STATEMENT
for the Year Ended December 31, Year 1

Consolidated net income is the same regardless of whether the parent used the cost method or equity method in its separate-entity records.

Sales (50,000 + 30,000)	$ 80,000
Cost of sales (26,500 + 14,700 + **(3a) 2,000**)	43,200
Goodwill impairment loss (0 + 0 + **(3b) 50**)	50
Expenses (misc.) (5,200 + 8,000)	13,200
	56,450
Net income	$ 23,550

COMPANY P
CONSOLIDATED STATEMENT OF RETAINED EARNINGS
for the Year Ended December 31, Year 1

Dividends on the consolidated statement of retained earnings are the dividends of the parent.

Balance, January 1	$ 85,000
Net income	23,550
	108,550
Dividends	6,000
Balance, December 31	$102,550

COMPANY P
CONSOLIDATED BALANCE SHEET
December 31, Year 1

The consolidated balance sheet accounts are the same regardless of whether the parent used the cost method or equity method in its separate-entity records.

Assets (misc.) (147,800 + 18,300)	$166,100
Inventory (30,000 + 14,000)	44,000
Goodwill (0 + 0 + **(3b) 950**)	950
	$211,050
Liabilities (47,000 + 11,500)	$ 58,500
Common stock	50,000
Retained earnings	102,550
	$211,050

Consolidated Statements, End of Year 2

On December 31, Year 2, Company S reported a net income of $10,000 for the year and paid a cash dividend of $3,000. Company P's net income for the year was $19,000 at this time (not including income from its investment in Company S). An impairment test conducted on December 31, Year 2, indicated that the goodwill had a fair value of $870. As a result a loss of $80 has occurred.

On December 31, Year 2, Company P makes the following cost-method journal entry:

Cash	3,000	
Dividend income		3,000
Dividend received by Company S		

The dividend income ($3,000) combined with the previous operating earnings ($19,000) gives Company P a final net income for Year 2 of $22,000.

The financial statements of the two companies as at December 31, Year 2, are presented in Exhibit 6.5.

Exhibit 6.5

YEAR 2 INCOME STATEMENTS

	Company P	Company S
Sales	$ 60,000	$40,000
Dividend income	3,000	—
Total revenue	63,000	40,000
Cost of sales	32,000	18,000
Expenses (misc.)	9,000	12,000
Total expenses	41,000	30,000
Net income	$ 22,000	$10,000

The parent's income includes dividend income from the subsidiary, which can be reconciled to dividends paid by the subsidiary.

YEAR 2 RETAINED EARNINGS STATEMENTS

	Company P	Company S
Balance, January 1	$ 99,800	$10,800
Net income	22,000	10,000
	121,800	20,800
Dividends	8,000	3,000
Balance, December 31	$113,800	$17,800

BALANCE SHEETS — December 31, Year 2

	Company P	Company S
Assets (misc.)	$131,800	$21,000
Inventory	35,000	16,000
Investment in S (cost method)	19,000	—
	$185,800	$37,000
Liabilities	$ 22,000	$ 9,200
Common stock	50,000	10,000
Retained earnings	113,800	17,800
	$185,800	$37,000

The investment account still remains at the original cost.

The purchase discrepancy amortization schedule at the end of Year 2 is shown in Exhibit 6.6.

Exhibit 6.6

PURCHASE DISCREPANCY AMORTIZATION SCHEDULE

	Balance Jan. 1, Year 1	Amort. to end of Year 1	Balance Dec. 31, Year 1	Amort. Year 2	Balance Dec. 31, Year 2
Inventory (1a)	$2,000	$2,000	$ —	$—	$ — (a)
Goodwill (1b)	1,000	50	950	80	870 (b)
	$3,000	$2,050	$950	$80	$870 (c)

The amortization of the purchase discrepancy is not reflected in the investment account when the parent uses the cost method.

Because Company P has used the cost method, it is necessary to make two preliminary calculations before preparing the consolidated income statement and retained earnings statement. We first calculate consolidated net income for Year 2, as follows:

Only the Year 2 amortization of the purchase discrepancy is deducted when calculating consolidated net income for Year 2.

Company P net income — cost method		$22,000
Less: dividend income from Company S		3,000
Company P net income, own operations		19,000
Company S net income	10,000	
Company P ownership	100%	10,000
Purchase discrepancy amortization **(6c)**	(80)	
Company P ownership	100%	(80)
Consolidated net income		$28,920

As discussed previously, this calculation is simply adjusting Company P's Year 2 net income under the cost method to what it would have been under the equity method; it gives us a net income number to work toward when we prepare the consolidated income statement.

Because we are consolidating more than one year after the date of acquisition, an additional calculation is required. Company P's retained earnings on January 1, Year 2, are not equal to consolidated retained earnings. A calculation must be made to adjust these retained earnings to the balance that would result if Company P had used the equity method.

The calculation of consolidated retained earnings as at January 1, Year 2, is as follows:

This calculation converts from the cost method to the equity method at a point in time.

Company P retained earnings, Jan. 1, Year 2 (cost method)		$ 99,800
Company S retained earnings, Jan. 1, Year 2	10,800	
Company S retained earnings, acquisition date	6,000	
Increase since acquisition	4,800	
Company P ownership	100%	4,800
Purchase discrepancy amortization to end of Year 1 **(6c)**	2,050	
Company P ownership	100%	(2050)
Consolidated retained earnings (which is equal to Company P's retained earnings under the equity method)		$102,550

Retained earnings reflects the balance *at a point in time*. It reflects the cumulative effect of all adjustments to a point in time.

The points that follow are presented as further explanation of why a calculation of this nature adjusts a parent's retained earnings under the cost method to retained earnings under the equity method. These points require careful reading, because it is very important for you to understand fully why this particular process actually works.

1. Consolidated retained earnings at acquisition date consist only of the retained earnings of the parent company.
2. Consolidated net income in any single year since acquisition date consists of the net income of the parent company (from its own operations), plus the parent's share of the net income of the subsidiary, less the purchase discrepancy amortization for that year.
3. It should logically follow that the consolidated retained earnings balance at any time subsequent to the acquisition date must contain the parent's share of the subsidiary's net incomes earned since acquisition date less the total of the amortization of the purchase discrepancy to that date.
4. If the parent has used the equity method, the parent's retained earnings balance at any time subsequent to acquisition does contain, as required, the parent's share of the subsidiary's net incomes less the total purchase discrepancy amortization to date.
5. If the parent has used the cost method, the parent's retained earnings contain

The parent's retained earnings under the cost method includes dividend income from the subsidiary since the date of acquisition.

The change in retained earnings plus cumulative dividends paid is equal to cumulative net income.

The consolidated financial statements present the combined position of the parent and subsidiary as if the parent had acquired the subsidiary's assets and liabilities directly.

only the parent's share of the dividends that the subsidiary has declared since acquisition date.

6. The sum of net incomes less the sum of dividends — both measured from the acquisition date — equals the change (increase or decrease) in retained earnings measured from the same date.

7. When we add the parent's share of the change in the retained earnings of the subsidiary to the retained earnings of the parent (which contain the parent's share of the subsidiary's dividends under the cost method), the resulting calculated amount now contains the parent's share of the subsidiary's net income earned since the date of acquisition. By deducting the total amortization of the purchase discrepancy to date from this amount, we arrive at a retained earnings number that represents the retained earnings of the parent under the equity method, which of course is equal to consolidated retained earnings.

The consolidated income statement is prepared — using the income statements of the two companies (Exhibit 6.5), the Year 2 purchase discrepancy amortization schedule, and the calculation of consolidated net income for Year 2 — by adding the revenues and expenses of the two companies, adjusting the expenses for the Year 2 amortization, excluding the dividend income, and verifying that the net income on the statement equals the calculated net income.

The consolidated retained earnings statement for Year 2 is prepared using the calculated amount for consolidated retained earnings for January 1, by adding consolidated net income and deducting the dividends of Company P.

The consolidated balance sheet is prepared in the usual manner except that the amount for retained earnings is taken from the consolidated retained earnings statement.

Exhibit 6.7 shows the preparation of the Year 2 consolidated financial statements using the direct approach.

DISCUSSION QUESTION

How Do We Value Goodwill?

BIO Company is a private company. It employs 30 engineers and scientists who are involved with research and development of various biomedical devices. All of the engineers and scientists are highly paid and regarded in the field of biomedical research. BIO is 50 percent owned by Rod Smart who started the company in Year 3 and 50 percent by a group of venture capitalists who contributed $10 million of equity capital in Year 4 to fund the R & D activity of the group.

On January 1, Year 6, REX Ltd., a public company listed on the TSX Venture Exchange, acquired 100 percent of the shares of BIO by issuing 5 million of its own shares. Its shares were trading at $4 per share on the date of this transaction.

The balance sheet for BIO on January 1, Year 6 was as follows:

Cash and marketable securities	$ 2,500,000
Tangible capital assets — net	800,000
Development costs	3,000,000
	$ 6,300,000
Liabilities	$ 900,000
Common shares	10,100,000
Deficit	(4,700,000)
	$ 6,300,000

The cash, marketable securities, tangible capital assets and liabilities have fair values equal to carrying values. Prior to Year 5, all of the research and development costs were expensed. Starting in Year 5, the developments costs were capitalized because the management of BIO felt that they were getting close to patenting some of their products.

The management of REX is aware that BIO will need to be included in REX's consolidated financial statements. Management has the following questions related to these consolidated financial statements.

Required:

1. Will any of the purchase price be allocated to BIO's skilled workers? If so, how will this asset be valued and how will it be amortized or checked for impairment on an annual basis?
2. Will any of the purchase price be allocated to identifiable intangible assets? If so, how will this asset be valued and how will it be amortized or checked for impairment on an annual basis?
3. How much of the purchase price will be allocated to goodwill and how will goodwill be evaluated for impairment on an annual basis?

Exhibit 6.7	**Year 2 Consolidated Financial Statements**

(direct approach)

COMPANY P
CONSOLIDATED INCOME STATEMENT
for the Year Ended December 31, Year 2

Consolidated net income is the same regardless of whether the parent used the cost method or equity method in its separate-entity records.	Sales (60,000 + 40,000)	$100,000
	Cost of sales (32,000 + 18,000)	50,000
	Goodwill impairment loss (0 + 0 + **(6b) 80**)	80
	Expenses (misc.) (9,000 + 12,000)	21,000
		71,080
	Net income	$ 28,920

COMPANY P
CONSOLIDATED STATEMENT OF RETAINED EARNINGS
for the Year Ended December 31, Year 2

Consolidated retained earnings is the same regardless of whether the parent used the cost method or equity method in its separate-entity records.	Balance, January 1	$102,550
	Net income	28,920
		131,470
	Dividends	8,000
	Balance, December 31	$123,470

COMPANY P
CONSOLIDATED BALANCE SHEET
December 31, Year 2

The unamortized purchase discrepancy related to goodwill is reported on the consolidated balance sheet and is the same amount regardless of whether the parent used the cost method or equity method in its separate-entity records.	Assets (misc.) (131,800 + 21,000)	$152,800
	Inventory (35,000 + 16,000)	51,000
	Goodwill (0 + 0 + **(6b) 870**)	870
		$204,670
	Liabilities (22,000 + 9,200)	$ 31,200
	Common stock	50,000
	Retained earnings	123,470
		$204,670

Consolidation of an 80 Percent Owned Subsidiary — Direct Approach

We now illustrate the consolidation of Company P and its 80 percent owned subsidiary Company S over a two-year period when the cost method has been used to account for the investment.

Assume that on January 1, Year 1, instead of purchasing 100 percent of Company S for $19,000, Company P purchased 80 percent for $15,200. All other facts about the two companies are the same as in the previous example. The journal entry of Company P on January 1, Year 1, is as follows:

Investment in S	15,200	
Cash		15,200

The calculation and allocation of the purchase discrepancy and the calculation of the noncontrolling interest on January 1, Year 1, are shown in Exhibit 6.8.

Exhibit 6.8

COMPANY P
CALCULATION OF PURCHASE DISCREPANCY
January 1, Year 1

The imputed value of the subsidiary is derived by taking the purchase price and dividing by the percentage ownership acquired by the parent.	Cost of 80 percent of Company S		$15,200
	Imputed value of 100 percent of Company S		$19,000
	Book value of Company S, Jan. 1, Year 1		
	Common stock	10,000	
	Retained earnings	6,000	
			16,000
	Purchase discrepancy		3,000
	Allocated:	(FV – BV)	
	Inventory	2,000	2,000 **(a)**
	Balance — goodwill		$ 1,000 **(b)**

CALCULATION OF NONCONTROLLING INTEREST — January 1, Year 1

NCI is based on the imputed fair value of the subsidiary as a whole.	Imputed shareholders' equity, Company S (above)	$19,000
	Noncontrolling interest's ownership	20%
	Noncontrolling interest	$ 3,800 **(c)**

The following are the individual balance sheets of Company P and Company S, as well as Company P's consolidated balance sheet on January 1, Year 1, prepared using the direct approach.

BALANCE SHEETS — January 1, Year 1

	Company P	*Company S*	*Consolidated*
Assets (misc.)	$142,800	$17,000	$159,800
Inventory	22,000	10,000	34,000
Investment in S	15,200	—	—
Goodwill	—	—	1,000
	$180,000	$27,000	$194,800
Liabilities	$ 45,000	$11,000	$ 56,000
Common stock	50,000	10,000	50,000
Retained earnings	85,000	6,000	85,000
Noncontrolling interest	—	—	3,800
	$180,000	$27,000	$194,800

The subsidiary's assets and liabilities are brought onto the consolidated financial statements at 100 percent of their fair values.

The consolidated balance sheet was prepared as follows:

1. Eliminate the investment account and Company S's shareholders' equity.
2. Add the imputed purchase price discrepancy to Company S's assets and liabilities in order to use 100 percent of the fair values for Company S's assets and liabilities.
3. Report noncontrolling interest as a component of shareholders' equity at a value representing the noncontrolling interest's share of Company S's imputed value.

Consolidated Statements, End of Year 1

On December 31, Year 1, Company S reported a net income of $7,300 for the year and paid a cash dividend of $2,500. Company P's net income for the year was $18,300 at this time (not including income from its investment in Company S).

The cost method journal entry of Company P on December 31, Year 1 is:

Dividend income is 80 percent of dividends paid by subsidiary.

Cash	2,000	
Dividend income		2,000
80% of the dividend paid by Company S		

Exhibit 6.9

YEAR 1 INCOME STATEMENTS

	Company P	Company S	
Sales	$50,000	$30,000	
Dividend income	2,000	—	**(a)**
Total revenue	52,000	30,000	
Cost of sales	26,500	14,700	
Expenses (miscellaneous)	5,200	8,000	
Total expenses	31,700	22,700	
Net income	$20,300	$ 7,300	**(b)**

The parent's income includes dividend income from the subsidiary, which can be reconciled to dividends paid by the subsidiary.

YEAR 1 RETAINED EARNINGS STATEMENTS

	Company P	Company S	
Balance, January 1	$85,000	$ 6,000	**(c)**
Net income	20,300	7,300	
	105,300	13,300	
Dividends	6,000	2,500	
Balance, December 31	$99,300	$10,800	

The parent's retained earnings include the parent's income under the cost method, which includes dividend income from the subsidiary.

BALANCE SHEETS — December 31, Year 1

	Company P	Company S	
Assets (misc.)	$151,100	$18,300	
Inventory	30,000	14,000	
Investment in S (cost method)	15,200	—	
	$196,300	$32,300	
Liabilities	$ 47,000	$11,500	
Common stock	50,000	10,000	**(d)**
Retained earnings	99,300	10,800	**(e)**
	$196,300	$32,300	

These are the separate-entity balance sheets of the two legal entities.

Company P's net income for Year 1 is reported as $20,300 after the receipt of the dividend from Company S. An impairment test on goodwill conducted on December 31, Year 1, indicated that a $40 loss had occurred. The financial statements of Company P and Company S as at December 31, Year 1, are shown in Exhibit 6.9.

The Year 1 amortizations and consolidated net income must be calculated before the consolidated financial statements can be prepared, as shown in Exhibit 6.10.

Exhibit 6.10

PURCHASE DISCREPANCY AMORTIZATION SCHEDULE

	Balance Jan. 1, Year 1	Amortization Year 1	Balance Dec. 31, Year 1
Inventory **(8a)**	$2,000	$2,000	$ — **(a)**
Goodwill **(8b)**	1,000	50	950 **(b)**
	$3,000	$2,050	$950 **(c)**
Company P's share (80%)	$2,400	$1,640	$760 **(d)**
Noncontrolling interest's share (20%)	600	410	190 **(e)**

The purchase price discrepancy is allocated between the parent and noncontrolling interest.

CALCULATION OF CONSOLIDATED NET INCOME — Year 1

Consolidated net income is equal to the parent's separate-entity income accounted for under the equity method.

Company P net income — cost method **(9b)**		$20,300
Less: dividend income from Company S **(9a)**		2,000
Company P net income, own operations		18,300
Company S net income	7,300	
Less: Purchase discrepancy amortization	(2,050)	
	5,250	
Company P ownership	80%	
		4,200 **(f)**
Consolidated net income		$22,500 **(g)**
Noncontrolling interest in Company S net income (20% × 5,250)		$ 1,050 **(h)**

These calculations form the basis for preparing the Year 1 consolidated financial statements for both the direct and the working paper approaches (see Appendix 6A for the latter).

Exhibit 6.11 shows the preparation of the consolidated financial statements when the direct approach is used.

The consolidated income statement combines the income statements of the separate legal entities and incorporates consolidation adjustments for the amortization of the purchase discrepancy.

The consolidated income statement is prepared by combining the revenues and expenses of the two companies, adjusted for the Year 1 amortization of the purchase discrepancy. Company P's dividend income is excluded, and the noncontrolling interest in the income of Company S is shown in the statement as an allocation of the income of the single entity.

The consolidated retained earnings statement contains the retained earnings of Company P at the beginning of the year, consolidated net income, and the dividends of Company P.

The consolidated balance sheet is prepared by combining the assets and liabilities of the two companies, adjusted for the unamortized purchase discrepancy. The parent's investment account is excluded, and the noncontrolling interest in the net assets of the subsidiary is shown as a component of shareholders' equity. This amount is 20 percent of the December 31 shareholders' equity of Company S plus 20 percent of the unamortized purchase discrepancy.

Exhibit 6.11	Year 1 Consolidated Financial Statements
	(direct approach)

COMPANY P
CONSOLIDATED INCOME STATEMENTS
for the Year Ended December 31, Year 1

Consolidated net income and retained earnings are the same as they were in Chapter 5 when the parent used the equity method.

Sales (50,000 + 30,000)	$ 80,000
Cost of sales (26,500 + 14,700 + **(10a) 2,000**)	43,200
Goodwill impairment loss (0 + 0 + **(10b) 50**)	50
Expenses (miscellaneous) (5,200 + 8,000)	13,200
	56,450
Net income — entity	23,550
Less noncontrolling interest **(10h)**	1,050
Net income **(10g)**	$ 22,500

COMPANY P
CONSOLIDATED STATEMENT OF RETAINED EARNINGS
for the Year Ended December 31, Year 1

Balance, January 1	$ 85,000
Net income	22,500
	107,500
Dividends	6,000
Balance, December 31	$101,500

COMPANY P
CONSOLIDATED BALANCE SHEET
December 31, Year 1

Assets (miscellaneous) (151,100 + 18,300)	$169,400
Inventory (30,000 + 14,000)	44,000
Goodwill (0 + 0 + **(10b) 950**)	950
	$214,350

Noncontrolling interest is shown as a component of shareholders' equity.

Liabilities (47,000 + 11,500)	$ 58,500
Noncontrolling interest (20% × [**(9d) 10,000** + **(9e) 10,800** + **(10c) 950**)]	4,350
Common stock	50,000
Retained earnings	101,500
	$214,350

Consolidated Statements, End of Year 2

On December 31, Year 2, Company S reported earnings of $10,000 for the year and paid a cash dividend of $3,000. Company P's earnings for the year were $19,000 at this time (excluding any income from its investment in Company S). Company P's journal entry to record the dividend received from Company S is:

Under the cost method, investment income is reported when dividends are received or receivable from the investee company.

Cash	2,400	
Dividend income		2,400
80% of the dividend paid by Company S		

Company P reports earnings of $21,400 in Year 2. That amount includes this dividend income. An impairment test conducted on December 31, Year 2, indicated that the goodwill had a fair value of $870, and therefore a $80 impairment loss had occurred. The financial statements of the two companies as at December 31, Year 2, are shown in Exhibit 6.12.

Exhibit 6.12

YEAR 2 INCOME STATEMENTS

	Company P	Company S	
Sales	$ 60,000	$40,000	
Dividend income	2,400	—	(a)
Total revenue	62,400	40,000	
Cost of sales	32,000	18,000	
Expenses (misc.)	9,000	12,000	
Total expenses	41,000	30,000	
Net income	$ 21,400	$10,000	(b)

These statements are the separate-entity statements of the parent and subsidiary.

YEAR 2 RETAINED EARNINGS STATEMENTS

	Company P	Company S	
Balance, Jan. 1	$ 99,300	$10,800	(c)
Net income	21,400	10,000	
	120,700	20,800	
Dividends	8,000	3,000	
Balance, Dec. 31	$112,700	$17,800	(d)

The parent's retained earnings includes dividend income received from the subsidiary since the date of acquisition.

BALANCE SHEETS — December 31, Year 2

	Company P	Company S	
Assets (misc.)	$134,500	$21,000	
Inventory	35,000	16,000	
Investment in S (cost method)	15,200	—	
	$184,700	$37,000	
Liabilities	$ 22,000	$ 9,200	
Common stock	50,000	10,000	(e)
Retained earnings	112,700	17,800	(f)
	$184,700	$37,000	

The parent has used the cost method on its separate-entity financial statements.

Regardless of the approach to be used (direct or working paper), the four calculations shown in Exhibit 6.13 must be made before the consolidated financial statements are prepared.

Exhibit 6.13

PURCHASE DISCREPANCY AMORTIZATION SCHEDULE

This schedule is used to support adjustments made when preparing consolidated financial statements.

	Balance Jan. 1, Year 2	Amortization Year 2	Balance Dec. 31, Year 2	
Inventory (10a)	$ —	$ —	$ —	
Goodwill (10b)	950	80	870	
	$950	$80	$870	(a)
Company P's share (80%)	$760	$64	$696	
Noncontrolling interest's share (20%)	190	16	174	(b)

CALCULATION OF CONSOLIDATED NET INCOME — Year 2

This schedule calculates the bottom line for the consolidated income statement.

Company P net income — cost method		$21,400
Less dividend income from Company S		2,400
Company P net income, own operations		19,000
Company S net income (12b)	10,000	
Less purchase discrepancy amortization (13a)	(80)	
	9,920	
Company P ownership	80%	
		7,936 (c)
Consolidated net income		$26,936 (c)
Noncontrolling interest in Company S net income (20% × 9,920)		$ 1,984 (d)

CALCULATION OF CONSOLIDATED RETAINED EARNINGS
as at January 1, Year 2

This schedule incorporates cumulative adjustments to a point in time.

Company P retained earnings, Jan. 1, Year 2 (cost method) (12c)		$ 99,300
Company S retained earnings, Jan. 1, Year 2 (12c)	10,800	
Company S retained earnings, acquisition date (9c)	6,000	
Increase since acquisition	4,800	
Less purchase discrepancy amortization to end of Year 1 (10c)	(2,050)	
	2,750	
Company P's ownership	80%	
		2,200
Consolidated retained earnings (which is equal to retained earnings — equity method)		$101,500 (e)

CALCULATION OF NONCONTROLLING INTEREST
December 31, Year 2

This schedule calculates noncontrolling interest on the balance sheet at a point in time.

Shareholders' equity — Company S	
Common stock (12e)	$10,000
Retained earnings (12f)	17,800
	27,800
Unamortized purchase discrepancy (13a)	870
	28,670
Noncontrolling interest's ownership	20%
	$ 5,734 (f)

These four calculations are the starting point for the preparation of the consolidated financial statements whether the direct or the working paper approach is used.

Exhibit 6.14 shows the consolidated financial statements prepared using the direct approach. The concepts involved are the same as were outlined earlier for a 100 percent owned subsidiary. The only difference here is that the noncontrolling interest is reflected in the consolidated income statement and balance sheet.

Exhibit 6.14	

Year 2 Consolidated Financial Statements
(direct approach)

COMPANY P
CONSOLIDATED INCOME STATEMENT
for the Year Ended December 31, Year 2

The income statement includes adjustments for only one year and noncontrolling interest's share of income for only one year.

Sales (60,000 + 40,000)	$100,000
Cost of sales (32,000 + 18,000)	50,000
Goodwill impairment loss (0 + 0 + **(13a) 80**)	80
Expenses (misc.) (9,000 + 12,000)	21,000
	71,080
Net income — entity	28,920
Less noncontrolling interest **(13d)**	1,984
Net income **(13c)**	$ 26,936

COMPANY P
CONSOLIDATED STATEMENT OF RETAINED EARNINGS
for the Year Ended December 31, Year 2

Balance, January 1 **(13e)**	$101,500
Net income	26,936
	128,436
Dividends	8,000
Balance, December 31	$120,436

COMPANY P
CONSOLIDATED BALANCE SHEET
December 31, Year 2

The balance sheet reflects adjustments at the end of the year and noncontrolling interest's share of net assets at the end of the year.

Assets (misc.) (134,500 + 21,000)	$155,500
Inventory (35,000 + 16,000)	51,000
Goodwill (0 + 0 + **(13a) 870**)	870
	$207,370
Liabilities (22,000 + 9,200)	$ 31,200
Common stock	50,000
Retained earnings	120,436
Noncontrolling interest **(13f)**	5,734
	$207,370

Additional Calculations The preparation of the consolidated financial statements of companies P and S for Year 2 has been illustrated. Because the parent, Company P, used the cost method, additional calculations had to be made to determine certain consolidated amounts. One more calculation can be made to verify the consolidated retained earnings shown on the balance sheet. This calculation is shown below.

CALCULATION OF CONSOLIDATED RETAINED EARNINGS
as at December 31, Year 2

This schedule incorporates cumulative adjustments to the end of Year 2 and is used to verify retained earnings at the end of Year 2.

Company P retained earnings, Dec. 31, Year 2 — cost method **(12d)**		$112,700
Company S retained earnings, Dec. 31, Year 2 **(12d)**	17,800	
Company S retained earnings, acquisition date **(9c)**	6,000	
Increase since acquisition	11,800	
Less purchase discrepancy amortization to the end of Year 2		
((10c) **2,050** + (13a) **80**)	(2,130)	
	9,670	
Company P's ownership	80%	7,736
Consolidated retained earnings which is equal to Company P retained earnings — equity method		$120,436

This concludes our basic illustrations of the preparation of consolidated financial statements subsequent to the date that a parent company purchased a subsidiary. Before we proceed to Chapter 7, there are two additional topics that need to be addressed.

Subsidiary Acquired on Date Other Than Year-end

In all of our examples to date, we have assumed that the parent acquired the subsidiary on the last day of the fiscal year. As a result, when we prepared the first consolidated income statement at the end of the next fiscal year it contained all of the subsidiary's revenue and expenses for that year. We will now describe the consolidation process if the acquisition took place *during* the year.

Assume that Parent Inc. (which has a December 31 year-end) acquired 80% of Subsidiary Ltd. on September 30, Year 2. The Year 2 operations of Subsidiary would impact the December 31, Year 2, consolidated income statement in the following manner:

Revenues: Subsidiary's revenues October 1 to December 31

Expenses: Subsidiary's expenses October 1 to December 31

The consolidated financial statements should include the subsidiary's income only from the date of acquisition.

Noncontrolling interest: 20% × Subsidiary's net income for period October 1 to December 31

Net impact on consolidated net income: Increased by 80% of Subsidiary's net income for last three months.

This form of presentation makes subsequent-year comparisons difficult for readers. To solve this problem, a pro-forma consolidated income statement could be prepared as if the subsidiary had been acquired at the beginning of the fiscal year. This pro-forma consolidated income statement could be presented in summary form in the notes to the financial statements.

An International Perspective

The Canadian standards for consolidations subsequent to the date of acquisition are basically the same as IASB standards with one exception. The NCI's share of income is typically shown as a deduction on the consolidated income statement under Canadian standards. Under IASB standards, the NCI's share of income is shown on the statement of shareholders' equity as an allocation of net income between the controlling entity and noncontrolling interest. These standards should be converged once a new section on consolidated financial statements is exposed for public comment and approved by the IASB and CICA.

SUMMARY

This chapter has illustrated the preparation of consolidated financial statements covering a two-year period after the date of acquisition when the parent has used the cost method to account for its investment. The same examples that were used in Chapter 5, under the equity method, were used here. When the cost method has been used, additional calculations must be made for consolidated net income and consolidated retained earnings.

The basic steps in the consolidation process when the parent has used the equity and cost methods are outlined in Exhibit 6.15. It is important to have a good grasp of the procedures under both methods because Chapters 5 and 6 are the foundation for the consolidation issues we will introduce in the chapters that follow.

Exhibit 6.15

PREPARATION OF CONSOLIDATED FINANCIAL STATEMENTS
Basic Steps

	Parent company uses	
	Cost method	*Equity method*
1. Calculate and allocate the purchase discrepancy on the date of acquisition.	Yes	Yes
2. Prepare a purchase discrepancy amortization schedule (date of acquisition to present date).	Yes	Yes
3. Calculate consolidated net income—current year.	Yes	No*
4. Prepare the consolidated income statement.	Yes	Yes
5. Calculate the start-of-year balance of consolidated retained earnings.	Yes	No*
6. Prepare the consolidated retained earnings statement.	Yes	Yes
7. Calculate the end-of-year balance of consolidated retained earnings (optional).	Yes	No*
8. Calculate noncontrolling interest at the end of the year (for the consolidated balance sheet).	Yes	Yes
9. Prepare a statement of changes in noncontrolling interest (optional).	Yes	Yes
10. Prepare a consolidated balance sheet.	Yes	Yes

* If the parent company uses the equity method of accounting, the parent's net income equals consolidated net income, and the parent's retained earnings always equal consolidated retained earnings. Therefore, the calculations in steps 3, 5, and 7 are not necessary.

SELF-STUDY PROBLEM

On January 1, Year 1, Allen Company acquired 70% of the outstanding common shares of Bell Company for $87,500 in cash. On that date Bell had common stock of $50,000 and retained earnings of $45,000. At acquisition the identifiable assets and liabilities of Bell had fair values that were equal to book values except for plant assets, which had a fair value $30,000 greater than book value; inventory, which had a fair value $8,000 less than book value; and bonds payable, which had a fair value $12,420 greater than book value. The plant assets had a remaining useful life of 8 years on January 1, Year 1, and are amortized on a straight-line basis. The bonds payable mature on December 31, Year 8, and are amortized using the effective interest method. The market rate of interest for similar bonds is 6%.

Financial statements for the Year 6 fiscal year are as follows:

	Allen	Bell
Income statements		
Sales	$ 400,000	$100,000
Rent revenue	15,000	—
Dividend revenue	3,500	—
	418,500	100,000
Cost of sales	200,000	45,000
Depreciation	55,000	20,000
Interest expense	32,000	8,000
Other expenses	28,000	17,000
	315,000	90,000
Net income	$ 103,500	$ 10,000

	Allen	Bell
Retained earnings statements		
Balance, January 1	$ 400,000	$135,000
Net income	103,500	10,000
	503,500	145,000
Dividends	30,000	5,000
Balance, December 31	$ 473,500	$140,000
Balance sheets		
Cash	$ 12,500	$ 10,000
Accounts receivable	60,000	25,000
Inventory	200,000	40,000
Investment in Bell — cost method	87,500	—
Plant and equipment	1,200,000	470,000
Accumulated depreciation	(300,000)	(220,000)
	$1,260,000	$325,000
Accounts payable	$ 86,500	$ 35,000
Bonds payable, 8%	400,000	100,000
Common stock	300,000	50,000
Retained earnings	473,500	140,000
	$1,260,000	$325,000

Other Information

In Year 2, a goodwill impairment loss of $10,000 was recorded. Subsequent goodwill testing yielded no further evidence of impairment until Year 6, when a decline in the fair value of Bell Company occurred and management decided to reflect an impairment loss of $7,650 in the year's consolidated statements.

On December 31, Year 6, Bell Company owes Allen Company $9,000.

Required:

1. Using the direct approach, prepare the following Year 6 consolidated financial statements:
   (a) Income statement.
   (b) Retained earnings statement.
   (c) Balance sheet.
2. Prepare a schedule of the Year 6 changes in noncontrolling interest.

Solution to Self-study Problem

Cost of 70% of Bell		$ 87,500
Imputed value of 100% of Bell		$125,000
Book value of Bell		
Common stock	50,000	
Retained earnings	45,000	
		95,000
		30,000
Purchase discrepancy — January 1, Year 1		
Allocated:	FV – BV	
Plant assets	30,000 **(a)**	
Inventory	– 8,000 **(b)**	
	22,000	
Bonds payable	12,420	9,580 **(c)**
Goodwill		$20,420 **(d)**

BOND AMORTIZATION SCHEDULE

Date	Cash paid	Interest expense	Bond premium amortization	Carrying amount of bonds
Jan 1/ Year 1				$112,420
Dec 31/ Year 1	$ 8,000	$ 6,745	$ 1,255	111,165
Dec 31/ Year 2	8,000	6,670	1,330	109,835
Dec 31/ Year 3	8,000	6,590	1,410	108,425
Dec 31/ Year 4	8,000	6,506	1,494	106,931
Dec 31/ Year 5	8,000	6,416	1,584	105,347
	40,000	32,927	7,073	
Dec 31/ Year 6	8,000	6,321	1,679	103,668 **(e)**
Dec 31/ Year 7	8,000	6,220	1,780	101,888
Dec 31/ Year 8	8,000	6,112	1,888	100,000
	$64,000	$51,580	$12,420	

PURCHASE DISCREPANCY AMORTIZATION

	Balance Jan. 1/Year 1	Amortization To end of Year 5	Year 6	Balance Dec. 31/Year 6
Plant assets **(a)**	$30,000	$18,750	$ 3,750	$ 7,500 **(e)**
Inventory **(b)**	– 8,000	– 8,000	—	— **(f)**
Goodwill **(d)**	20,420	10,000	7,650	2,770 **(g)**
	42,420	20,750	11,400	10,270
Bonds payable **(c)**	12,420	7,073	1,679	3,668 **(h)**
	$30,000	$13,677	$ 9,721	$ 6,602 **(i)**

CALCULATION OF CONSOLIDATED NET INCOME — Year 6

Net income — Allen		$103,500
Less dividend from Bell		3,500 **(j)**
		100,000
Net income — Bell	10,000	
Less purchase discrepancy amort. **(i)**	9,721	
	279 **(k)**	
Allen's ownership	70%	195
		$100,195 **(l)**

CALCULATION OF CONSOLIDATED RETAINED EARNINGS
January 1, Year 6

Retained earnings — Allen		$400,000
Retained earnings — Bell	135,000	
Retained earnings — Bell, acquisition date	45,000	
Increase since acquisition	90,000	
Less purchase discrepancy amort. **(i)**	13,677	
	76,323	
Allen's ownership	70%	
		53,426
		$453,426 **(m)**

CALCULATION OF CONSOLIDATED RETAINED EARNINGS
December 31, Year 6

Retained earnings — Allen		$473,500
Retained earnings — Bell	140,000	
Retained earnings — Bell, acquisition date	45,000	
Increase since acquisition	95,000	
Less purchase discrepancy amort. (**(i) 13,677 + 9,721**)	23,398	
	71,602	
Allen's ownership	70%	50,121
		$523,621 **(n)**

CALCULATION OF NONCONTROLLING INTEREST
December 31, Year 6

Common stock — Bell	$ 50,000
Retained earnings — Bell	140,000
	190,000
Unamortized purchase discrepancy **(i)**	6,602
	196,602
	30%
	$ 58,981 **(o)**

1.(a)

ALLEN COMPANY
CONSOLIDATED INCOME STATEMENT
for the Year Ended December 31, Year 6

Sales (400,000 + 100,000)	$500,000
Rent revenue	15,000
Dividend revenue (3,500 + 0 – **(j) 3,500**)	—
	515,000

Cost of sales (200,000 + 45,000)	245,000
Depreciation (55,000 + 20,000 + **(e) 3,750**)	78,750
Interest expense (32,000 + 8,000 **– (h) 1,679**)	38,321
Other expenses (28,000 + 17,000)	45,000
Goodwill impairment loss **(g)**	7,650
	414,721
Net income — entity	100,279
Less noncontrolling interest (30% x **(k) 279**)	84 **(p)**
Net income	$100,195

(b)

ALLEN COMPANY
CONSOLIDATED RETAINED EARNINGS STATEMENT
for the Year Ended December 31, Year 6

Balance, January 1 **(m)**	$453,426
Net income	100,195
	553,621
Dividends	30,000
Balance, December 31 **(n)**	$523,621

(c)

ALLEN COMPANY
CONSOLIDATED BALANCE SHEET
December 31, Year 6

Cash (12,500 + 10,000)	$ 22,500
Accounts receivable (60,000 + 25,000 – ***9,000**)	76,000
Inventory (200,000 + 40,000)	240,000
Plant and equipment (1,200,000 + 470,000 ₁ **(a) 30,000**)	1,700,000
Accumulated depreciation	
(300,000 + 220,000 + **(e) 18,750 + (e) 3,750**)	(542,500)
Goodwill **(g)**	2,770
	$1,498,770
Accounts payable (86,500 + 35,000 – ***9,000**)	$ 112,500
Bonds payable (400,000 + 100,000 + **(h) 3,668**)	503,668
	616,168
Common stock	300,000
Retained earnings **(n)**	523,621
Noncontrolling interest **(o)**	58,981
	$1,498,770

*Intercompany receivable/payable

2.   **YEAR 6 CHANGES IN NONCONTROLLING INTEREST**

Balance, January 1 (30% × *201,323)	$60,397
Allocation of entity net income **(p)**	84
	60,481
Dividends (30% × 5,000)	1,500
Balance, December 31 **(o)**	$58,981

* Common stock	$ 50,000
Retained earnings, January 1	135,000
	185,000
Unamortized purchase discrepancy (**(i) 30,000 – 13,677**)	16,323
	$201,323

APPENDIX 6A

Preparing Consolidated Financial Statements Using the Working Paper Approach

In this chapter, we have illustrated the direct approach for preparing consolidated financial statements when the parent has used the cost method to account for its investment. In the examples used, we first examined the situation where the subsidiary was 100 percent owned, and then the situation where the parent's ownership was 80 percent. We will now illustrate the working paper approach using the same examples.

Year 1 Consolidated Financial Statement Working Paper

A number of methods can be used to prepare consolidated financial statement working papers when the parent has used the cost method. All methods used must result in identical consolidated amounts. The approach that we will illustrate adjusts the parent's accounts on the working paper to what they would have been if the equity method had been used to account for the investment. This requires the same additional calculations used in the direct approach. After the accounts have been adjusted, the working paper eliminations illustrated in Chapter 5 under the equity method are repeated. Exhibit 6A.1 shows the preparation of the consolidated financial statements for Year 1 using a working paper, assuming Company S is a 100 percent owned subsidiary of Company P. To compare it with the direct approach, see Exhibit 6.4.

First, convert the parent's income statement from the cost method to equity method.

Entry #a adjusts the accounts of Company P as at December 31, Year 1, to what they would have been under the equity method. The information for this entry is contained in the calculation of consolidated net income for Year 1.

#a	Dividend income — Company P	2,500	
	Investment in S — Company P	2,750	
	Investment income — Company P		5,250

All relevant items in the financial statements of Company P except the December 31, Year 1, retained earnings contain balances arrived at using the equity method.

The remaining working paper entries are the same equity method elimination entries used in Exhibit 5A.1 and are reproduced next without further elaboration:

Then, record the same consolidation entries recorded under the equity method.

#1	Investment income — Company P	5,250	
	Dividends — Company S		2,500
	Investment in S — Company P		2,750
#2	Retained earnings, Jan. 1 — Company S	6,000	
	Common stock — Company S	10,000	
	Purchase discrepancy	3,000	
	Investment in S — Company P		19,000
#3	Cost of sales — Company S	2,000	
	Goodwill impairment loss (expense)	50	
	Goodwill	950	
	Purchase discrepancy		3,000

Exhibit 6A.1

CONSOLIDATED FINANCIAL STATEMENT WORKING PAPER
December 31, Year 1 (cost method)

	P	S	Eliminations Dr.	Cr.	Consolidated
Sales	$ 50,000	$30,000			$ 80,000
Dividend income	2,500		**(a)** $ 2,500		
Investment income			**(1)** 5,250	**(a)** $ 5,250	
	52,500	30,000			80,000
Cost of sales	26,500	14,700	**(3)** 2,000		43,200
Goodwill impair. loss			**(3)** 50		50
Misc. expenses	5,200	8,000			13,200
	31,700	22,700			56,450
Net income	$ 20,800	$ 7,300	$ 9,800	$ 5,250	$ 23,550
Retained earnings, Jan. 1	$ 85,000	$ 6,000	**(2)** $ 6,000		$ 85,000
Net income	20,800	7,300	9,800	$ 5,250	23,550
	105,800	13,300			108,550
Dividends	6,000	2,500		**(1)** 2,500	6,000
Retained earnings, Dec. 31	$ 99,800	$10,800	$15,800	$ 7,750	$102,550
Assets, misc.	$147,800	$18,300			$166,100
Inventory	30,000	14,000			44,000
Investment in S	19,000		**(a)** $ 2,750	**(1)** $ 2,750	
				(2) 19,000	
Purchase discrepancy			**(2)** 3,000	**(3)** 3,000	
Goodwill			**(3)** 950		950
	$196,800	$32,300			$211,050
Liabilities	$ 47,000	$11,500			$ 58,500
Common stock	50,000	10,000	**(2)** 10,000		50,000
Retained earnings	99,800	10,800	15,800	7,750	102,550
	$196,800	$32,300	$32,500	$32,500	$211,050

Investment income is replaced by the subsidiary's revenues and expenses plus the amortization of the purchase discrepancy.

The investment account is replaced by the carrying value of the subsidiary's assets and liabilities plus the unamortized purchase discrepancy.

Year 2 Consolidated Financial Statement Working Paper

The working papers for the preparation of the Year 2 consolidated financial statements are presented in Exhibit 6A.2. See Exhibit 6.7 to compare the direct approach.

The elimination entries #a and #b adjust the accounts of Company P to equity method balances. These entries are reproduced below.

#a Investment in S — Company P	2,750	
Retained earnings, Jan. 1 — Company P		2,750

First, convert the parent's income statement and beginning retained earnings from the cost method to equity method.

This entry adjusts the investment in S account and the January 1 retained earnings of Company P to the equity method balances at the beginning of the year. The amount used is readily apparent in the calculation of consolidated retained earnings as at January 1, Year 2.

Exhibit 6A.2

CONSOLIDATED FINANCIAL STATEMENT WORKING PAPER
December 31, Year 2 (cost method)

	P	S	Eliminations Dr.	Eliminations Cr.	Consolidated
Sales	$ 60,000	$40,000			$100,000
Dividend income	3,000		**(b)** $ 3,000		
Investment income			**(1)** 9,920	**(b)** $ 9,920	
	63,000	40,000			100,000
Cost of sales	32,000	18,000			50,000
Goodwill impair. loss			**(3)** 80		80
Expenses, misc.	9,000	12,000			21,000
	41,000	30,000			71,080
Net income	$ 22,000	$10,000	$13,000	$ 9,920	$ 28,920
Retained earnings, Jan. 1	$ 99,800	$10,800	**(2)** $10,800	**(a)** $ 2,750	$102,550
Net income	22,000	10,000	13,000	9,920	28,920
	121,800	20,800			131,470
Dividends	8,000	3,000		**(1)** 3,000	8,000
Retained earnings, Dec. 31	$113,800	$17,800	$23,800	$15,670	$123,470
Assets, misc.	$131,800	$21,000			$152,800
Inventory	35,000	16,000			51,000
Investment in S	19,000		**(a)** $ 2,750	**(1)** $ 6,920	
			(b) 6,920	**(2)** 21,750	
Purchase discrepancy			**(2)** 950	**(3)** 950	
Goodwill			**(3)** 870		870
	$185,800	$37,000			$204,670
Liabilities	$ 22,000	$ 9,200			$ 31,200
Common stock	50,000	10,000	**(2)** 10,000		50,000
Retained earnings	113,800	17,800	23,800	15,670	123,470
	$185,800	$37,000	$45,290	$45,290	$204,670

The entries on the income statement are adjustments for one period to bring the accounts to the desired balance for one period of time i.e., for one year.

The entries on the balance sheet are cumulative adjustments to bring the accounts to the desired balance at the end of the period i.e., at a point in time.

#b	Dividend income — Company P	3,000	
	Investment in S — Company P	6,920	
	Investment income — Company P		9,920

Entry #b adjusts the accounts of Company P to the equity method balances at the end of Year 2. The calculation of consolidated net income for Year 2 provides the amount for this entry.

After these entries have been made in the working paper, all of the accounts of Company P contain balances arrived at using the equity method. The remaining elimination entries recorded in the working paper, which are reproduced below, are identical to those that were discussed in Chapter 5 (see Exhibit 5A.2).

Then, record the same consolidation entries recorded under the equity method.

#1 Investment income — Company P	9,920	
Dividends — Company S		3,000
Investment in S — Company P		6,920

#2 Retained earnings, Jan. 1 — Company S	10,800	
Common stock — Company S	10,000	
Purchase discrepancy	950	
Investment in S — Company P		21,750

#3 Goodwill impairment loss (expense)	80	
Goodwill	870	
Purchase discrepancy		950

80 Percent Owned Subsidiary — Year 1

Exhibit 6A.3 shows the preparation of the consolidated financial statements as at December 31, Year 1, using a working paper. See Exhibit 6.11 to compare the direct approach.

Working paper elimination entry #a adjusts the accounts of Company P as at December 31, Year 1, to what they would have been under the equity method. The information for this entry is contained in the calculation of consolidated net income for Year 1.

These entries convert the parent's income statement and beginning retained earnings from the cost method to equity method.

#a Dividend income — Company P	2,000	
Investment in S — Company P	2,200	
Investment income — Company P		4,200

After this entry has been entered in the working paper, all relevant items in the financial statements of Company P, except retained earnings as of December 31, Year 1, contain balances arrived at under the equity method.

The remaining working paper entries are the same equity method elimination entries as were used in Exhibit 5A.3. These entries are reproduced below, without further elaboration.

#1 Investment income — Company P	4,200	
Dividends — Company S		2,000
Investment in S — Company P		2,200

These entries are the same consolidation entries when the parent used the equity method.

#2 Retained earnings, Jan. 1 — Company S	6,000	
Common stock — Company S	10,000	
Purchase discrepancy	3,000	
Investment in S — Company P		15,200
Noncontrolling interest		3,800

#3 Cost of sales — Company S	2,000	
Goodwill impairment loss	50	
Goodwill	950	
Purchase discrepancy		3,000

| #4 Noncontrolling interest (income statement) | 1,050 | |
| Noncontrolling interest (balance sheet) | | 1,050 |

| #5 Noncontrolling interest (balance sheet) | 500 | |
| Dividends — Company S | | 500 |

Exhibit 6A.3

CONSOLIDATED FINANCIAL STATEMENT WORKING PAPER
December 31, Year 1 (cost method)

		P	S	Eliminations Dr.	Eliminations Cr.	Consolidated
The entries on the worksheet are recorded only on the worksheet and are not recorded in the separate-entity books of the parent or subsidiary.	Sales	$ 50,000	$30,000			$ 80,000
	Dividend income	2,000		**(a)** $ 2,000		
	Investment income			**(1)** 4,200	**(a)** $ 4,200	
		52,000	30,000			80,000
	Cost of sales	26,500	14,700	**(3)** 2,000		43,200
	Goodwill impair. loss			**(3)** 50		50
	Misc. expenses	5,200	8,000			13,200
		31,700	22,700			56,450
	Net income — entity					23,550
	Noncontrolling interest			**(4)** 1,050		1,050
	Net income	$ 20,300	$ 7,300	$ 9,300	$ 4,200	$ 22,500
	Retained earnings, Jan. 1	$ 85,000	$ 6,000	**(2)** $ 6,000		$ 85,000
	Net income	20,300	7,300	9,300	$ 4,200	22,500
		105,300	13,300			107,500
	Dividends	6,000	2,500		**(1)** 2,000	6,000
					(5) 500	
	Retained earnings, Dec. 31	$ 99,300	$10,800	$15,300	$ 6,700	$101,500
	Assets, misc.	$151,100	$18,300			$169,400
	Equipment (net)	30,000	14,000			44,000
	Investment in S	15,200		**(a)** $ 2,200	**(1)** $ 2,200	
					(2) 15,200	
Noncontrolling interest appears both on the income statement (for a period of time) and on the balance sheet (at a point in time).	Purchase discrepancy			**(2)** 3,000	**(3)** 3,000	
	Goodwill			**(3)** 950		950
		$196,300	$32,300			$214,350
	Liabilities	$ 47,000	$11,500			$ 58,500
	Common stock	50,000	10,000	**(2)** 10,000		50,000
	Retained earnings	99,300	10,800	15,300	6,700	101,500
	Noncontrolling interest				**(2)** 3,800	
				(5) 500	**(4)** 1,050	4,350
		$196,300	$32,300	$31,950	$31,950	$214,350

80 Percent Owned Subsidiary — Year 2

Exhibit 6A.4 shows the working paper approach to the preparation of the Year 2 consolidated financial statements. See Exhibit 6.14 to compare the direct approach.

The elimination entries #a and #b adjust the accounts of Company P to equity method balances. These entries are reproduced below.

#a   Investment in S — Company P   2,200
      Retained earnings, Jan. 1 — Company P   2,200

Exhibit 6A.4

CONSOLIDATED FINANCIAL STATEMENT WORKING PAPER
December 31, Year 2 (cost method)

	P	S	Eliminations Dr.	Eliminations Cr.	Consolidated
Consolidated net income is equal to the parent's separate entity income under the equity method.					
Sales	$ 60,000	$40,000			$100,000
Dividend income	2,400		**(b)** $ 2,400		
Investment income			**(1)** 7,936	**(b)** $ 7,936	
	62,400	40,000			100,000
Cost of sales	32,000	18,000			50,000
Goodwill impair. loss			**(3)** 80		80
Expenses, misc.	9,000	12,000			21,000
	41,000	30,000			71,080
Net income — entity					28,920
Noncontrolling interest			**(4)** 1,984		1,984
Net income	$ 21,400	$10,000	$12,400	$ 7,936	$ 26,936
Retained earnings, Jan. 1	$ 99,300	$10,800	**(2)** $10,800	**(a)** $ 2,200	$101,500
Net income	21,400	10,000	12,400	7,936	26,936
	120,700	20,800			128,436
Dividends	8,000	3,000		**(1)** 2,400	8,000
				(5) 600	
Retained earnings, Dec. 31	$112,700	$17,800	$23,200	$13,136	$120,436
Assets, misc.	$134,500	$21,000			$155,500
Inventory	35,000	16,000			51,000
Investment in S	15,200		**(a)** $ 2,200	**(1)** $ 5,536	
			(b) 5,536	**(2)** 17,400	
Consolidated retained earnings is equal to the parent's separate entity retained earnings under the equity method.					
Purchase discrepancy			**(2)** 950	**(3)** 950	
Goodwill			**(3)** 870		870
	$184,700	$37,000			$207,370
Liabilities	$ 22,000	$ 9,200			$ 31,200
Common stock	50,000	10,000	**(2)** 10,000		50,000
Retained earnings	112,700	17,800	23,200	13,136	120,436
Noncontrolling interest				**(2)** 4,350	5,734
			(5) 600	**(4)** 1,984	
	$184,700	$37,000	$43,356	$43,356	$207,370

This entry adjusts the investment account and the January 1 retained earnings of Company P to the equity method balances at the beginning of the year. The amount used is readily apparent in the calculation of consolidated retained earnings as at January 1, Year 2.

#b	Dividend income — Company P	2,400	
	Investment in S — Company P	5,536	
	Investment income — Company P		7,936

Entry #b adjusts the accounts of Company P to the equity method balances at the end of Year 2. The calculation of consolidated net income for Year 2 provides the amount for this entry.

After these entries have been made in the working paper, all of the accounts of Company P contain balances arrived at using the equity method. The remaining elimination entries recorded in the working paper, which are reproduced below, are identical to those that were discussed in Chapter 5 (see Exhibit 5A.4).

#1	Investment income — Company P	7,936	
	Investment in S — Company P		5,536
	Dividends — Company S		2,400

These journal entries appear only on the consolidated worksheet and are not posted to the separate-entity accounting records.

#2	Retained earnings, January 1 — Company S	10,800	
	Common stock — Company S	10,000	
	Purchase discrepancy	950	
	Investment in S — Company P		17,400
	Noncontrolling interest		4,350

#3	Goodwill impairment loss	80	
	Goodwill	870	
	Purchase discrepancy		950

#4	Noncontrolling interest (income statement)	1,984	
	Noncontrolling interest (balance sheet)		1,984

#5	Noncontrolling interest (balance sheet)	600	
	Dividends — Company S		600

REVIEW QUESTIONS

Questions, cases, and problems that deal with the appendix material are denoted with an asterisk.

1. Outline the calculation of the following when the parent company accounts for its investment using the cost method:
    (a) Consolidated net income.
    (b) Consolidated retained earnings.

2. What accounts in the financial statements of the parent company have balances that differ depending on whether the cost or equity method has been used?

3. Why does adding the parent's share of the increase in retained earnings of the subsidiary and the parent's retained earnings under the cost method result in consolidated retained earnings? Assume that there is no purchase discrepancy.

*4. What are the initial entries on the working paper when the parent has used the cost method to account for its investment?

5. A subsidiary was acquired during the fiscal year of the parent. Describe the preparation of the consolidated income statement for the year. What additional disclosures are required?

6. When the parent company uses the cost method, an adjustment must be made to the parent's retained earnings on consolidation in every year after the year of acquisition. Why is this entry necessary? Why is a similar entry not required when the parent utilized the equity method?

7. Why is the income assigned to the noncontrolling interest treated as a deduction in computing consolidated net income?

8. How would the consolidation of a parent-founded subsidiary differ from the consolidation of a purchased subsidiary?

MULTIPLE-CHOICE QUESTIONS

1. When a company uses the cost method to record its investment in a subsidiary during the year, which of the following will be included in the journal entry to record the parent's share of the subsidiary's dividends when they are declared?
   a. Debit dividend revenue.
   b. Credit dividend income.
   c. Debit cash.
   d. Credit investment in subsidiary.

2. Which of the following best describes why a company would use the cost method to record its investment in a subsidiary rather than the equity method?
   a. It results in the same net income and retained earnings as consolidation.
   b. It is easy and inexpensive to use.
   c. It is required by the *CICA Handbook*.
   d. It is required by the Canada Revenue Agency (CRA) for tax purposes.

3. AG acquired 80% of the shares of its subsidiary LM on January 1, Year 4. On this date the fair value of the land of LM was greater than its carrying value. Which of the combinations of LM's net book value (NBV) and fair value increments (FVI) would be included in its consolidated asset values for land on December 31, Year 6?
   a. 80% of NBV and 80% of FVI
   b. 100% of NBV and 80% of FVI
   c. 100% of NBV and 100% of FVI
   d. 80% of NBV and 100% of FVI

Use the following data for Questions 4 to 8.

On January 1, Year 4, Place Inc. acquired an 80% interest in Setting Co. for $800,000 cash. At that time, Setting's assets and liabilities had book values equal to fair values, except for the following:

Inventory	Undervalued by $75,000	Turns over 6 times a year
Plant and equipment	Undervalued by $50,000	Remaining useful life: 10 years
Bonds payable	Overvalued by $40,000	Maturity Date: December 31, Year 8

The premium/discount on bonds payable is amortized on a straight-line basis.

At January 1, Year 4, Setting had 100,000 no-par-value common shares outstanding with a book value of $550,000 and retained earnings of $50,000.

The abbreviated financial statements of Place and Setting on December 31, Year 6, are as follows:

BALANCE SHEETS

	Place	Setting
Current assets	$ 950,000	$ 800,000
Investment in Setting	800,000	—
Plant and equipment (net)	1,250,000	1,555,000
	$3,000,000	$2,355,000

Current liabilities	$ 500,000	$ 280,000
10% bonds payable	—	800,000
Common stock	1,000,000	550,000
Retained earnings	1,500,000	725,000
	$3,000,000	$2,355,000

COMBINED INCOME AND RETAINED EARNINGS STATEMENTS

Sales	$2,500,000	$900,000
Cost of goods sold	1,200,000	330,000
Expenses	400,000	220,000
	1,600,000	550,000
Net operating income	900,000	350,000
Dividends received from Setting	100,000	—
Net income	1,000,000	350,000
Retained earnings, Jan. 1, Year 6	800,000	500,000
	1,800,000	850,000
Dividends declared and paid	300,000	125,000
Retained earnings, Dec. 31, Year 6	$1,500,000	$725,000

4. Which of the following is the amount of the inventory fair value increment that will be recognized on Place's consolidated income statement for the year ended December 31, Year 4?
   a. $0
   b. $56,250
   c. $60,000
   d. $75,000

5. Which of the following is the amount of the fair value increment relating to plant and equipment (net) that will be recognized as an increase to depreciation expense on Place's consolidated income statement for the year ended December 31, Year 5?
   a. $4,000
   b. $5,000
   c. $8,000
   d. $32,000

6. Which of the following is the correct adjustment to interest expense for the amortization of the bond fair value increment on Place's consolidated income statement for the year ended December 31, Year 4?
   a. $8,000 increase.
   b. $6,400 increase.
   c. $8,000 decrease.
   d. $6,400 decrease.

7. How many years' worth of fair value increment amortizations must be used to calculate consolidated beginning retained earnings at January 1, Year 6, from Place's cost-basis accounting records?
   a. 0
   b. 1
   c. 2
   d. 3

8. At December 31, Year 4, Place's consolidated balance sheet reported a non controlling interest of $260,000. Setting did not declare any dividends during Year 4. What did Place's consolidated income statement for the year ended

December 31, Year 4, report as the noncontrolling interest's portion of consolidated income?

a. $60,000
b. $70,000
c. $140,000
d. $180,000

9. Bailey Inc. owns 75 percent of the shares of Neville Corp. Neville owes Bailey
$600,000 for inventory purchased. In preparing consolidated statements
what amount of this account payable should be eliminated?

a. $0
b. $150,000
c. $450,000
d. $600,000

10. On January 1, Year 4, Donald Corp. reported net assets of $880,000 on its
balance sheet, although a building (with a 10-year life) having a book value
of $330,000 is now worth $400,000. Ober Ltd. paid $840,000 on that date
for 80% of Donald's outstanding shares. The balance of the purchase discrepancy was allocated to intangible assets other than goodwill to be written off
over 20 years. The December 31, Year 6, income statement of Donald showed
total expenses of $621,000, while the income statement of Ober showed total
expenses of $714,000. What is the amount of total expenses (excluding non-
controlling interest) on the Year 6 consolidated income statement?

a. $1,335,000
b. $1,340,000
c. $1,344,600
d. $1,347,000

Use the following Information for Questions 11 to 13.

On January 1, Year 6, AB Inc. purchased 80% of the common shares of CD
Corp. for $1,400,000. On the date of acquisition, CD's shareholders' equity was as
follows:

Common shares	$600,000
Retained earnings	608,000

Any purchase price discrepancy was allocated to goodwill. During Year 6, CD
earned a net income of $400,000 and paid dividends of $300,000. On December
31, Year 6, a goodwill impairment loss of $30,000 was recorded.

11. What is the amount of noncontrolling interest on the consolidated balance
sheet as at December 31, Year 6?

a. $241,600
b. $255,600
c. $261,600
d. $364,000

12. What is the amount of noncontrolling interest on the consolidated income
statement for the year ended December 31, Year 6?

a. $20,000
b. $60,000
c. $74,000
d. $80,000

13. What is the amount of goodwill on the consolidated balance sheet as at December 31, Year 6?
    a. $403,600
    b. $409,600
    c. $433,600
    d. $512,000

14. On January 1, Year 2, Law Corporation acquired 90% of the common shares of Yer Ltd. On that date, Yer's equipment had a book value of $300,000 and a fair value of $400,000. How would the account balance for equipment on the consolidated balance sheet at the end of Year 4 differ if Law had used the cost method rather than the equity method in accounting for its investment in Yer?
    a. There would be no difference.
    b. The consolidated equipment account would be higher under the cost method.
    c. The consolidated equipment account would be lower under the cost method.
    d. Further information is needed to determine the difference.

CASES

Case 1 It should have surprised few that, with compound annual growth in revenue at nearly 24 percent yet profits steadily declining, Nortel Networks' bubble burst during 2001. Waves of acquisitions, generally in exchange for inflated stock, were "suddenly" overvalued. In the face of mounting losses from operations, 2001 saw the discontinuance of significant operations plus other special charges to income totalling over US$16 billion as assets were adjusted to more realistic values.

Significant among these charges was the write-off of goodwill that had been an important component of acquisitions consummated over the past several years. Exhibit 1 on the following page contains summary information regarding several of the large acquisitions made by Nortel Networks Corporation.

Canada's new rules for business combinations came into effect as follows:

- Section 1581, "Business Combinations," January 2002.
- Section 3062, "Goodwill and Other Intangible Assets," January 2002.
- Section 3063, "Impairment of Long Lived Assets," April 2003.

Required:

PART A

(a) If the new business combination rules had been introduced two or three years earlier, would Nortel's accounting for its acquisitions as indicated in Exhibit 1 have been any different? Explain.

(b) Would the accounting results have been different? Explain.

PART B

Different suggestions have been proposed in the past regarding the accounting for goodwill. The alternatives offered were:

1. Goodwill should be capitalized and reviewed for impairment.

2. Goodwill should be capitalized and amortized.

3. Goodwill should be written off directly through income.

4. Goodwill should be written off directly against shareholders' equity.
Outline the pros and cons for each alternative.

(Case developed by Peter Secord, St. Mary's University)

Exhibit 1

NORTEL NETWORKS CORPORATION
INTANGIBLE ASSETS ACQUIRED
Selected Acquisitions, 2000 & 2001

Acquisition	Purchase price	Acquired goodwill	Acquired technology	Acquired IPR&D	Net tangible assets (liabilities)
980 NPLC	$2,453	$2,054	$402	$ 15	$ (18)
Alteon	6,025	5,262	391	403	(31)
CoreTek	1,530	1,342	115	176	(103)
Xros	3,115	2,966	29	191	(71)
Clarify	4,851	4,573	210	64	4
Qtera	3,003	2,629	–	559	(185)

Source: www.sedar.com, Nortel Networks Corporation, *Annual Report*, March 11, 2002.
Legend: IPR&D is in progress research and development
US Dollar amounts in millions

Case 2　For the past five years you have been employed as a staff accountant for a medium-sized public accounting firm. The nature of the firm's client base has been such that virtually no consolidation work has been required of the partners and the staff accountants. However, the recent acquisition of a few new large clients has changed all of this because these clients have subsidiaries and prepare consolidated financial statements.

To prepare for this, it has been decided that the firm will put on a series of professional development seminars each Friday afternoon to act as a refresher for the firm's staff and partners. Each session will consist of slide presentations involving the consolidation process and procedures. In addition, some case problems will be handed out, and after the attendees have had 30 minutes or so to come up with a solution, the seminar leader will lead the discussion. You will be the seminar leader when the following mini-case is handed out.

> Darnell Ltd. has just bought 80 percent of the shares of Norton Technologies Inc. for $3,500,000 cash plus 150,000 newly issued common shares. This share issue will increase the number of outstanding shares of Darnel by approximately 20 percent. The accountants of Darnell have examined the records of Norton and have determined that all of the assets and liabilities that appear on its balance sheet have a net fair value of approximately $5,000,000.

The seminar participants will be told that, based on this information, they are to outline how they would proceed with the consolidation process and to indicate any further information they require.

Required:

Prepare the notes that you will use as you lead the discussion.

Case 3   Gerry's Fabrics Ltd. (GFL), a private company, manufactures a variety of clothing for women and children and sells it to retailers across Canada. Until recently, the company has operated from the same plant since its incorporation under federal legislation 40 years ago. Over the years, the profits of the company have varied widely, and there have been periods of losses.

In the year ended March 31, Year 1, the company entered into an arrangement whereby it issued common shares from treasury to a group of new shareholders. At the same time, the existing shareholders were given the option of exchanging their common shares for preferred shares, which are redeemable at the option of the company and retractable at the option of the shareholder. One shareholder who had held 25% of the common shares elected to accept the preferred shares, while the other shareholders elected to retain their common shares.

A "Preferred Share Agreement" (the Agreement), was signed by the shareholder who had accepted the preferred shares (the "preferred shareholder"). Under the Agreement, the preferred shareholder can require GFL to redeem all of his shares in any year, after giving at least 90 days notice prior to the fiscal year end. The Agreement does not provide for partial redemptions. The total redemption price for all shares is 1.25 times "income before taxes" for that year. The term "income before taxes" is defined in the Agreement as follows:

1. Income before taxes for the year of redemption must be calculated:
   - in accordance with the accounting policies set forth in this Agreement; or
   - where no accounting policy has been clearly specified, in accordance with policies consistent in intent with the policies contained in this Agreement.
2. Income before taxes for the year of redemption need not, for the purposes of the Agreement, be the same as that which is reported to shareholders or that which is used for calculating income taxes payable.

The Agreement specifies the applicable accounting policies as follows:

A. Revenue recognition:
   1. In cases where a deposit of 10% or more of the sales price has been received from the customer, revenue shall be recognized on completion of the manufacturing of the goods ordered.
   2. In all other cases, revenue shall be recognized upon shipment to the customer, and no allowance shall be made for returned merchandise or adjustments.
B. Cost of goods sold and inventory:
   1. All inventory on hand at the end of a fiscal year (excluding raw materials) shall be costed at actual production costs, including its full share of all overhead expenditures.
   2. Raw materials inventory shall include all expenditures that were needed to make the inventory available for use, including unpacking and storing costs.
C. Amortization:
   1. All applicable amortization shall be computed on a straight-line basis using realistic residual values.
   2. Amortization shall be recorded over the physical life of the assets, regardless of their useful life to the company.

     3.   No amortization shall be recorded on assets that are increasing in value.

D. Capitalization:

     1.   All expenditures shall be capitalized as assets unless their life is limited to the current financial period. All maintenance and repair costs that extend an asset's useful life shall be capitalized.

     2.   Assets shall be recorded at cost and amortized in accordance with C above.

E. Liabilities:

     1.   Each liability shall be recorded at the amount required to settle the obligation. A debt-to-equity ratio of 1:1 is assumed to exist. Interest incurred on debt in excess of this ratio will not be deductible in computing income before taxes.

F. Errors and adjustments:

     1.   All errors, adjustments, and changes in value shall be attributed to the year to which the error or adjustment or change relates.

G. Compensation and related transactions:

     1.   Average compensation per employee shall be in accordance with levels used in fiscal Year 1 adjusted by the Consumer Price Index.

     2.   All related party transactions must be measured at fair value or values established in the market place for transactions between GFL and unrelated third parties.

The Agreement also contains a separate clause that deals with "arbitration procedures." These procedures allow an independent arbitrator to calculate the share redemption price after having obtained full access to the books and records of GFL.

The preferred shareholder has advised GFL of his intention to have GFL redeem his preferred shares and has provided GFL with the required 90 days notice. The redemption price, calculated by GFL, was based on the March 31, Year 5, financial statements. However, the preferred shareholder disagrees with GFL's figure for income before taxes.

Since the price is being disputed, the matter is to be resolved by an independent arbitrator. Both parties have agreed to engage Cook & Co., Chartered Accountants, to make a binding decision. You, CA, are employed by Cook & Co. The engagement partner has asked you to prepare a memo providing complete analyses required for and recommendations to be considered in the calculation of the share-redemption price. Your notes from your investigations are contained in Exhibit I.

Required:

Prepare the memo to the partner.   *(CICA adapted)*

EXHIBIT I

NOTES FROM INVESTIGATION OF GFL

1. The disputed share-redemption price calculation was prepared by the vice-president of finance of GFL and is 1.25 times the company's unaudited income before taxes of $895,420 for the year ended March 31, Year 5.

2. The unaudited financial statements for the year ended March 31, Year 5, reflect the following transactions and accounting policies:

    •   During fiscal Year 4, GFL acquired all the shares of a competing company (J Ltd.) for $8 million. Most of the amount by which the purchase price exceeded the book value of the assets and liabilities acquired was recorded as goodwill and is being amortized over 10 years. The purchase was financed almost entirely by debt at 10% interest for five years.

    •   On January 1, Year 5, a volume discount policy was introduced. At March 31, Year 5, an estimated liability of $95,500 was provided for volume discounts that may become due.

- In fiscal Year 4, the manufacturing processes were altered to introduce more mechanization, and standard costing was adopted. All variances from standard costs are being expensed.
- In order to reduce taxable income and save cash, all employee incentives are being accrued at year-end and paid five months later.
- In Year 3, GFL decided to account for one of its successful investments on the equity basis. During fiscal Year 5, the directors of GFL chose to revert to the cost basis for the investment.
- In fiscal Year 5, GFL commenced construction of another manufacturing facility at a cost of $1.8 million, including equipment. Some manufacturing occurred in a part of the new facility before the whole facility was ready for use. To be conservative, any costs that were incurred after manufacturing had commenced were expensed, except for new equipment installations.
- Land that has been held for several years for future expansion of the company was recorded at cost plus carrying costs (property taxes, maintenance, and similar) until fiscal Year 5. The land was reclassified in late fiscal Year 5 as inventory and was written down to the lower of cost and market.
- In March Year 5, GFL sold some of its capital assets under a deferred payment arrangement. Gains on disposal will be recorded as payment is received, on a proportional basis.
- In April Year 5, an enhanced executive pension plan was introduced. The March 31, Year 5 financial statements include pension expenses that reflect the additional costs resulting from the new pension plan enhancements.

3. Notes to the financial statements for fiscal Year 5 disclose the following:
- During the year, GFL sold $4 million worth of goods to DGR Ltd. DGR is owned by several of the common shareholders of GFL. DGR paid a special price for goods that was about $380,000 lower than the price paid by other retailers.
- A $200,000 liability has been recorded for legal costs pertaining to a patent infringement case that is before the courts.

PROBLEMS

Problem 1   When Pill Ltd. acquired 85% of Sill Corporation on January 1, Year 1, for $238,000, the imputed purchase discrepancy of $60,000 was allocated entirely to goodwill. On December 31, Year 1, a goodwill loss of $1,500 was recognized. Pill uses the cost method to account for its investment. Pill reported a separate entity Year 1 net income of $25,000 and declared no dividends. Sill reported a separate entity net income of $40,000 and paid dividends of $9,000 in Year 1.

Required:

Compute the following:
(a) Consolidated net income for Year 1.
(b) Noncontrolling interest that would appear on the Year 1 consolidated income statement.
(c) Investment in Sill at December 31, Year 1 (equity method).

Problem 2   Large Ltd. purchased 75% of Small Company on January 1, Year 1, for $600,000, when the balance sheet of Small showed common stock of $400,000 and retained earnings of $100,000. On that date, the inventory of Small was undervalued by $40,000, and a patent with an estimated remaining life of 5 years was overvalued by $70,000.

Small reported the following subsequent to January 1, Year 1:

	Net income	Dividends
Year 1	$ 80,000	$25,000
Year 2 (loss)	(35,000)	10,000
Year 3	100,000	40,000

A test for goodwill impairment on December 31, Year 3, indicated a loss of $19,300 being recorded for Year 3. Large uses the cost method to account for its investment in Small and reported the following for Year 3 for its separate-entity statement of retained earnings:

Retained earnings, beginning	$500,000
Net income	200,000
Dividends	(70,000)
Retained earnings, end	$630,000

Required:

PART A
Prepare the cost-method journal entries of Large for each year.

PART B
Compute the following on the consolidated financial statements for the year ended December 31, Year 3:
(a) Goodwill.
(b) Noncontrolling interest on the balance sheet.
(c) Retained earnings, beginning of year.
(d) Net income.
(e) Noncontrolling interest on the income statement.

Problem 3 On January 1, Year 2, Gros Corporation acquired 70% of the outstanding common shares of Petite Company for a total cost of $84,000. On that date, Petite had $35,000 of common shares and $25,000 of retained earnings. The book values of each of Petite's identifiable assets and liabilities were equal to their fair values except for the following:

	Book value	Fair value
Inventory	$ 45,000	$ 55,000
Equipment	70,000	90,000

The equipment had an estimated useful life of 10 years as at January 1, Year 2, and the entire inventory was sold during Year 2.

Selected account balances from the records of Gros and Petite for the year ended December 31, Year 6 were as follows:

	Gros	Petite
Inventory	$150,000	$ 80,000
Equipment, net	326,000	160,000
Goodwill		
Noncontrolling interest on balance sheet		
Retained earnings, end of year	270,000	50,000
Cost of goods sold	500,000	450,000
Amortization expense	35,000	20,000
Noncontrolling interest on income statement		
Net income	90,000	48,000
Dividends paid	30,000	10,000

Additional Information

- Gros uses the cost method to account for its investment in Petite.
- An independent valuator has estimated that the goodwill associated with Gros's acquisition of Petite had a fair value of $28,000 as of December 31, Year 6. (Note: No impairment losses have been recognized in all years prior to Year 6.)

Required:

(a) Determine the amounts on the Year 6 consolidated financial statements for the above noted accounts.

(b) If the independent appraisal of the fair value of goodwill as at December 31, Year 6, showed an amount of $8,000 instead of the $28,000 indicated above, what would be the impact on the following:
1. Consolidated net income.
2. Consolidated retained earnings.
3. Noncontrolling interest in net income.

Problem 4 Summarized balance sheets of Corner Company and its subsidiary Brook Corporation on December 31, Year 4, are as follows:

	Corner	Brook	Consolidated
Current assets	$ 160,000	$ 700,000	$ 860,000
Investment in Brook (cost)	640,000		
Other assets	600,000	900,000	1,500,000
	$1,400,000	$1,600,000	$2,360,000
Liabilities	$ 800,000	$ 200,000	$1,000,000
Noncontrolling interest	—	—	280,000
Common stock	900,000	600,000	900,000
Retained earnings	(300,000)	800,000	180,000
	$1,400,000	$1,600,000	$2,360,000

On the date that Corner acquired its interest in Brook, there was no purchase discrepancy and the book values of Brook's net assets were equal to fair values. During Year 4, Corner reported a net loss of $60,000 while Brook reported a net income of $140,000. No dividends were declared by either company during Year 4. Corner uses the cost method to account for its investment.

Required:

Compute the following:

(a) The percentage of Brook's shares owned by Corner.

(b) Consolidated net income for Year 4.

(c) Corner's December 31, Year 3, retained earnings if it had used the equity method to account for its investment.

(d) The retained earnings of Brook on the date that Corner acquired its interest in Brook.

Problem 5 Pen Ltd. acquired an 85% interest in Silk Corp. on December 31, Year 1, for $646,000. On that date Silk had common stock of $500,000 and retained earnings of $100,000. The imputed purchase discrepancy was allocated $70,000 to inventory, with the balance to patents being amortized over 10 years. Silk reported net income of $30,000 in Year 2 and $52,000 in Year 3. While no dividends were declared in Year 2, Silk declared a dividend of $15,000 in Year 3.

Pen, which uses the cost method, reported a net income of $28,000 in Year 2 and a net *loss* of $45,000 in Year 3. Pen's retained earnings on December 31, Year 3, were $91,000.

Required:

Compute the following:
(a) Noncontrolling interest in net income for Year 2 and Year 3.
(b) Consolidated net income for Year 2 and Year 3.
(c) Consolidated retained earnings at December 31, Year 3.
(d) Noncontrolling interest at December 31, Year 3.
(e) Investment in Silk at December 31, Year 3, if Pen had used the equity method.
(f) Consolidated patents at December 31, Year 3.

Problem 6 On January 1, Year 3, Grant Corporation bought 80% of the outstanding common shares of Lee Company for $70,000 cash. On that date, Lee had $25,000 of common shares outstanding and $30,000 retained earnings. Also on that date, the book value of each of Lee's identifiable assets and liabilities was equal to its fair value except for the following:

	Book value	Fair value
Inventory	$50,000	$55,000
Patent	10,000	20,000

The patent had an estimated useful life of 5 years at January 1, Year 3, and all of the inventory was sold during Year 3. Grant uses the cost method to account for its investment.

Other Information

- The fair value of goodwill was determined to be $10,000 on December 31, Year 6. Any goodwill impairment occured in Year 6.
- Grant's accounts receivable contain $30,000 owing from Lee.

The following are the separate entity financial statements of Grant and Lee as at December 31, Year 6.

BALANCE SHEETS
December 31, Year 6

	Grant	Lee
Assets		
Cash	$ 5,000	$ 18,000
Accounts receivable	185,000	82,000
Inventory	310,000	100,000
Investment in Lee	70,000	—
Equipment, net	230,000	205,000
Patent, net	—	2,000
	$800,000	$407,000
Liabilities and Shareholders' equity		
Accounts payable	$190,000	$195,000
Other accrued liabilities	60,000	50,000
Income taxes payable	80,000	72,000
Common shares	170,000	25,000
Retained earnings	300,000	65,000
	$800,000	$407,000

STATEMENTS OF INCOME AND RETAINED EARNINGS
Year ended December 31, Year 6

	Grant	Lee
Sales	$900,000	$360,000
Cost of goods sold	(340,000)	(240,000)
Gross margin	560,000	120,000
Amortization expense	(30,000)	(25,000)
Other expenses	(180,000)	(56,000)
Income tax expense	(120,000)	(16,000)
Net income	230,000	23,000
Retained earnings, January 1, Year 6	70,000	42,000
Retained earnings, December 31, Year 6	$300,000	$ 65,000

Required:
Prepare consolidated financial statements.

Problem 7   The following statements of income and retained earnings were prepared by Paris Corporation and Slater Company on December 31 of the current year:

	Paris	Slater
Sales	$900,000	$500,000
Dividend income	60,000	—
	960,000	500,000
Cost of sales	600,000	300,000
Operating expenses	200,000	80,000
	800,000	380,000
Net income	160,000	120,000
Retained earnings, January 1	301,000	584,000
	461,000	704,000
Dividends	150,000	75,000
Retained earnings, December 31	$311,000	$629,000

Paris obtained its 80% interest in Slater eight years ago when Slater had retained earnings of $53,000. The $100,000 purchase discrepancy on acquisition date was allocated entirely to intangible assets with an estimated remaining life of 10 years. Paris uses the cost method to account for its investment.

Required:
Prepare the following statements for the current year:
(a) Consolidated income statement.
(b) Consolidated retained earnings statement.

Problem 8   On July 1, Year 5, Big purchased 80% of the outstanding common shares of Little for $82,080. On that date Little's equipment had a fair value that was $21,600 less than book value. The equipment had an estimated remaining useful life of 8 years. All other assets and liabilities had book values equal to fair values. On June 30, Year 6, goodwill had a fair value of $20,000.

On June 30, Year 6, the following financial statements were prepared. Big uses the cost method to account for its investment.

INCOME STATEMENTS

	Big	Little
Sales	$270,000	$162,000
Investment income	10,800	—
	280,800	162,000
Cost of sales	140,100	94,380
Expenses (misc.)	31,080	28,200
	171,180	122,580
Net income	$109,620	$ 39,420

RETAINED EARNINGS STATEMENTS

	Big	Little
Balance, July 1	$459,000	$ 32,400
Net income	109,620	39,420
	568,620	71,820
Dividends	32,400	13,500
Balance, June 30	$536,220	$ 58,320

BALANCE SHEETS — June 30, Year 6

	Big	Little
Miscellaneous assets	$ 875,940	$128,820
Equipment (net)	102,000	45,600
Investment in Little	82,080	—
	$1,060,020	$174,420
Liabilities	$ 253,800	$ 62,100
Common stock	270,000	54,000
Retained earnings	536,220	58,320
	$1,060,020	$174,420

Required:

(a) Prepare the consolidated financial statements of Big as at June 30, Year 6.

(b) Prepare a schedule showing the changes in noncontrolling interest during the year.

Problem 9   On December 31, Year 2, Palm Inc. purchased 80% of the outstanding common shares of Storm Company for $310,000. At that date, Storm had common shares of $200,000 and retained earnings of $60,000. In negotiating the purchase price, it was agreed that the assets on Storm's balance sheet were fairly valued except for capital assets, which had a $40,000 excess of fair value over net book value. It was also agreed that Storm had unrecognized intangible assets consisting of customer lists that had an estimated value of $24,000.The capital assets had a remaining useful life of 8 years at the acquisition date and the customer lists would be amortized over a 12-year period. Any goodwill arising from this business combination would be tested periodically for impairment. Palm accounts for its investment using the cost method.

Other Information

Impairment tests performed at the end of Year 6 indicated that the goodwill had a fair value of $50,000 and the customer lists had a fair value of $13,750. The impairment loss on these assets occurred entirely in Year 6.

Financial statements for Palm and Storm for the year ended December 31, Year 6, were as follows:

BALANCE SHEETS
December 31, Year 6

	Palm	Storm
Assets		
Cash	$ 20,000	$ 30,000
Accounts receivable	88,000	160,000
Notes receivable	—	10,000
Inventory	100,000	180,000
Capital assets — net	230,000	160,000
Other investments	82,000	22,000
Investment in Storm Company	310,000	—
	$830,000	$562,000
Liabilities and Shareholders' Equity		
Accounts payable	$ 80,000	$ 62,000
Other current liabilities	10,000	50,000
Notes payable	130,000	100,000
Common shares	500,000	200,000
Retained earnings	110,000	150,000
	$830,000	$562,000

STATEMENTS OF INCOME AND RETAINED EARNINGS
Year ended December 31, Year 6

	Palm	Storm
Sales	$870,000	$515,000
Cost of goods sold	(638,000)	(360,000)
Gross profit	232,000	155,000
Amortization expense	(22,000)	(35,000)
Other expenses	(144,000)	(72,000)
Interest and dividend income	30,000	2,000
Net income	96,000	50,000
Retained earnings, beginning of year	50,000	120,000
Dividends declared	(36,000)	(20,000)
Retained earnings, end of year	$110,000	$150,000

Required:

Prepare consolidated financial statements.

Problem 10 On July 1, Year 4, Aaron Co. purchased 80% of the voting shares of Bondi Ltd. for $543,840. The balance sheet of Bondi on that date appears below.

The accounts receivable of Bondi were collected in October Year 4, and the inventory was completely sold by May Year 5. Bondi's fixed assets had a remaining life of 15 years on July 1, Year 4, and the bonds payable mature on June 30, Year 8. The bonds were issued at par on July 1, Year 1. The stated rate of interest on the bonds is 6% payable semi-annually. The market rate of interest was 8% on July 1, Year 4. Tests for impairment of goodwill indicated a loss of $8,329 in Year 5 and $5,553 in Year 6.

BONDI LTD.
BALANCE SHEET
as at July 1, Year 4

	Net book value	Fair market value
Cash	$ 96,000	$ 96,000
Accounts receivable	120,000	144,004
Inventory	180,000	228,000
Fixed assets (net)	540,000	450,000
	$936,000	
Current liabilities	$107,200	107,200
Bonds payable	200,000	186,534
Common shares	120,000	
Retained earnings	508,800	
	$936,000	

The financial statements for Aaron and Bondi at December 31, Year 6, are presented below. Aaron has used the cost method to account for its investment in Bondi.

BALANCE SHEETS

	Aaron	Bondi
Cash	$ 120,000	$ 84,000
Accounts receivable	180,000	114,000
Inventory	300,000	276,000
Fixed assets (net)	720,000	540,000
Investment in Bondi — *same as purch price did not pay div*	543,840	—
Other investments	250,666	—
	$2,114,506	$1,014,000
Current liabilities	$ 180,200	$ 135,800
Bonds payable	315,000	200,000
Common shares	300,600	120,000
Retained earnings	1,318,706	558,200
	$2,114,506	$1,014,000

INCOME STATEMENTS

	Aaron	Bondi
Sales	$1,261,000	$1,200,000
Dividend income from Bondi	4,000	—
Income from other investments	25,000	—
	1,290,000	1,200,000
Cost of goods sold	840,000	1,020,000
Depreciation	60,000	54,000
Interest expense	37,000	26,400
Other expenses	227,000	91,200
	1,164,000	1,191,600
Net income	$ 126,000	$ 8,400

Required:

(a) Prepare the consolidated financial statements for the year ended December 31, Year 6.

(b) Calculate goodwill impairment loss and noncontrolling interest on the consolidated income statement for the year ended December 31, Year 6, under the parent company extension theory.

(c) Calculate goodwill and noncontrolling interest on the consolidated balance sheet at December 31, Year 6, under the parent company extension theory.

Problem 11   Foxx Corp. purchased 75% of the outstanding shares of Rabb Ltd. on January 1, Year 3, at a cost of $117,000. On that date, Rabb had common shares of $50,000 and retained earnings of $30,000. Fair values were equal to carrying values for all the net assets except the following:

	Carrying value	Fair value
Inventory	$30,000	$19,000
Equipment	45,000	69,000
Software	—	15,000

The equipment had an estimated remaining life of 6 years on January 1, Year 3, and the software was to be amortized over 10 years. Foxx uses the cost method to account for its investment. The testing for impairment at December 31, Year 6, yielded the following fair values:

Software	$ 8,000
Goodwill	20,000

The impairment loss on these assets occurred entirely in Year 6.

The following are the financial statements of Foxx Corp. and its subsidiary Rabb Ltd. as at December 31, Year 6:

BALANCE SHEETS
December 31, Year 6

	Foxx Corp.	Rabb Ltd.
Cash	$ —	$ 10,000
Accounts receivable	40,000	30,000
Note receivable	—	40,000
Inventory	66,000	44,000
Equipment, net	220,000	76,000
Land	150,000	30,000
Investment in Rabb	117,000	—
	$593,000	$230,000
Bank indebtedness	$ 90,000	$ —
Accounts payable	70,000	60,000
Notes payable	40,000	—
Common shares	150,000	50,000
Retained earnings	243,000	120,000
	$593,000	$230,000

STATEMENTS OF RETAINED EARNINGS
Year ended December 31, Year 6

	Foxx Corp.	Rabb Ltd.
Retained earnings, January 1, Year 6	$153,000	$ 92,000
Net income	120,000	48,000
Dividends	(30,000)	(20,000)
Retained earnings, December 31, Year 6	$243,000	$120,000

INCOME STATEMENTS
Year ended December 31, Year 6

	Foxx Corp.	Rabb Ltd.
Sales	$821,000	$320,000
Investment income	15,000	3,600
	836,000	323,600
Cost of sales	480,000	200,000
Amortization	40,000	12,000
Miscellaneous expenses	116,000	31,600
Income taxes	80,000	32,000
	716,000	275,600
Net Income	$120,000	$ 48,000

Other Information

The notes payable are intercompany.

Required:

(a) Prepare the Year 6 consolidated financial statements.
(b) Calculate goodwill impairment loss and noncontrolling interest on the consolidated income statement for the year ended December 31, Year 6, under the parent company extension theory.
(c) Calculate goodwill and noncontrolling interest on the consolidated balance sheet at December 31, Year 6, under the parent company extension theory.

Problem 12 The following financial statements were prepared on December 31, Year 6.

BALANCE SHEET

	Pearl	Silver
Cash	$ 300,000	$ 100,000
Accounts receivable	200,000	—
Inventory	2,000,000	420,000
Plant and equipment	3,000,000	2,690,000
Accumulated depreciation	(750,000)	(310,000)
Investment in Silver Company — at cost	2,400,000	—
	$7,150,000	$2,900,000
Liabilities	$ 900,000	$ 300,000
Capital stock	2,850,000	1,600,000
Retained earnings	3,400,000	1,000,000
	$7,150,000	$2,900,000

INCOME STATEMENT

Sales	$4,000,000	$1,000,000
Dividend income	150,000	—
	4,150,000	1,000,000
Cost of sales	2,500,000	400,000
Miscellaneous expenses	320,000	70,000
Depreciation expense	80,000	10,000
Income tax expense	250,000	120,000
	3,150,000	600,000
Net income	$1,000,000	$ 400,000

RETAINED EARNINGS STATEMENT

Balance, January 1	$2,900,000	$ 800,000
Net income	1,000,000	400,000
	3,900,000	1,200,000
Dividends	500,000	200,000
Balance, December 31	$3,400,000	$1,000,000

Other Information

Pearl purchased 75% of the outstanding voting shares of Silver for $2,400,000 on July 1, Year 2, at which time Silver's retained earnings were $400,000. The purchase discrepancy on this date was allocated as follows:

- 30% to undervalued inventory.
- 40% to equipment — remaining life 8 years.
- Balance to goodwill.

During Year 3, a goodwill impairment loss of $70,000 was recognized, and an impairment test conducted as at December 31, Year 6, indicated that a further loss of $20,000 had occurred.

Silver owes Pearl $75,000 on December 31, Year 6.

Required:

(a) Prepare consolidated financial statements on December 31, Year 6.
(b) Calculate goodwill impairment loss and noncontrolling interest on the consolidated income statement for the year ended December 31, Year 6, under the parent company extension theory.
(c) Calculate goodwill and noncontrolling interest on the consolidated balance sheet at December 31, Year 6, under the parent company extension theory.

Problem 13 Balance sheet and income statement data for two affiliated companies for the current year appear below.

Other Information

- Albeniz acquired an 80% interest in Bach on January 1, Year 1, for $272,000. On that date the following information was noted about specific net assets of Bach:

	Book value	Fair value
Inventory	$20,000	$50,000
Land	25,000	45,000
Equipment (estimated life 15 years)	60,000	78,000
Misc. intangibles (estimated life 20 years)	—	42,000

- On January 1, Year 1, Bach had a retained earnings balance of $30,000.
- Albeniz carries its investment at cost.

BALANCE SHEET DATA
as at December 31, Year 4

	Albeniz	Bach
Cash	$ 40,000	$ 21,000
Receivables	92,000	84,000
Inventories	56,000	45,000
Land	20,000	60,000
Plant and equipment	200,000	700,000
Accumulated depreciation	(80,000)	(350,000)
Investment in Bach Company (cost)	272,000	—
Advances to Bach Company	100,000	—
Total assets	$700,000	$560,000
Accounts payable	$130,000	$ 96,500
Advances payable	—	100,000
Common stock	400,000	200,000
Retained earnings	170,000	163,500
Total liabilities and shareholders' equity	$700,000	$560,000

INCOME STATEMENT DATA
Year Ended December 31, Year 4

	Albeniz	Bach
Sales revenues	$600,000	$400,000
Interest income	6,700	—
Dividend income from Bach	6,400	—
Total revenues	613,100	400,000
Cost of goods sold	334,000	225,000
Depreciation expense	20,000	70,000
Selling and administrative expense	207,000	74,000
Interest expense	1,700	6,000
Income taxes expense	20,700	7,500
Total expenses	583,400	382,500
Net income	$ 29,700	$ 17,500

Required:

Prepare the following:
(a) Consolidated income statement.
(b) Consolidated balance sheet.

Problem 14 On January 2, Year 1, Brady Ltd. purchased 80% of the outstanding shares of Partridge Ltd. for $4,120,000. On that date, Partridge's balance sheet and the fair values of its identifiable assets and liabilities appear below.

   The patents had a remaining life of 10 years on the acquisition date. The bonds were issued at par on January 1, Year 1, and mature on December 31, Year 10. Goodwill impairment losses were recorded as follows:

- Year 1: $25,000.
- Year 3: $12,500.

	Book value	Fair value
Cash	$ 500,000	$ 500,000
Accounts receivable	1,500,000	1,500,000
Inventory	2,000,000	2,200,000
Plant and equipment (net)	4,500,000	4,500,000
Patents (net)	1,000,000	1,500,000
	$9,500,000	
Accounts payable	$2,000,000	2,000,000
10% bonds payable	3,000,000	3,300,000
Common stock	2,000,000	
Retained earnings	2,500,000	
	$9,500,000	

On December 31, Year 3, the financial statements of the two companies are as follows:

BALANCE SHEETS

	Brady	Partridge
Cash	$ 400,000	$ 600,000
Accounts receivable	1,000,000	1,300,000
Inventory	4,600,000	1,900,000
Plant and equipment (net)	8,000,000	5,000,000
Patents (net)	—	700,000
Investment in Partridge Ltd. (cost)	4,120,000	—
	$18,120,000	$9,500,000
Accounts payable	$ 3,000,000	$1,400,000
Bonds payable	4,000,000	3,000,000
Common stock	5,000,000	2,000,000
Retained earnings	6,120,000	3,100,000
	$18,120,000	$9,500,000

INCOME STATEMENTS

	Brady	Partridge
Sales	$10,000,000	$5,000,000
Dividend revenue from Partridge	80,000	—
	10,080,000	5,000,000
Cost of goods sold	7,000,000	3,000,000
Depreciation expense	900,000	400,000
Patent amortization expense	—	100,000
Interest expense	480,000	300,000
Other expenses	680,000	850,000
Income taxes	600,000	150,000
	9,660,000	4,800,000
Net income	$ 420,000	$ 200,000

Required:

(a) Prepare consolidated financial statements on December 31, Year 3.
(b) If Brady had used the equity method, which financial statement items would have amounts different from those shown? Compute the equity-method balances of these items.

Chapter ⑦ Intercompany Inventory and Land Profits

LEARNING OBJECTIVES

After studying this chapter, you should be able to do the following:

- Describe the effect on consolidated net income of the elimination of both intercompany revenues (and expenses) and intercompany asset profits.
- Prepare consolidated financial statements that reflect the elimination of upstream and downstream intercompany profits in inventory and land.
- Prepare consolidated financial statements that reflect the realization of upstream and downstream intercompany profits in inventory and land that were held back in previous periods.
- Explain how the revenue recognition and matching principles are used to support adjustments for intercompany transactions when preparing consolidated financial statements.
- Prepare the journal entries under the equity method to reflect the elimination and subsequent realization of intercompany profits in inventory and land.

INTRODUCTION

In previous discussions we stressed that consolidated financial statements report the activities of a group of affiliated companies as if they constitute a single company. While these companies may transact business with one another as well as with nonaffiliated companies, all intercompany transactions are eliminated so that the final consolidated statements reflect only transactions with entities outside the group. The elimination of intercompany transactions and unrealized profit is one of the most significant problems encountered in the consolidation process. The volume of transfers within most large enterprises can be quite large. For example, Inco Limited, a world leader in nickel production, reported intersegment revenue of $709 million in 2005. Such transactions are especially common in companies that have been constructed as a vertically integrated chain of organizations. These entities reduce their costs by developing affiliations in which one operation furnishes products to another.

Intercompany transactions are also used to shift income from one jurisdiction to another to minimize or avoid paying income taxes. As a result, the Canadian federal government in 2006 introduced legislation to prevent Canadian companies from trying to avoid paying income tax by using offshore tax havens such as non-resident trusts and foreign investment entities. The government felt that multinational companies operating in Canada have avoided "hundreds of millions" of dollars in taxes over the past decade through the use of tax havens.

Chapter 5 illustrated the elimination of intercompany receivables and payables. The next two chapters focus on the elimination of all other transactions that occur between a parent and its subsidiaries or between two or more subsidiaries that have a common parent.

Intercompany Revenue and Expenses

Intercompany Sales and Purchases

The following simple example will be used to illustrate the basic idea behind the elimination of intercompany sales and purchases in the preparation of a consolidated income statement.

The transaction with the dealer is an arm's-length transaction (i.e., with an outsider).

Let your imagination stray a bit and suppose that when you went shopping for groceries, the change you received from the cashier included some dollar coins. When you got home you noticed that the loon on one of these coins was upside down. You took the coin to a dealer and learned that some coins with this flaw had been accidentally released into circulation by the Royal Canadian Mint and as a result were worth substantially more than their face value. The dealer offered you $41 for this dollar coin, which you accepted. It is obvious that you made a profit of $40 on this transaction. An income statement showing only this transaction would appear as follows:

Revenue is recognized when it is earned in a transaction with an outsider in accordance with the revenue recognition principle.

INCOME STATEMENT — COIN TRANSACTION

Sales	$41
Cost of sales	1
Net income	$40

Now let your imagination stray even farther and assume that the following events took place between the time you received the coin from the supermarket and the time you sold it to the coin dealer. Your pants have four pockets. Let's call them pocket 1, pocket 2, pocket 3, and pocket 4. Pocket 1 received the coin from the supermarket and sold it to pocket 2 for $10. Pocket 2 sold the coin to pocket 3 for $15. Pocket 3 sold the coin to pocket 4 for $25, and then pocket 4 sold the coin to the dealer for $41. Has any part of the transaction changed as far as you (as an entity) are concerned? The answer of course is no. You still had sales of $41, cost of goods sold of $1, and a net income of $40. But assume that each of your pockets recorded its part in the transaction and prepared an income statement:

The cost of the coin is expensed in the same period as the revenue in accordance with the matching principle.

Income was recorded when the coin was moved from one pocket to another.

INCOME STATEMENTS OF FOUR POCKETS

	Pocket 1	Pocket 2	Pocket 3	Pocket 4
Sales	$10	$15	$25	$41
Cost of goods sold	1	10	15	25
Net income	$ 9	$ 5	$10	$16

The arrows indicate the interpocket transactions that took place. Also, the sum of the net incomes of your four pockets is equal to your net income of $40. We should therefore be able to prepare an income statement for you (as an entity) by combining the components of the income statements of your four pockets as follows:

COMBINED INCOME STATEMENT

Sales (10 + 15 + 25 + 41)	$91
Cost of goods sold (1 + 10 + 15 + 25)	51
Net income	$40

Income should only be recognized when it is earned in a transaction with an outsider.

However, sales and cost of goods sold are not the correct amounts because they contain the interpocket sales and purchases. Both items should reflect only sales to and purchases from *outside* the entity. If we eliminate the interpocket sales and purchases, we will have an income statement that reflects only transactions that you as an entity incurred with others outside the entity. This statement can be prepared as follows:

COMBINED INCOME STATEMENT — ENTITY

	Total of four pockets	Interpocket sales & purchases	Total
Sales	$91	$50	$41
Cost of goods sold	51	50	1
Net income	$40	$ 0	$40

Notice that if we eliminate an equal amount of revenue and expense from an income statement, the resultant net income remains unchanged.

Your four pockets in this example are similar in all respects to a parent company and its subsidiary companies. Let us assume that a parent company (P) has holdings in three subsidiaries as follows: P owns 80 percent of S1, 90 percent of S2, and 75 percent of S3. The coin transactions previously illustrated were carried out by P and its three subsidiaries. These were the only transactions that took place during the current year. At the year-end the parent and its subsidiaries prepared the following income statements:

Only S3 had a transaction with an outsider.

INCOME STATEMENTS — PARENT AND SUBSIDIARIES

	P	S1	S2	S3
Sales	$10	$15	$25	$41
Cost of goods sold	1	10	15	25
Net income	$ 9	$ 5	$10	$16

We are assuming that P uses the equity method but has made no entries during the current year and that all purchase discrepancies have been fully amortized in prior years.

Before preparing a consolidated income statement, we can calculate consolidated net income as follows:

P's net income $ 9

	S1	S2	S3	Total	
Subsidiary net income	$ 5	$10	$16	$31	
P's ownership	80%	90%	75%		
Share of subsidiary's net income	$ 4	$ 9	$12		25
Consolidated net income					$34

Suppose we prepare a consolidated income statement without eliminating intercompany sales and purchases, in the following manner:

P AND SUBSIDIARIES
CONSOLIDATED INCOME STATEMENT
for Current Year

Sales and cost of sales are overstated because intercompany sales and purchases have not yet been eliminated.

Sales (10 + 15 + 25 + 41)	$91
Cost of goods sold (1 + 10 + 15 + 25)	51
Net income — entity	40
Less noncontrolling interest (see calculation below)	6
Net income	$34

CALCULATION OF NONCONTROLLING INTEREST

S1 (20% × 5)	$1
S2 (10% × 10)	1
S3 (25% × 16)	4
	$6

Note that the net income of the consolidated entity is made up of the net incomes of the parent and its three subsidiaries. But we have not eliminated the intercompany sales and purchases that took place during the year. If we eliminate these intercompany transactions, the bottom-line net income earned by the consolidated entity will not change. Noncontrolling interest and consolidated net income are only *allocations* of the entity's net income, so they also will not be affected by the elimination of these intercompany sales and purchases. The consolidated income statement after the elimination of intercompany sales and purchases would be as follows:

CONSOLIDATED INCOME STATEMENT
(after elimination of intercompany items)

The consolidated income statement now reflects only the transactions with outsiders.

Sales	(91 – 50)	$41
Cost of goods sold	(51 – 50)	1
Net income — entity		40
Less noncontrolling interest		6
Net income		$34

Other Examples of Intercompany Revenue and Expenses

Suppose the parent company loans $100,000 to the subsidiary company and receives a note payable on demand with interest at 10 percent. The transactions would be recorded as follows:

	Parent Company			**Subsidiary Company**		
These transactions are recorded on the separate-entity books of the parent and subsidiary.	Note receivable	100,000		Cash	100,000	
	Cash		100,000	Note payable		100,000

To record intercompany borrowings on January 1 of the current year

	Cash	10,000		Interest expense	10,000	
	Interest revenue		10,000	Cash		10,000

To record the intercompany payment of interest on December 31 of the current year

From the consolidated entity's point of view, all that has happened is that cash has been transferred from one bank account to another. No revenue has been earned, no expense has been incurred, and there are no receivables or payables with parties outside of the consolidated entity. The elimination of $10,000 interest revenue and interest expense on the consolidated income statement does not change the net income of the consolidated entity. If total net income is not affected, then the amount allocated to the noncontrolling and controlling interest is also not affected. On the consolidated balance sheet, we eliminate $100,000 from notes receivable and notes payable. An equal elimination of assets and liabilities on a balance sheet leaves the amounts of the two equities (noncontrolling interest and controlling interest) unchanged.

Consolidated net income does not change when we eliminate an equal amount of revenue and expense.

Note also that if the roles are reversed and the *subsidiary* loans $100,000 to the *parent*, the eliminations on the consolidated income statement and balance sheet are the same and have no effect on the amount of the noncontrolling interest appearing on each statement.

Intercompany Management Fees Often the parent will charge its subsidiary companies a yearly management fee as a means of allocating head office costs to all the companies within the group. (We will not discuss the pros and cons of this procedure here. Readers who are interested in the reasons for, and effectiveness of, allocations of this nature are advised to consult a management accounting textbook.) From an external reporting point of view, we have intercompany revenues and expenses that must be eliminated on the consolidated income statement.

Intercompany Rentals Occasionally buildings or equipment owned by one company are used by another company within the group. Rather than transfer legal title, the companies agree on a yearly rental to be charged. In such cases, intercompany rental revenues and expenses must be eliminated from the consolidated income statement.

In summary, the following intercompany revenues and expenses are eliminated from the consolidated income statement:

The elimination entries are recorded on the consolidated working papers and not in the separate-entity books of the parent and subsidiary.

- Intercompany sales and purchases;
- Intercompany interest revenue and expense;
- Intercompany management fee revenue and expense;
- Intercompany rental revenue and expense.

These items are eliminated to ensure that revenue is only recognized when it is earned with a party outside of the consolidated entity and to stop the double-counting of revenues and expenses. This has no effect on the calculation of the noncontrolling interest in the net income of the subsidiary companies.

DISCUSSION QUESTION

Why Is It Not Revenue?

You, the controller, recently had the following discussion with the president:

President: I just don't understand why we can't recognize the revenue from the intercompany sale of inventory on the consolidated financial statements. The subsidiary company sold the goods to the parent at fair value and received the cash for the sale. We need to record the profit on this sale in order to maintain a steady earnings growth for our company. Otherwise, the bank will be concerned about our ability to repay the loan.

Controller: You are right that the sub has received the cash but that is not the main criterion for determining when to recognize the revenue. Furthermore, you need to understand that the consolidated financial statements are different than the individual financial statements for the parent and subsidiary.

President: I have never understood why we need to prepare consolidated financial statements. It is just extra work. Who uses these statements? Furthermore, the profit on the intercompany transaction should be reported on the income statement because tax had to be paid on this profit. Surely, if tax is paid, the profit is legitimate.

Controller: Once again, cash payments do not determine when we report income tax expense on the income statement. How about we get together for lunch tomorrow? I will prepare a brief presentation to illustrate the difference between the income for the parent and subsidiary compared to income for the consolidated entity and will explain how all of these statements properly apply generally accepted accounting principles for revenue and expense recognition.

As part of the presentation, you decided to prepare monthly income statements for the parent, subsidiary, and consolidated entity for the following situation:

* Parent owns 100% of the subsidiary
* Subsidiary buys goods for $100 in July and sells them to the parent in August at a markup of 20% of cost
* In September, Parent sells these goods at a markup of 20% of selling price
* Both companies pay income tax at the rate of 40%

Required:

Prepare your presentation to the president.

Intercompany Profits in Assets

The consolidated financial statements should reflect only the results of transactions with outsiders.

When one affiliated company sells assets to another affiliated company, it is possible that the profit or loss recorded on the transaction has not been realized from the point of view of the consolidated entity. If the purchasing affiliate has sold these assets outside the group, all profits (losses) recorded are realized. If, however, all or a portion of these assets have not been sold outside the group, we must eliminate the remaining intercompany profit (loss) from the consolidated statements. The intercompany profit (loss) will be realized for consolidation purposes during the accounting period in which the particular asset is sold to outsiders. The sale to outsiders may also result in an additional profit (loss) that is not adjusted in the consolidation process. Three types of unrealized intercompany profits (losses) are eliminated:

- Profits in inventory;
- Profits in nondepreciable assets;
- Profits in depreciable assets.

The first two of these will be discussed in this chapter; the last one in Chapter 8.

The examples that follow illustrate the holdback of unrealized intercompany profits in one accounting period and the realization of the profit in a subsequent period. The holdback and realization of intercompany losses will not be illustrated. Note, however, that the same principles apply.

Downstream and upstream are defined by who the seller is.

When the parent sells to the subsidiary, the transaction is referred to as a downstream transaction. When the subsidiary sells to the parent or another subsidiary, the transaction is referred to as an upstream transaction.

As a means of illustrating the concepts involved in the elimination of intercompany profits, we will use as a simple example the financial statements of a parent and its 90-percent owned subsidiary one year after the acquisition date. We will prepare the consolidated financial statements as if there were no intercompany transactions between the two companies. We will then introduce the concept of unrealized profits that were "overlooked" when we prepared the consolidated statements, and redo the consolidation so that the effects and differences can be observed.

On January 1, Year 1, Parent Company acquired 90 percent of the common shares of Sub Incorporated for $11,250. On that date Sub had common stock of $8,000 and retained earnings of $4,500, and there were no differences between the fair values and the book values of its identifiable net assets. The purchase discrepancy was calculated as follows:

Cost of 90% of Sub		$11,250
Imputed value of 100% of Sub		$12,500
Book value of Sub		
Common stock	8,000	
Retained earnings	4,500	
		12,500
Purchase discrepancy		$ 0

On December 31, Year 1, Parent reported earnings from its own operations of $3,400 and declared dividends of $2,000. Sub reported a net income of $1,700 and did not declare dividends during the year. Parent accounts for its investment using the cost method, and because there were no dividends declared by Sub, no entry was made on December 31, Year 1.

The financial statements of Parent and Sub as at December 31, Year 1, are presented in Exhibit 7.1.

Because Parent has used the cost method, we calculate consolidated net income and the noncontrolling interest's share of the entity's net income before preparing the consolidated income statement. We also need to calculate noncontrolling interest on the consolidated balance sheet at the end of Year 1. These calculations are shown in Exhibit 7.2.

Exhibit 7.1

YEAR 1 INCOME STATEMENTS

	Parent	Sub
Sales	$20,000	$ 8,000
Cost of sales	13,000	4,300
Miscellaneous expenses	1,400	900
Income tax expense	2,200	1,100
	16,600	6,300
Net income	$ 3,400	$ 1,700

These are the separate-entity statements of the parent and subsidiary.

YEAR 1 RETAINED EARNINGS STATEMENTS

	Parent	Sub
Balance, January 1	$12,000	$ 4,500
Net income	3,400	1,700
	15,400	6,200
Dividends	2,000	—
Balance, December 31	$13,400	$ 6,200

BALANCE SHEETS — December 31, Year 1

	Parent	Sub
Assets (miscellaneous)	$21,650	$19,200
Inventory	7,500	4,000
Investment in Sub Inc.	11,250	—
	$40,400	$23,200
Liabilities	$12,000	$ 9,000
Common stock	15,000	8,000
Retained earnings	13,400	6,200
	$40,400	$23,200

The parent uses the cost method in its separate-entity records.

Exhibit 7.2

CALCULATION OF CONSOLIDATED NET INCOME — Year 1

NCI on the income statement is based on the subsidiary's income for the year.

Net income — Parent Co.		$3,400
Net income — Sub Inc.	1,700	
Parent Co.'s share	90%	1,530
Consolidated net income		$4,930 (a)
Noncontrolling interest (10% × 1,700)		$ 170 (b)

CALCULATION OF NONCONTROLLING INTEREST
December 31, Year 1

NCI on the balance sheet is based on the subsidiary's shareholders' equity at the end of the year.

Shareholders' equity — Sub Inc.	
Common stock	$8,000
Retained earnings	6,200
	14,200
Noncontrolling interest's share	10%
	$1,420 (c)

The consolidated income statement is prepared by combining the revenues and expenses of the two companies and deducting the noncontrolling interest from the income of the entity (Exhibit 7.3). In examining both the consolidated income statement (Exhibit 7.3) and the calculation of consolidated net income (Exhibit 7.2), the reader will note the following:

Net income — Parent Co.	$3,400
Plus net income — Sub Inc.	1,700
Equals net income — entity	$5,100

The consolidated retained earnings statement is made up of the following: the January 1 retained earnings of Parent, consolidated net income, and the dividends of Parent (see Exhibit 7.3).

Exhibit 7.3

Year 1 Consolidated Statements
(direct approach)

PARENT COMPANY
CONSOLIDATED INCOME STATEMENT
for the Year Ended December 31, Year 1

The subsidiary's income is added to the parent's income on a line-by-line basis.

Sales (20,000 + 8,000)	$28,000
Cost of sales (13,000 + 4,300)	17,300
Miscellaneous expenses (1,400 + 900)	2,300
Income tax expenses (2,200 + 1,100)	3,300
	22,900
Net income — entity	5,100
Less noncontrolling interest **(2b)**	170
Net income **(2a)**	$ 4,930

PARENT COMPANY
CONSOLIDATED RETAINED EARNINGS STATEMENT
for the Year Ended December 31, Year 1

Balance, January 1	$12,000
Net income	4,930
	16,930
Dividends	2,000
Balance, December 31	$14,930

PARENT COMPANY
CONSOLIDATED BALANCE SHEET
December 31, Year 1

The subsidiary's assets and liabilities are added to the parent's assets and liabilities on a line-by-line basis.

Assets — miscellaneous (21,650 + 19,200)	$40,850
Inventory (7,500 + 4,000)	11,500
	$52,350
Liabilities (12,000 + 9,000)	$21,000
Common stock	15,000
Retained earnings	14,930
Noncontrolling interest **(2c)**	1,420
	$52,350

The consolidated balance sheet is prepared by ignoring the parent's investment account and the shareholders' equity of the subsidiary, and combining the assets and liabilities of the two companies. Shareholders' equity is made up of the common stock of the parent and consolidated retained earnings. The calculated amount for noncontrolling interest is presented as a component of shareholders' equity in the balance sheet (see Exhibit 7.3).

Intercompany Inventory Profits: Subsidiary Selling (Upstream Transactions)

From the Sub's separate entity perspective, it earned the income on the sale to the Parent.

We now assume that there were intercompany transactions during Year 1 that were overlooked when the consolidated statements were prepared. These transactions were as follows:

1. During Year 1, Sub made sales to Parent amounting to $5,000 at a gross profit rate of 30 percent.

2. At the end of Year 1, Parent's inventory contained items purchased from Sub for $2,000.

3. Sub paid (or accrued) income tax on its taxable income at a rate of 40 percent.

Holdback of Inventory Profits — Year 1   It should be noted that the subsidiary recorded a gross profit of $1,500 (30% × $5,000) on its sales to the parent during the year and paid income tax of $600 (40% × $1,500) on this profit. If the parent had sold all of its intercompany purchases to customers outside the entity, this $1,500 gross profit would be considered realized from the point of view of this consolidated single entity. But the parent's inventory contains items purchased from the subsidiary for $2,000. There is an unrealized intercompany profit of $600 (30% × $2,000) in this inventory, which must be held back from consolidated income in Year 1 and realized in the period in which it is sold to outsiders. In addition, the $240 tax expense relating to this profit must also be held back from the Year 1 consolidated income statement. When this $600 gross profit is realized on a future consolidated income statement, the income tax expense will be matched on that statement with the profit realized.

From the consolidated perspective, some of Sub's income was not realized with an outsider.

Not only do we have to hold back an unrealized profit for consolidation purposes, but also we must make an adjustment for the income taxes relating to that profit. Since income taxes are computed at the individual company level rather than at the consolidated entity level, the company that recorded the profit also paid (or accrued) income taxes on that profit, and the income tax expense on its income statement reflects this. The matching of expenses with revenues is a basic accounting concept; the adjustment made for income taxes on intercompany profits is a perfect example of this matching process. Section 1000 of the *Handbook* reinforces this concept as follows:

Income tax should be expensed in the same period as revenue.

> Expenses that are linked to revenue generating activities in a cause-and-effect relationship are normally matched with revenue in the accounting period in which the revenue is recognized. [1000.51]

The difference between the buyer's tax basis and the cost of transferred assets as reported in the consolidated financial statements technically meets the definition of

From a consolidated perspective, some of the tax paid by the subsidiary was prepaid since the income was not yet earned.

a temporary difference and would normally give rise to future income taxes. However, Section 3465[1] explicitly states:

> a future income tax liability or asset should not be recognized in the consolidated financial statements for a temporary difference arising between the tax basis of the asset in the buyer's tax jurisdiction and its cost as reported in the consolidated financial statements. Any taxes paid or recovered by the transferor as a result of the transfer should be recorded as an asset or liability in the consolidated financial statements until the gain or loss is recognized by the consolidated entity. [3465.35]

We will refer to the tax assets and liabilities arising from intercompany transactions as deferred charge–income taxes for the assets and deferred credit–income taxes for the liabilities.

Using the direct approach, we will now prepare the Year 1 consolidated statements after making the consolidation adjustments shown in Exhibit 7.4.

Exhibit 7.4

INTERCOMPANY TRANSACTIONS

Intercompany sales and purchases		$5,000 **(a)**
Intercompany inventory profits:		
Ending inventory — Sub Inc. selling		$ 600 **(b)**
Income tax (40%)		240 **(c)**
After-tax profit		$ 360 **(d)**

CALCULATION OF CONSOLIDATED NET INCOME — Year 1

The unrealized profit is always deducted from the selling company's income

Net income — Parent Co.		$3,400
Net income — Sub Inc.	1,700	
Less after-tax profit in ending inventory **(4d)**	360	
Adjusted net income — Sub Inc.	1,340	
Parent Co.'s share	90%	1,206
Consolidated net income		$4,606 **(e)**
Noncontrolling interest (10% × 1,340)		$ 134 **(f)**

CALCULATION OF NONCONTROLLING INTEREST
December 31, Year 1

NCI on the consolidated balance sheet is affected when there are unrealized profits on upstream transactions at the end of the year.

Shareholders' equity — Sub Inc.	
Common stock	$ 8,000
Retained earnings	6,200
	14,200
Less after-tax profit in ending inventory	360
Adjusted shareholders' equity	13,840
Noncontrolling interest's share	10%
	$ 1,384 **(g)**

Remember that the purpose of the calculation of consolidated net income is to

---

[1] Section 3465 also adds some complications to the valuation of assets in a business combination that is accounted for as a purchase. These requirements with respect to business combinations will be discussed in Chapter 10.

NCI is affected when there is unrealized profit on upstream transactions.

adjust the parent's cost-method net income to what it would have been under the equity method. Notice that the after-tax profit is deducted from the net income of Sub, because the subsidiary was the selling company and its net income contains this profit being held back for consolidation purposes. Note also that the noncontrolling interest's share of the Year 1 income is based on the *adjusted income* of Sub.

Exhibit 7.5 illustrates the preparation of the Year 1 consolidated financial statements.

The first two numbers in brackets are from the statements of Parent and Sub. Any additional numbers, which are in boldface and labelled, are adjustments made to eliminate the intercompany transactions. The eliminations made on the income statement require further elaboration:

Exhibit 7.5

Year 1 Consolidated Statements
Elimination of Intercompany Profits in Inventory
(direct approach)

PARENT COMPANY
CONSOLIDATED INCOME STATEMENT
for the Year Ended December 31, Year 1

The unrealized profits are eliminated on the consolidated financial statements.

Sales (20,000 + 8,000 – **(4a) 5,000**)	$23,000
Cost of sales (13,000 + 4,300 **– (4a) 5,000 + (4b) 600**)	12,900
Miscellaneous expenses (1,400 + 900)	2,300
Income tax expense (2,200 + 1,100 – **(4c) 240**)	3,060
	18,260
Net income — entity	4,740
Less noncontrolling interest **(4f)**	134
Net income **(4e)**	$ 4,606

PARENT COMPANY
CONSOLIDATED RETAINED EARNINGS STATEMENT
for the Year Ended December 31, Year 1

Balance, January 1	$12,000
Net income	4,606
	16,606
Dividends	2,000
Balance, December 31	$14,606

PARENT COMPANY
CONSOLIDATED BALANCE SHEET
December 31, Year 1

By eliminating the unrealized profit, inventory is now stated at cost to the consolidated entity.

Assets — miscellaneous (21,650 + 19,200)	$40,850
Inventory (7,500 + 4,000 **– (4b) 600**)	10,900
Deferred charge — income taxes (0 + 0 **+ (4c) 240**)	240
	$51,990
Liabilities (12,000 + 9,000)	$21,000
Common stock	15,000
Retained earnings	14,606
Noncontrolling interest **(4g)**	1,384
	$51,990

1. The eliminations of intercompany sales and purchases are equal reductions of revenues and expenses that do not change the net income of the consolidated entity or the amount allocated to the noncontrolling and controlling equities.

2. To hold back the gross profit of $600 from the consolidated entity's net income, we increase cost of goods sold by $600. The reasoning is as follows:

   (a) Cost of goods sold is made up of opening inventory, plus purchases, less ending inventory.

   (b) The ending inventory contains the $600 gross profit.

   (c) If we subtract the $600 profit from the ending inventory, the resulting amount represents cost to the consolidated entity.

   (d) A reduction of $600 from ending inventory increases cost of goods sold by $600.

   (e) This increase to cost of goods sold reduces the before-tax net income earned by the entity by $600.

   The $600 adjustment is similar to the adjustment we studied in Intermediate Accounting to correct errors in inventory. If you have difficulty understanding the adjustments for unrealized profits in inventory, you may want to go back to your intermediate accounting text to review the adjustment for errors in inventory.

3. Because the entity's before-tax net income has been reduced by $600, it is necessary to reduce the income tax expense (the tax paid on the profit held back) by $240.

4. A reduction of income tax expense increases the net income of the consolidated entity.

5. A $600 increase in cost of goods sold, together with a $240 reduction in income tax expense, results in the after-tax profit of $360 being removed from the entity's net income.

When ending inventory is overstated, cost of sales is understated.

When cost of sales is increased, income decreases, and income tax expense should decrease.

The unrealized profits are not eliminated on the separate-entity financial statements.

It is important to realize that all of the above adjustments are being made on the consolidated working papers and not on the separate entity financial statements. What was recorded on the subsidiary's own books was legitimate from its own perspective. But from the consolidated perspective, some of the profit was not yet realized. It must be eliminated from the consolidated financial statements.

Again it is important to note the following components of the entity's net income:

Net Income — Parent Co.	$3,400
Adjusted net income — Sub Inc.	1,340
Net income — entity	$4,740

The consolidated retained earnings statement has been prepared in the normal manner. Retained earnings at the beginning of the year are the parent's retained earnings at the date of acquisition; net income is taken from the consolidated income statement; and dividends are the parent's dividends.

The only new concepts relating to the preparation of the consolidated balance sheet involve the adjustments made on the asset side (a) to eliminate the unrealized profit in inventory and (b) to set up the deferred charge — income taxes on this profit. These adjustments are shown in boldface in Exhibit 7.5 and are labelled to correspond with the calculations in Exhibit 7.4. The reasons for these adjustments can be further explained as follows:

The unrealized profit is deducted from the inventory to bring inventory back to its original cost in accordance with the historical cost principle.

1. The holdback of the $600 gross profit on the consolidated income statement was accomplished by reducing the amount of ending inventory in calculating the cost of goods sold. (A reduction in ending inventory increases cost of goods sold.) The ending inventory in the cost of goods sold calculation is the inventory balance on the consolidated balance sheet. Removing the $600 gross profit from the asset results in the consolidated inventory being reflected at cost to the entity.

Income tax will be expensed when the profit is realized in accordance with the matching principle.

2. On the consolidated income statement, we reduced income tax expense by $240, representing the tax paid on the gross profit. As far as the consolidated entity is concerned, this tax of $240 was paid prematurely because the income was not yet earned. The tax will become an expense when the inventory is sold to outsiders. These deferred charge–income taxes are "added into" the assets on the consolidated balance sheet. (The illustration assumes that neither the parent nor the subsidiary had deferred income taxes on their individual balance sheets.)

3. A reduction of $600 from inventory and a $240 increase in deferred charge–income taxes results in a net reduction to consolidated assets of $360, which equals the $360 reduction that has been made on the equity side.

Equity Method Journal Entries   While our example has assumed that Parent uses the cost method to account for its investment, it is useful to see where the differences would lie if the equity method were used. If Parent was using the equity method, the following journal entries would be made on December 31, Year 1:

The equity method captures the net effect of all consolidation entries.

Investment in Sub Inc.	1,530	
Investment income		1,530
90% of the net income of Sub Inc.		
(90% × 1,700 = 1,530)		
Investment income	324	
Investment in Sub Inc.		324
To hold back 90% of the after-tax inventory profit recorded		
by Sub Inc. (90% × 360 = 324)		

After these entries were posted, the two related equity-method accounts of Parent would show the following changes and balances:

	Investment in Sub Inc.	Investment income
January 1, Year 1	$11,250	$ —
December 31, Year 1		
Income from Sub Inc.	1,530	1,530
After-tax inventory profit (held back)	(324)	(324)
Balance, December 31, Year 1	$12,456	$1,206

The parent's income under the equity method should be equal to consolidated net income.

Parent's total income under the equity method would be $4,606 consisting of $3,400 from their own operations as reported in Exhibit 7.1 plus investment income of $1,206 as reported above. This income of $4,606 should be and is equal to consolidated net income.

Appendix 7A at the end of this chapter illustrates the working-paper approach to the preparation of the Year 1 consolidated financial statements when the equity and cost methods are used.

In Year 2, the parent sold its Year 1 inventory to outsiders.

Realization of Inventory Profits — Year 2 The previous example illustrated the holdback of an unrealized intercompany inventory profit in Year 1. We will continue our example of Parent Company and Sub Inc. by looking at the events that transpired in Year 2. On December 31, Year 2, Parent reported earnings from its own operations of $4,050 and declared dividends of $2,500. Sub reported a net income of $3,100 and again did not declare a dividend. Using the cost method, Parent made no journal entries with respect to the operations of Sub. During Year 2, there were no intercompany transactions, and at year end, the inventory of Parent contained no items purchased from Sub. In other words, the December 31, Year 1, inventory of Parent was sold during Year 2, and the unrealized profit that was held back for consolidated purposes in Year 1 will have to be realized in Year 2.

The financial statements of Parent and Sub are presented in Exhibit 7.6.

Exhibit 7.6

YEAR 2 INCOME STATEMENTS

	Parent	Sub
	Parent	*Sub*
Sales	$25,000	$12,000
Cost of sales	16,000	5,500
Miscellaneous expenses	2,350	1,400
Income tax expense	2,600	2,000
	20,950	8,900
Net income	$ 4,050	$ 3,100

Cost of sales for the parent includes the inflated inventory value at the beginning of the year.

YEAR 2 RETAINED EARNINGS STATEMENTS

	Parent	Sub
Balance, January 1	$13,400	$ 6,200
Net income	4,050	3,100
	17,450	9,300
Dividends	2,500	—
Balance, December 31	$14,950	$ 9,300

The sub's retained earnings at the beginning of the year includes the unrealized profit at the end of Year 1.

BALANCE SHEETS — December 31, Year 2

	Parent	Sub
Assets (miscellaneous)	$22,800	$20,800
Inventory	9,900	7,500
Investment in Sub Inc.	11,250	—
	$43,950	$28,300
Liabilities	$14,000	$11,000
Common stock	15,000	8,000
Retained earnings	14,950	9,300
	$43,950	$28,300

Inventory at the end of Year 2 does not include any unrealized profit.

Before we prepare the Year 2 consolidated income statement, we must carry out the calculations shown in Exhibit 7.7.

Exhibit 7.7

INTERCOMPANY INVENTORY PROFITS — Year 2

Intercompany inventory profits:	
Opening inventory — Sub Inc. selling	$600 (a)
Income tax (40%)	240 (b)
After-tax profit	$360 (c)

CALCULATION OF CONSOLIDATED NET INCOME — Year 2

When the profits are realized, they are credited to the income of the original seller.

Net income — Parent Co.		$4,050
Net income — Sub Inc.	3,100	
Add after-tax profit in opening inventory (7c)	360	
Adjusted net income — Sub Inc.	3,460	
Parent Co.'s share	90%	3,114
Consolidated net income		$7,164 (d)
Noncontrolling interest (10% × 3,460)		$ 346 (e)

CALCULATION OF CONSOLIDATED RETAINED EARNINGS
January 1, Year 2

The unrealized profit at the end of Year 1 must be eliminated when calculating consolidated retained earnings at the beginning of Year 2.

Retained earnings — Parent Co.		$13,400
Retained earnings — Sub Inc.	6,200	
Acquisition retained earnings	4,500	
Increase since acquisition	1,700	
Less profit in opening inventory (7c)	360	
Adjusted increase since acquisition	1,340	
Parent Co.'s share	90%	1,206
Consolidated retained earnings		$14,606 (f)

CALCULATION OF NONCONTROLLING INTEREST
December 31, Year 2

All of subsidiary's shareholders' equity is legitimate from a consolidated perspective at the end of Year 2.

Capital stock — Sub Inc.	$ 8,000
Retained earnings — Sub Inc.	9,300
	17,300
	10%
	$ 1,730 (g)

The after-tax inventory profit of $360 that was held back in Year 1 is being realized in Year 2 and is added to the net income of Sub, because the subsidiary was the company that originally recorded the profit. Note that the noncontrolling interest share of the Year 2 net income of Sub is based on the *adjusted net income* of that company.

Exhibit 7.8 illustrates the preparation of the Year 2 consolidated financial statements using the *direct* approach.

In preparing the Year 2 consolidated income statement, we make consolidation adjustments that bring the original before-tax profit into the income statement and increase income tax expense for the tax on this profit. The eliminations (i.e., adjustments) made are shown in boldface and are labelled. The elimination entries are explained as follows:

1. There were no intercompany sales or purchases in Year 2, and therefore no elimination is required on the income statement.

2. To realize the gross profit of $600 in Year 2, we decrease cost of goods sold by $600. The reasoning behind this is as follows:

(a) Cost of goods sold is made up of opening inventory, plus purchases, less ending inventory.

Since beginning inventory was inflated, cost of sales for Year 2 was inflated.

(b) The opening inventory contains the $600 gross profit. After we reduce it by $600, the opening inventory is at cost to the entity.

(c) A reduction of $600 from opening inventory decreases cost of goods sold by $600.

(d) This decrease in cost of goods sold increases the before-tax net income earned by the entity by $600.

Exhibit 7.8		

Year 2 Consolidated Statements
(direct approach)

PARENT COMPANY
CONSOLIDATED INCOME STATEMENT
for the Year Ended December 31, Year 2

The unrealized profits from the end of Year 1 are recognized in consolidated income in Year 2.

Sales (25,000 + 12,000)	$37,000
Cost of sales (16,000 + 5,500 **– (7a) 600**)	20,900
Miscellaneous expenses (2,350 + 1,400)	3,750
Income tax expense (2,600 + 2,000 **+ (7b) 240**)	4,840
	29,490
Net income — entity	7,510
Less noncontrolling interest **(7e)**	346
Net income **(7d)**	$ 7,164

PARENT COMPANY
CONSOLIDATED RETAINED EARNINGS STATEMENT
for the Year Ended December 31, Year 2

Balance, January 1 **(7f)**	$14,606
Net income	7,164
	21,770
Dividends	2,500
Balance, December 31	$19,270

PARENT COMPANY
CONSOLIDATED BALANCE SHEET
December 31, Year 2

There are no unrealized profits at the end of Year 2.

Assets — miscellaneous (22,800 + 20,800)	$43,600
Inventory (9,900 + 7,500)	17,400
	$61,000
Liabilities (14,000 + 11,000)	$25,000
Common stock	15,000
Retained earnings	19,270
Noncontrolling interest **(7g)**	1,730
	$61,000

When cost of sales is decreased, income increases and tax expense should increase.

3. Using the concepts of matching, we increase income tax expense by $240 in order to match it with the $600 gross profit being realized. Note that the deferred charge–income tax on the December 31, Year 1, consolidated balance sheet (see Exhibit 7.5) becomes an expense on the Year 2 consolidated income statement, because the December 31, Year 1, inventory was sold in Year 2.

4. A $600 decrease in cost of goods sold, together with a $240 increase in income tax expense, results in the after-tax intercompany Year 1 profit of $360 being realized for consolidation purposes in Year 2.

Because the parent has used the cost method, we must calculate consolidated retained earnings as at January 1, Year 2, before preparing the Year 2 consolidated retained earnings statement. This calculation was shown in Exhibit 7.7. Note that this calculation adjusts the retained earnings of the parent from cost method to the equity-method balance.

The Year 2 consolidated retained earnings statement is prepared using the January 1 calculated balance, the net income from the consolidated income statement, and the dividends of the parent.

Before the consolidated balance sheet is prepared, we must calculate noncontrolling interest at December 31, Year 2. This calculation was shown in Exhibit 7.7.

The preparation of the consolidated balance sheet on December 31, Year 2, is straightforward because no inventory profit eliminations are required. The inventory of Parent does not contain any unrealized profit, and there is no related deferred charge–income taxes on the balance sheet. All previous unrealized inventory profits have now been realized for consolidation purposes.

When you view the adjustments that were made to prepare the Year 2 consolidated statements (see Exhibit 7.8) it may strike you that the adjustments made on the income statement have not been reflected in the rest of the consolidated statements, and that as a result the statements should not balance. But they *do* balance, so the $360 increase in the after-tax net income of the entity must have been offset by a $360 change in the retained earnings statement and balance sheet.

To see where this $360 difference ended up, it is useful to prepare a calculation that shows the changes in noncontrolling interest during Year 2. This calculation is shown below:

CHANGES IN NONCONTROLLING INTEREST — Year 2

NCI is based on the sub's shareholders' equity after it has been adjusted for unrealized profit on upstream transactions.

Sub Inc.

Capital stock	8,000	
Retained earnings — January 1	6,200	
	14,200	
Less unrealized inventory profit	360	
Adjusted	13,840	
	10%	
Noncontrolling interest, January 1		$1,384
Allocation of Year 2 entity net income		346
Noncontrolling interest, December 31		$1,730

The intercompany profit of $360 was recorded in the Sub's separate-entity income in Year 1 but reported in consolidated income in Year 2.

In examining this calculation and the calculation of consolidated retained earnings on January 1 in Exhibit 7.7, we see that the $360 increase in the entity's Year 2 consolidated net income was offset by a $360 *decrease* in the January 1 balances of noncontrolling interest and retained earnings, allocated as follows:

To noncontrolling interest (10% × 360)	$ 36
To controlling interest (90% × 360)	324
	$360

Equity Method Journal Entries

The equity method captures the net effect of all consolidation entries including the adjustment for realized profits.

If Parent had used the equity method, the following journal entries would have been made on December 31, Year 2:

Investment in Sub Inc.	2,790	
Investment income		2,790

To record 90% of the reported income of Sub Inc. (90% × 3,100)

Investment in Sub Inc.	324	
Investment income		324

To realize in Year 2 the after-tax inventory profit held back in Year 1 (90% × 360)

After these entries are posted, the two related equity-method accounts of Parent show the following changes and balances:

	Investment in Sub Inc.	Investment income
January 1, Year 2	$12,456	$ —
December 31, Year 2		
Income from Sub Inc.	2,790	2,790
After-tax inventory profit (realized)	324	324
Balance, Dec. 31, Year 2	$15,570	$3,114

Note that the January 1 balance ($12,456) included the $324 holdback, and that this amount was realized during the year with a journal entry. It should be obvious that the December 31 balance ($15,570) does not contain any holdback.

Appendix 7A illustrates the working-paper approach to preparing the Year 2 consolidated financial statements when the equity and cost methods are used.

Intercompany Inventory Profits: Parent Selling (Downstream Transactions)

In our previous example, the subsidiary was the selling company in the intercompany profit transaction (an upstream transaction). This resulted in the $360 after-tax profit elimination being allocated to the controlling and noncontrolling equities. Recall that our example was based on the assumption that we had forgotten to take intercompany transactions into account when we originally prepared the consolidated statements. We then corrected the statements by eliminating the intercompany revenues and expenses and the unrealized inventory profit.

Suppose we had assumed that it was the parent company that sold the inventory to the subsidiary (a downstream transaction). The calculation of consolidated net income for each of the two years should indicate where the differences would lie.

CALCULATION OF CONSOLIDATED NET INCOME — Year 1

Unrealized profits on downstream transactions are deducted from the parent's separate-entity income.

Net income — Parent Co.		$3,400
Less after-tax profit in ending inventory		360
Adjusted net income — Parent Co.		3,040
Net income — Sub Inc.	1,700	
Parent Co.'s share	90%	1,530
Consolidated net income		$4,570
Noncontrolling interest (10% × 1,700)		$ 170

Notice that the after-tax profit is deducted from the net income of Parent because it was the selling company, and that Parent's net income contains this profit being held back for consolidation purposes. Notice also that "Net income — entity" remains unchanged, as the following calculation indicates:

Adjusted net income — Parent Co.	$3,040
Net income — Sub Inc.	1,700
Net income — entity	$4,740

The eliminations on the consolidated income statement for intercompany sales and purchases and for unrealized profit in inventory, and the related adjustment to income tax expense, would not change. This means that consolidated revenues and expenses are identical to those in the previous example (see Exhibit 7.3). But consolidated net income is different, as the following partial consolidated income statement indicates:

PARENT COMPANY
PARTIAL CONSOLIDATED INCOME STATEMENT — Year 1

NCI is not affected by the elimination of unrealized profits on downstream transactions.

Net income — entity	$4,740
Less noncontrolling interest	170
Net income	$4,570

Because Parent was the selling company, all of the $360 holdback was allocated to the parent and none was allocated to the noncontrolling interest.

On the December 31, Year 1, consolidated balance sheet, the elimination entries to adjust inventory and deferred charge–income taxes would be the same as before. However, the noncontrolling interest on the consolidated balance sheet is based on the December 31, Year 1, balances of the common stock and retained earnings of Sub. The after-tax inventory holdback is *not* allocated to noncontrolling interest; because Parent was the selling company, it has been allocated entirely to consolidated retained earnings.

Year 2 consolidated net income would be calculated as follows:

When unrealized profits on downstream transactions are realized, they are added to the parent's separate-entity income.

Net income — Parent Co.		$4,050
Add after-tax profit in opening inventory		360
Adjusted net income — Parent Co.		4,410
Net income — Sub Inc.	3,100	
Parent Co.'s share	90%	2,790
Consolidated net income		$7,200
Noncontrolling interest (10% × 3,100)		$ 310

"Net income — entity" for Year 2 has not changed and is made up of:

Adjusted net income — Parent Co.	$4,410
Net income — Sub Inc.	3,100
Net income — entity	$7,510

The elimination entries on the Year 2 consolidated income statement would be the same as in the previous illustration (see Exhibit 7.8), but because the amount for noncontrolling interest is $310, the consolidated net income is a higher amount, as the following partial consolidated income statement indicates:

PARENT COMPANY
PARTIAL CONSOLIDATED INCOME STATEMENT — Year 2

Net income — entity	$7,510
Less noncontrolling interest	310
Net income	$7,200

To summarize, the holdback and subsequent realization of intercompany profits in assets is allocated to the noncontrolling and controlling equities *only if* the subsidiary was the original seller in the intercompany transaction. If the parent was the original seller, the allocation is entirely to the controlling equity.

Equity Method Journal Entries If Parent used the equity method to account for its investment, it would make the following entries as at December 31, Year 1:

Investment in Sub Inc.	1,530	
Investment income		1,530
To record 90% of the reported Year 1 net income of Sub Inc. (90% × 1,700)		

The parent absorbs the full charge for unrealized profits on downstream transactions in Year 1.

Investment income	360	
Investment in Sub Inc.		360
To hold back the after-tax inventory profit recorded by Parent Co. in Year 1		

An astute reader will notice that because the parent was the selling company, the second entry is removing the profit from accounts that did not contain it in the first place. This of course is quite true. However, it is the investment income account that establishes the equality between Parent's net income (under the equity method) and consolidated net income. In the same manner, the investment in Sub on the balance sheet of Parent establishes the equality between Parent's retained earnings (under the equity method) and consolidated retained earnings. This means that all adjustments that affect consolidated net income are reflected in these two accounts.

The equity method is referred to as the one-line consolidation.

On December 31, Year 2, Parent would make the following journal entries if it used the equity method:

Investment in Sub Inc.	2,790	
Investment income		2,790
To record 90% of the reported net income of Sub Inc.		

The parent receives the full benefit when unrealized profits on downstream transactions are realized in Year 2.

Investment in Sub Inc.	360	
Investment income		360
To realize in Year 2 the after-tax inventory profit held back in Year 1		

Intercompany Land Profit Holdback

The holdback and realization of an intercompany profit in land is accomplished in a more straightforward manner on the consolidated income statement. Suppose that in Year 1 there was an intercompany sale of land for $2,600 on which a before-tax profit of $600 was recorded, that $240 tax was accrued, and that on December 31,

Year 1, the land was still held by the purchasing company. (Throughout the text and end-of-chapter material, we assume that these gains are not capital gains.)

The selling company would make the following entry to record the intercompany transaction:

Cash	2,600	
Land		2,000
Gain on sale of land		600

The purchasing company would record the intercompany transaction as follows:

The purchasing company's cost is $600 higher than the selling company's cost.

| Land | 2,600 | |
| Cash | | 2,600 |

When consolidated financial statements are prepared, the profit elimination and the related income-tax adjustment will take place as follows:

PARENT COMPANY
CONSOLIDATED INCOME STATEMENT
Year 1

Gain on sale of land (600 – **600**)	$ 0
Income tax expense (P + S – **240**)	XXX
Net income — entity	XXX
Less noncontrolling interest	XXX
Net income	$XXX

The after-tax profit is deducted from the selling company's separate entity income.

It should be obvious that the holdback of the gain, along with the reduction of the income tax expense, has reduced the entity's net income by $360. If the subsidiary is the selling company, the $360 after-tax profit held back will be used to calculate noncontrolling interest in the consolidated income statement; in this manner it will be allocated to the two equities. If the parent is the selling company, noncontrolling interest will not be affected and the entire after-tax holdback will be allocated to the controlling entity.

The following shows the eliminations required in the preparation of the Year 1 balance sheet:

After eliminating the profit, the land is stated at the original cost to the consolidated entity.

PARENT COMPANY
CONSOLIDATED BALANCE SHEET
December 31, Year 1

Assets	
Land (2,600 – **600**)	$2,000
Deferred charge–income taxes (+ **240**)	240
Total assets	$ XXX

The balance sheet eliminations for a land profit are very similar to those for an inventory profit. The before-tax profit is deducted from land rather than inventory. The tax asset is added into the consolidated balance sheet. Since the land is not expected to be sold in the next year, the difference between the accounting and tax value of this asset will not reverse for at least one year. Therefore, the tax asset should be presented as a non-current asset. We will refer to this tax asset as deferred charge–income taxes.

The equity side of the balance sheet is not presented. If the subsidiary is the selling company, the calculation of noncontrolling interest on December 31, Year 1, will have to reflect this fact. If the parent is the selling company, the entire $360 after-tax profit hold-back is automatically reflected in the retained earnings shown on the balance sheet.

Realization of Intercompany Land Profits

An unrealized intercompany inventory profit held back for consolidated purposes in Year 1 is considered realized in Year 2 because any inventory on hand at the beginning of a year has usually been sold by the end of that year.

When are intercompany land profits considered realized for consolidation purposes? The answer is this: when the land is sold to outsiders, which may be many years later. At the end of each successive year prior to the sale to outsiders, the preparation of the consolidated balance sheet requires the same adjustments as those of Year 1. Consolidated income statements require no adjustment until the year of the sale to outsiders because, in each year prior to that event, the income statements of both affiliates will not contain any transactions with regard to the land.

However, assuming that Parent Company uses the cost method, the calculation of beginning consolidated retained earnings each year will have to include an adjustment to hold back the $360 unrealized land profit. The calculation would be identical to that shown in Exhibit 7.7 except that it would be described as land profit rather than profit in opening inventory. (This particular calculation is based on the assumption that Sub Inc. was the selling company.) Each successive year would require the same adjustment until the land is sold to outsiders.

In this case, let us assume that the land was sold to outsiders during Year 8 at a profit of $1,300. The company making the sale in Year 8 would record the following journal entry:

Cash	3,900	
Land		2,600
Gain on sale of land		1,300

> The unrealized profits will be eliminated from retained earnings of the selling company on the consolidated working papers each year until the land is sold to outsiders.

> The gain on the separate-entity income statement is $1,300.

While the selling company recorded a gain of $1,300, the gain to the entity is $1,900 (1,300 + 600). On the Year 8 consolidated income statement, the gain held back in Year 1 is realized and the income tax expense adjusted as follows:

PARENT COMPANY
CONSOLIDATED INCOME STATEMENT
Year 8

Gain on sale of land (1,300 + **600**)	$1,900
Income tax expense (P + S + **240**)	XXX
Net income — entity	XXX
Less noncontrolling interest	XXX
Net income	$ XXX

> The gain on the consolidated income statement is $1,900 ($1,300 + $600 previously held back).

The entity's net income is increased by $360 ($600 – $240). If the subsidiary was the original selling company, the net income of the noncontrolling interest is affected in Year 8; the entire $360 is allocated to the controlling interest if the parent was the original seller.

Equity Method Journal Entries Parent Co.'s equity journal entries for the land gain in years 1 and 8 would be identical to the entries illustrated previously for inventory in years 1 and 2, depending of course on which company was the original seller in the intercompany profit transaction.

Intercompany Transfer Pricing

In our coin example at the beginning of this chapter, we saw a loonie sold for a gross profit of $40, which was allocated to the four related companies as follows:

Parent	$ 9
Sub 1	5
Sub 2	10
Sub 3	16
Total	$40

Intercompany transactions are sometimes undertaken to transfer profit from high-tax to low-tax jurisdictions.

From a financial reporting point of view we are not concerned with the amount of profit earned by each company; but only with eliminating intercompany transactions and profits that are unrealized because they have not been sold outside the consolidated "single entity." From a taxation point of view, the consolidated entity is not subject to tax; rather each company pays tax on its taxable income. It should seem obvious that the management of the parent company would be interested in maximizing the after-tax profit of this single entity if possible. If all of the companies are in one taxation jurisdiction, there is nothing that management can do to increase the after-tax profit. However, if some of the companies are in jurisdictions with low rates of corporate income tax while others are in high tax rate jurisdictions, management may try to structure each company's transfer price so that the majority (or all) of the $40 profit is earned in low tax rate jurisdictions. This will often bring companies into conflict with the governments of the high tax rate jurisdictions.

The examples in this chapter regarding the elimination of unrealized intercompany profits follow the dictates of entity theory. The entity method is also required when valuing the subsidiary's assets and liabilities at fair value at the date of acquisition as we learned in Chapter 4. Therefore, the CICA standard-setters are consistent in requiring the use of the entity method in many different aspects of preparing consolidated financial statements.

An International Perspective

Canadian GAAP for intercompany transactions is substantially similar to the requirements of the IASB.

The elimination of unrealized intercompany profits is such an integral part of the consolidation process, that one must assume that countries requiring the preparation of consolidated statements also require the elimination of these profits. In fact, some countries only eliminate the parent's share of the unrealized profits (net income remains the same but the amount reported for noncontrolling interest is affected). The IASB requires that unrealized profits be completely eliminated as does FASB in the United States. IAS 16 permits the revaluation of land to fair value whereas it must be recorded at cost under Canadian GAAP.

SUMMARY

To ensure that consolidated financial statements reflect only transactions between the single entity and those outside the entity, all intercompany transactions are eliminated. The elimination of intercompany revenues and expenses does not affect the net income of this entity; therefore, it cannot affect the amounts allocated to the two equities in the balance sheet.

Intercompany profits in assets are not recognized in the consolidated financial statements until the assets have been sold outside the group or consumed. (The concept of realization as a result of consumption is discussed in the next chapter.)

The elimination of unrealized intercompany profits in assets reduces the net income of the entity. Also, it will affect the amount allocated to noncontrolling interest only if the subsidiary was the selling company. The income tax recorded on the unrealized profit is also removed from the consolidated income statement, and is shown as deferred charge–income taxes until a sale to outsiders takes place.

When the assets that contain the intercompany profit are sold outside (or consumed), the profit is considered realized and is reflected in the consolidated income statement. The appropriate income tax is removed from the consolidated balance sheet and reflected as an expense in the income statement. The adjustments for income tax ensure that income tax expense is properly matched to income recognized on the consolidated income statement.

SELF-STUDY PROBLEM

The following are the Year 5 financial statements of Peter Corporation and its subsidiary, Salt Company:

	Peter	Salt
Year 5 income statements		
Sales	$900,000	$250,000
Management fees	25,000	—
Interest	—	3,600
Gain on land sale	—	20,000
Dividends	12,000	—
	937,000	273,600
Cost of sales	540,000	162,000
Interest expense	3,600	—
Other expenses	196,400	71,600
Income tax expense	80,000	16,000
	820,000	249,600
Net income	$117,000	$ 24,000
Year 5 retained earnings statements		
Balance, January 1	$153,000	$ 72,000
Net income	117,000	24,000
	270,000	96,000
Dividends	50,000	15,000
Balance, December 31	$220,000	$ 81,000
Balance sheets — December 31, Year 5		
Cash	$ 12,000	$ 8,000
Accounts receivable	70,000	10,000
Notes receivable	—	60,000
Inventory	32,000	27,000
Land	175,000	19,000
Plant and equipment (net)	238,000	47,000
Investment in Salt Co.	65,000	—
	$592,000	$171,000

Notes payable	$ 60,000	$ —
Other liabilities	212,000	40,000
Common stock	100,000	50,000
Retained earnings	220,000	81,000
	$592,000	$171,000

Other Information

1. On January 1, Year 3, Peter purchased 80% of the common shares of Salt for $65,000. On that date, Salt had retained earnings of $10,000 and the book values of its identifiable net assets were equal to fair values.

2. The companies sell merchandise to each other. Peter sells to Salt at a gross profit rate of 35%; Salt earns a gross profit of 40% from its sales to Peter.

3. The December 31, Year 4, inventory of Peter contained purchases made from Salt amounting to $7,000. There were no intercompany purchases in the inventory of Salt on this date.

4. During Year 5 the following intercompany transactions took place:

   (a) Salt made a $25,000 payment to Peter for management fees, which was recorded as "other expense."

   (b) Salt made sales of $75,000 to Peter. The December 31, Year 5, inventory of Peter contained merchandise purchased from Salt amounting to $16,500.

   (c) Peter made sales of $100,000 to Salt. The December 31, Year 5, inventory of Salt contained merchandise purchased from Peter amounting to $15,000.

   (d) On July 1, Year 5, Peter borrowed $60,000 from Salt and signed a note bearing interest at 12% per annum. Interest on this note was paid on December 31, Year 5.

   (e) In Year 5, Salt sold land to Peter, recording a gain of $20,000. This land is being held by Peter on December 31, Year 5.

5. Goodwill impairment tests have been conducted yearly since the date of acquisition. Losses due to impairment were as follows: Year 3, $2,600; Year 4, $800; Year 5, $1,700.

6. Peter accounts for its investment using the cost method.

7. Both companies pay income tax at a rate of 40%.

Required:

(a) Prepare the Year 5 consolidated financial statements.

(b) Prepare the following:
   (i)   A calculation of consolidated retained earnings as at December 31, Year 5.
   (ii) A statement of changes in noncontrolling interest for Year 5.
   (iii) A statement of changes in deferred charge–income taxes for Year 5.

(c) Assume that Peter uses the equity method.
   (i) Calculate the balance in the investment account as at December 31, Year 4.
   (ii) Prepare Peter's equity-method journal entries for Year 5.

Solution to Self-study Problem

(a) Supporting Schedules

CALCULATION AND AMORTIZATION OF THE PURCHASE DISCREPANCY

Cost of 80% of Salt, Jan. 1, Year 3		$ 65,000
Imputed value of 100% of Salt		$ 81,250
Book value of Salt, Jan. 1, Year 3		
Common stock	50,000	
Retained earnings	10,000	
		60,000
Purchase discrepancy		21,250
Allocated to revalue the net assets of Salt		–0–
Goodwill, Jan. 1, Year 3		21,250
Amortized (impairment losses):		
Year 3–Year 4	3,400 **(a)**	
Year 5	1,700 **(b)**	5,100
Goodwill, Dec. 31, Year 5		$ 16,150 **(c)**

INTERCOMPANY ITEMS

Notes receivable and payable	$ 60,000 **(d)**
Management fee revenue and expense	$ 25,000 **(e)**
Sales and purchases (100,000 + 75,000)	$175,000 **(f)**
Interest revenue and expense (12% × 60,000 × 1/2 yr.)	$ 3,600 **(g)**
Dividend from Salt (80% × 15,000)	$ 12,000 **(h)**

UNREALIZED PROFITS

	Before tax	40% tax	After tax
Inventory			
Opening (7,000 × 40%) — Salt selling	$ 2,800	$1,120	$ 1,680 **(i)**
Ending			
Salt selling (16,500 × 40%)	$ 6,600	$2,640	$ 3,960 **(j)**
Peter selling (15,000 × 35%)	5,250	2,100	3,150 **(k)**
	$11,850	$4,740	$ 7,110 **(l)**
Land — Salt selling	$20,000	$8,000	$12,000 **(m)**

CALCULATION OF CONSOLIDATED NET INCOME — Year 5

Income of Peter			$117,000
Less: Dividends from Salt **(h)**		12,000	
Ending inventory profit **(k)**		3,150	15,150
Adjusted net income			101,850
Income of Salt		24,000	
Less: Ending inventory profit **(j)**	3,960		
Land gain **(m)**	12,000		
Amortization of purchase discrepancy	1,700		
		17,660	
		6,340	
Add opening inventory profit **(i)**		1,680	
Adjusted net income		8,020	
		80%	6,416
Consolidated net income			$108,266 **(n)**
Noncontrolling interest (20% × 8,020)			$ 1,604 **(o)**

CALCULATION OF CONSOLIDATED RETAINED EARNINGS
January 1, Year 5

Retained earnings — Peter		$153,000
Retained earnings — Salt	72,000	
Acquisition retained earnings	10,000	
Increase	62,000	
Less opening inventory profit **(i)**	1,680	
Less purchase discrepancy amortization Year 3—Year 4 **(a)**	3,400	
Adjusted increase	56,920 **(p)**	
Peter's share	80%	45,536 **(p)**
Consolidated retained earnings, Jan. 1, Year 5		$198,536 **(q)**

CALCULATION OF DEFERRED CHARGE–INCOME TAXES — December 31, Year 5

Ending inventory	$ 4,740
Land	8,000
	$12,740 **(r)**

CALCULATION OF NONCONTROLLING INTEREST — December 31, Year 5

Common stock — Salt		$50,000
Retained earnings — Salt		81,000
		131,000
Add: Unamortized purchase discrepancy **(c)**		16,150
Less: Ending inventory profit **(j)**	3,960	
Land gain **(m)**	12,000	(15,960)
Adjusted		131,190
Noncontrolling interest's share		20%
		$26,238 **(s)**

PETER CORPORATION
CONSOLIDATED INCOME STATEMENT — Year 5

Sales (900,000 + 250,000 – **(f) 175,000**)	$975,000*
Cost of sales (540,000 + 162,000 – **(f) 175,000** – (i) **2,800** + (l) **11,850**)	536,050**
Other expenses (196,400 + 71,600 – **(e) 25,000**)	243,000
Goodwill impairment loss **(b)**	1,700
Income tax (80,000 + 16,000 – **(m) 8,000** + (i) **1,120** – (l) **4,740**)	84,380
Total expense	865,130
Net income — entity	109,870
Less noncontrolling interest **(o)**	1,604
Net income **(n)**	$108,266

* Revenue items completely eliminated from statement:	
Management fees	$25,000
Interest	3,600
Land gain	20,000
Dividends	12,000
** Expense items completely eliminated from statement:	
Interest	$ 3,600

PETER CORPORATION
CONSOLIDATED RETAINED EARNINGS STATEMENT — Year 5

Balance, January 1 **(q)**	$198,536
Net income	108,266
	306,802
Dividends	50,000
Balance, Dec. 31	$256,802

PETER CORPORATION
CONSOLIDATED BALANCE SHEET — December 31, Year 5

Cash (12,000 + 8,000)	$ 20,000
Accounts receivable (70,000 + 10,000)	80,000
Inventory (32,000 + 27,000 – **(l) 11,850**)	47,150
Land (175,000 + 19,000 – **(m) 20,000**)	174,000
Plant and equipment (net) (238,000 + 47,000)	285,000
Goodwill **(c)**	16,150
Deferred charge–income taxes **(r)**	12,740
	$635,040
Other liabilities (212,000 + 40,000)	$252,000
Common stock	100,000
Retained earnings	256,802
Noncontrolling interest **(s)**	26,238
	$635,040

(b)(i) **CALCULATION OF CONSOLIDATED RETAINED EARNINGS,**
December 31, Year 5

Retained earnings, Dec. 31, Year 5 — Peter			$220,000
Less: Ending inventory profit **(k)**			3,150
Adjusted			216,850
Retained earnings, Dec. 31, Year 5 — Salt		81,000	
Acquisition retained earnings		10,000	
Increase		71,000	
Less: Purchase discrepancy amortization **(a)** + **(b)**	5,100		
Ending inventory profit **(j)**	3,960		
Land gain **(m)**	12,000	21,060	
Adjusted increase		49,940	
Peter's share		80%	39,952
Consolidated retained earnings, December 31, Year 5			$256,802

(ii) **CHANGES IN NONCONTROLLING INTEREST** — Year 5

Common stock — Salt	$50,000
Retained earnings, Jan. 1, Year 5 — Salt	72,000
	122,000
Add: Unamortized purchase discrepancy (21,250 – **(a) 3,400**)	17,850
Less profit in inventory **(i)**	(1,680)
	138,170
Noncontrolling interest's share	20%
Noncontrolling interest, Jan. 1, Year 5	27,634
Allocation of entity income, Year 5 **(o)**	1,604
	29,238
Dividends (20% × 15,000)	3,000
Noncontrolling interest, December 31, Year 5	$26,238

(iii)   **CHANGES IN DEFERRED CHARGE–INCOME TAXES** — Year 5

Balance, Jan. 1, Year 5 (inventory) **(i)**			$ 1,120
Taxes paid in Year 5 but deferred			
Inventory **(l)**		4,740	
Land **(m)**		8,000	12,740
			13,860
Expensed Year 5 **(i)**			1,120
Balance, Dec. 31, Year 5			$ 12,740

(c)(i)

Investment in Salt, Dec. 31, Year 4 (cost method)			$ 65,000
Retained earnings, Dec. 31, Year 4 — Salt		72,000	
Acquisition retained earnings		10,000	
Increase		62,000	
Less inventory profit **(i)**	1,680		
Amort. of purchase discrepancy	**(a)** 3,400	5,080	
Adjusted increase		56,920	
Peter's share		80%	45,536
Investment in Salt, December 31, Year 4			
(equity method)			$110,536

(ii)   **Year 5 EQUITY–METHOD JOURNAL ENTRIES**
                          (See Calculation of Consolidated Net Income)

Investment in Salt Co.	6,416	
Investment income		6,416
80% of adjusted net income of Salt Co.		
Cash	12,000	
Investment in Salt Co.		12,000
Dividends from Salt Co.		
Investment income	3,150	
Investment in Salt Co.		3,150
Ending inventory profit — Peter selling		

APPENDIX 7A

Preparing Consolidated Financial Statements Using the Working Paper Approach

In this chapter we have illustrated the direct approach for preparing the consolidated financial statements of Parent Company over a two-year period. In the example used, an inventory profit recorded by Sub Inc. was held back for consolidated purposes in Year 1, and realized in the consolidated statements in Year 2. The example assumed that Parent had used the cost method, but the journal entries that would have been made if Parent had used the equity method were also illustrated.

We will now illustrate the preparation of the consolidated financial statements for Years 1 and 2 using the working-paper approach. For each year, we will present the working paper under the equity method, followed by the working paper under the cost method. The reason for proceeding in this particular order is that when the cost method has been used, the first working paper entries adjust the accounts of the parent to equity method balances. The working paper elimination entries are then made that are appropriate for the equity method.

Year 1 Working Paper (equity method) Exhibit 7A.1 illustrates the working paper for the preparation of the Year 1 consolidated financial statements when Parent Co. has used the equity method.

Exhibit 7A.1

CONSOLIDATED FINANCIAL STATEMENT WORKING PAPER
Equity Method
ELIMINATION OF INVENTORY PROFIT — December 31, Year 1

	Parent	Sub	Eliminations Dr.	Cr.	Consolidated
Sales	$20,000	$ 8,000	**(i)** $ 5,000		$23,000
Investment income	1,206		**(1)** 1,206		
	21,206	8,000			23,000
Cost of sales	13,000	4,300	**(ii)** 600	**(i)** $ 5,000	12,900
Misc. expenses	1,400	900			2,300
Income tax exp.	2,200	1,100		**(iii)** 240	3,060
	16,600	6,300			18,260
Net income — entity					4,740
Noncontrolling interest			**(4)** 134		134
Net income	$ 4,606	$ 1,700	$ 6,940	$ 5,240	$ 4,606
Retained earnings, Jan. 1	$12,000	$ 4,500	**(2)** $ 450 **(3)** 4,050		$12,000
Net income	4,606	1,700	6,940	$ 5,240	4,606
	16,606	6,200			16,606
Dividends	2,000	—			2,000
Retained earnings, Dec. 31	$14,606	$ 6,200	$11,440	$ 5,240	$14,606
Assets, misc.	$21,650	$19,200			$40,850
Inventory	7,500	4,000		**(ii)** $ 600	10,900
Deferred charge — income taxes			**(iii)** $ 240		240
Investment in Sub	12,456			**(3)** 11,250 **(1)** 1,206	
	$41,606	$23,200			$51,990
Liabilities	$12,000	$ 9,000			$21,000
Common stock	15,000	8,000	**(2)** 800 **(3)** 7,200		15,000
Retained earnings	14,606	6,200	11,440	5,240	14,606
Noncontrolling interest				**(2)** 1,250 **(4)** 134	1,384
	$41,606	$23,200	$19,680	$19,680	$51,990

Sidebar notes:

Consolidated net income is equal to the parent's income under the equity method.

Consolidated retained earnings are equal to the parent's retained earnings under the equity method.

The elimination entries used were as follows:

Investment income is eliminated since the subsidiary's revenues and expenses plus adjustments for unrealized profits will replace it.

#1 Investment income — Parent Co. 1,206
    Investment in Sub Inc. — Parent Co. 1,206

This entry eliminates the investment income from the income statement and restates the investment account to the balance at the beginning of the year.

This entry establishes NCI at the start of the year.

#2	Retained earnings, January 1 — Sub Inc.	450	
	Common stock — Sub Inc.	800	
	Noncontrolling interest (balance sheet)		1,250

This entry eliminates 10 percent of the shareholders' equity of Sub Inc. at the beginning of the year and establishes the noncontrolling interest as at that date.

The investment account is eliminated since it will be replaced by the carrying value of the subsidiary's assets and liabilities plus adjustments for unrealized profits.

#3	Retained earnings, January 1 — Sub Inc.	4,050	
	Common stock — Sub Inc.	7,200	
	Investment in Sub Inc. — Parent Co.		11,250

This entry eliminates the parent's share of the shareholders' equity of the subsidiary at the beginning of the year against the parent's investment account. Usually the difference represents the unamortized purchase discrepancy on that date, but in this particular example there is no purchase discrepancy.

| #4 | Noncontrolling interest (income statement) | 134 | |
| | Noncontrolling interest (balance sheet) | | 134 |

This entry allocates the applicable portion of the net income of the entity to the noncontrolling interest. The amount requires a separate calculation, as follows:

Net income — Sub Inc.	$1,700
Less after-tax profit in ending inventory	360
Adjusted net income — Sub Inc.	1,340
	10%
Noncontrolling interest	$ 134

The remaining working paper entries eliminate the intercompany transactions for Year 1.

These two entries eliminate the intercompany transactions and unrealized profits in ending inventory.

| #i | Sales | 5,000 | |
| | Cost of sales | | 5,000 |

To eliminate intercompany sales and purchases.

| #ii | Cost of sales | 600 | |
| | Inventory | | 600 |

To hold back the before-tax profit, on the consolidated income statement and (from inventory) on the consolidated balance sheet.

This entry removes the income tax expense related to the unrealized profit.

| #iii | Deferred charge–income taxes | 240 | |
| | Income tax expense | | 240 |

The income tax effect of the inventory profit held back in #(ii).

Year 1 Working Paper (cost method)   Exhibit 7A.2 illustrates the working paper for the preparation of the Year 1 consolidated financial statements, assuming that Parent has used the cost method to account for its investment.

Entry #a adjusts Parent's accounts from the cost to the equity method. The numbers used are obtained from the calculation of consolidated net income for Year 1 in Exhibit 7.4.

This entry converts the parent's income from the cost method to the equity method.

| #a | Investment in Sub Inc. — Parent Co. | 1,206 | |
| | Investment income — Parent Co. | | 1,206 |

Now that Parent's accounts have been adjusted to the equity method, the remaining working paper entries are identical to those presented in Exhibit 7A.1.

Year 2 Working Paper (equity method) The working paper for the preparation of the Year 2 consolidated financial statements when the parent has used the equity method are shown in Exhibit 7A.3. The inventory profit held back in Year 1 is realized in Year 2; because the subsidiary was the original selling company, the resulting increase in after-tax income is allocated to the controlling and noncontrolling equities.

Exhibit 7A.2

CONSOLIDATED FINANCIAL STATEMENT WORKING PAPER
Cost Method
ELIMINATION OF INVENTORY PROFIT — December 31, Year 1

		Parent	Sub	Eliminations Dr.		Cr.		Consolidated
Consolidated net income is the same as when the parent used the equity method.	Sales	$20,000	$ 8,000	**(i)** $ 5,000				$23,000
	Investment income			**(1)** 1,206	**(a)** $ 1,206			
		20,000	8,000					23,000
	Cost of sales	13,000	4,300	**(ii)** 600	**(i)** 5,000			12,900
	Misc. expenses	1,400	900					2,300
	Income tax exp.	2,200	1,100		**(iii)** 240			3,060
		16,600	6,300					18,260
	Net income — entity							4,740
	Noncontrolling interest			**(4)** 134				134
	Net income	$ 3,400	$ 1,700	$ 6,940	$ 6,446			$ 4,606
	Retained earnings, Jan. 1	$12,000	$ 4,500	**(2)** $ 450				$12,000
				(3) 4,050				
	Net income	3,400	1,700	6,940	$ 6,446			4,606
		15,400	6,200					16,606
	Dividends	2,000	—					2,000
	Retained earnings, Dec. 31	$13,400	$ 6,200	$11,440	$ 6,446			$14,606
	Assets, misc.	$21,650	$19,200					$40,850
	Inventory	7,500	4,000		**(ii)** $ 600			10,900
	Deferred charge– income taxes			**(iii)** $ 240				240
	Investment in Sub	11,250			**(3)** 11,250			
				(a) 1,206	**(1)** 1,206			
		$40,400	$23,200					$51,990
Consolidated retained earnings is the same as when the parent used the equity method.	Liabilities	$12,000	$ 9,000					$21,000
	Common stock	15,000	8,000	**(2)** 800				15,000
				(3) 7,200				
	Retained earnings	13,400	6,200	11,440	6,446			14,606
	Noncontrolling interest				**(2)** 1,250			
					(4) 134			1,384
		$40,400	$23,200	$20,886	$20,886			$51,990

The working paper entries are reproduced below, with brief explanations:

#1 Investment income — Parent Co.   3,114
        Investment in Sub Inc. — Parent Co.   3,114

The investment income account is eliminated against the investment account, which establishes the start-of-year balance in this account.

#2 Retained earnings, January 1 — Sub Inc.   620
        Common stock — Sub Inc.   800
            Noncontrolling interest (balance sheet)   1,420

Exhibit 7A.3

CONSOLIDATED FINANCIAL STATEMENT WORKING PAPER
Equity Method Realization of Inventory Profit
December 31, Year 2

		Parent	Sub	Eliminations Dr.	Cr.	Consolidated
Cost of sales is decreased because beginning inventory was inflated.	Sales	$25,000	$12,000			$37,000
	Investment income	3,114		**(1)** $ 3,114		
		28,114	12,000			37,000
	Cost of sales	16,000	5,500		**(i)** $ 600	20,900
	Misc. expenses	2,350	1,400			3,750
	Income tax exp.	2,600	2,000	**(i)** 240		4,840
		20,950	8,900			29,490
	Net income — entity					7,510
	Noncontrolling interest			**(4)** 346		346
	Net income	$ 7,164	$ 3,100	$ 3,700	$ 600	$ 7,164
	Retained earnings, Jan. 1	$14,606	$ 6,200	**(2)** $ 620		$14,606
				(3) 5,580		
	Net income	7,164	3,100	3,700	$ 600	7,164
		21,770	9,300			21,770
	Dividends	2,500				2,500
	Retained earnings, Dec. 31	$19,270	$ 9,300	$ 9,900	$ 600	$19,270
There is no unrealized profit in inventory at the end of the year.	Assets, misc.	$22,800	$20,800			$43,600
	Inventory	9,900	7,500			17,400
	Investment in Sub	15,570		**(i)** $ 324	**(1)** $ 3,114	
					(3) 12,780	
		$48,270	$28,300			$61,000
	Liabilities	$14,000	$11,000			$25,000
	Common stock	15,000	8,000	**(2)** 800		15,000
				(3) 7,200		
	Retained earnings	19,270	9,300	9,900	600	19,270
	Noncontrolling interest			**(i)** 36	**(2)** 1,420	1,730
					(4) 346	
		$48,270	$28,300	$18,260	$18,260	$61,000

This entry eliminates 10 percent of the shareholders' equity of Sub Inc. as at the beginning of the year, with the amount used to establish the noncontrolling interest as at January 1, Year 2. Note that this opening balance is not the same as the closing balance at the end of Year 1, because it does not contain a portion of the inventory profit being held back at that time. This difference is adjusted in entry #i as follows:

Income tax expense is increased to match against the gain being realized.

#i	Income tax expense	240	
	Investment in Sub Inc. — Parent Co.	324	
	Noncontrolling interest (balance sheet)	36	
	Cost of sales		600

There are two parts to this entry. The credit to cost of sales is made in order to realize in the Year 2 consolidated income statement the inventory profit that was held back in Year 1. The debit to income tax expense matches the expense to the profit realized. (Remember that the Year 1 consolidated balance sheet contained a deferred tax asset of this amount.) These two entries increase the after-tax income of the consolidated entity by $360. The debit of $36 (10% × 360) establishes the correct opening balance in noncontrolling interest. The debit of $324 (90% × 360) establishes the investment account with a balance of $12,780 as at the beginning of the year. Before this entry, the investment account had a correct equity-method balance of $12,456, which included the holdback of 90 percent of the unrealized inventory profit at the end of Year 1. This entry reverses the holdback so that the next entry can be made.

#3	Retained earnings, January 1 — Sub Inc.	5,580	
	Common stock — Sub Inc.	7,200	
	Investment in Sub Inc. — Parent Co.		12,780

The parent's share (90 percent) of the shareholders' equity of the subsidiary at the beginning of the year is eliminated against the parent's investment account.

NCI is increased for its share of the after-tax gain on the sale of the inventory.

#4	Noncontrolling interest (income statement)	346	
	Noncontrolling interest (balance sheet)		346

This final entry allocates the applicable portion of the entity's Year 2 net income to the noncontrolling interest, based on the adjusted income of the subsidiary, calculated as follows:

Net income — Sub Inc.	$3,100
Add after-tax profit in opening inventory	360
Adjusted net income — Sub Inc.	3,460
Noncontrolling interest's share	10%
	$ 346

Year 2 Working Paper (cost method) Exhibit 7A.4 contains the Year 2 working paper based on the assumption that the parent has used the cost method.

Entry #a adjusts the investment account of the parent to the equity method balance at the beginning of Year 2. The source of the amounts used can be found in the calculation of consolidated retained earnings as at January 1, Year 2, presented in Exhibit 7.7.

Entry #b adjusts the investment account to the equity method balance as at December 31, Year 2. (See the calculation of Year 2 consolidated net income in Exhibit 7.7.)

Once the parent's accounts have been adjusted to reflect the equity method, the remaining entries are identical to those shown in Exhibit 7A.3.

Exhibit 7A.4

CONSOLIDATED FINANCIAL STATEMENT WORKING PAPER
Cost Method
REALIZATION OF INVENTORY PROFIT
December 31, Year 2

		Parent	Sub	Eliminations Dr.	Eliminations Cr.	Consolidated
	Sales	$25,000	$12,000			$37,000
	Investment income			**(1)** $ 3,114	**(b)** $ 3,114	
		25,000	12,000			37,000
	Cost of sales	16,000	5,500		**(i)** 600	20,900
	Misc. expenses	2,350	1,400			3,750
	Income tax exp.	2,600	2,000	**(i)** 240		4,840
		20,950	8,900			29,490
	Net income — entity					7,510
	Noncontrolling interest			**(4)** 346		346
	Net income	$ 4,050	$ 3,100	$ 3,700	$ 3,714	$ 7,164
	Retained earnings, Jan. 1	$13,400	$ 6,200	**(2)** $ 620	**(a)** $ 1,206	$14,606
				(3) 5,580		
	Net income	4,050	3,100	3,700	3,714	7,164
		17,450	9,300			21,770
	Dividends	2,500	—			2,500
	Retained earnings, Dec. 31	$14,950	$ 9,300	$ 9,900	$ 4,920	$19,270
	Assets — miscellaneous	$22,800	$20,800			$43,600
	Inventory	9,900	7,500			17,400
	Investment in Sub	11,250		**(b)** $ 3,114		
				(i) 324	**(1)** $ 3,114	
				(a) 1,206	**(3)** 12,780	
		$43,950	$28,300			$61,000
	Liabilities	$14,000	$11,000			$25,000
	Common stock	15,000	8,000	**(2)** 800		15,000
				(3) 7,200		
	Retained earnings	14,950	9,300	9,900	4,920	19,270
	Noncontrolling interest			**(i)** 36	**(2)** 1,420	1,730
					(4) 346	
		$43,950	$28,300	$22,580	$22,580	$61,000

The entries on the income statement are adjustments for one period to bring the accounts to the desired balance for one period of time, i.e., for one year.

The entries on the balance sheet are cumulative adjustments to bring the accounts to the desired balance at the end of the period, i.e., at a point in time.

REVIEW QUESTIONS

1. In what way are an individual's pants with four pockets similar to a parent company with three subsidiaries? Explain, with reference to intercompany revenues and expenses.

2. List the types of intercompany revenue and expenses that are eliminated in the preparation of a consolidated income statement, and indicate the effect that each elimination has on the amount of noncontrolling interest in net income.

3. "From a single-entity point of view, intercompany revenue and expenses and intercompany borrowings do nothing more than transfer cash from one bank account to another." Explain.

4. If an intercompany profit is recorded on the sale of an asset to an affiliate within the consolidated entity in Period 1, when should this profit be considered realized? Explain.

5. Explain how the revenue recognition principle supports the elimination of intercompany transactions when preparing consolidated financial statements.

6. "The reduction of a $1,000 intercompany gross profit from ending inventory should be accompanied by a $400 increase to deferred charge–income taxes in consolidated assets." Do you agree? Explain.

7. Explain how the matching principle supports adjustments to income tax expense when eliminating intercompany profits from consolidated financial statements.

8. A parent company rents a sales office to its wholly owned subsidiary under an operating lease requiring rent of $2,000 a month. What adjustments to income tax expense should accompany the elimination of the parent's $24,000 rent revenue and the subsidiary's $24,000 rent expense when a consolidated income statement is being prepared? Explain.

9. "Intercompany losses recorded on the sale of assets to an affiliate within the consolidated entity should always be eliminated when consolidated financial statements are prepared." Do you agree with this statement? Explain.

10. Describe the effects that the elimination of intercompany sales and intercompany profits in ending inventory will have on the various elements of the consolidated financial statements.

11. What difference does it make on the consolidated financial statements if there are unrealized profits in ending inventory resulting from a downstream transaction as compared to an upstream transaction?

12. When there are unrealized profits in inventory at the end of Year 1, consolidated net income would normally be affected for Years 1 and 2. Explain.

13. An intercompany gain on the sale of land is eliminated in the preparation of the consolidated statements in the year that the gain was recorded. Will this gain be eliminated in the preparation of subsequent consolidated statements? Explain.

MULTIPLE-CHOICE QUESTIONS

Use the following data for Questions 1 to 7.

The financial statements of Post Company and Stamp Company on December 31, Year 5, were as follows:

BALANCE SHEETS

	Post	Stamp
Assets		
Cash	$ 50,000	$ 10,000
Current receivables	250,000	100,000
Inventories	3,000,000	520,000
Equipment (net)	6,150,000	2,500,000
Buildings (net)	2,600,000	500,000
Investment in Stamp (at cost)	850,000	—
	$12,900,000	$3,630,000
Liabilities and shareholders' equity		
Current liabilities	$ 300,000	$ 170,000
Long-term liabilities	4,000,000	1,100,000
No-par common stock	3,000,000	500,000
Retained earnings	5,600,000	1,860,000
	$12,900,000	$3,630,000

STATEMENTS OF INCOME AND RETAINED EARNINGS

	Post	Stamp
Sales revenue	$ 3,500,000	$ 900,000
Other revenues	300,000	30,000
	3,800,000	930,000
Cost of goods sold	1,700,000	330,000
Depreciation expense	300,000	100,000
Other expenses	200,000	150,000
Income tax expense	300,000	70,000
	2,500,000	650,000
Net income	1,300,000	280,000
Retained earnings, beginning balance	4,500,000	1,600,000
	5,800,000	1,880,000
Dividends declared	200,000	20,000
Retained earnings, ending balance	$ 5,600,000	$1,860,000

Additional Information

- Post owns 70% of Stamp and carries its investment in Stamp on its books by the cost method.
- During Year 4, Post sold Stamp $100,000 worth of merchandise, of which $60,000 was resold by Stamp in the year. During Year 5, Post had sales of $200,000 to Stamp, of which 40% was resold by Stamp. Intercompany sales are priced to provide Post with a gross profit of 30% of the sales price.
- On December 31, Year 4, Post had in its inventories $150,000 of merchandise purchased from Stamp during Year 4. On December 31, Year 5, Post had in its ending inventories $100,000 of merchandise that had resulted from purchases of $350,000 from Stamp during Year 5. Intercompany sales are priced to provide Stamp with a gross profit of 60% of the sale price.
- Both companies are taxed at 25%.

1. What amount of sales revenue would appear on Post's consolidated income statement for the year ended December 31, Year 5?
    a. $3,850,000
    b. $4,050,000
    c. $4,200,000
    d. $4,400,000

2. What amount of other revenue would appear on Post's consolidated income statement for the year ended December 31, Year 5?
   a. $300,000
   b. $310,000
   c. $316,000
   d. $330,000

3. To calculate Post's consolidated cost of goods sold, the first step is to add together the unadjusted totals from Post's and Stamp's separate entity financial statements. What is the amount of adjustment necessary to this figure for unrealized profits in beginning inventory for the year ended December 31, Year 5?
   a. −$102,000
   b. −$96,000
   c. −$76,500
   d. −$6,000

4. Refer to Question #3. What is the total amount of adjustment necessary to consolidated cost of goods sold for intercompany sales for Year 5 and unrealized profits in ending inventory at December 31, Year 5?
   a. −$448,000
   b. −$454,000
   c. −$478,000
   d. −$556,000

5. To calculate Post's consolidated income tax expense, first add together the unadjusted totals from Post's and Stamp's separate entity financial statements. What amount of adjustment is necessary to this figure for the unrealized profit in beginning inventory for the year ended December 31, Year 5?
   a. $22,500
   b. $24,000
   c. $25,500
   d. $28,000

6. Which of the following would appear on Post's consolidated income statement for the year ended December 31, Year 5, for noncontrolling interest?
   a. $77,250
   b. $84,000
   c. $90,750
   d. $99,000

7. Which of the following would appear on Post's consolidated balance sheet at December 31, Year 5, for noncontrolling interest?
   a. $694,500
   b. $708,000
   c. $714,750
   d. $721,500

8. Pedro Company owns 80% of Sunita Ltd. During Year 2, Pedro sold goods with a 40% gross margin to Sunita. Sunita sold all of these goods in Year 2. How should the Year 2 consolidated income statement be adjusted?
   a. Sales and cost of goods sold should be reduced by the intercompany sales.
   b. Sales and cost of goods sold should be reduced by 80% of the intercompany sales.

   c. Net income should be reduced by 80% of the gross profit of the intercompany sales.

   d. No adjustment is necessary.

9. In Year 2, an 80%-owned subsidiary sold land to the parent at a gain of $50,000. The parent still owns this land at the end of Year 5. Which of the following consolidation adjustments is appropriate for the Year 5 consolidated financial statements?

   a. Decrease gain on sale of land by $50,000.

   b. Decrease noncontrolling interest on the income statement by $10,000.

   c. Increase noncontrolling interest on the balance sheet by $10,000.

   d. Decrease land by $50,000.

10. If unrealized inventory profits have occurred, what is the impact on consolidated financial statements between upstream and downstream transfers?

   a. Downstream transfers may be ignored since they are made by the parent company.

   b. Downstream transfers affect the computation of the noncontrolling interest's share of the subsidiary's net income but upstream transfers do not.

   c. No difference exists in consolidated financial statements between upstream and downstream transfers.

   d. Upstream transfers affect the computation of the noncontrolling interest's share of the subsidiary's net income but downstream transfers do not.

11. Castle Corp. owns 75% of the outstanding shares of Moat Ltd. During Year 5, Moat sold merchandise to Castle for $200,000. At December 31, Year 5, 50% of this merchandise remains in Castle's inventory. For Year 5, gross profit percentages were 40% for Castle and 30% for Moat. How much unrealized profit should be eliminated from ending inventory in the consolidation process at December 31, Year 5?

   a. $30,000

   b. $40,000

   c. $45,000

   d. $60,000

12. Bell Co. owns 90% of Tower Inc. During Year 4, Tower sold inventory costing $75,000 to Bell for $100,000. A total of 16 percent of this inventory was not sold to outsiders until Year 5. During Year 5, Bell sold inventory which cost $96,000 to Tower for $120,000. Thirty-five percent of this inventory was not sold to outsiders until Year 6. Bell reported cost of goods sold of $380,000 in Year 5, while Tower reported an amount of $210,000. What amount should be reported as cost of goods sold on the Year 5 consolidated income statement?

   a. $465,600

   b. $473,440

   c. $474,400

   d. $522,400

13. Hardwood Inc. owns 90% of the outstanding shares of Softwood Corp. During Year 4, Softwood sold inventory which cost $77,000 to Hardwood for $110,000. A total of $40,000 of this inventory was still on hand on December 31, Year 4, and was sold in Year 5. During Year 5, Softwood sold inventory costing $72,000 to Hardwood for $120,000. On December 31, Year 5, $50,000 of this inventory was still on hand. In Year 5 Hardwood reported a net income of $150,000 while Softwood reported $90,000. Assuming a 40%

tax rate, what is the amount of the noncontrolling interest that would be reported on the Year 5 consolidated income statement?
a. $8,200
b. $8,520
c. $9,000
d. $9,800

14. When preparing the consolidated balance sheet, any unrealized profit is removed from ending inventory. Which of the following financial statement concepts best supports this accounting practice?
a. Recognition criteria
b. Historical cost measurement assumption
c. Timeliness
d. Full disclosure principle

(CGA-Canada, from 2002 to 2007)

15. You are preparing the consolidated financial statements for PALE Corp. and its 80%-owned subsidiary, SALE Inc., for the year ended July 31, Year 5. Which of the following transactions would give rise to a deferred income tax asset being recorded on the consolidated balance sheet?
a. PALE sells inventory to SALE at a markup of 30%, and SALE resells all of this inventory prior to year-end.
b. PALE sells inventory to SALE at a markup of 30%, and SALE resells 60% of this inventory prior to year-end.
c. SALE sells inventory that it had acquired from PALE in the previous year to an unrelated party at a markup of 30%.
d. SALE sells inventory that it had acquired from PALE in the previous year to an unrelated party at a loss of $1,000.

(CGA-Canada, from 2002 to 2007)

CASES

Case 1 Beaver Ridge Oilers' Players Association and Mr. Slim, the CEO of the Beaver Ridge Oilers Hockey Club (Club), ask for your help in resolving a salary dispute. Mr. Slim presents the following income statement to the player representatives:

BEAVER RIDGE OILERS HOCKEY CLUB
INCOME STATEMENT

Ticket revenues		$3,000,000
Player salaries	$600,000	
Stadium rent	2,100,000	
Staff salaries	500,000	
Promotion	100,000	3,300,000
Net income (loss)		$ (300,000)

Mr. Slim argues that the Club loses money and cannot afford a salary increase. After further investigation, you determine that the Club owns 90% of the voting shares of Oilers Stadium Inc. (Stadium), which is used primarily by the Oilers. The Club accounts for its investment in the Stadium under the cost method. The Stadium has not declared any dividends since its inception three years ago. As such, the Club has never reported any income on its investment in the Stadium.

Mr. Slim insists that the income for the Stadium should not be a factor in the negotiation of the players' salaries since the Stadium is a separate legal entity and is taxed as a separate legal entity. The income statement for the Stadium is as follows:

OILERS STADIUM INC.
INCOME STATEMENT

Stadium rent revenue	$2,100,000	
Concession revenue	1,200,000	
Parking revenue	100,000	$3,400,000
Cost of concessions	400,000	
Depreciation of stadium	500,000	
Staff salaries	700,000	1,600,000
Net income		$1,800,000

Required:

(a) What advice would you provide to the negotiating parties regarding the issue of whether to consider the Stadium's income in the salary negotiations? Give supporting arguments. Indicate what other pertinent information you would need to provide specific recommendations.

(b) How would your advice change if the Stadium were 90% owned by Mr. Slim directly rather than the Club? Explain.

Case 2   In early September, Year 1, your firm's audit client, D Ltd. (D), acquired in separate transactions, an 80% interest in N Ltd. (N) and a 40% interest in K Ltd. (K). All three companies are federally incorporated Canadian companies and have August 31 year-ends. They all manufacture small appliances but they do not compete with each other.

You are the senior on the audit of D. The partner has just received the preliminary consolidated financial statements from the controller of D along with unconsolidated statements for the three separate companies. Extracts from these statements are summarized in Exhibit I. The partner has requested that you provide him with a memorandum discussing the important financial accounting issues of D. Account balances for the consolidated financial statements should be recalculated to the extent that information is available.

D acquired the 80% interest in N for $4,000,000 paid as follows:

(1) $2,000,000 in cash and,
(2) 160,000 common shares of D recorded in the books of D at $2,000,000.

D acquired its 40% interest in K at a cost of $2,100,000 paid as follows:

(1) $100,000 in cash and,
(2) 160,000 common shares of D recorded in the books of D at $2,000,000.

During the course of the audit, the following information was obtained:

1. The book value of 80% of N's net assets at the date of acquisition was $2,280,000. The purchase discrepancy consisted of the following:

The excess of current value of land over book value	$ 800,000
The excess of current value of plant and equipment over book value	700,000
20% NCI's share of excess of current value over book value	(300,000)
Goodwill of N written off	(48,000)
Deferred research and development expenditures written off	(72,000)
Unallocated excess	640,000
	$1,720,000

The plant and equipment had a remaining useful life of 10 years when D acquired N.

2. The price paid by D for its investment in K was 10% lower than 40% of the fair value of K's identifiable net assets.

3. During August Year 2, K sold goods to D as follows:

Cost to K	$1,000,000
Normal selling price	1,250,000
Price paid by D	1,200,000

D had not sold these goods as of August 31, Year 2.

N also sold goods to D in August Year 2 and D had not sold them by August 31, Year 2.

Cost to N	$600,000
Normal selling price	750,000
Price paid by D	850,000

4. For the year ended August 31, Year 2, D's sales were $8,423,300 and N's sales were $6,144,500.

Required:

Prepare the memorandum requested by the partner.

(CICA adapted)

EXHIBIT I

EXTRACTS FROM FINANCIAL STATEMENTS
At August 31, Year 2
(in 000s)

	Unconsolidated			Consolidated
	D	N	K	D
Investment in N Ltd., at cost	$4,000			
Investment in K Ltd., at cost	2,100			$2,100
Deferred development costs		$ 90		
Goodwill		60		
Noncontrolling interest				590
Common shares	6,000	1,000	$2,000	6,000
Retained earnings, beginning	618	1,850	1,760	618
Net income	600	300	100	660
Dividends	(400)	(200)	(150)	(400)
Retained earnings, end of year	$ 818	$1,950	$1,710	$ 878

PROBLEMS

Problem 1   On January 1, Year 2, PAT Ltd. acquired 90% of SAT Inc. and accounts for its investment under the cost method. SAT sells inventory to PAT on a regular basis at a markup of 30% of selling price. The intercompany sales were $150,000 in Year 2 and $180,000 in Year 3. The total amount owing by PAT related to these intercompany sales was $50,000 at the end of Year 2 and $40,000 at the end of Year 3. On January 1, Year 3, the inventory of PAT contained goods purchased from SAT amounting to $60,000, while the December 31, Year 3, inventory contained goods purchased from SAT amounting to $70,000. Both companies pay income tax at the rate of 40%.

Selected account balances from the records of PAT and SAT for the year ended December 31, Year 3 were as follows:

Inventory	$ 500,000	$ 300,000
Accounts payable	600,000	320,000
Retained earnings, beginning of year	2,400,000	1,100,000
Sales	4,000,000	2,500,000
Cost of sales	3,100,000	1,700,000
Income tax expense	80,000	50,000

Required:

(a) Determine the amount to report on the Year 3 consolidated financial statements for the above noted accounts.

(b) Indicate how noncontrolling interest on the Year 3 consolidated income statement and Year 3 consolidated balance sheet will be affected by the intercompany transactions noted above.

Problem 2   The consolidated income statement of a parent and its 90%-owned subsidiary appears below. It was prepared by an accounting student before reading this chapter.

The following items were overlooked when the statement was prepared:

- The opening inventory of the parent contained an intercompany profit of $5,000.
- During the year, intercompany sales (at a 30% gross profit rate) were made as follows:

By the parent	$100,000
By the subsidiary	80,000

- At the end of the year, half of the items purchased from the parent remained in the inventory of the subsidiary.
- All of the rental revenue and 70% of the interest revenue were intercompany and appeared on the income statement of the parent.
- Assume a 40% rate for income tax.

CONSOLIDATED INCOME STATEMENT

Sales	$500,000
Rental revenue	24,000
Interest revenue	50,000
Total revenue	574,000
Cost of goods sold	350,000
Rental expense	24,000
Interest expense	35,000
Miscellaneous administration expense	45,000
Income tax expense	42,000
Noncontrolling interest in net income	9,000
Total costs and expenses	505,000
Net income	$ 69,000

Required:

Prepare a correct consolidated income statement.

Problem 3   On January 1, Year 1, Spike Ltd. purchased land for $100,000. On December 31, Year 1, Pike Co. acquired all of the common shares of Spike. The fair value of Spike's land on this date was $115,000.

On December 31, Year 2, Spike sold their land to Pike for $125,000. On December 31, Year 3, Pike sold the land to an arm's-length party for $130,000.

Both companies pay income tax at the rate of 40%. Assume that any gain on sale of land is fully taxable. The only land owned by these two companies is the land purchased by Spike in Year 1.

Required:

Determine the account balances for land, gain on sale of land, and income tax on gain for Years 1, 2, and 3 for three sets of financial statements (i.e., separate-entity statements for Pike and Spike and consolidated statements) by completing the following table:

	Land	Gain on Sale	Income Tax on Gain
December 31, Year 1 Pike Spike Consolidated			
December 31, Year 2 Pike Spike Consolidated			
December 31, Year 3 Pike Spike Consolidated			

Problem 4 The statements of income and retained earnings of Paste Company and its subsidiaries, Waste Company and Baste Company, were prepared for the year ended December 31, Year 6, and are shown below:

	Paste	Waste	Baste
Revenues			
Sales	$450,000	$270,000	$190,000
Dividends	43,750	—	—
Rent	—	130,000	—
Interest	10,000	—	—
	503,750	400,000	190,000
Expenses			
Cost of sales	300,000	163,000	145,000
General and administrative	50,000	20,000	15,000
Interest	—	10,000	—
Depreciation	18,000	28,000	—
Rent	25,000	—	14,000
Income tax	27,000	75,000	7,000
	420,000	296,000	181,000
Net income	83,750	104,000	9,000
Retained earnings, Jan. 1, Year 6	800,000	92,000	75,000
	883,750	196,000	84,000
Dividends	180,000	50,000	5,000
Retained earnings, Dec. 31, Year 6	$703,750	$146,000	$ 79,000

Additional Information

- Paste purchased its 80% interest in Waste on January 1, Year 1. On this date, Waste had a retained earnings balance of $40,000 and the purchase discrepancy amounting to $15,000 was allocated entirely to plant and equipment with an estimated remaining life of 8 years.
- Paste purchased its 75% interest in Baste on December 31, Year 3. On this date, Baste had a retained earnings balance of $80,000. The purchase discrepancy amounting to $19,000 was allocated to goodwill; however, because Baste had failed to report adequate profits, the goodwill was entirely written off for consolidated purposes by the end of Year 5.
- Paste has established a policy that any intercompany sales will be made at a gross profit rate of 30%.
- On January 1, Year 6, the inventory of Paste contained goods purchased from Waste for $15,000.
- During Year 6, the following intercompany sales took place:

Paste to Waste	$ 90,000
Waste to Baste	170,000
Baste to Paste	150,000

- On December 31, Year 6, the inventories of each of the three companies contained items purchased on an intercompany basis in the following amounts:

Inventory of:	
Paste	$90,000
Waste	22,000
Baste	60,000

- In addition to its merchandising activities, Waste is in the office equipment rental business. Both Paste and Baste rent office equipment from Waste, and the rental expense on their Year 6 income statements is entirely from this type of transaction.
- During Year 6, Waste paid $10,000 interest to Paste for intercompany advances.
- Paste Company uses the cost method to account for its investments, and uses tax allocation at a rate of 40% when it prepares consolidated financial statements.

Required:

(a) Prepare a statement of consolidated income and retained earnings for Year 6.
(b) Use the criteria for revenue recognition as stated in Section 3400 of the *CICA Handbook* to support the adjustments for unrealized profits on intercompany sales when preparing consolidated financial statements.
(c) Now assume that Paste uses the equity method. Prepare Paste's equity-method journal entries for Year 6.

Problem 5   X Co. acquired 75% of Y Co. on January 1, Year 1, when Y Co. had common stock of $100,000 and retained earnings of $70,000. The purchase discrepancy was allocated as follows on this date:

Inventory	$ 60,000
Equipment (15-year life)	45,000
Total purchase discrepancy	$105,000

Since this date the following events have transpired:

Year 1

- Y Co. reported a net income of $130,000 and paid dividends of $25,000.

- On July 1, X Co. sold land to Y Co. for $102,000. This land was carried in the records of X Co. at $75,000.
- On December 31, Year 1, the inventory of X Co. contained an intercompany profit of $30,000.
- X Co. reported a net income of $400,000 from its own operations.

Year 2

- Y Co. reported a net loss of $16,000 and paid dividends of $5,000.
- Y Co. sold the land that it purchased from X Co. to an unrelated company for $130,000.
- On December 31, Year 2, the inventory of Y Co. contained an intercompany profit of $12,000.
- X Co. reported a net income from its own operations of $72,000.

Required:

Assume a 40% tax rate.
(a) Prepare X Co.'s equity method journal entries for each of Years 1 and 2.
(b) Calculate consolidated net income for each of Years 1 and 2.
(c) Prepare a statement showing the changes in noncontrolling interest in each of Years 1 and 2.
(d) Calculate the balance in X Co.'s account "Investment in Y Co. (equity method)" as at December 31, Year 2.

Problem 6 L Co. owns a controlling interest in M Co. and Q Co. L Co. purchased an 80% interest in M Co. at a time when M Co. reported retained earnings of $500,000. L Co. purchased a 70% interest in Q Co. at a time when Q Co. reported retained earnings of $50,000.

An analysis of the changes in retained earnings of the three companies during the current year appears below:

	Parent L Co.	Sub M Co.	Sub. Q Co.
Retained earnings balance, beginning of current year	$ 976,000	$ 843,000	$ 682,000
Net income	580,000	360,000	240,000
Dividends paid or declared	(250,000)	(200,000)	(150,000)
Retained earnings balance, end of current year	$1,306,000	$1,003,000	$ 772,000

Q Co. sells parts to L Co., which after further processing and assembly are sold by L Co. to M Co., where they become a part of the finished product sold by M Co. Intercompany profits included in inventories at the beginning and end of the current year are estimated as follows:

	Beginning inventory	Ending inventory
Intercompany profit in inventory		
On sales from Q to L	$90,000	$ 35,000
On sales from L to M	52,000	118,000

L Co. uses the cost method to account for its investments, and income tax allocation at a 40% rate when it prepares consolidated financial statements.

Required:

(a) Calculate consolidated net income for the current year.
(b) Prepare a statement of consolidated retained earnings for the current year.

Problem 7 On January 1, Year 3, the Most Company purchased 80% of the outstanding voting shares of the Least Company for $1.6 million in cash. On that date, Least's balance sheet and the fair values of its identifiable assets and liabilities were as follows:

	Carrying value	Fair value
Cash	$ 25,000	$ 25,000
Accounts receivable	310,000	290,000
Inventories	650,000	600,000
Plant and equipment (net)	2,015,000	2,050,000
Total assets	$3,000,000	
Current liabilities	$ 300,000	$ 300,000
Long-term liabilities	1,200,000	1,100,000
Common stock	500,000	
Retained earnings	1,000,000	
Total liabilities and shareholders' equity	$3,000,000	

On January 1, Year 3, Least's plant and equipment had a remaining useful life of eight years. Its long-term liabilities matured on January 1, Year 7. Goodwill, if any, is to be tested yearly for impairment.

The balance sheets as at December 31, Year 9, and the retained earnings statements for the year ending December 31, Year 9, for the two companies are as follows:

BALANCE SHEETS
December 31, Year 9

	Most	Least
Cash	$ 500,000	$ 40,000
Accounts receivable	1,700,000	500,000
Inventories	2,300,000	1,200,000
Plant and equipment (net)	8,200,000	4,000,000
Investment in Least (at cost)	1,600,000	—
Land	700,000	260,000
Total assets	$15,000,000	$6,000,000
Current liabilities	$ 600,000	$ 200,000
Long-term liabilities	3,000,000	3,000,000
Common stock	1,000,000	500,000
Retained earnings	10,400,000	2,300,000
Total liabilities and shareholders' equity	$15,000,000	$6,000,000

RETAINED EARNINGS — Year 9

Balance, January 1, Year 9	$ 9,750,000	$2,000,000
Net income, Year 9	1,000,000	400,000
	10,750,000	2,400,000
Dividends, Year 9	350,000	100,000
Balance, December 31, Year 9	$10,400,000	$2,300,000

Additional Information

- The inventories of both companies have a maximum turnover period of one year. Receivables have a maximum turnover period of 62 days.

- On July 1, Year 7, Most sold a parcel of land to Least for $100,000. Most had purchased this land in Year 4 for $150,000. On September 30, Year 9, Least sold the property to another company for $190,000.
- During Year 9, $2 million of Most's sales were to Least. Of these sales, $500,000 remain in the December 31, Year 9, inventories of Least. The December 31, Year 8, inventories of Least contained $312,500 of merchandise purchased from Most. Most's sales to Least are priced to provide it with a gross profit of 20%.
- During Year 9, $1.5 million of Least's sales were to Most. Of these sales, $714,280 remain in the December 31, Year 9, inventories of Most. The December 31, Year 8, inventories of Most contained $857,140 of merchandise purchased from Least. Least's sales to Most are priced to provide it with a gross profit of 30%.
- Dividends declared on December 31, Year 9, were:

Most	$350,000
Least	100,000

- Goodwill impairment tests resulted in losses of $52,200 in Year 4, and $8,700 in Year 9.
- Assume a 40% tax rate for both companies.

Required:

(a) Prepare the consolidated retained earnings statement.
(b) Prepare the consolidated balance sheet.
(c) Explain how the matching principle supports the adjustments to cost of goods sold when eliminating intercompany sales from the consolidated financial statements.
(d) Calculate goodwill and noncontrolling interest on the consolidated balance sheet at December 31, Year 9, under the parent company extension theory.

Problem 8 H Co. has controlling interests in three subsidiaries, as shown in the data below:

	H Co.	L Co.	Subsidiaries J Co.	K Co.
Retained earnings at acquisition		$30,000	$40,000	$25,000
Percent of ownership		95%	90%	85%
Retained earnings, Jan. 1, Year 5	$12,000	50,000	43,000	30,000
Net income (loss), Year 5		20,000	(5,000)	30,000
Dividends paid, Year 5	10,000	5,000	3,000	15,000
Intercompany sales		50,000	70,000	

K Co. had items in its inventory on January 1, Year 5, on which L Co. had made a profit of $5,000.

J Co. had items in its inventory on December 31, Year 5, on which K Co. had made a profit of $10,000.

J Co. rents premises from L Co. at an annual rental of $8,500.

The parent company has no income (other than from its investments) and no expenses. It uses the equity method of recording its investments but has made no entries during Year 5. Assume a 40% tax rate.

Required:

Prepare the following:
(a) Entries that H Co. would make in Year 5.
(b) A calculation of consolidated net income for Year 5.
(c) A statement of consolidated retained earnings for Year 5.

Problem 9

Purple Company purchased a 70% interest in Sand Company several years ago in order to obtain retail outlets for its major products. Since that time Purple has sold to Sand a substantial portion of its merchandise requirements. At the beginning of the current year, Sand's inventory of $690,000 was composed 60% of goods purchased from Purple at markups averaging 30% on Purple's cost. Sales from Purple to Sand during the current year were $5,600,000. The estimated intercompany profit in Sand's ending inventory was $194,000.

Purple owns buildings and land used in Sand's retail operations and rented to Sand. Rentals paid by Sand to Purple during the current year amounted to $743,000. At the end of the current year, Purple sold to Sand for $250,000 land to be used in the development of a shopping centre that had cost Purple $203,500. The gain was included in Purple's net income for the current year. Purple also holds a one-year, 6% note of Sand on which it has accrued interest revenues of $22,500 during the current year.

During the current year, Purple reported net income of $568,100 and Sand reported net income of $248,670. Purple uses the cost method to account for its investment.

Required:

Calculate the current year's consolidated net income (assume a 40% tax rate).

Problem 10

The income statements of Evans Company and Falcon Company for the current year are shown below:

	Evans	Falcon
Sales revenues	$450,000	$600,000
Dividend revenues	32,000	—
Rental revenues	33,600	—
Interest revenues	—	18,000
	515,600	618,000
Cost of goods sold	288,000	353,000
Operating expenses	104,000	146,000
Interest expense	30,000	—
Income taxes	31,700	43,500
	453,700	542,500
Net income	61,900	75,500
Beginning retained earnings	632,000	348,000
Dividends	(30,000)	(40,000)
Ending retained earnings	$663,900	$383,500

Evans owns 80% of the outstanding common stock of Falcon, purchased at the time the latter company was organized.

Evans sells parts to Falcon at a price that is 25% above cost. Total sales from Evans to Falcon during the year were $85,000. Included in Falcon's inventories were parts purchased from Evans amounting to $21,250 in beginning inventories and $28,750 in the ending inventory.

Falcon sells back to Evans certain finished goods, at a price that gives Falcon an average gross profit of 30% on these intercompany sales. Total sales from Falcon to Evans during the year were $177,000. Included in the inventories of Evans were parts acquired from Falcon amounting to $11,000 in beginning inventories and $3,000 in ending inventories.

Falcon rents an office building from Evans, and pays $2,800 per month in rent. Evans has borrowed $600,000 through a series of 5% notes, of which Falcon holds $360,000 as notes receivable. Use income tax allocation at a 40% rate.

Required:

(a) Prepare a consolidated income statement.
(b) Prepare a consolidated statement of retained earnings.
(c) Calculate goodwill impairment loss and noncontrolling interest on the consolidated income statement for the year ended December 31, Year 6, under the parent company extension theory.

Problem 11   The partial trial balance of P Co. and S Co. at December 31, Year 5, was:

	P Co.		S Co.	
	Dr.	Cr.	Dr.	Cr.
Investment in S. Co.	90,000			
Common stock		150,000		60,000
Retained earnings (charged with dividends, no other changes during the year)		101,000		34,000

Additional Information

- The investment in the shares of S Co. (a 90% interest) was acquired January 2, Year 1, for $90,000. At that time, the shareholders' equity of this company was as follows: capital stock, $60,000; retained earnings, $20,000.
- Net incomes of the two companies for the year were:

P Co.	$60,000
S Co.	48,000

- During Year 5, sales of P Co. to S Co. were $10,000, and sales of S Co. to P Co. were $50,000. Rates of gross profit on intercompany sales in Year 4 and Year 5 were 40% of sales.
- On December 31, Year 4, the inventory of P Co. included $7,000 of merchandise purchased from S Co., and the inventory of S Co. included $3,000 of merchandise purchased from P Co. On December 31, Year 5, the inventory of P Co. included $20,000 of merchandise purchased from S Co. and inventory of S Co. included $5,000 of merchandise purchased from P Co.
- During the year ended December 31, Year 5, P Co. paid dividends of $12,000 and S Co. paid dividends of $10,000.
- At the time that P Co. purchased the stock of S Co., the purchase discrepancy was allocated to patents of S Co. These patents are being amortized for consolidation purposes over a period of five years.
- In Year 3, land that originally cost $45,000 was sold by S Co. to P Co. for $50,000. The land is still owned by P Co.
- Assume a corporate tax rate of 40%.

Required:

Prepare the following:

(a) A statement of consolidated retained earnings for the year ended December 31, Year 5.
(b) Your calculations of the amount of noncontrolling interest that would appear in the consolidated balance sheet at December 31, Year 5

Problem 12

On January 2, Year 1, Road Ltd. acquired 70% of the outstanding voting shares of Runner Ltd. The purchase discrepancy of $280,000 on that date was allocated in the following manner:

Inventory	$100,000	
Land	50,000	
Plant and equipment	60,000	estimated life 5 years
Patent	40,000	estimated life 8 years
Goodwill	30,000	
	$280,000	

The Year 5 income statements and retained earnings statements for the two companies were as follows:

	Road	Runner
Sales	$4,000,000	$2,100,000
Intercompany investment income	210,700	—
Rental revenue	—	70,000
Total revenue	4,210,700	2,170,000
Cost of goods sold	2,000,000	800,000
Selling and administrative expense	550,000	480,000
Interest expense	250,000	140,000
Depreciation	450,000	225,000
Patent amortization	—	25,000
Rental expense	35,000	—
Income tax	300,000	200,000
Total expenses	3,585,000	1,870,000
Net income	$ 625,700	$ 300,000
Retained earnings, January 1	$2,000,000	$ 900,000
Add net income	625,700	300,000
	2,625,700	1,200,000
Less dividends	100,000	50,000
Retained earnings, December 31	$2,525,700	$1,150,000

Additional Information

- Runner regularly sells merchandise to Road. Intercompany sales in Year 5 totalled $400,000.
- Intercompany profits in the inventories of Road were as follows:

January 1, Year 5	$75,000
December 31, Year 5	40,000

- Road's entire rental expense relates to equipment rented from Runner.
- A goodwill impairment loss of $3,000 occurred in Year 5.
- Road uses the equity method to account for its investment, and uses income tax allocation at the rate of 40% when it prepares consolidated statements.

Required:

(a) Prepare the following consolidated financial statements for Year 5:
   (i) Income statement.
   (ii) Retained earnings statement.
(b) Calculate goodwill impairment loss and noncontrolling interest on the consolidated income statement for the year ended December 31, Year 6, under the parent company extension theory.

Problem 13 The following are the financial statements of Post Corporation and its subsidiary Sage Company as at December 31, Year 3:

BALANCE SHEETS
December 31, Year 3

	Post	Sage
Cash	$ 12,200	$ 12,900
Accounts receivable	17,200	9,100
Notes receivable	—	55,000
Inventory	34,000	27,000
Land	175,000	19,000
Plant and equipment	520,000	65,000
Accumulated depreciation	(229,400)	(17,000)
Investment in Sage, at cost	63,000	—
	$592,000	$171,000
Accounts payable	$212,000	$ 40,000
Notes payable	55,000	—
Capital stock	100,000	50,000
Retained earnings	225,000	81,000
	$592,000	$171,000

STATEMENTS OF INCOME AND RETAINED EARNINGS — Year 3

	Post Corp.	Sage Co.
Sales	$900,000	$240,000
Management fee revenue	26,500	—
Interest revenue	—	6,800
Gain on sale of land	—	30,000
Dividend revenue	10,500	—
	937,000	276,800
Cost of goods sold	540,000	162,000
Interest expense	20,000	—
Other expenses	180,000	74,800
Income tax expense	80,000	16,000
	820,000	252,800
Net income	117,000	24,000
Retained earnings, January 1	158,000	72,000
Dividends	(50,000)	(15,000)
Retained earnings, December 31	$225,000	$ 81,000

Additional Information

- Post purchased 70% of the outstanding shares of Sage on January 1, Year 1, at a cost of $63,000, and has used the cost method to account for its investment. On that date Sage had retained earnings of $15,000, and fair values were equal to carrying values for all its net assets except inventory (overvalued by $12,000) and equipment (undervalued by $18,000). The equipment had an estimated remaining life of five years.
- The companies sell merchandise to each other at a gross profit rate of 25%.
- The December 31, Year 2, inventory of Post contained purchases made from Sage amounting to $14,000. There were no intercompany purchases in the inventory of Sage on this date.

- During Year 3 the following intercompany transactions took place:
  - Sage made a payment of $26,500 to Post for management fees, which was recorded under the category "other expenses."
  - Sage made sales of $90,000 to Post. The December 31, Year 3, inventory of Post contained merchandise purchased from Sage amounting to $28,000.
  - Post made sales of $125,000 to Sage. The December 31, Year 3, inventory of Sage contained merchandise purchased from Post amounting to $18,000.
  - On July 1, Year 3, Post borrowed $55,000 from Sage and signed a note bearing interest at 12% per annum. The interest on this note was paid on December 31, Year 3.
  - During the year, Sage sold land to Post and recorded a gain of $30,000 on the transaction. This land is being held by Post on December 31, Year 3.
- Goodwill impairment losses occurred as follows: Year 1, $2,600; Year 2, $460; Year 3, $1,530.
- Both companies pay income tax at 40% on their taxable incomes.

Required:

(a) Prepare the following consolidated financial statements for Year 3:
  (i) Income statement
  (ii) Retained earnings statement
  (iii) Balance sheet
(b) Calculate goodwill impairment loss and noncontrolling interest on the consolidated income statement for the year ended December 31, Year 3, under the parent company extension theory.
(c) Calculate goodwill and noncontrolling interest on the consolidated balance sheet at December 31, Year 3, under the parent company extension theory.

Problem 14 On January 1, Year 1, the Vine Company purchased 60,000 of the 80,000 common shares of the Devine Company for $80 per share. On that date, Devine had common stock of $3,500,000, and retained earnings of $2,100,000. When acquired, Devine had inventories with fair values $100,000 less than carrying value, a parcel of land with a fair value $200,000 greater than the carrying value, and equipment with a fair value $200,000 less than carrying value. There are also internally generated patents with an estimated market value of $400,000 and a five-year remaining life. A long-term liability had a market value $100,000 greater than book value; this liability was paid off December 31, Year 4. All other identifiable assets and liabilities of Devine had fair values equal to their carrying values. At the acquisition date, the equipment had an expected remaining useful life of 12 years. Goodwill is to be treated in accordance with the provisions of the *CICA Handbook*, Section 3062. Both companies use the straight-line method for all depreciation and amortization calculations and the FIFO inventory cost flow assumption. Assume a 40% income tax rate on all applicable items.

On September 1, Year 5, Devine sold a parcel of land to Vine, and recorded a total nonoperating gain of $400,000.

Sales from Vine to Devine totalled $1,000,000 in Year 4 and $2,000,000 in Year 5. These sales were priced to provide a gross profit margin on selling price of 33 $^1/_3$% to the Vine Company. Devine's December 31, Year 4, inventory contained $300,000 of these sales; December 31, Year 5, inventory contained $600,000.

Sales from Devine to Vine were $800,000 in Year 4 and $1,200,000 in Year 5. These sales were priced to provide a gross profit margin on selling price of 40% to the Devine Company. Vine's December 31, Year 4, inventory contained $100,000 of these sales; the December 31, Year 5, inventory contained $500,000.

Vine's investment in Devine's account is carried in accordance with the cost method, and includes advances to Devine of $200,000.

There are no intercompany amounts other than those noted, except for the dividends of $500,000 (total amount) declared and paid by Devine.

INCOME STATEMENTS
for Year Ending December 31, Year 5
(in $000s)

	Vine	Devine
Sales	$11,600	$3,000
Dividends, investment income, and gains	400	1,000
Total revenues	12,000	4,000
Cost of goods sold	8,000	1,500
Other expenses	500	300
Income taxes	500	200
Total expenses	9,000	2,000
Net income	$ 3,000	$2,000

BALANCE SHEETS
December 31, Year 5
(in $000s)

	Vine	Devine
Cash and current receivables	$ 900	$ 300
Inventories	4,600	2,400
Investment in Devine (cost)	5,000	
Plant and equipment	13,000	6,800
Land	6,000	2,500
Total assets	$29,500	$12,000
Current liabilities	$ 700	$ 300
Long-term liabilities	6,600	1,100
Future income taxes	200	100
Common stock	10,000	3,500
Retained earnings	12,000	7,000
Total liabilities and equity	$29,500	$12,000

Required:

(a) Show the allocation of the purchase price at acquisition and the related amortization schedule. Show and label all calculations.

(b) Compute the investment income under the equity method that would be reported if Vine had been permitted to use the equity method, rather than consolidate, in Year 5.

(c) Prepare a consolidated income statement for the Vine Company and its subsidiary for the year ending December 31, Year 5.

(d) Prepare a consolidated balance sheet for Vine Company at December 31, Year 5.

(e) Prepare a proof of consolidated retained earnings at December 31, Year 5.

(Adapted from a problem prepared by Peter Secord, St. Mary's University.)

Problem 15   Paper Corp. purchased 70% of the outstanding shares of Sand Ltd. on January 1, Year 2, at a cost of $84,000. Paper has always used the cost method to account for its investments. On January 1, Year 2, Sand had common shares of $50,000 and retained earnings of $30,000, and fair values were equal to carrying values for all its net assets except inventory (fair value was $9,000 less than book value) and equipment (fair value was $24,000 greater than book value). The equipment had an estimated remaining life of 6 years on January 1, Year 2.

The following are the financial statements of Paper Corp. and its subsidiary Sand Ltd. as at December 31, Year 5:

BALANCE SHEETS
December 31, Year 5

	Paper Corp.	Sand Ltd.
Cash	$ —	$ 10,000
Accounts receivable	36,000	30,000
Note receivable	—	40,000
Inventory	66,000	44,000
Equipment, net	220,000	76,000
Land	150,000	30,000
Investment in Sand	84,000	—
	$556,000	$230,000
Bank indebtedness	$ 90,000	$ —
Accounts payable	50,000	60,000
Notes payable	40,000	—
Common shares	150,000	50,000
Retained earnings	226,000	120,000
	$556,000	$230,000

STATEMENTS OF RETAINED EARNINGS
for the year ended December 31, Year 5

	Paper Corp.	Sand Ltd.
Retained earnings, January 1, Year 5	$106,000	$ 92,000
Net income	120,000	48,000
Dividends	—	(20,000)
Retained earnings, December 31, Year 5	$226,000	$120,000

INCOME STATEMENTS
for the year ended December 31, Year 5

	Paper Corp.	Sand Ltd.
Sales	$798,000	$300,000
Management fee revenue	24,000	—
Investment income	14,000	3,600
Gain on sale of land	—	20,000
	836,000	323,600
Cost of sales	480,000	200,000
Amortization	40,000	12,000
Interest expense	10,000	—
Miscellaneous expenses	106,000	31,600
Income taxes	80,000	32,000
	716,000	275,600
Net income	$120,000	$ 48,000

Additional Information

1. During Year 5, Sand made a cash payment of $2,000 per month to Paper for management fees, which is included in Sand's "Miscellaneous expenses."
2. During Year 5, Paper made intercompany sales of $100,000 to Sand. The December 31, Year 5, inventory of Sand contained goods purchased from Paper amounting to $30,000. These sales had a gross profit of 35%.
3. On April 1, Year 5, Paper acquired land from Sand for $40,000. This land has been recorded on Sand's books at a net book value of $20,000. Paper paid for the land by signing a $40,000 notes payable to Sand, bearing yearly interest at 8%. Interest for Year 5 was paid by Paper in cash on December 31, Year 5. This land was still being held by Paper on December 31, Year 5.
4. The fair value of consolidated goodwill remained unchanged from January 1, Year 5, to July, Year 5. On July 1, Year 5, a valuation was performed, indicating that the fair value of consolidated goodwill was $3,500.
5. Sand and Paper pay taxes at a 40% rate. Assume that none of the gains or losses were capital gains or losses.

Required:

(a) Prepare, in good form, a calculation of goodwill and any unamortized purchase price discrepancy as of December 31, Year 5.
(b) Prepare Paper's consolidated income statement for the year ended December 31, Year 5.
(c) Calculate the following balances that would appear on Paper's consolidated balance sheet as at December 31, Year 5.
  (i)   Inventory
  (ii)   Land
  (iii) Notes payable
  (iv)   Noncontrolling interest
  (v)   Common shares
(d) Now assume that Paper switches to the equity method. Calculate the balance in the Investment in Sand account as at December 31, Year 5.

(CGA Canada, from 2002 to 2007)

Chapter 8

(A) Intercompany Profits in Depreciable Assets
(B) Intercompany Bondholdings

LEARNING OBJECTIVES

After studying this chapter, you should be able to do the following:

- Prepare consolidated financial statements that reflect the elimination and subsequent realization of upstream and downstream intercompany profits in depreciable assets.
- Explain how the historical cost principle supports the elimination of unrealized profits resulting from intercompany transactions when preparing consolidated financial statements.
- Prepare the journal entries under the equity method to reflect the elimination and subsequent realization of intercompany profits in depreciable assets.
- Calculate the gain or loss that results from the elimination of intercompany bondholdings and the allocation of such gain or loss to the equities of the controlling and noncontrolling interests.
- Explain how the recognition of gains on the elimination of intercompany bondholdings is consistent with the principle of recording gains only when they are realized.
- Prepare consolidated financial statements that reflect the gains or losses that are the result of intercompany bondholdings.

INTRODUCTION

The elimination of intercompany transactions and unrealized profit is one of the most significant problems encountered in the consolidation process. The volume of transfers within most large enterprises can be quite large. For example, Petro-Canada, one of Canada's largest oil and gas companies, reported intersegment revenue of $1,484[1] million in 2006, which represented more than 7 percent of total revenues.

In this chapter we complete our examination of intercompany profits in assets; we also examine the consolidation issues that arise from intercompany bondholdings. Because these transactions are so distinctly different in their impact on the consolidated statements, this chapter is divided into two parts.

Part (A) looks at the elimination and realization of intercompany profits (losses) in depreciable assets. The concepts involved in the holdback of profits

---

[1]Petro-Canada 2006 Annual Report, www.petrocanada.ca/annualreport2006/en/ investor/notes/3.htm, accessed September 11, 2007.

(losses) are similar to those examined previously with regard to intercompany land profits (losses), but the realization concepts are different because they are based on consumption rather than a sale.

Part (B) examines the gains (losses) that are created in the consolidated financial statements when intercompany bondholdings are eliminated.

(A) Intercompany Profits in Depreciable Assets

Holdback and Realization — Year 1

Profit is recognized when the goods are sold to outsiders.

In Chapter 7, we illustrated the holdback of an intercompany profit in inventory and land. In both cases, the before-tax profit of $600 and the corresponding income tax of $240 were held back in the year of the intercompany transaction and realized in the year that the asset was sold to outsiders. In both cases, the profit was eventually recognized in both the financial statements of the individual companies and in the consolidated financial statements. Only the timing of the recognition was different. We will now examine the holdback and the realization in the consolidated statements of an intercompany profit in a depreciable asset.

We return to the Chapter 7 example of Parent Company and its 90-percent owned subsidiary, Sub Inc. The Year 1 financial statements of the two companies are shown in Exhibit 8.1 on the following page. Parent has used the cost method to account for its investment.

Notice that although the net incomes and total assets of the two companies are unchanged, the details on each statement have been changed so that we can focus on the following intercompany transaction involving equipment that occurred during the year.

On July, 1 Year 1, Sub sold highly specialized equipment with a very short useful life to Parent and recorded a profit of $600 on the transaction. We are assuming that Sub purchased this equipment for $1,500 on this date with the intention of using it, but instead immediately sold it to Parent for $2,100. This intercompany transaction was recorded in the following manner by the two companies:

Parent Company			*Sub Inc.*		
Equipment	2,100		Cash	2,100	
Cash		2,100	Equipment		1,500
			Gain on sale of		
			equipment		600

It is also assumed that this transaction was not a capital gain for tax purposes, and that Sub's tax rate is 40 percent. This means that Sub paid $240 (40% × 600) income tax on this profit. We further assume that this is the only depreciable asset held by either company and that the equipment is expected to be obsolete in one-and-a-half years. On December 31, Year 1, Parent recorded depreciation expense on this equipment in the following manner:

The parent's depreciation expense is based on the parent's cost.

Depreciation expense	700	
Accumulated depreciation		700
To record depreciation for half a year		
(2,100 ÷ 1½ = 1,400 × ½ = 700)		

Exhibit 8.1

INCOME STATEMENTS — for Year 1

	Parent	Sub
Sales	$20,000	$ 7,400
Gain on sale of equipment	—	600
	20,000	8,000
Depreciation expense	700	—
Miscellaneous expenses	13,700	5,200
Income tax expense	2,200	1,100
	16,600	6,300
Net income	$ 3,400	$ 1,700

The gain on sale is recorded on the separate-entity books of Sub.

RETAINED EARNINGS STATEMENTS — for Year 1

	Parent	Sub
Balance, January 1	$12,000	$ 4,500
Net income	3,400	1,700
	15,400	6,200
Dividends	2,000	—
Balance, December 31	$13,400	$ 6,200

BALANCE SHEETS — at December 31, Year 1

	Parent	Sub
Assets (miscellaneous)	$27,750	$23,200
Equipment	2,100	—
Accumulated depreciation	(700)	—
Investment in Sub Inc.	11,250	—
	$40,400	$23,200
Liabilities	$12,000	$ 9,000
Common stock	15,000	8,000
Retained earnings	13,400	6,200
	$40,400	$23,200

The equipment is recorded at the parent's cost on the separate-entity books of Parent.

The cost of the equipment to the single entity was $1,500.

It should be noted that if Sub had sold the equipment at its cost, Parent's Year 1 depreciation expense would have been $500 ($1,500 \div 1\frac{1}{2} \times \frac{1}{2} = 500$). This is the amount of depreciation expense that should appear in the income statement of the entity (i.e., in the consolidated income statement) for Year 1, in that it represents depreciation based on the historical cost of the equipment to the entity.

When we examine the separate income statements of the two companies (Exhibit 8.1), it should be obvious that the $600 gain is not a gain from a single-entity point of view, and that the $700 depreciation expense does not represent historical cost depreciation to the entity. Two adjustments need to be made when the Year 1 consolidated income statement is prepared; these have opposite effects on the before-tax income of the entity. The first adjustment eliminates the gain on sale of equipment recorded on July 1, Year 1, because as of that date the gain is unrealized from the single-entity point of view. This adjustment reduces before-tax income by $600 and holds back this profit for consolidation purposes. A corresponding reduction of $240 should be made to income tax expense so that a net after-tax gain of $360 is held back. This concept is similar in all respects to the holdback of the land gain that was illustrated in Chapter 7.

The depreciation expense for the single entity was $500.

The second adjustment reduces depreciation expense by $200 ($600 ÷ 1½ × ½). The amount of the reduction represents the depreciation taken in Year 1 on this $600 gain, and results in a consolidated depreciation expense of $500 based on historical cost, as required. This reduction of depreciation expense increases the before-tax income of the entity by $200. In other words, the parent uses the equipment to carry out its business of selling goods or providing services to its customers. Even though the equipment is not sold to outsiders, the products or services are sold to outsiders. Therefore, the gain from the intercompany sale of the equipment is realized over the life of the equipment as the parent uses the equipment to produce goods or provide services for outsiders. This concept bases the realization of the gain on the consumption (by depreciation) of the asset that contains the unrealized gain. A corresponding increase of $80 should be made to income tax expense to match the tax with the portion of the gain realized. The result will be a net after-tax realization of $120 for consolidation purposes.

The net effect of the two after-tax adjustments results in the entity's Year 1 net income being reduced by $240 (360 – 120). Because Sub was the selling company, this $240 reduction is allocated to the noncontrolling and controlling interests in the same manner as was illustrated in Chapter 7.

The preceding paragraphs have briefly outlined the concepts involved in the holdback and realization of an intercompany gain in a depreciable fixed asset. We will now apply these concepts by preparing the Year 1 consolidated financial statements of Parent using the direct approach. It is useful to start by preparing the three calculations shown in Exhibit 8.2.

Exhibit 8.2

EQUIPMENT GAIN — SUB INC. SELLING

	Before tax	40% tax	After tax
This is an upstream transaction since the Sub sold to the Parent.			
Gain, July 1, Year 1	$600	$240	$360 **(a)**
Less realized by depreciation for Year 1	200	80	120 **(b)**
Balance, unrealized at Dec. 31, Year 1	$400	$160	$240 **(c)**

CALCULATION OF CONSOLIDATED NET INCOME — for Year 1

The Sub's income is adjusted for both the unrealized gain and the realization of the gain through depreciation by the parent.	Net income — Parent Co.		$3,400
Net income — Sub Inc.	1,700	
Less after-tax gain on sale of equipment **(2a)**	360	
	1,340	
Add after-tax gain realized by depreciation **(2b)**	120	
Adjusted net income — Sub Inc.	1,460	
Parent Co.'s share	90%	1,314
Consolidated net income		$4,714 **(d)**
Noncontrolling interest (10% × 1,460)		$ 146 **(e)**

CALCULATION OF NONCONTROLLING INTEREST
at December 31, Year 1

NCI is affected by unrealized profits on upstream transactions. (left margin note)	

Shareholders' equity — Sub Inc.

Common stock	$8,000
Retained earnings	6,200
	14,200
Less net unrealized equipment gain after tax **(2c)**	240
Adjusted shareholders' equity	13,960
Noncontrolling interest's share	10%
	$1,396 **(f)**

It should be noted that the calculation of consolidated net income is made to adjust the net income of the parent from the cost method to the equity method. If the parent had used the equity method, we would still have to adjust for unrealized profits from intercompany transactions.

DISCUSSION QUESTION

Is Income Under The Equity Method Always Equal to Consolidated Net Income?

Enron Corporation's 2000 financial statements disclosed the following transaction with LIM2, a nonconsolidated special purpose entity (SPE) that was formed by Enron:

> In June 2000, LIM2 purchased dark fiber optic cable from Enron for a purchase price of $100 million. LIM2 paid Enron $30 million in cash and the balance in an interest-bearing note for $70 million. Enron recognized $67 million in pre-tax earnings in 2000 related to the asset sale.

Investigators later discovered that LIM2 was in many ways controlled by Enron. In the wake of the bankruptcy of Enron, both the American and Canadian standard-setters introduced accounting standards that require the consolidation of SPEs that are essentially controlled by their sponsor firm.

By selling goods to SPEs that it controlled but did not consolidate, did Enron overstate its earnings?

How should this transaction have been accounted for assuming that:

(a) Enron controlled LIM2 and used consolidated financial statements to report its investment in LIM2.

(b) Enron had significant influence over LIM2 and used the equity method to report its investment.

(c) Enron did not have control or significant influence over LIM2 but LIM2 was considered a related party and Enron had to apply Section 3840, "Related Party Transactions."

Exhibit 8.3 illustrates the preparation of the consolidated financial statements using the direct approach.

The consolidated income statement was prepared by combining, line by line, the revenues and expenses of the two companies. The amount for noncontrolling interest is based on the *adjusted income* of Sub. The intercompany eliminations are shown in Exhibit 8.3 in boldface and are summarized as follows:

(i) The $600 gain on the equipment and the income tax expense for the tax on this gain are eliminated. The net effect is to reduce the after-tax income of the entity by $360.

(ii) The excess depreciation to the single entity in Year 1 is eliminated. Consolidated depreciation is now based on historical cost. Because this elimination results in a realization of $200 of the original gain, income tax expense is increased by $80 to match the tax with the gain realized. The net result is an after-tax realization of $120.

The two eliminations decreased the entity's net income by $240, which was allocated to the two equities as follows:

To noncontrolling interest (10% × 240)	$ 24
To controlling interest (90% × 240)	216
	$240

Exhibit 8.3	**Year 1 Consolidated Statements** **Adjusted for Intercompany Equipment Profit** (direct approach)

PARENT COMPANY
CONSOLIDATED INCOME STATEMENT
for the Year Ended December 31, Year 1

Income tax expense is matched to the income of the consolidated entity.

Sales (20,000 + 7,400)	$27,400
Gain on sale of equipment (0 + 600 – **(2a) 600**)	–0–
	27,400
Depreciation expense (700 + 0 – **(2b) 200**)	500
Miscellaneous expenses (13,700 + 5,200)	18,900
Income tax expense (2,200 + 1,100 – **(2a) 240** + **(2b) 80**)	3,140
	22,540
Net income — entity	4,860
Less noncontrolling interest **(2e)**	146
Net income **(2d)**	$ 4,714

PARENT COMPANY
CONSOLIDATED RETAINED EARNINGS STATEMENT
for the Year Ended December 31, Year 1

Balance, January 1	$12,000
Net income	4,714
	16,714
Dividends	2,000
Balance, December 31	$14,714

PARENT COMPANY
CONSOLIDATED BALANCE SHEET
at December 31, Year 1

The equipment is reported at the cost when it was purchased from outsiders.

Assets — miscellaneous (27,750 + 23,200)	$50,950
Equipment (2,100 + 0 – **(2a) 600**)	1,500
Accumulated depreciation (700 + 0 – **(2b) 200**)	(500)
Deferred charge–income taxes (0 + 0 + **(2a) 240** – **(2b) 80**)	160
	$52,110
Liabilities (12,000 + 9,000)	$21,000
Common stock	15,000
Retained earnings	14,714
Noncontrolling interest	1,396
	$52,110

The consolidated retained earnings statement has been prepared in the normal manner. Because we are consolidating one year after acquisition, the parent's retained earnings at the beginning of the year are equal to consolidated retained earnings on that date.

The consolidated balance sheet was prepared by combining the assets and liabilities of the two companies and making the following adjustments (shown in Exhibit 8.3 in boldface) for the equipment gain:

The tax paid on the unrealized profits represents a prepayment from a consolidated viewpoint.

Accumulated depreciation is based on the original cost to the consolidated entity.

(i)   When the before-tax gain of $600 is removed from the equipment, the resulting balance of $1,500 represents the original cost to the entity. The $240 increase to deferred charge–income taxes represents the tax on this gain and corresponds with the reduction of tax expense in the income statement.

(ii) Removes the amount of the gain contained in accumulated depreciation. The resulting amount ($500) is the accumulated depreciation on the original cost. The $80 decrease to deferred charge–income taxes corresponds with the increase in income tax expense made in the income statement.

Note that the $400 reduction of the net book value of the equipment ($600 – $200), together with an increase in deferred charge–income taxes of $160 (40% × $400), results in total consolidated assets being reduced by $240, which corresponds to the reduction made to the entity's net income in the consolidated income statement. The fact that this reduction was allocated to the two equities was noted on page 333.

Equity Method Journal Entries

Our example has assumed that Parent uses the cost method to account for its investment. If Parent was using the equity method, the following journal entries would be made on December 31, Year 1:

The equity method captures the net effect of all consolidation entries.

Investment in Sub Inc.	1,530	
Investment income		1,530
90% of the net income of Sub Inc. (90% × 1,700 = 1,530)		
Investment income	324	
Investment in Sub Inc.		324
To hold back 90% of the equipment profit recorded by Sub (90% × 360 = 324)		
Investment in Sub Inc.	108	
Investment income		108
To realize 90% of the profit realized by depreciation (90% × 120 = 108)		

After these entries are posted, the two related equity-method accounts of Parent will show the following changes and balances:

The investment account is a balance sheet account at the end of the year whereas investment income is an income statement account for one period of time.

	Investment in Sub Inc.	Investment income
Balance, January 1, Year 1	$11,250	
Income from Sub Inc.	1,530	$1,530
Equipment profit (held back)	(324)	(324)
Equipment profit realized	108	108
Balance, December 31, Year 1	$12,564	$1,314

The parent's income under the equity method should be equal to consolidated net income.

Parent's total income under the equity method would be $4,714, consisting of $3,400 from its own operations as reported on page 330 plus investment income of $1,314 as reported above. This income of $4,714 should be and is equal to consolidated net income.

Appendix 8A, at the end of this chapter, illustrates the working-paper approach to the preparation of the Year 1 consolidated financial statements. Because the cost-method approach first adjusts the parent's accounts to the equity method, cost-method working papers are the only ones illustrated.

Realization of Remaining Gain — Year 2

The equipment sold to the parent on July 1, Year 1, had a remaining life of $1\frac{1}{2}$ years on that date. When the Year 1 consolidated income statement was prepared, both the holdback of the total gain and the realization of one-third of the gain took place. When the Year 2 consolidated income statement is prepared, adjustments will be made to realize the remaining two-thirds of the gain. This intercompany gain will be fully realized for consolidation purposes at the end of Year 2, only because the equipment had an unusually short remaining life of $1\frac{1}{2}$ years on the date of the intercompany sale.

The Year 2 financial statements for the two companies are shown in Exhibit 8.4.

Before the consolidated financial statements are prepared, we must make the four calculations shown in Exhibit 8.5.

Exhibit 8.4

INCOME STATEMENTS — for Year 2

	Parent	Sub
Sales	$25,000	$12,000
Depreciation expense	1,400	—
Miscellaneous expenses	16,950	6,900
Income tax expense	2,600	2,000
	20,950	8,900
Net income	$ 4,050	$ 3,100

The parent reports depreciation expense for one full year on its separate-entity income statement.

RETAINED EARNINGS STATEMENTS — for Year 2

	Parent	Sub
Balance, January 1	$13,400	$ 6,200
Net income	4,050	3,100
	17,450	9,300
Dividends	2,500	—
Balance, December 31	$14,950	$ 9,300

BALANCE SHEETS — at December 31, Year 2

	Parent	Sub
Assets (miscellaneous)	$32,700	$28,300
Equipment	2,100	—
Accumulated depreciation	(2,100)	—
Investment in Sub Inc.	11,250	—
	$43,950	$28,300
Liabilities	$14,000	$11,000
Common stock	15,000	8,000
Retained earnings	14,950	9,300
	$43,950	$28,300

The parent reports accumulated depreciation for $1\frac{1}{2}$ years on its separate-entity balance sheet.

Exhibit 8.5

EQUIPMENT GAIN — SUB INC. SELLING

	Before tax	40% tax	After tax
Gain, July 1, Year 1	$600	$240	$360 **(a)**
Less realized by depreciation for Year 1	200	80	120 **(b)**
Balance unrealized, at Dec. 31, Year 1	400	160	240 **(c)**
Less realized by depreciation for Year 2	400	160	240 **(d)**
Balance unrealized, at Dec. 31, Year 2	$ –0–	$ –0–	$ –0–

Differentiate between adjustments for a period of time (i.e., for Year 2) versus a point in time (i.e., at the end of Year 1).

CALCULATION OF CONSOLIDATED NET INCOME — for Year 2

This schedule shows the calculation for a period of time, i.e., for Year 2.

Net income — Parent Co.		$4,050
Net Income — Sub Inc.	3,100	
Add after-tax equipment gain realized by depreciation **(5d)**	240	
Adjusted net income — Sub Inc.	3,340	
Parent Co.'s share	90%	3,006
Consolidated net income		$7,056 **(e)**
Noncontrolling interest (10% × 3,340)		$ 334 **(f)**

CALCULATION OF CONSOLIDATED RETAINED EARNINGS
at January 1, Year 2

This schedule shows the calculation at a point in time, i.e., at the beginning of Year 2, which is the same as at the end of Year 1.

Retained earnings — Parent Co.		$13,400
Retained earnings — Sub Inc.	6,200	
Acquisition retained earnings	4,500	
Increase since acquisition	1,700	
Less unrealized after-tax equipment gain, Jan. 1 **(5c)**	240	
Adjusted increase since acquisition	1,460	
Parent Co.'s share	90%	1,314
Consolidated retained earnings		$14,714 **(g)**

CALCULATION OF NONCONTROLLING INTEREST
at December 31, Year 2

At the end of Year 2, the intercompany gain has been fully realized and no adjustment is necessary from a consolidated viewpoint.

Capital stock — Sub Inc.	$ 8,000
Retained earnings — Sub Inc.	9,300
	17,300
	10%
	$ 1,730 **(h)**

In the first table in Exhibit 8.5, you should note that the $600 gain on sale in Year 1 is fully realized from a consolidated perspective by the end of Year 2. From a consolidated perspective, the $600 gain was eliminated in Year 1 but was realized by adjusting depreciation expense over the remaining life of the equipment. Since the remaining life of the equipment was only 1½ years at the date of the intercompany sale, the $600 gain was brought into consolidated income over 1½ years. If the remaining useful life were 5 years, the $600 gain would be brought into consolidated income over 5 years.

The Year 2 consolidated financial statements prepared using the direct approach are shown in Exhibit 8.6. (Eliminations required for the intercompany equipment gain are shown in boldface.)

Exhibit 8.6

Year 2 Consolidated Statements
Adjusted for Intercompany Equipment Profit
(direct approach)

PARENT COMPANY
CONSOLIDATED INCOME STATEMENT
for the Year Ended December 31, Year 2

Depreciation expense for one year is based on the original cost to the consolidated entity.

Sales (25,000 + 12,000)	$37,000
Depreciation expense (1,400 + 0 – **(5d) 400**)	1,000
Miscellaneous expense (16,950 + 6,900)	23,850
Income tax expense (2,600 + 2,000 + **(5d) 160**)	4,760
	29,610
Net income — entity	7,390
Less noncontrolling interest **(5f)**	334
Net income **(5e)**	$ 7,056

PARENT COMPANY
CONSOLIDATED RETAINED EARNINGS STATEMENT
for the Year Ended December 31, Year 2

Balance, January 1	$14,714
Net income	7,056
	21,770
Dividends	2,500
Balance, December 31	$19,270

PARENT COMPANY
CONSOLIDATED BALANCE SHEET
at December 31, Year 2

Accumulated depreciation is total depreciation taken to the end of Year 2 based on the original cost to the consolidated entity.

Assets — miscellaneous (32,700 + 28,300)	$61,000
Equipment (2,100 + 0 – **(5a) 600**)	1,500
Accumulated depreciation (2,100 + 0 – **(5b + 5c) 600**)	(1,500)
	$61,000
Liabilities (14,000 + 11,000)	$25,000
Common stock	15,000
Retained earnings	19,270
Noncontrolling interest **(5h)**	1,730
	$61,000

When the consolidated income statement is prepared, the depreciation expense is reduced by $400. The result is a consolidated depreciation expense of $1,000 based on the entity's cost. This adjustment realizes $400 of the equipment gain for consolidation purposes. Income tax expense is increased by $160 to match expense with the gain realized. The net effect of the two adjustments in the income statement is to increase the entity's net income by an after-tax realization amounting to $240.

The Year 2 consolidated retained earnings statement is prepared using the calculated January 1 balance, consolidated net income, and the dividends of Parent Company.

At the end of Year 2, the equipment's net book value is zero on the Parent's separate-entity balance sheet and on the consolidated balance sheet.

Two adjustments are required in the preparation of the consolidated balance sheet. A reduction of $600 in equipment removes the gain and restates the equipment to the $1,500 historical cost to the entity. This equipment is fully depreciated on December 31, Year 2; therefore, accumulated depreciation should be equal to the historical cost of $1,500. When the accumulated depreciation is reduced by $600, the resulting balance ($1,500) is equal to the entity's historical cost.

Note that when both the equipment and the accumulated depreciation are reduced by $600, total consolidated assets are not changed. The net gain held back on the Year 1 consolidated balance sheet has been realized as at the end of Year 2. If no unrealized gains are being held back, there will be no deferred income tax adjustments made in the consolidated balance sheet. The deferred charge of $160 that appeared in the December 31, Year 1, consolidated balance sheet became an expense in the Year 2 consolidated income statement.

The unrealized profit at the end of Year 1 was realized in income for Year 2.

As discussed above, the adjustments made in the consolidated income statement increased the entity's net income by $240, while the adjustments made in the asset side of the consolidated balance sheet did not change total assets. In order for this to balance out, there must have been both an increase and a decrease of $240 on the liability side of the consolidated balance sheet. The $240 increase occurred in the income statement and was allocated to the two equities in the balance sheet. The $240 decrease occurred in the Sub's retained earnings at the beginning of the year and was allocated to the two equities. In the calculation of consolidated retained earnings on page 336, Parent absorbs $216 (90% × 240). In the following schedule showing the changes in noncontrolling interest for the year, it is obvious where the remaining $24 (10% × 240 = 24) decrease went.

CHANGES IN NONCONTROLLING INTEREST — for Year 2

Sub Inc.:	
Common stock	$ 8,000
Retained earnings, Jan. 1	6,200
	14,200
Less after-tax equipment profit **(5c)**	240
Adjusted	13,960
	10%
Noncontrolling interest Jan. 1	1,396
Year 2 entity net income allocated	334
Noncontrolling interest, Dec. 31 **(5h)**	$ 1,730

Equity Method Journal Entries   If Parent had been using the equity method, the following journal entries would have been made on December 31, Year 2:

Investment in Sub Inc.	2,790	
Investment income		2,790
90% of Sub Inc.'s Year 2 net income (90% × 3,100 = 2,790)		

Investment in Sub Inc.   216

    Investment income   216

90% of the portion of the equipment gain realized by depreciation in Year 2
(90% × 240 = 216)

After these entries are posted, the two related equity method accounts of Parent show the following changes and balances:

	Investment in Sub Inc.	Investment income
Balance, January 1, Year 2	$12,564	
Income from Sub Inc.	2,790	$2,790
Equipment gain realized	216	216
Balance, December 31, Year 2	$15,570	$3,006

The investment account contains all adjustments to the end of the period whereas the investment income account contains adjustments for only one period.

Appendix 8A of this chapter illustrates the working-paper approach to the preparation of the Year 2 consolidated financial statements.

Comparison of Realization of Inventory and Equipment Profits over Two-year Period

In Chapter 7, the holdback and realization of an intercompany profit in inventory was illustrated. In this chapter, we have illustrated the holdback and realization of an intercompany gain in equipment. In both cases, the after-tax profit (gain) was $360 (60% × 600), and the subsidiary was the selling company. The following summarizes the effect on the entity's net income over a two-year period.

INTERCOMPANY INVENTORY PROFIT

	Year 1	Year 2	Total
Parent Co., net income	$3,400	$4,050	$ 7,450
Sub Inc., net income	1,700	3,100	4,800
	5,100	7,150	12,250
After-tax profit (held back) realized	(360)	360	–0–
Net income — consolidated entity	$4,740	$7,510	$12,250
Allocated to the two equities:			
Noncontrolling interest	$ 134	$ 346	$ 480
Consolidated retained earnings	4,606	7,164	11,770
	$4,740	$7,510	$12,250

The intercompany profits are eventually realized from a consolidated viewpoint.

INTERCOMPANY EQUIPMENT GAIN

	Year 1	Year 2	Total
Parent Co., net income	$3,400	$4,050	$ 7,450
Sub Inc., net income	1,700	3,100	4,800
	5,100	7,150	12,250
After-tax gain (held back)	(360)	–0–	(360)
After-tax gain realized	120	240	360
Net income — consolidated entity	$4,860	$7,390	$12,250
Allocated as follows:			
Noncontrolling interest	$ 146	$ 334	$ 480
Consolidated retained earnings	4,714	7,056	11,770
	$4,860	$7,390	$12,250

Intercompany profits on depreciable assets are realized as the assets are used over their useful lives.

The two-year summaries shown above help illustrate a number of significant points in relation to consolidated financial statements:

Differentiate between point-in-time (balance sheet) versus period-of-time (income statement) adjustments.

1. The consolidated entity's net income is measured for periods of time that are usually one year in length.

2. During this measurement process, the holdback and subsequent realization of profits (losses) resulting from intercompany transactions takes place.

3. The realization of previously held back profits (losses) occurs during the period in which the acquiring company either sells the asset containing the profit (loss) to outsiders, or depreciates the asset, therefore consuming the asset while it produces other products or services for outsiders.

4. If we examine a time period longer than one year, and if, at the end of that period, the assets of the constituent companies do not contain intercompany profits, the following becomes evident:

    The consolidated entity's net income for this longer period consists of

    (a) the reported net income of the parent company, exclusive of intercompany investment or dividend income, *plus*

    (b) the reported net income of the subsidiary company (or companies), *minus*

    (c) the purchase discrepancy amortization.

    In the above illustration, we assumed that the purchase discrepancy was zero.

5. The entity's net income measurement for this longer time period is not affected by the fact that assets were sold at intercompany profits (losses) during the period. (See the two-year total column.) The same is true of the allocation to the two equities.

Adjustments for unrealized and realized profits from intercompany transactions are always charged/credited to the original seller.

6. When consolidated statements are prepared at the end of an intervening time period (for example Year 1, Year 2) we have to determine whether there were profits (losses) recorded by any of the constituent companies that were not realized by the end of the period.

7. The profit holdbacks and realizations are used in the measurement of the entity's net income and are adjustments to the reported net income of the selling constituent in the allocation of that net income.

In Chapter 7, we also illustrated the holdback and realization of a $360 after-tax intercompany gain in land. In this case, the realization process took place in Year 8; however, the overall concepts discussed above remain the same.

(B) Intercompany Bondholdings

Our discussions so far have focused on gains (losses) resulting from the intercompany sale of inventory, land, and depreciable assets. The treatment of these gains (losses) in the preparation of consolidated financial statements can be summarized as follows: gains (losses) resulting from the intercompany sale of assets are realized subsequent to the recording of the intercompany transaction by the selling affiliate.

Occasionally, one affiliate will purchase all or a portion of the bonds issued by another affiliate. When consolidated financial statements are being prepared, the elimination of the intercompany accounts (investment in bonds and bonds payable; interest revenue and interest expense) may result in a gain (loss) being reflected in those statements. The treatment of this type of gain (loss) can be summarized in the

Gains/losses on intercompany bondholdings are reported on consolidated statements prior to recording them on the separate-entity statements.

following manner: gains (losses) arising because of the elimination of intercompany bondholding accounts are realized prior to the recording of these gains (losses) by the affiliates. Before we examine how these gains and losses occur in the elimination of the intercompany accounts, let us look at intercompany bondholding situations that do not result in gains or losses.

Intercompany Bondholdings — No Gain or Loss

Not all intercompany bondholdings result in gains or losses being reflected in the consolidated statements. For example, let us assume that one affiliate issued $10,000 in bonds, and that another affiliate acquired the whole issue.

(The amounts used are unrealistically low for a bond issue, but are realistic in relation to the size of Parent Company and Sub Inc., the two companies that we have been using in our illustrations. In any case, the concepts are the same regardless of the amounts used.)

Immediately after the issue, the records of the two companies would show the following accounts:

The asset and liability appear on the separate-entity financial statements.

Acquiring Affiliate's Records		*Issuing Affiliate's Records*	
Investment in bonds	10,000	Bonds payable	10,000

From the entity's point of view, the two accounts are similar to intercompany receivables and payables and would be eliminated by the following working paper entry when the consolidated balance sheet is being prepared:

This entry is made on the consolidation worksheet.

Bonds payable	10,000	
Investment in bonds		10,000

It is important to note that the eliminations are equal, and because of this, there is no gain or loss resulting from the working paper elimination of these two intercompany accounts. At the end of each succeeding year, this working paper elimination is repeated until the bonds mature. After that date, the two accounts no longer exist in the affiliates' records and further working paper eliminations are not required.

The consolidated balance sheet is not the only statement requiring working paper eliminations. If we assume that the bonds pay interest at the rate of 10 percent, the income statement of the issuing affiliate will show interest expense of $1,000, while the income statement of the acquiring affiliate will show interest revenue of $1,000. These intercompany revenue and expense accounts are eliminated by the following working paper entry when the consolidated income statement is being prepared:

This entry does not change the net income of the consolidated entity.

Interest revenue	1,000	
Interest expense		1,000

Again, it is important to note that the amounts are equal, and that because of this there is no gain or loss resulting from this working paper elimination. The consolidated income statement working paper elimination is repeated each year until the bonds mature.

Our example has assumed that the bonds were issued at par. Suppose, now, that the bonds were issued to the purchasing affiliate at a premium or discount. Provided that both affiliates use the same methods to amortize the issue premium or discount, and the purchase premium or discount, the amounts in the intercompany accounts on all successive balance sheets and income statements will be equal. The important concept of equal eliminations on both statements would still be true.

DISCUSSION QUESTION

Who Lost This $300,000?

Several years ago, the Penston Company purchased 90 percent of the outstanding shares of Swansan Corporation. The acquisition was made because Swansan produced a vital component used in Penston's manufacturing process. Penston wanted to ensure an adequate supply of this item at a reasonable price. The former owner, James Swansan, who agreed to continue managing this organization, retained the remaining 10 percent of Swansan's stock. He was given responsibility over the subsidiary's daily manufacturing operations but not for any of the financial decisions.

At a recent meeting, the president of Penston and the company's chief financial officer began discussing Swansan's debt position. The subsidiary had a debt-to-equity ratio that seemed unreasonably high considering the significant amount of cash flows being generated by both companies. Payment of the interest expense, especially on the subsidiary's outstanding bonds, was a major cost, one that the corporate officials hoped to reduce. However, the bond indenture specified that Swansan could retire this debt prior to maturity only by paying 107 percent of face value.

This premium was considered prohibitive. Thus, to avoid contractual problems, Penston acquired a large portion of Swansan's liability on the open market for 101 percent of face value. Penston's purchase created an effective loss on the debt of $300,000: the excess of the price over the book value of the debt as reported on Swansan's books.

Company accountants currently are computing the noncontrolling interest's share of consolidated net income to be reported for the current year. They are unsure about the impact of this $300,000 loss. The subsidiary's debt was retired, but officials of the parent company made the decision. Who lost this $300,000? How should it be allocated on the consolidated financial statements?

Intercompany Bondholdings — With Gain or Loss

The market price of bonds moves inversely with changes in interest rates.

When the market rate is different from the coupon rate on the date of a bond issue, the bonds will be issued at a price that is different from the par or face value. If the interest rates are higher (lower) than the coupon rate, the bonds will be issued at a discount (premium). Subsequent to the issue, bond market prices will rise (fall) if the market interest rate falls (rises). It is the market price differential on the date of an intercompany purchase, combined with any unamortized issue discount or premium, that causes the consolidated gains or losses that result from the elimination of intercompany bondholdings. Let us change our example slightly to illustrate this.

Parent Co. has a $10,000 bond issue outstanding that pays 10 percent interest annually on December 31. The bonds were originally issued at a premium, which is being amortized by the company on a straight-line basis at the rate of $50 per year.[2]

---

[2]We will use the straight-line method in the first few illustrations because it is easier to understand. Later in the chapter, we will illustrate the effective-interest method, which is required by GAAP.

On December 31, Year 1, the unamortized issue premium amounts to $200. The bonds mature on December 31, Year 5.

On December 31, Year 1, Sub purchases all of the outstanding bonds of Parent on the open market at a cost of $9,600. Immediately after Sub acquires these bonds, the records of the two companies would show the following accounts.

Sub purchased the bonds in the market for $9,600, which is $600 less than the net book value of these bonds on Parent's books.

Sub Inc.'s Records		Parent Co.'s Records	
Investment in bonds of		Bonds payable	$10,000
Parent Co.	$10,000	Add unamortized issue	
Less discount on purchase	400	premium	200
Net	$ 9,600	Net	$10,200

The net amounts reflect how the asset and the liability would be presented on the respective balance sheets of the two companies on December 31, Year 1. The preparation of the consolidated balance sheet on this date would require the elimination of the two intercompany amounts by the following working paper entry:

A gain of $600 is recorded on the consolidation worksheet.

Bonds Payable — Parent Co.	10,200	
Investment in bonds of Parent Co. — Sub. Inc.		9,600
Gain on bond retirement		600

To eliminate the intercompany bond accounts and to recognize the resulting gain on the retirement of bonds

From the consolidated perspective, Parent's bonds have been retired; Parent no longer has a bond payable to outsiders.

The eliminations of the asset and liability would appear in the consolidated balance sheet working paper. The balancing amount of the elimination entry "Gain on bond retirement" appears in the consolidated income statement working paper. From the consolidated entity's point of view, the bonds of the entity have been purchased on the open market and retired. The retirement gain can be calculated in the following manner:

Carrying amount of the bond liability	$10,200
Cost of investment in bonds	9,600
Gain on bond retirement	$ 600

The gain on bond retirement was realized on a transaction with outsiders.

The gain should be recognized because the benefits and risks of the consolidated entity have substantially changed in a transaction with outsiders. From a consolidated perspective, the entity has retired a liability of $10,200 by paying $9,600. Its financial position has improved; the gain has been realized and should be recognized.

Note that if Parent had acquired and retired its own bonds in the same manner, it would have recorded a gain on bond retirement of the same amount. This gain would appear on Parent's income statement and would also appear on the consolidated income statement. The actual event was different (Sub purchased the bonds), but because the two companies are a single economic entity, the gain will still appear on the consolidated income statement. The only difference is that the gain on the consolidated income statement does not appear on the income statement of the parent. Instead, it appears on the consolidated income statement as a result of the unequal elimination of the intercompany asset and liability accounts in the preparation of the consolidated balance sheet.

The gain is reported on the consolidated statements, not on the single-entity statements.

An examination of the make-up of the asset and liability accounts will indicate why there is a gain of $600. If the bonds had originally been issued at par (face value), and if the bonds had been acquired on the open market at a price equal to par, there would be no gain on retirement. It is the unamortized issue premium and the discount on the bond purchase that cause the gain. This premium and discount will be amortized by the two companies in Years 2 to 5, and thus will be reflected in the individual income statements of the two companies in those future periods. This will become clearer when we examine the consolidation procedures in Year 2. The important point to note at this stage is that the constituent companies will pay tax on this gain in future periods when the actual recording of the gain takes place. The consolidated entity is realizing the gain in Year 1; therefore, this timing difference requires income tax allocation if a proper matching is to take place. Assuming a 40 percent tax rate, the following additional working paper elimination entry is required:

Income tax expense is reported on the consolidated statements in accordance with the matching principle.

Income tax expense	240	
Deferred credit–income taxes		240

To record the deferred income tax liability and expense on the Year 1 intercompany bond gain (40% × 600 = 240)

The effect of eliminations (i) and (ii) on the Year 1 consolidated income is to increase the net income of the entity by $360 (600 – 240 = 360). The entity's net income consists of the net income of the parent, plus the net income of the subsidiary; therefore, the after-tax increase must affect one or the other, or perhaps both.

There are four possible approaches that could be taken:

There are various approaches to allocate the gain between the two companies.

1. Allocate the gain to the issuing company, because the company purchasing the bonds is acting as an agent for the issuing company.

2. Allocate the gain to the purchasing company, because its investment led to the retirement of the bonds for consolidation purposes.

3. Allocate the gain to the parent company, because its management controls the actions of all the affiliated companies in the group. This would only be a separate alternative if both parties to the transaction were subsidiaries of that parent.

4. Allocate the gain between the issuing and purchasing companies, because each will record its portion of the gain in future periods.

An allocation of the gain would not be required in the case of 100 percent owned subsidiaries because there would be no noncontrolling interest in the consolidated financial statements. The approach adopted is very important when the subsidiaries are less than 100 percent owned, because approaches 1, 2, and 4 could result in all or a portion of the gain being allocated to the subsidiary company, and this would affect noncontrolling interest. The *CICA Handbook* is silent regarding the approach to be taken. However, an exposure draft issued prior to the release of Section 1600 indicated a preference for alternative 4. When Section 1600 was released in 1975, the preference indicated in the exposure draft had been deleted. In the illustrations that follow, any gains (losses) from the elimination of intercompany bondholding will be allocated to the purchasing and issuing affiliates (approach 4), because it reflects how each company will actually record the transaction in future years. The agency approach is briefly discussed on page 357.

We will use approach 4 because it is consistent with the income measurement by the separate entities in future years.

Calculation of the Portion of the Gain Allocated to the Affiliates

From the point of view of the purchasing affiliate, the cost of the acquisition is compared with the par value of the bonds acquired, the difference being a gain or loss. From the point of view of the issuing affiliate, the cost to retire the bonds is the par value of the bonds; the difference between the par value and the carrying value is the gain or loss.

The gain and its allocation can be calculated in the following manner:

Par (face) value of bond liability	$10,000
Cost of investment in bonds	9,600
Gain allocated to purchasing affiliate — before tax	$ 400
Carrying amount of bond liability	$10,200
Par (face) value of bond liability	10,000
Gain allocated to issuing affiliate — before tax	$ 200

The $600 gain is allocated to the affiliates based on the premium or discount on their separate-entity books.

Notice that the gain to the consolidated entity of $600 is made up of the two gains allocated to the affiliates (400 + 200 = 600). The gain allocated to the purchasing affiliate is equal to the discount on the purchase affiliate's books and the gain allocated to the issuing affiliate is equal to the premium on the issuing affiliate's books. Both the entity's gain and the amounts allocated are expressed in before-tax dollars. The chart in Exhibit 8.7 is useful in calculating the after-tax amounts required when the entity's after-tax net income is being allocated to the two equities.

Exhibit 8.7

This chart shows how the after-tax gains are allocated for consolidation purposes.

ALLOCATION OF GAIN ON BOND

	Entity			Parent Co.			Sub Inc.		
	Before tax	40% tax	After tax	Before tax	40% tax	After tax	Before tax	40% tax	After tax
Gain on bond retirement — Dec. 31, Year 1	$600	$240	$360	$200	$80	$120	$400	$160	$240
	(a)	(b)	(c)	(d)	(e)	(f)	(g)	(h)	(i)

The Year 1 financial statements of the two companies are shown in Exhibit 8.8. Parent Co. has used the cost method to account for its investment.

Parent has interest expense of $950 on its separate-entity books.

The net incomes and total assets of the two companies are unchanged from previous examples. However, the details on each statement have been changed to reflect the intercompany bond transaction that occurred on December 31, Year 1. Remember that the intercompany bond purchase occurred on that date, and that the interest expense of Parent for Year 1 was paid to bondholders outside the consolidated entity. The amount of expense ($950) is made up of the $1,000 interest paid less the $50 amortization of the issue premium.

Before the Year 1 consolidated financial statements are prepared, the three calculations in Exhibit 8.9 are made.

Exhibit 8.10 illustrates the direct approach to the preparation of the Year 1 consolidated financial statements.

Exhibit 8.7 which was prepared to allocate the gain in both before-tax and after-tax dollars was used in preparing the consolidated income statement and in calculating consolidated net income and retained earnings, as follows:

1. The entity column reflects the amounts used in preparing the consolidated income statement. Note that the after-tax column is not used.

2. Both of the allocation columns (Parent Co. and Sub Inc.) were used to calculate consolidated net income and noncontrolling interest for the year, and to calculate noncontrolling interest and consolidated retained earnings at the end of the year, but only in after-tax amounts. This is because they are used to adjust the after-tax net incomes and equities of the two companies. The before-tax and tax columns are presented only to show that the columns cross-add.

Exhibit 8.8

INCOME STATEMENTS — for Year 1

	Parent	Sub
Sales	$20,000	$ 8,000
Interest expense	950	—
Miscellaneous expenses	13,450	5,200
Income tax expense	2,200	1,100
	16,600	6,300
Net income	$ 3,400	$ 1,700

Sub has no interest revenue because it purchased the bonds on the last day of the year.

RETAINED EARNINGS STATEMENTS — for Year 1

	Parent	Sub
Balance, January 1	$12,000	$ 4,500
Net income	3,400	1,700
	15,400	6,200
Dividends	2,000	—
Balance, December 31	$13,400	$ 6,200

BALANCE SHEETS — at December 31, Year 1

	Parent	Sub
Assets (miscellaneous)	$29,150	$13,600
Investment in Parent Co. bonds	—	9,600
Investment in Sub Inc.	11,250	—
	$40,400	$23,200
Miscellaneous liabilities	$ 1,800	$ 9,000
Bonds payable	10,200	—
Common stock	15,000	8,000
Retained earnings	13,400	6,200
	$40,400	$23,200

The investment in bonds and bonds payable are reported on the separate-entity balance sheets.

In summary, the eliminations made for the intercompany bondholdings had the following effect on the consolidated statements:

1. The elimination of $9,600 in assets and $10,200 in liabilities resulted in a $600 before-tax gain, which was reflected in the income statement.

Income tax is accrued on the consolidated financial statements to match to the gain on bond retirement.

2. An increase of $240 (40% × 600) to income tax expense and to a deferred tax liability reflected the tax effects of the gain.

3. The two adjustments in the income statement increased the net income of the entity by $360; this was allocated to the two equities in the balance sheet, as follows:

	Total	Noncontrolling interest	Controlling interest
Gain allocated to Parent Co.	$120	$ —	$120
Gain allocated to Sub Inc.	240	24	216
	$360	$24	$336

The after-tax gain is allocated to NCI and controlling interest.

4. The adjustments made in preparing the consolidated balance sheet can be summarized conceptually as follows:

Asset side:
Investment in bonds	– 9,600

Liability side:
Bonds payable	–10,200
Deferred credit–income taxes	+ 240
Noncontrolling interest	+ 24
Consolidated retained earnings	+ 336
	– 9,600

Exhibit 8.9

CALCULATION OF CONSOLIDATED NET INCOME — for Year 1

The gain on bond retirement is allocated to the two affiliates as a consolidation adjustment.

Net income — Parent Co.		$3,400
Add after-tax bond gain allocated **(7f)**		120
Adjusted		3,520
Net income — Sub Inc.	1,700	
Add after-tax bond gain allocated **(7i)**	240	
Adjusted	1,940	
Parent Co. ownership	90%	1,746
Consolidated net income		$5,266 **(a)**
Noncontrolling interest (10% × 1,940)		$ 194 **(b)**

CALCULATION OF NONCONTROLLING INTEREST
at December 31, Year 1

The gain allocated to Sub affects NCI at the end of the year.

Sub Inc.	
Common stock	$ 8,000
Retained earnings	6,200
	14,200
Add after-tax bond gain allocated **(7i)**	240
Adjusted	14,440
	10%
	$ 1,444 **(c)**

CALCULATION OF CONSOLIDATED RETAINED EARNINGS
at December 31, Year 1

This schedule shows the calculation at a point in time, i.e., at the end of Year 1.

Retained earnings — Parent Co.		$13,400
Add after-tax bond gain allocated **(7f)**		120
Adjusted		13,520
Retained earnings — Sub Inc.	6,200	
Acquisition retained earnings	4,500	
Increase since acquisition	1,700	
Add after-tax bond gain allocated **(7i)**	240	
Adjusted	1,940	
	90%	1,746
		$15,266 **(d)**

Exhibit 8.10	Year 1 Consolidated Statements

Year 1 Consolidated Statements
Adjusted for Intercompany Bondholdings
(direct approach)

PARENT COMPANY
CONSOLIDATED INCOME STATEMENT
for the Year Ended December 31, Year 1

The gain on bond retirement appears on the consolidated income statement because the gain was realized with a transaction with outsiders.

Sales (20,000 + 8,000)	$28,000
Gain on bond retirement (0 + 0 + **(7a) 600**)	600
	28,600
Interest expense (950 + 0)	950
Miscellaneous expenses (13,450 + 5,200)	18,650
Income tax expense (2,200 + 1,100 + **(7b) 240**)	3,540
	23,140
Net income — entity	5,460
Less noncontrolling interest **(9b)**	194
Net income	$ 5,266

PARENT COMPANY
CONSOLIDATED RETAINED EARNINGS STATEMENT
for the Year Ended December 31, Year 1

Balance, January 1	$12,000
Net income	5,266
	17,266
Dividends	2,000
Balance, December 31	$15,266

PARENT COMPANY
CONSOLIDATED BALANCE SHEET
at December 31, Year 1

The bonds payable are zero on the consolidated balance sheet because outsiders no longer hold them.

Assets — miscellaneous (29,150 + 13,600)	$42,750
Investment in Parent Co. bonds (0 + 9,600 – **9600**)	–0–
	$42,750
Miscellaneous liabilities (1,800 + 9,000)	$10,800
Bonds payable (10,200 + 0 – **10,200**)	–0–
Deferred credit–income taxes (0 + 0 + **(7b) 240**)	240
Total liabilities	11,040
Common stock	15,000
Retained earnings	15,266
Noncontrolling interest **(9c)**	1,444
	$42,750

Equity Method Journal Entries   If Parent has used the equity method, the following entries are made on December 31, Year 1:

These entries capture the net effect of all consolidation adjustments.

Investment in Sub Inc.	1,530	
Investment income		1,530

90% of the Year 1 net income of Sub Inc.
(90% × 1,700 = 1,530)

Investment in Sub Inc.	120	
Investment income		120
Bond gain allocated to Parent Co.		
Investment in Sub Inc.	216	
Investment income		216
90% of bond gain allocated to Sub Inc.		
(90% × 240 = 216)		

The related equity-method accounts of Parent will show the following changes and balances in Year 1:

	Investment in Sub Inc.	Investment income
January 1, Year 1	$11,250	
December 31, Year 1		
Income from Sub Inc.	1,530	$1,530
Bond gain to parent	120	120
90 percent of bond gain to subsidiary	216	216
Balance, December 31, Year 1	$13,116	$1,866

The investment account contains cumulative adjustments to the end of the period whereas the investment income account contains adjustments for only one period.

Appendix 8B illustrates the working-paper approach to the preparation of the Year 1 consolidated financial statements.

Accounting for Gain in Subsequent Years

We will now focus on Year 2 so that we can illustrate the consolidation eliminations that must be made in years subsequent to the original intercompany bond purchase.

At the end of Year 2, the two companies prepared the financial statements shown in Exhibit 8.11.

Focus initially on the items "interest revenue" and "interest expense," which each company recorded in the following manner:

Parent Company

These entries are made on the separate-entity books of Parent and Sub.

Interest expense	1,000	
Cash		1,000
To record payment of Year 2 interest		
Bonds payable	50	
Interest expense		50
To amortize issue premium		
(200 ÷ 4 = 50)		

Sub Inc.

Cash	1,000	
Interest revenue		1,000
To record receipt of Year 2 interest		
Investment in bonds of		
Parent Co.	100	
Interest revenue		100
To amortize discount on the purchase		
of bonds (400 ÷ 4 = 100)		

The income being reported by the separate entities has already been reported on the consolidated financial statements.

Notice that the entry recording the amortization of the issue premium and the purchase discount increased the respective net incomes of the two companies. Thus, in Year 2, Parent recorded one-quarter of the original gain allocated to it in Year 1 (200 × 1/4 = 50); in the same manner, Sub also recorded one-quarter of the original gain allocated to it in Year 1 (400 × 1/4 = 100). Because the bonds mature four years after the date of the intercompany purchase, and because the original gain on bond retirement was created because of the existence of the unamortized issue premium and the discount on the intercompany purchase of bonds (200 + 400 = 600), the concept that the gain is realized on the consolidated financial statements before it is recorded by the constituent companies becomes evident.

Exhibit 8.11

INCOME STATEMENTS — for Year 2

	Parent	Sub
Sales	$25,000	$10,900
Interest revenue	—	1,100
	25,000	12,000
Interest expense	950	—
Miscellaneous expenses	17,400	6,900
Income tax expense	2,600	2,000
	20,950	8,900
Net income	$ 4,050	$ 3,100

The separate-entity income statements show interest revenue and expense for bonds that were retired from a consolidated viewpoint.

RETAINED EARNINGS STATEMENTS — for Year 2

	Parent	Sub
Balance, January 1	$13,400	$ 6,200
Net income	4,050	3,100
	17,450	9,300
Dividends	2,500	—
Balance, December 31	$14,950	$ 9,300

BALANCE SHEETS — at December 31, Year 2

	Parent	Sub
Assets (miscellaneous)	$32,700	$18,600
Investment in Parent Co. bonds	—	9,700
Investment in Sub Inc.	11,250	—
	$43,950	$28,300
Miscellaneous liabilities	$ 3,850	$11,000
Bonds payable	10,150	—
Common stock	15,000	8,000
Retained earnings	14,950	9,300
	$43,950	$28,300

The separate-entity balance sheets show investment and bonds payable for bonds that were retired from a consolidated viewpoint.

Both Sub's interest revenue of $1,100 (1,000 + 100) and Parent's interest expense of $950 (1,000 – 50) represent intercompany revenues and expenses that are eliminated on the Year 2 consolidated income statement with the following *incomplete* working paper entry:

The difference between interest revenue and interest expense is due to the difference in amortization of the bond premium and discount.

Interest revenue	1,100	
Interest expense		950
To eliminate Year 2 intercompany interest revenue and expense		

In past examples, the elimination of intercompany revenues and expenses (sales and purchases, rental revenue and expense, etc.) had no effect on the net income of the entity, because the amounts eliminated were always equal. Referring back to the journal entries made by both companies, you will see that this equal component is still present. We are still eliminating $1,000 interest revenue and expense in the working paper elimination. However, we are also eliminating the

The intercompany interest must be eliminated on consolidation to avoid double-counting of the gain on bond retirement.

portions of the gain on bond retirement that were recorded by both companies as a result of the amortization of the premium and discount in Year 2. Failure to do this would result in the gain on bond retirement being recorded twice over the life of the bonds. It is because we do not allow this portion of the gain to be reflected in the Year 2 consolidated income statement that we have an unequal elimination of intercompany revenue and expense on the working paper elimination entry. The elimination of $1,100 intercompany interest revenue and $950 intercompany interest expense decreases the before-tax net income of the entity by $150. We will describe this reduction of the entity's before-tax net income as the "interest elimination loss."

The realization of a gain on bond retirement on the consolidated income statement in the year of acquisition of intercompany bonds will always result in an "interest elimination loss" affecting the entity's before-tax net income in all subsequent consolidated income statements until the bonds mature. This "interest elimination loss" does not appear as such in the consolidated income statement, because it results from eliminating an amount of intercompany interest revenue that is larger than the amount of intercompany interest expense eliminated. Conversely, the realization of a loss on bond retirement in the year of acquisition of intercompany bonds will always result in an "interest elimination gain" in all subsequent consolidated income statements, because the amount of interest expense eliminated will always be larger than the amount of interest revenue eliminated.

Income tax expense must be eliminated on consolidation to match with the elimination of the interest revenue and interest expense.

As stated previously, the entity's Year 2 before-tax net income has been decreased by $150. This results from eliminating the portion of the gain on bond retirement recorded by the constituent companies in Year 2. Recall that the entire before-tax gain was realized for consolidated purposes in Year 1; and also, that to satisfy the matching process an income tax expense was recorded and a deferred tax liability was set up on the consolidated balance sheet. Both companies paid (or accrued) income tax on a portion of this gain in Year 2 — a total of $60 (150 × 40%). These companies also recorded the income tax paid (or accrued) as an expense, but from a consolidated point of view, the payment was a reduction of the deferred tax liability previously set up. We must therefore decrease income tax expense when preparing the consolidated income statement[3] because it is not a consolidated expense. The *incomplete* income statement working paper elimination entry is as follows:

Interest revenue	1,100	
Interest expense		950
Income tax expense		60

To eliminate Year 2 intercompany interest revenue and expense and to adjust for the income tax effect of the elimination

The addition of the income tax expense entry still leaves us with an unequal elimination on the consolidated income statement. However, this "interest elimination loss" is now in after-tax dollars and amounts to $90 (1,100 – 950 – 60). A reconstruction of the intercompany bond chart for the life of the bonds as shown in Exhibit 8.12 will illustrate how this loss is allocated to the two constituents each year.

---

[3] We must also reduce the amount of the deferred tax liability that was set up in Year 1 by $60.

Exhibit 8.12

ALLOCATION OF GAIN ON BOND

	Entity			Parent Co.			Sub Inc.		
	Before tax	40% tax	After tax	Before tax	40% tax	After tax	Before tax	40% tax	After tax
Gain on bond, Dec. 31, Year 1	$600	$240	$360	$200	$80	$120	$400	$160	$240 **(a)**
Interest elimination loss — Year 2	150	60	90	50	20	30	100	40	60 **(b)**
Balance — gain — Dec. 31, Year 2	450	180	270	150	60	90	300	120	180 **(c)**
Interest elimination loss — Year 3	150	60	90	50	20	30	100	40	60
Balance — gain — Dec. 31, Year 3	300	120	180	100	40	60	200	80	120
Interest elimination loss — Year 4	150	60	90	50	20	30	100	40	60
Balance — gain — Dec. 31, Year 4	150	60	90	50	20	30	100	40	60
Interest elimination loss — Year 5	150	60	90	50	20	30	100	40	60
Balance, Dec. 31, Year 5	$–0–	$–0–	$–0–	$–0–	$–0–	$–0–	$–0–	$–0–	$–0–

The interest elimination loss for each year is equal to the amortization of the bond premium and bond discount on the separate-entity books.

To further illustrate this, examine the interest accounts of the two companies from the date of the intercompany purchase to the date of maturity of the bonds.

By the end of Year 5, the cumulative income recorded on the separate-entity books of Parent and Sub is equal to the $600 gain on bond retirement which was reported in the Year 1 consolidated income statement.

Year ended Dec. 31	Parent's interest expense	Sub's interest revenue	Difference
Year 2	$ 950	$1,100	$150
Year 3	950	1,100	150
Year 4	950	1,100	150
Year 5	950	1,100	150
	$3,800	$4,400	$600

The preparation of a bond chart would be the first step in the preparation of the Year 2 consolidated statements. This chart would have the same format as the one shown above, but would be comprised of only the first three lines from that particular chart. Before the Year 2 consolidated financial statements are prepared, the three calculations in Exhibit 8.13 are made.

The Year 2 consolidated financial statements prepared using the direct approach are shown in Exhibit 8.14.

The unequal elimination of the intercompany interest revenue and expense, and the income tax adjustment made in the preparation of the consolidated income statement, were explained on the previous page. This created the "hidden" after-tax interest elimination loss of $90, in this statement. This loss is depicted and allocated in the chart above.

Exhibit 8.13

CALCULATION OF CONSOLIDATED NET INCOME — Year 2

The interest elimination loss is allocated to Parent and Sub based on Exhibit 8.12.

Net income — Parent Co.		$4,050
Less after-tax interest elimination loss allocated **(12b)**		30
Adjusted		4,020
Net income — Sub Inc.	3,100	
Less after-tax interest elimination loss allocated **(12b)**	60	
Adjusted	3,040	
Parent Co. ownership	90%	2,736
Consolidated net income		$6,756 **(a)**
Noncontrolling interest (10% × 3,040)		$ 304 **(b)**

CALCULATION OF CONSOLIDATED RETAINED EARNINGS
at January 1, Year 2

This schedule shows the calculation at a point in time, i.e., at the beginning of Year 2, which is the same as at the end of Year 1.

Retained earnings — Parent Co.		$13,400
Add after-tax bond gain allocated (Dec. 31, Year 1) **(12a)**		120
Adjusted		13,520
Retained earnings — Sub Inc.	6,200	
Acquisition retained earnings	4,500	
Increase since acquisition	1,700	
Add after-tax bond gain allocated (Dec. 31, Year 1) **(12a)**	240	
Adjusted	1,940	
Parent Co. ownership	90%	1,746
Consolidated retained earnings		$15,266 **(c)**

CALCULATION OF NONCONTROLLING INTEREST
at December 31, Year 2

Only the portion of the gain on bond retirement allocated to the Sub affects NCI.

Sub Inc.	
Common stock	$ 8,000
Retained earnings	9,300
	17,300
Add after-tax bond gain allocated as at Dec. 31, Year 2 **(12c)**	180
Adjusted shareholders' equity	17,480
	10%
	$ 1,748 **(d)**

Exhibit 8.14	**Year 2 Consolidated Statements**

Year 2 Consolidated Statements
Adjusted for Intercompany Bondholdings
(direct approach)

PARENT COMPANY
CONSOLIDATED INCOME STATEMENT
for the Year Ended December 31, Year 2

There was no interest revenue earned from outsiders and no interest expense paid to outsiders *during the year.*	

Sales (25,000 + 10,900)	$35,900
Interest revenue (0 + 1,100 – **1,100**)	–0–
	35,900
Interest expense (950 + 0 – **950**)	–0–
Miscellaneous expenses (17,400 + 6,900)	24,300
Income tax expense (2,600 + 2,000 – **(12b) 60**)	4,540
	28,840
Net income — entity	7,060
Less noncontrolling interest **(13b)**	304
Net income **(13a)**	$ 6,756

PARENT COMPANY
CONSOLIDATED RETAINED EARNINGS STATEMENT
for the Year Ended December 31, Year 2

Balance, January 1 **(13c)**	$15,266
Net income	6,756
	22,022
Dividends	2,500
Balance, December 31	$19,522

PARENT COMPANY
CONSOLIDATED BALANCE SHEET
at December 31, Year 2

There is no bond payable to outsiders and no investment in bonds of outsiders *at the end of the year.*	

Assets — miscellaneous (32,700 + 18,600)	$51,300
Investment in Parent Co. bonds (0 + 9,700 – **9,700**)	–0–
	$51,300
Miscellaneous liabilities (3,850 + 11,000)	$14,850
Bonds payable (10,150 + 0 – **10,150**)	–0–
Deferred credit–income taxes (0 + 0 + **(12c) 180**)	180
Total liabilities	15,030
Shareholders' equity	
Common stock	15,000
Retained earnings	19,522
Noncontrolling interest **(13d)**	1,748
	$51,300

The eliminations made in the preparation of the Year 2 consolidated balance sheet require elaboration. The item "Investment in Parent Co. bonds" in the balance sheet of Sub has a balance of $9,700 after the Year 2 amortization of the discount on purchase (9,600 + 100). Bonds payable in the balance sheet of Parent Co. has a balance of $10,150 after the Year 2 amortization on the issue premium (10,200 − 50). When the consolidated balance sheet is being prepared, these two intercompany accounts are eliminated by the following *incomplete* entry:

Bonds payable	10,150	
Investment in Parent Co. bonds		9,700
To eliminate the intercompany bonds on December 31, Year 2		

This entry is somewhat similar to the entry made on December 31, Year 1 (see page 343), except that the before-tax amount needed to balance at this time is a gain of $450 instead of the $600 gain that was required a year ago. Furthermore, the $450 gain does not appear as such in the consolidated income statement in Year 2. Recall that the $600 gain appeared on the Year 1 consolidated income statement. A gain on bond retirement appears as such only once in the year of the intercompany purchase. Recall also that a portion of the gain was recorded in Year 2 by Parent and Sub, was eliminated in preparing the Year 2 consolidated income statement, and is not reflected again. The $450 needed to balance is a before-tax gain as at December 31, Year 2. A referral to the bond chart (page 352) indicates that the entity's deferred income tax liability with respect to this gain is $180 as at this date. We can now extend the working paper entry by including the deferred tax component as follows:

At the end of Year 2, the deferred tax liability is the 40 percent tax on the difference between income recognized for consolidation purposes ($600) compared to income recognized by the separate entities ($150).

Bonds payable	10,150	
Investment in Parent Co. bonds		9,700
Deferred credit–Income taxes		180
To eliminate the intercompany bond accounts and set up the deferred tax liability as at December 31, Year 2		

The after-tax gain needed to balance is now $270. The bond chart shows this gain as allocated $90 to Parent and $180 to Sub.

To summarize, the Year 2 elimination entries made for the intercompany bondholdings had the following effect on the consolidated statements:

1. The adjustments made in the income statement created an after-tax interest elimination loss of $90, which decreased the entity's net income and was allocated to the two equities as follows:

The interest elimination loss for the year is first allocated to Parent and Sub and then to NCI and controlling interest *for the year*.

	Total	Noncontrolling interest	Controlling interest
Loss allocated to Parent Co.	$30	$—	$30
Loss allocated to Sub Inc.	60	6	54
	$90	$ 6	$84

2. The elimination of $9,700 in assets and $10,150 in bond liabilities, together with the adjustment to reflect the $180 deferred tax liability, resulted in an after-tax increase of $270 in the equity side of the balance sheet. This was allocated to the two equities, at December 31, Year 2, as follows:

The difference between gain on bond retirement versus interest elimination loss for all years to date is first allocated to Parent and Sub and then to NCI and controlling interest *at the end of the year*.

	Total	Noncontrolling interest	Controlling interest
Gain allocated to Parent Co.	$ 90	$ —	$ 90
Gain allocated to Sub Inc.	180	18	162
	$270	$18	$252

Remember that the original $600 gain in Year 1 was allocated to the two equities in the consolidated balance sheet as at December 31, Year 1 (see page 345).

3. The adjustments made in the preparation of both the December 31, Year 2, balance sheet and the Year 2 income statement can be summarized conceptually with respect to their effect on the consolidated balance sheet as follows:

This chart shows the adjustments to the consolidated balance sheet at the end of Year 2.

Asset side: Investment in bonds			− $ 9,700
Liability side:			
Bonds payable			− $10,150
Deferred credit–income taxes			+ 180
Noncontrolling interest			
Balance, Dec. 31, Year 1	+	24	
Year 2 entity net income	−	6	+ 18
Consolidated retained earnings			
Balance, Dec. 31, Year 1	+	336	
Year 2 entity net income	−	84	+ 252
			− $ 9,700

The $252 increase in consolidated retained earnings is automatically reflected when the consolidated income and retained earnings statements are prepared. The $18 increase in noncontrolling interest is captured in the calculation of the amount of this equity (see page 355).

Equity Method Journal Entries

If Parent has used the equity method, the following entries will be made on December 31, Year 2:

These entries should cause Parent's separate-entity income under the equity method to be equal to consolidated net income.

Investment in Sub Inc.	2,790	
Investment income		2,790
90% of the Year 2 net income of Sub Inc. (90% × 3,100 = 2,790)		
Investment income	30	
Investment in Sub Inc.		30
Interest elimination loss allocated to Parent Co.		
Investment income	54	
Investment in Sub Inc.		54
90% of interest elimination loss allocated to Sub Inc. (90% × 60 = 54)		

The related equity-method accounts of Parent will show the following changes and balances in Year 2:

The investment account under the equity method ($15,822) is different than the investment account under the cost method ($11,250 as per page 350).

	Investment in Sub Inc.	Investment income
December 31, Year 1	$13,116	
December 31, Year 2		
Income from Sub Inc.	2,790	$2,790
Interest loss to parent	(30)	(30)
90% of interest loss to subsidiary	(54)	(54)
Balance, December 31, Year 2	$15,822	$2,706

Appendix 8B, later in this chapter, illustrates the working paper approach to preparing the Year 2 consolidated financial statements.

Less Than 100 Percent Purchase of Affiliate's Bonds

Our example assumed that Sub purchased 100 percent of Parent's bonds for $9,600 on December 31, Year 1. Suppose we changed the assumption so that only

40 percent of Parent's bonds were purchased, for $3,840. The elimination needed to prepare the Year 1 consolidated statements would be:

Bonds payable (40% × 10,200)	4,080	
Investment in bonds of Parent Co.		3,840
Gain on bond retirement		240

A gain on bond retirement is only recognized on the portion of the bonds being retired from a consolidated perspective.

If only 40 percent of the bond liability has been eliminated, the consolidated balance sheet will show bonds payable amounting to $6,120, representing the 60 percent that is not intercompany and is payable to bondholders outside the entity.

When consolidated income statements are later prepared, only 40 percent of the interest expense will be eliminated; the remaining 60 percent will be left as consolidated interest expense.

Intercompany Purchases During the Fiscal Year

Our previous example also assumed that the intercompany purchase of bonds took place on the last day of the fiscal year. If the purchase took place *during* the fiscal year, the Year 1 consolidated income statement contains both the gain on bond retirement and the hidden loss resulting from the elimination of intercompany interest revenue earned and expense incurred for the period subsequent to the acquisition.

Gains (losses) Not Allocated to the Two Equities

The other approaches would allocate the gain on bond retirement differently to Parent and Sub, which changes the amounts allocated to NCI.

On page 344 the four approaches that can be taken to allocate bond gains (losses) were outlined. The illustrations used approach 4; the calculations for this approach are more complicated than for approaches 1 to 3. Because the *CICA Handbook* is silent in this matter, any of these approaches may be used. Under approaches 1 to 3, the gain or loss is allocated to only one of the companies, and the bond chart (page 352) is much simpler, as it needs only the entity columns.

The "agency" method (#1) may well have the greatest merit: because only a company that has issued bonds can logically retire them, allocating the gain or loss to the issuing company puts the emphasis on the economic substance of the transaction rather than on its actual form. In the example used, the entire $600 gain would be allocated to Parent Co. If the example used was changed so that the bonds were originally issued by Sub. Inc., and the agency method was followed, the $600 gain would at first be allocated to the subsidiary; however, because Parent owns 90 percent of Sub, noncontrolling interest would reflect 10 percent of this gain.

Gains (losses) Allocated to Two Equities — Loss to One, Gain to the Other

Suppose that the issuing affiliate had $10,000 in bonds outstanding with a carrying value of $10,700, and the purchasing affiliate paid $10,100 to acquire all of the issue on the open market. From the entity point of view there is a before-tax gain on bond retirement of $600, calculated as follows:

The gain is equal to the difference between the cost to retire the bonds as compared to the carrying value of the bonds when they are retired.

Carrying amount of bonds	$10,700
Cost of investment in bonds	10,100
Gain on bond retirement	$ 600

If we allocate the gain to the two affiliates (approach 4), we see that the issuing affiliate is allocated a gain of $700, while the purchasing affiliate is allocated a loss of $100. This can be verified by the following calculation:

The $600 gain is allocated to the affiliates based on the premium or discount on their separate-entity books.

Carrying amount of bond liability	$10,700
Par value of bond liability	10,000
Gain to issuing affiliate	$ 700
Cost of investment in bonds	$10,100
Par value of bond liability	10,000
Loss to purchasing affiliate	$ 100

In subsequent years the entity's "interest elimination loss" will be allocated as a *loss* to the issuing affiliate and a *gain* to the purchasing affiliate.

Effective Yield Method of Amortization

Our previous examples have assumed that both companies use the straight-line method to amortize the premiums and discounts. All of the end-of-chapter problems assume the straight-line method unless stated otherwise. This method leads to fairly easy calculations because the yearly amortizations are equal. If one or both companies use the effective interest method of amortization, the calculations become more complex, but the concepts remain the same.

The following examples illustrate the effective interest method.

On December 31, Year 0 Subco issued $100,000 face value bonds for a price of $92,791. The bonds pay interest on December 31 each year at a stated rate of 10 percent and mature on December 31, Year 5. The market rate of interest was 12 percent on December 31, Year 0. Given that the stated rate of interest was lower than the market rate, the bonds were issued at a discount. The issue price of the bonds can be determined by taking the present value of future cash flows using a discount rate of 12 percent as follows:

The effective rate used in the present value calculations and bond amortization tables is the market rate of 12 percent.

Principal $100,000 × (P/F, 12%, 5 years) (0.56743)	$56,743
Interest 10,000 × (P/A, 12%, 5 years) (3.60478)	36,048
	$92,791

The following schedule shows how Subco would amortize the discount for its separate-entity financial statements and shows that the amortization of the bond discount increases interest expense (decreases income) each year over the term of the bonds:

The bond discount is amortized on Subco's separate-entity books over the remaining term of the bonds using the effective rate of 12 percent.

Period	Interest paid	Interest expense	Amortization of bond discount	Unamortized bond discount	Bond carrying value
Year 0				$7,209	$ 92,791
Year 1	$10,000[1]	$11,135[2]	$1,135[3]	6,074[4]	93,926
Year 2	10,000	11,271	1,271	4,803	95,197
Year 3	10,000	11,424	1,424	3,379	96,621
Year 4	10,000	11,594	1,594	1,785	98,215
Year 5	10,000	11,785	1,785	0	100,000

[1] $100,000 × 10% = $10,000   [2] $92,791 × 12% = $11,135
[3] $10,000 – $11,135 = $1,135   [4] $7,209 – $1,135 = $6,074

The market value of the bonds will increase when the market rate decreases.

The market rate of interest for these bonds decreased to 8 percent and these bonds were trading at a price of $105,154 on December 31, Year 2. If Subco redeems the bonds on this date, it would prepare the following journal entry:

Loss on bond redemption	9,957	
Bonds payable	95,197	
Cash		105,154

Now assume that Subco did not redeem its own bonds but Pubco purchased Subco's bonds in the open market on December 31, Year 2, for $105,154. The following schedule shows the amortization of this premium by Pubco using the effective interest method and shows that the amortization of the bond premium decreases interest revenue (decreases income) each year over the remaining term of the bonds:

Pubco amortizes its bond premium on its separate-entity books using its effective rate of 8 percent.

Period	Interest received	Interest revenue	Amortization of bond premium	Unamortized bond premium	Bond carrying value
Year 2				$5,154	$105,154
Year 3	$10,000[1]	$8,412[2]	$1,588[3]	3,566[4]	103,566
Year 4	10,000	8,285	1,715	1,851	101,851
Year 5	10,000	8,149	1,851	0	100,000

[1] $100,000 × 10% = $10,000
[3] $10,000 − $8,412 = $1,588
[2] $105,154 × 8% = $8,412
[4] $5,154 − $1,588 = $3,566

From a consolidated perspective, the bonds were retired at a loss of $9,957.

From a separate legal entity perspective, Subco has bonds payable on its balance sheet while Pubco has an investment in bonds on its balance sheet. From a consolidated perspective, these bonds were redeemed when Pubco purchased these bonds in the open market. A loss on redemption of $9,957 (105,154 − 95,197) should be recorded on the consolidated income statement. In subsequent years, Subco and Pubco will amortize the bond discount and premium on their separate-entity books. From a consolidated perspective, the amortization of the bond discount and premium should be eliminated because the bonds no longer exist. The following bond chart shows how the loss on bond redemption and the elimination of bond amortization is allocated to Pubco and Subco each year over the remaining life of the bonds:

	Entity	Pubco	Subco
Loss on bond, Dec. 31, Yr 2	$9,957	$5,154	$4,803
Interest elimination gain — Yr 3	3,012	1,588	1,424
Balance — loss — Dec. 31, Yr 3	6,945	3,566	3,379
Interest elimination gain — Yr 4	3,309	1,715	1,594
Balance — loss — Dec. 31, Yr 4	3,636	1,851	1,785
Interest elimination gain — Yr 5	3,636	1,851	1,785
Balance — loss — Dec. 31, Yr 5	$ –0–	$ –0–	$ –0–

To further illustrate, examine the interest accounts of the two companies from the date of the intercompany purchase to the date of maturity of the bonds:

From the separate-entity perspectives, Pubco and Subco continue to amortize the bond discount or premium using their effective rates.

Year ended Dec. 31	Pubco's interest revenue	Subco's interest expense	Difference
Year 3	$ 8,412	$11,424	$3,012
Year 4	8,285	11,594	3,309
Year 5	8,149	11,785	3,636
	$24,846	$34,803	$9,957

The loss on retirement was recognized in Year 2 from a consolidated perspective and over the 3-year period ending in Year 5 from a single-entity perspective.

Under the effective interest method, the difference between interest revenue and interest expense changes over time. Under the straight-line method, the difference would be $3,319 ($9,957 / 3) each year for three years. Under both methods, a loss on bond redemption of $9,957 is recorded on the consolidated income statement in Year 2. In turn, consolidated income is increased by a total of $9,957 over the 3-year remaining term of the bonds as the amortization of the bond premium and discount is eliminated.

An International Perspective

The Canadian standards for eliminating profit on intercompany profits are basically the same as IASB standards unless the reporting entity uses IAS 16 to revalue property, plant, and equipment (PPE) to fair value. If PPE is valued at fair value under IAS 16, the gains are recorded as the fair value changes not when the assets are sold to outsiders. If the reporting entity values PPE at cost less accumulated amortization under IAS 16, then the profit made on intercompany transactions must be accounted for in the same manner as illustrated in this chapter under Canadian GAAP.

SUMMARY

This chapter completed the illustrations of the holdback and realization of intercompany profits and gains in assets, by examining the consolidation procedures involved when the profit is in an asset subject to amortization. The gain is held back in order to state the depreciable asset at its undepreciated historical cost from a consolidated perspective. The intercompany profit is subsequently realized as the assets are used or consumed in generating revenues over the remaining life of the assets. Because there are differences between the periods in which the tax is paid and the periods in which the gains are realized in the consolidated statements, income tax must be allocated.

The second part of the chapter examined the gains and losses that are created in the consolidated statements by the elimination of intercompany bondholdings. When the investing company purchases the bonds from outsiders, the bonds are effectively retired from a consolidated perspective. The difference between the price paid to retire the bonds and the book value of the bonds is a gain or loss. These gains and losses can occur only if there were premiums or discounts involved in the issue or purchase of these bonds. In the case of intercompany bondholdings, the gains or losses are recognized in the consolidated statements before they are recorded by the affiliated companies; whereas intercompany asset gains are recorded by the affiliated companies before they are recognized in the consolidated statements.

Our initial examination of consolidations in earlier chapters focused first on the working-paper approach and then on the direct approach. As the concepts became more complex we concentrated on the direct approach, and working papers were shifted to end-of-chapter appendices. This change of focus was intentional. Examination problems often contain complex purchase discrepancy allocations as well as intercompany asset and bond transactions. Readers who have mastered the direct approach will probably find that they can answer exam questions more quickly with it.

SELF-STUDY PROBLEM 1

The following are the Year 15 financial statements of Penn Company and its subsidiary Sill Corp.

	Penn	Sill
Year 15 income statements		
Miscellaneous revenues	$500,000	$300,000
Investment income	9,194	—
Gain on sale of equipment	14,000	—
Gain on sale of patent	—	7,500
	523,194	307,500
Miscellaneous expenses	309,600	186,500
Depreciation expense	120,000	80,000
Patent amortization expense	800	—
Income tax expense	33,000	16,000
	463,400	282,500
Net income	$ 59,794	$ 25,000
Year 15 retained earnings statements		
Balance, January 1	$162,000	$154,000
Net income	59,794	25,000
	221,794	179,000
Dividends	25,000	8,000
Balance, December 31	$196,794	$171,000
Balance sheets, December 31, Year 15		
Miscellaneous assets	$271,600	$131,000
Land and buildings	200,000	656,000
Equipment	—	44,000*
Accumulated depreciation	(80,000)	(250,000)
Patent (net)	19,200	—
Investment in Sill Corp.	285,994	—
	$696,794	$581,000
Miscellaneous liabilities	$100,000	$210,000
Common stock	400,000	200,000
Retained earnings	196,794	171,000
	$696,794	$581,000

* For illustrative purposes, we are assuming that this is the only equipment owned by either company.

Other Information

Penn owns 80% of Sill and has used the equity method to account for its investment. The purchase discrepancy on acquisition date has been fully amortized for consolidation purposes prior to Year 15, and there were no unrealized intercompany profits or losses in the assets of the companies on December 31, Year 14. During Year 15, the following intercompany transactions took place:

1. On January 1, Year 15, Penn sold used equipment to Sill and recorded a $14,000 gain on the transaction as follows:

Selling price of equipment		$44,000
Book value of equipment sold		
Cost	60,000	
Accumulated depreciation — Dec. 31, Year 14	30,000	30,000
Gain on sale of equipment		$14,000

This equipment had an estimated remaining life of eight years on this date.

2. On January 1, Year 5, Sill developed a patent at a cost of $34,000. It has been amortizing this patent 17 years. On October 1, Year 15, Sill sold the over patent to Penn and recorded a $7,500 gain, calculated as follows:

Selling price of patent over			$20,000
Book value of patent sold			
Cost		34,000	
Amortization:			
To December 31, Year 14 (10 × 2,000)	20,000		
Year 15 (¾ × 2,000)	1,500	21,500	12,500
Gain on sale of patent			$ 7,500

Penn is amortizing this patent over its remaining legal life of 6¼ years.

3. Both gains were assessed income tax at a rate of 40%.

Required:

(a) Using the reported net incomes of both companies, prepare a calculation that shows that Penn's net income is equal to consolidated net income.

(b) Using Penn's investment account, prepare a calculation that shows that the purchase discrepancy is fully amortized.

(c) Prepare the following Year 15 consolidated financial statements:
   (i)   Income statement.
   (ii) Retained earnings statement.
   (iii) Balance sheet.

Solution to Self-study Problem 1

UNREALIZED PROFITS

	Before tax	40% tax	After tax	
Equipment (Penn selling):				
Gain recorded, Jan. 1, Year 15	$14,000	$5,600	$8,400	**(a)**
Depreciation, Year 15 (14,000 ÷ 8)	1,750	700	1,050	**(b)**
Balance unrealized, Dec. 31, Year 15	$12,250	$4,900	$7,350	**(c)**
Patent (Sill selling):				
Gain recorded, Oct. 1, Year 15	$ 7,500	$3,000	$4,500	**(d)**
Amortization, Year 15 (7,500 ÷ 6¼ × ¼)	300	120	180	**(e)**
Balance unrealized Dec. 31, Year 15	$ 7,200	$2,880	$4,320	**(f)**
Deferred charge–income taxes — December 31, Year 15:				
Equipment profit			$4,900	**(g)**
Patent profit			2,880	**(h)**
			$7,780	**(i)**

(a)

Net income, Penn Co.		$59,794
Less investment income		9,194
Net income, Penn Co. — own operations		50,600
Less January 1 equipment gain **(a)**		8,400
		42,200
Add after-tax equipment gain realized in Year 15 **(b)**		1,050
Adjusted net income		43,250
Net income, Sill Corp.	25,000	
Less October 1 patent gain **(d)**	4,500	
	20,500	
Add after-tax patent gain realized in Year 15 **(e)**	180	
Adjusted net income	20,680	
Penn's ownership	80%	16,544
Consolidated net income		$59,794 **(j)**
Noncontrolling interest (20% × 20,680)		$ 4,136 **(k)**

(b) Investment in Sill Corp. (equity method):

Balance, Dec. 31, Year 15		$285,994
Add unrealized after-tax equipment gain, Dec. 31, Year 15 **(c)**		7,350
		293,344
Sill Corp., Dec. 31, Year 15:		
Common stock	200,000	
Retained earnings	171,000	
	371,000	
Less unrealized after-tax patent gain, Dec. 31, Year 15 **(f)**	4,320	
Adjusted shareholders' equity	366,680	
Penn's ownership	80%	293,344
Unamortized purchase discrepancy		$ –0–

(c) (i)

CONSOLIDATED INCOME STATEMENT — for Year 15

Miscellaneous revenues (500,000 + 300,000)	$800,000
Gain on sale of equipment (14,000 + 0 – **(a) 14,000**)	–0–
Gain on sale of patents (0 + 7,500 – **(d) 7,500**)	–0–
Miscellaneous expenses (309,600 + 186,500)	496,100
Depreciation expense (120,000 + 80,000 – **(b) 1,750**)	198,250
Patent amortization expense (800 – **(e) 300**)	500
Income tax expense (33,000 + 16,000 – **(c) 4,900 – (f) 2,880**)	41,220
	736,070
Net income — entity	63,930
Less noncontrolling interest **(k)**	4,136
Net income	$ 59,794

(ii)

CONSOLIDATED RETAINED EARNINGS STATEMENT — for Year 15

Balance, January 1	$162,000
Net income	59,794
	221,794
Dividends	25,000
Balance, December 31	$196,794

(iii)   **CONSOLIDATED BALANCE SHEET** — at December 31, Year 15

Miscellaneous assets (271,600 + 131,000)	$402,600
Land and buildings (200,000 + 656,000)	856,000
Equipment (44,000 – **(a) 14,000** + **30,000***)	60,000
Accumulated depreciation (80,000 + 250,000 – **(b) 1,750** + **30,000***)	(358,250)
Patent (19,200 – **(f) 7,200**)	12,000
Deferred charge–income taxes (0 + 0 + **(i) 7,780**)	7,780
	$980,130
Miscellaneous liabilities (100,000 + 210,000)	$310,000
Common stock	400,000
Retained earnings	196,794
Noncontrolling interest**	73,336
	$980,130

*   It is necessary to increase equipment and accumulated depreciation by $30,000 in order to re-establish the original historical cost of the equipment and the accumulated depreciation as at the date of the intercompany sale.

** Sill Corp. —

Adjusted shareholders' equity (see part (b))	$366,680
	20%
Noncontrolling interest	$ 73,336

SELF-STUDY PROBLEM 2

The financial statements of Parson Corp. and Sloan Inc. for the year ended December 31, Year 5, appear on the next page.

Other Information

1. Parson acquired 75% of Sloan on January 1, Year 1, at a cost of $96,000. On this date Sloan's retained earnings amounted to $40,000, and the purchase discrepancy was allocated entirely to goodwill. Impairment tests conducted yearly since acquisition yielded a loss of $3,200 in Year 2 and a further loss of $800 in Year 5. Parson uses the cost method to account for the investment.
2. Sloan has a 10%, $100,000 bond issue outstanding. These bonds were originally issued at a premium and mature on December 31, Year 8. On January 1, Year 5, the unamortized issue premium amounted to $1,200. Sloan uses the straight-line method to amortize the premium.
3. On January 1, Year 5, Parson acquired $60,000 face value of Sloan's bonds at a cost of $61,500. The purchase premium is being amortized by Parson using the straight-line method.
4. Both companies pay income tax at a rate of 40%.
5. Gains and losses from intercompany bondholdings are to be allocated to the two companies when consolidated statements are prepared.

Required:

(a) Prepare the following Year 5 consolidated financial statements:
    (i) Income statement.
    (ii) Retained earnings statement.
    (iii) Balance sheet.
(b) Prepare a calculation of consolidated retained earnings on December 31, Year 5.
(c) Prepare the Year 5 journal entries that would be made by Parson if the equity method was used to account for the investment in Sloan's shares.

(d) Calculate the balance in the "Investment in Sloan shares" account as at December 31, Year 5, if Parson had used the equity method.

INCOME STATEMENTS — for Year 5

	Parson	Sloan
Miscellaneous revenues	$650,000	$200,000
Interest revenue	5,625	—
Dividend revenue	7,500	—
	663,125	200,000
Miscellaneous expenses	432,000	129,600
Interest expense	—	9,700
Income tax expense	92,000	24,000
	524,000	163,300
Net income	$139,125	$ 36,700

RETAINED EARNINGS STATEMENTS — for Year 5

	Parson	Sloan
Balance, January 1	$245,000	$ 90,000
Net income	139,125	36,700
	384,125	126,700
Dividends	70,000	10,000
Balance, December 31	$314,125	$116,700

BALANCE SHEETS — at December 31, Year 5

	Parson	Sloan
Miscellaneous assets	$607,000	$372,600
Investment in Sloan shares	96,000	—
Investment in Sloan bonds	61,125	—
	$764,125	$372,600
Miscellaneous liabilities	$300,000	$ 75,000
Bonds payable	—	100,000
Premium on bonds	—	900
Common stock	150,000	80,000
Retained earnings	314,125	116,700
	$764,125	$372,600

Solution to Self-study Problem 2

Cost of 75% of Sloan		$ 96,000
Implied value of 100% of Sloan		$128,000
Book value of Sloan, January 1, Year 1		
Common stock	80,000	
Retained earnings	40,000	
		120,000
Purchase discrepancy — January 1, Year 1		8,000
Allocated to revalue Sloan's net assets		–0–
Balance — goodwill		8,000
Impairment losses		
Year 1 to Year 4		3,200 **(a)**
Year 5		800 **(b)**
Balance — goodwill, December 31, Year 5		$ 4,000 **(c)**
NCI's share (25%)		$ 1,000 **(d)**

INTERCOMPANY TRANSACTIONS
YEAR 5 BEFORE-TAX BOND LOSS

Cost of 60% of Sloan's bonds acquired Jan. 1, Year 5		$61,500
Carrying amount of liability		
Bonds payable	100,000	
Bond premium	1,200	
	101,200	
Amount acquired by Parson	60%	60,720
Bond loss to be reflected in the Year 5 income statement		$ 780 **(e)**

Allocated as follows:		
Cost of bonds		$61,500
Face value of bonds (intercompany portion)		60,000
Before-tax loss — Parson		$ 1,500 **(f)**

Face value of bonds		$60,000
Carrying amount of bonds (intercompany portion)		60,720
Before-tax gain — Sloan		$ 720 **(g)**

INTERCOMPANY INTEREST REVENUE AND EXPENSE

Interest expense		
10% × 100,000	10,000	
Premium amortization (1,200 ÷ 4) *Jan1/r5 – Dec 31/r8*	300	
Total expense	9,700	
Intercompany portion	60%	$5,820 **(h)**
Interest revenue		
10% × 60,000	6,000	
Premium amortization (1,500 ÷ 4)	375	5,625 **(i)**
Before tax interest elimination gain to entity		$ 195 **(j)**

Allocated:		
Before tax loss to Sloan (300 × 60%) *1200/4*		$ 180 **(k)**
Before tax gain to Parson (1500/4)		375 **(l)**
Total gain allocated (before-tax dollars)		$ 195 **(m)**

SUMMARY

	Entity			Parson Co.			Sloan Inc.		
	Before tax	40% tax	After tax	Before tax	40% tax	After tax	Before tax	40% tax	After tax
Jan. 1/Year 5 bond loss (gain)	$780	$312	$468	$1,500	$600	$900	$(720)	$(288)	$(432) **(n)**
Int. elim. gain (loss) Year 5	195	78	117	375	150	225	(180)	(72)	(108) **(o)**
Dec. 31/ Year 5 balance loss (gain)	$585	$234	$351	$1,125	$450	$675	$(540)	$(216)	$(324) **(p)**

(a) (i)   **CALCULATION OF CONSOLIDATED NET INCOME** — for Year 5

Net income — Parson		$139,125
Less: Dividend from Sloan	7,500	
January 1 after-tax bond loss allocated **(n)**	900	8,400
		130,725
Add Year 5 after-tax interest elimination gain allocated **(o)**		225
Adjusted net income		130,950
Net income — Sloan	36,700	
Add January 1 after-tax bond gain allocated **(n)**	432	
Less: Year 5 after-tax interest elimination loss allocated **(o)**	(108)	
Purchase discrepancy amortization **(b)**	(800)	
Adjusted net income	36,224	
Parson's ownership	75%	27,168
Consolidated net income		$158,118 **(q)**
Noncontrolling interest (25% × 36,224)		$ 9,056 **(r)**

CONSOLIDATED INCOME STATEMENT — for Year 5

Miscellaneous revenues (650,000 + 200,000)	$850,000
Interest revenue (5,625 + 0 – **(i) 5,625**)	
Dividend revenue (7,500 + 0 – **7,500**)	
Miscellaneous expenses (432,000 + 129,600)	561,600
Loss on bond retirement **(n)**	780
Interest expense (9,700 – **(h) 5,820**)	3,880
Goodwill impairment loss **(b)**	800
Income tax expense (92,000 + 24,000 – **(p) 234**)	115,766
	682,826
Net income, entity	167,174
Less: Noncontrolling interest **(r)**	9,056
Net income **(q)**	$158,118

(ii)   **CALCULATION OF CONSOLIDATED RETAINED EARNINGS**
at January 1, Year 5

Retained earnings — Parson		$245,000
Retained earnings — Sloan	90,000	
Acquisition retained earnings	40,000	
Increase since acquisition	50,000	
Less: Goodwill impairment loss **(a)**	3,200	
	46,800	
Parson's ownership	75%	35,100
Consolidated retained earnings, Jan. 1, Year 5		$280,100 **(s)**

CONSOLIDATED RETAINED EARNINGS STATEMENT — for Year 5

Balance, January 1 **(s)**	$280,100
Net income	158,118
	438,218
Dividends	70,000
Balance, December 31	$368,218

(iii)

CALCULATION OF NONCONTROLLING INTEREST
at December 31, Year 5

Shareholders' equity — Sloan	
Common stock	$ 80,000
Retained earnings	116,700
	196,700
Add net Year 5 after-tax bond gain allocated **(p)**	324
Less: Unimpaired goodwill **(c)**	(4,000)
Adjusted shareholders' equity	193,024
	25%
	$ 48,256 **(t)**

CONSOLIDATED BALANCE SHEET — at December 31, Year 5

Miscellaneous assets (605,000 + 372,600)	$977,600
Investment in Sloan bonds (61,125 + 0 – 61,125)	
Deferred charge–income taxes **(p)**	234
Goodwill **(c)**	4,000
	$981,834
Miscellaneous liabilities (300,000 + 75,000)	$375,000
Bonds payable (100,000 – 60,000)	40,000
Premium on bonds (900 – **(p) 540**)	360
Total liabilities	415,360
Noncontrolling interest **(f)**	48,256
Common stock	150,000
Retained earnings	368,218
	566,474
	$981,834

(b)

PROOF — CONSOLIDATED RETAINED EARNINGS
at December 31, Year 5

Retained earnings — Parson		$314,125
Less: Net Year 5 after-tax bond loss allocated **(p)**		675
Adjusted retained earnings		313,450
Retained earnings — Sloan	116,700	
Acquisition retained earnings	40,000	
Increase since acquisition	76,700	
Less: Goodwill impairment losses ((**a**) **3,200** + (**b**) **800**)	(4,000)	
Add net Year 5 after-tax bond gain allocated **(p)**	324	
Adjusted increase	73,024	
Parsons' ownership	75%	54,768
Consolidated retained earnings		$368,218

(c)

EQUITY METHOD JOURNAL ENTRIES

Investment in Sloan	27,525	
Investment income		27,525
75% of Sloan's Year 5 net income (75% × 36,700)		
Investment in Sloan	243	
Investment income		243
75% of the net Year 5 bond gain allocated to Sloan (75% × 324)		

Cash	7,500	
Investment in Sloan		7,500
Dividends received from Sloan		
Investment income	600	
Investment in Sloan		600
Year 5 goodwill impairment loss (75% × 800)		
Investment income	675	
Investment in Sloan		675
Year 5 net bond loss allocated to Parson		

(d)

	Investment in Sloan shares
Balance, December 31, Year 4 — cost method	$ 98,000
Increase in retained earnings to Jan. 1, Year 5 (46,800 × 75%)	35,100
Balance, December 31, Year 4 — equity method	133,100
Investment income, Year 5 (see equity method journal entries)	26,493
Dividends from Sloan	(7,500)
Balance, December 31, Year 5 — equity method	$152,093

APPENDIX 8A

Working Papers for Intercompany Profits in Depreciable Fixed Assets

Exhibit 8A.1 illustrates the working paper for the preparation of Year 1 consolidated financial statements when Parent Company has used the cost method to account for its investment.

The following working paper entries were made to arrive at the consolidated amounts:

Convert Parent's separate entity figures to the equity method.

#a	Investment in Sub Inc. — Parent Co.	1,314	
	Investment income — Parent Co.		1,314
	To adjust the financial statements of Parent to the equity method (see the calculation of consolidated net income on page 331)		
#1	Investment income — Parent Co.	1,314	
	Investment in Sub Inc. — Parent Co.		1,314
	To restate the investment account to the balance at the beginning of the year		
#2	Retained earnings, January 1 — Sub Inc.	450	
	Common stock — Sub Inc.	800	
	Noncontrolling interest (balance sheet)		1,250
	To eliminate 10% of the shareholders' equity of the subsidiary as at the beginning of the year and establish the noncontrolling interest at that date		
#3	Retained earnings, January 1 — Sub Inc.	4,050	
	Common stock — Sub Inc.	7,200	
	Investment in Sub Inc. — Parent Co.		11,250
	To eliminate the parent's share of the shareholders' equity of the subsidiary at the beginning of the year against the parent's investment account		

Exhibit 8A.1

**CONSOLIDATED FINANCIAL STATEMENT WORKING PAPER —
COST METHOD
ELIMINATION OF EQUIPMENT PROFIT** — December 31, Year 1

	Parent	Sub	Eliminations Dr.	Eliminations Cr.	Consolidated
The gain on sale is eliminated on consolidation. Sales	$20,000	$ 7,400			$27,400
Gain on sale of equipment		600	**(i)** $ 600		
Investment income			**(1)** 1,314	**(a)** $ 1,314	
	20,000	8,000			27,400
Depreciation exp.	700			**(ii)** 200	500
Misc. expenses	13,700	5,200			18,900
Income tax exp.	2,200	1,100		**(iii)** 160	3,140
	16,600	6,300			22,540
Consolidated net income is equal to the parent's income under the equity method ($3,400 + $1,314). Net income, entity					4,860
Noncontrolling interest			**(4)** 146		146
Net income	$ 3,400	$ 1,700	$ 2,060	$ 1,674	$ 4,714
Retained earnings, Jan. 1	$12,000	$ 4,500	**(2)** $ 450		$12,000
			(3) 4,050		
Net income	3,400	1,700	2,060	$ 1,674	4,714
	15,400	6,200			16,714
Dividends	2,000				2,000
Retained earnings, Dec. 31	$13,400	$ 6,200	$ 6,560	$ 1,674	$14,714
Equipment is restated to historical cost to the consolidated entity. Assets, misc.	$27,750	$23,200			$50,950
Equipment	2,100			**(i)** $ 600	1,500
Accumulated depreciation	(700)		**(ii)** $ 200		(500)
Deferred charge–income taxes			**(iii)** 160		160
Investment in Sub	11,250		**(a)** 1,314	**(1)** 1,314	
				(3) 11,250	
	$40,400	$23,200			$52,110
Liabilities	$12,000	$ 9,000			$21,000
Common stock	15,000	8,000	**(2)** 800		15,000
			(3) 7,200		
Retained earnings	13,400	6,200	6,560	1,674	14,714
Noncontrolling interest				**(2)** 1,250	1,396
				(4) 146	
	$40,400	$23,200	$16,234	$16,234	$52,110

#4   Noncontrolling interest (income statement)   146
         Noncontrolling interest (balance sheet)   146
     To allocate the applicable portion of the net income of the entity to the
     noncontrolling interest (see the calculation of consolidated net income on
     page 331)

#i Gain on sale of equipment — Sub Inc.   600
        Equipment — Parent Co.   600
    To eliminate the unrealized gain on the income statement and balance sheet

#ii Accumulated depreciation — Parent Co.   200
        Depreciation expense — Parent Co.   200
    To eliminate the excess depreciation

#iii Deferred charge–income taxes   160
        Income tax expense   160
    To recognize the tax effect of the unrealized gain being held back

Exhibit 8A.2 contains the Year 2 consolidated financial statement working papers.

The following working paper entries were used:

Convert Parent's separate entity figures to the equity method.

#a Investment in Sub Inc. — Parent Co.   4,320
        Investment income — Parent Co.   3,006
        Retained earnings, Jan. 1 — Parent Co.   1,314
    To adjust the statements of Parent to the equity method (see calculation of
    consolidated net income and calculation of consolidated retained
    earnings, page 336)

#1 Investment income — Parent Co.   3,006
        Investment in Sub Inc. — Parent Co.   3,006
    To adjust investment account to start-of-year balance

#2 Retained earnings, Jan. 1 — Sub Inc.   620
    Common stock — Sub Inc.   800
        Noncontrolling interest (balance sheet)   1,420
    To eliminate 10% of the shareholders' equity of Sub Inc. at the beginning
    of the year

The excess depreciation expense is eliminated.

#i Investment In Sub Inc. — Parent Co.   216
    Noncontrolling interest (balance sheet)   24
    Income tax expense   160
        Depreciation expense   400
    The Year 2 realization of the after-tax equipment profit of $240, and the
    holdback of the profit from start-of-year noncontrolling interest, and the
    reversal of the holdback from the start-of-year balance in the investment
    account

#ii Accumulated depreciation   600
        Equipment   600
    To establish the two accounts to cost

#3 Retained earnings, Jan. 1 — Sub Inc.   5,580
    Common stock — Sub Inc.   7,200
        Investment in Sub Inc. — Parent Co.   12,780
    To eliminate parent's share of start-of-year shareholders' equity of subsidiary
    against the investment account

#4 Noncontrolling interest (income statement)   334
        Noncontrolling interest (balance sheet)   334
    Allocation of entity's Year 2 net income (see calculation of consolidated
    net income, page 336)

Exhibit 8A.2

CONSOLIDATED FINANCIAL STATEMENT WORKING PAPER — COST METHOD
REALIZATION OF EQUIPMENT PROFIT — December 31, Year 2

	Parent	Sub	Eliminations Dr.	Eliminations Cr.	Consolidated
One year of excess depreciation is eliminated on the consolidated income statement.					
Sales	$25,000	$12,000			$37,000
Investment income			(1) $ 3,006	(a) $ 3,006	
	25,000	12,000			37,000
Depreciation expense	1,400			(i) 400	1,000
Miscellaneous expenses	16,950	6,900			23,850
Income tax expense	2,600	2,000	(i) 160		4,760
	20,950	8,900			29,610
Net income — entity					7,390
Noncontrolling interest			(4) 334		334
Net income	$ 4,050	$ 3,100	$ 3,500	$ 3,406	$ 7,056
Retained earnings, Jan. 1	$13,400	$ 6,200	(2) $ 620 (3) 5,580	(a) $ 1,314	$14,714
Net income	4,050	3,100	3,500	3,406	7,056
	17,450	9,300			21,770
Dividends	2,500				2,500
Retained earnings, Dec. 31	$14,950	$ 9,300	$ 9,700	$ 4,720	$19,270
Cumulative excess depreciation (1½ years) is eliminated on the consolidated balance sheet.					
Assets — miscellaneous	$32,700	$28,300			$61,000
Equipment	2,100			(ii) $ 600	1,500
Accumulated depreciation	(2,100)		(ii) $ 600		(1,500)
Investment in Sub Inc.	11,250		(a) 4,320 (i) 216	(1) 3,006 (3) 12,780	
	$43,950	$28,300			$61,000
Liabilities	$14,000	$11,000			$25,000
Common stock	15,000	8,000	(2) 800 (3) 7,200		15,000
Retained earnings	14,950	9,300	9,700	4,720	19,270
Noncontrolling interest			(i) 24	(2) 1,420 (4) 334	1,730
	$43,950	$28,300	$22,860	$22,860	$61,000

APPENDIX 8B

Working Papers for Intercompany Bondholdings

Exhibit 8B.1 illustrates the working paper for the preparation of the Year 1 consolidated financial statements when Parent Company has used the cost method to account for its investment.

The following working paper entries were used:

Convert Parent's separate entity figures to the equity method.

#a Investment in Sub Inc. — Parent Co.   1,866
     Investment income — Parent Co.   1,866
To adjust the financial statements of Parent to the equity method as follows:
    Adjusted net income — Sub Inc. (see page 347) $1,940
       90%
       1,746
     Add bond gain allocated to Parent Co.   120
       $1,866

#1 Investment income — Parent Co.   1,866
     Investment in Sub Inc. — Parent Co.   1,866
To restate the investment account to the balance at the beginning of the year

#2 Retained earnings, January 1 — Sub Inc.   4,500
Common stock — Sub Inc.   8,000
     Investment in Sub Inc. — Parent Co.   11,250
     Noncontrolling interest (balance sheet)   1,250
To eliminate the investment account and the shareholders' equity of the subsidiary, and establish the noncontrolling interest; at the beginning of the year

#3 Noncontrolling interest (income statement)   194
     Noncontrolling interest (balance sheet)   194
To allocate entity net income to noncontrolling interest (see calculation of consolidated net income, page 347)

These entries are made on the consolidation working papers.

#i Bonds payable — Parent Co.   10,200
     Investment in Parent Co. bonds (Sub Inc.)   9,600
     Gain on bond retirement   600
To eliminate the intercompany bonds and record the resultant gain as at December 31, Year 1

#ii Income tax expense (income statement)   240
     Deferred charge–income taxes (balance sheet)   240
To record the income tax on the bond gain recorded

Exhibit 8B.2, on page 376, contains the working papers for the preparation of the Year 2 consolidated financial statements.

The working paper entries are as follows:

#a Investment in Sub Inc. — Parent Co.   4,572
     Investment income — Parent Co.   2,706
     Retained earnings, Jan. 1 — Parent Co.   1,866
To adjust the statements of Parent Co. to the equity method (see calculations of consolidated net income and consolidated retained earnings, page 353)

Exhibit 8B.1

**CONSOLIDATED FINANCIAL STATEMENT WORKING PAPER —
COST METHOD
ELIMINATION OF INTERCOMPANY BONDHOLDINGS**
December 31, Year 1

	Parent	Sub	Eliminations Dr.	Cr.	Consolidated
The gain on bond retirement appears on the consolidated income statement. Sales	$20,000	$ 8,000			$28,000
Gain on bond retirement				**(i)** $ 600	600
Investment income			**(1)** $ 1,866	**(a)** 1,866	
	20,000	8,000			28,600
Interest expense	950				950
Miscellaneous expenses	13,450	5,200			18,650
Income tax expense	2,200	1,100	**(ii)** 240		3,540
	16,600	6,300			23,140
Net income — entity					5,460
Noncontrolling interest			**(3)** 194		194
Net income	$ 3,400	$ 1,700	$ 2,300	$ 2,466	$ 5,266
Retained earnings, Jan. 1	$12,000	$ 4,500	**(2)** $ 4,500		$12,000
Net income	3,400	1,700	2,300	$ 2,466	5,266
	15,400	6,200			17,266
Dividends	2,000				2,000
Retained earnings, Dec. 31	$13,400	$ 6,200	$ 6,800	$ 2,466	$15,266
The investment in bonds and bonds payable are eliminated on consolidation. Assets — miscellaneous	$29,150	$13,600			$42,750
Investment in Parent bonds		9,600		**(i)** $ 9,600	
Investment in Sub Inc.	11,250		**(a)** $ 1,866	**(1)** 1,866	
				(2) 11,250	
	$40,400	$23,200			$42,750
Income tax on the gain on bond retirement is reported on the consolidated balance sheet. Miscellaneous liabilities	$ 1,800	$ 9,000			$10,800
Bonds payable	10,200		**(i)** 10,200		
Deferred credit— income taxes				**(ii)** 240	240
Common stock	15,000	8,000	**(2)** 8,000		15,000
Retained earnings	13,400	6,200	6,800	2,466	15,266
Noncontrolling interest				**(2)** 1,250	1,444
				(3) 194	
	$40,400	$23,200	$26,866	$26,866	$42,750

#1	Investment income — Parent Co.	2,706	
	Investment in Sub Inc. — Parent Co.		2,706
	To adjust the investment account to start-of-year balance		

#2	Retained earnings, Jan. 1 — Sub Inc.	6,200	
	Common stock — Sub Inc.	8,000	
	Noncontrolling interest (balance sheet)		1,420
	Investment in Sub Inc. — Parent Co.		12,780

To eliminate the shareholders' equity of the subsidiary at the beginning of the year, of which 10% is allocated to the noncontrolling interest, and 90% to reduce the investment account as at the beginning of the year

The various accounts related to bonds are adjusted to the desired balances for the consolidated financial statements.

#i	Interest revenue	1,100	
	Bonds payable	10,150	
	Interest expense		950
	Income tax expense		60
	Investment in Parent Co. bonds		9,700
	Deferred credit–income taxes		180
	Investment in Sub Inc. — Parent Co.		336
	Noncontrolling interest (balance sheet)		24

This involved elimination entry is explained in the following manner. The elimination of interest revenue (1,100) and interest expense (950), and the adjustment to income tax (60), made on the income statement reduces the entity's after-tax net income by $90. We have described this previously as the "interest elimination loss" for the year. These income statement entries reverse the bond gain recorded by the constituent companies in Year 2.

The elimination of bonds payable (10,150) and investment in bonds (9,700), and the related adjustment to deferred credit–income taxes (180), made on the balance sheet, increases the equity side of the balance sheet by $270, and thus establishes the bond gain as at December 31, Year 2.

The two remaining entries reverse the bond gain allocated to Parent at the end of Year 1 from the investment account and allocate the Year 1 bond gain to noncontrolling interest. Noncontrolling interest now contains the correct balance as at December 31, Year 1.

NCI is adjusted for their share of Sub's adjusted net income for the year.

#3	Noncontrolling interest (income statement)	304	
	Noncontrolling interest (balance sheet)		304
	To allocate entity Year 2 net income to noncontrolling interest (see calculation of consolidated net income, page 353)		

REVIEW QUESTIONS

1. Explain how an intercompany gain of $2,700 on the sale of a depreciable asset is held back on the consolidated income statement in the year of sale and realized on subsequent consolidated income statements. What income tax adjustments should be made in each instance?

2. "The realization of intercompany inventory and depreciable asset profits is really an adjustment made in the preparation of consolidated income statements to arrive at historical cost numbers." Explain.

Exhibit 8B.2

CONSOLIDATED FINANCIAL STATEMENT WORKING PAPER
COST METHOD
ELIMINATION OF INTERCOMPANY BONDHOLDINGS
December 31, Year 2

		Parent	Sub	Eliminations Dr.		Eliminations Cr.		Consolidated
Interest revenue and interest expense are eliminated on consolidation.	Sales	$25,000	$10,900					$35,900
	Interest revenue		1,100	**(i)**	$ 1,100			
	Investment income			**(1)**	2,706	**(a)**	$ 2,706	
		25,000	12,000					35,900
	Interest expense	950				**(i)**	950	
	Miscellaneous expenses	17,400	6,900					24,300
	Income tax expense	2,600	2,000			**(i)**	60	4,540
		20,950	8,900					28,840
	Net income — entity							7,060
	Noncontrolling interest			**(3)**	304			304
	Net income	$ 4,050	$ 3,100		$ 4,110		$ 3,716	$ 6,756
	Retained earnings, Jan. 1	$13,400	$ 6,200	**(2)**	$ 6,200	**(a)**	$ 1,866	$15,266
	Net income	4,050	3,100		4,110		3,716	6,756
		17,450	9,300					22,022
	Dividends	2,500						2,500
	Retained earnings, Dec. 31	$14,950	$ 9,300		$10,310		$ 5,582	$19,522
	Assets — miscellaneous	$32,700	$18,600					$51,300
	Invest. in bonds of Parent		9,700			**(i)**	$ 9,700	
						(1)	2,706	
	Investment in Sub Inc.	11,250		**(a)**	$ 4,572	**(2)**	12,780	
						(i)	336	
		$43,950	$28,300					$51,300
Deferred income taxes are $60 less than they were at the end of the previous year.	Liabilities	$ 3,850	$11,000					$14,850
	Bonds payable	10,150		**(i)**	10,150			
	Deferred credit— income taxes					**(i)**	180	180
	Common stock	15,000	8,000	**(2)**	8,000			15,000
	Retained earnings	14,950	9,300		10,310		5,582	19,522
	Noncontrolling interest					**(i)**	24	1,748
						(2)	1,420	
						(3)	304	
		$43,950	$28,300		$33,032		$33,032	$51,300

3. An intercompany inventory profit is realized when the inventory is sold outside the entity. Is this also the case with respect to an intercompany profit in a depreciable asset? Explain.

4. An intercompany gain on a depreciable asset resulting from a sale by the parent company is subsequently realized by an adjustment to the subsidiary's depreciation expense in the preparation of consolidated income statements. Should this adjustment be taken into account in the calculation of noncontrolling interest in net income? Explain.

5. Why does an intercompany sale of a depreciable asset (such as equipment or building) require subsequent adjustments to depreciation expense within the consolidation process?

6. If an intercompany sale of a depreciable asset has been made at a price above book value, the beginning retained earnings of the seller are reduced when preparing each subsequent consolidation. Why does the amount of the adjustment change from year to year?

7. Four approaches could be used to allocate gains (losses) on the elimination of intercompany bondholdings in the preparation of consolidated financial statements. Outline these four approaches. Which approach is conceptually superior? Explain.

8. An "interest elimination gain (loss)" does not appear as a distinguishable item on a consolidated income statement. Explain.

9. The adjustment for the holdback of an intercompany gain in assets requires a corresponding adjustment to a consolidated deferred tax asset. The adjustment for a gain from intercompany bondholdings requires a corresponding adjustment to a consolidated deferred tax liability. In both cases the tax adjustment is made because of a gain. Why is the tax adjustment different? Explain.

10. "Some intercompany gains (losses) are realized for consolidation purposes subsequent to their actual recording by the affiliates, while others are recorded by the affiliates subsequent to their realization for consolidation purposes." Explain, referring to the type of gains (losses) that apply in each case.

11. Explain how the recognition of gains on the elimination of intercompany bondholdings is consistent with the principle of recording gains only when they are realized.

12. Explain how the matching principle supports the recognition of deferred income tax expense when a gain is recognized on the elimination of intercompany bondholdings.

MULTIPLE-CHOICE QUESTIONS

Use the following data to answer Questions 1 to 8.

On January 1, Year 1, Present Inc. purchased 80% of the outstanding voting shares of Sunrise Co. for $3,000,000. On that date, Sunrise's shareholders' equity consisted of retained earnings of $1,500,000 and common stock of $1,000,000. Sunrise's identifiable assets and liabilities had fair values that were equal to their carrying values on January 1, Year 1.

Account balances for selected accounts for the Year 5 financial statements were as follows:

	Present	Sunrise
Property, plant, and equipment (net)	$2,100,000	$3,500,000
Common stock	1,500,000	1,000,000
Retained earnings, beginning of Year 5	2,600,000	2,800,000
Amortization expense	250,000	300,000
Income tax expense	300,000	350,000
Net income	450,000	525,000
Dividends paid	300,000	0

Additional Information

- Present carries its investment in Sunrise on its books by the cost method.
- At the beginning of Year 4, Sunrise sold Present a machine for its fair value of $800,000. Sunrise had purchased the machine in Year 1. The book value at the time of the sale to Present was $640,000. The machine had an estimated remaining useful life of 8 years on the date of the intercorporate sale.
- Any goodwill arising from the business combination is to be tested annually for impairment. Goodwill has not been impaired in any year since the date of acquisition.
- Both companies use the straight-line method for depreciation.
- Both companies are taxed at 40%.

1. What was the amount of goodwill that arose from Present's acquisition of Sunrise?
   a. $400,000
   b. $500,000
   c. $1,000,000
   d. $1,250,000

2. What is the amount that would appear on Present's consolidated balance sheet at December 31, Year 5, for property, plant, and equipment (net)?
   a. $5,440,000
   b. $5,480,000
   c. $5,504,000
   d. $5,600,000

3. What is amortization expense on the consolidated income statement for Year 5?
   a. $530,000
   b. $538,000
   c. $550,000
   d. $570,000

4. What is income tax expense on the consolidated income statement for Year 5?
   a. $642,000
   b. $650,000
   c. $658,000
   d. $666,000

5. What is noncontrolling interest on the consolidated income statement for Year 5?

    a. $ 85,800
    b. $102,600
    c. $105,000
    d. $107,400

6. What is noncontrolling interest on the consolidated balance sheet at the end of Year 5?
    a. $850,600
    b. $995,600
    c. $1,100,600
    d. $1,148,600

7. Which of the following statements is true related to deferred income tax on the consolidated financial statements for Year 5?
    a.   There will be a deferred tax expense of $48,000 on the consolidated income statement.
    b.   There will be a deferred tax recovery of $48,000 on the consolidated income statement.
    c.   There will be a deferred tax asset of $48,000 on the consolidated balance sheet.
    d.   There will be a deferred tax liability of $48,000 on the consolidated balance sheet.

8. Which of the following is (are) the consolidation adjustment(s) to retained earnings, beginning of Year 5, as a result of the intercompany sale of machinery?
    a.   Decrease Sunrise's retained earnings by $84,000.
    b.   Decrease Sunrise's retained earnings by $140,000.
    c.   Decrease Sunrise's retained earnings by $160,000.
    d.   Decrease Sunrise's retained earnings by $96,000 and increase Present's retained earnings by $12,000.

9. Black Ltd. owns all of the outstanding shares of White Inc. On January 1, Year 5, White sold equipment to Black and recorded a before-tax profit of $20,000 on the transaction. (White's tax rate is 40%.) Black is depreciating this equipment over 5 years, using the straight-line method. The net adjustments to calculate the Year 5 and Year 6 consolidated net income would be an increase of how much?

	Year 5	Year 6
a.	$20,000	$0
b.	$ 9,600	$2,400
c.	$16,000	$4,000
d.	$20,000	$4,000

10. A parent company has bonds outstanding that were originally issued at a premium. At the beginning of the current year, a subsidiary purchased all of the parent's bonds on the open market at a discount. Which of the following statements is true?
    a.   The interest income and expense will agree in amount and should be offset when the consolidated income statement is prepared.
    b.   Whether the balances agree or not, both the bond interest income and expense should be reported in the consolidated income statement.
    c.   In computing noncontrolling interest, the interest expense should be included but the interest income should not.

d. Whether the balances agree or not, both the bond interest income and expense should be eliminated when preparing the consolidated income statement.

11. A subsidiary issues bonds directly to its parent at a discount. Both use the same amortization method. Which of the following statements is true?
   a. Because of the discount, the bond interest accounts on the two sets of financial statements will not agree.
   b. Since the bond was issued by the subsidiary, the amount of noncontrolling interest must be affected.
   c. Bond interest income and expense will be equal in amount and must be eliminated when preparing the consolidated income statement.
   d. Elimination is not necessary for consolidation purposes because the bond was acquired directly from the subsidiary.

12. A bond that had been issued by a subsidiary at a premium was acquired several years ago by its parent on the market at a discount. The bond issue is still outstanding. Which of the following statements is true?
   a. The bond issue has no impact on the preparation of current consolidated financial statements because the bond acquisition was made in the past.
   b. The original gain would be reported in the current year's consolidated income statement.
   c. The interest income and interest expense balances exactly offset so that no adjustment to retained earnings or to income is necessary.
   d. For consolidated purposes, retained earnings must be increased at the beginning of the current year, but by an amount that is smaller than the original gain.

Use the following data to answer Questions 13 to 15.

Ravens owns 90 percent of the outstanding common shares of Gaels. On January 1, Year 2, Gaels issued $200,000 of five percent, 10-year bonds payable for $240,000. The interest is paid annually on December 31. On December 31, Year 8, Ravens purchased 30 percent of these bonds in the open market for $56,000. Both companies use the straight-line method to amortize any bond premium or discount. The bond accounts for Ravens and Gaels on their separate-entity financial statements at December 31, Year 8 were as follows:

	Ravens	Gaels
Investment in bonds	$56,000	
Bonds payable		$200,000
Premium on bonds		12,000

13. What is the net book value of the bonds payable on the consolidated balance sheet at December 31, Year 8?
   a. $140,000
   b. $148,400
   c. $156,000
   d. $212,000

14. What is the noncontrolling interest's share of the adjustment on the consolidated income statement for the year ended December 31, Year 8?
   a. $360
   b. $760
   c. $3,600
   d. $7,600

15. Assume that Gaels' bonds were the only bonds payable for the consolidated entity. Which of the following statements is true related to bond interest expense for the consolidated income statements?
    a. There will be no interest expense on the Year 8 consolidated income statement.
    b. There will be no adjustments for interest expense on consolidation for the Year 8 income statement.
    c. There will be no interest expense on the Year 9 income statement.
    d. There will be no adjustments for interest expense on consolidation for the Year 9 income statement.

CASES

Case 1   On January 1, Year 1, Plum purchased 100 percent of the common shares of Slum. On December 31, Year 2, Slum purchased a machine for $90,000 from an external supplier. The machine had an estimated useful life of six years with no residual value. On December 31, Year 4, Plum purchased the machine from Slum for $100,000. The estimated remaining life at the time of the intercompany sale was 4 years. Plum pays income tax at the rate of 40 percent whereas Slum is taxed at a rate of 30 percent.

When preparing the consolidated statements for Year 5, the controller and manager of accounting at Plum got into a heated debate as to the proper tax rate to use when eliminating the tax on the excess depreciation being taken by Plum. The controller thought that Slum's tax rate should be used since Slum was the owner of this machine before the intercompany sale. The manager of accounting thought that Plum's tax rate should be used since Plum was the actual company saving the tax at the rate of 40 percent.

In Year 6, the Canada Revenue Agency (CRA) audited Plum. It questioned the legitimacy of the intercompany transaction for the following reasons:

1. Was the selling price of $100,000 a fair reflection of market value?

2. Was Plum trying to gain a tax advantage by saving tax at a rate of 40 percent rather than the 30 percent saving which Slum used to realize?

Plum argued that, under the terms of the sale, CRA was better off because CRA received tax in Year 4 from the gain on the intercompany sale. Had the intercompany sale not occurred, CRA would not have received this tax.

Required:

a. Determine the economic benefits, if any, to the consolidated entity from tax savings as a result of this intercompany transaction. Was it a good financial decision to undertake this transaction? Explain.

b. Would your answer to (a) be any different if Plum only owned 60 percent of the common shares of Slum? Explain.

c. Indicate what amount of tax savings would be reported for the depreciation expense on the consolidated income statement under the various reporting alternatives. Which method would you recommend? Explain your answer using basic accounting principles.

Case 2   Stephanie Baker is an audit senior with the public accounting firm of Wilson & Lang. It is February Year 9 and the audit of Canadian Development Limited (CDL) for the year ended December 31, Year 8, is proceeding. Stephanie has identified several transactions that occurred in the Year 8 fiscal year that have major accounting implications. The engagement partner has asked Stephanie to draft a memo to him addressing the accounting implications, financial statement disclosure issues, and any other important matters regarding these transactions.

CDL is an important player in many sectors of the economy. The company has both debt and equity securities that trade on a Canadian stock exchange. Except for a controlling interest (53%) owned by the Robichaud family, CDL's shares are widely held. The company has interests in the natural resources, commercial and residential real estate, construction, transportation, and technology development sectors among others.

Changes in capital structure

During Year 8, CDL's underwriters recommended some changes to the company's capital structure. As a result, the company raised $250 million by issuing one million convertible, redeemable debentures at $250 each. Each debenture is convertible into one common share at any time. CDL's controlling shareholders acquired a sizeable block of the one million debentures issued; a few large institutional investors took up the remainder.

The company proposes to partition the balance sheet in a manner that will include a section entitled "Shareholders' Equity and Convertible Debentures." The company views this classification as appropriate because the convertible debt, being much more akin to equity than debt, represents a part of the company's permanent capital. Maurice Richard, the controller of CDL, has emphasized that the interest rate on the debentures is considerably lower than on normal convertible issues and that it is expected that the majority of investors will exercise their conversion privilege. The company has the option of repaying the debt at maturity in 20 years' time, through the issuance of common shares. The option will be lost if the company is unable to meet certain solvency tests at the maturity date. The company's intention was to raise additional permanent capital, and convertible debt was chosen because of the attractive tax savings. The debentures are redeemable at $250 from January 1, Year 15, to January 1, Year 18.

At the same time as the company issued the convertible debentures, two million common shares were converted into two million preferred, redeemable shares. The net book value of the two million common shares was $20 million. The preferred shares do not bear dividends and are mandatorily redeemable in five years at $20 per share. They have been recorded at their redemption value of $40 million and the difference between this redemption value and the net book value of the common shares ($20 million) has been charged against retained earnings.

Disposal of residential real estate segment

Intercity Real Estate Corporation (IRE) is a wholly owned subsidiary of CDL and has two operating divisions: a money-losing residential real estate division and a highly profitable commercial real estate division. The two divisions had been combined in one legal entity for tax purposes as the losses arising from the residential real estate division have more than offset the profits from the commercial real estate division.

During Year 8, CDL decided to dispose of its shares of IRE. However, CDL wished to retain the commercial real estate division and decided to transfer the division's assets to another corporation prior to selling the shares of IRE. As part of the sale agreement, just before the closing, the commercial real estate assets were transferred out of IRC to CDL who then transferred the assets to a newly created subsidiary, Real Property Inc. (RPI). In order to maximize the asset base of RPI, the commercial real estate assets were transferred at fair values, which greatly increased their tax base and created considerable income for tax purposes.

Maurice has explained to Stephanie that, since the transfer would create income for tax purposes, it was necessary for both CDL and the purchaser to agree on the fair value of the commercial real estate assets, even though they were not part of the IRC sale. IRC's purchaser agreed to the values used, because the loss carry-forwards, that would have otherwise expired, offset the income for tax purposes.

CDL is planning to take RPI public sometime this year. The commercial real estate assets of RPI have been recorded at the values established in the sale of IRC because management believes that this amount represents the cost of acquiring the business from IRC. Maurice has stressed that the transfer between IRC and RPI is very different from the majority of transactions between companies under common control. He argues that the transfer of the commercial real estate assets to RPI represents a bona fide business combination since there is a change of substance and not just of form. CDL maintains a policy of granting subsidiaries a high degree of autonomy and, in substance, they do not function "under common control." Maurice indicated that the real estate assets are worth more to CDL as a result of this transaction because of the increase in the tax values of the assets. Finally, an unrelated party was involved in the transaction and in the determination of the fair value of the assets.

Stephanie noted that after the transfer, the real estate business changed. RPI has undertaken a major refurbishing program and has just bought a large chain of shopping centres that has doubled the company's asset base.

Required:

Assume the role of Stephanie Baker and prepare the memo for the partner.

(CICA adapted)

PROBLEMS

Problem 1   X Company owns 80% of Y Company and uses the equity method to account for its investment. On January 1, Year 2, the investment in Y Company account had a balance of $86,900, and Y Company's capital stock and retained earnings totalled $100,000. The unamortized purchase discrepancy had an estimated remaining life of 6 years at this time. The following intercompany asset transfers took place in Years 2 and 3: January 1, Year 2, sale of asset to X at a profit of $45,000; April 30, Year 3, sale of asset to Y at a profit of $60,000. Both assets purchased are being depreciated over 5 years. In Year 2, Y reported a net income of $125,000 and dividends paid of $70,000, while in Year 3 its net income and dividends were $104,000 and $70,000 respectively.

Required:

Calculate the December 31, Year 3, balance in the account "Investment in Y." (Assume a 40% tax rate.)

Problem 2   Peggy Company owns 75% of Sally Inc. and uses the cost method to account for its investment. The following data were taken from the Year 4 income statements of the two companies:

	Peggy	Sally
Gross profit	$580,000	$270,000
Miscellaneous expenses	110,000	85,000
Depreciation expense	162,000	97,000
Income tax expense	123,000	35,000
Total expenses	395,000	217,000
Net income	$185,000	$ 53,000

In Year 2, Sally sold equipment to Peggy at a profit of $15,000. Peggy has been depreciating this equipment over a 5-year period. Use income tax allocation at a rate of 40%.

Required:

(a) Calculate consolidated net income for Year 4.
(b) Prepare a consolidated income statement for Year 4.
(c) Calculate the amount of the asset "deferred charge–income taxes" that would appear on the Year 4 consolidated balance sheet.

Problem 3   The comparative consolidated income statements of a parent and its 75%-owned subsidiary were prepared incorrectly as at December 31 and are shown below. The following items were overlooked when the statements were prepared:

- The Year 5 gain on sale of assets resulted from the subsidiary selling equipment to the parent on September 30. The parent immediately leased the equipment back to the subsidiary at an annual rental of $12,000. This was the only intercompany rent transaction that occurred each year. The equipment had a remaining life of 5 years on the date of sale.
- The Year 6 gain on sale of assets resulted from the January 1 sale of a building, with a remaining life of 7 years, by the subsidiary to the parent.
- Both gains were taxed at a rate of 40%.

CONSOLIDATED INCOME STATEMENTS

	Year 5	Year 6
Miscellaneous revenues	$750,000	$825,000
Gain on sale of assets	8,000	42,000
Rental revenue	3,000	12,000
	761,000	879,000
Miscellaneous expenses	399,800	492,340
Rental expense	52,700	64,300
Depreciation expense	75,000	80,700
Income tax expense	81,000	94,500
Noncontrolling interest	32,500	5,160
	641,000	737,000
Net income	$120,000	$142,000

Required:

Prepare correct consolidated income statements for Years 5 and 6.

Problem 4   On December 31, Year 2, HABS Inc. sold equipment to NORD at its fair value of $2,000,000 and recorded a gain of $500,000. This was HABS's only income (other than any investment income from NORD) during the year. NORD reported income (other than any investment income from HABS) of $200,000 for Year 2. Both companies paid dividends of $100,000 during Year 2.

Required:

(a) Calculate NORD's income before taxes for Year 2 assuming that
   (i)   HABS and NORD are not related.
   (ii) NORD owns 75% of HABS and reports its investment in HABS on a consolidated basis.
   (iii) NORD owns 75% of HABS and reports its investment in HABS using the equity method.

(iv) NORD owns 75% of HABS and reports its investment in HABS using the cost method.

(b) Calculate HABS's income before taxes for Year 2 assuming that
  (i) NORD and HABS are not related.
  (ii) HABS owns 75% of NORD and reports its investment in NORD on a consolidated basis.
  (iii) HABS owns 75% of NORD and reports its investment in NORD using the equity method.
  (iv) HABS owns 75% of NORD and reports its investment in NORD using the cost method.

(c) Compare and contrast the income reported under the different reporting methods. Which method best reflects the economic reality of the business transaction?

Problem 5 The balance sheets of Forest Company and Garden Company are presented below as at December 31, Year 8.

BALANCE SHEETS — at December 31, Year 8

	Forest	Garden
Cash	$ 13,000	$ 48,800
Receivables	25,000	86,674
Inventories	80,000	62,000
Investment in stock of Garden	207,900	—
Plant and equipment	740,000	460,000
Accumulated depreciation	(625,900)	(348,400)
Patents	—	4,500
Investment in bonds of Forest	—	58,426
	$440,000	$372,000
Current liabilities	$ 59,154	$ 53,000
Dividends payable	6,000	30,000
Bonds payable 6%	94,846	—
Capital stock	200,000	150,000
Retained earnings	80,000	139,000
	$440,000	$372,000

Additional Information

- Forest acquired 90% of Garden for $207,900 on July 1, Year 1, and accounts for its investment under the <u>cost method</u>. At that time, the shareholders' equity of Garden amounted to $175,000, and the assets of Garden were undervalued by the following amounts:

Inventory	$12,000	
Buildings	$10,000	remaining life 10 years
Patents	$16,000	remaining life 8 years

- During Year 8, Forest reported net income of $41,000 and paid dividends of $25,000 whereas Garden reported net income of $63,000 and paid dividends of $50,000.

- During Years 2 to 7, goodwill impairment losses totalled $1,950. An impairment test conducted in Year 8 indicated a further loss of $7,150.

- Forest sells goods to Garden on a regular basis at a gross profit of 30%. During Year 8, these sales totalled $150,000. On January 1, Year 8, the inventory of

Garden contained goods purchased from Forest amounting to $18,000, while the December 31, Year 8, inventory contained goods purchased from Forest amounting to $22,000.

- On August 1, Year 6, Garden sold land to Forest at a profit of $16,000. During Year 8, Forest sold one-quarter of the land to an unrelated company.
- Forest's bonds have a par value of $100,000, pay interest annually on December 31 at a stated rate of 6% and mature on December 31, Year 11. Forest incurs an effective interest cost of 8% on these bonds. These bonds had a carrying value of $93,376 on January 1, Year 8. On that date, Garden acquired $60,000 of these bonds on the open market at a cost of $57,968. Garden will earn an effective rate of return of 7% on these bonds. Both companies use the effective-interest method to account for their bonds.

The Year 8 income statements of the two companies show the following with respect to bond interest.

	Forest	Garden
Interest expense	$7,470	
Interest revenue		$4,058

- Garden owes Forest $22,000 on open account on December 31, Year 8.
- Assume a 40% corporate tax rate and allocate bond gains (losses) between the two companies.

Required:

(a) Prepare the following statements:
   (i) Consolidated balance sheet.
   (ii) Consolidated retained earnings statement.
(b) Prepare the Year 8 journal entries that would be made on the books of Forest if the equity method was used to account for the investment.
(c) Explain how a loss on the elimination of intercompany bondholdings is viewed as a temporary difference and gives rise to a deferrred income tax asset.
(d) Calculate goodwill and noncontrolling interest on the consolidated balance sheet at December 31, Year 8, under the parent company extension theory.

Problem 6   Income statements of M Co. and K Co. for the year ended December 31, Year 6, are presented below:

	M Co.	K Co.
Sales	$600,000	$350,000
Rent revenue	—	50,000
Interest revenue	6,700	—
Income from subsidiary	30,320	—
Gain on land sale	—	8,000
	637,020	408,000
Cost of goods sold	334,000	225,000
Depreciation expense	20,000	70,000
Administrative expense	207,000	74,000
Interest expense	1,700	6,000
Income tax expense	20,700	7,500
	583,400	382,500
Net income	$ 53,620	$ 25,500

Additional Information

- M Co. uses the equity method to account for its investment in K Co.
- M Co. acquired its 80% interest in K Co. on January 1, Year 1. On that date the

purchase discrepancy of $25,000 was allocated entirely to buildings; it is being amortized over a 20-year period.

- M Co. made an advance of $100,000 to K Co. on July 1, Year 6. This loan is due on demand and requires the payment of interest at 12% per year.
- M Co. rents marine equipment from K Co. During Year 6, $50,000 rent was paid and was charged to administrative expense.
- In Year 4, M Co. sold land to K Co. and recorded a profit of $10,000 on the sale. K Co. held the land until October, Year 6, when it was sold to an unrelated company.
- During Year 6, K Co. made sales to M Co. totalling $90,000. The December 31, Year 6, inventories of M Co. contain an unrealized profit of $5,000. The January 1, Year 6, inventories of M Co. contained an unrealized profit of $12,000.
- On January 1, Year 4, M Co. sold machinery to K Co. and recorded a profit of $13,000. The remaining useful life on that date was 5 years. Assume straight-line depreciation.
- Tax allocation is to be used, and you are to assume a 40% average corporate tax rate for this purpose.

Required:

Prepare a consolidated income statement for Year 6.

Problem 7   The Pure Company purchased 70% of the capital stock of Gold Company on January 1, Year 6, for $483,000 when the latter company's capital stock and retained earnings were $500,000 and $40,000, respectively. On this date, an appraisal of the assets of Gold disclosed the following differences:

	Carrying value	Fair value
Inventory	$120,000	$108,000
Land	150,000	200,000
Plant and equipment	700,000	770,000

The plant and equipment had an estimated life of 20 years on this date.

The balance sheets of Pure and Gold, prepared on December 31, Year 11, follow:

	Pure	Gold
Cash	$ 41,670	$ 57,500
Accounts receivable	212,150	170,000
Inventory	225,000	180,000
Investment in Gold Co. stock (equity method)	544,710	—
Investment in Gold Co. bonds	227,000	—
Land	100,000	150,000
Plant and equipment	625,000	940,000
Less accumulated depreciation	(183,000)	(220,000)
Patent (net of amortization)	31,500	—
	$1,824,030	$1,277,500
Accounts payable	$ 56,030	$ 100,000
Bonds payable (due Year 20)	—	477,500
Capital stock	750,000	500,000
Retained earnings	1,018,000	200,000
	$1,824,030	$1,277,500

Other Information

- Goodwill impairment tests have resulted in losses totalling $28,000.
- On January 1, Year 1, Gold issued $500,000 of 8 ½% bonds at 90, maturing in 20 years (on December 31, Year 20).
- On January 1, Year 11, Pure acquired $200,000 of Gold's bonds on the open market at a cost of $230,000.
- On July 1, Year 8, Gold sold a patent to Pure for $63,000. The patent had a carrying value on Gold's books of $42,000 on this date and an estimated remaining life of 7 years.
- Pure uses tax allocation (rate 40%) and allocates bond gains between affiliates when it consolidates Gold.
- Pure uses the equity method to account for its investment.

Required:

Prepare a consolidated balance sheet as at December 31, Year 11.

Problem 8   On January 2, Year 1, Poplar Ltd. purchased 80% of the outstanding shares of Spruce Ltd. for $2,000,000. At that date, Spruce had common stock of $500,000 and retained earnings of $1,250,000. Poplar acquired the Spruce stock to obtain control of copyrights held by Spruce. These copyrights, with a remaining life of 8 years, had a fair value of $750,000 in excess of their carrying value. Except for the copyrights, the carrying values of the recorded assets and liabilities of Spruce were equal to their fair values. On December 31, Year 4, the trial balances of the two companies were as follows:

	Poplar	Spruce
Cash	$ 1,000,000	$ 500,000
Accounts receivable	2,000,000	356,000
Inventory	3,000,000	2,250,000
Plant and equipment	14,000,000	2,500,000
Copyrights (net)	—	400,000
Investment in Spruce (cost)	2,000,000	—
Investment in Poplar bonds	—	244,000
Cost of goods sold	2,400,000	850,000
Other expenses	962,000	300,000
Interest expense	38,000	—
Income tax expense	600,000	350,000
Dividends	600,000	250,000
	$26,600,000	$8,000,000
Accounts payable	$ 2,492,000	$2,478,500
Accumulated depreciation: plant and equipment	4,000,000	1,000,000
Bonds payable	500,000	—
Premium on bonds payable	8,000	—
Common stock	4,500,000	500,000
Retained earnings, January 1	10,000,000	2,000,000
Sales	4,900,000	2,000,000
Dividend revenue	200,000	—
Interest revenue	—	21,500
	$26,600,000	$8,000,000

Additional Information

- The Year 4 net incomes of the two companies are as follows:

Poplar Ltd.	$1,100,000
Spruce Ltd.	521,500

- On January 2, Year 2, Spruce sold equipment to Poplar for $500,000. The equipment had a net book value of $400,000 at the time of the sale. The remaining useful life of the equipment was 5 years.

- The Year 4, opening inventories of Poplar contained $500,000 of merchandise purchased from Spruce during Year 3. Spruce had recorded a gross profit of $200,000 on this merchandise.

- During Year 4, Spruce's sales to Poplar totalled $1,000,000. These sales were made at a gross profit rate of 40%.

- Poplar's ending inventory contains $300,000 of merchandise purchased from Spruce.

- Other expenses include depreciation expense and copyright amortization expense.

- On January 2, Year 2, Poplar issued 8%, 7-year bonds with a face value of $500,000 for $514,000. Interest is paid annually on December 31. On January 2, Year 4, Spruce purchased one-half of this issue in the open market at a cost of $242,500. Intercompany bond gains (losses) are to be allocated between the two affiliates.

- Tax allocation will be at a rate of 40%.

Required:

(a) Prepare the following consolidated financial statements:
  (i) Income statement.
  (ii) Retained earnings statement.
  (iii) Balance sheet.
(b) Calculate the December 31, Year 4, balance in the account "Investment in Spruce" if Poplar had used the equity method to account for its investment.

Problem 9 On January 1, Year 1, Porter Inc. purchased 85% of the voting shares of Sloan Ltd. for $3,026,000 in cash. On this date, Sloan had no-par common stock outstanding in the amount of $2,200,000 and retained earnings of $1,100,000. The identifiable assets and liabilities of Sloan had fair values that were equal to their carrying values except for the following:

- Plant and equipment (net) had a fair value $200,000 greater than its carrying value. The remaining useful life on January 1, Year 1, was 20 years with no anticipated salvage value.

- Accounts receivable had a fair value $75,000 less than carrying value.

- Long-term liabilities had a fair value $52,680 less than carrying value. These liabilities were issued at par and mature on December 31, Year 10.

Other Information

- Between January 1, Year 1, and December 31, Year 3, Sloan earned $345,000 and paid dividends of $115,000.

- Goodwill impairment tests yielded losses as follows: Year 1, $30,300; Year 2, $6,075; Year 4, $12,125.

- On January 1, Year 2, Sloan sold a patent to Porter for $165,000. On this date, the patent had a carrying value on the books of Sloan of $185,000, and a remaining useful life of 5 years.
- On September 1, Year 3, Porter sold land to Sloan for $93,000. The land had a carrying value on the books of Porter of $72,000. Sloan still owned this land on December 31, Year 4.
- For the year ending December 31, Year 4, the statements of income revealed the following:

	Porter	Sloan
Total revenues	$2,576,000	$973,000
Cost of goods sold	1,373,000	467,000
Amortization expense	483,000	176,000
Interest expense	115,000	44,700
Other expenses (including income tax)	237,000	108,300
Total expenses	2,208,000	796,000
Net income	$ 368,000	$177,000

Porter records its investment in Sloan using the cost method and includes dividend income from Sloan in its total revenues.

- Porter and Sloan paid dividends of $125,000 and $98,000 respectively in Year 4.
- Sloan issued no common stock subsequent to January 1, Year 1. Selected balance sheet accounts for the two companies as at December 31, Year 4, were:

	Porter	Sloan
Accounts receivable (net)	$ 987,000	$ 133,000
Inventories	1,436,000	787,000
Plant and equipment (net)	3,467,000	1,234,000
Patent (net)	263,000	–0–
Land	872,000	342,000
Long-term liabilities	1,876,000	750,000
Retained earnings	4,833,000	1,409,000

- During Year 4, Porter's merchandise sales to Sloan were $150,000. The unrealized profits in Sloan's inventory on January 1 and December 31, Year 4, were $14,000 and $10,000 respectively. At December 31, Year 4, Sloan still owed Porter $5,000 for merchandise purchases.
- During Year 4, Sloan's merchandise sales to Porter were $55,000. The unrealized profits in Porter's inventory on January 1 and December 31, Year 4, were $1,500 and $2,500 respectively. At December 31, Year 4, Porter still owed Sloan $2,000 for merchandise purchases.
- Use income tax allocation at a rate of 40% and straight-line method for amortization of capital assets and long-term liabilities.

Required:

(a) Compute the balances that would appear in the consolidated balance sheet of Porter and Sloan as at December 31, Year 4, for the following:
  (i) Patent (net).
  (ii) Goodwill.
  (iii) Noncontrolling interest.
  (iv) Retained earnings.
  (v) Long-term liabilities.
(b) Porter has decided not to prepare consolidated financial statements and will report its investment in Sloan by the equity method. Calculate the total revenues, including

investment income, that would be disclosed in the income statement drawn up by Porter for the year ended December 31, Year 4.

(c) Assume that Sloan pays interest annually at the rate of 6% on its long-term liabilities. When Porter acquired Sloan on January 1, Year 1, the fair value of Sloan's long-term liabilities would have produced an effective yield of 7%. Calculate long-term liabilities on the consolidated financial statements assuming that Porter and Sloan use the effective interest method to account for their long-term liabilities.

(SMA adapted)

Problem 10   Alpha Corporation owns 90% of the common stock of Beta Corporation and uses the equity method to account for its investment.

On January 1, Year 4, Alpha purchased $160,000 par of Beta's 10% bonds for $150,064. Beta's bond liability on this date consisted of $800,000 par 10% bonds due January 1, Year 8, and unamortized discount of $73,065. Interest payment dates are June 30 and December 31. The effective rate of interest on Alpha's bond investment is 6% every six months and 6.5% every six months for Beta's bond liability.

Both companies have a December 31 year-end and use the effective interest method to account for bonds. Alpha uses income tax allocation at 40% tax rate when it prepares consolidated financial statements.

Beta reported a net income of $114,000 in Year 4 and declared a dividend of $30,000 on December 31.

Required:

(a) Calculate the amount of the gain or loss that will appear as a separate item on the Year 4 consolidated income statement, as a result of the bond transaction that occurred during the year.

(b) Prepare the equity method journal entries that Alpha would make on December 31, Year 4.

(c) Calculate the amount of the bond liability that will appear on the December 31, Year 4, consolidated balance sheet.

Problem 11   Parent Co. owns 75% of Sub Co. and uses the cost method to account for its investment. The following are summarized income statements for the year ended December 31, Year 7. (Sub Co. did not declare or pay dividends in Year 7.)

INCOME STATEMENTS — for Year 7

	Parent	Sub
Interest revenue	$ 8,750	$ —
Other misc. revenues	900,000	500,000
	908,750	500,000
Interest expense	—	44,000
Other misc. expenses	600,000	350,000
Income tax expense	124,000	42,000
	724,000	436,000
Net income	$184,750	$ 64,000

Other Information

On July 1, Year 7, Parent purchased 40% of the outstanding bonds of Sub for $152,500. On that date, Sub had $400,000 of 10% bonds payable outstanding, which mature in 5 years. The bond discount on the books of Sub on July 1, Year 7, amounted to $20,000. Interest is payable January 1 and July 1. Any gains (losses) are to be allocated to each company. Both companies use the straight-line method to account for bonds.

Required:

Prepare a consolidated income statement for Year 7 using a 40% tax rate.

Problem 12   Palmer Corporation owns 70% of the common stock of Scott Corporation and uses the equity method to account for its investment.

Scott purchased $80,000 par of Palmer's 10% bonds on October 1, Year 5, for $76,000. Palmer's bond liability on October 1, Year 5, consisted of $400,000 par of 10% bonds due on October 1, Year 9, with unamortized discount of $8,000. Interest payment dates are April 1 and October 1 of each year and straight-line amortization is used. Intercompany bond gains (losses) are to be allocated to each affiliate.

Both companies have a December 31 year-end. Scott's financial statements for Year 5 indicate that it earned a net income of $70,000 and that on December 31, Year 5, it declared a dividend of $15,000.

Required:

(a) Prepare the journal entries under the equity method that Palmer would make in Year 5. (Assume a 40% tax rate.)
(b) Compute the amount of the bond liability that will appear on the December 31, Year 5, consolidated balance sheet.

Problem 13   On December 31, Year 1, RAV Company purchased 60% of the outstanding common shares of ENS Company for $780,000. On that date, ENS had common shares of $500,000 and retained earnings of $120,000. In negotiating the purchase price, it was agreed that assets and liabilities were fairly valued except for equipment, which had a $30,000 excess of carrying value over fair value and land, which had a $120,000 excess of fair value over carrying value. The equipment had a remaining useful life of six years at the acquisition date and no salvage value. ENS did not record the fair value deficiency on the equipment because ENS felt that it would recover the carrying value of this equipment through future cash flows.

The adjusted trial balances for RAV and ENS for the year ended December 31, Year 5, were as follows:

	RAV	ENS
Cash	$ 150,000	$ 75,000
Accounts receivable	275,000	226,000
Inventory	570,000	257,000
Land	600,000	170,000
Building – net	710,000	585,000
Equipment – net	690,000	349,000
Investment in ENS	540,000	
Cost of goods sold	2,400,000	2,107,000
Amortization expense	240,000	120,000
Income taxes and other expenses	960,000	432,000
Dividends paid	540,000	304,000
Total debits	$7,675,000	$4,625,000
Accounts payable	$ 465,000	$ 296,000
Long-term debt	900,000	540,000
Common shares	1,200,000	500,000
Retained earnings, beginning	600,000	279,000
Sales	4,220,000	3,010,000
Other revenues	80,000	
Investment income from ENS	210,000	
Total credits	$7,675,000	$4,625,000

Other Information

1. Each year, goodwill is evaluated to determine if there has been a permanent impairment. ENS's goodwill was valued at $100,000 at the end of Year 4 and $75,000 at the end of Year 5.
2. RAV's inventories contained $200,000 of merchandise purchased from ENS at December 31, Year 5, and $250,000 at December 31, Year 4. During Year 5, sales from ENS to RAV were $600,000. Merchandise was priced at the same profit margin as applicable to other customers. RAV owed $150,000 to ENS at December 31, Year 5 and $157,000 at December 31, Year 4.
3. On July 1, Year 2, ENS purchased a building from RAV for $750,000. The building had an original cost of $800,000 and a net book value of $600,000 on RAV's books on July 1, Year 2. ENS estimated the remaining life of the building was 15 years at the time of the purchase from RAV.
4. ENS rented another building from RAV throughout the year for $5,000 per month.
5. RAV uses the equity method of accounting for its long-term investments.
6. Both companies pay tax at the rate of 40%. Ignore future income taxes when allocating and amortizing the purchase price discrepancy.

Required:

(a) Prepare a consolidated income statement for the year ended December 31, Year 5.
(b) Prepare the current assets and capital assets sections of the consolidated balance sheet at December 31, Year 5.
(c) Calculate noncontrolling interest on the consolidated balance sheet at December 31, Year 4.
(d) If RAV had used the cost method instead of the equity method of accounting for its investment in ENS, would RAV's net income for Year 5 increase, decrease, or remain the same on
(i) its separate entity income statement, and
(ii) the consolidated income statement.
Briefly explain.

(CGA-Canada, from 2002 to 2007)

Problem 14 Shown below are selected ledger accounts from the trial balance of a parent and its subsidiary as of December 31, Year 9.

Other Information

- P Company purchased its 90% interest in S Company in Year 1, on the date that S Company was incorporated, and has followed the equity method to account for its investment since that date.
- On April 1, Year 5, land that had originally cost $15,000 was sold by S Company to P Company for $21,000. P purchased the land with the intention of developing it, but in Year 9 it decided that the location was not suitable and the land was sold to a chain of drug stores.
- On January 1, Year 2, P Company issued $200,000 face value bonds due in 10 years. The proceeds from the bond issue amounted to $190,000.
- On July 1, Year 9, S Company purchased $40,000 of these bonds on the open market at a cost of $38,750. Intercompany bondholding gains (losses) are allocated between the two affiliates.
- S Company had $75,000 in sales to P Company during Year 9.
- Use income tax allocation at a 40% tax rate.

	P Co.	S Co.
Investment in bonds of P	$ —	$ 39,000
Investment in stock of S (equity method)	139,899	—
Sales	630,000	340,000
Interest income	—	1,850
Investment income	15,339	—
Gain on sale of land	7,000	—
Capital stock	300,000	100,000
Retained earnings	85,000	50,000
Bonds payable 8 percent	198,000	—
Cost of sales	485,000	300,000
Interest expense	17,000	—
Selling and administrative expense	50,000	20,000
Income tax expense	34,000	8,740
Dividends	10,000	8,000

Required:

(a) Prepare a statement of consolidated net income for Year 9.

(b) Prepare a consolidated statement of retained earnings for Year 9.

Problem 15 Financial statements of Champlain Ltd. and its 80%-owned subsidiary Samuel Ltd. as at December 31, Year 5, are presented on the next page.

Other Information

- Champlain acquired its 80%-interest in Samuel on January 1, Year 1. The retained earnings of Samuel were $12,000 on that date, and there have been no subsequent changes in the capital stock accounts. On January 1, Year 1, fair values were equal to carrying values except for the following:

	Carrying value	Fair value
Inventory	$50,000	$32,000
Patent	–0–	14,000

- The patent of Samuel had a remaining legal life of 8 years on January 1, Year 1, and any goodwill was to be tested annually for impairment. As a result, impairment losses occurred as follows: Year 2, $20,000; Year 4, $13,120; Year 5, $18,280.
- On January 1, Year 5, the inventories of Champlain contained items purchased from Samuel on which Samuel had made a profit of $1,900. During Year 5, Samuel sold goods to Champlain for $92,000, of which $21,000 remained unpaid at the end of the year. Samuel made a profit of $3,300 on goods remaining in Champlain's inventory at December 31, Year 5.
- On January 1, Year 3, Samuel sold equipment to Champlain at a price that was $21,000 in excess of its book value. The equipment had an estimated remaining life of 6 years on that date.
- Champlain sold a tract of land to Samuel in Year 2 at a profit of $7,000. This land is still held by Samuel at the end of Year 5.
- Assume a corporate tax rate of 40%.

BALANCE SHEETS — at December 31, Year 5

	Champlain	Samuel
Cash	$ 18,100	$ 20,600
Accounts receivable	60,000	55,000
Inventories	35,000	46,000
Investment in Samuel — at cost	129,200	—
Land, building, and equipment	198,000	104,000
Accumulated depreciation	(86,000)	(30,000)
	$354,300	$195,600
Accounts payable	$ 56,000	$ 70,100
Dividends payable	5,000	5,500
Capital stock	225,000	50,000
Retained earnings	68,300	70,000
	$354,300	$195,600

STATEMENTS OF INCOME AND RETAINED EARNINGS
for the Year Ended December 31, Year 5

	Champlain	Samuel
Sales	$535,400	$270,000
Dividend and miscellaneous income	9,900	—
	545,300	270,000
Cost of sales	364,000	206,000
Selling expense	78,400	24,100
Administrative expense (including depreciation)	46,300	20,700
Income taxes	13,800	6,200
	502,500	257,000
Net income	42,800	13,000
Retained earnings, January 1	45,500 42,800	68,000
Dividends paid	(20,000)	(11,000)
Retained earnings, December 31	$ 68,300	$ 70,000

Required:

(a) Prepare the following consolidated financial statements:
  (i) Income statement.
  (ii) Retained earnings statement.
  (iii) Balance sheet.

(b) Explain how the historical cost principle supports the elimination of the profit on the sale of the equipment from Samuel to Champlain when preparing Samuel's consolidated financial statements.

(c) Calculate goodwill impairment loss and noncontrolling interest on the consolidated income statement for the year ended December 31, Year 5, under the parent company extension theory.

(d) Calculate goodwill and noncontrolling interest on the consolidated balance sheet at December 31, Year 5, under the parent company extension theory.

Problem 16   On December 31, Year 1, the Peach Company purchased 80% of the outstanding voting shares of the Orange Company for $964,000 in cash. The balance sheet of Orange on that date and the fair values of its tangible assets and liabilities were as follows:

	Book value	Fair value
Cash and accounts receivable	$ 200,000	$175,000
Inventories	300,000	300,000
Plant and equipment	600,000	800,000
Accumulated depreciation	(100,000)	
	$1,000,000	
Current liabilities	$ 100,000	$100,000
Long-term liabilities	200,000	216,850
No-par common stock	500,000	
Retained earnings	200,000	
	$1,000,000	

The difference between the fair value and book value of cash and accounts receivable of the subsidiary at December 31, Year 1, was adjusted by Orange in Year 2. At the acquisition date, the plant and equipment had an estimated remaining useful life of 10 years with no net salvage value. The long-term liabilities mature on December 31, Year 6. Any goodwill arising from the business combination will be tested for impairment. Peach uses the cost method to account for its investment in Orange. Both Peach and Orange use the straight-line method to calculate all depreciation for depreciable assets and amortization of premiums or discounts on long-term liabilities.

The statements of income and changes in retained earnings of the two companies for the year ending December 31, Year 5, were as follows:

	Peach	Orange
Sales of merchandise	$6,000,000	$1,000,000
Other revenues	200,000	20,000
Total revenues	6,200,000	1,020,000
Cost of goods sold	2,500,000	400,000
Depreciation expense	500,000	80,000
Interest expense	400,000	16,000
Other expenses (including income tax)	1,300,000	194,000
Total expenses	4,700,000	690,000
Net income	1,500,000	330,000
Retained earnings, 1/1/Year 5	4,200,000	300,000
Dividends	(200,000)	(50,000)
Retained earnings, 31/12/Year 5	$5,500,000	$ 580,000

Other Information

- Goodwill impairment losses were recorded as follows: Year 2, $3,600; Year 4, $30,000; Year 5, $11,200.
- On December 31, Year 4, Orange sold a warehouse to Peach for $54,000. It had been purchased on January 1, Year 3, for $100,000 and had an estimated 20-year life on that date with no salvage value.
- During Year 4, Orange sold merchandise that it had purchased for $120,000 to Peach for $250,000. None of this merchandise had been resold by Peach by December 31, Year 4. Both companies account for inventories on the first-in, first-out basis.
- Peach had sales of $200,000 to Orange during Year 4, which gave rise to a gross profit of $125,000. This inventory was resold by Orange during Year 4 for $225,000.

- During Year 5, Orange sold merchandise that had been purchased for $160,000 to Peach for $300,000. Since the sales occurred in December of Year 5, all of this merchandise remained in the December 31, Year 5, inventories of Peach and had not been paid for by Peach.
- During September of Year 5, Peach had sales of $280,000 to Orange, which increased Peach's gross profit by $160,000. By December 31, Year 5, one-half of this merchandise had been sold to the public by Orange.
- On January 1, Year 5, Peach sold to Orange for $28,000 a machine that had cost $40,000. On January 1, Year 5, it had been depreciated for 6 years of its estimated 8-year life. This sale was not considered an extraordinary transaction by Peach.
- During Year 5, Peach charged Orange $25,000 for management fees.
- Assume a 40% corporate tax rate.

Required:

(a) Prepare a consolidated income statement for Peach and its subsidiary, Orange, for the year ending December 31, Year 5, in accordance with the recommendations of the *CICA Handbook*. Assume that the loss from sale of the warehouse will be eliminated.

(b) Prepare a consolidated statement of retained earnings for Peach and its subsidiary, Orange, for the year ending December 31, Year 5.

(c) Explain the rationale for not always eliminating losses on intercompany sales of depreciable assets when preparing consolidated financial statements.

(d) Assume that Orange pays interest annually at the rate of 8% on its long-term liabilities. When Peach acquired Orange on December 31, Year 1, the fair value of Sloan's long-term liabilities would have produced an effective yield of 6%. Calculate interest expense and noncontrolling interest on the consolidated income statement assuming that Peach and Orange use the effective interest method to account for their long-term liabilities.

(SMA adapted)

Problem 17 On January 1, Year 1, Handy Company (Handy) purchased 70% of the outstanding common shares of Dandy Limited (Dandy) for $7,000. On that date, Dandy's shareholders' equity consisted of common shares of $250 and retained earnings of $4,500.

The financial statements for Handy and Dandy for Year 6 were as follows:

BALANCE SHEET
at December 31, Year 6

	Handy	Dandy
Cash	$ 1,340	$ 780
Accounts receivable	2,800	1,050
Inventory	3,400	2,580
Capital assets — net	4,340	3,010
Investment in Dandy	7,000	—
Total	$18,880	$7,420
Current liabilities	$ 4,200	$ 540
Long-term liabilities	3,100	1,230
Common shares	1,000	250
Retained earnings	10,580	5,400
Total	$18,880	$7,420

STATEMENT OF INCOME AND RETAINED EARNINGS
year ended December 31, Year 6

	Handy	Dandy
Sales	$21,900	$7,440
Cost of sales	14,800	3,280
Gross profit	7,100	4,160
Other revenue	1,620	—
Amortization expense	(840)	(420)
Other expenses	(5,320)	(2,040)
Income before income taxes	2,560	1,700
Income tax expense	800	680
Net income	1,760	1,020
Retained earnings, beginning of year	10,420	5,180
Dividends paid	(1,600)	(800)
Retained earnings, end of year	$10,580	$5,400

Other Information

1. In negotiating the purchase price at the date of acquisition, it was agreed that the fair values of all of Dandy's assets and liabilities were equal to their book values, except for the following:

	Book Value	Fair value
Inventory	$2,100	$2,200
Equipment	2,500	3,000

2. Both companies use FIFO to account for their inventory and the straight-line method for amortizing their capital assets. Dandy's equipment had a remaining useful life of 10 years at the acquisition date.

3. Goodwill is not amortized on a systematic basis. However, each year, goodwill is evaluated to determine if there has been a permanent impairment. It was determined that goodwill on the consolidated balance sheet should be reported at $1,100 on December 31, Year 5, and at $1,030 on December 31, Year 6.

4. During Year 6, inventory sales from Dandy to Handy were $5,000. Handy's inventories contained merchandise purchased from Dandy for $2,000 at December 31, Year 5, and $2,500 at December 31, Year 6. Dandy earns a gross margin of 40% on its intercompany sales.

5. On January 1, Year 2, Handy sold some equipment to Dandy for $1,000 and recorded a gain of $200 before taxes. This equipment had a remaining life of 8 years at the time of the purchase by Dandy.

6. Handy charges $50 per month to Dandy for consulting services.

7. Handy uses the cost method of accounting for its long-term investment.

8. Both companies pay taxes at the rate of 40%.

Required:

(a) Prepare a consolidated statement of income for the year ended December 31, Year 6. Show supporting calculations.

(b) Calculate consolidated retained earnings at January 1, Year 6, and then prepare a consolidated statement of retained earnings for the year ended December 31, Year 6. Show supporting calculations.

(c) Explain how the historical cost principle supports the adjustments made on consolidation when there has been an intercompany sale of equipment.

(d) Calculate goodwill impairment loss and noncontrolling interest on the consolidated income statement for the year ended December 31, Year 6, under the parent company extension theory.

(CGA-Canada, from 2002 to 2007)

Chapter 9

Consolidated Cash Flows and Ownership Issues

LEARNING OBJECTIVES

After studying this chapter, you should be able to do the following:

- Prepare a consolidated cash flow statement by applying concepts learned in prior courses and unique consolidation concepts discussed here.
- Prepare consolidated financial statements in situations where the parent's ownership has increased (step purchase).
- Prepare consolidated financial statements after parent's ownership has decreased.
- Prepare consolidated financial statements in situations where the subsidiary has preferred shares in its capital structure.
- Calculate consolidated net income and noncontrolling interest in situations where a parent has direct and indirect control over a number of subsidiary companies.

INTRODUCTION

While it is still the norm for the capital structure of a company to consist of common and/or preferred shares, some companies no longer use the terms *common shares* or *preferred shares* to describe their shares. Instead, they may use terms such as *Class A* and *Class B* shares and then describe the essential features of the shares. Celestica Inc., a world leader in the delivery of innovative electronics manufacturing services, refers to its two classes of shares as *subordinate voting shares* and *multiple voting shares*. The subordinate shares entitle the holder to one vote per share whereas the multiple voting shares entitle the holder to 25 votes per share. The holders of the subordinate voting shares and multiple voting shares are entitled to share ratably in any dividends of the company. Onex Corporation, one of Canada's largest corporations with global operations in the services, manufacturing, and technology industries, owns the multiple voting shares of Celestica while the noncontrolling shareholders own most of the subordinated voting shares. This share distribution gives Onex Corporation 79 percent of the votes but only 13 percent of the dividends. The noncontrolling interest gets 21 percent of the votes but 87 percent of the dividends.

Up to now in this text, the companies involved in the business combination only had common shares outstanding and the parent obtained control over the subsidiary in one purchase. Later in this chapter, we will consider situations where the subsidiary also has preferred shares outstanding and situations where the parent's ownership interest changes. We commence the chapter with a discussion of certain factors that are unique to the overall consolidation process and that must be considered when the consolidated cash flow statement is prepared.

Consolidated Cash Flow Statement

In the previous chapters we illustrated the direct approach to preparing the consolidated balance sheet and the consolidated income and retained earnings statements. In this approach, the individual statements of the parent and its subsidiaries are combined. We will now focus on the preparation of the final consolidated statement — the cash flow statement. While this statement could be prepared by combining the separate cash flow statements of the parent and its subsidiaries, this would involve eliminating all intercompany transactions, including intercompany transfers of cash. It is much easier to prepare the cash flow statement using comparative consolidated balance sheets and the consolidated income statement, because these statements do not contain any intercompany transactions. In all the illustrations in this chapter, we will assume that cash flows from operations are presented using the indirect method, whereby net income is adjusted for the effects of noncash items such as amortizations and changes in working capital items, and for gains and losses associated with investing and financing cash flows. If the direct method were used, only the items affecting cash would be presented in the first place. Therefore, we would not need to adjust for noncash items.

> **Under the indirect method, we start with net income and show the adjustments to convert it to a cash basis.**

The preparation of the cash flow statement for a single unconsolidated company is well covered in introductory and intermediate accounting texts. The basic process used to determine the reasons for the change in cash or cash equivalents is one of analyzing the changes that have occurred in all noncash items on the balance sheet. The procedures used to carry out this analysis (a working paper or a series of T-accounts) will not be repeated here. Instead, we will describe items that are unique to consolidated statements and that must be taken into account in the analysis. The major items that require special attention are summarized below:

> **The change in cash can be determined by analyzing the change in non-cash items during the period.**

1. Acquisition-date fair value differences are amortized in the consolidated income statement. While some of the amortizations may be obvious from their descriptions in the income statement, others may be buried in some expense accounts. Because amortizations have no effect on cash flows, we must adjust the year's net income for them in order to arrive at cash flow from operations.

2. Noncontrolling interest in the consolidated income statement is an allocation of the entity's net income and does not affect cash flows. We must add it back to net income in the same manner as depreciation in order to arrive at the operating cash flow.

> **The consolidated CFS contains adjustments for items, which are unique to consolidated financial statements such as NCI and amortization of purchase discrepancy.**

3. Dividends paid by subsidiaries to the parent company do not change the entity's cash. Dividends paid by the parent to its shareholders, and dividends paid by the subsidiaries to noncontrolling shareholders, reduce the cash of the consolidated entity. The *Handbook* requires separate disclosure of dividends paid to noncontrolling shareholders.[1]

4. A change in the parent's ownership percentage during the year requires a careful analysis to determine its effect on consolidated assets, liabilities, and equities. This will be illustrated in a later section of this chapter (on ownership changes).

---

[1] *CICA Handbook*, paragraph 1540.35.

5. In the year that a subsidiary is acquired, special disclosures are required in the cash flow statement. The following example illustrates this.

The consolidated balance sheet of Parent Company and its five subsidiaries as at December 31, Year 1, is shown below.

PARENT COMPANY
CONSOLIDATED BALANCE SHEET
at December 31, Year 1

Cash	$ 500,000
Other assets	900,000
Goodwill	120,000
	$1,520,000
Liabilities	$ 500,000
Common shares	200,000
Retained earnings	720,000
Noncontrolling interest	100,000
	$1,520,000

On January 2, Year 2, Parent acquired 80 percent of the outstanding common shares of its sixth subsidiary, Sable Ltd., for a total cost of $140,000. The shareholders of Sable received cash of $90,000 and common shares of Parent with a market value of $50,000 in this transaction. The management of Parent determined that the other assets of Sable had a fair value of $205,000 on this date. The balance sheet of Sable on December 31, Year 1, is shown below:

SABLE LTD.
BALANCE SHEET
at December 31, Year 1

This is the separate-entity balance sheet of Sable.

Cash	$ 30,000
Other assets	200,000
	$230,000
Liabilities	$ 70,000
Common shares	100,000
Retained earnings	60,000
	$230,000

Parent's journal entry to record the acquisition of 80 percent of the common shares of Sable would be as follows on January 2, Year 2:

This entry is recorded on the separate-entity records for Parent.

Investment in Sable Ltd.	140,000	
Common shares		50,000
Cash		90,000

We will now prepare the consolidated balance sheet of Parent on January 2, Year 2, incorporating the latest acquisition.

The calculation and allocation of the purchase discrepancy for the Sable investment is shown below:

<table>
<tr><td rowspan="9">The components of the purchase discrepancy are reported on the consolidated balance sheet.</td><td>Cost of 80% investment in Sable</td><td>$140,000</td></tr>
<tr><td>Implied value of 100% of Sable</td><td>$175,000</td></tr>
<tr><td>Book value of Sable</td><td>160,000</td></tr>
<tr><td>Purchase discrepancy</td><td>15,000</td></tr>
<tr><td>Allocated:</td><td></td></tr>
<tr><td>   Other assets</td><td>5,000</td></tr>
<tr><td>   Goodwill</td><td>10,000</td></tr>
<tr><td>Noncontrolling interest (175,000 × 20%)</td><td>$ 35,000</td></tr>
</table>

The consolidated balance sheet appears below:

**PARENT COMPANY
CONSOLIDATED BALANCE SHEET**
at January 2, Year 2

<table>
<tr><td rowspan="4">The assets and liabilities of the subsidiary are added to the consolidated balance sheet.</td><td>Cash (500,000 + 30,000 – **90,000**)</td><td>$ 440,000</td></tr>
<tr><td>Other assets (900,000 + 200,000 + **5,000**)</td><td>1,105,000</td></tr>
<tr><td>Goodwill (120,000 + **10,000**)</td><td>130,000</td></tr>
<tr><td></td><td>$1,675,000</td></tr>
<tr><td></td><td>Liabilities (500,000 + 70,000)</td><td>$ 570,000</td></tr>
<tr><td></td><td>Common shares (200,000 + **50,000**)</td><td>250,000</td></tr>
<tr><td></td><td>Retained earnings</td><td>720,000</td></tr>
<tr><td></td><td>Noncontrolling interest (100,000 + **35,000**)</td><td>135,000</td></tr>
<tr><td></td><td></td><td>$1,675,000</td></tr>
</table>

Preparing the Consolidated Cash Flow Statement

We can now prepare the consolidated cash flow statement for the two-day period that has elapsed by analyzing the changes in the two consolidated balance sheets. We know that the only transaction that has taken place is Parent's acquisition of 80 percent of Sable. The journal entry of Parent to record the acquisition was illustrated earlier. If we were preparing the cash flow statement of the parent company, we would use our knowledge of this entry in our analysis. But we are preparing the consolidated cash flow statement, and the account "Investment in Sable" does not appear in the consolidated balance sheet. In order to do the proper analysis we need to visualize the effect of this new acquisition on the consolidated balance sheet. We can depict this effect in the form of a "consolidating entry" in the following manner:

<table>
<tr><td rowspan="8">This entry shows the incremental effect of purchasing the subsidiary.</td><td>**Cash**</td><td>**30,000**</td><td></td></tr>
<tr><td>**Other assets (200,000 + 5,000)**</td><td>**205,000**</td><td></td></tr>
<tr><td>**Goodwill**</td><td>**10,000**</td><td></td></tr>
<tr><td>   **Liabilities**</td><td></td><td>**70,000**</td></tr>
<tr><td>   **Noncontrolling interest**</td><td></td><td>**35,000**</td></tr>
<tr><td>   Cash</td><td></td><td>90,000</td></tr>
<tr><td>   Common shares</td><td></td><td>50,000</td></tr>
</table>

Notice that the portion of the entry shown in boldface is the amount of the account "Investment in Sable" that made up the parent's acquisition journal entry shown on page 402. Using this analysis, we would normally show the purchase of other assets and goodwill as cash outflows from investing activities and the increase in liabilities, noncontrolling interest, and common shares as cash inflows from

The investment account is replaced by the underlying assets and liabilities in the consolidation process.

financing activities. However, the *Handbook* requires that only the net cash outflow from a business combination be presented on the cash flow statement and the details of the changes in noncash accounts arising from the business combination be disclosed in the notes to financial statements.[2] Therefore, the consolidated cash flow statement for Parent Company would be presented as follows:

PARENT COMPANY
CONSOLIDATED CASH FLOW STATEMENT
for the Two-day Period Ended January 2, Year 2

Only the net change in cash is presented on the consolidated CFS.

Operating cash flow:	$ nil
Investing cash flow:	
Acquisition of Sable, less cash acquired in acquisition $30,000 [note 1]	60,000
Financing cash flow:	nil
Net change in cash for the two-day period	(60,000)
Cash, December 31, Year 1	500,000
Cash, January 2, Year 2	$440,000

Note 1: Effective January 2, Year 2, the company acquired 80% of the common shares of Sable for a total consideration of $140,000. The acquisition, which was accounted for by the acquisition method, is summarized as follows:

The details of the changes in noncash items are described in the notes to the consolidated CFS.

Net assets acquired:	
Other assets	$205,000
Goodwill	10,000
Liabilities	(70,000)
Noncontrolling interest	(35,000)
	$110,000
Consideration given:	
Common shares	$ 50,000
Cash	90,000
	140,000
Less cash acquired on acquisition	30,000
	$110,000

Notice that the only item appearing on the cash flow statement is a $60,000 cash outflow under investing activities. The $60,000 is the difference between the cash paid for the shares of the subsidiary ($90,000) and the cash held by the subsidiary on the date of acquisition ($30,000). The other assets acquired and liabilities assumed in the business acquisition are not shown on the face of the cash flow statement as investing and financing activities but are disclosed in the notes to the financial statements. So, when we prepare a cash flow statement, we must differentiate between those changes in noncash items arising from a business combination and those changes arising from other activities. Those changes arising from the business combination are netted and given one line on the cash flow statement with the details disclosed in the notes to the financial statements. The other changes are presented on the face of the cash flow statement according to normal practices.

In our discussion of the consolidated cash flow statement, we have focused entirely on items unique to consolidated statements, on the assumption that the

---

[2] *CICA Handbook*, paragraphs 1540.42 and .43.

overall process for preparing such statements has been covered in earlier financial accounting courses. The next major topic in this chapter, *ownership change*, also presents items that require analysis as to their effects on consolidated cash flows. The cash flow effects will be discussed in the appropriate sections.

Changes in Parent's Ownership Interest

The parent's percentage of ownership can change when the parent buys or sells shares of the subsidiary or when the subsidiary issues or repurchases shares.

A parent's ownership interest will change if:

(a) the parent purchases additional holdings in its subsidiary (block acquisitions); *or*

(b) the parent sells some of its holdings in its subsidiary; *or*

(c) the subsidiary issues additional common shares to the public, and the parent does not maintain its previous ownership percentage; *or*

(d) the subsidiary repurchases some of its common shares from the noncontrolling interest.

Any time the parent's percentage of ownership increases, we will account for the transaction as a purchase. Any time the parent's percentage decreases, we will account for the transaction as a sale.

When the parent's ownership changes, the percentage of subsidiary common stock held by the noncontrolling interest also changes. The major consolidation problem involved with ownership change is the effect such changes have on the valuation of subsidiary net assets and noncontrolling interest in the consolidated statements. When the parent's ownership percentage *increases*, there will be an additional purchase discrepancy that must be allocated to revalue the net assets of the subsidiary as at that date. When the parent's ownership *decreases*, a portion of the unamortized purchase discrepancy will be transferred from the parent to the noncontrolling interest. We will use a comprehensive example to illustrate various changes in a parent's ownership interest. We will begin with step-by-step acquisitions.

Block Acquisitions of Subsidiary (Step Purchases)

The subsidiary is valued at fair value on the consolidated balance at the date of acquisition.

The consolidation illustrations that we have used in previous chapters have assumed that the parent company achieved its control in a subsidiary by making a single purchase of the subsidiary's common shares. On the date of acquisition, the fair values of the subsidiary's assets (including goodwill) and liabilities were determined and then brought on to the consolidated balance sheet along with the book values of the parent's assets and liabilities. The noncontrolling interest at the date of acquisition was also valued at fair value. In periods subsequent to the date of acquisition, the subsidiary's net assets were accounted for based on the values determined at the date of acquisition. They were not revalued to fair value at each reporting date.

We will now consider a situation where the parent achieves its control position through a series of block acquisitions (sometimes described as step purchases).

Purchase of First Block of Shares
On January 1, Year 1, Par Company acquires 1,000 common shares (10 percent of the outstanding shares) of Star Company for $20,000. The 10 percent voting interest does not give Par control or significant influence. The investment is classified as available-for-sale. On this date, the shareholders' equity of Star consists of common shares of $100,000 and retained earnings of $70,000. During Year 1, Star reported net income of $10,000 and did not declare any dividends. At the end of Year 1, the fair value of Star's shares was $22 per share.

Par's journal entries for Year 1 for the available-for-sale investment would be as follows:

Available-for-sale investments are reported at fair value at each reporting date.

Investment in Star	20,000	
Cash		20,000
To record purchase of 1,000 shares of Star for $20 per share		

Investment in Star	2,000	
Other comprehensive income — unrealized gain on Star		2,000
To record unrealized gain on available-for-sale investment in Star		

The purchase price discrepancy at the date of acquisition is ignored. Par's share of Star's income for the year is also ignored because the investment is reported at its fair value of $22,000 at the end of Year 1.

Purchase of Second Block of Shares

On January 1, Year 2, Par acquires another 2,000 common shares of Star for $44,000. The book values of Star's net assets are equal to fair values except for specialized equipment, which is undervalued by $10,000. The equipment has an estimated remaining life of 5 years. During Year 2, Star reported a net income of $30,000 and paid dividends of $20,000. At December 31, Year 2, the fair value of Star's shares was $25 per share.

The equity method is used once the investor obtains significant influence.

Par now owns 30 percent of Star and has obtained significant influence in the key decisions for Star. As a result, Par will now adopt the equity method of accounting for its 30 percent interest. The change in reporting method will be accounted for prospectively as a change in estimate because the circumstances changed from not having significant influence to having significant influence.

Under the equity method, a purchase discrepancy is calculated and subsequently amortized similar to the process used for consolidation. The purchase discrepancy is first calculated when the equity method first becomes applicable and is calculated as if the entire 30 percent was purchased on this date. The purchase price incorporates the cost of the current purchase plus the carrying value of prior purchases.

The calculation and allocation of the purchase discrepancy as at January 1, Year 2, is as follows:

The purchase discrepancy must be allocated and amortized under the equity method.

Amount paid for 30% of Star (20,000 + 2,000 + 44,000)		$66,000
Book value of Star's net assets:		
Common stock	100,000	
Retained earnings (70,000 + 10,000)	80,000	
Total shareholders' equity	180,000	
Par's ownership interest	30%	54,000
Purchase discrepancy		12,000
Allocated:		
Equipment (10,000 × 30%)		3,000
Goodwill		$ 9,000

Since the fair value of Star's shares went up during Year 2, there appears to be no impairment in Star's goodwill. The fair value excess attributed to the equipment must be amortized over its useful life of 5 years. Par's journal entries for Year 2 for the significant-influence investment would be as follows:

Investment in Star	44,000	
Cash		44,000
To record purchase of 2,000 shares of Star for $22 per share		

Investment in Star	9,000	
Investment income		9,000
To record 30% of reported income for the year (30% × 30,000)		

| Investment income | | 600 | |
| Investment in Star | | | 600 |

To record amortization of purchase discrepancy related to equipment (3,000 / 5 years)

| Cash | | 6,000 | |
| Investment in Star | | | 6,000 |

To record dividends received during the year (30% × 20,000)

The investment is not reported at fair value under the equity method.

The balance in the investment account at the end of Year 2 is $68,400 (22,000 + 44,000 + 9,000 – 600 – 6,000). The fair value of the investment is $75,000 (3,000 shares × $25 per share) but is ignored under the equity method.

Purchase of Third Block of Shares On January 1, Year 3, Par acquires another 1,000 common shares of Star for $25,000. The book values of Star's net assets are equal to fair values except for specialized equipment, which is undervalued by $8,000. The equipment has an estimated remaining life of 4 years. During Year 3, Star reported a net income of $40,000 and paid dividends of $20,000. At December 31, Year 3, the fair value of Star's shares was $29 per share.

Par now owns 40 percent of Star, still has significant influence in the key decisions for Star and will continue using the equity method. A purchase discrepancy for this 10 percent step is calculated and allocated as follows:

A separate allocation of the purchase discrepancy should be prepared for each incremental investment.

Cost of 10% of Star			$25,000
Book value of Star's net assets:			
Common stock		100,000	
Retained earnings (80,000 + 30,000 – 20,000)		90,000	
Total shareholders' equity		190,000	
Par's ownership interest	10%	19,000	
Purchase discrepancy			6,000
Allocated:			
Equipment (8,000 × 10%)			800
Goodwill			$ 5,200

There are now two separate and incremental calculations and allocations of purchase discrepancy based on the purchase price for each step. The allocation for the 30 percent step is carried forward with its previous values and is not revalued to fair value on the date of the third step. The following purchase discrepancy amortization schedule is prepared to keep track of the allocation and amortization of the purchase discrepancy for each step:

PURCHASE DISCREPANCY AMORTIZATION SCHEDULE

	Second Step		Third Step		
	Equip.	Goodwill	Equip.	Goodwill	Total
Jan 1, Year 2 purchase	$3,000	$9,000			$12,000
Amortization for Year 2	(600)				(600)
Balance, December 31, Year 2	2,400	9,000			11,400
Jan 1, Year 3 purchase			$800	$5,200	6,000
Amortization for Year 3	(600)		(200)		(800)
Balance, December 31, Year 3	$1,800	$9,000	$600	$5,200	$16,600

The previous block acquisitions are not normally revalued when there is a new acquisition.

Since the fair value of Star's shares went up during Year 3, there appears to be no impairment in Star's goodwill. The fair value excess attributed to the equipment is being amortized over its useful life.

Par's journal entries for Year 3 for the significant-influence investment would be as follows:

Investment in Star	25,000	
Cash		25,000
To record purchase of 1,000 shares of Star for $25 per share		

Investment in Star	16,000	
Investment income		16,000
To record 40% of reported income for the year (40% × 40,000)		

The amortization of the purchase discrepancy is recorded in the investment account under the equity method.

Investment income	800	
Investment in Star		800
To record amortization of purchase discrepancy related to equipment		

Cash	8,000	
Investment in Star		8,000
To record dividends received during the year (40% × 20,000)		

The balance in the investment account at the end of Year 3 is $100,600 (68,400 + 25,000 + 16,000 − 800 − 8,000). The fair value of the investment is $116,000 (4,000 shares × $29 per share) but is ignored under the equity method.

Purchase of Fourth Block of Shares   On January 1, Year 4, Par acquires another 3,000 common shares of Star for $87,000. The book values of Star's net assets are equal to fair values except for specialized equipment, which is undervalued by $7,500. The equipment has an estimated remaining life of 3 years. During Year 4, Star reported a net income of $50,000 and paid dividends of $20,000. At December 31, Year 4, the fair value of Star's shares was $34 per share.

The investment account is adjusted to fair value when the investor obtains control of the investee.

Par now owns 70 percent of Star and has control over Star. The business combination should be reported on a consolidated basis. The change in reporting method will be accounted for prospectively as a change in estimate because the circumstances changed from not having control to having control. *Handbook* section 1582.86 states the subsidiary should be valued at fair value as of the acquisition date and any gains or losses resulting from adjusting the investment to fair value should be recognized in income. If, before the business combination, the acquirer recognized changes in the value of its noncontrolling equity investment in other comprehensive income, the amount that was recognized in other comprehensive income is reclassified and included in the calculation of any gain or loss as of the acquisition date. Therefore, Par will make the following entries on January 1, Year 4:

Any unrealized gains in other comprehensive income are transferred to regular income on the date of a business combination.

Investment in Star	15,400	
Unrealized gain on investment		15,400
To adjust investment in Star to fair value (116,000 − 100,600)		

Other comprehensive income — unrealized gain	2,000	
Unrealized gain on investment		2,000
To reclassify other comprehensive income into regular income		

Investment in Star	87,000	
Cash		87,000
To record purchase of 3,000 shares at $29 per share		

The investment in Star now contains a balance of $203,000 (100,600 + 15,400 + 87,000), which is equal to the fair value of the 7,000 shares. When the parent first obtains control of the subsidiary, we must prepare a new calculation and allocation

Any previous purchase price allocations are replaced by a new purchase price allocation on the date of a business combination.

of the purchase discrepancy for the percentage ownership at the time of the purchase to reflect the revaluation of the entire subsidiary to fair value. In so doing, we will ignore the purchase price allocations and amortizations from the previous steps. The purchase discrepancy calculation and amortization for the 70 percent interest as at January 1, Year 4 is as follows:

The purchase discrepancy is calculated and allocated to value the subsidiary at 100 percent of its fair value.

Value of 70% of Star		$203,000
Implied value of 100% of Star		$290,000
Book value of Star's net assets:		
Common stock	100,000	
Retained earnings (90,000 + 40,000 – 20,000)	110,000	
Total shareholders' equity		210,000
Purchase discrepancy		80,000
Allocated:		
Equipment		7,500
Goodwill		$ 72,500

Since the fair value of Star's shares went up during Year 4, there appears to be no impairment in Star's goodwill. The fair value excess attributed to the equipment must be amortized over its useful life of 3 years. The following purchase discrepancy amortization schedule is prepared to keep track of the allocation and amortization of the purchase discrepancy for both the controlling and noncontrolling interest:

PURCHASE DISCREPANCY AMORTIZATION SCHEDULE

	Equipment		Goodwill		Total
	Parent	NCI	Parent	NCI	
	70%	30%	70%	30%	
Jan 1, Year 4, purchase	$5,250	$2,250	$50,750	$21,750	$80,000
Amortization for Year 4	(1,750)	(750)			(2,500)
Balance, December 31, Year 4	$3,500	$1,500	$50,750	$21,750	$77,500

Assuming that Par continues to use the equity method on its separate-entity books, the journal entries for Year 4 would be as follows:

Investment in Star	35,000	
Investment income		35,000
To record 70% of reported income for the year (70% × 50,000)		
Investment income	1,750	
Investment in Star		1,750
To record Par's share of amortization of purchase discrepancy related to equipment		
Cash	14,000	
Investment in Star		14,000
To record dividends received during the year (70% × 20,000)		

Only the parent's share of the amortization of the purchase discrepancy is recorded in the parent's books.

The investment account is not adjusted to fair value subsequent to the date of acquisition.

The balance in the investment account at the end of Year 4 is $222,250 (203,000 + 35,000 – 1,750 –14,000). The fair value of the investment is $238,000 (7,000 shares × $34 per share) but is ignored under the equity method and under consolidation.

Purchase of Fifth Block of Shares   On January 1, Year 5, Par acquires another 2,000 common shares of Star for $68,000. The book values of Star's net assets are equal to fair values except for specialized equipment, which is undervalued by $6,000. The equipment has an estimated remaining life of 2 years. During Year 5, Star reported a net income of $60,000 and paid dividends of $20,000. At December 31, Year 5, the fair value of Star's shares was $38 per share.

Par now owns 90 percent of Star, continues to have control over Star and continues to report its investment on a consolidated basis. However, it does not revalue the entire subsidiary to market value on this fifth purchase. The revaluation to market value only occurs when the parent obtains control over the subsidiary, which happened in the fourth step. Nevertheless, we must calculate and allocate the purchase discrepancy for this 20 percent purchase as an incremental step as follows:

A separate allocation of the purchase discrepancy should be prepared for each incremental investment subsequent to the date of acquisition.

Cost of 20% of Star		$68,000
Book value of Star's net assets:		
Common stock	100,000	
Retained earnings (110,000 + 50,000 – 20,000)	140,000	
Total shareholders' equity	240,000	
Par's ownership interest	20%	48,000
Purchase discrepancy		20,000
Allocated:		
Equipment (6,000 × 20%)		1,200
Goodwill		$18,800

Since the fair value of Star's shares went up during the year, there appears to be no impairment in Star's goodwill. The purchase discrepancy amortization schedule for Year 5 is shown in Exhibit 9.1:

Exhibit 9.1

PURCHASE DISCREPANCY AMORTIZATION SCHEDULE

The previous block acquisitions are not revalued when there is a new acquisition subsequent to the date of acquisition.

	Equipment Parent	Equipment NCI	Goodwill Parent	Goodwill NCI	Total
Balance, December 31, Year 4	$3,500	$1,500	$50,750	$21,750	$77,500
NCI sold 20/30 of its interest		(1,000)		(14,500)	(15,500)
	3,500	500	50,750	7,250	62,000
Amortization for Year 5 – re Step 4	(1,750)	(250)			(2,000)
Unamortized relating to step 4	1,750	250	50,750	7,250	60,000
Jan 1, Year 5, purchase	1,200		18,800		20,000
Amortization for Year 5 – re Step 5	(600)				(600)
Balance, December 31, Year 5	$2,350	$ 250	$69,550	$ 7,250	$79,400
	(a)	(b)	(c)	(d)	(e)

At the end of Year 5, Par owns 90 percent and the NCI owns 10 percent. The purchase discrepancy for Par has two components — the 70 percent component and the 20 percent component. Each component is kept track of separately. The purchase discrepancy for the NCI is based on the 10 percent component remaining from when the business combination first occurred.

Assuming that Par continues to use the equity method on its separate-entity books, the journal entries for Year 5 would be as follows:

These entries are recorded on the separate-entity books of the parent.	Investment in Star Cash To record purchase of 2,000 shares at $34 per share	68,000 	 68,000
	Investment in Star Investment income To record 90% of reported income for the year (90% × 60,000)	54,000	 54,000

	Investment income
	    Investment in Star
	To record Par's share of amortization of purchase discrepancy
	    related to equipment (1,750 + 600)
		2,350	
			2,350

	Cash Investment in Star To record dividends received during the year (90% × 20,000)	18,000	 18,000

The balance in the investment account at the end of Year 5 is $323,900 (222,250 + 68,000 + 54,000 – 2,350 – 18,000). The investment account can be segregated into three components as follows:

The investment account can be reconciled to the subsidiary's equity at any point in time when the parent uses the equity method.

Book value of Star's net assets:		
Common stock	$100,000	
Retained earnings (140,000 + 60,000 – 20,000)	180,000	
Total shareholders' equity	280,000	
Par's ownership interest	90%	$252,000
Unamortized purchase discrepancy		
Equipment **(1a)**		2,350
Goodwill **(1c)**		69,550
Total		$323,900

Similarly, the noncontrolling interest can be calculated using these same three components as follows:

NCI on the balance sheet is comprised of the NCI's share of the subsidiary's equity and the unamortized purchase discrepancy at the balance sheet date.

Book value of Star's net assets:	$280,000	
NCI's ownership interest	10%	$28,000
Unamortized purchase discrepancy		
Equipment **(1b)**		250
Goodwill **(1d)**		7,250
Total		$35,500

We will now illustrate the consolidation process by using the following condensed balance sheets for Par and Star at the end of Year 5:

The parent's retained earnings under the equity method are equal to consolidated retained earnings.

	Par	Star
Investment in Star (equity method)	$ 323,900	
Equipment — net	500,000	$140,000
Other assets	700,000	490,000
	$1,523,900	$630,000
Liabilities	$ 450,000	$350,000
Common shares	500,000	100,000
Retained earnings	573,900	180,000
	$1,523,900	$630,000

The consolidated balance sheet at December 31, Year 5, will be as follows:

PAR COMPANY
CONSOLIDATED BALANCE SHEET
at December 31, Year 5

Both the parent's and NCI's share of the unamortized purchase discrepancy appear on the consolidated balance sheet.

Equipment — net (500,000 + 140,000 + **(1a) 2,350** + **(1b) 250**)	$ 642,600
Other assets (700,000 + 490,000)	1,190,000
Goodwill (**(1c) 69,550** + **(1d) 7,250**)	76,800
	$1,909,400
Liabilities (450,000 + 350,000)	$ 800,000
Common shares	500,000
Retained earnings	573,900
Noncontrolling interest	35,500
	$1,909,400

Numerous small purchases can be grouped into one block purchase when calculating and allocating the purchase discrepancy.

Numerous Small Purchases   Assume that Par attempts to purchase the remaining outstanding shares of Star by making daily open market purchases of the subsidiary's shares. At the end of two months it abandons the idea. During this period it has made 35 separate share purchases that in total represent 4 percent of the subsidiary's outstanding shares. Since it would be impractical to calculate 35 purchase discrepancies, the *Handbook* recommends taking the total cost of these purchases and treating it as a single block purchase of 4 percent.

Repurchase of Shares by Subsidiary   When the subsidiary repurchases and cancels some or all of the common shares being held by the noncontrolling shareholders, the parent's percentage ownership in the common shares will increase. The increase in ownership will be accounted for in a similar manner to a step-by-step acquisition.

Consolidated Retained Earnings — Cost Method   The examples used to illustrate block purchases have assumed that the parent company uses the equity method to account for its investment. When the parent has used the cost method, a calculation adjusting to the equity method is required when consolidated statements are prepared. This calculation has been extensively illustrated in earlier chapters and requires only slight modification when block acquisitions have been made.

In our comprehensive example, we noted that the investment in the subsidiary was valued at fair value of $203,000 on the date of the business combination, January 1, Year 4. If Par had been using the cost method, the investment account would have to be adjusted to $203,000 as at January 1, Year 4, on the consolidation worksheet. The other side of the entry would be credited to retained earnings. From there, we can illustrate the basic idea behind the calculation of consolidated retained earnings at the end of Year 5 in the following manner:

CALCULATION OF CONSOLIDATED RETAINED EARNINGS
at December 31, Year 5

Consolidated retained earnings should recognize the parent's percentage ownership for each step of the step-by-step acquisitions.

Retained earnings of parent — cost method		$ xxx
Adjust investment account to fair value at date of business combination		xxx
Adjusted retained earnings of parent at date of business combination, Jan. 1, Year 4		xxx
Less: Parent's share of purchase discrepancy amortizations		
Year 4 purchase	xxx	
Year 5 purchase	xxx	xxx
Adjusted		xxx

Retained earnings of subsidiary at the time of Year 5 purchase	xxx	
Retained earnings of subsidiary at the time of Year 4 purchase	xxx	
Increase since Year 4 purchase	xxx	
Parent's ownership percentage	70%	xxx
Retained earnings of subsidiary — Dec. 31, Year 5	xxx	
Retained earnings of subsidiary at the time of Year 5 purchase	xxx	
Increase since Year 5 purchase	xxx	
Parent's ownership percentage	90%	xxx
Consolidated retained earnings		$ xxx

Consolidated Cash Flow Analysis Par Company's fifth block purchase of shares (on January 1, Year 5, for $68,000) requires further analysis to determine the effect on the Year 5 consolidated balance sheet. This cash has left the consolidated entity, so the effect of the transaction must appear on the Year 5 consolidated cash flow statement. By examining the purchase discrepancy amortization schedule above, we note that the parent paid $1,200 for the fair value excess pertaining to equipment which is $200 more than the carrying value ($1,000) of equipment deemed sold by the NCI. Similarly, the parent paid $18,800 for goodwill on the fifth step that is $4,300 more than the carrying value ($14,500) of goodwill deemed sold by the NCI. The total carrying value of the NCI to be removed from the consolidated balance sheet is $63,500 which consists of the following:

20% of book value of Star's shareholders' equity (20% × $240,000)	$48,000
Unamortized fair value excess of equipment sold by NCI	1,000
Goodwill sold by NCI	14,500
Total carrying value of NCI removed from consolidated balance sheet	$63,500

NCI on the consolidated balance sheet decreases when the parent purchases additional shares of the subsidiary.

We can depict the effect of the fifth purchase on the consolidated balance sheet with the following entry:

Equipment (1,200 – 1,000)	200	
Goodwill (18,800 – 14,500)	4,300	
Noncontrolling interest	63,500	
Cash		68,000

The cost of purchasing additional shares in the subsidiary should be reported in investing activities on the consolidated cash flow statement.

The $68,000 cash outflow should appear and be described on the consolidated cash flow statement under the caption "Investing activities." The details of the changes in noncash accounts on the consolidated balance sheet arising from the fifth block purchase of shares would be disclosed in the notes to financial statements.

Parent Sells Some of Its Holdings in Subsidiary

Let's continue with the previous illustration involving Par and Star. Assume that on January 1, Year 6, Par sold 900 shares in Star Company on the open market for $34,200.

Note that after the sale, Par's ownership percentage is 81 percent (8,100 ÷ 10,000). Note also that Par has disposed of 10 percent of its investment in Star (900 ÷ 9,000). Another way of calculating the percentage of investment disposed is as follows:

Ownership before sale	90%
Ownership after sale	81%
Change	9%

Percentage of investment sold: 9 ÷ 90 = 10%.

The gain on sale of shares of subsidiary as reported on the parent's separate-entity books under the equity method would also be reported on the consolidated income statement.

Par would make the following journal entry to record the sale of 900 shares:

Cash	34,200	
Investment in Star (10% × $323,900)		32,390
Gain on sale of shares		1,810

The $1,810 gain on sale would appear on Par's current income statement and would also appear on the consolidated income statement.

The total unamortized purchase discrepancy to be reported on the consolidated financial statements would remain the same in total. However, the portion belonging to the noncontrolling interest would increase because the noncontrolling interest now owns 19% of the subsidiary. The portion belonging to the controlling interest would decrease because the parent has sold 10 percent of its interest.

In this example, there are two unamortized purchase discrepancies relating to the fourth and fifth block purchases. Does the reduction in the unamortized purchase discrepancy for the parent come from the fourth block or fifth block or both? The answer is that the reduction affects both, because paragraph 1600.42 of the *Handbook* requires that the reduction of the carrying amount of the investment should be based on the average carrying value. Therefore, because we have reduced the investment account by 10 percent, we have also reduced the two unamortized purchase discrepancies by 10 percent.

NCI is increased by the carrying value of the shares sold by the parent.

It is debateable whether the increase in the noncontrolling interest should be valued at fair value or carrying value. One could argue that the noncontrolling interest should be increased by $38,000 because that is the amount paid by the noncontrolling interest for these 900 shares. On the other hand, one could argue that Star's net assets on the consolidated statements should not be revalued because there has not been a change in control and the cost of allocating the purchase price is not worth the benefit derived from this information. For illustrative purposes, we will use the latter approach and increase the noncontrolling interest by the carrying value of the shares being sold by the parent.[3] The following schedule shows the change in values for the controlling and noncontrolling interest as a result of Par's sale of 900 shares:

	Controlling Interest			Noncontrolling Interest		
	Before	*Sold*	*After*	*Before*	*Bought*	*After*
Percentage ownership	90%	9%	81%	10%	9%	19%
Share of Star's shareholders' equity	$252,000	$25,200	$226,800	$28,000	$25,200	$53,200
Unamortized purchase discrepancy						
Equipment	2,350	235	2,115	250	235	485
Goodwill	69,550	6,955	62,595	7,250	6,955	14,205
Total	$323,900	$32,390	$291,510	$35,500	$32,390	$67,890

[3] At the time of writing this text, there was no guidance in the *CICA Handbook* as to the method of valuing the NCI for this type of situation. The CICA will be issuing an exposure draft on Consolidated Financial Statements in 2008. The exposure draft should clarify the accounting for this situation.

We will now illustrate the consolidation process by using the following condensed balance sheets for Par and Star at January 1, Year 6. The previous balance sheets have been updated for the entry to record the sale of 900 shares by Par.

	Par	Star
Investment in Star (323,900 – 32,390)	$ 291,510	
Equipment — net	500,000	$140,000
Other assets (700,000 + 34,200)	734,200	490,000
	$1,525,710	$630,000
Liabilities	$ 450,000	$350,000
Common shares	500,000	100,000
Retained earnings (573,900 + 1,810)	575,710	180,000
	$1,525,710	$630,000

The consolidated balance sheet at January 1, Year 6, will be as follows:

PAR COMPANY
CONSOLIDATED BALANCE SHEET
At January 1, Year 6

Equipment — net (500,000 + 140,000 + **2,115** + **485**)	$ 642,600
Other assets (734,200 + 490,000)	1,224,200
Goodwill (**62,595** + **14,205**)	76,800
	$1,943,600
Liabilities (450,000 + 350,000)	$ 800,000
Common shares	500,000
Retained earnings	575,710
Noncontrolling interest	67,890
	$1,943,600

The subsidiary's net assets are not revalued when the parent sells a portion of its investment in the subsidiary.

Consolidated Cash Flow Analysis   Par's journal entry to record the sale of 900 shares is shown on page 414. We can see that this transaction increased the entity's cash by $34,200, and we know that the gain appears on the consolidated income statement. But "Investment in Star" does not appear on the consolidated balance sheet. By examining the schedule above showing the change in controlling and noncontrolling interest or by comparing the consolidated balance sheets at December 31, Year 5, and January 1, Year 6, we can see that noncontrolling interest increased by $32,390. Accordingly, we can prepare the following entry, which shows the effect of the transaction on the consolidated financial statements:

Cash	34,200	
Noncontrolling interest		32,390
Gain on sale of investment		1,810

The proceeds from selling shares in the subsidiary should be reported in investing activities on the consolidated cash flow statement.

The *Handbook* requires that only the net cash inflow from a disposal of business units be presented on the cash flow statement and the details of the changes in non-cash accounts arising from the disposal of business units be disclosed in the notes to financial statements. Therefore, the $34,200 increase in cash would appear as an investing activity in the Year 6 consolidated cash flow statement, and the $1,810 gain would be deducted from net income to arrive at cash flow from operating activities.

Income Statement Analysis

On December 31, Year 6, Star reported a net income of $40,000 and paid dividends amounting to $15,000. A goodwill impairment test conducted on December 31, Year 6, indicated that an impairment loss of $6,000 had occurred. The following purchase discrepancy amortization schedule would be made on December 31, Year 6:

PURCHASE DISCREPANCY AMORTIZATION SCHEDULE

	Equipment		Goodwill		Total
	Parent	NCI	Parent	NCI	
Balance, December 31, Year 5	$2,350	$250	$69,550	$ 7,250	$79,400
Sale of 10% to NCI on Jan 1, Year 6	(235)	235	(6,955)	6,955	
Adjusted	2,115	485	62,595	14,205	79,400
Amortization for Year 6	(2,115)	(485)			(2,600)
Goodwill impairment (81% to parent)			(4,860)	(1,140)	(6,000)
Balance, December 31, Year 6	$ 0	$ 0	$57,735	$13,065	$70,800

A portion of the parent's unamortized purchase discrepancy is transferred to the NCI.

Note that the Year 6 amortization completely eliminates the purchase discrepancy related to the equipment because this is the last year of the equipment's useful life.

Par's equity-method journal entries for Year 6 would be as follows:

Investment in Star	32,400	
Investment income		32,400
To record 81% of Star's net income for Year 6 (40,000 × 81%)		
Cash	12,150	
Investment in Star		12,150
To record dividends received from Star in Year 6 (15,000 × 81%)		
Investment income	6,975	
Investment in Star		6,975
To record Par's share of amortization of the purchase discrepancy for Year 6 (2,115 + 4,860)		

Dividends received from the subsidiary are recorded as a reduction in the investment account under the equity method.

The following are the Year 6 income statements of Par and Star:

	Par	Star
Miscellaneous revenue	$200,000	$150,000
Gain on sale of investment	1,810	—
Investment income	25,425	—
	227,235	150,000
Miscellaneous expense	130,000	90,000
Equipment depreciation expense	—	20,000
	130,000	110,000
Net income	$ 97,235	$ 40,000

The gain on sale of investment is not eliminated and therefore appears on the consolidated income statement. Investment income is replaced with the revenues and expenses of Star, the amortization of the purchase discrepancies, and the noncontrolling interest. The Year 6 consolidated income statement prepared using the direct approach appears below:

PAR COMPANY
CONSOLIDATED INCOME STATEMENT
Year Ended December 31, Year 6

Miscellaneous revenues (200,000 + 150,000)	$350,000
Gain on sale of investment (1,810 + 0)	1,810
	351,810
Miscellaneous expenses (130,000 + 90,000)	220,000
Equipment depreciation (0 + 20,000 + **2,600**)	22,600
Goodwill impairment loss (0 + 0 + **6,000**)	6,000
	248,600
Net income — entity	103,210
Less noncontrolling interest (19% × 40,000 – 485 – **1,140**)	5,975
Net income	$ 97,235

The NCI is charged with its share of the amortization of the purchase discrepancy.

DISCUSSION QUESTION

What Is the Goodwill Really Worth?

On December 31, Year 7, Pepper Company, a public company, agreed to a business combination with Salt Limited, an unrelated private company. Pepper issued 72 of its common shares for all (50) of the outstanding common shares of Salt. This transaction increased the number of outstanding Pepper shares from 100 to 172. Pepper's shares were trading around $10 per share in days leading up to the business combination. The condensed balance sheets for the two companies on this date were as follows (in 000s):

	Pepper Book Value	Pepper Fair Value	Salt Book Value	Salt Fair Value
Tangible assets	$500	$600	$100	$120
Intangible assets (excluding goodwill)	200	500	250	350
	$700		$350	
Liabilities	$400	410	$170	200
Shareholders' equity	300		180	
	$700		$350	

On January 1, Year 8, Pepper sold 40 percent of its investment in Salt to an unrelated third party for $500 in cash. The CFO at Pepper stated that Salt must have been worth $1,250 if the unrelated third party was willing to pay $500 for a 40 percent interest in Salt. If so, Pepper saved $530 by buying Salt for only $720. Accordingly, the CFO wants to recognize a gain of $530 in the Year 7 income statement to reflect the true value of the Salt shares.

You have been asked by the CFO to prepare a presentation to senior management on the accounting implications for the business combination and subsequent sale of 40 percent of the investment. She would like you to consider two alternative methods of valuing Salt on the consolidated balance at the date of acquisition — one based on cost of purchase and one based on fair value of subsidiary. Your presentation should answer the following questions:

1. How is a subsidiary usually valued on the consolidated balance sheet at the date of acquisition?

2. How would Pepper's consolidated balance sheet differ at the date of acquisition under the two different valuation alternatives? Which method best reflects economic reality? Which method is required by GAAP?

3. How is a subsidiary usually valued on the consolidated balance sheet after the parent sells a portion of its interest in the subsidiary?

4. How would Pepper's consolidated balance sheet look after the sale of the 40 percent interest in Salt to the unrelated third party?

Subsidiary Issues Additional Shares to Public

Let us assume that Par did not sell 900 shares on January 1, Year 6, and that, instead, Star Company issued an additional 2,500 shares for $95,000 on January 1, Year 3. Star would record this transaction as follows:

Cash	95,000	
Common stock		95,000
To record the issuance of 2,500 shares		

The parent's percentage interest decreases when the subsidiary issues additional shares and the parent does not purchase any of the additional shares.

Star now has 12,500 common shares issued. Because Par did not buy any of the new issue, its holdings have remained constant (9,000 shares), but its ownership interest has declined to 72 percent (9,000 ÷ 12,500). This represents a 20 percent reduction in its investment, calculated as follows:

Ownership before share issue	90%
Ownership after share issue	72%
Change	18%
Percentage of investment reduced: 18 ÷ 90 = 20%	

The effect of this reduction on the unamortized purchase discrepancy is the same as if the parent had sold a portion of its holding in the subsidiary to the noncontrolling interest (*CICA Handbook*, paragraphs 1600.46–47). In this case, 20 percent of the parent's share of the unamortized purchase discrepancy has been "disposed of" as a result of the share issue. However, at this point the only entry made to record the transaction is the entry made by Star. Parent must also adjust its investment account to record the effect of this transaction on its investment. The following analysis indicates the amount of the adjustment:

The parent gave up 20 percent of its old investment and received 72 percent of the increase in the subsidiary's equity.

Loss due to reduction of investment account — 20% × 323,900	$64,780
Gain due to ownership of new assets resulting from subsidiary	
share issue — 72% × 95,000	68,400
Net gain to parent due to share issue	$ 3,620

In our previous example, we explained the reasoning for removing 20 percent from the investment account. The unamortized purchase discrepancy is included in the $323,900 amount, and if this discrepancy has been reduced by 20 percent, a logical extension is to remove 20 percent from the total investment balance. If the subsidiary had issued the 2,500 shares for no consideration, the investment account would have to be reduced by $64,780, and a loss equal to that amount would be recorded by Par. But Star received $95,000 for its new share issue, and Par now controls 72 percent of the net assets of its subsidiary, including the additional cash received as a result of the new share issue. Par has gained by the 72 percent ownership interest in the assets received by Star. It should be obvious that net gain or loss resulting from the transaction depends on the amount that the subsidiary received from its new share issue. Given the facts of this particular example, Par would make the following journal entry on January 1, Year 6:

Investment in Star	3,620	
Gain from subsidiary share issue		3,620
To record the effect of subsidiary's issue of 2,500 shares on parent's investment		

As in our previous example, we assume that in Year 6, Star reported a net income of $40,000 and paid $15,000 in dividends. The following purchase discrepancy amortization schedule would be prepared on December 31, Year 6:

PURCHASE DISCREPANCY AMORTIZATION SCHEDULE

	Equipment		Goodwill		Total
	Parent	NCI	Parent	NCI	
Balance, December 31, Year 5	$2,350	$250	$69,550	$ 7,250	$79,400
Sale of 20% to NCI on Jan. 1, Year 6	(470)	470	(13,910)	13,910	
Adjusted	1,880	720	55,640	21,160	79,400
Amortization for Year 6	(1,880)	(720)			(2,600)
Goodwill impairment (72% to parent)			(4,320)	(1,680)	(6,000)
Balance, Dec. 31, Year 6	$　0	$　0	$51,320	$19,480	$70,800

Twenty percent of the parent's unamortized purchase discrepancy is transferred to the NCI. There is no attempt to incorporate fair values at the date of this transaction.

Par's equity method journal entries for Year 6 would be as follows:

Investment in Star	28,800	
Investment income		28,800
To record 72% of Star's net income for Year 6 (40,000 × 72%)		

Cash	10,800	
Investment in Star		10,800
To record dividends received from Star in Year 6 (15,000 × 72%)		

The parent absorbs 72 percent of the goodwill impairment.

Investment income	6,200	
Investment in Star		6,200
To record Par's share of the amortization of the purchase discrepancy for Year 6 (1,880 + 4,320)		

The elimination of the parent's interest in the subsidiary's shareholders' equity against the parent's investment account leaves a balance equal to the unamortized purchase discrepancy. This will now be illustrated.

Investment in Star	
Balance, December 31, Year 5	$323,900
Increase due to subsidiary share issue	3,620
Star net income (40,000 × 72%)	28,800
Star dividends (15,000 × 72%)	(10,800)
Purchase discrepancy amortization	(6,200)
Balance, December 31, Year 6	339,320

The investment account is comprised of the parent's share of the subsidiary's equity plus the unamortized purchase discrepancy.		
Shareholders' equity of Star		
Common stock — December 31, Year 5	100,000	
Share issue — Year 6	95,000	
Common stock, December 31, Year 6	195,000	
Retained earnings, December 31, Year 6		
(180,000 + 40,000 − 15,000)	205,000	
Total, December 31, Year 6	400,000	
Par's ownership interest	72%	288,000
Balance — unamortized purchase discrepancy		$ 51,320

The amortization schedule on page 419 shows how the unamortized purchase discrepancy would be allocated to equipment and goodwill in the preparation of the consolidated balance sheet on December 31, Year 6. Noncontrolling interest would appear in the amount of $131,480 (28% × 400,000 + 19,480).

The Year 6 income statements of Par and Star are shown below, and are followed by the consolidated income statement.

	Par	*Star*
Miscellaneous revenue	$200,000	$150,000
Gain from subsidiary share issue	3,620	—
Investment income	22,600	—
	226,220	150,000
Miscellaneous expense	130,000	90,000
Equipment depreciation expense	—	20,000
	130,000	110,000
Net income	$ 96,220	$ 40,000

PAR COMPANY
CONSOLIDATED INCOME STATEMENT
Year Ended December 31, Year 6

The parent's gain from the subsidiary's issuance of additional shares appears on the consolidated income statement.	Miscellaneous revenues (200,000 + 150,000)	$350,000
	Gain from subsidiary share issue	3,620
		353,620
	Miscellaneous expense (130,000 + 90,000)	220,000
	Equipment depreciation (0 + 20,000 + **2,600**)	22,600
	Goodwill impairment loss (0 + 0 + **6,000**)	6,000
		248,600
	Net income — entity	105,020
	Less noncontrolling interest (28% × 40,000 − 720 − 1,680)	8,800
	Net income	$ 96,220

Consolidated Cash Flow Analysis   To recap, the issue of 2,500 shares on January 1, Year 6, was recorded by Star Company with the following journal entry:

Cash	95,000	
Common stock		95,000

Also, in order to record the effect of the reduction on its investment, Par made the following journal entry on this date:

Investment in Star	3,620	
Gain from subsidiary share issue		3,620

The effect of this transaction on the consolidated financial statements can be depicted as follows:

The consolidated entity received cash from the NCI.

Cash	95,000	
Noncontrolling interest*		91,380
Gain from subsidiary share issue		3,620

*CHANGES IN NONCONTROLLING INTEREST

Balance after subsidiary share issue		
Shareholders' equity before issue	$280,000	
New share issue	95,000	
	375,000	
	28%	
Share of Star's shareholders' equity	105,000	
Unamortized purchase discrepancy — equipment	720	
Goodwill	21,160	126,880
Balance before subsidiary share issue		35,500
Increase in noncontrolling interest		$ 91,380

The gain must be deducted from net income on the cash flow statement because the full amount of cash received is shown in the investing activities section.

The $95,000 increase in cash would appear as a financing activity in the Year 6 consolidated cash flow statement; the $3,620 gain would be deducted from net income to arrive at cash flow from operating activities. The details of the changes in noncash accounts on the consolidated balance sheet arising from the deemed disposal of business units would be disclosed in the notes to financial statements.

Subsidiary with Preferred Shares Outstanding

All of the consolidation examples that we have used up to this point have assumed that the subsidiary companies have only one class of shares — common shares — in their capital structures. We now examine situations where the subsidiary also has preferred shares. The basic concepts of consolidation do not change, but when there is more than one class of shares outstanding, there is an additional problem involved in determining the amount of noncontrolling interest in the net assets and net income of the subsidiary. The following example will illustrate the approach that is used.

Illustration — Preferred Shareholdings

On December 31, Year 1, the shareholders' equity of Sonco Inc. was as follows:

If the subsidiary were wound up today, how much of its equity would go to the preferred shareholders?

Preferred shares, $10 dividend, cumulative, redeemable at $105 per share	
Issued and outstanding 1,000 shares	$100,000
Common shares	
Issued and outstanding 30,000 shares	360,000
Total share capital	460,000
Retained earnings (note 1)	140,000
	$600,000

Note 1: On December 31, Year 1, dividends on preferred shares were one year in arrears.

On January 1, Year 2, Parco Ltd. purchased 27,000 common shares of Sonco for $450,000. The purchase discrepancy was allocated entirely to franchise agreements, to be amortized over a 10-year period.

Because the parent company acquired control by purchasing 90 percent of the voting common shares, the noncontrolling interest consists of the shareholdings represented by 10 percent of the common shares and 100 percent of the preferred shares. In order to calculate any purchase discrepancy associated with the common share purchase, and the amount of the noncontrolling interest in both classes of shares, it is necessary to split the shareholders' equity of Sonco into its preferred and common share capital components in the following manner:

	Total	Preferred	Common
Preferred shares	$100,000	$100,000	$ —
Redemption premium on preferred	—	5,000	(5,000)
Common shares	360,000	—	360,000
Total share capital	460,000	105,000	355,000
Retained earnings	140,000	10,000	130,000
	$600,000	$115,000	$485,000

The preferred shareholders would get the first $115,000 and the common shareholders would get the rest.

The $115,000 allocated to preferred share capital represents the total amount that the company would have to pay to the preferred shareholders if the preferred shares were redeemed on this date. It is made up of the redemption price on 1,000 shares ($105,000) and the one year's dividends in arrears ($10,000) on these shares.

By using the two components of shareholders' equity, both the purchase discrepancy and the noncontrolling interest on the date of acquisition can be calculated, as follows:

The purchase discrepancy on the common shares is calculated in the same way as before.

Cost of 90 percent of common shares	$450,000
Implied value of 100% of Sonco	$500,000
Book value of common shares of Sonco	485,000
Purchase discrepancy	15,000
Allocated: franchise agreement	15,000
Balance	$ –0–
Noncontrolling interest, January 1, Year 2	
Preferred shares (115,000 × 100%)	$115,000
Common shares (500,000 × 10%)	50,000
	$165,000

The preparation of the consolidated balance sheet on January 1, Year 2, will not be illustrated, but it should be obvious that the only difference from previous examples lies in how the noncontrolling interest is calculated on this date.

The financial statements of Parco and Sonco on December 31, Year 2, are shown in Exhibit 9.2.

In order to prepare the Year 2 consolidated financial statements, it is again necessary to split the shareholders' equity of Sonco into its preferred and common share components. Because there has been no change in total share capital, the allocation of this component is identical to the one made as at January 1 (see above). But retained earnings *has* changed, and so we will allocate the retained earnings statement in the following manner:

	Total	Preferred	Common
Any calculations involving the subsidiary's equity must be split between common and preferred shareholders.			
Balance, January 1, Year 2	$140,000	$10,000	$130,000
Net income (see point #2)	60,000	10,000	50,000
	200,000	20,000	180,000
Dividends (see point #1)	50,000	20,000	30,000
Balance, December 31, Year 2	$150,000	$ –0–	$150,000

It is important to note the following regarding the allocation process:

1. All dividends in arrears plus the current year's dividends must be paid to preferred shareholders before any dividends are paid to common shareholders. In this situation the dividends paid by Sonco were:

Preferred	$20,000
Common	30,000
	$50,000

The preferred shareholders' claim on income is one year's worth of dividends in any given year whether or not dividends are declared in that year.

2. When preferred shares are cumulative, the preferred shareholders are entitled to income equal to the yearly dividend even when the company has no income or has suffered a loss for the year. This means that the net income (or loss) for a particular year must be allocated to its preferred and common components. In the situation we are examining, the Year 2 net income is allocated this way:

To preferred equity	$10,000
To common equity	50,000
Total net income	$60,000

Exhibit 9.2

YEAR 2 INCOME STATEMENTS

	Parco	Sonco
The parent received 90 percent of the dividends paid to common shareholders.		
Revenues — miscellaneous	$750,000	$420,000
Dividends from Sonco	27,000	—
	777,000	420,000
Expenses — miscellaneous	688,000	360,000
Net income	$ 89,000	$ 60,000

YEAR 2 RETAINED EARNINGS STATEMENTS

	Parco	Sonco
Balance, January 1	$381,000	$140,000
Net income	89,000	60,000
	470,000	200,000
Dividends	90,000	50,000
Balance, December 31	$380,000	$150,000

BALANCE SHEETS — December 31, Year 2

	Parco	Sonco
The parent has an investment in the common shares of the subsidiary but no investment in the preferred shares.		
Assets — miscellaneous	$510,000	$810,000
Investment in Sonco — at cost	450,000	—
	$960,000	$810,000
Liabilities	$180,000	$200,000
Preferred shares	—	100,000
Common shares	400,000	360,000
Retained earnings	380,000	150,000
	$960,000	$810,000

The allocation of total shareholders' equity as at December 31, Year 2, can now be prepared as shown below:

	Total	Preferred	Common
Share capital	$460,000	$105,000	$355,000
Retained earnings	150,000	–0–	150,000
	$610,000	$105,000	$505,000

Because Parco has used the cost method to account for its investment, we must make the two calculations shown in Exhibit 9.3 before preparing the Year 2 consolidated financial statements:

Exhibit 9.3

CALCULATION OF CONSOLIDATED NET INCOME, YEAR 2

The preferred shareholders' claim on income is one year's worth of dividends.

Net income, Parco		$ 89,000
Less common dividends from Sonco (90% × 30,000)		27,000
		62,000
Net income, Sonco	60,000	
Less allocated to preferred shares	10,000	
Net income, common shares	50,000	
Less purchase discrepancy amortization (15,000 ÷ 10)	1,500 **(a)**	
Adjusted income	48,500	
Parco's share	90%	43,650
Consolidated net income		$105,650 **(b)**
Noncontrolling interest in net income		
Preferred net income (100% × 10,000)		$ 10,000
Common net income (10% × 48,500)		4,850
		$ 14,850 **(c)**

The NCI owns all of the preferred shares and 10 percent of the common shares of the subsidiary.

CALCULATION OF NONCONTROLLING INTEREST
at December 31, Year 2

Preferred equity	105,000 × 100%	$105,000
Common equity	(505,000 + 15,000 – **(3a) 1,500**) × 10%	51,850
		$156,850 **(d)**

The Year 2 consolidated financial statements are shown in Exhibit 9.4.

Exhibit 9.4

Year 2 Consolidated Statements
(when subsidiary has preferred shares)

PARCO LTD.
CONSOLIDATED INCOME STATEMENT
for the Year Ended December 31, Year 2

The NCI includes all of the income pertaining to the preferred shares and 10 percent of the income pertaining to the common shares.

Revenues (750,000 + 420,000)	$1,170,000
Expenses (688,000 + 360,000 + **(3a) 1,500**)	1,049,500
Net income — entity	120,500
Less noncontrolling interest **(3c)**	14,850
Net income **(3b)**	$ 105,650

PARCO LTD.
CONSOLIDATED RETAINED EARNINGS STATEMENT
for the Year Ended December 31, Year 2

Balance, January 1	$ 381,000
Net income	105,650
	486,650
Dividends	90,000
Balance, December 31	$ 396,650

PARCO LTD.
CONSOLIDATED BALANCE SHEET
at December 31, Year 2

Assets — miscellaneous (510,000 + 810,000)	$1,320,000
Franchise agreements (15,000 – **(3a) 1,500**)	13,500
	$1,333,500

Liabilities (180,000 + 200,000)	$ 380,000
Common shares	400,000
Retained earnings	396,650
Noncontrolling interest **(3d)**	156,850
	$1,333,500

> The subsidiary's common and preferred shares do not appear on the consolidated balance sheet.

Other Types of Preferred Shares

> The amount of income, dividends, and equity belonging to the preferred shareholders is dependent on the rights of the preferred shareholders.

In the example above, the preferred shares are cumulative. If the shares were non-cumulative, net income would be allocated to the preferred shares only if preferred dividends were declared during the year, and of course dividends are never in arrears with this type of preferred share. If dividends are not declared in a particular year, no income would be allocated to the preferred shares because the preferred shareholders would never get a dividend for that year. If the preferred shares are participating, the allocation of net income will follow the participation provisions.

Subsidiary Preferred Shares Owned by Parent

> Any purchase discrepancy related to the preferred shares should be treated similar to a retirement of the preferred shares by the subsidiary itself.

A parent company may own all or a portion of its subsidiary's preferred shares in addition to its common share investment. When the cost of the investment in preferred shares is different from the book value of the stock acquired, a problem arises as to how to treat the preferred stock purchase discrepancy in the consolidated financial statements. Since preferred shares do not share in the value changes that take place in the subsidiary (the exception would be fully participating shares), market price changes in preferreds result from changes in interest rates. Because of this, the purchase discrepancy should not be used to revalue the subsidiary's identifiable net assets or goodwill. Instead, the purchase of the preferred shares should be treated as a retirement of the preferred shares, which is a capital transaction. Consequently, the purchase price discrepancy should be adjusted to consolidated contributed surplus or retained earnings. For example, assume that in addition to its common share investment in its subsidiary, a parent owns 30 percent of the subsidiary's noncumulative preferred shares. The parent uses the equity method to account for both investments, and on December 31, Year 9, had retained earnings amounting to $136,500 and no contributed surplus. On this date, the purchase discrepancy from the 30 percent interest in preferred shares amounted to $11,865. Instead of presenting this amount among the assets on the consolidated balance sheet, we should deduct it from retained earnings so that consolidated retained earnings on December 31, Year 9, will be reported at $124,635 (136,500 – 11,865).

Indirect Shareholdings

When one company has control over another company, financial reporting by means of consolidated financial statements is required. The *Handbook* describes the concept of control as follows:

Control of another company can be achieved through direct or indirect ownership.

> An enterprise is presumed to control another enterprise when it owns, directly or indirectly, an equity interest that carries the right to elect the majority of the members of the other enterprise's board of directors, and is presumed not to control the other enterprise without such ownership. In a particular situation, these presumptions may be overcome by other factors that clearly demonstrate that control exists or does not exist.[4]

In all examples that we have used up to this point, the parent has had a direct ownership of over 50 percent of the common shares of the subsidiary. We continue to assume that over 50 percent ownership of the voting shares is necessary for control, but we now modify the assumption to allow this percentage to be achieved by both direct and indirect ownership. The following diagrams illustrate both direct and indirect holdings. In this first diagram, B and C are subsidiaries of A through direct control:

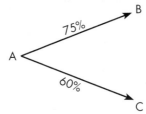

The second example, below, illustrates indirect control. G is a subsidiary of F, but F in turn is a subsidiary of E. Because E can control the voting shares of G through its control of F, G is also a subsidiary of E.

Both F and G are considered to be subsidiaries of E and therefore should be consolidated with E.

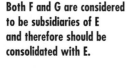

In the third example, K is a subsidiary of J through direct control. L is also a subsidiary of J through indirect control, because 55 percent of its voting shares are controlled directly or indirectly by J, even though only 43 percent [25% + (60% × 30%)] of L's net income will flow to J under the equity method of accounting.

J can control L because it has control of 55 percent of the votes at L's shareholders' meetings.

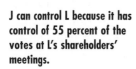

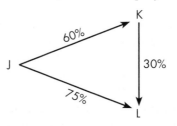

---

[4]   *CICA Handbook*, paragraph 1590.08.

While many Canadian companies have intercorporate structures that are far more complex than those illustrated, the consolidation procedures for indirect holdings are not as complicated as the diagrams might indicate. Remember that if a parent company has 50 subsidiaries, the amount of cash appearing on the consolidated balance sheet is the sum of the cash from 51 separate balance sheets. This basic concept applies to most items appearing in the consolidated statements. In addition, we emphasized in past chapters the following statements that describe the fundamental relationships resulting from the parent's use of the equity method to account for its investment:

1. Parent's net income equals consolidated net income.

2. Parent's retained earnings equal consolidated retained earnings.

3. The elimination of the parent's share of the shareholders' equity of the subsidiary against the investment account leaves a balance consisting of the parent's share of the unamortized purchase discrepancy. This balance is used to revalue the net assets of the subsidiary when the consolidated balance sheet is prepared.

4. The portion of the shareholders' equity of the subsidiary that is not eliminated and the noncontrolling interest's share of the unamortized purchase discrepancy appear on the consolidated balance sheet as noncontrolling interest.

Since these fundamental relationships also apply when we have indirect holdings, the key to the preparation of consolidated statements when control is achieved by a mixture of direct and indirect investments is the use of the equity method of accounting for each investment. (If the cost method has been used, adjustments to the equity method must be made.) The following example will illustrate these concepts.

Parent Inc. owns 80 percent of the common shares of Subone Ltd. (which is sufficient for control) and 45 percent of the common shares of Subtwo Ltd. (which we assume is not sufficient for control). However, Subone owns 25 percent of the common shares of Subtwo. This investment combined with the parent's 45 percent investment gives the parent control of 70 percent of the voting shares; therefore, Subtwo is considered to be a subsidiary of Parent.

Each investment is accounted for using the equity method. In order to simplify the illustration, we assume that on acquisition date the fair values of the identifiable net assets of the investee corporations were equal to their book values, with the purchase discrepancies from each investment being allocated to unrecorded computer databases.

We will illustrate the preparation of consolidated financial statements for Year 6, during which Parent had a net income from its own operations amounting to $135,000. Subone had a net income from its own operations amounting to $75,000, while the net income of Subtwo was $40,000. Exhibit 9.5, which shows the calculation of the Year 6 consolidated net income, is useful because it illustrates the use of the equity method of accounting by both Subone and Parent.

Regarding the preparation and interpretation of Exhibit 9.5, the following should be noted:

1. Purchase discrepancy amortizations are recorded by each company owned by another company in the group. This is the first adjustment shown. The amounts have been assumed. Any adjustments required for intercompany gains and losses would also be made here (as would the deduction for intercompany dividends if the cost method had been used by Parent and Subone).

2. Because Parent cannot record its 80 percent share of Subone's net income until Subone has recorded its 25 percent share of Subtwo's net income, Subtwo's net income is allocated first.

The principles applied when consolidating directly controlled subsidiaries apply equally well when consolidating indirectly controlled subsidiaries.

The allocation of income to investors must start at the lowest level of the corporate hierarchy and work its way up.

3. Subone's net income using the equity method can now be determined.

4. After Subone's net income has been allocated, Parent's net income using the equity method is determined. This amount, of course, equals consolidated net income.

5. The portion of the net income of Subtwo and Subone that was not allocated is the noncontrolling interest in that net income.

6. The "Total" column shows amounts that appear in the consolidated income statement. Consolidated net income is $220,645, while noncontrolling interest is $28,855.

Exhibit 9.5

CALCULATION OF CONSOLIDATED NET INCOME — Year 6

Subone accrues its share of Subtwo's income before Parent accrues its share of Subone's income.

	Parent	Subone	Subtwo	Total
Net income before investment income	$135,000	$75,000	$40,000	$250,000
Less database amortization — Subtwo			(300)	(300) **(a)**
Allocate Subtwo				
25% to Subone		9,925	(9,925)	
45% to Parent	17,865		(17,865)	
Subone net income — equity method		84,925		
Less database amortization — Subone		(200)		(200) **(b)**
		84,725		
Allocate Subone				
80% to Parent	67,780	(67,780)		
Unallocated — NCI		$16,945	$11,910	28,855 **(c)**
Parent net income — equity method	$220,645			
Consolidated net income				$220,645 **(d)**

Exhibit 9.6 shows the Year 6 financial statements of the three companies.

In preparing the Year 6 consolidated income statement, we eliminate the three investment income accounts and replace them with the revenues and expenses of the two subsidiaries, the database amortization expense, and the noncontrolling interest in the net incomes of the subsidiaries. The consolidated retained earnings statement is identical to that of Parent and requires no preparation.

Exhibit 9.6

INCOME STATEMENTS — Year 6

For these separate-entity statements, the investor has used the equity method to account for its investment.

	Parent	Subone	Subtwo
Miscellaneous revenues	$475,000	$285,000	$ 90,000
Investment income — Subone	67,780	—	—
Investment income — Subtwo	17,865	9,925	—
	560,645	294,925	90,000
Miscellaneous expenses	340,000	210,000	50,000
Net income	$220,645	$ 84,925	$ 40,000

RETAINED EARNINGS STATEMENTS — Year 6

	Parent	Subone	Subtwo
Balance, January 1	$279,120	$116,400	$ 80,000
Net income	220,645	84,925	40,000
	499,765	201,325	120,000
Dividends	45,000	30,000	10,000
Balance, December 31	$454,765	$171,325	$110,000

BALANCE SHEETS — December 31, Year 6

	Parent	Subone	Subtwo
Other assets	$608,500	$402,925	$460,000
Investment in Subone	281,900	—	—
Investment in Subtwo	104,365	53,400	—
	$994,765	$456,325	$460,000
Liabilities	$300,000	$110,000	$250,000
Common shares	240,000	175,000	100,000
Retained earnings	454,765	171,325	110,000
	$994,765	$456,325	$460,000

In preparing the consolidated balance sheet, we eliminate the investors' portion of the shareholders' equity of the investee companies against the investment accounts; this leaves a balance consisting of the unamortized purchase discrepancies. The amount of shareholders' equity not eliminated represents noncontrolling interest. The following calculations illustrate this:

The unamortized purchase discrepancy can be derived by backing out the parent's share of the subsidiary's equity from the investment account.

Parent:

Investment in Subone		$281,900
Shareholders' equity, Subone		
Common shares	175,000	
Retained earnings	171,325	
	346,325	
Parent ownership	80%	277,060
Balance — Parent's share of unamortized databases		4,840
NCI's share of unamortized databases (assumed)		1,210
Total unamortized databases from Subone		$ 6,050
Investment in Subtwo		$104,365
Shareholders' equity, Subtwo		
Common shares	100,000	
Retained earnings	110,000	
	210,000	
Parent's ownership	45%	94,500
Balance — Parent's share of unamortized databases		9,865

The unamortized purchase discrepancy relating to the NCI is an assumed figure, which must be incorporated, in the consolidated financial statements.

Subone:

Investment in Subtwo		53,400
Shareholders' equity, Subtwo (above)	210,000	
Subone ownership	25%	52,500
Balance — Investor's share of unamortized databases		900
Parent's total share of unamortized databases		10,765
NCI's share of unamortized databases (assumed)		4,615
Total unamortized databases from Subtwo		$ 15,380

CALCULATION OF NONCONTROLLING INTEREST
at December 31, Year 6

Shareholders' equity, Subone (346,325 × 20% + 1,210)	$ 70,475
Shareholders' equity, Subtwo (210,000 × 30% + 4,615)	67,615
	$138,090

Exhibit 9.7 shows the preparation of the Year 6 consolidated financial statements using the direct approach.

Exhibit 9.7

PARENT INC.
CONSOLIDATED FINANCIAL STATEMENTS
December 31, Year 6

CONSOLIDATED INCOME STATEMENT

The consolidated income statement includes the amortization of the purchase discrepancy for a period of time for the directly controlled and indirectly controlled subsidiaries.

Miscellaneous revenues (475,000 + 285,000 + 90,000)	$850,000
Miscellaneous expense (340,000 + 210,000 + 50,000)	600,000
Database amortization ((5a) 300 + (5b) 200)	500
	600,500
Net income — entity	249,500
Less noncontrolling interest (5c)	28,855
Net income (5d)	$220,645

CONSOLIDATED RETAINED EARNINGS STATEMENT

Balance, January 1	$279,120
Net income	220,645
	499,765
Dividends	45,000
Balance, December 31	$454,765

CONSOLIDATED BALANCE SHEET

The consolidated balance sheet includes the unamortized purchase discrepancy at a point in time for the directly controlled and indirectly controlled subsidiaries.

Other assets (608,500 + 402,925 + 460,000)	$1,471,425
Databases (6,050 + 15,380)	21,430
	$1,492,855
Liabilities (300,000 + 110,000 + 250,000)	$ 660,000
Common shares	240,000
Retained earnings	454,765
Noncontrolling interest	138,090
	$1,492,855

International Perspective

The Canadian standards for the cash flow statements are converged with IASB except that IAS 7 allows the disclosure of cash flow per share whereas Canadian standards allow disclosure of only earnings per share information. The standards for changes in ownership are converged except that IFRS have less detail on dilution gains and step acquisitions. These differences should be eliminated within a few years once the work on consolidations is completed.

SUMMARY

In this chapter we examined four topics that present special problems in consolidated financial statement preparation. While the consolidated balance sheet and income statement are prepared by combining the statements of the parent and its subsidiaries, the consolidated statement of cash flows is best prepared by analyzing the changes in successive consolidated balance sheets.

The next topic was concerned with changes in the parent's percentage ownership and the effect that such changes have on the noncontrolling interest and particularly on unamortized purchase discrepancies. These ownership changes also require special attention when the consolidated cash flow statement is prepared.

Preferred shares in the capital structure of subsidiary companies present unique problems in calculating noncontrolling interest if the parent's ownership of the preferred shares is not the same as its ownership of the common shares. The problem is solved by allocating shareholders' equity and any changes therein to preferred and common share components.

Control by a parent company can be achieved through direct ownership of the subsidiary's voting shares or through indirect ownership by other subsidiaries or investees. If the equity method is used for all of the investment accounts, the consolidation process is fairly easy, because the major problem involved with indirect holdings is how to determine the amount for noncontrolling interest. If the cost method is used to account for the investments, we would apply the basic procedure of adjusting from cost to equity, and then continue preparing the consolidated statements in the normal manner. This adjustment from cost to equity can be very involved when the affiliation structure is complex.

Self-Study Problem

On January 1, Year 1, X Company acquired 800 shares of Y Company's common stock for $24,000 and 180 shares of its $5 cumulative, nonparticipating preferred stock for $19,800. On this date, the shareholders' equity accounts of Y Company were:

Common shares (1,000 no par value shares issued)	$10,000
Preferred shares (200 no par value shares issued)	20,000
Retained earnings (note 1)	12,000

Note 1 — Preferred dividends were two years in arrears on January 1, Year 1.

The income statements for the two companies for the year ended December 31, Year 5, are presented on the next page.

Additional Information

- Any purchase discrepancy is allocated to brand names, to be amortized over 40 years.
- In Year 5, Y paid dividends totalling $9,000. Preferred dividends were 2 years in arrears on December 31, Year 4.
- X uses the cost method to account for its investment in Y.
- Y purchases merchandise for resale from X. In Year 5, Y purchased $33,000 in merchandise from X and had items in inventory on December 31, Year 5, on which X

had made a profit of $2,500. The January 1, Year 5, inventory contained an inter-company profit of $1,400.

- X rents equipment from Y and in Year 5 paid a rental charge of $3,000 and record-ed an account payable to Y of $2,000 for the balance of the rentals.
- On July 1, Year 3, Y sold a building to X at a profit of $13,000. X is depreciating this building on a straight-line basis over a 10-year life.
- Y paid $20,000 to X for management fees in Year 5.
- Assume a corporate tax rate of 40%.

	X Company	Y Company
Sales	$600,000	$400,000
Dividend and management fees	27,500	—
Rental revenue	—	11,200
	627,500	411,200
Cost of sales	343,900	234,700
Depreciation expense	20,000	70,000
Rental expense	5,000	—
Selling and admin expense	207,000	74,000
Interest expense	1,700	6,000
Income tax expense	20,000	9,000
	597,600	393,700
Net income	$ 29,900	$ 17,500

Required:

Prepare a consolidated income statement for Year 5.

Solution to Self-study Problem

Calculation of purchase discrepancy

Cost of 90% of preferred shares (180/200)		$19,800
Book value of preferred:		
Share capital	$20,000	
Dividends in arrears (200 × 5 × 2)	2,000	
	22,000	
	90%	19,800
Purchase discrepancy		–0–

Cost of 80% of common shares (800/1,000)		$24,000
Implied value of 100% of common shares		$30,000
Book value of common:		
Share capital	10,000	
Retained earnings	12,000	
Less preferred dividend arrears	(2,000)	
		20,000
Purchase discrepancy — brand names		$10,000

Intercompany revenues and expenses

Dividends — preferred (90% × 1,000 × 3)	$ 2,700
— common (80% × [9,000 – 3,000])	4,800
	$ 7,500 (a)
Management fees	$20,000 (b)
Rent (3,000 + 2,000)	$ 5,000 (c)
Sales	$33,000 (d)

Intercompany profits	Before Tax	Tax 40%	After Tax	
Opening inventory -- X selling	$1,400	$ 560	$ 840	**(e)**
Closing inventory — X selling	$2,500	$1,000	$1,500	**(f)**
Building realized — Y selling	$1,300	$ 520	$ 780	**(g)**

Calculation of consolidated net income — for Year 5

X net income		$29,900
Less: Dividends from Y **(a)**	7,500	
Closing inventory profit **(f)**	1,500	9,000
		20,900
Add: opening inventory profit **(e)**		840
		21,740

	Total	Preferred	Common
Y net income	17,500	1,000	16,500
Less: Brand name amortization (10,000 ÷ 40)			(250)**(h)**
Add: building profit **(g)**			780
		1,000	17,030 **(i)**
Company X's ownership interest		90%	80%
		900	13,624

	14,524
	$36,264

CONSOLIDATED INCOME STATEMENT — For Year 5

Sales (600,000 + 400,000 – **(d) 33,000**)	$967,000
Dividend and management fees (27,500 + 0 – **(a) 7,500** – **(b) 20,000**)	0
Rental revenue (11,200 – **(c) 5,000**)	6,200
	973,200
Cost of sales (343,900 + 234,700 – **(d) 33,000** – **(e) 1,400** + **(f) 2,500**)	546,700
Depreciation (20,000 + 70,000 – **(g) 1,300**)	88,700
Rental expense (5,000 + 0 – **(c) 5,000**)	0
Selling and admin (207,000 + 74,000 – **(b) 20,000**)	261,000
Interest (1,700 + 6,000)	7,700
Brand name amortization **(h)**	250
Income tax (20,000 + 9,000 + **(e) 560** + **(g) 520** – **(f) 1,000**)	29,080
	933,430
Net income – entity	39,770
Less: noncontrolling interest **(i) (10% × 1,000) + (20% × 17,030)**	3,506
Net income	$ 36,264

REVIEW QUESTIONS

1. Is the consolidated cash flow statement prepared in the same manner as the consolidated balance sheet and income statement? Explain.

2. A parent company acquired a 75% interest in a subsidiary company in Year 4. The acquisition price was $1,000,000, made up of cash of $700,000 and the parent's common shares with a current market value of $300,000. Explain how this acquisition should be reflected in the Year 4 consolidated cash flow statement.

3. Why are the amortization of the purchase price discrepancy and income assigned to the noncontrolling interest added back to consolidated net income to compute net cash flow from operating activities in the consolidated cash flow statement?

4. Why are dividend payments to noncontrolling shareholders treated as an outflow of cash in the consolidated cash flow statement but not included as dividends paid in the consolidated retained earnings statement?

5. When should the change in accounting for a long-term investment from the cost method to the equity method be accounted for retroactively and when should it be accounted for prospectively?

6. When a parent increases its investment in a subsidiary from 60% to 75% should the purchase discrepancy from the 60% purchase be revalued to fair value? Explain.

7. When a parent decreases its investment in a subsidiary from 76% to 60% should the noncontrolling interest be revalued to fair value? Explain.

8. A parent company will realize a loss or gain when its subsidiary issues common shares at a price per share that differs from the carrying amount per share of the parent's investment, and the parent's ownership percentage declines. Explain why this is so.

9. If a gain or loss is realized by a parent company as a result of the sale of a portion of the investment in a subsidiary, should the gain or loss be eliminated in the preparation of the consolidated income statement? Explain.

10. The shareholders' equity of a subsidiary company contains preferred and common shares. The parent company owns 100% of the subsidiary's common shares. Will the consolidated financial statements show noncontrolling interest? Explain.

11. A company's net income for the year was $17,000. During the year, the company paid dividends on its noncumulative preferred shares amounting to $12,000. Calculate the amount of the year's net income that "belongs to" the common shares.

12. Explain how a purchase discrepancy from an investment in preferred shares should be reflected in the consolidated financial statements.

13. Explain how the noncontrolling interest in the net assets and net income of a subsidiary is reported when the parent owns 90% of the subsidiary's common shares and 30% of the subsidiary's cumulative preferred shares.

14. Explain the difference in the calculation of consolidated net income and consolidated retained earnings depending on whether the preferred shares of a subsidiary are cumulative or noncumulative.

15. What is the major consolidation problem associated with indirect shareholdings?

MULTIPLE-CHOICE QUESTIONS

Use the following information to answer Questions 1 to 6.

The abbreviated consolidated financial statements of Print Inc. and its subsidiary, Set Inc., for the two years ended December 31, Year 5 and Year 6, are presented on the next page.

Additional Information

- Set is a 75%-owned subsidiary of Print.
- Print owns a 25% interest in Run that is accounted for using the equity method.
- During Year 6, Set declared and paid $200,000 in dividends and Run declared and paid $40,000 in dividends.

BALANCE SHEETS

	Year 6	Year 5	Increase (decrease)
Cash	$ 150,000	$ 290,000	$(140,000)
Accounts receivable	1,415,000	1,350,000	65,000
Inventory	380,000	400,000	(20,000)
Investment in Run Inc.	185,000	160,000	25,000
Plant and equipment (net)	1,270,000	900,000	370,000
	$3,400,000	$3,100,000	$ 300,000
Current liabilities	$ 520,000	$ 750,000	$(230,000)
10% debentures	800,000	600,000	200,000
Common stock	1,000,000	900,000	100,000
Retained earnings	900,000	700,000	200,000
Noncontrolling interest	180,000	150,000	30,000
	$3,400,000	$3,100,000	$ 300,000

COMBINED INCOME AND RETAINED EARNINGS STATEMENT
for the Year Ended December 31, Year 6

Sales	$2,500,000
Cost of goods sold	1,140,000
Depreciation expense	440,000
Administration expenses	375,000
	1,955,000
Net operating income	545,000
Investment income from Run	35,000
Total net income	580,000
Less: noncontrolling interest	80,000
Consolidated net income	500,000
Retained earnings at January 1, Year 6	700,000
	1,200,000
Dividends declared and paid	300,000
Retained earnings at December 31, Year 6	$ 900,000

The questions are based on Print's consolidated cash flow statement for the year ended December 31, Year 6.

1. Which of the following would be shown as an adjustment to Print's consolidated net income for investment income from Run?
   a. $0
   b. +$25,000
   c. +$35,000
   d. −$35,000

2. Which of the following would be shown as an adjustment to Print's consolidated net income for noncontrolling interest on the consolidated income statement?
   a. −$80,000
   b. −$30,000
   c. +$30,000
   d. +$80,000

3. Which of the following is the correct disclosure for the change in property, plant, and equipment in the investing section of Print's consolidated cash flow statement for the year ended December 31, Year 6?

    a. Purchase of property, plant, and equipment, –$370,000.

    b. Purchase of property, plant, and equipment, –$810,000.

    c. Proceeds from sale of property, plant, and equipment, +$370,000.

    d. Proceeds from sale of property, plant, and equipment, +810,000.

4. Print classifies all dividend payments to and received from affiliated corporations as financing activities, along with its own dividend payments. Which of the following is the correct amount that must be disclosed for dividends paid to noncontrolling interests on Print's consolidated cash flow statement for the year ended December 31, Year 6?

    a. $10,000

    b. $50,000

    c. $60,000

    d. $240,000

5. Which of the following is the correct amount that must be disclosed for dividends received from Run on Print's consolidated cash flow statement for the year ended December 31, Year 6?

    a. $0

    b. +$10,000

    c. +$30,000

    d. +$40,000

6. Which of the following best describes the disclosure required on the cash flow statement in the year a parent corporation acquires a controlling interest in a subsidiary corporation?

    a. The net investment should be presented as an operating activity.

    b. The net assets acquired, other than cash and cash equivalents, should be presented as an investing activity, and the method of financing the acquisition should be presented separately.

    c. The working capital assets acquired, other than cash and cash equivalents, should be presented as an operating activity, the long-term assets acquired should be presented as an investing activity, and the financing acquired should be presented as a financing activity.

    d. The net increase in the investment account should be presented as an investing activity, and no other disclosure is required.

7. For which of the following situations would it be appropriate to prepare a consolidated statement for VAN, COU and VER?

    a. VAN owns 60% of COU and COU owns 40% of VER.

    b. VAN owns 40% of COU and COU owns 60% of VER.

    c. VAN owns 20% of COU and 40% of VER and COU owns 60% of VER.

    d. VAN owns 60% of COU, COU owns 40% of VER and VER owns 60% of VAN.

(CGA-Canada, from 2002 to 2007)

8. For which of the following situations would the subsidiary's assets and liabilities be valued at 100% of their fair value on the consolidated balance sheet?

    a. When the parent purchased additional shares of the subsidiary to increase its percentage ownership from 40% to 60%.

    b. When the parent purchased additional shares of the subsidiary to increase its percentage ownership from 60% to 80%.

    c. When the parent sold shares of the subsidiary to decrease its percentage ownership from 90% to 60%.

    d. All of the above.

Use the following information to answer Questions 9 to 14.

Pot Inc. acquired an 80% interest in the common shares of Shot Inc. on July 1, Year 5, for $264,000. The equity sections of Pot and Shot at December 31, Year 4, were as follows:

	Pot	Shot
Common shares	$400,000	$200,000
Preferred shares (10,000 8% shares redeemable at $13 each)	—	100,000
Retained earnings	70,000	60,000
	$470,000	$360,000

Additional Information
- The after-tax net income of Shot for Year 5 amounted to $60,000 and was earned evenly throughout the year.
- The preferred shares are cumulative and nonvoting.
- Dividends on the preferred shares are payable on June 30 and December 31 each year. Dividends were 2 years in arrears at December 31, Year 4, and were not paid on June 30, Year 5.

For Questions 9 to 12, assume Pot did not purchase any of Shot's preferred shares on July 1, Year 5.

9. When Pot Inc. calculates goodwill arising from its purchase of Shot Inc., which of the following represents the claim of the preferred shareholders on Shot's net asset position for dividends in arrears?
   a. $0
   b. $4,000
   c. $16,000
   d. $20,000

10. When Pot Inc. calculates goodwill arising from its purchase of Shot Inc., which of the following represents the claim of the preferred shareholders at redemption (other than dividends in arrears) on Shot's net asset position?
    a. $80,000
    b. $100,000
    c. $108,000
    d. $10,000

11. When Pot Inc. consolidates Shot Inc. immediately after acquisition, what amount will be disclosed as noncontrolling interest related to common shares?
    a. $48,000
    b. $52,000
    c. $58,000
    d. $66,000

12. When Pot Inc. consolidates Shot Inc. immediately after acquisition, what amount will be disclosed as noncontrolling interest related to preferred shares?
    a. $100,000
    b. $120,000
    c. $150,000
    d. $160,000

For Questions 13 and 14, assume that on July 1, Year 5, Pot purchases 40% of Shot's preferred shares in addition to the 80% of common shares. Pot pays an additional $40,000 for these shares.

13. Which method will be used to report the investment in preferred shares on Pot's separate entity financial statements?
    a. Cost.
    b. Equity.
    c. Modified equity.
    d. Consolidation.

14. On December 31, Year 5, Shot pays $24,000 in dividends to preferred shareholders. What amount will Pot disclose as dividend revenue from preferred shares on its consolidated income statement for the year ended December 31, Year 5?
    a. $0
    b. $1,600
    c. $3,200
    d. $9,600

Use the following information to answer Questions 15 to 19.

On August 31, Year 6, Plow Inc. purchased 75% of the outstanding common shares of Share Inc. for $750,000. At January 1, Year 6, Share had common shares of $500,000 and retained earnings of $240,000. At the date of acquisition, plant and equipment on Share's books was undervalued by $40,000. This plant had a remaining useful life of 5 years. The balance of the purchase discrepancy was allocated to unrecorded trademarks of Share to be amortized over a 10-year period. Net income for Year 6 was $90,000, earned evenly throughout the year. On December 15, Year 6, Share declared and paid dividends of $10,000.

On December 31, Year 6, Plow sold 20% of its 75% interest in Share for $160,000.

15. What is the amount of the gain or loss that will arise from Plow's disposition of Share at December 31, Year 6?
    a. $8,200
    b. $8,700
    c. $10,000
    d. $46,150

16. Which one of the following is the correct amount of trademarks that should appear on Plow's consolidated statements at December 31, Year 6 (assuming Share is Plow's only subsidiary)?
    a. $92,800
    b. $108,000
    c. $123,733
    d. $154,667

17. What percentage of Share does Plow own after the disposition?
    a. 55%
    b. 60%
    c. 67.5%
    d. 85%

18. What is the amount of the unamortized purchase discrepancy related to plant and equipment on the consolidated balance sheet at December 31, Year 6?
    a. $24,000
    b. $28,000

c. $32,000

d. $37,333

19. How will the gain or loss from partial disposition of ownership in Share be disclosed on Plow's consolidated financial statements at December 31, Year 6?
    a. It will not appear on the consolidated financial statements.
    b. It will appear in the notes only.
    c. It will appear in the retained earnings section of the consolidated balance sheet.
    d. It will appear on the consolidated income statement.

20. On January 1, 2003, PEAL Corporation acquired 60 percent of the common shares of SEAL Inc. for $1,000,000. On that date, the fair value of land owned by SEAL was $200,000 greater than its carrying value. On December 31, Year 5, the fair value of the land was $300,000 greater than its carrying value. Which of the following transactions on December 31, Year 5, would cause an increase in the value assigned to land on the consolidated balance sheet?
    a. SEAL sells the land to PEAL at its fair value.
    b. SEAL sells the land to one of PEAL's other subsidiaries at its fair value.
    c. SEAL sells the land to an unrelated party at its fair value.
    d. PEAL repurchases an additional 20% of SEAL's shares.

(CGA-Canada, from 2002 to 2007)

CASES

Case 1 For the past 10 years, Prince Company (Prince) has owned 75,000 or 75 percent of the common shares of Stiff Inc. (Stiff). Mrs. Winer owns another 20 percent and the other 5 percent are widely held. Although Prince has the controlling interest, you would never know it during the annual shareholders' meetings. Mrs. Winer keeps the board of directors on its toes by asking a lot of tough questions and continuously threatening legal action if her rights as a minority shareholder are not protected.

Mr. Impatient owns 100 percent of the shares of Prince. After Prince's latest shareholders' meeting, he decided that Prince would offer to purchase Mrs. Winer's shares in Stiff or Prince would sell its interest in Stiff as he was tired of all of the heckling from Mrs. Winer. The shares of Stiff were recently trading for $100 per share.

On November 13, Year 13, Prince offered to pay $110 per share to Mrs. Winer for her 20 percent interest in Stiff. To Mr. Impatient's surprise, Mrs. Winer accepted the offer and the transaction was consummated on December 31, Year 13. On the closing date, the shares of Stiff had a book value of $70 per share and all identifiable net assets had a fair value equal to book value except for unrecognized patents, which had a fair value of $1.3 million and an estimated useful life of 4 years.

The CFO of Prince wants to recognize the entire purchase price discrepancy as goodwill in order to minimize the impact on earnings for Years 13 and 14. The controller, on the other hand, believes that some of the purchase price discrepancy should be charged to income in Year 13 as a loss because of the excessive price paid for the shares.

Required:

How would you resolve the dispute? Provide the arguments to support your position and indicate the impact of your decision on consolidated net income for Years 13 and 14. State your assumptions.

Case 2   Traveller Bus Lines Inc. (TBL) is a wholly owned subsidiary of Canada Transport Enterprises Inc. (CTE). CTE is a publicly traded transportation and communications conglomerate. TBL is primarily in the business of operating buses over short and long-distance routes in central and western Canada and the United States. TBL also has a school bus division operating in Eastern Canada. CTE and its subsidiaries are audited by DeBoy Shoot, which issued an unqualified audit opinion on CTE's June 30 year-end consolidated financial statements. This was the only audit opinion issued on the CTE group of companies. TBL has a July 31 year-end. It is now September 8, Year 7. CTE has been reporting operating losses for several years and has put TBL up for sale as part of a strategy to change its focus. This is the first of several planned divestitures, designed to restore CTE's lacklustre stock price.

Currently, the only interested party is an employee group led by TBL's president, Dan "Driver" Williams. Williams' management buy-out team consists of the vice-president of operations and the chief financial officer. Handling the negotiations at CTE's corporate office is Andrew Joel, vice-president of strategic divestitures.

The buy-out team has submitted the first draft agreement of purchase and sale for review. Exhibit I contains extracts from the draft agreement; notes made by CTE's lawyer are shown in italics. You, a CA at Heatley Dan LLP, have gathered some additional background information (Exhibit II).

Andrew wants to maximize the total selling price. He asked the partner in charge of the advisory services at Heatley Dan LLP to review the information given and provide recommendations on how CTE can maximize the total selling price and how the agreement should be changed to minimize possible disputes in the future. In addition, he would like a summary of the accounting issues of significance to CTE that will arise on the sale of TBL. The partner has asked you to prepare the draft report to Andrew.

Required:

Prepare the draft report.

(CICA adapted)

EXHIBIT I

EXTRACTS OF DRAFT PURCHASE AND SALE AGREEMENT

Agreement of purchase and sale between the employee group (hereinafter the Purchaser) and Canada Transport Enterprises Inc. (hereinafter CTE) for the assets and liabilities of the business known as Traveller Bus Lines Inc. (TBL)

1. The assets and liabilities of TBL are those included in its draft July 31, Year 7, financial statements.
2. Excluded from the liabilities to be assumed by the purchaser are all environmental liabilities including, but not limited to, gasoline and diesel fuel spills and tank leakage, pesticide residues, and all other chemical contamination.
3. The purchase price is determined by the sum of: (A) the book value of the net assets at July 31, Year 7, which is twelve million dollars, ($12 million), plus (B) 55% of the net reported income after taxes, for the twelve month period ending July 31, Year 8 (the contingent consideration). *Lawyer's Note — The contingent consideration should be worth at least $3.6 million since the division's earnings computed on this basis have averaged more than $6.6 million for the last four years before deducting head office charges.*
4. This agreement is conditional on the Purchaser obtaining adequate financing and, after inspection, finding TBL's records satisfactory.
5. CTE agrees not to compete with the Purchaser for 10 years.
6. CTE will provide a loan guarantee for up to 25% of the purchase price for the Purchaser.

7. The Purchaser agrees to provide full maintenance services to the truck and trailer fleet of one of CTE's other subsidiaries for five years. Charges will be based on cost plus 10%.

8. The central bus station will be restored by CTE to its original condition by December 31, Year 7.

9. CTE will provide free advertising to the Purchaser, on request, for one year following the closing date. The Purchaser will create all the advertising material, including TV commercials.

10. All bus route rights will be assigned to the Purchaser.

11. The purchase price will be allocated based on book values.

12. The sale will close on October 1, Year 7, at 12:01 a.m., and the entire consideration with the exception of the contingent consideration will be due and payable one (1) month after closing. The contingent consideration is due one (1) month after the July 31, Year 8, financial statements are finalized.

13. Overdue amounts will be charged interest at a rate of 11% per annum.

14. CTE will act in a consulting capacity to advise the Purchaser for a fee of $25,000 per annum.

EXHIBIT II

INFORMATION GATHERED

1. Exclusive rights to most bus routes were obtained almost 40 years ago when the provincial governments were handing out the routes at no cost to the local bus lines. They had no competition at that time. Other similar bus routes were subsequently purchased for significant amounts.

2. TBL's summary draft financial statements for July 31, Year 7, are as follows (in thousands of dollars):

Revenue	$48,123
Expenses (including $2,403 of head office charges)	40,239
Income before income taxes	7,884
Current taxes	2,995
Future taxes	567
Net income	$ 4,322
Current assets	$14,133
Long-term assets	25,131
Liabilities	(21,264)
Future taxes	(6,000)
Equity	$12,000

3. The TBL Maintenance Department has recently completed a study that demonstrated that the school buses would last 15 years rather than the 10 years on which the straight-line depreciation rates have always been based.

4. All school boards pay a non-refundable deposit, three months before the beginning of the school year in September, to guarantee bus service for the coming school year.

5. TBL ran a "Travel the Country" promotion in June Year 7. Sales of the three-month passes for unlimited travel, costing $400, were brisk. The driver punches the passes each time the holders take a trip. To compensate travellers who use their passes fewer than 10 times in the three-month period, TBL permits them to trade in their passes for either a pair of skis or a pair of in-line skates or the cash value of these items ($150).

6. CTE's consolidation entries for Year 7 related to TBL are a fair value increment of $432,300 for capital assets and $2,332,000 for goodwill, which is being amortized for 27 more years.

7. Included in TBL's long-term assets is a note receivable for $3.1 million, secured by the real property of a chain of four gas stations. Because of fierce competition from stations owned by the large oil companies, the value of the properties has declined from $4.2 million, the amount stated in the May Year 6 appraisal, to $2.4 million, according to the May Year 7 appraisal released on July 22, Year 7. The payments on the note are being made on schedule.

8. On August 18, Year 7, the Panamee School District announced the cancellation of all school bus services previously contracted for Year 7/8 in the school district.

9. The management buyout team plans to spend $500,000 on TV advertisements that promote bus travel in a national advertising campaign starting in early Year 8. The team also plans to retrofit all long-distance buses at substantial cost.

10. TBL moved all maintenance operations to a new facility in June Year 7. The building was purchased for $3.4 million, and the company had to vacate a leased facility 18 months before the end of the lease. The prospects of sub-letting the facility do not look good.

PROBLEMS

Problem 1   The following Year 1 consolidated statement was prepared for Standard Manufacturing Corp. and its 60%-owned subsidiary, Pritchard Windows Inc.:

STANDARD MANUFACTURING CORP.
CONSOLIDATED STATEMENT OF CASH FLOWS
for the Year Ended December 31, Year 1

Cash flows from operating activities:		
Consolidated net income	120,000	
Noncash items included in income		
Depreciation	45,200	
Goodwill impairment loss	1,000	
Bond premium amortization	(2,000)	
Noncontrolling interest	9,800	
Loss on sale of equipment	23,000	
Decrease in inventory	20,000	
Increase in accounts receivable	(12,000)	
Net cash provided by operating activities		$205,000
Cash flows from investing activities		
Purchase of buildings	(150,000)	
Sale of equipment	60,000	
Net cash used in investing activities		(90,000)
Cash flows from financing activities		
Dividends paid		
To Standard shareholders	(50,000)	
To noncontrolling shareholders	(6,000)	
Bond issue	100,000	
Preferred share redemption	(120,000)	
Net cash used in financing activities		(76,000)
Net increase in cash		39,000
Cash balance, January 1		50,000
Cash balance, December 31		$ 89,000

Required:

(a) Did the loss on the sale of equipment shown above result from a sale to an affiliate or a nonaffiliate? Explain.

(b) Explain why the amortization of bond premium is treated as a deduction from net income in arriving at net cash flow from operations.

(c) Determine the net income of Pritchard Windows for Year 1 (assume no intercompany transactions or unrealized profits and that the only change in the unamortized purchase discrepancy during the year was the goodwill impairment loss.).

(d) Explain why dividends to noncontrolling shareholders are not shown as a dividend in the consolidated retained earnings statement but are shown as a distribution of cash in the consolidated cash flow statement.

(e) Determine the amount of dividends paid by Pritchard Windows in Year 1.

Problem 2   Financial statements of Par Corp. and its subsidiary Star Inc. on December 31, Year 12, are shown below:

BALANCE SHEETS
at December 31, Year 12

	Par	Star
Cash	$ 40,000	$ 1,000
Accounts receivable	100,000	85,000
Inventories	55,000	48,000
Land	30,000	70,000
Plant and equipment	400,000	700,000
Accumulated depreciation	(180,000)	(300,000)
Investment in Star common shares	280,000	—
	$725,000	$604,000
Accounts payable	$ 92,000	$180,000
Accrued liabilities	8,000	10,000
Preferred shares	—	50,000
Common shares	450,000	200,000
Retained earnings	175,000	164,000
	$725,000	$604,000

RETAINED EARNINGS STATEMENTS
for the Year Ended December 31, Year 12

	Par	Star
Balance, January 1	$180,000	$208,000
Net income (loss)	30,000	(24,000)
	210,000	184,000
Dividends	35,000	20,000
Balance, December 31	$175,000	$164,000

Other Information

- On January 1, Year 5, the balance sheet of Star showed the following shareholders' equity:

$8 cumulative preferred stock, 500 shares issued	$ 50,000
Common stock, 2,000 shares issued	200,000
Deficit [note 1]	(80,000)
	$170,000

Note 1: Dividends on preferred shares are two years in arrears.

On this date, Par acquired 1,400 common shares of Star for a cash payment of $280,000.

The fair values of Star's identifiable net assets differed from carrying values only with respect to the following:

	Carrying amount	Fair value
Accounts receivable	$ 42,000	$ 40,000
Inventory	65,000	72,000
Plant	600,000	650,000
Long-term liabilities	400,000	420,000

The plant had an estimated remaining life of 5 years on this date, and the long-term liabilities had a maturity date of December 30, Year 12. Any goodwill is to be tested annually for impairment.

- Both Par and Star make substantial sales to each other at an intercompany selling price that yields the same gross profit as the sales they make to unrelated customers. Intercompany sales in Year 12 were:

Par to Star	$400,000
Star to Par	330,000

- During Year 12, Par billed Star $2,000 per month in management fees. At year-end, Star has not remitted the December billing to Par.
- The January 1, Year 12, inventories of the two companies contained unrealized intercompany profits as follows:

Inventory of Par	$30,000
Inventory of Star	21,000

- The December 31, Year 12, inventories of the two companies contained unrealized intercompany profits as follows:

Inventory of Par	$35,000
Inventory of Star	37,000

- On July 1, Year 7, Star sold equipment to Par for $82,000. The equipment had a carrying value in the records of Star of $60,000 on this date and an estimated remaining life of 5 years.
- Goodwill impairment losses were recorded as follows: Year 7, $92,500; Year 9, $46,470; and Year 12, $19,710.
- Assume a 40% corporate tax rate.
- Par has accounted for its investment in Star by the cost method.
- All dividends in arrears were paid by December 31, Year 11.

Required:

PART A

Prepare, with all necessary calculations, the following:
(a) The Year 12 consolidated retained earnings statement.
(b) The consolidated balance sheet as at December 31, Year 12.

PART B

How would consolidated net income for Year 12 change if Star's preferred shares were non-cumulative instead of cumulative?

PART C

On January 1, Year 13, Star issued common shares for $100,000 in cash. Because Par did not purchase any of these shares, Par's ownership percentage declined from 70% to 56%.

Calculate the gain or loss that would appear on the Year 13 consolidated income statement as a result of this transaction.

Problem 3

On December 31, Year 5, the accountant of Regent Corporation prepared a reconciliation (see below), which was used in the preparation of the consolidated financial statements on that date.

Investment in Argyle Ltd. — equity method balance		$315,000
Shareholders' equity of Argyle		
8,000 common shares	50,000	
Retained earnings	175,000	
	225,000	
Regent's ownership	90%	202,500
Regent's share of unamortized purchase discrepancy		112,500
NCI's share of unamortized purchase discrepancy		12,500
Total unamortized purchase discrepancy		$125,000
Allocated: Land		$ 28,333
Equipment — remaining life 8 years		44,444
Trademarks — remaining life 10 years		52,223
		$125,000

Other Information

- On December 31, Year 6, Argyle reported a net income of $50,000 (earned evenly throughout the year) and declared dividends of $20,000.
- On April 1, Year 6, Argyle issued an additional 2,000 common shares at a price of $75 each. Regent did not acquire any of these shares.
- On October 1, Year 6, because the market price of Argyle's common shares had fallen, Regent purchased 1,300 shares of Argyle on the open market at $60 per share. The decline in value is not believed to be permanent. Any purchase discrepancy was allocated 20% to land, 35% to equipment and 45% to trademark.

Required:

(a) Calculate the equity method balance in the investment in Argyle account on December 31, Year 6.
(b) Calculate the balance of the unamortized purchase discrepancy, and its allocation, as at December 31, Year 6. Assume that Regent had purchased its 90% interest in one block acquisition on January 1, Year 2.

Problem 4

The comparative consolidated balance sheets at December 31, Year 2, and the consolidated income statement for Year 2, of Parent Ltd. and its 70%-owned subsidiary are shown below.

	Year 2	Year 1
Cash	$ 810,000	$ 335,000
Accounts receivable	600,000	710,000
Inventory	989,500	490,000
Plant and equipment	5,350,000	5,100,000
Accumulated depreciation	(2,350,000)	(1,980,000)
Goodwill	530,000	565,000
	$5,929,500	$5,220,000

Current liabilities	$ 598,400	$1,300,000
Long-term liabilities	3,100,000	2,600,000
Capital stock	800,000	800,000
Retained earnings	916,000	520,000
Noncontrolling interest	515,000	—
	$5,929,500	$5,220,000

Revenues	$8,500,000
Gain on sale of investment in Sub	123,500
	8,623,500
Cost of sales and expenses	7,680,100
Depreciation	370,000
Goodwill impairment loss	35,000
	8,085,100
Net income—entity	538,400
Noncontrolling interest	38,400
Net income	$ 500,000

Additional Information

- On December 31, Year 1, Parent owned 100% of Sub. On this date, the shareholders' equity of Sub amounted to $1,120,000 and the parent's unamortized purchase discrepancy of $565,000 was allocated entirely to the goodwill of Sub.
- On January 1, Year 2, Parent sold 30% of its shares of Sub for $629,000 cash and recorded a gain of $123,500 on the transaction. Parent uses the equity method to account for its investment.
- Parent paid $104,000 in dividends during Year 2.

Required:

Prepare in good form a consolidated cash flow statement for Year 2 in accordance with the requirements of the *CICA Handbook*.

Problem 5   On April 1, Year 7, Princeton Corp. purchased 70% of the common shares of Simon Ltd. for $910,000. On this same date, Simon purchased 60% of the common shares of Fraser Inc. for $600,000. On April 1, Year 7, the purchase discrepancies from the two investments were allocated entirely to broadcast rights to be amortized over 10 years. The cost method is being used to account for both investments.

During Year 7, the three companies sold merchandise to each other. On December 31, Year 7, the inventory of Princeton contained merchandise on which Simon recorded a profit of $32,000. On the same date, the inventory of Fraser contained merchandise on which Princeton recorded a profit of $18,000. (Assume a 40% tax rate.)

The following information is available:

	Princeton	Simon	Fraser
Common shares	$600,000	$550,000	$300,000
Retained earnings — Jan. 1, Year 7	650,000	400,000	300,000
Net income — Year 7*	100,000	200,000	150,000
Dividends declared — Dec. 31	25,000	30,000	70,000

* Earned evenly throughout the year.

Required:

Calculate the following:

(a) Consolidated net income — Year 7.

(b) Noncontrolling interest as at December 31, Year 7.

(c) Consolidated broadcast rights as at December 31, Year 7.

Problem 6   On January 1, Year 5, PET Company acquired 800 shares of SET Company's common stock for $56,000. On this date, the shareholders' equity accounts of SET Company were:

Common shares (1,000 no par value shares issued)	$20,000
Preferred shares (4,000 no par value shares issued) (Note 1)	40,000
Retained earnings	30,000
	$90,000

Note 1 — The preferred shares are $1, cumulative, nonparticipating with a liquidation value of 1.05. They were two years in arrears on January 1, Year 5.

The following are the statements of retained earnings for the two companies for Year 5:

	PET	SET
Retained earnings, beginning of year	$50,000	$30,000
Net income	30,000	20,000
Dividends	(25,000)	(15,000)
Retained earnings, end of year	$55,000	$35,000

Additional Information

- PET uses the cost method to account for its investment in SET.
- Any purchase discrepancy is allocated to patents with an estimated useful life of 6 years as at January 1, Year 5. Neither company has any patents recorded on their separate-entity records.

Required:

(a) Prepare a consolidated statement of retained earnings for Year 5.

(b) Prepare an independent calculation of retained earnings at the end of Year 5.

(c) Calculate noncontrolling interest for the consolidated income statement for Year 5 and noncontrolling interest for the consolidated balance sheet at the end of Year 5.

Problem 7   On January 1, Year 8, Summer Company's shareholders' equity was as follows:

Common shares	$20,000
Retained earnings	70,000
	$90,000

Plumber Company held 90% of the 4,000 outstanding shares of Summer on January 1, Year 8, and its investment in Summer Company account had a balance of $126,000 on that date. Plumber accounts for its investment by the equity method. Any purchase difference was allocated to unrecorded trademarks with a remaining life on January 1, Year 8, of 10 years.

The following events took place subsequent to January 1, Year 8:

- On July 1, Year 8, Plumber sold 720 of the Summer Company shares it held at a price of $30 per share.

- During Year 8, Summer reported a net income of $20,000 (earned equally throughout the year) and declared dividends of $5,000 on December 31.
- During Year 9, Summer reported a net income of $28,000 and paid dividends of $8,000 on November 15.
- On December 29, Year 9, Summer issued an additional 500 shares to third parties at a price of $46 per share.

Required:

(a) Calculate the gain or loss in Year 8 and Year 9 as a result of the ownership change that took place each year.
(b) Would the gain or loss appear on the consolidated income statement each year? Explain.
(c) Calculate the consolidated trademarks as at December 31, Year 9.
(d) Does the value for the trademarks on the consolidated balance sheet as calculated in part (c) comply with the historical cost principle? Explain.

Problem 8   The accountant of Consolidated Enterprises has just finished preparing the consolidated balance sheet, income statement, and retained earnings statement for Year 2, and has asked you for assistance in preparing the consolidated cash flow statement. Consolidated has only one subsidiary, which is 80% owned, and in addition has a long-term investment of 45% of the outstanding shares of Pacific Finance Co.

The following items have been prepared from the analysis of the Year 2 consolidated statements:

Decrease in accounts receivable	$ 23,000
Increase in accounts payable	5,000
Increase in inventory	15,000
Equity earnings from Pacific Finance	90,000
Increase in bonds payable	120,000
Building purchased for cash	580,000
Depreciation reported for current period	73,000
Gain recorded on sale of equipment	8,000
Carrying value of equipment sold	37,000
Goodwill impairment loss	3,000
Dividends received from Pacific Finance	25,000
Consolidated net income for the year	450,000
Entity net income allocated to noncontrolling interest	14,000
Dividends paid by parent company	60,000
Dividends paid by subsidiary company	30,000
Cash balance, January 1, Year 2	42,000

Required:

Prepare the consolidated cash flow statement.

Problem 9   Parent Co. owns 9,500 shares of Sub Co. and accounts for its investment by the equity method. On December 31, Year 5, the shareholders' equity of Sub was as follows:

Common shares (10,000 shares issued)	$100,000
Retained earnings	170,000

On January 1, Year 6, Parent sold 1,900 shares from its holdings in Sub for $66,500. On this date and prior to the sale, the balance in the investment in Sub account was $320,000, and the unamortized purchase discrepancy was allocated in the following manner:

35% to land
40% to equipment (remaining life 4 years)
25% to patents (remaining life 10 years)

During Year 6, Sub reported a net income of $150,000 and paid dividends totalling $70,000.

Required:

PART A

(a) Prepare the journal entry that Parent would make on January 1, Year 6, to record the sale of the 1,900 shares.
(b) Calculate the amount of the unamortized purchase discrepancy that would be allocated to land, equipment, and patents on December 31, Year 6.
(c) Prepare an independent proof of the unamortized purchase discrepancy on December 31, Year 6.

PART B

The accountant of Parent is going to prepare a consolidated cash flow statement for Year 6 by analyzing the changes in the consolidated balance sheets from December 31, Year 5, to December 31, Year 6. She needs some assistance in determining what effect Parent's sale of 1,900 shares had on the consolidated financial statements.

Prepare a journal entry to record the effect that the January 1, Year 6, sale of shares had on the consolidated entity.

Problem 10 On January 1, Year 5, Pic Company acquired 7,500 shares of Sic Company's common stock for $600,000. On January 1, Year 6, Pic Company acquired an additional 2,000 shares of Sic Company's common stock for $166,000. On January 1, Year 5, the shareholders' equity of Sic was:

Common shares (10,000 no par value shares issued)	$200,000
Retained earnings	300,000
	$500,000

The following are the statements of retained earnings for the two companies for Years 5 and 6:

	Pic		Sic	
	Year 5	Year 6	Year 5	Year 6
Retained earnings, beginning of year	$500,000	$530,000	$300,000	$310,000
Net income	130,000	140,000	100,000	110,000
Dividends	(100,000)	(120,000)	(90,000)	(90,000)
Retained earnings, end of year	$530,000	$550,000	$310,000	$330,000

Additional Information
- Pic uses the cost method to account for its investment in Sic.
- Any purchase discrepancy is allocated to patents with a life expectancy until December 31, Year 9. Neither company has any patents recorded on their separate-entity records.
- There were no unrealized profits from intercompany transactions since the date of acquisition.

Required:
a. Calculate consolidated net income for Year 6.

b. Calculate the following account balances for the consolidated balance sheet at December 31, Year 6:
   i.   Patents
   ii. Noncontrolling interest
   iii. Retained earnings

Problem 11 Intercompany shareholdings of an affiliated group during the year ended December 31, Year 2, were as follows:

York Ltd.	Queen's Company	McGill Company
90% of Queen's Company	70% of Carleton Ltd.	60% of Trent Ltd.
80% of McGill Company	10% of McGill Company	

The equity method is being used for intercompany investments, but no entries have been made in Year 2. The net incomes before equity method earnings for Year 2 were as follows:

	Net income
York Ltd.	$54,000
Queen's Company	22,000
McGill Company	26,700
Carleton Ltd.	15,400
Trent Ltd.	11,600

Intercompany profits before taxes in the December 31, Year 2, inventories and the affiliated companies involved were:

Selling corporation	Profit made by selling corporation
York Ltd.	$10,000
McGill Company	1,000
Carleton Ltd.	2,400

Use income tax allocation at a 40% rate. Assume that there is no purchase discrepancy for any of the intercompany shareholdings.

Required:

(a) Calculate consolidated net income for Year 2.
(b) Calculate the amount of noncontrolling interest in subsidiary net income that would appear on the Year 2 consolidated income statement.
(c) Will the consolidation adjustment for unrealized profits be any different if McGill Company sold inventory to Carleton Ltd. or York Ltd.? Use the revenue recognition principle to explain your answer.

Problem 12 Craft Ltd. held 80% of the outstanding common shares of Delta Corp. as at December 30, Year 12. Balance sheets for the two companies on that date appear on the next page.

In order to establish a closer relationship with Nonaffiliated Corporation, a major supplier to both Craft and Delta, all three companies agreed that Nonaffiliated would take an equity position in Delta. Accordingly, for a cash payment of $30 per share, Delta issued 6,125 additional common shares to Nonaffiliated on December 31, Year 12. This was the only transaction that occurred on this date.

CRAFT LTD.
BALANCE SHEET
at December 30, Year 12

Cash	$ 50,000	Accounts payable	$ 70,000
Accounts receivable	90,000	Mortgage payable	250,000
Inventory	180,000	Common shares	480,000
Buildings and equipment (net)	600,000	Retained earnings	610,000
Investment in Delta	490,000		
	$1,410,000		$1,410,000

DELTA CORP.
BALANCE SHEET
at December 30, Year 12

Cash	$ 65,000	Accounts payable	$100,000
Accounts receivable	120,000	Accrued liabilities	85,000
Inventory	200,000	Common shares [note]	250,000
Buildings and equipment (net)	400,000	Retained earnings	350,000
	$785,000		$785,000

Note: 24,500 common shares outstanding on December 30, Year 12.

Other Information

- Craft has used the equity method of accounting for its investment in Delta since it acquired its 80% interest in Delta in Year 2. At that time, the purchase discrepancy was entirely allocated to inventory and patent which still exists but is not recorded on Delta's separate-entity books.
- There were no unrealized intercompany asset profits as at December 30, Year 12.

Required:

Prepare a consolidated balance sheet as at December 31, Year 12 (show calculation details for all items on the balance sheet).

Problem 13 A Company owns 75% of B Company and 40% of C Company. B Company owns 40% of C Company. The following information was assembled at December 31, Year 7.

	A Company	B Company	C Company
Cash	$ 117,800	$ 49,300	$ 20,000
Accounts receivable	200,000	100,000	44,000
Inventory	277,000	206,000	58,000
Investment in C	85,000	92,000	—
Investment in B	409,250	—	—
Property, plant, and equipment	2,800,000	1,500,000	220,000
Accumulated depreciation	(1,120,000)	(593,000)	(90,000)
	$2,769,050	$1,354,300	$252,000
Accounts payable	$ 206,000	$ 88,000	$ 2,000
Bonds payable	1,000,000	700,000	—
Preferred stock	—	50,000	—
Common stock	1,200,000	400,000	200,000
Retained earnings, January 1	314,250	61,000	30,000
Net income	118,800	55,300	20,000
Dividends	(70,000)	—	—
	$2,769,050	$1,354,300	$252,000

Other Information

- A Company purchased its 40% interest in C Company on January 1, Year 4. On that date, the negative purchase discrepancy of $10,000 on the 40% investment was allocated to equipment with an estimated life of 10 years.
- A Company purchased its 75% of B Company's common shares on January 1, Year 6. On that date, the 100% implied purchase discrepancy was allocated $40,000 to buildings with an estimated life of 20 years, and $53,333 to patents to be amortized over 8 years. The preferred shares of B Company are noncumulative.
- On January 1, Year 7, B Company purchased its 40% interest in C Company for $92,000. The book value of C Company's net assets approximated fair value on this date.
- The inventory of B Company contains a profit of $2,400 on merchandise purchased from A Company. The inventory of A Company contains a profit of $3,000 on merchandise purchased from C Company.
- On December 31, Year 7, A Company owes $20,000 to C Company and B Company owes $2,000 to A Company.
- Both A Company and B Company use the equity method to account for their investments but have made no equity method adjustments in Year 7.
- An income tax rate of 40% is used for consolidation purposes.

Required:

(a) Calculate noncontrolling interest in net income for Year 7.
(b) Prepare a consolidated statement of retained earnings for Year 7.
(c) Prepare a consolidated balance sheet on December 31, Year 7.
Show all calculations.

Problem 14   Parento Inc. owns 80% of Santana Corp. The consolidated financial statements of Parento are shown below:

PARENTO INC.
CONSOLIDATED BALANCE SHEET
December 31, Year 4

	Year 4	Year 3
Cash	$118,600	$ 49,800
Accounts receivable	115,000	126,000
Inventory	232,000	192,000
Land	86,000	114,000
Buildings and equipment	598,000	510,000
Accumulated depreciation	(205,000)	(168,000)
Databases	16,800	19,200
	$961,400	$843,000
Accounts payable	$ 54,400	$ 31,200
Accrued liabilities	7,200	27,000
Bonds payable	320,000	240,000
Bond premium	9,600	10,800
Common shares	180,000	180,000
Retained earnings	363,480	330,000
Noncontrolling interest	26,720	24,000
	$961,400	$843,000

PARENTO INC.
CONSOLIDATED INCOME STATEMENT
For the Year Ended December 31, Year 4

Sales		$360,000
Cost of sales	235,000	
Depreciation	37,000	
Interest expense	31,400	
Loss on land sale	2,000	
Database amortization	2,400	307,800
Net income — entity		52,200
Noncontrolling interest		4,320
Net income		$ 47,880

Parento Inc. purchased its 80% interest in Santana Corp. on January 1, Year 2, for $114,000 when Santana had net assets of $90,000. The purchase discrepancy was allocated $24,000 to databases (10-year life), with the balance allocated to equipment (20-year life).

Parento issued $80,000 in bonds on December 31, Year 4. Santana reported a net income of $24,000 for Year 4 and paid dividends of $8,000.

Parento reported a Year 4 equity method income of $47,880 and paid dividends of $14,400.

Required:

(a) Prepare a consolidated statement of cash flows for Year 4.
(b) Why are 100% of the dividends paid by Santana not shown as a cash outflow on the cash flow statement?

Problem 15   On January 1, Year 5, Wellington Inc. owned 90% of the outstanding common shares of Sussex Corp. Wellington accounts for its investment using the equity method. The balance in the investment account on January 1, Year 5, amounted to $235,800. The unamortized purchase discrepancy on this date was allocated entirely to vacant land held by Sussex.

The shareholders' equity of Sussex on January 1, Year 5, was as follows:

Common shares (7,200 shares outstanding)	$ 28,000
Retained earnings	134,000
	$162,000

The following events occurred in Year 5:
* The net income of Sussex for Year 5 amounted to $36,000, earned equally throughout the year.
* On April 1, Year 5, Sussex issued 1,800 shares at a price of $25 per share. Wellington did not acquire any of these shares.
* On June 30, Year 5, Sussex paid dividends amounting to $12,000.
* On September 15, Year 5, Sussex sold 30% of its vacant land at its own carrying value.
* On December 31, Year 5, Wellington sold 648 shares from its investment in Sussex for $22,000.

Required:

Calculate the following as at December 31, Year 5:
(a) The purchase discrepancy allocated to vacant land and the split in value between the parent and the NCI.
(b) The balance in the investment account using the equity method.
(c) The amount of noncontrolling interest.

Problem 16

On January 1, Year 8, Panet Company acquired 40,000 common shares of Saffer Corporation for $500,000. This purchase represented 8% of the outstanding shares of Saffer. It was the intention of Panet to acquire more shares in the future in order to eventually gain control of Saffer.

On January 1, Year 10, Panet purchased an additional 135,000 common shares of Saffer for $2,500,000. Saffer's shareholders' equity section was:

10% noncumulative preferred shares	$ 500,000
Common shares, no par value,	
500,000 shares outstanding	3,000,000
Retained earnings	2,700,000

On this date, the fair values of Saffer's assets were equal to book values, except for inventory, which was undervalued by $120,000, and land, which was undervalued by $1,000,000.

On January 1, Year 11, Panet purchased an additional 225,000 common shares of Saffer for $3,600,000. The shareholders' equity section for Saffer was:

10% noncumulative preferred shares	$ 500,000
Common shares, no par value,	
500,000 shares outstanding	3,000,000
Retained earnings	3,200,000

On January 1, Year 11, the fair values of Saffer's assets were equal to book values except for the following:

	Book value	Fair value
Accounts receivable	$ 200,000	$ 140,000
Plant and equip. (net)	10,000,000	10,900,000
Long-term liabilities	2,000,000	2,200,000

The plant and equipment had a remaining life of 20 years. The long-term liabilities mature on December 31, Year 20.

The balance sheets as at December 31, Year 12, and the income statements for the year ending December 31, Year 12, for the two companies are as follows:

BALANCE SHEET

	Panet	Saffer
Assets:		
Cash	$ 500,000	$ 200,000
Accounts receivable	2,400,000	300,000
Inventories	500,000	400,000
Plant and equipment (net)	10,000,000	9,000,000
Investment in Saffer (at cost)	6,600,000	—
Land	5,500,000	1,000,000
	$25,500,000	$10,900,000
Liabilities:		
Current liabilities	$ 3,000,000	$ 500,000
Long-term liabilities	4,000,000	2,000,000
	7,000,000	2,500,000
Shareholders' equity:		
10% noncumulative preferred shares	—	500,000
Common shares	9,000,000	3,000,000
Retained earnings	9,500,000	4,900,000
	18,500,000	8,400,000
Total liabilities and shareholders' equity	$25,500,000	$10,900,000

INCOME STATEMENT

	Panet	Saffer
Sales	$15,000,000	$9,000,000
Dividend revenue	120,000	—
	15,120,000	9,000,000
Cost of goods sold	9,500,000	6,200,000
Depreciation expense	2,500,000	530,000
Income tax	1,032,000	730,000
Other expenses	468,000	440,000
	13,500,000	7,900,000
Net Income	$ 1,620,000	$1,100,000

Additional Information

- Dividends declared and paid during Year 12:

Panet	$500,000
Saffer	200,000

- On January 1, Year 12, the inventory of Panet contained an $85,000 intercompany profit, and the inventory of Saffer contained an intercompany profit amounting to $190,000.
- During Year 12, Saffer sold inventory to Panet for $2,600,000 at a gross profit margin of 35%. Sales of $400,000 remained in Panet's inventory at December 31, Year 12.
- During Year 12, Panet sold inventory to Saffer for $3,900,000 at a gross profit margin of 45%. Sales of $250,000 remained in Saffer's inventory at December 31, Year 12.
- Saffer sold a piece of equipment to Panet on July 1, Year 12, for $450,000. At that time, the carrying value of the equipment in Saffer's books was $240,000, and it had a remaining life of 10.5 years. Panet still owes Saffer for 30% of the purchase price of the equipment. The gain on sale has been netted against other expenses in Saffer's Year 12 income statement.
- Both companies follow the straight-line method for depreciating fixed assets and premiums or discounts on long-term liabilities.
- A goodwill impairment loss of $92,000 was recorded in Year 11, and a further loss of $58,000 occurred in Year 12.
- Assume a 40% tax rate.

Required:

(a) Prepare the following Year 12 consolidated financial statements:
  (i) Income statement.
  (ii) Balance sheet.
(b) Calculate goodwill impairment loss and noncontrolling interest on the consolidated income statement for the year ended December 31, Year 12, under the parent company extension theory.
(c) Calculate goodwill and noncontrolling interest on the consolidated balance sheet at December 31, Year 12, under the parent company extension theory.

Problem 17   On December 31, Year 6, Ultra Software Limited purchased 70,000 common shares (70%) of a major competitor, Personal Program Corporation (PPC), at $30 per share. The remaining common and the preferred shares were owned by several shareholders who were unwilling to sell at that time.

The preferred shares, which are noncumulative, are entitled to a $12 dividend. Each is convertible into two shares of common stock. Immediate conversion of these preferred shares has been, and will continue to be, highly unlikely due to the current market conditions for the shares. Management is concerned, however, about the effect that any future conversion would have.

At December 31, Year 6, PPC's net assets had a book value of $1,525,000. The identifiable assets and liabilities had book values equal to fair values, with the following exceptions:

- Land, with a book value of $200,000, had a fair value of $295,000.
- Software patents and copyrights had a total market value estimated as $300,000 above book value. These were expected to have a 5-year life.
- Inventories of packaged software had a cost to PPC of $20,000 and an estimated selling price of $140,000. Estimated future selling expenses for these items were $15,000.
- An unrecorded brand name had an estimated fair value of $2,375,000. This will be amortized over 40 years.

The trial balances at December 31, Year 8, for these two companies are provided as Exhibit 9.8, which appears on page 457.

In Year 7, PPC sold packaged software costing $30,000 to Ultra at a price of $45,000. Of this software, 60% was still in Ultra's inventory at December 31, Year 7. During Year 8, packaged software costing $42,000 was sold by PPC to Ultra for $60,000. Ultra's inventory at December 31, Year 8, included $22,000 of goods purchased in this sale. Neither of these packaged software inventories sold to Ultra had a fair value difference at acquisition.

Included in the Year 8 income of PPC was a gain of $50,000 on the sale of patents to another company. This sale took place on June 30, Year 8. These patents had a fair value difference of $20,000 at acquisition.

On September 30, Year 8, Ultra sold surplus computer hardware to PPC. This equipment had a cost of $6,000,000, was one-half depreciated, and was sold for its fair value of $2,000,000. Disassembly and shipping costs of $80,000 were paid by Ultra. There was estimated to be a 9-year remaining life in its new use.

Preferred dividends were paid in all years, and no new shares have been issued since the acquisition date.

Assume a 40% tax rate.

Required:

PART A
In accordance with GAAP, prepare the following (assume a 40% tax rate):
(a) A consolidated income statement for the period ended December 31, Year 8.
(b) A consolidated statement of retained earnings for the period ended December 31, Year 8.
(c) A schedule showing the values of the following consolidated balance sheet accounts as at December 31, Year 8:
   (i)   Software patents and copyrights.
   (ii) Packaged software inventory.
   (iii) Noncontrolling interest.

PART B
Write a brief note to the management of Ultra in which you outline the financial reporting implications in the event that the preferred shareholders of PPC exercise their conversion privilege.

(Prepared by Peter Secord, St. Mary's University.)

Exhibit 9.8

TRIAL BALANCES
December 31, Year 8 ($000s)

	Ultra Software		Personal Program	
Cash	$ 320		$ 150	
Accounts receivable	300		280	
Inventory	350		380	
Patents and copyrights	350		450	
Furniture and equipment (net)	540		675	
Building (net)	800		925	
Land	450		200	
Investment in PPC	2,100		—	
Accounts payable		$ 340		$ 138
Mortgage payable		350		
Bank loan payable				320
Preferred shares (12,500 outstanding)				1,400
Common shares (300,000 outstanding)		3,000		
Common shares (100,000 outstanding)				100
Retained earnings		1,300		117
Sales		6,200		4,530
Other income		120		7
Gain on sale of patent				50
Loss on sale of computer	1,080			
Cost of sales	4,050		2,600	
Other expenses (incl. tax)	850		675	
Depreciation	75		142	
Interest	45		35	
Dividends			150	
	$11,310	$11,310	$6,662	$6,662

Problem 18

The summarized trial balances of Phase Limited and Step Limited as of December 31, Year 5, are as follows (amounts in thousands):

	Phase	Step
Current assets	$ 173	$ 89
Investment in Step	257	—
Property, plant, and equipment	540	298
Dividends declared	80	40
Cost of goods sold	610	260
Other expenses	190	55
	$1,850	$742
Liabilities	$ 88	$ 38
Capital stock	400	200
Retained earnings, beginning	360	104
Sales, gains, and other revenue	1,002	400
	$1,850	$742

Phase had acquired the investment in Step in three stages:

Date	Shares	Cost	Step retained earnings
Jan 1/Year 2	4,000	$ 50,700	$ 28,000
Jan 1/Year 4	6,000	98,300	69,000
Jan 1/Year 5	6,000	108,000	104,000

The January 1, Year 2, acquisition enabled Phase to elect 3 members to the 10-member board of directors of Step. The January 1, Year 4 acquisition did not give Phase control over Step. Any difference between cost and the underlying book value for each acquisition is attributable equally to land and to patents, which are expected to produce benefits until December 31, Year 11. Step had issued 20,000 shares of stock on July 1, Year 1, the date of incorporation, and has neither issued nor retired shares since that date. Other information follows:

- Sale of depreciable assets (6-year remaining life), from Phase to Step, on June 30, Year 5, at a gain of $60,000.
- Intercompany sales:

Year 4	Phase to Step	$50,000
	Step to Phase	20,000
Year 5	Phase to Step	80,000
	Step to Phase	10,000

- Opening inventory of Phase contained merchandise purchased from Step for $10,000. Company policy was for a 20% gross margin on intercompany sales. Ending inventory of Phase contained merchandise purchased from Step for $5,000. One-half of the goods sold intercompany during Year 5 had not been paid for by year-end.
- Assume a 40% tax rate.

Required:

Compute the following consolidated amounts as of December 31, Year 5:
(a) Patents.
(b) Property, plant, and equipment.
(c) Current assets (ignore deferred charges — income taxes).
(d) Noncontrolling interest on balance sheet.
(e) Retained earnings, beginning.
(f) Cost of goods sold.
(g) Net income (statement not required).

(Adapted from problem prepared by Peter Secord, St. Mary's University.)

Problem 19   On January 1, Year 3, Hoola Company purchased 60,000 shares of Soop Ltd. for $540,000. On January 1, Year 6, Hoola purchased another 30,000 shares of Soop for $420,000. During the entire period, Soop had a total of 100,000 shares outstanding. Hoola accounts for its investment in Soop using the equity method.

The following information was extracted from the financial records of Soop:

	January 1, Year 3	January 1, Year 6	December 31, Year 7
Net book value of patent	$110,000	$ 80,000	$ 60,000
Fair value of patent	165,000	240,000	240,000
Common shares	100,000	100,000	100,000
Retained earnings	400,000	550,000	710,000
Remaining useful life of patent in years	11	8	6

All net identifiable assets had a fair value equal to book value on the date of acquisition except for the patent. Any goodwill arising on the dates of acquisition has not been amortized. Furthermore, the annual tests for goodwill impairment have indicated no impairment of goodwill since the dates of acquisition. Hoola and Soop do not have any goodwill recorded on their own separate-entity balance sheets. Hoola does not have any patents on its own balance sheet.

There have not been any intercompany transactions between Hoola and Soop.

Required:

(a) Calculate the balances of the following accounts on the consolidated balance sheet at December 31, Year 7:
   (i)   patents
   (ii) goodwill
   (iii) noncontrolling interest
(b) Calculate the balance in the investment in Soop account at December 31, Year 7.
(c) On January 1, Year 8, Hoola sold 20,000 shares of Soop for $280,000 in cash. Prepare the journal entry for Hoola to record this sale.
(d) Calculate goodwill and noncontrolling interest on the consolidated balance sheet at December 31, Year 7 under the parent company extension theory.

(CGA-Canada, from 2002 to 2007)

10 **Other Consolidation Reporting Issues**

LEARNING OBJECTIVES

After studying this chapter, you should be able to do the following:

- Identify a variable interest entity and prepare consolidated statements for a primary beneficiary and its variable interest entity.
- Explain how the definitions of assets and liabilities can be used to support the consolidation of variable interest entities.
- Describe and apply the current accounting standards that govern the reporting of interests in joint ventures.
- Explain how the gain recognition principle supports the recognition of a portion of gains occurring on transactions between the venturer and the joint venture.
- Understand the future income tax implications to the accounting for a business combination.
- Describe the *Handbook*'s requirements for segment disclosures and apply the quantitative thresholds to determine reportable segments.

INTRODUCTION

In this chapter, we discuss some additional consolidation issues that were not previously covered. We will start by discussing situations where control exists through means other than share ownership. Then, we will examine the accounting for joint ventures. After that, we look at how *Handbook* Section 3465 on future income taxes affects the accounting for a business combination. This chapter concludes with the disclosure requirements associated with a company's business segments.

Variable Interest Entities

A variable interest entity is a type of special purpose entity that requires consolidation.

Special purpose entities (SPEs) have long been used by businesses as a vehicle to carry out specific activities. Until recently the only financial reporting involvement for a company establishing a SPE was the disclosure requirements regarding related party transactions. Now GAAP requires that some types of SPEs (described as variable interest entities) are subject to consolidation in the same manner as is a subsidiary.

For the past seven chapters, we have been preparing consolidated financial statements in situations where the parent company has control over the subsidiary company by owning the majority of the voting shares. We will now study situations where a special purpose entity (SPE) is subject to control on a basis other than ownership of voting interests.

What Is an SPE?

An SPE is an entity created to accomplish a very specific business activity.

An SPE is a proprietorship, partnership, corporation, or trust set up to accomplish a very specific and limited business activity. Over the past decade, SPEs have been used to lease manufacturing assets, hedge financial instruments, borrow against high-quality receivables, conduct research and development activities, and carry out a variety of other specified functions.

SPEs are often able to obtain debt financing at very favourable interest rates.

Low-cost financing of asset purchases is often a major benefit of establishing an SPE. Rather than engaging in the business transaction directly, the sponsoring business sets up an SPE to purchase and finance the asset acquisition. The SPE then leases the asset to the sponsor. This strategy saves the business money because the SPE is often eligible for a lower interest rate. This advantage is achieved for several reasons. First, the SPE typically operates with a very limited set of assets—in many cases just one asset. By isolating an asset in an SPE, the risk of the asset is isolated from the overall risk of the sponsoring firm. Thus, the SPE's creditors remain protected by the specific collateral in the asset. Second, the business activities of an SPE can be strictly limited by its governing documents. These limits further protect lenders by preventing the SPE from engaging in any activities not specified in its agreements.

Before GAAP was changed, many companies used SPEs as a vehicle for "off balance sheet financing."

Another apparent reason for establishing an SPE was to avoid the consolidation of the SPE with the sponsoring enterprise and thereby avoid having to show additional debt on the consolidated balance sheet. Because governing agreements limited the activities and decision making in most SPEs, the sponsoring enterprise was able to control the activities of the SPEs through the governing agreements. They did not have to own a majority of the voting stock to maintain control. In fact, a sponsoring enterprise usually owned very little, if any, of the voting stock of the SPE. Therefore, the sponsoring enterprise did not control the SPE through a voting interest and did not have to consolidate the SPE under the *Handbook* section on business combinations. Like all business entities, SPEs generally have assets, liabilities, and investors with equity interests. Unlike most businesses, the role of the equity investors can be fairly minor. They may serve simply as a technical requirement to allow the SPE to function as a legal entity. Because they bear relatively low economic risk, equity investors are typically provided only a small rate of return.

The risks and rewards are not distributed in accordance with equity ownership but rather with some other variable interest attaching to a sponsoring firm as a result of contractual arrangements.

The small equity investments normally are insufficient to induce lenders to provide a low-risk interest rate for the SPE. As a result, another party (often the sponsoring firm that benefits from the SPE's activities) must be prepared to contribute substantial resources to enable the SPE to secure additional financing needed to accomplish its purpose. For example, the sponsoring firm may guarantee the debt of the SPE. Other contractual arrangements may limit returns to equity holders while participation rights provide increased profit potential and risks to the sponsoring firm. Risks and rewards such as these cause the sponsor's economic interest to vary depending on the success of the created entity—hence the term variable interest entity. In contrast to a traditional entity, an SPE's risks and rewards are not distributed according to stock ownership, but according to other variable interests. Exhibit 10.1 provides several examples of variable interest entities.

A firm with variable interests in an SPE increases its risk with the level (or potential level in the case of a guarantee) of resources provided. With increased risks come

Exhibit 10.1

EXAMPLES OF VARIABLE INTERESTS

The following are some examples of variable interests and the related potential for losses or returns accruing to the sponsor:

Variable interests	*Potential losses or returns*
• Guarantees of debt	• If an SPE cannot repay liabilities, sponsor will pay and incur a loss.
• Subordinated debt instruments	• If an SPE cannot repay its senior debt, the sponsor as subordinated debt holder may be required to absorb the loss.
• Variable rate liability	• Sponsor as holder of debt may participate in returns of SPE.
• Lease residual guarantee	• If leased asset declines below the residual value, sponsor as lessee will make up the shortfall.
• Non-voting equity instruments	• Sponsor as holder of debt or equity may participate in residual profits.
• Services	• Sponsor as service provider receives portion of residual profits.

increased incentives to exert greater influence over the decision making of the SPE. In fact, a firm with variable interests will regularly limit the decision-making power of the equity investors through the governance documents that establish the SPE. Although, technically, the equity investors are the owners of the SPE, in reality they may retain little of the traditional responsibilities, risks, and benefits of ownership. In fact, the equity investors often cede financial control of the SPE to those with variable interest in exchange for a guaranteed rate of return.

The equity investors of an SPE typically receive a guaranteed rate of return as reward for ceding control to the SPE's sponsor.

Enron Corp. provided what was undoubtably the most famous example in recent memory of the improper use of SPEs. In the investigation of its bankruptcy, in which its creditors and employees lost an estimated $60 billion, the following questionable accounting practices came to light:

- not consolidating SPEs and thereby keeping billions of dollars of debt off of its balance sheet;
- recognizing inflated profits on sales to the nonconsolidated SPEs;
- recognizing revenue from sales of forward contracts which were, in effect, disguised loans;
- inflating the fair value of investments;
- not adequately disclosing related party transactions.

The collapse of Enron shed light on many questionable accounting practices.

In the wake of the Enron collapse, the American and Canadian accounting standards boards adopted accounting standards for the consolidation of variable interest entities. These standards have been commonly referred to as the "Enron standards."

Consolidation of Variable Interest Entities

Prior to the CICA's issuance of Accounting Guideline 15, "Consolidation of Variable Interest Entities" (AcG-15) in June 2003, the assets, liabilities, and results of operations for SPEs frequently were not consolidated with those of the firm that controlled the SPE through variable interests. The firms relied on *Handbook* Section 1590 on subsidiaries, which states that control is achieved by owning the majority of the voting shares.

AcG-15 first describes how to identify a variable interest entity (VIE) that is not subject to control through voting ownership interests, but is nonetheless controlled by another enterprise. Each enterprise involved with a VIE must determine whether the financial support provided by that enterprise makes it the primary beneficiary of the VIE's activities. The primary beneficiary of the VIE is then required to include the assets, liabilities, and results of the VIE in its consolidated financial statements.

According to AcG-15, an entity qualifies as a VIE if either of the following conditions exists:[1]

In order to determine if consolidation is required, it is first necessary to determine if there is a primary beneficiary of the VIE.

A variable interest entity (VIE) is one in which the equity interest is insufficient to allow the entity to finance its activities, or in which the equity interest lacks any one of three characteristics that define a controlling interest.

A primary beneficiary is one that, through governing documents, obtains the characteristics of ownership that the equity investors do not have. A VIE has only one primary beneficiary.

In accordance with GAAP, the primary beneficiary is required to consolidate the VIE.

- The total equity investment at risk is not sufficient to permit the entity to finance its activities without additional subordinated financial support provided by any parties. In most cases, if equity at risk is less than 10 percent of total assets, the risk is deemed insufficient.
- The equity investors in the VIE lack any of the following three characteristics of a controlling financial interest:

  (1) the direct or indirect ability to make decisions about an entity's activities through voting or similar rights;
  (2) the obligation to absorb the expected losses of the entity if they occur (e.g. another firm may guarantee a return to the equity investors);
  (3) the right to receive the expected residual returns of the entity (e.g. the investors' returns may be capped by the entity's governing documents).

In assessing whether an enterprise should consolidate the assets, liabilities, revenues, and expenses of a VIE, AcG-15 next relies on an expanded notion of a controlling financial interest. The following characteristics are indicative of an enterprise qualifying as a primary beneficiary with a controlling financial interest in a VIE:

- the direct or indirect ability to make decisions about the entity's activities;
- the obligation to absorb the expected losses of the entity if they occur; or
- the right to receive the expected residual returns of the entity if they occur.

Note that these characteristics mirror those that the equity investors lack in a VIE. Since the primary beneficiary controls the resources of the VIE and will obtain the future economic benefits from these resources, these resources meet the definition of an asset and should be included on the consolidated balance sheet of the primary beneficiary. Similarly, since the primary beneficiary usually bears the risk of absorbing any expected loss of the VIE, it effectively is assuming responsibility for the liabilities of the VIE. Accordingly, these liabilities should be included on the consolidated balance of the primary beneficiary. The fact that the primary beneficiary may own no voting shares whatsoever becomes inconsequential because such shares do not effectively allow the equity investors to exercise control. Thus, in assessing control, a careful examination of the VIE's governing documents and the contractual arrangements among the parties involved is necessary to determine who bears the majority of the risks.

The following scenario provides an example of a primary beneficiary and variable interest entity and its primary beneficiary.

---

[1] CICA Accounting Guideline 15, paragraph .07

Example   Fleur Co. is a Quebec-based utility company. It is negotiating to acquire a power-generating plant from Rouyn Inc. for $105 million. If Fleur purchases the plant directly, it would finance the acquisition with a 5 percent bank loan for $100 million and $5 million of cash. Alternatively, it could set up a separate legal entity whose sole purpose would be to own the power-generating plant and lease it back to Fleur. Because the separate entity would isolate the plant from Fleur's other risky assets and liabilities and provide specific collateral, the interest rate of the financing would be 4 percent, which would save the company one million dollars per year. To obtain the lower interest rate, Fleur must guarantee the separate entity's debt and must also maintain certain predefined debt-to-equity ratios on its own balance sheet.

To take advantage of the lower interest rate, on January 1, Year 1, Fleur establishes Power Co., for the sole purpose of owning and leasing the power plant to Fleur. An outside investor will provide $5 million of cash in exchange for 100 percent of the common shares of Power Co. Fleur and Power sign an agreement with the following terms:

- Fleur has veto power on all key operating, investing, and financing decisions;
- Fleur will lease the power plant for five years for annual payments of $4.5 million to cover the cost of the interest and provide a 10 percent return on the $5 million investment by the outside investor;
- At the end of five years (or any extension), Fleur can renew the lease for a further five years, purchase the power plant for $105 million, or pay $5 million to buy the common shares from the outside investor.

It appears that Power is a VIE for three reasons:

Three reasons why Power Co. is a VIE.

1. Its owner's equity comprises less than 5 percent of total assets and is far short of the 10 percent benchmark provided in AcG-15;

2. Power lacks the ability to make key decisions because of Fleur's veto power;

3. The outside investor appears to bear almost no risk with respect to the operations of the power plant because Fleur guarantees the debt and guarantees a 10 percent return on the common shares.

Furthermore, the last two reasons indicate that Fleur is the primary beneficiary. It has control over Power and is exposed to the major risks, even though it has invested no assets in Power. Accordingly, Power should be consolidated with Fleur.

With two exceptions the initial consolidation records the assets and liabilities of a VIE at fair values.

An implied value of the VIE has to be determined in order to perform the initial consolidation.

Initial Measurement Issues   The financial reporting principles for consolidating VIEs require assets, liabilities, and noncontrolling interests (NCI) to be initially recorded at fair values with two notable exceptions. First, if any of the SPE's assets have been transferred from the primary beneficiary, these assets will be measured at the carrying value before the transfer. Second, the asset valuation procedures in AcG-15 also rely in part on the allocation principles described in *Handbook* Section 1581, "Business Combinations." Recall that Section 1581 requires an allocation of the cost of an acquisition based on the underlying fair values of its assets and liabilities. In a VIE, control is not obtained by incurring a cost, but through governance agreements and contractual arrangements. Therefore, an implied value substitutes for the acquisition cost in determining the valuation of a VIE. The implied value for what is viewed as a 100 percent purchase of the VIE is the sum of:

- consideration paid by the primary beneficiary (plus the reported values of any previously held interests), and
- the fair value of the noncontrolling interests of the VIE.

The implied value (which becomes the acquisition cost) is the sum of the amount invested by the primary beneficiary and the fair value of the noncontrolling interests.

The consideration received (referred to as assessed value) is the sum of the fair value of the VIE's net assets and the amount invested by the primary beneficiary.

The amounts of the implied value and the consideration received are compared to determine the amount of any goodwill or negative goodwill.

The implied value is compared to the value of consideration received, which is the sum of:

- carrying value of amount invested by primary beneficiary, and
- fair value of VIE's own net assets prior to investment by primary beneficiary.

If the implied value is less than the value of consideration received (which we will refer to as assessed value), then the assets are proportionately reduced using the same rules as for negative goodwill. If the implied value is greater than the assessed value, the difference is reported as goodwill when the VIE is a business or as a loss when the VIE is not a business. AcG-15 paragraph 5(f) defines a *business* as a self-sustaining, integrated set of activities and assets conducted and managed for the purpose of providing a return to investors. A business consists of inputs, processes applied to those inputs, and resulting outputs that are used to generate revenues. For a set of activities and assets to be a business, it must contain all of the inputs and processes necessary for it to conduct normal operations, including the ability to sustain a revenue stream by providing its outputs to customers.

The following example will illustrate the consolidation process for a variable interest entity.

Example XYZ Co. invests $5 million of cash in VAR Inc. on January 1, Year 3. VAR is deemed to be a variable interest entity and XYZ is the primary beneficiary. The balance sheet of VAR at the date of acquisition after XYZ's investment is as follows (in millions):

	Book Value	Fair Value
Cash	$ 5	$ 5
Capital assets	60	80
Total assets	$65	
Liabilities	40	40
Owners' equity		
XYZ	5	5
Noncontrolling interest	20	??
Total liabilities and equity	$65	

In this example the fair value of the noncontrolling interest is varied on the date of initial consolidation.

The allocations to be used in the consolidation of XYZ and VAR depend on the value assigned to noncontrolling interest (NCI). We will demonstrate these valuation principles using the following fair values for noncontrolling interest:

Situation	Fair Value of NCI
A	$40
B	37
C	44

	A	B	C
Implied Value of VAR's net assets			
Fair value of amount invested by XYZ	5	5	5
Fair value of NCI in VAR	40	37	44
Total implied value	45	42	49

In situation A, the implied value and the assessed value are equal.

	A	B	C
Assessed Value of VAR's net assets			
Carrying value of amount invested by XYZ	5	5	5
Fair value of VAR's own assets	80	80	80
Less: Fair value of VAR's liabilities	(40)	(40)	(40)
Total assessed value	45	45	45
Difference between implied and assessed values	0	(3)	4

In situation B, the implied value is less than the assessed value resulting in negative goodwill which is used to revalue capital assets.

In situation C, the implied value is greater than the assessed value resulting in goodwill which appears on the consolidated balance sheet.

Assigned on consolidation to:

Goodwill			4
Capital assets		(3)	
Balance to assign	0	0	0

Note that the value assigned to the noncontrolling interest is used to determine the value as a whole of VAR Inc. This amount becomes the equivalent of the acquisition cost for XYZ Co. In situation A, the value of the entity equals the sum of fair values of the entity's assets and liabilities. In situation B, the value of the whole is less than the sum of the values of the net assets resulting in a "negative goodwill" situation which is accounted for as prescribed in Section 1581. In situation C, the value of the whole is greater than the sum of the net assets and the difference is reflected as goodwill. The following journal entries summarize the values for VAR to be consolidated with XYZ under the three different scenarios:

The amounts used in the consolidation are summarized for each situation.

	A	B	C
Goodwill			4
Cash	5	5	5
Capital assets	80	77	80
Liabilities	(40)	(40)	(40)
Noncontrolling interest	(40)	(37)	(44)
Owners' equity re XYZ	(5)	(5)	(5)

The credit to owners' equity of $5 million will be eliminated against the debit balance for the investment in VAR on XYZ's books when preparing the consolidated balance sheet.

In subsequent years the normal consolidation procedures are followed.

Consolidation Issues Subsequent to Initial Measurement   After the initial measurement, consolidations of VIEs with their primary beneficiary should follow the same process as if the entity were consolidated based on voting interests. The implied purchase price discrepancy must be amortized. All intercompany transactions must be eliminated. The income of the VIE must be allocated among the parties involved (i.e., equity holders and the primary beneficiary). For a VIE, contractual arrangements, as opposed to ownership percentages, typically specify the distribution of its income.

Disclosure Requirements

A primary beneficiary of a VIE should disclose the following in its consolidated financial statements:

- The carrying amount and classification of consolidated assets that are collateral for the VIE's obligations;
- Lack of recourse if creditors (or beneficial interest holders) of a consolidated VIE have no recourse to the general credit of the primary beneficiary.

An enterprise that holds a significant variable interest in a VIE but is not the primary beneficiary should disclose the following:

- The nature of its involvement with the VIE and when that involvement began;
- The nature, purpose, size, and activities of the VIE;
- The enterprise's maximum exposure to loss as a result of its involvement with the VIE.

Clearly, the CICA wishes to enhance disclosures for all SPEs. Given that in the past, SPEs were often created in part to keep debt off a sponsoring firm's balance sheet, these enhanced disclosures are a significant improvement in financial reporting transparency.

The first fiscal year in which the requirements of AcG-15 became operative was 2005. The 2006 edition of *Financial Reporting in Canada* reported that of the 200 companies surveyed, 187 referred to VIEs in their disclosures, but only 35 indicated that they were primary beneficiaries and that the consolidation had a material effect on their financial statements.

Many companies that grant franchise agreements to operators of their retail store outlets determined that these independent franchisees were in fact VIEs under the provisions of AcG 15, and as a result consolidated these entities effective with their 2005 annual statements. In previous years, their statements contained basically accounts receivable from these independent franchisees, and franchise fee revenue. Upon consolidation, the receivables and franchise revenues were eliminated and were replaced by the assets, liabilities, sales, and expenses of each franchisee. The 2005 financial statements of Loblaw Companies Limited showed that 123 franchise stores were consolidated, while Sobeys Inc. reported the consolidation of 300 franchise affiliate stores. Shoppers Drug Mart Corporation was required to consolidate approximately 950 associate-owned stores under AcG 15.

In an interesting departure from the examples above, Gildan Activewear Inc. determined that its joint venture company, CanAm Yarns LLC, met the criteria of being a VIE, requiring full consolidation instead of proportionate consolidation as was used in previous years. (The consolidation of joint ventures is discussed in the next section of this chapter.) This required change resulted in increases of $8 million to assets, $5 million to liabilities, and $3 million to noncontrolling interests.

Differential Reporting When a qualifying enterprise is the primary beneficiary of one or more VIEs, it may use the cost or equity method instead of consolidating the financial statements.

Interests in Joint Ventures

In a joint venture arrangement, venturers contribute resources to carry out a specific undertaking.

A joint venture is a business arrangement whereby several venturers agree to contribute resources for a specific undertaking. A common example: one venturer provides the technical expertise, and the other provides marketing and/or financial expertise. Joint venture organizations are often formed for expensive and risky projects. They are fairly common in the oil-and-gas exploration sector and in large real-estate developments. Also, a Canadian company will often form a joint venture with a foreign company or the government of a foreign country as a means of expanding into international markets. For example Bombardier produces trains for China by operating under a joint venture agreement with a Chinese car manufacturer.

ATCO Group, an Alberta-based utilities and power generation company, has significant joint venture investments in power-generating plants. ATCO's income before taxes on the joint ventures represents more than 50 percent of the company's total income.

Joint ventures are not always separate entities.

A joint venture need not be a separate entity. Under a situation of jointly controlled operations, each venturer contributes the use of assets or resources to the joint venture activity but maintains individual title to and control of these assets and resources. An example would be a case in which one venturer manufactures part of a product, a second venturer completes the manufacturing process, and a third venturer handles the marketing of the product. Revenue and expenses are shared in accordance with the joint venture agreement. Some joint ventures involve only the joint control of assets used in the joint venture. An oil pipeline is an example of this: each oil-producing venturer uses the pipeline to transfer its oil and shares the cost in accordance with an agreement. If the separate-entity form is used, the joint venture may be created as a partnership; or it may be incorporated, with the venturers being shareholders.

Of the 200 companies that made up the sample used in the 2006 edition of *Financial Reporting in Canada*, 80 reported investments in joint ventures. Our discussions will focus on situations where a venturer has an investment in a separate-entity joint venture. The basic concepts discussed for this situation would apply with slight modifications to the non-separate-entity examples discussed earlier.

The accounting principles involved for reporting an investment in a joint venture are contained in Section 3055 of the *Handbook*. This section is complementary to Sections 3051, "Investments," and 1590, "Subsidiaries." Section 3055 presents the following descriptions relevant to our discussions:[2]

> **Joint control** of an economic activity is the contractually agreed sharing of the continuing power to determine its strategic operating, investing, and financing policies.

> A **joint venture** is an economic activity resulting from a contractual arrangement whereby two or more venturers jointly control the economic activity.

> A **venturer** is a party to a joint venture, has joint control over that joint venture, has the right and ability to obtain future economic benefits from the resources of the joint venture and is exposed to the related risks.

According to GAAP, joint control is the key feature in a joint venture which means no one venturer can unilaterally control the venture regardless of the size of its equity contribution.

A distinctive feature of these descriptions is the concept of *joint control*, which must be present for a joint venture to exist. Joint control is established by an agreement between the venturers (usually in writing), whereby no one venturer can unilaterally control the joint venture regardless of the number of assets it contributes. For example, a single venturer (Company L) could own more than 50 percent of the voting shares of Company M. This would normally indicate that Company M is a subsidiary; however, if there was an agreement establishing joint control, Company M would be a joint venture and not a subsidiary, and Company L would be a venturer and not a parent. To change the percentages, Company L could also own 32 percent of Company M. Without a further examination of the facts, this percentage would initially indicate that Company L has a significant influence investment, to be reported using the equity method. However, because of the joint control agreement, it must report its joint venture investment using proportionate consolidation.

Accounting for an Investment in a Joint Venture

Under Section 3055, a venturer must consolidate each of its joint ventures using the proportionate consolidation method.

Section 3055 is concerned only with the financial reporting for an interest in a joint venture by a venturer; it does not cover the accounting for the joint venture itself.[3] This section requires the venturer to report an investment in a joint venture by the *proportionate consolidation method*, which is an application of the proprietary theory of consolidation, which was discussed in Chapter 4. You will recall that under this concept, no amount for

---

[2] *CICA Handbook*, paragraph 3055.03.

[3] In July 1992, the Emerging Issues Committee issued EIC-38, "Accounting by Newly Formed Joint Ventures," which examines the accounting by the joint venture of assets contributed to it by the venturers.

Only the venturer's share of the joint venture's financial statement items are used in the consolidation process.

noncontrolling interest is shown in the consolidated financial statements. Applying this concept to an investment in a joint venture, consolidated statements using the proportionate consolidation method would be prepared by combining, on a line-by-line basis, the financial statement items of the venturer with the venturer's share of the financial statement items of the joint venture. By definition there must be at least two venturers; thus, we have a situation where a joint venture's assets, liabilities, revenues, and expenses are apportioned among the financial statements of each of the venturers.

Intercompany Transactions You will recall from our discussions in past chapters that intercompany profits in assets are fully eliminated from the consolidated statements of a parent and its subsidiaries. If the subsidiary was the selling company, 100 percent of the profit, net of income tax, is eliminated and allocated to both noncontrolling interest and consolidated retained earnings in the consolidated balance sheet. If the parent was the selling company, the entire net-of-tax profit is eliminated and allocated to consolidated retained earnings. This is not the case when we proportionately consolidate a venturer and a joint venture.

In the consolidation of a parent and subsidiary, 100 percent of the intercompany profits in assets are eliminated. If the sale was upstream, the amount eliminated affects both noncontrolling interest and retained earnings. If the sale was downstream, the amount eliminated affects only retained earnings.

If the joint venture sells assets at a profit to the venturer, and these assets have not been resold by the venturer to independent third parties, only the venturer's share of this after-tax profit is eliminated because there is no noncontrolling interest to allocate the remaining percentage to. Paragraph 3055.40 of the *Handbook* presents an alternative explanation, suggesting that the venturer cannot recognize a profit on a transaction with itself.

In consolidating a joint venture, only the venturer's share of any intercompany asset profits are eliminated regardless of whether the sale was upstream or downstream.

If the venturer sells assets at a profit to the joint venture, which the joint venture has not resold to independent third parties, it would be possible to eliminate 100 percent of the profit from consolidated retained earnings (i.e., the venturer's) because these retained earnings contain all of this profit. However, Section 3055 suggests that because the joint venture agreement does not allow a particular venturer to exercise control, a venturer selling to the venture is considered to be dealing at arm's length with the other venturers, and therefore a portion of the profit equal to the other venturers' ownership interest can be considered realized. However, if any of the other venturers are affiliated with the selling venturer, only the portion of the profit equal to the nonaffiliated venturers' interest should be considered realized.

In a downstream sale, the venturer realizes a profit selling to the other unrelated venturers.

The same treatment is prescribed for the sale of assets at a loss, except in situations where the transaction provides evidence of a reduction in the net realizable value of the asset, in which case the full amount of the loss is immediately recognized.

Only the venturer's share of intercompany revenues, expenses, receivables and payables, are eliminated in the consolidation process.

Intercompany revenues and expenses are not specifically mentioned in Section 3055, nor are *intercompany receivables and payables*. To be consistent with the general concept of consolidations, it would seem logical that they should be eliminated. However, due to the nature of the proportionate consolidation process, only the venturer's ownership percentage can be eliminated. To eliminate 100 percent of these items, as is done under full consolidation, would result in negative amounts because only the venturer's proportion of a joint venture's receivables or payables, revenues or expenses, is available for elimination under the proportionate method.

Purchase Discrepancies The formation of a joint venture by its venturers cannot result in purchase discrepancies in the investment accounts of the venturers. However, if one of the founding venturers sells its ownership interest, the new venturer could pay an amount different from its interest in the carrying value of the joint venture's net assets, resulting in a purchase discrepancy. This purchase discrepancy would be allocated and amortized in the same manner illustrated previously for parent–subsidiary affiliations.

Consolidation of a Venturer and a Joint Venture

Explor Ltd., a Calgary-based oil exploration company, is a joint venture in which A Company has a 45 percent ownership interest. A Company, an original founder of Explor, uses the equity method to account for its investment but has made no entries to its investment account for Year 4. The following are the financial statements of the two companies on December 31, Year 4:

INCOME STATEMENTS — Year 4

	A Company	Explor
Sales	$900,000	$300,000
Cost of sales	$630,000	$180,000
Miscellaneous expenses	100,000	40,000
	$730,000	$220,000
Net income	$170,000	$ 80,000

BALANCE SHEETS — December 31, Year 4

	A Company	Explor
Miscellaneous assets	$654,500	$277,000
Inventory	110,000	90,000
Investment in Explor	85,500	—
	$850,000	$367,000
Miscellaneous liabilities	$130,000	$ 97,000
Capital stock	300,000	100,000
Retained earnings, January 1	250,000	90,000
Net income — Year 4	170,000	80,000
	$850,000	$367,000

Financial statements of a venturer and a joint venture.

During Year 4, A Company sold merchandise totalling $110,000 to Explor and recorded a gross profit of 30 percent on these sales. On December 31, Year 4, the inventory of Explor contained items purchased from A Company for $22,000, and Explor had a payable of $5,000 to A Company on this date. A Company will use the proportionate consolidation method when it reports its investment in Explor for Year 4.

The following are the calculations of the amounts that are used in the elimination of intercompany transactions in the preparation of the consolidated financial statements:

Intercompany sales and purchases:	
Total for the year	$110,000
A Company's ownership interest	45%
Amount eliminated	$ 49,500

Intercompany receivables and payables:	
Total at end of year	$ 5,000
A Company's ownership interest	45%
Amount eliminated	$ 2,250

Intercompany profits in inventory:

Total at end of year (22,000 × 30%)	$ 6,600
Profit considered realized — 55%	3,630
Unrealized — 45 percent	$ 2,970

The following explanations will clarify the calculations made:

Only the venturer's share of intercompany transactions are eliminated when consolidation takes place.

1. Because the proportionate consolidation method will use 45 percent of Explor's financial statement items, we eliminate only 45 percent of the intercompany revenues, expenses, receivables, and payables. If we eliminated 100 percent of these items, we would be eliminating more than we are using in the consolidation process.

2. The inventory of Explor contains an intercompany profit of $6,600 recorded by A Company. Because there is joint control, A Company has realized $3,630 of this profit by selling to the other unaffiliated venturers, and therefore only A Company's 45 percent ownership interest is considered unrealized.

3. Income tax allocation is required when timing differences occur. Assuming that A Company pays income tax at a rate of 40 percent, the income tax effects of the inventory profit elimination can be calculated as follows:

	Before tax	40% tax	After tax
Inventory — A selling	$2,970	$1,188	$1,782

Because A Company has not recorded this year's equity method journal entries, we must calculate consolidated net income for Year 4 as follows:

Unrealized profit is always eliminated from the selling company's income.

Income of A Company		$170,000
Less after-tax unrealized inventory profit		1,782
Adjusted net income		168,218
Income of Explor	$80,000	
A's ownership interest	45%	36,000
Consolidated net income		$204,218

A Company has used the equity method prior to this year, and therefore its retained earnings at the beginning of the year are equal to consolidated retained earnings. We can prepare the consolidated retained earnings statement for Year 4 as follows:

A COMPANY
CONSOLIDATED STATEMENT OF RETAINED EARNINGS
for the Year Ended December 31, Year 4

Balance, January 1	$250,000
Net income	204,218
Balance, December 31	$454,218

The preparation of the remaining Year 4 consolidated statements without the use of a working paper is illustrated as follows:

A COMPANY
CONSOLIDATED INCOME STATEMENT
for the Year Ended December 31, Year 4

Sales (900,000 + [45% × 300,000] – **(a) 49,500**)	$985,500
Cost of sales	
(630,000 + [45% × 180,000] – **(a) 49,500** + **(c) 2,970**)	$664,470
Miscellaneous expenses	
(100,000 + [45% × 40,000] – **(d) 1,188**)	116,812
	$781,282
Net income	$204,218

A COMPANY
CONSOLIDATED BALANCE SHEET
December 31, Year 4

Intercompany revenues and expenses, receivables and payables, and unrealized profits in assets are eliminated in the preparation of the consolidated financial statements.

Miscellaneous assets		
(654,500 + [45% × 277,000] – **(b) 2,250**)		$776,900
Inventory (110,000 + [45% × 90,000] – **(c) 2,970**)		147,530
Deferred charge–income taxes	(d)	1,188
Total assets		$925,618
Miscellaneous liabilities		
(130,000 + [45% × 97,000] – **(b) 2,250**)		$171,400
Shareholders' equity		
Capital stock	300,000	
Retained earnings	454,218	754,218
Total liabilities and shareholders' equity		$925,618

The amounts used in the preparation are explained as follows:

Under the proportionate consolidation process, only the venturer's share of the joint venture's financial statement items are used.

1. With the exception of shareholders' equity and deferred charge–income tax, the first two amounts used come from the individual financial statements and consist of 100 percent of A Company plus 45 percent of Explor.

2. The adjustments labelled (a) through (d) eliminate the intercompany revenues and expenses, receivables and payables, unrealized inventory profit, and income tax on the unrealized inventory profit. It is assumed that miscellaneous expenses include income tax expense.

3. The investment account and shareholders' equity of Explor were eliminated in the following manner:

Investment in Explor		$85,500
Shareholders' equity of Explor		
Capital stock	$100,000	
Retained earnings, January 1	90,000	
	$190,000	
A Company's ownership interest	45%	85,500
Purchase discrepancy		–0–

4. Consolidated shareholders' equity consists of the capital stock of A Company plus consolidated retained earnings.

Unrealized intercompany profits are held back when equity method journal entries are prepared.

The calculation of consolidated net income (page 471) yields the amounts that A Company uses when it prepares the following Year 4 equity method journal entry:

| Investment in Explor | 34,218 | |
| Equity earnings from Explor | | 34,218 |

To record 45% of the net income of Explor less the holdback of after-tax
unrealized profit in inventory (36,000 – 1,782 = 34,218)

Gains on Assets Contributed as an Investment in a Joint Venture

Suppose that on the date of formation of a joint venture, instead of contributing cash, a venturer contributes nonmonetary assets and receives an interest in the joint venture, and that the assets contributed have a fair value that is greater than their carrying value in the records of the venturer. Would it be appropriate for the venturer to record a gain from investing in the joint venture? And if so, how much gain should be realized, and when should it be recognized? The requirements set out in Section 3055 of the *Handbook* regarding this matter are as follows:

1. The investment should be recorded at the fair value of the nonmonetary assets transferred to the joint venture.

2. Only the gain represented by interests of the other nonrelated venturers should be realized in the financial statements. This gain should be recognized in a systematic manner over the life of the contributed assets, or if nondepreciable, on a basis appropriate to the expected services provided or revenues earned.

3. The portion of the gain represented by the venturer's own interest should be deferred until the asset has been sold to unrelated outsiders by the joint venture. This deferred gain will be deducted from the venturer's share of the related joint venture asset, so that the asset appears on the consolidated balance sheet at an amount equal to the venturer's share of the cost of the asset transferred.

4. If a loss results from the recording of the investment, the portion of the loss represented by the interest of the other unrelated venturers is recognized immediately into income. An exception: when it is evident that the loss is permanent, the entire loss is immediately recognized.

5. When the venturer transfers assets to the joint venture and receives cash in addition to an interest in the joint venture, the cash received can be considered the proceeds from the partial sale of the assets to the other unrelated venturers, provided that the cash came from the investment of the other venturers or from the other venturers' share of joint venture borrowings.

The following examples will illustrate these concepts.

Example 1 A Co. and B Inc. formed JV Ltd. on January 1, Year 1. A Co. invested land with a book value of $200,000 and a fair value of $700,000 for a 40 percent interest in JV Ltd., while B Inc. contributed assets with a total fair value of $1,050,000, for a 60 percent interest in JV Ltd. Cash of $130,000 was included in the assets invested by B Inc. We will concern ourselves only with the recording by A Co. of its 40 percent interest in JV Ltd., and we will assume that the land contributed will provide services for an estimated 10-year period. On December 31, Year 1, JV Ltd. reported a net income of $204,000. The deferred gains are calculated as follows:

Fair value of land transferred to JV Ltd.	$700,000
Carrying value of land on A Co.'s books	200,000
Gain on transfer to JV Ltd.	500,000
A Co.'s portion to be netted against land (40%)	200,000
B Inc.'s portion to be deferred and amortized (60%)	$300,000

Margin notes:

If an investor contributes assets other than cash, the investment is recorded at the fair value of these assets and the gain is split between the portion represented by the venturer's own interest and the portion represented by the interests of the other unrelated venturers. Both gains are initially deferred, and taken into income on different basis.

The deferred gain represented by the interest of the other venturers is taken into income over the service life of the particular asset.

The venturer's portion of the gain is taken into income only when the asset is sold to unrelated outsiders.

If cash is received by the venturer in addition to an equity interest in the joint venture, the cash is considered to be proceeds of a partial sale to the other venturers.

A Co.'s journal entry to record the initial investment on January 1, Year 1, is as follows:

A Co.'s $500,000 gain from investing land is split between the two founding venturers. Both gains are deferred.

Investment in JV Ltd.	700,000	
Land		200,000
Deferred (contra) gain, A Co.		200,000
Deferred gain, B Inc.		300,000

Using the equity method of accounting, A Co. will record its 40 percent share of the yearly net incomes or losses reported by JV Ltd.; in addition, it will recognize a portion of the $300,000 gain it realized by selling to the unrelated venturer, B Inc. The portion recognized will be based on an estimate that the land will provide equal services each year for 10 years.

The December 31, Year 1, entries are as follows:

A portion of the other venturer's deferred gain is taken into income each year as part of the equity method journal entries prepared by A Co.

Investment in JV Ltd.	81,600	
Equity earnings from JV Ltd. (40% × 204,000)		81,600
Deferred gain, B Inc.	30,000	
Gain on transfer of land to JV Ltd. (300,000 ÷ 10 years)		30,000

Equity earnings of $81,600 will be eliminated in the preparation of the Year 1 consolidated income statement; they will be replaced with 40 percent of the revenues and expenses of JV Ltd. The $30,000 gain on transfer of land to JV Ltd. will appear in the consolidated income statement, and the unamortized balance of the deferred gain to B Inc. of $270,000 will appear in the consolidated balance sheet. The $200,000 deferred (contra) gain to A Co. is referred to as a contra gain because it is like a contra account. It will be deducted from land in the preparation of the consolidated balance sheet. Note that if the land transferred to JV Ltd. had been recorded at the carrying value of A Co., it would appear in the balance sheet of JV Ltd. at $200,000. On A Co.'s consolidated balance sheet it would appear at $80,000 (40% × 200,000). The land appears on JV's balance sheet at $700,000 and will appear on the consolidated balance sheet as follows:

A Co.'s deferred gain serves as a contra asset account and is deducted from land when the consolidated balance sheet is prepared. It will be taken into income only when the joint venturer sells the land.

40% × 700,000	$280,000
Less deferred (contra) gain, A Co.	200,000
Consolidated land	$ 80,000

This method of recognizing the gain from investing will be repeated over the next nine years, unless JV Ltd. sells this land before that period expires. If it does, A Co. will immediately take the balances in the two deferred gains accounts into income.

Example 2 The facts from this example are identical in all respects to those from the previous example except that we assume that A Co. receives a 40 percent interest in JV Ltd. plus $130,000 in cash in return for investing land with a fair value of $700,000 while B Inc. contributed assets with a total fair value of $855,000.

The original gain on the transfer ($500,000) and the allocation to A Co. ($200,000) and B Inc. ($300,000) is the same as in Example 1. However, because the $130,000 in cash received by A Co. came entirely from the cash invested by B Inc., it is considered to be the sale proceeds of the portion of the land deemed to have been sold. In other words, A Co. is considered to have sold a portion of the land to B Inc. (through the joint venture) and will immediately record a gain from selling, computed as follows:

When A Co. invests land in the joint venture for a 40 percent interest and receives cash of $130,000, this amount is considered the sale proceeds from selling a portion of the land to B Co.

The amount of the gain from selling to B Co. is deducted from B Co.'s portion of the deferred gain ($300,000) and is taken immediately into income by A Co.

Sale proceeds	$130,000
Carrying value of land sold (130 ÷ 700 × 200,000)	37,143
Immediate gain from selling land to B Inc.	$ 92,857

A Co.'s January 1, Year 1, journal entry to record the investment of land and the receipt of cash would be as follows:

Cash	130,000	
Investment in JV Ltd.	570,000	
Land		200,000
Deferred (contra) gain, A Co.		200,000
Gain on transfer of land to JV Ltd.		92,857
Deferred gain, B Inc.		207,143

The December 31, Year 1, entries are as follows:

Investment in JV Ltd.	81,600	
Equity earnings from JV Ltd. (40% × 204,000)		81,600
Deferred gain, B Inc.	20,714	
Gain on transfer of land to JV Ltd. (207,143 ÷ 10 years)		20,714

Assuming a December 31 year-end, the $113,571 (92,857 + 20,714) gain on transfer of land to JV Ltd. will appear in the Year 1 consolidated income statement. The unamortized balance of the deferred gain to B Inc. of $186,429 (207,143 − 20,714) will appear on the consolidated balance sheet. The $200,000 deferred (contra) gain to A Co. will be deducted from land in the consolidated balance sheet in the same manner as was illustrated in Example 1.

Example 3 In this last example, we will increase the amount of cash that A Co. received when it invested land for a 40 percent interest in JV Ltd. Let us assume that the cash received was $150,000 instead of the $130,000 that we used in Example 2. Because B Inc. only invested $130,000 cash in the joint venture, the additional $20,000 was borrowed by JV Ltd. In this situation, the $150,000 cash received is considered to be partly sale proceeds and partly a return of equity to A Co. The allocation of the cash between sale proceeds and return of equity is made as follows:

When some of the cash received by A Co. comes from joint venture borrowings, only B Co.'s share of the cash borrowed is considered proceeds from the sale of land.

Sale proceeds:		
From B Inc.'s investment in JV Ltd.		$130,000
From borrowings of JV Ltd.	20,000	
B Inc.'s proportion	60%	12,000
		142,000
Return of equity to A Co.:		
A Co.'s proportion of JV borrowings	40%	8,000
Total cash received		$150,000

The gain from selling is computed as follows:

Sale proceeds	$142,000
Carrying value of assets sold (142/700 × 200,000)	40,571
Immediate gain from selling land to B Inc.	$101,429

A Co.'s January 1, Year 1, journal entry would be as follows:

<table>
<tr><td>**This entry records A Co.'s investment of land and the receipt of $150,000 in cash. The resultant deferred gain of $500,000 is allocated to A Co. and B Co. with a portion of B Co.'s gain realized as a result of the cash proceeds.**</td><td>

Cash	150,000	
Investment in JV Ltd.	550,000	
Land		200,000
Deferred (contra) gain, A Co.		200,000
Gain from transfer of land to JV Ltd.		101,429
Deferred gain, B Inc.		198,571

</td></tr>
</table>

On December 31, Year 1, A Co.'s journal entries would be:

| Investment in JV Ltd. | 81,600 | |
| Equity earnings from JV Ltd. (40% × 204,000) | | 81,600 |

| Deferred gain, B Inc. | 19,857 | |
| Gain from transfer of land to JV Ltd. (198,571 ÷ 10 years) | | 19,857 |

The $121,286 gain on transfer of land to JV Ltd. will appear on the Year 1 consolidated income statement, while the unamortized balance of the deferred gain to B Inc. of $178,714 will appear on the consolidated balance sheet. The $200,000 deferred (contra) gain to A Co. will be deducted from land in the preparation of the consolidated balance sheet in exactly the same manner as was previously illustrated, as follows:

40% × 700,000	$280,000
Less deferred (contra) gain, A Co.	200,000
Consolidated land	$ 80,000

Differential Reporting　A qualifying enterprise may elect to use either the equity method or the cost method to report its interests in joint ventures so long as all interests in joint ventures are accounted for using the same method. Interests in joint ventures not proportionately consolidated and income or loss from those interests should be presented separately in the balance sheet and income statement.

Future Directions　While the IASB currently allows a venturer the option of using either the equity method or the proportionate consolidation method to report its interest in a joint venture, it has an exposure draft outstanding which would eliminate the use of proportionate consolidation. With this in mind, it is quite possible that when Canada adopts international standards in 2011, the equity method will be the only method allowed to report an investment in a joint venture.

Future Income Taxes and Business Combinations

Our previous discussions of the accounting for business combinations have ignored the effects of income tax allocation.

Up to this point, we have ignored the income tax implications associated with business combinations. Corporate tax law in this area is quite complex and can be fully understood only by readers who have been exposed to the topic through in-depth tax courses. There is always the danger that essential accounting concepts associated with business combinations and consolidated financial statements could be overshadowed if an attempt is made to combine basic accounting issues with the complex tax allocation procedures. Attentive readers will now have achieved a reasonable understanding of the broad accounting concepts behind consolidated statements. To complete our coverage of this financial reporting process, we now turn our attention to the additional effects that income tax allocation can have on the accounting for a business combination. But before we do this, we provide the following useful background material.

Future Income Tax Concepts

A temporary difference occurs when the carrying amount of an asset or liability does not equal its tax basis. Under *Handbook* Section 3465, when temporary differences exist future tax assets or liabilities must be set up on the balance sheet by multiplying the amount of the difference by the tax rate.

When the carrying amount of an asset is less than its tax basis, or some portion of a liability can be deducted for tax purposes in the future, the result is a future tax asset. When the carrying amount of an asset is greater than its tax basis the result is a future tax liability.

Handbook Section 3465, "Income Taxes," uses the balance sheet (or liability) approach. This approach requires that the differences between the carrying value of an asset or liability and its tax basis be accounted for. These differences are called *temporary differences*. The tax basis of an asset is described as the amount that could be deducted in determining taxable income if the asset was recovered for its carrying value. The tax basis of a liability is its carrying amount *less* the amount that will be deductible for tax purposes with respect to that liability in future periods.

Under Section 3465, there are two basic types of temporary differences: deductible and taxable. A *deductible temporary difference* is one that can be deducted in determining taxable income in the future when the asset or liability is recovered or settled for its carrying amount. These differences exist when (a) the carrying amount of an asset is less than its tax basis, or (b) an amount related to a liability can be deducted for tax purposes. Accounting for these differences results in *future income tax assets*.

A *taxable temporary difference* is one that will result in future taxable amounts when the carrying amount of the asset or liability is recovered or settled. Such differences, which result in *future income tax liabilities*, occur mainly when the carrying amount of an asset is greater than its tax basis.

A few examples will illustrate some of these concepts. We assume a 40 percent tax rate in each case.

Example 1 A company has an account payable of $3,000 on its balance sheet at the end of Year 1, for unpaid expenses that were deducted for tax purposes during Year 1. The carrying amount is $3,000. The tax basis of the liability is:

Carrying amount	$3,000
Less: amount deductible for tax in future periods	–0–
Tax basis	$3,000

Because the carrying amount and the tax basis are equal, a temporary difference does not exist.

Example 2 At the end of Year 1, a company has an account receivable of $1,000 from sales made during the year. This receivable is expected to be collected through a series of instalments during Years 2 and 3. For tax purposes, the revenue is taxable in the year of collection. The carrying amount at the end of Year 1 is $1,000, while the tax basis is zero. This creates a taxable temporary difference of $1,000, requiring a future tax liability of $400.

Example 3 At the end of Year 1, a company has a warranty liability of $1,500. Warranty costs are only deductible for tax purposes when they have been paid. The carrying value is $1,500, while the tax basis is zero, We have a deductible temporary difference of $1,500, requiring a future tax asset of $600.

Example 4 An asset is purchased at a cost of $2,000. For financial statement purposes, it will be depreciated using the straight-line method over a five-year life, with no estimated salvage value. For tax purposes, capital cost allowance will be taken at a 30 percent rate, subject to the half-year rule in the first year. The following illustrates the yearly depreciation and capital cost allowance over the first three years:

When the amount of CCA taken exceeds book depreciation, the result is a future tax liability. A future tax asset occurs when book depreciation exceeds CCA.

		Carrying value	Tax basis
Year 1 cost		$2,000	$2,000
Year 1:	Depreciation	400	—
	CCA	—	300
Balance, end of Year 1		1,600	1,700
Year 2:	Depreciation	400	—
	CCA	—	510
Balance, end of Year 2		1,200	1,190
Year 3:	Depreciation	400	—
	CCA	—	357
Balance, end of Year 3		$ 800	$ 833

Note that at the end of Year 1, there is a deductible temporary difference of $100, requiring a future tax asset of $40. At the end of Year 2, we have a taxable temporary difference of $10, requiring a future tax liability of $4. By the end of Year 3, we are back to a deductible temporary difference of $33, requiring a future tax asset of approximately $13. Note also that while the carrying value of this asset becomes zero at the end of Year 5, it will have a positive tax basis for an infinite number of future years. In other words, the reversing that inevitably must occur is often a very long time happening.

These examples have focused on some of the basics behind the balance sheet approach, and will be useful in understanding some of the business combination illustrations that follow. However, before we examine the future income tax effects associated with a business combination, there is one other interesting provision of Section 3465 that needs to be examined.

The Acquisition of an Asset at a Price Different Than the Tax Basis (other than in a business combination)   Because the balance sheet approach requires the recording of a future tax asset or liability whenever the carrying value of an asset or liability differs from its tax basis, a unique situation exists when a single asset is purchased and its tax basis is different from its cost on the date that it was acquired. The required accounting is outlined in the *Handbook* as follows:

> When an asset is acquired other than in a business combination and the tax basis of the asset is less than its cost, the cost of future income taxes recognized at the time of the acquisition should be added to the cost of the asset. When an asset is acquired other than in a business combination and the tax basis of that asset is greater than its cost, the benefit related to future income taxes recognized at the time of acquisition should be deducted from the cost of the asset [3465.43]
>
> In some circumstances, an asset acquired, other than an asset acquired in a business combination, has a tax basis which is less than its cost. This gives rise to a taxable temporary difference that results in the recognition of a future income tax liability. Adding the cost of future income taxes to the cost of the asset reflects the following:
>
> (a) the carrying amount of the asset would include the cost to acquire the asset and the unavoidable income tax consequences of utilizing the asset; and
>
> (b) the carrying amount will represent the minimum future cash flows necessary to recover the investment in the asset including any tax consequences associated with the asset [3465.44].

An example of the application of this section follows.

Example   A company purchases a piece of equipment for $1,000. Because of the special nature of the asset, only 25 percent of its cost is deductible for tax purposes. Therefore, the tax basis of this equipment is $250. The initial carrying value of the asset is determined by the following formula:

$$\text{Cost of the asset} \quad + \quad \frac{[(\text{Cost} - \text{Tax basis}) \times \text{tax rate}]}{(1 - \text{tax rate})}$$

In this example, if we assume a 40% tax rate, the calculation to determine the initial carrying value of this equipment is:

$$1,000 \quad + \quad \frac{[(1,000 - 250) \times .40]}{(1 - .40)} \quad = \quad \$1,500$$

The journal entry required to record the acquisition of this equipment is as follows:

Equipment	1,500	
Future income taxes		500
Cash		1,000

If we compare the carrying value of the equipment with its tax basis and calculate the tax liability, we can see that the amount recorded for the asset satisfies the requirements of this section as follows:

Carrying amount of equipment	$1,500
Tax basis	250
Taxable temporary difference	1,250
Tax rate	40%
Future income tax liability	$ 500

It should be noted that this gross-up of cost applies only to the purchase of a single asset and does not apply to the acquisition of assets in a business combination. Particularly, it does not apply to goodwill that normally results from such a combination.

Business Combination Illustrations

Section 3465 not only requires application of the balance sheet approach, but also requires that future income taxes associated with the purchase discrepancy be accounted for.

We use the following simple illustrations to convey the basic concepts involved and the reasoning behind them.

Illustration 1   Sub Co. has a single productive asset. The balance sheet of this company is shown below:

SUB CO. — BALANCE SHEET
December 31, Year 3

Asset	$800
Future income taxes	12
	$812

This example illustrates the unique situation when the acquisition of an asset results in its cost being recorded in an amount greater than its acquisition price.

Liabilities	$300
Shareholders' equity	512
	$812

The tax basis of the single asset and the liabilities is:

Asset	$830
Liabilities	300
Net	$530

Using a 40 percent tax rate, Sub Co. has correctly applied the provisions of Section 3465 by setting up in its separate entity statements a future tax asset of $12 for the deductible temporary difference of $30.

On January 1, Year 4, Parent Inc. purchased 100 percent of Sub Co. for $1,000 cash. Parent determines that the fair value of Sub's single asset is $950 and that the fair value of its liabilities is $300. The calculation of the purchase discrepancy is made in the following manner:

When a business combination occurs, the acquirer records the net assets acquired at fair values, and when the tax basis of these net assets are a different amount, a future tax asset or liability becomes part of the allocation of the acquisition cost.

Cost of 100% of Sub Co.		$1,000
Shareholders' equity of Sub Co.	512	
Parent's ownership	100%	512
Purchase discrepancy		488
Allocated:		
Asset (950 – 800)	150	
Future income tax asset/liability (see calculation below)	(60)	90
Balance, goodwill		$ 398

Paragraph 1581.47 requires that the provisions of Section 3465 be followed with respect to the differences between the fair values assigned to the assets and liabilities of the acquired company and their tax basis. These differences, multiplied by the tax rate of the subsidiary, produce future income tax assets and liabilities, which are to be included as part of the allocation of the purchase cost. Paragraph 1581.46 also requires that the fair values be determined without reference to their values for tax purposes.

Returning to this particular example, the calculation of the future tax liability to be used for consolidation purposes is as follows:

In this example, a subsidiary's future tax asset is replaced by a future tax liability upon consolidation.

Asset fair value used in consolidation	$950
Tax basis of the asset	830
Taxable temporary difference	120
Tax rate of Sub Co.	40%
Future income tax liability – as recalculated for consolidation	48
Future income tax asset – as previously stated by Sub	12
Fair value adjustment required on consolidation	$ 60

Because the fair value and the tax basis of Sub's liabilities are both $300, no future income tax implications are associated with these liabilities. Note that in applying these concepts, we are replacing a $12 future income tax asset on the balance sheet of Sub Co. with a future income tax liability of $48 on the consolidated balance sheet with respect to the same asset. Note also that no future income taxes are recorded in relation to the goodwill of $398. The following paragraph from Section 3465 explains why:

Any difference between the carrying amount of goodwill and its tax basis is a taxable temporary difference that would usually result in a future income tax liability. This section does not permit such a future income tax liability because goodwill itself is a residual and recognition of the future income tax liability would merely increase the carrying amount of that residual. [3465.23]

The *Handbook* does not allow the recording of future tax liabilities that would normally be associated with goodwill.

Note that because this paragraph does not allow the recording of a future tax liability for the taxable temporary difference that is associated with goodwill, the provisions of paragraph 3465.43 (discussed previously) do not apply. If those provisions did apply, goodwill would have to be grossed up in a manner similar to the case where a single asset is purchased and the cost and tax basis are different.

Let us assume that Parent Inc. was formed on December 31, Year 3, by the issuance of common stock for $1,000 in cash. The nonconsolidated balance sheet of Parent is shown below, followed by the consolidated balance sheet (with bracketed amounts indicating its preparation using the direct approach):

PARENT INC. — BALANCE SHEET
January 1, Year 4

Investment in Sub Co.	$1,000
Common stock	$1,000

PARENT INC. — CONSOLIDATED BALANCE SHEET
January 1, Year 4

Assets (800 + 150)	$ 950
Goodwill	398
	$1,348
Liabilities	$ 300
Future income taxes	48
Common stock	1,000
	$1,348

The future income tax liability that appears on the consolidated balance sheet can be verified as follows:

Carrying value of assets above (excluding goodwill)	$950
Tax basis of assets	830
Taxable temporary difference	120
Tax rate	40%
Future income tax liability	$ 48

Illustration 2 We will use the same facts about the two companies as in Illustration 1, except that we assume that Parent Inc. purchased 90 percent of Sub Co. for $900 cash. Parent's nonconsolidated balance sheet is presented below:

PARENT INC. — BALANCE SHEET
January 1, Year 4

Cash	$ 100
Investment in Sub Co.	900
	$1,000
Common stock	$1,000

The balance sheet of Sub Co. is unchanged (see page 479). The purchase discrepancy is calculated as follows:

Cost of 90% of Sub Co.		$900.0
Shareholders' equity of Sub Co.	512.0	
Parent's ownership	90%	460.8
Purchase discrepancy		439.2
Allocated:		
Asset (950 – 800) × 90%	135.0	
Future income tax asset/liability	(54.0)	81.0
Balance, goodwill		$358.2

The future tax liability associated with this single asset of Sub Co. used in the allocation is calculated as follows:

Value used for consolidation (800 + 135)	$935
Tax basis	830
Taxable temporary difference	105
Tax rate	40%
Future tax liability as recalculated for consolidation	42
Future tax asset – as previously stated by Sub	12
Fair value adjustment required on consolidation	$ 54

The consolidated balance sheet of Parent is prepared as follows:

PARENT INC. — CONSOLIDATED BALANCE SHEET
January 1, Year 4

Cash	$ 100.0
Assets (800 + 135)	935.0
Goodwill	358.2
	$1,393.2
Liabilities	$ 300.0
Future income taxes	42.0
Noncontrolling interest (10% × 512)	51.2
Common stock	1,000.0
	$1,393.2

In preparing consolidated financial statements in subsequent periods, the values used for each subsidiary's net assets have to be compared each year to their tax basis in order to determine new values for future tax assets and liabilities.

Note that the amount for noncontrolling interest is based on the carrying value of the net assets of the subsidiary used in the consolidation process.

The allocation of the purchase price at the date of acquisition is fairly complicated in situations involving future income taxes. In subsequent periods, we must compare the carrying value of an asset or liability to its tax basis on each date that a balance sheet is prepared, and make an adjustment to previously recorded future income tax balances. When we prepare a consolidated balance sheet subsequent to acquisition, we will have to compare the values used in the consolidation for a subsidiary's net assets with the tax basis of these assets in the records of the subsidiary.

Operating Loss Carry-forwards

Under Section 3465, accounting recognition can be given to the carry-forward of unused tax losses if it is "more likely than not that a future income tax asset will be realized." If the acquired company has already recognized a future tax asset due to the potential carry-forward of unused tax losses, this future tax asset will be allowed

The tax benefits of operating loss carry-forwards, that were not previously recognizable by either party to the business combination, form part of the allocation of the purchase cost; if due to the combination, they now satisfy the recognition test.

to stand on the date of the business combination. The combining of the two companies does not ordinarily change this status. However, if the acquired company was not able to recognize unused tax losses, the fact that it is combining with the acquiring company may provide the additional impetus to satisfy the "more likely than not" criterion. This could result because the two companies combined will do business with each other or will be able to reduce future costs, all of which could result in greater possibilities of having future taxable incomes than was the case before the combination. The acquirer could also benefit in the future, in that its previously unrecognized tax losses could be recognized at the time of the combination. In both situations, the future income tax asset would be included when the cost of the purchase is allocated. Note that recognizing such a future tax asset as part of the allocation of the acquisition cost reduces the amount that otherwise would have been allocated to goodwill. This concept must also be taken into account in situations where a future tax asset was *not* recognized as an allocation of the acquisition cost, but subsequently becomes recognizable. In this situation the future tax asset would be set up in the consolidated statements; the amount so recognized would be used first to reduce the amount of goodwill from the combination, then to reduce any unamortized intangible properties from the combination; any amount left would then be used to reduce (consolidated) income tax expense.

Differential Reporting   A qualifying enterprise may elect to use the taxes-payable basis to account for income taxes. However, the enterprise must disclose details about income tax expense including a reconciliation of the income tax rate or expense-related-to-income to the statutory income tax rate or the dollar amount that would result from its application.

The Exposure Draft on Business Combinations   If passed by the Accounting Standards Board, this exposure draft will change two areas that we have just discussed. In Illustration 2 (page 481) the amount shown for noncontrolling interest is based on the carrying value of Sub Co.'s net assets. Under the proposed new Section 1582, it would be based on the fair value of the subsidiary's net assets including goodwill. Tax benefits from operating loss carry-forwards (as just discussed) form part of the allocation of the purchase cost. Under the exposure draft, Section 3465 would be amended so that the tax benefits would still be recognized but would not form part of the allocation. As at November 2007, this exposure draft was still outstanding as were similar drafts issued by the IASB and FASB.

Segment Disclosures

For simplicity, most of the examples used in previous chapters were unrealistic, in that they consisted of a parent company and a single subsidiary. When you consider all companies that trade on the Toronto Stock Exchange, very few are made up of only two companies, and many of the larger ones consist of the parent and a substantial number of subsidiaries. The consolidation process treats these separate legal entities as a single economic entity by aggregating the components of their financial statements. In past years, all companies comprising a given consolidated group were often in a single line of business and were located in Canada, so this aggregation of statements provided useful information to the users of the consolidated statements. However, the tremendous corporate expansion that started in

Section 1701 "Segment Disclosures" attempts to provide useful information which by nature of the consolidation process is hidden from the statement's users.

the 1970s created companies engaged in diversified activities in many parts of the world, and it became obvious that the basic consolidated financial statements were not providing adequate information. Financial statement users needed information about a company that would allow them to assess all of its different components, which have different growth potentials, profitability characteristics, and inherent risks, which vary with the products and services being provided and the markets being entered. Consolidated financial statements do not provide this information.

In 1979, *Handbook* Section 1700, "Segmented Information," was issued as a response to this user need. This section required footnote disclosures that disaggregated the consolidated financial statements into industry segments and geographic segments. It also required that information be provided about the company's export sales. This section remained unchanged until 1998, when a new Section 1701 was issued to replace it. This new section was the result of the joint efforts of the Accounting Standards Board of the CICA and the Financial Accounting Standards Board in the United States, and is identical to FASB #131, issued at approximately the same time.

Section 1701, "Segment Disclosures"

Public companies are required to disclose information about their lines of business, products and services, countries where they operate, and major customers.

Section 1701 was introduced in January 1998 as a replacement for the old Section 1700. It requires a public company to disclose information about its operating segments and, in addition, information about its products and services, the countries in which it operates, and its major customers. It is expected that such information will provide users with a better understanding of a company's performance and its prospects for future cash flows.

The term used in the previous section, *industry segment*, has been replaced by a new term, *operating segment*. This is more than a cosmetic change; it also signals a change in approach. This new *management approach* is based on the way that a company's management organizes its components internally for assessing performance and making strategic decisions. It focuses on the financial information that the company's decision makers use for that purpose. Each component is called an operating segment and is defined as one:

(a) that engages in business activities from which it may earn revenues and incur expenses (including revenues and expenses relating to transactions with other components of the same enterprise),

(b) whose operating results are regularly reviewed by the enterprise's chief operating decision maker to make decisions about resources to be allocated to the segment and assess its performance, and

(c) for which discrete financial information is available. [1701.10]

The presentation of management's operating breakdown, and of related information generated for internal assessment purposes, should provide more useful information to external users than was provided under the old section. However, it should also be noted that full comparability between two companies is still not likely, because definitions of operating segments still vary. Even so, additional comparability will be achieved through the requirement for disclosures about products and their associated revenues, and about countries in which the company earns revenues and holds assets.

Identification of Reportable Operating Segments

Section 1701 requires information to be disclosed about all operating segments that meet certain *quantitative thresholds*. This requirement is described as follows:

Three tests (revenue, profit, and assets) are used to determine whether or not a particular operating segment is reportable. Each test applies a 10% rule.

An enterprise should disclose separately information about an operating segment that meets *any* of the following quantitative thresholds:

(a) Its reported revenue, including both sales to external customers and intersegment sales or transfers, is 10 percent or more of the combined revenue, internal and external, of all reported operating segments.

(b) The absolute amount of its reported profit or loss is 10 percent or more of the greater, in absolute amount, of:
  (i) the combined reported profit of all operating segments that did not report a loss, or
  (ii) the combined reported loss of all operating segments that did report a loss.

(c) Its assets are 10 percent or more of the combined assets of all operating segments. [1701.19]

These quantitative thresholds establish which reportable operating segments require separate disclosures. Any segments falling outside these guidelines may be combined under the category "Other," provided that at least 75 percent of a company's total external revenue is included in reportable segments. If it is not, additional operating segments must be disclosed. The section also suggests that from a practical point of view, the total number of operating segments reported will probably not exceed 10 or 11 segments.

Illustration   The following illustrates an application of quantitative thresholds. For internal evaluation purposes, JK Enterprises Inc. generates information from its six divisions. In terms of Section 1701, these divisions are operating segments. The following amounts (stated in millions) have been assembled to determine which of these operating segments are reportable in accordance with the section's quantitative thresholds.

Operating segments	Revenues	Operating profit (loss)	Assets
Autoparts	$53.9	$18.1	$10.9
Office furnishings	8.6	1.3	1.2
Publishing	6.5	(2.1)	1.4
Retail	5.0	(2.8)	3.2
Finance	11.8	3.7	14.0
Software	7.9	3.9	0.9
	$93.7	$22.1	$31.6

Revenue Test

10% × $93.7 = $9.37

From this test, Autoparts and Finance are identified.

Operating Profit (loss) Test

To apply this test, first compute separate totals for all profits and all losses. Then choose the largest of the absolute amount of the two totals, as follows:

Total of all operating profits	$27.0
Total of all operating losses	4.9

10% × $27.0 = $2.7

Autoparts, Retail, Finance, and Software are identified.

Asset Test

10% × $31.6 = $3.16

Autoparts, Retail, and Finance are identified.

Following is a summary of all three quantitative tests for JK Enterprises:

Operating segments	Revenues	Operating profit (loss)	Assets
Autoparts	X	X	X
Office furnishings			
Publishing			
Retail		X	X
Finance	X	X	X
Software		X	

Thus, separate disclosures are required for Autoparts, Retail, Finance, and Software, as each satisfies at least one of the tests. Office furnishings and Publishing can be combined and reported under the heading "Other."

Separate disclosure is required if a segment satisfies any one test.

Information To Be Disclosed

The *Handbook* section outlines intensive disclosures required for each reportable segment.

The following disclosures are required for *each reportable segment* that has been identified by the quantitative thresholds:

1. Factors used by management to identify segments.
2. The types of products and services that generate revenues.
3. A measure of profit (loss).
4. Total assets.
5. Each of the following *if* the specific amounts are included in the measure of profit (loss) above:
   (a) Revenues from external customers.
   (b) Intersegment revenues.
   (c) Interest revenue and expense. (This may be netted for a particular segment only if that segment receives a majority of its revenues from interest *and* if the chief operating decision maker uses the net number to assess performance.)
   (d) Amortization of capital assets.
   (e) Unusual revenues, expenses, and gains (losses).
   (f) Equity income from significant influence investments.
   (g) Income taxes.
   (h) Extraordinary items.
   (i) Significant noncash items other than the amortization above.
6. The amount of significant influence investments, if such investments are included in segment assets.

7. Total expenditures for additions to capital assets and goodwill.

8. An explanation of how a segment's profit (loss) and assets have been measured, and how common costs and jointly used assets have been allocated, and of the accounting policies that have been used.

9. Reconciliations of the following:
   (a) Total segment revenue to consolidated revenues.
   (b) Total segment profit (loss) to consolidated net income (loss).
   (c) Total segment assets to consolidated assets.

The following information must also be disclosed, unless such information has already been clearly provided as part of the segment disclosures. This additional information is also required in situations where the company has only a single reportable segment.

1. The revenue from external customers for each product or service, or for each group of similar products and services, whenever practical.

2. The revenue from external customers broken down between those from the company's country of domicile (i.e., Canada) and those from all foreign countries. Where revenue from an individual country is material, it must be separately disclosed.

3. Goodwill and capital assets broken down between those located in Canada and those located in foreign countries. Where assets located in an individual country are material, they must be separately disclosed.

4. When a company's sales to a single external customer are 10 percent or more of total revenues, the company must disclose this fact, as well as the total amount of revenues from each customer and which operating segment reported such revenues. The identity of the customer does not have to be disclosed.

As with all financial reporting, comparative amounts for at least the last fiscal year must also be presented.

The disclosures required by the new Section 1701 are a radical departure from those of the old Section 1700. This new approach seems to be a better one because it provides external users with the information that top management uses to assess performance.

The presentation of a measure of profit, revenue, and assets for each reportable segment allows a statement user to calculate a measure of return on assets, margin and turnover, so that the relative contribution of each segment to the overall profitability of the company can be assessed and compared with that of the previous year.

Exhibit 10.2 shows the segment disclosures from the 2006 financial statements of Rogers Communications Inc. (amounts are in millions of dollars). Product revenue from each operating segment is also provided. Because the majority of its business is conducted in Canada, no information has to be provided about revenues and assets in foreign countries.

Exibit 10.2

ROGERS COMMUNICATIONS INC.
SEGMENTED INFORMATION
Year Ended December 31, 2006 and 2005

(a) Operating segments:

All of the Company's reportable segments are substantially in Canada. Information by reportable segment for the years ended December 31, 2006 and 2005 is as follows:

	2006					2005				
	Wireless	Cable and Telecom	Media	Corporate Items and Eliminations	Consolidated Totals	Wireless (Restated—note 2(b))	Cable and Telecom	Media	Corporated Items and Elimination	Consolidated totals (Restated—Note 2(b))
Operating revenue	$4,580	$3,201	$1,210	$(153)	$8,838	$3,860	$2,492	$1,097	$(115)	$7,334
Cost of sales	628	153	175	—	956	625	158	157	—	940
Sales and marketing expenses	604	412	206	4	1,226	604	320	198	—	1,122
Operating, general and administrative expenses	1,376	1,731	678	(22)	3,763	1,240	1,244	614	(36)	3,062
Integration and store closure expenses	3	15	—	—	18	54	5	—	7	66
	1,969	890	151	(135)	2,875	1,337	765	128	(86)	2,144
Management fees (recovery)	12	64	17	(93)	—	12	41	15	(68)	—
	1,957	826	134	(42)	2,875	1,325	724	113	(18)	2,144
Depreciation and amortization	630	662	52	240	1,584	624	558	52	255	1,489
Operating income (loss)	1,327	164	82	(282)	1,291	701	166	61	(273)	655
Interest:										
Long-term debt	(398)	(223)	(14)	15	(620)	(397)	(249)	(9)	(44)	(699)
Intercompany	89	(35)	(2)	(52)	—	37	(24)	(4)	(9)	—
Foreign exchange gain (loss)	1	1	—	—	2	26	12	1	(4)	35
Gain (loss) on repayment of long-term debt	—	—	—	(1)	(1)	—	(27)	—	—	(27)
Change in fair value of derivative instruments	(5)	—	—	1	(4)	(27)	2	—	16	(9)
Other income (expense)	(2)	1	6	5	10	(6)	3	1	4	2
Income tax reduction (expense)	(274)	269	68	(119)	(56)	84	(5)	14	(95)	(2)
Net income (loss) for the year	$ 738	$ 177	$ 140	$(433)	$ 622	$ 418	$ (122)	$ 64	$(405)	$(45)
Additions to PP&E	$ 684	$ 794	$ 48	$ 186	$1,712	$ 585	$ 714	$ 40	$ 16	$ 1,355
Goodwill	$ 926	$ 926	$ 703	$ —	$2,779	$1,212	$1,118	$ 706	$ —	$ 3,036
Total assets	$7,471	$5,216	$1,459	$(41)	$14,105	$8,793	$4,627	$1,321	$(907)	$13,834

Source: www.sedar.com, Rogers Communications Inc., Audited Annual Financial Statements, March 30, 2007.

Exhibit 10.2 (continued)

In addition, Cable and Telecom consists of the following reportable segments. Information by reportable segment for the years ended December 31, 2006 and 2005 is as follows:

2006

	Cable and Internet	Rogers Home Phone	Rogers Business Solutions	Rogers Retail	Corporate items and eliminations	Total Cable and Telecom
Operating revenue	$1,944	—	$596	$310	$ (4)	$3,201
Cost of sales	—	—	—	153	—	153
Sales and marketing expenses	123	96	70	123	—	412
Operating, general and administrative expenses	988	249	477	21	(4)	1,731
Integration and store closure expenses	—	—	—	6	9	15
	$ 833	$ 10	$ 49	$ 7	$ (9)	$ 890
Additions to PP&E	$ 492	$193	$ 98	$ 11	—	$ 794

2005

	Cable and Internet	Rogers Home Phone	Rogers Business Solutions	Rogers Retail	Corporate items and eliminations	Total Cable and Telecom
Operating revenue	$1,735	$150	$284	$327	$ (4)	$2,492
Cost of sales	—	—	—	158	—	158
Sales and marketing expenses	123	27	38	132	—	320
Operating, general and administrative expenses	889	114	226	19	(4)	1,244
Integration and store closure expenses	—	—	—	—	5	5
	$ 723	$ 9	$ 20	$ 18	$ (5)	$ 765
Additions to PP&E	$ 515	$121	$ 63	$ 15	—	$ 714

In late December 2006 and January 2007, the Company's real estate properties and related leases were transferred to RCI from its subsidiaries. This transfer of real estate is not anticipated to have a material impact on the future results of these operating segments.

Effective January 2007, the Rogers Retail segment of the Company acquired the assets of approximately 170 Wireless retail locations with a carrying value of approximately $20 million, for cash consideration of $73 million, which represented fair value. The combined operations continue to be in the Rogers Retail segment of the company.

Beginning in 2007, the Cable and Internet and Rogers Home Phone segments will be combined to align with changes in management and internal reporting implemented in 2007.

(b)   Product revenue:
Revenue from external customers is comprised of the following:

	2006	2005
		(Restated— note 2(b))
Wireless:		
Post paid (voice and data)	$4,084	$3,384
Prepaid	214	210
One-way messaging	15	20
Network revenue	4,313	3,614
Equipment sales	267	246
	4,580	3,860
Cable and Telecom:		
Cable and Internet	1,944	1,735
Rogers Home Phone	355	150
Rogers Business Solutions	596	284
Rogers Retail	310	327
Intercompany eliminations	(4)	(4)
	3,201	2,492
Media:		
Advertising	555	503
Circulation and subscription	149	137
Retail	279	252
Blue Jays	163	149
Other	64	56
	1,210	1,097
Corporate items and intercompany eliminations	(153)	(115)
	$8,838	$7,334

SUMMARY

In this chapter, we have examined four different topics, which almost wind up our study of business combinations and the preparation of consolidated financial statements. Consolidation is required for a variable interest entity, which is controlled by a primary beneficiary on a basis of control other than through ownership of a voting interest. The proportionate, line-by-line consolidation of a joint venture has some unique features associated with it, particularly in the areas of the elimination of intercompany profits and of the accounting for assets contributed as equity investments in the venture.

The consolidated expenses resulting from the allocation of the purchase discrepancy are not deductible for tax purposes, but under the balance sheet approach the reflection of future tax assets and liabilities is required for the differences between the carrying values and the tax bases of subsidiary company net assets shown on consolidated balance sheets.

Consolidation hides information about the lines of business conducted by multinational conglomerates. Required segment disclosures are designed to provide financial statement users with relevant information that will aid them in assessing company results.

REVIEW QUESTIONS

1. Explain the similarities and differences between a subsidiary and a variable interest entity.

2. Explain the similarities and differences between a majority shareholder for a subsidiary and a primary beneficiary for a variable interest entity.

3. Explain how the definitions of assets and liabilities can be used to support the consolidation of variable interest entities.

4. In what way is the proportionate consolidation method different from the full consolidation method?

5. Y Company has a 62 percent interest in Z Company. Are there circumstances where this would not result in Z Company being a subsidiary of Y Company? Explain.

6. The consolidating treatment of an unrealized intercompany inventory profit differs between a parent–subsidiary affiliation and a venturer–joint venture affiliation. Explain where the differences lie.

7. A venturer invested nonmonetary assets in the formation of a new joint venture. The fair value of the assets invested was greater than the book value in the accounting records of the venturer. Explain how the venturer should account for the investment.

8. Explain how the gain recognition principle supports the recognition of a portion of gains occurring on transactions between the venturer and the joint venture.

9. X Company recently acquired control over Y Company. On the date of acquisition the fair values of Y Company's assets exceeded their tax bases. How does this difference affect the consolidated balance sheet?

10. A parent company has recently acquired a subsidiary. On the date of acquisition, both the parent and the subsidiary had unused income tax losses that were unrecognized in their financial statements. How would this affect the consolidation figures on the date of acquisition?

11. What is the difference between a *deductible* temporary difference and a *taxable* temporary difference?

12. Explain how it is possible to have a future tax liability with regard to the presentation of a subsidiary's assets in a consolidated balance sheet, whereas on the subsidiary's balance sheet the same assets produce a future tax asset.

13. Explain how the definition of a liability supports the recognition of a future income tax liability when the fair value of an asset acquired in a business combination is greater than the tax basis of this asset.

14. Describe the three tests for identifying reportable operating segments.

15. For each of its operating segments that require separate disclosure, what information must an enterprise report?

16. In accordance with Section 1701, "Segment Disclosures":
    (a) What information must be disclosed about business carried out in other countries?
    (b) What information must be disclosed about a company's products or services?
    (c) What information must be provided about a company's customers?

17. What sort of reconciliations are required for segmented reporting?

18. Explain how the use of the information provided in segment disclosures can aid in the assessment of the overall profitability of a company.

MULTIPLE-CHOICE QUESTIONS

1. Which of the following is not a characteristic of a primary beneficiary of a variable interest entity?
   a. Its equity at risk in the variable interest entity is more than 90% of the total assets of the entity.
   b. It has the direct or indirect ability to make decisions about the entity's activities.
   c. It has an obligation to absorb the expected losses of the entity if they occur.
   d. It has the right to receive the expected residual returns of the entity if they occur.

2. Which of the following conditions must exist for an entity to qualify as a variable interest entity?
   a. The equity at risk in the variable interest entity is less than 10% of the total assets of the entity.
   b. The equity at risk in the variable interest entity is more than 90% of the total assets of the entity.
   c. The equity investor has the direct or indirect ability to make decisions about the entity's activities.
   d. The equity investor has the right to receive the expected residual returns of the entity if they occur.

3. Which of the following could occur at the date of acquisition when consolidating a variable interest entity that is not a business but not when consolidating a subsidiary?
   a. Negative goodwill
   b. Positive goodwill
   c. A loss on purchase
   d. A gain on purchase

Use the following data for Questions 4 and 5.

Pastry Company has a 40% interest in the joint venture Dough Corporation. Pastry was an original founder of Dough on January 1, Year 5, and Pastry uses the cost method to account for its investment on its nonconsolidated financial statements. The income statements and accounts payable of Pastry and Dough for the year ended December 31, Year 5 were as follows:

	Pastry	Dough
Sales	$1,000,000	$400,000
Cost of sales	700,000	240,000
Other expenses	160,000	100,000
Net income	$ 140,000	$ 60,000
Accounts payable	$ 180,000	$ 95,000

Additional Information
- During Year 5, Pastry sold $100,000 of merchandise to Dough at a gross profit on sales of 20%. On December 31, Year 5, Dough owed Pastry $35,000 relating to these purchases.

- On December 31, Year 5, the inventory of Dough contained $30,000 of goods purchased from Pastry.
- Ignore income taxes for this question

4. What would be the amount of consolidated cost of sales for Pastry for the year ended December 31, Year 5?
    a. $756,000
    b. $758,400
    c. $768,000
    d. $796,000

    (CGA-Canada, from 2002 to 2007)

5. What would be the amount of consolidated accounts payable for Pastry as at December 31, Year 5?
    a. $204,000
    b. $215,200
    c. $218,000
    d $240,000

    (CGA-Canada, from 2002 to 2007)

6. PRI has a 40% interest in NCE, a joint venture. During Year 5, NCE reported net income of $100,000 and paid a dividend of $60,000. NCE's inventory includes goods purchased from PRI on which PRI had made a profit of $10,000. What is the amount of income PRI should report on its investment in NCE for Year 5 under the equity method? (Ignore income taxes)
    a. $24,000
    b. $30,000
    c. $36,000
    d $40,000

    (CGA-Canada, from 2002 to 2007)

Use the following data for Questions 7 and 8.

Golden Company has assembled the following data regarding its operating segments (000s omitted):

Segment	Revenues	Operating profit	Assets
A – Prepackaged food	$ 77,000	$ 4,500	$ 180,000
B – Canned food	465,000	29,000	235,000
C – Frozen food	156,000	12,400	900,000
D – Frozen beverages	820,000	(35,000)	750,000
E – Canned beverages	1,200,000	305,000	350,000
	$2,718,000	$315,900	$2,415,000

7. Using only the operating profit test, which of the operating segments would be reportable?
    a. B, E.
    b. D, E.
    c. E.
    d. B, D, E.

8. Using all of the tests for operating segments in Section 1701, which of the above would be reportable?
    a. A, B, C, D, E.
    b. B, C, D, E.

    c. B, D, E.

    d. D, E.

9. Which of the following is true regarding the differential reporting section of the *CICA Handbook*?

    a. Differential reporting pertains only to publicly accountable enterprises whose owners unanimously give their consent.

    b. All alternatives selected in accordance with differential reporting must be fully disclosed in the financial statements.

    c. Differential reporting permits the use of proportionate consolidation rather than full consolidation where control exists.

    d. Differential reporting allows the testing for goodwill impairment every three years, rather than annually.

(CGA-Canada, from 2002 to 2007)

10. On January 1, Year 6, REK Ltd. contributed land to a joint venture and received a 40% interest in the joint venture. The land had a net book value of $200,000 and a fair value of $240,000 on the date of the transfer. What is the amount of the gain related to the transfer of the land that would be reported by REK on the consolidated financial statements on the date of the transfer?

    a. No gain will be recognized regardless of cash received from the joint venture.

    b. 40% will be recognized regardless of cash received from the joint venture.

    c. 40% will be recognized if cash received from the joint venture is 40% of the fair value of the land.

    d. 60% will be recognized regardless of cash received from the joint venture.

(CGA-Canada, from 2002 to 2007)

11. When a company is an investor in a joint venture, it uses proportionate consolidation to report its interest in the joint venture. Which of the following statements is true with respect to proportional consolidation?

    a. Proportionate consolidation will report less net income than will full consolidation.

    b. Proportionate consolidation presents the underlying net assets owned by the venturer.

    c. Proportionate consolidation presents the underlying net assets controlled by the venturer.

    d. Profits from intercompany transactions are not eliminated under proportionate consolidation.

(CGA-Canada, from 2002 to 2007)

12. On January 1, Year 3, Gaspe Ltd. purchased an asset for $500,000. The company amortizes the capital asset on a straight-line basis over its useful life of 5 years. The residual value is expected to be $150,000. The capital cost allowance rate is 30% and the tax rate for Year 3 is 30%. Which one of the following statements best describes the items and amounts that would be shown on the balance sheet of Gaspe Ltd. as at December 31, Year 3, if the asset acquired was the company's only capital asset and the company uses the half-year rule?

    a. A capital asset with a net carrying amount of $280,000 and a future income tax liability of $1,500.

b. A capital asset with a net carrying amount of $350,000 and a future income tax liability of $1,500.

c. A capital asset with a net carrying amount of $430,000 and a future income tax liability of $1,500.

d. A capital asset with a net carrying amount of $430,000 and a future income tax asset of $1,500.

(CICA adapted)

13. Which of the following would not be a criterion for identifying a reportable operating segment for segmented reporting purposes?
    a. Discrete financial information is available for the segment, which is reviewed by the company's chief operating decision maker.
    b. The activities of the segment fall into a different Statistics Canada industry classification than other company operations.
    c. The segment incurs both revenues and expenses.
    d. Revenue of the segment is 10% or more of the total revenues from all segments.

Use the following data for Questions 14 and 15.

On January 1, Year 3, a joint venture named JV Corporation was formed. At this time, A Ltd. contributed cash of $75,000 and took back a 20% interest in JV Corporation. During Year 3, A Ltd. sold merchandise to JV Corporation at a profit of $15,000 before taxes. Half of this remained in JV Corporation's inventory at December 31, Year 3. With respect to these sales, JV Corporation owed A Ltd. $10,000 at December 31, Year 3. Both companies are subject to 40% tax rates. Year-end balance sheets of both companies follow:

BALANCE SHEETS — December 31, Year 3

	A Ltd.	JV Corporation
Cash and accounts receivable	$ 80,000	$ 60,000
Inventory	240,000	110,000
Fixed assets (net)	500,000	350,000
Investment in JV Corp.	75,000	—
	$895,000	$520,000
Liabilities	$495,000	$ 95,000
Common shares	100,000	375,000
Retained earnings	300,000	50,000
	$895,000	$520,000

14. What would be the inventory reported on A Ltd.'s consolidated balance sheet at December 31, Year 3?
    a. $257,500
    b. $260,500
    c. $261,100
    d. $345,500

15. What would be the liabilities reported on A Ltd.'s consolidated balance sheet at December 31, Year 3?
    a. $580,000
    b. $514,000
    c. $512,000
    d. $504,000

16. Robertson Inc. purchased all of Gaddy Corp. for $420,000. On that date, Gaddy had net assets with a $400,000 fair market value and a carrying value

of $300,000. The tax basis of the net assets was $270,000. Assuming a 30% tax rate, what amount of goodwill should be recognized for this acquisition?

a. $20,000
b. $59,000
c. $120,000
d. $129,000

17. On January 1, Year 5, Holiday Corporation purchased a 100% interest in the common shares of Card Ltd. for $270,000. At this date, Card Ltd.'s balance sheet included the following:

	Book Value	Fair Value	Tax Basis
Assets	$560,000	$600,000	$375,000
Current liabilities	360,000	360,000	360,000
Future income tax liability	74,000		
Common shares	50,000		
Retained earnings	72,000		

Assume that Holiday has a future income tax liability of $98,000 on its January 1, Year 5, balance sheet. Both companies are subject to 40% income tax rates. If a consolidated balance sheet was prepared for Holiday immediately following the acquisition of Card Ltd., what would be reported for a future income tax liability?

a. $90,000
b. $172,000
c. $176,000
d. $188,000

CASES

Case 1   Mr. Landman has spent the last 10 years developing small commercial strip malls and has been very successful. He buys a residential property in a high traffic area, rezones the property, and then sells the property to a contractor who builds the plaza and sells it to investors. Mr. Landman has often been hired to manage the commercial plazas for a fee.

Mr. Landman now wants to become a real estate baron. Rather than just developing the plazas for resale, he wants to form partnerships with builders and/or investors to build commercial properties and keep them as long-term investments.

He has found two properties suitable for development and has made offers to the present owners to purchase these properties on January 1, Year 2. The offers are conditional upon arranging suitable financing for the acquisition of these properties.

Mr. Landman intends to set up two separate companies to buy, develop, and hold the properties. Elgin Company will purchase the property on Elgin Street for $1,200,000 and build a small office building at an expected cost of $2,800,000. Mr. Landman's holding company, Holdco, will invest $1,200,000 in Elgin for 30 percent of its common shares. Mr. Richer will invest $2,800,000 for a 70 percent interest in Elgin. According to the terms of the shareholders' agreement, Mr. Landman and Mr. Richer must agree on all major operating, investing, and financing decisions. Otherwise, the property will be sold in the open market and the company will be wound up.

The second company, Metcalfe Inc., will buy a recently developed strip mall on Metcalfe Street for $2,000,000. The purchase will be financed with a first mortgage of $1,500,000 and $500,000 of equity. Mr. Landman's holding company will invest $200,000 in Metcalfe for 40 percent of its common shares and will manage the property. Mr. Richer will invest $300,000 for a 60 percent interest in Metcalfe. The shareholders' agreement contains the following terms:

- Mr. Richer will be guaranteed a return of his investment of $300,000 plus cumulative dividends of $24,000 a year.
- Mr. Landman has veto power on all key operating, investing, and financing decisions.
- Mr. Landman's holding company would guarantee the payment of dividends to Mr. Richer on an annual basis. After both shareholders have received cumulative dividends equal to 8 percent of their initial investments, Mr. Richer would receive 10 percent and Mr. Landman's holding company would receive 90 percent of the undistributed profits.

Required:

How should these two investments be reported on the financial statements of Holdco? Provide arguments to support your recommendations.

Case 2 P Co. is looking for some additional financing in order to renovate one of the company's manufacturing plants. It is having difficulty getting new debt financing because its debt-to-equity ratio is higher than the 3:1 limit stated in its bank covenant. It is unable to attract an equity partner because the sole owner of P Co. has set conditions for an equity partner that make it practically impossible to find a new equity investor.

Part of the problem results from the use of historical cost accounting. If the company's assets were recorded at fair value, the debt-to-equity ratio would be much lower. In order to get around the rules for historical cost accounting, the CFO for P Co. came up with the following plan.

On September 2, Year 5, P Co will sell its manufacturing facility to SPE for $600,000 in the form of a non interest bearing note receivable. SPE will be set up for the sole purpose of renovating the manufacturing facility. No other activities may be carried out by SPE without the approval of P Co. Mr. Renovator, who will invest $360,000 in cash to cover the estimated cost of the renovation, will be the sole owner of SPE. On January 1, Year 6, after the renovation is complete and one day after P Co.'s year end, SPE will sell the manufacturing facility back to P. Co. at $1,000,000 and will be wound up. P will finance the repurchase with a $400,000 bank loan and by offsetting the remaining $600,000 against the note receivable from SPE from the original sale of the manufacturing facility to SPE. By selling the unrenovated facility and repurchasing the renovated facility, P Co. will be able to reflect the facility at its fair value, borrow the money to finance the renovation, and improve its debt-to-equity position.

The existing and pro forma balance sheets (in 000s) and debt-to-equity ratios for P Co. and SPE are presented below in condensed form:

	P Co Sep 1/5	P Co Dec 31/5	P Co Jan 1/6	SPE Dec 31/5
Note receivable from SPE		$ 600		
Manufacturing facility	$ 100		$1,000	$960
Other assets	900	900	900	0
	$1,000	$1,500	$1,900	$960
Note payable to P Co.				$600
Other liabilities	$ 800	$ 800	$1,200	
Common shares	10	10	10	360
Retained earnings	190	690	690	0
	$1,000	$1,500	$1,900	$960
Debt to equity ratio	4:1	1.14:1	1.71:1	1.67:1

The CFO would like you to prepare a memo in which you discuss the accounting issues related to these proposed transactions.

Required:

Prepare the memo requested by the CFO. Ignore income taxes.

Case 3   The Coca-Cola Company (see www.cocacola.com) is a world leader in the beverage industry; an estimated one billion servings of Coca-Cola products are consumed every day. Coca-Cola manufactures syrups, concentrates, and beverage bases; bottling is carried out under contract by authorized local businesses, which have rights to particular territories. With some exceptions, these bottling and distribution operations are locally owned and operated by independent businesspeople who are native to the nations in which they are located, and who often also bottle other local or international brands of soft drinks. The Coca-Cola Company has an equity position in a significant proportion of these bottlers, especially 10 strategically aligned business partners, referred to as the "anchor bottlers." These anchor bottlers are also distinguished by:

- a pursuit of the same strategic aims as the Coca-Cola Company in developing the nonalcoholic beverage business;
- a commitment to long-term growth;
- commitment to the Coca-Cola system;
- service to a large, geographically diverse area;
- sufficient financial resources to make long-term investments;
- managerial expertise and depth.

Among these anchor bottlers, Coca-Cola Enterprises (see www.cokecce.com) is the largest soft drink bottler in the world; 44% of the common shares of Coca-Cola Enterprises are owned by the Coca-Cola Company, the only significant shareholder. Sales of US$2.5 billion (13% of revenue) were made in 1997 by the Coca-Cola Company to Coca-Cola Enterprises. The Company provides certain administrative and other services to Coca-Cola Enterprises under negotiated fee arrangements; it also provides direct support for certain marketing activities of Coca-Cola Enterprises and participates in cooperative advertising and other marketing programs (amounting to $604 million in 1997). In addition, during 1997 and 1996 the Company committed approximately $190 million to Coca-Cola Enterprises under a company program that encourages bottlers to invest in building and supporting beverage infrastructure.

Coca-Cola Enterprises, with 56,000 employees and operations in 46 American states, in Canada, and in several European Union countries, is publicly traded on the New York Stock Exchange. Revenues in 1997 totalled $11.2 billion, of which over 90% arose from the sale of Coca-Cola Company products. The Coca-Cola Company uses the equity method to account for its investment in Coca-Cola Enterprises. If valued at the December 31, 1997, quoted closing price for Coca-Cola Enterprises shares, the calculated value of this investment in Coca-Cola Enterprises would have exceeded the 1997 carrying value of US$184 million, by approximately $5.8 billion.

Technical Note:

It is clear that certain assumptions as to the nature of significant influence and control are being employed in the accounting policy choices of the Coca-Cola Company, which follows U.S. rules. Since 1988, U.S. GAAP has required consolidation of all majority-owned subsidiaries unless control is temporary or does not rest with the majority owner. FASB Statement #94 requires consolidation of a majority-owned subsidiary even if it has "nonhomogeneous" operations, a large minority interest, or a foreign location.

However, accounting standards in North America (and indeed globally) are evolving so that the "old" standard of legal (*de jure*) control is being superseded by a standard based on "*de facto*" control (control as determined by the facts and circumstances of the relationship). Canadian standards have already moved significantly in this direction. U.S. GAAP (consult the FASB website, www.fasb.org, for current details) is also moving in this direction. North American harmonization of consolidation principles is the ultimate goal, so standards and practices in this and other areas should have a high degree of congruity throughout the NAFTA countries.

Required:

(a) Review the above facts, drawn from 1997 annual reports, carefully. Considering both the current and likely future state of accounting standards governing consolidation, analyze the financial reporting practices of the Coca-Cola Company with respect to its significant investments in the anchor bottlers.

(b) Consult the website of the Coca-Cola Company (www.cocacola.com) for information. The notes to the financial statements included at this site will contain information as to the current accounting practices for these investments. Determine how these financial reporting practices have evolved (if at all) and evaluate the results of your analysis in part (a) relative to current practices of the Company.

(Case prepared by Peter Secord, St. Mary's University.)

Case 4 AcG 15 affects many Canadian business enterprises that are involved with variable interest entities (VIEs). Retrieve the annual reports of any two of the following companies :

- Tim Hortons Inc.
- Air Canada
- George Weston Limited
- Petro-Canada
- Canadian Tire Corporation Limited
- Allied Hotel Properties Inc.

Required:

Write a brief report on each company that describes

1. The extent of its involvement with VIEs
2. The effect of the requirements of AcG 15 on its financial statements

PROBLEMS

Problem 1 Pharma Company (Pharma) is a pharmaceutical company operating in Winnipeg. It is developing a new drug for treating multiple sclerosis (MS). On January 1, Year 3, Benefit Ltd. (Benefit) signed an agreement to guarantee the debt of Pharma and guarantee a specified rate of return to the common shareholders. In return, Benefit will obtain the residual profits of Pharma. The agreement establishes Pharma as a variable interest entity and Benefit as the primary beneficiary.

The balance sheets (in 000,000s) of Benefit and Pharma on January 1, Year 3, were as follows:

	Benefit Book Value	Pharma Book Value	Pharma Fair Value
Current assets	$250	$ 50	$ 50
Property, plant, and equipment	400	80	90
Intangible assets	50	20	70
	$700	$150	$210

Current liabilities	$145	$ 60	$ 60
Long-term debt	325	120	125
Common shares	10	1	
Retained earnings	220	(31)	
	$700	$150	

An independent appraiser determined the fair values of Pharma's noncurrent assets. The appraiser indicated that he was quite confident with the appraised value for the property, plant, and equipment but had some reservations in putting a specific value on the intangible assets.

Required:

Prepare a consolidated balance sheet at January 1, Year 3, assuming that the agreement between Benefit and Pharma established the following fair values for the common shares of Pharma:
(a) $25
(b) $15
(c) $30

Problem 2 On January 1, Year 1, Able Ltd., Baker Ltd., and Drexal Ltd. entered into a joint venture agreement to form the Frontier Exploration Company. Able contributed 30% of the assets to the venture and agreed that its share of the venture would be the same percentage. Presented below are the financial statements of Able and Frontier as at December 31, Year 6:

BALANCE SHEETS

	Able	Frontier
Current assets	$247,000	$ 40,000
Investment in Frontier	27,000	—
Other assets	530,000	70,000
	$804,000	$110,000
Current liabilities	$ 94,000	$ 20,000
Long-term debt	400,000	—
Capital stock	200,000	10,000
Retained earnings	110,000	80,000
	$804,000	$110,000

INCOME STATEMENTS

	Able	Frontier
Revenues	$900,000	$100,000
Income from Frontier	9,000	—
Total revenues	909,000	100,000
Cost of sales and expenses	812,000	70,000
Net income	$ 97,000	$ 30,000

Able's investment has been accounted for by the partial equity method (no adjustments have been made for intercompany transactions).

Able acts as the sole supplier for certain materials used by Frontier in its exploration activities. The December 31, Year 6, inventory of Frontier contains items purchased from Able on which Able recorded a gross profit of $10,000. At December 31, Year 6, Frontier owed Able $12,000 representing invoices not yet paid. Frontier's Year 6 intercompany purchases amounted to $70,000.

Required:

Prepare the necessary financial statements for Able on a proportionate consolidated basis in accordance with Section 3055 of the *CICA Handbook*. (Use a rate of 40% for income tax effects.)

Problem 3   Leighton Corp. has just acquired 100% of the voting shares of Knightbridge Inc. and is now preparing the financial data needed to consolidate this new subsidiary. Leighton paid $700,000 for its investment. Details of all of Knightbridge's assets and liabilities on acquisition date were as follows:

	Fair market value	Tax basis
Instalment accounts receivable	$120,000	$ –0–
Inventory	150,000	150,000
Land	100,000	100,000
Buildings	180,000	110,000
Equipment	200,000	130,000
Trade liabilities	240,000	240,000

Required:

Determine the amounts that will be used to prepare a consolidated balance sheet on the date of acquisition, assuming that Knightbridge's tax rate is 45%. Knightbridge has not set up future tax amounts for any of its assets or liabilities.

Problem 4   On December 31, Year 4, Russell Inc. invested $20,000 in Charger Corp., a variable interest entity. Prior to this Russell had no interest in Charger. In the contractual agreements entered into that day with all parties involved, Russell was established as the primary beneficiary of Charger. Immediately after Russell's investment, Charger Corp. prepared the following balance sheet :

Cash	$ 20,000	Long-term debt	$120,000
Marketing software	140,000	Noncontrolling interest	60,000
Computer equipment	40,000	Russell equity interest	20,000
	$200,000		$200,000

Each of the above amounts represents an assessed value at December 31, Year 4, except for marketing software.

Required:

(a) If the marketing software was undervalued by $20,000, what reported amounts for Charger's financial statement items would appear in Russell's December 31, Year 4, financial statements.

(b) If the marketing software was overvalued by $20,000, what reported amounts for Charger's financial statement items would appear in Russell's December 31, Year 4, financial statements.

Problem 5   On January 1, Year 5, AB Company (AB) purchased 80% of the outstanding common shares of Dandy Limited (Dandy) for $8,000. On that date, Dandy's shareholders' equity consisted of common shares of $1,000 and retained earnings of $6,000.

In negotiating the purchase price at the date of acquisition, it was agreed that the fair values of all of Dandy's assets and liabilities were equal to their book values and tax basis except for the following:

	Fair value	Carrying value	Tax basis
Equipment	$950	$700	$600

Dandy has recorded future income taxes on its separate-entity balance sheet on all temporary differences. Dandy had a loss carry-forward of $800 as at December 31, Year 4. This carry-forward can be applied against taxable income in the future. Dandy did not previously recognize the benefit of the carry-forward because it was not sure whether it would earn $800 in taxable income in the future. Now that AB controls Dandy, AB is sure that Dandy will be able to utilize the loss carry-forwards because AB will transfer income-earning assets to Dandy if necessary to generate taxable income in Dandy. AB plans to utilize these loss carry-forwards as soon as possible.

Both companies use the straight-line method for amortizing their capital assets and pay taxes at the rate of 40%. Dandy's equipment had a remaining useful life of 10 years at the date of acquisition.

Dandy reported income before application of any loss carry-forwards as follows for the first three years after being acquired by AB:

Year	Net income
Year 5	$ 0
Year 6	100
Year 7	200

Required:

(a) Calculate goodwill at the date of acquisition. Be sure to consider the future tax implications on the purchase price discrepancy.

(b) Calculate noncontrolling interest at the date of acquisition.

(c) Prepare a schedule to show the amortization of the purchase price discrepancy for the three-year period ending December 31, Year 7. Assume that the goodwill impairment loss was $300 in Year 6, the future income tax liability is amortized at the same rate as the equipment, and the loss carry-forwards are applied against income as the income is earned.

(d) Explain why the purchase price discrepancy related to the equipment gives rise to a future income tax liability.

Problem 6   On January 1, Year 1, Green Inc. purchased 100% of the common shares of Mansford Corp. for $335,000. Green's balance sheet data on this date just prior to this acquisition are as follows:

	Book value	Tax basis
Cash	$ 340,000	$ 340,000
Accounts receivable	167,200	–0–
Inventory	274,120	274,120
Land	325,000	325,000
Buildings (net)	250,000	150,000
Equipment (net)	79,000	46,200
	$1,435,320	$1,135,320
Current liabilities	$ 133,000	133,000
Future income tax	120,000	—
Non-current liabilities	—	
Common stock	380,000	
Retained earnings	802,320	
	$1,435,320	

The balance sheet and other related data for Mansford are as follows:

MANSFORD CORP. — BALANCE SHEET
January 1, Year 1

	Book value	Fair value	Tax basis
Cash	$ 52,500	$ 52,500	$ 52,500
Accounts receivable	61,450	61,450	61,450
Inventory	110,000	134,000	110,000
Land	75,000	210,000	75,000
Buildings (net)	21,000	24,000	15,000
Equipment (net)	17,000	16,000	12,000
	$336,950	$497,950	$325,950
Current liabilities	$ 41,115	41,115	41,115
Non-current liabilities	150,000	155,000	150,000
Future income taxes	4,400		—
Common stock	100,000		
Retained earnings	41,435		
	$336,950		

For both companies, the income tax rate is 40%.

Required:

Prepare a consolidated balance sheet at January 1, Year 1.

Problem 7   Assume that all of the facts in Problem 6 remain unchanged except that Green paid $201,000 for 60% of the voting shares of Mansford.

Required:

(a) Prepare a consolidated balance sheet at January 1, Year 1.

(b) Explain how the definition of a liability supports the recognition of a future income tax liability when a parent purchases shares in a subsidiary and the fair values of the subsidiary's identifiable net assets are greater than their net book values.

Problem 8   The balance sheets of Prime Inc. and Variable Ltd. on December 31, Year 11 were as follows:

	Prime Book Value	Variable Ltd. Book Value	Fair Value
Cash	$ 200,000		
Accounts receivable	250,000	$ 50,000	$ 50,000
Land	400,000	80,000	200,000
Manufacturing facility	750,000	320,000	300,000
	$1,600,000	$450,000	$550,000
Current liabilities	$ 275,000	$ 60,000	$ 60,000
Long-term debt	525,000	290,000	280,000
Common stock	50,000	10,000	
Retained earnings	750,000	90,000	
	$1,600,000	$450,000	

Variable's manufacturing facility is old and very costly to operate. For the year ended December 31, Year 11, the company lost money for the first time in its history. Variable does not have the financial ability to refurbish the plant. It must either cease operations or find a partner to refurbish the plant.

On January 1, Year 12, Prime agreed to provide an interest-free loan of $200,000 to Variable on the following terms and conditions:

- Prime Inc. would be hired by Variable to refurbish the manufacturing facility at a fixed cost of $200,000 and would be retained to manage the plant for a minimum of five years.
- Prime Inc. would have full authority to make all major operating, investing, and financing decisions related to Variable over the five-year period.
- The common shares of Variable were valued at $180,000 as at January 1, Year 12. Prime has the option to buy the shares of Variable at any time after January 1, Year 17, at $180,000 plus any dividends in arrears.
- The existing shareholders of Variable would be guaranteed a cumulative dividend of 8 percent a year on the value of their shares. Prime would receive the residual profits after the dividends were paid to the common shareholders.

Variable earned income of $200,000 and paid dividends of $50,000 over the five-year period ended December 31, Year 16. The balance sheets of Prime Inc. and Variable Ltd. on December 31, Year 16 were as follows:

	Prime	Variable
Cash	$ 20,000	$180,000
Accounts receivable	275,000	70,000
Land	400,000	80,000
Manufacturing facility	650,000	260,000
	$1,345,000	$590,000
Current liabilities	$ 185,000	$ 50,000
Long-term debt	450,000	290,000
Common stock	50,000	10,000
Retained earnings	660,000	240,000
	$1,345,000	$590,000

Assume that Variable is a variable interest entity and Prime is the primary beneficiary. The manufacturing facility had an estimated remaining useful life of 10 years as at January 1, Year 12. The long-term debt matures on December 31, Year 21.

Required:

(a) Calculate consolidated retained earnings at December 31, Year 16.
(b) Prepare a consolidated balance sheet for Prime at December 31, Year 16.
(c) Use the definition of a liability to explain the rationale for including the liabilities of the variable interest entity on the consolidated balance sheet for the primary beneficiary.

Problem 9   The following information has been assembled about Casbar Corp. as at December 31, Year 5 (amounts are in thousands):

Operating segment	Revenues	Profit	Assets
A	$12,000	$2,100	$24,000
B	9,600	1,680	21,000
C	7,200	1,440	15,000
D	3,600	660	9,000
E	5,100	810	8,400
F	1,800	270	3,600

Required:

Determine which operating segments require separate disclosures.

Problem 10   The following are the December 31, Year 9, balance sheets of three related companies:

	Pro Ltd.	Forma Corp.	Apex Inc.
Cash	$ 70,000	$ 1,500	$200,000
Accounts receivable	210,000	90,000	110,000
Inventory	100,000	62,500	70,000
Investment in Forma Corp. — at cost	326,000	—	—
Investment in Apex Inc. — at cost	150,000	—	—
Land	100,000	110,000	60,000
Plant and equipment	726,000	550,000	290,000
Accumulated depreciation	(185,000)	(329,000)	(60,000)
	$1,497,000	$485,000	$670,000
Accounts payable	$ 175,000	$ 90,000	$130,000
Bonds payable	312,000	—	—
Common shares	800,000	100,000	500,000
$12 preferred shares	—	200,000	—
Retained earnings	210,000	95,000	40,000
	$1,497,000	$485,000	$670,000

Other Information

- On January 1, Year 5, Pro purchased 40% of Forma for $116,000. On that date, Forma's shareholders' equity was as follows:

Common shares	$100,000
Retained earnings	80,000
	$180,000

   All of the identifiable net assets of Forma had fair values equal to carrying values except for the following, for which fair values exceeded carrying values by:

Inventory	$20,000
Land	40,000
Plant and equipment	50,000

- On September 30, Year 7, Pro purchased the remaining 60% of Forma for $210,000. On that date, Forma's shareholders' equity was as follows:

Common shares	$100,000
Retained earnings	110,000
	$210,000

   On this date, the following net assets of Forma were undervalued by the amounts shown:

Inventory	$10,000
Plant and equipment	70,000

- For consolidation purposes, any purchase discrepancy allocated to plant and equipment is amortized over 20 years from each date of aquisition. A goodwill impairment loss amounting to $2,025 was recorded in Year 8.
- During Year 8, Forma issued 2,000 cumulative, $12, no-par-value preferred shares. Pro did not acquire any of these shares.

- The inventories of Pro contained intercompany profits from items purchased from Forma in the following amounts:

December 31, Year 8	$40,000
December 31, Year 9	45,000

- During Year 9, Pro and two other unrelated companies formed Apex, which is a joint venture. Pro invested $150,000 cash for its 30% interest in the venture.
- The year-end inventories of Apex contained a $12,000 intercompany profit from items purchased from Pro since its formation in Year 9.
- Forma paid dividends in all years prior to Year 9. The company's directors, in assessing the effect of the Year 9 operating loss on the company's liquidity position, did not declare dividends in Year 9.
- On December 31, Year 9, the accounts receivable of Pro contained the following:

Receivable from Forma	$13,000
Receivable from Apex	$40,000

Required:

Prepare the Year 9 consolidated balance sheet. (Use income tax allocation at a 40% rate as it applies to unrealized profits only. Ignore future income taxes on the purchase price discrepancy.)

Problem 11   The following are the Year 9 income statements of Kent Corp. and Laurier Ltd.

INCOME STATEMENTS
for the Year Ended December 31, Year 9

	Kent	Laurier
Sales	$3,000,000	$1,200,000
Other income	200,000	70,000
Gain on sale of land	—	100,000
	$3,200,000	$1,370,000
Cost of sales	$1,400,000	$ 560,000
Operating expenses	500,000	300,000
Depreciation expense	100,000	130,000
Income tax	400,000	150,000
	$2,400,000	$1,140,000
Net income	$ 800,000	$ 230,000

Other Information

- Kent acquired its 40% interest in the common shares of Laurier in Year 3 at a cost of $825,000 and uses the cost method to account for its investment.
- The purchase discrepancy amortization schedule showed the following write-off for Year 9:

Buildings	$ 9,000
Goodwill impairment loss	13,000
	22,000
Long-term liabilities	12,500
Purchase discrepancy amortization — Year 9	$ 9,500

- In Year 9, rent amounting to $125,000 was paid by Laurier to Kent. Kent has recorded this as other income.

- In Year 6, Kent sold land to Laurier and recorded a profit of $75,000 on the transaction. During Year 9, Laurier sold one-half of the land to an unrelated land development company.
- During Year 9, Laurier paid dividends totalling $80,000.
- It has been established that Kent's 40% interest would *not* be considered control in accordance with the *CICA Handbook*.
- Assume a 40% tax rate.

Required:

(a) Assume that Laurier is a joint venture that is owned by Kent and two other unrelated venturers. Also assume that Kent acquired its interest after Laurier's initial formation, and that the purchase discrepancies are therefore valid. Prepare the income statement of Kent for Year 9 in accordance with GAAP (show all calculations).

(b) Assume that Laurier is *not* a joint venture, and furthermore, that Kent's long-term investment in Laurier is a significant influence investment. Prepare the income statement of Kent for Year 9 in accordance with GAAP (show all calculations).

Problem 12   Connor Company and Sparks Company formed Banff Ltd. on January 1, Year 3. Banff is a joint venture according to Section 3055 of the *CICA Handbook*. Connor Company contributed $12,000 in cash for a 60% interest in the joint venture.

The following financial statements were prepared on December 31, Year 3:

BALANCE SHEETS

	Connor Company	Banff
Current assets	$ 75,000	$ 6,000
Investment in Banff Ltd. — cost	12,000	—
Fixed assets	190,000	72,000
Accumulated depreciation	(60,000)	(5,000)
Other assets	16,000	8,000
	$233,000	$81,000
Current liabilities	$ 33,000	$18,500
Long-term debt	45,000	40,000
Capital stock	85,000	20,000
Retained earnings, January 1	30,000	—
Net income for the year	40,000	2,500
	$233,000	$81,000

INCOME STATEMENTS

	Connor Company	Banff
Sales	$150,000	$20,000
Cost of sales	$ 90,000	$11,000
Expenses	20,000	6,500
	$110,000	$17,500
Net income	$ 40,000	$ 2,500

Additional Information

- During Year 3, Banff made purchases totalling $6,000 from Connor Company. Connor Company recorded a gross profit of $1,800 on its sales to Banff.

- On December 31, Year 3, the inventories of Banff contain 25% of the items purchased from Connor Company.
- Connor Company has used the cost method to account for its investment in Banff.
- Connor Company wishes to prepare consolidated statements in accordance with Section 3055 of the *Handbook*.
- Use income tax allocation at a rate of 40%.

Required:

(a) Prepare the consolidated financial statements for Connor Company as at December 31, Year 3.
(b) Use the gain recognition principle to explain why only a portion of the gain is eliminated on the sale of inventory by Connor Company to Banff.

Problem 13   Albert Company has an investment in the voting shares of Prince Ltd. On December 31, Year 5, Prince reported a net income of $860,000 and declared dividends of $200,000.

During Year 5, Albert had sales to Prince of $915,000, and Prince had sales to Albert of $500,000. On December 31, Year 5, the inventory of Albert contained an after-tax intercompany profit of $40,000, and the inventory of Prince contained an after-tax intercompany profit of $72,000.

On January 1, Year 4, Albert sold equipment to Prince and recorded an after-tax profit of $120,000 on the transaction. The equipment had a remaining life of 5 years on this date. Albert uses the equity method to account for its investment in Prince.

Required:

Prepare Albert's Year 5 equity method journal entries under each of the following two assumptions:

(a) Albert owns 64% of Prince.
(b) Albert owns 30% of Prince and Prince is a joint venture.

Problem 14   On January 1, Year 1, Amco Ltd. and Newstar Inc. formed Bearcat Resources, a joint venture. Newstar contributed miscellaneous assets with a fair value of $750,000 for a 60% interest in the venture. Amco contributed plant and equipment with a book value of $300,000 and a fair value of $1,000,000 and received a 40% interest in the venture plus $500,000 in cash. On December 31, Year 1, Bearcat reported a net income of $180,000 and declared a dividend of $75,000. Amco has a December 31 year-end and will account for its 40% interest using the equity method. (Assume a 20-year life for the plant and equipment.)

Required:

PART A
Assume that the miscellaneous assets contributed by Newstar included cash of $500,000.
(a) Prepare Amco's Year 1 journal entries.

PART B
Assume that there was no cash in the assets contributed by Newstar and that the cash received by Amco had been borrowed by Bearcat.
(a) Prepare Amco's Year 1 journal entries.
(b) For all accounts (except cash) that you used to answer Part B(a), state where each would appear in Amco's Year 1 consolidated financial statements.

Problem 15 The following are the Year 9 income statements of Poker Inc. and Joker Company

INCOME STATEMENTS
Year ended December 31, Year 9

	Poker	Joker
Sales	$1,000,000	$800,000
Other income	200,000	110,000
Gain on sale of trademark	—	40,000
	1,200,000	950,000
Cost of goods sold	600,000	550,000
Selling and administrative expenses	200,000	150,000
Amortization expense	50,000	40,000
Income before income taxes	350,000	210,000
Income taxes	105,000	63,000
Net income	$ 245,000	$147,000

Additional Information

- Poker acquired a 60% interest in the common shares of Joker on January 1, Year 4, at a cost of $420,000 and uses the cost method to account for its investment. At that time, Joker's net book value of shareholders' equity was $700,000 and the fair value of each of its assets and liabilities equalled book value (there was no goodwill).
- In Year 9, Joker paid a management fee of $50,000 to Poker. Poker recorded this as other income.
- In Year 5, Poker sold two trademarks with an indefinite life to Joker and recorded a total gain on sale of $60,000 ($30,000 for each trademark). During Year 9, Joker sold one of these trademarks to an unrelated company for a gain of $40,000.
- During Year 9, Joker declared and paid dividends totalling $200,000.
- The income tax rate is 30% for both companies.

Required:

(a) Assume that Joker is a joint venture that is jointly owned by Poker and several unrelated venturers. Prepare Poker's consolidated income statement for the year ended December 31, Year 9.

(b) Assume that Joker is not a joint venture, and furthermore, that Poker's long-term investment provides it with control over Joker. Provide a calculation of Poker's net income that should be reported in accordance with GAAP for the year ended December 31, Year 9.

Problem 16 Jager Ltd., a joint venture, was formed on January 1, Year 3. Cliffcord Corp., one of the three founding venturers, invested land for a 40% interest in the joint venture. The other two venturers invested equipment and cash for their 60% equity in Jager. All of the venturers agreed that the land had a fair market value of $2,000,000, and would provide services to the venture for approximately 8 years. This land had been acquired by Cliffcord over 20 years ago, and as a result, the carrying value on Cliffcord's records on January 1 was only $600,000. Cliffcord recorded its investment in the joint venture at $2,000,000. On December 31, Year 3, Jager recorded a net loss of $100,000.

Cliffcord uses the equity method to record its investment.

Required:

(a) Prepare Cliffcord's Year 3 journal entries.

(b) Describe how the accounts you created in (a) would be presented in Cliffcord's Year 3 consolidated financial statements.

(c) If Cliffcord had received a 40% interest and $1,000,000 in cash in return for investing this land in the venture, briefly explain how the entries that you made in (a) would be different. You may assume that the other venturers contributed cash in excess of $1,000,000 for their ownership interests.

Problem 17   The following balance sheets have been prepared as at December 31, Year 5, for Kay Corp. and Adams Co. Ltd.:

	Kay	Adams
Cash	$ 68,000	$ 30,000
Accounts receivable	80,000	170,000
Inventory	600,000	400,000
Property and plant	1,400,000	900,000
Investment in Adams	352,000	—
	$2,500,000	$1,500,000
Current liabilities	$ 400,000	$ 150,000
Bonds payable	500,000	600,000
Capital stock	900,000	450,000
Retained earnings	700,000	300,000
	$2,500,000	$1,500,000

Additional Information

- Kay acquired its 40% interest in Adams for $352,000 in Year 1, when Adams' retained earnings amounted to $170,000. The purchase discrepancy on that date was fully amortized by the end of Year 5.
- In Year 4, Kay sold land to Adams and recorded a gain of $60,000 on the transaction. This land is still being used by Adams.
- The December 31, Year 5, inventory of Kay contained a profit recorded by Adams amounting to $35,000.
- On December 31, Year 5, Adams owes Kay $29,000.
- Kay has used the cost method to account for its investment in Adams.
- Use income tax allocation at a rate of 40%.

Required:

Prepare *three* separate balance sheets for Kay as at December 31, Year 5, in accordance with GAAP, assuming that the investment in Adams:
(a) is a control investment.
(b) is a joint venture investment.
(c) is a significant influence investment.

Chapter 11 Foreign Currency Transactions

LEARNING OBJECTIVES

After studying this chapter, you should be able to do the following:

- Translate foreign currency transactions and balances into the reporting currency.
- Describe when to use the current rate and when to use the historical rate when translating assets and liabilities denominated in a foreign currency. Evaluate whether this practice produces results consistent with the normal measurement and valuation of assets and liabilities for domestic transactions and operations.
- Describe the concept of hedging, and prepare a list of items that could be used as a hedge.
- Prepare journal entries and subsequent financial statement presentation for forward exchange contracts that hedge existing monetary positions, firm commitments, or are entered into for speculative purposes.
- Apply the concept of hedge accounting to long-term debt acting as a hedge of a future revenue stream.
- Differentiate between the accounting for a fair value hedge and a cash flow hedge.

INTRODUCTION

Many Canadian companies conduct business in foreign countries as well as in Canada. For some companies, foreign business simply means purchasing products and services from foreign suppliers, or selling products and services to foreign customers. Other companies go far beyond importing and exporting; they borrow and lend money in foreign markets and conduct business in foreign countries through sales offices, branches, subsidiaries, and joint ventures. Of 200 Canadian public companies recently sampled, 123 made disclosures about geographic areas.[1] These companies are generating revenues, incurring costs, and employing assets in countries other than Canada. Bombardier, in its 2006 annual report, reported export revenues of $5.3 billion, representing 36 percent of total sales.

No specific accounting issues arise when the parties involved in an import or export transaction agree that the settlement will be in Canadian dollars. Because it is a *Canadian dollar denominated transaction*, the company will record the foreign purchase or sale in exactly the same manner as any domestic purchase or sale. In

[1] *Financial Reporting in Canada 2006*, 32nd edition. Toronto: CICA, chapter 13.

many situations, however, the agreement calls for the transaction to be settled in a foreign currency. This means one of two things: (a) the Canadian company will have to acquire foreign currency in order to discharge the obligations resulting from its imports; or (b) the Canadian company will receive foreign currency as a result of its exports, and will have to sell the foreign currency in order to receive Canadian dollars. Transactions such as these are called *foreign currency denominated transactions*.

As the foreign currency exchange rate fluctuates, so does the Canadian dollar value of these foreign transactions. Companies often find it necessary to engage in some form of hedging activity to reduce losses arising from fluctuating exchange rates. The Bank of Nova Scotia uses derivative financial instruments to accommodate the risk management needs of its customers, for proprietary trading, and for asset/liability management purposes. Derivative instruments designated as "asset/liability management" are those used to manage the bank's interest rate, foreign currency, and other exposures, which include instruments designated as hedges. At the end of fiscal year 2006, The Bank of Nova Scotia reported foreign exchange and gold derivative financial instruments with a notional value of $287 billion.[2] In 2006, these derivative financial instruments were simply disclosed in the notes to the financial statements. Under the new rules for financial instruments, effective October 1, 2006, publicly accountable enterprises must report these derivative financial instruments on the balance sheet at fair value on a net basis.

Aside from foreign currency risk, there are many other types of risk a company is exposed to and many different ways of hedging this risk. Bombardier used an innovative contract to increase sales by 38 percent. It offered buyers a $1,000 rebate on its snowmobiles if a pre-set amount of snow did not fall that season. The company was able to make such a guarantee by buying a weather derivative based on a snowfall index. When the season ended the level of snowfall had been such that no payment was received on the weather derivative. However, Bombardier did not have to pay any rebates to their customers either. Furthermore, the buyers purchased the snowmobiles earlier in the season because they did not wait for the snow to fall before making their purchase. This change led to a reduction in working capital requirements (due to lower inventory holding costs) and less strain on production capabilities. The company therefore benefited from lower costs as well as increased earnings.

This chapter covers accounting issues related to foreign currency transactions and foreign currency hedging activities. To provide background for subsequent discussions, the chapter begins with a brief look at exchange rates.

Currency Exchange Rates

An exchange rate is the price to change one currency into another currency.

Both the recording of foreign currency denominated transactions and the translation of foreign currency financial statements require the use of currency exchange rates. An exchange rate is simply the price of one currency in terms of another currency. Exchange rates fluctuate on a daily basis. Historically, governments have tried to stabilize rates between their currencies. Shortly after World War II, a group of the

---

[2] www.scotiabank.com/images/en/filesaboutscotia/14891.pdf, accessed September 11, 2007.

world's major trading nations agreed to "peg" the rates at which their currencies would be exchanged in terms of U.S. dollars. Since these pegged rates stayed reasonably steady, the accounting for foreign transactions was fairly simple. Differences in inflation rates and major changes in the balance of payments among the participating nations were contributing factors in the eventual demise of this agreement in the early 1970s.

The end of pegged rates led to the present system, in which long-term rates are determined by market forces. This system of floating exchange rates is not totally market driven in the short term, because governments often intervene in the marketplace to lessen the swings in the value of their currencies. It is not uncommon to hear that the Canadian dollar has weakened in relation to the U.S. dollar, and that the Bank of Canada has made massive purchases of Canadian dollars in order to soften the decline; or that the U.S. Federal Reserve Bank and the central banks of other countries intervened in the foreign currency markets by purchasing U.S. dollars because the U.S. dollar was declining in relation to other major currencies. Sometimes interventions of this nature are fruitless, as was the case in 1994, when Mexico's central bank abandoned its attempt to prop up the peso and allowed a substantial devaluation to take place.

Reasons for Fluctuating Exchange Rates Currencies trade in markets in such major cities as New York, London, Paris, and Tokyo; and transfers of enormous amounts of currency between countries can take place in a matter of seconds. The price of a currency will fluctuate in much the same manner as the price of any other commodity. There are many reasons why a country's currency price changes, of which the major ones are the following:

- *Inflation rates.* As a general rule, if country A has a higher rate of inflation than country B, the price of A's currency will weaken relative to B's. In a period of inflation, the purchasing power of a country's currency declines. If this currency will not buy as much in goods as it did before, then neither will it buy as much currency of another country as it did before.

- *Interest rates.* Higher interest rates attract foreign investment to a country and in so doing drive up the price of its currency.

- *Trade surpluses and deficits.* As a country exports more than it imports, its currency strengthens and becomes worth more.

Exchange Rate Quotations Exchange rates showing the value of the Canadian dollar in terms of other foreign currencies are quoted daily in many Canadian business newspapers. The amounts that usually appear are called *direct quotations*, which means that the amount represents the cost in Canadian dollars to purchase one unit of foreign currency. For example, a quotation of 1 pound = CDN$2.2972 means that it costs 2.2972 Canadian dollars to purchase 1 British pound. An *indirect quotation* would state the cost in a foreign currency to purchase one Canadian dollar. For example, a quotation of 1 dollar = 0.4353 pounds indicates that it costs 0.4353 British pounds to purchase 1 Canadian dollar. An indirect quotation can be obtained by computing the reciprocal of the *direct* quotation. Conversely, a direct quotation can be obtained by computing the reciprocal of the *indirect* quotation ($1 \div 2.2972 = 0.4353$, and $1 \div 0.4353 = 2.2972$).

Direct quotations are the most useful ones for recording transactions denominated in foreign currencies. Using the exchange rates quoted above, a Canadian

Exchange rates fluctuate over time due primarily to differences in inflation rates, interest rates, and trading practices between the two countries.

Exchange rates can be quoted directly or indirectly.

The direct method is the reciprocal of the indirect method.

company would record the purchase of £10,000 of inventory from a British supplier as $22,972.

Examples of foreign exchange quotations on a particular day for three countries' currencies are shown in Exhibit 11.1. These rates represent the amount in Canadian dollars that a commercial bank would charge if it sold one unit of foreign currency to a major customer. The first rate quoted is called the *spot rate*. If a customer wanted to purchase 5,000 euros on the date that these rates were quoted, the cost would be $8,544 (5,000 × 1.7088). Note that if the bank were to purchase euros from the customer, the amount that it would pay the customer would be slightly less than the amount quoted per euro. The bank's selling rate has to be greater than its purchasing rate if it is to make a profit dealing in foreign currencies. The forward rates quoted (1 month forward, 2 months forward, etc.) are the rates for forward exchange contracts. A *forward exchange contract* is an agreement between a bank and a customer to exchange currencies on a specified future date at a specified rate. For example, when a bank enters into a forward exchange contract with a customer to purchase 5,000 euros six months forward, the bank is committing itself to take delivery of this quantity of euros six months from this date, and to pay the customer $8,528 (5,000 × 1.7055) at that time. Of course, there is also a commitment on the part of the customer to sell 5,000 euros to the bank in six months' time. The use of forward exchange contracts in hedging transactions will be illustrated later in this chapter.

Exhibit 11.1

FOREIGN EXCHANGE DIRECT QUOTATIONS

Country		Currency	CDN$ per unit
United States		Dollar	1.0345
	1 month forward		1.0355
	2 months forward		1.0365
	3 months forward		1.0368
	6 months forward		1.0378
	12 months forward		1.0390
European Union		Euro	1.7088
	1 month forward		1.7086
	3 months forward		1.7076
	6 months forward		1.7055
	12 months forward		1.7041
Japan		Yen	0.012787
	1 month forward		0.012823
	3 months forward		0.012889
	6 months forward		0.012996
	12 months forward		0.013214

Accounting for Foreign Currency Transactions

We will now focus on the issues associated with import/export transactions and foreign currency denominated debt. Accounting problems arise when there are exchange rate changes between the date of a transaction and the eventual settlement in foreign currency. During this period, the company holds foreign currency denominated monetary assets and liabilities, and questions arise as to how to measure these items if financial statements need to be prepared in the intervening period, and what to do with any gains or losses that may result from such measurements. A monetary asset or liability is one that is fixed by contract or otherwise in terms of a monetary unit. Accounts receivable and investments in bonds are examples of monetary assets; accounts payable and bond liabilities are monetary liabilities. A foreign currency denominated monetary position is a net asset position if monetary assets exceed monetary liabilities, or a net liability position if monetary liabilities exceed monetary assets.

> **The historical rate is the rate on the date of the transaction, and the current rate is the rate on the reporting date.**

For accounting purposes, there are basically three rates used in translating foreign currency into the reporting currency: the current rate, the historical rate, and the forward rate. The spot rate on the reporting date of the financial statements is called the current rate. The spot rate on the date of a transaction is called the historical rate for that transaction. The agreed rate for exchange of currencies at a future date is called the forward rate. To illustrate the use of these terms, consider the following example.

Example   ABC Co. has a year-end of December 31. On November 13, Year 1, ABC purchased inventory from a French supplier when the spot rate for one euro (€) was €1 = $1.70. On November 14, Year 1, ABC entered into a contract with a bank to sell euros in 60 days at a rate of €1 – $1.68. The spot rate on December 31, Year 1 was €1 = $1.69. The financial statements for Year 1 were finalized on March 14, Year 2, and released to users on March 15, Year 2. In this example, the current rate is $1.69, the historical rate for the purchase of the inventory is $1.70 and the forward rate for the planned sale of euros is $1.68.

If some inventory was purchased every day throughout the year, the historical rate for each purchase should technically be used to translate the purchase for each day. This procedure is very costly and usually not worth the cost–benefit trade-off. From a practical point of view, it is usually sufficient to use an average rate for the period. The average rate represents the average of the historical rates throughout the period.

When foreign transactions are translated into Canadian dollars, the translation method should produce results consistent with the valuation practices for domestic operations. If Canadian GAAP requires a financial statement item to be reported at historical cost, the historical cost of the item in foreign currency should be multiplied by the historical rate to derive the historical cost in Canadian dollars. If Canadian GAAP requires a financial statement item to be reported at current value at the end of the year, the current value of the item in foreign currency should be multiplied by the current rate to derive the current value in Canadian dollars. If historical cost in foreign currency is multiplied by the current rate or if the current value in foreign currency is multiplied by the historical rate, the Canadian dollar figure is neither historical cost nor current value.

> **The translation method should produce either historical cost in dollars or current value in dollars consistent with normal measurement rules for the financial statement items.**

According to Canadian GAAP, monetary assets and monetary liabilities are valued at current value, non-monetary assets are usually valued at the lower of historical cost and market value, and non-monetary liabilities and shareholders' equity are usually valued at historical amounts. Revenues and expenses are usually measured at historical amounts. As we study the different translation methods in this chapter and the next chapter, we should evaluate whether the translation methods preserve the normal measurement rules under Canadian GAAP.

Import/Export Transactions Denominated in Foreign Currency

Unless otherwise noted, all examples in the text assume that the entity will present its financial statements using the Canadian dollar as the reporting currency.

When a Canadian company purchases goods from a foreign supplier, it usually is billed in the currency of the foreign country. However, the transaction is recorded in the company's accounting records in the currency used in the company's financial statements. Unless noted otherwise, all examples in this book assume that the Canadian dollar is the reporting currency. With this in mind, let's consider the following example to illustrate the accounting for an import transaction.

Example   On June 1, Year 1, Maritime Importers Inc. purchased merchandise from a supplier in Switzerland at a cost of 10,000 Swiss francs, with payment in full to be made in 60 days. The exchange rate on the date of purchase was SF1 = $0.941 and SFI = $0.949 on June 30, Year 1, the company's year-end. Maritime paid its supplier on July 30, Year 1, when the exchange rate was SF1 = $0.953. The following journal entries, recorded in Canadian dollars, illustrate the company's purchase of merchandise, year-end adjustments, and subsequent payment.

June 1, Year 1

Inventory	9,410	
Accounts payable (10,000 × 0.941)		9,410

The cost of the purchase is finalized when the item is purchased.

The purchase of the inventory at a cost of 10,000 Swiss francs and the related liability are translated at the spot rate on the date of purchase. The value of the inventory has been fixed at its historical cost and is not exposed to exchange fluctuations, except in the situation where the market price in Swiss francs declines and the lower of cost and market rule is applied.[3] In such a case, the lower of cost and market rule would be applied by comparing the Canadian dollar historical cost of the inventory with the market price in Swiss francs translated at the current exchange rate.[4]

On the other hand, Maritime now has a monetary position that is exposed to exchange fluctuations. The Canadian dollar amount required to pay the 10,000 Swiss francs will change as the exchange rate changes. To better reflect the cost of settling this obligation, this liability should be revalued to current value at each reporting date.

On the company's year-end, the account payable of 10,000 Swiss francs must be translated at the current rate. The previously recorded amount ($9,410) is increased by $80 to reflect a translated liability of $9,490 (10,000 × 0.949).

June 30, Year 1

Exchange loss	80	
Accounts payable		80
To adjust the account payable to the current rate		

Foreign exchange adjustments are included in income in the period in which they occur.

The resulting foreign exchange loss would appear on the income statement for the year ended June 30, Year 1.

On the settlement date, the exchange rate has increased from $0.949 to $0.953. The SF10,000 account payable is increased by $40 to reflect its translation at the

---

[3] See *CICA Handbook*, paragraph 1651.18.

[4] For example, if the market price of the inventory purchased had declined to SF9,950 on June 30 (assuming that none of the inventory purchased had been sold by year-end), the market price in Canadian dollars would be $9,443 (SF9,950 × 0.949). Because the translated market price is greater than the previous translated historical cost of $9,410, a write down would not be required.

spot rate at this date ($10,000 \times 0.953 = 9,530$). The company purchases 10,000 Swiss francs from its bank at a cost of $9,530 and remits the francs to its Swiss supplier. The foreign exchange loss of $40 will appear on the income statement for the year ended June 30, Year 2. The following journal entries record the transactions:

July 30, Year 1

Exchange loss	40	
Accounts payable		40
To adjust the account payable to the spot rate		

Accounts payable	9,530	
Cash ($10,000 \times 0.953$)		9,530
Payment to supplier		

An Export Example We will now consider an example of the export of goods by a Canadian company.

On November 15, Year 1, Regina Malt Producers Ltd. shipped a carload of malt to a brewery in the United States, with full payment to be received on January 31, Year 2. The selling price of the malt was US$26,000. Regina Malt has a December 31 year-end. The following exchange rates existed on the dates significant for accounting purposes:

Transaction date — Nov. 15, Year 1
    Selling price US$26,000
    Exchange rate US$1 = CDN$1.325
Year end — Dec. 31, Year 1
    Exchange rate US$1 = CDN$1.329
Settlement date — Jan. 31, Year 2
    Exchange rate US$1 = CDN$1.319

The journal entries required on the dates noted above are as follows:

The sale is translated at the historical rate to produce a historical price in Canadian dollars. This is consistent with normal measurement rules to record sales at historical values.

Nov. 15, Year 1

Accounts receivable	34,450	
Sales		34,450

The accounts receivable and the sales are recorded at the November 15 spot rate (US$26,000 $\times$ 1.325 = CDN$34,450). The sales amount has been established at historical value and is unaffected by future exchange rate fluctuations. The accounts receivable (a monetary item) is at risk to exchange rate fluctuations. Note that while accounts receivable has been recorded at CDN$34,450, it is in fact a receivable of US$26,000.

At the company's year-end, the exchange rate has changed to US$1 = CDN$1.329, and the receivable must appear in the financial statements at $34,554 (US$26,000 $\times$ 1.329 = CDN$34,554). The following journal entry adjusts the accounts receivable to the year-end spot rate:

The accounts receivable is translated at the current rate to produce a current value in Canadian dollars. This is consistent with normal measurement rules to record monetary items at current values.

Dec. 31, Year 1

Accounts receivable	104	
Exchange gain		104

This exchange gain will appear in the company's Year 1 income statement.

By January 31, Year 2, which is the settlement date, the value of the U.S. dollar has declined relative to the Canadian dollar. When Regina Malt collects US$26,000 from its customer and delivers the U.S. dollars to its bank, it only receives CDN$34,294 ($26,000 \times 1.319$). The journal entry to record the receipt of

US$26,000, and its conversion to Canadian dollars and the resultant loss, is as follows:

Jan. 31, Year 2

Cash	34,294	
Exchange loss	260	
Accounts receivable		34,554
Payment from U.S. customer		

The exchange loss of $260 will appear in the Year 2 income statement. Note that the actual exchange loss between the transaction date and the settlement date was $156 (34,450 – 34,294). Because the company's year-end occurred between these two dates, the exchange loss will appear in two income statements in the following manner:

Year 1 income statement	
Exchange gain	$104
Year 2 income statement	
Exchange loss	260
Total exchange loss on the transaction	$156

Exchange gains are reported in income even though they are unrealized.

The previous examples have illustrated the concept that exchange gains and losses resulting from the translation of a *current monetary position* (i.e., a receivable or payable that is due within one year from the date of a balance sheet) are reflected in income in the year in which they occur. Note that these exchange gains and losses are actually unrealized in the sense that they result from the translation of a liability or a receivable. This practice places representational faithfulness as a higher priority than conservatism. The actual exchange gain or loss results from the settlement of the position, as was illustrated above. The same concept is applied to *non-current monetary positions* which is discussed in the next section.

Transaction Gains and Losses from Non-current Monetary Items

Many Canadian companies borrow money in foreign markets, mainly because the capital markets in Canada are relatively small. The following example illustrates the accounting for foreign currency denominated debt.

Example Sable Company has a calendar year-end. On January 1, Year 1, the company borrowed 2,000,000 Swiss francs from a Swiss bank. The loan is to be repaid on December 31, Year 4, and requires interest at 8 percent to be paid each December 31. Both the annual interest payments and the loan repayment are to be made in Swiss francs.

During the term of the loan, the following exchange rates necessary for our analysis were in effect:

Jan. 1, Year 1	SF1 = $0.945
Average, Year 1	SF1 = $0.942
Dec. 31, Year 1	SF1 = $0.939
Dec. 31, Year 2	SF1 = $0.942
Dec. 31, Year 3	SF1 = $0.941
Dec. 31, Year 4	SF1 = $0.946

Sable Company would record the transactions as follows:

Jan. 1, Year 1

Cash	1,890,000	
Loan payable (2,000,000 × 0.945)		1,890,000

Interest expense is translated at the average of the historical rates to produce a historical price in Canadian dollars. This is consistent with normal measurement rules to record interest expense at historical values.

This entry records the incurrence of a four-year loan of SF2,000,000 translated at the spot rate. On December 31, the company purchases 160,000 Swiss francs (2,000,000 × 8 percent) from its bank to make the interest payment, at a cost of $150,240 (160,000 × 0.939). A question arises as to whether the amount paid should be reflected as the interest expense for the past year. Remember that interest expense was SF160,000, which accrued throughout the year. It seems logical, therefore, to translate the interest expense using the average of the Year 1 exchange rates, or better still to translate the monthly interest at the average for each month. In either case, when the interest is actually paid at the end of the year an exchange gain or loss will have to be recorded. Using the average exchange rate for Year 1, the journal entries to record the interest expense and payment are as follows:

Dec. 31, Year 1

Interest expense	150,720	
Exchange gain		480
Cash		150,240

To record interest expense at the average Year 1 rate of SF1 = $0.942, and the payment of interest at the year-end rate of SF1 = $0.939

The loan payable is translated at the current rate to produce a current value in Canadian dollars. This is consistent with normal measurement rules to record monetary items at current values.

On December 31, the loan is translated for financial statement purposes at $1,878,000 (2,000,000 × 0.939). The next entry adjusts the loan payable to the amount required on that date:

Dec. 31, Year 1

Loan payable	12,000	
Exchange gain		12,000

Exchange gains and losses occur on items translated at the current rate but not on items translated at historical rates.

The $12,480 total exchange gain resulting from the interest payment and the translation of the loan will appear in the Year 1 income statement.

Journal entries for years 2 through 4 will not be illustrated; however, the following summarizes the yearly exchange gains and losses from translating this loan liability.

	Total	Year 1	Year 2	Year 3	Year 4
Exchange gain (loss)	$(2,000)	$12,000	$(6,000)	$2,000	$(10,000)

Speculative Forward Exchange Contracts

In a forward exchange contract, two parties agree to exchange currencies at a future date at a specified exchange rate.

A forward exchange contract is one in which an exchange broker (usually a bank) and its customer agree to exchange currencies at a set price on a future date. Forward contracts can be either fixed dated or option dated. A fixed-dated contract specifies a fixed date such as June 18, for example. An option-dated contract specifies a certain period such as the month of June. A company may enter into a forward exchange contract purely to speculate on future exchange movements. For example, a company might enter into a contract to purchase foreign currency at a 60-day forward rate in anticipation that the spot rate in 60 days' time will be greater than the original forward rate. If its projection turns out to be accurate, it would purchase the foreign currency from the bank at the contracted price, and immediately sell the currency to the bank at the higher spot rate. The following example deals with a speculative forward exchange contract.

Example   On December 1, Year 1, Raven Company enters into a forward contract to sell 1 million Philippines pesos (PP) to its bank on March 1, Year 2, at the market rate for a 90-day forward contract of PP1 = $0.0227. On December 31, Year 1, Raven's year-end, the 60-day forward rate to sell Philippines pesos on March 1 has changed to PP1 = $0.0222. On March 1, Year 2, the currencies are exchanged when the spot rate is PP1 = $0.0220.

According to Section 3855, this forward contract is considered to be a financial instrument. It must be recorded at fair value on the date of the transaction and be revalued at fair value throughout its life, with any gains or losses reflected in income as they occur. There are two methods of recording this forward contract: the gross method and the net method. Under the gross method, the receivable from the bank and payable to the bank are each recorded separately at fair value. Under the net method, the receivable and payable are netted against each other and only the net receivable or net payable is recorded. The entries for this contract under the gross and net methods are shown in Exhibit 11.2.

The receivable and payable under the forward contract will be offset against each other and only the net amount will be reported on the balance sheet at each reporting date.

Exhibit 11.2

JOURNAL ENTRIES FOR SPECULATIVE FORWARD CONTRACT

		Gross Method		Net Method	
A forward contract is a financial instrument, which must be valued at fair value throughout its life.	*December 1, Year 1*				
	Receivable from bank ($)	22,700			
	Payable to bank (PP)		22,700		
	Record forward contract at forward rate (PP1,000,000 × 0.0227 = $22,700)				
	December 31, Year 1				
	Forward contract			500	
	Payable to bank (PP)	500			
	Exchange gain		500		500
	Revalue forward contract at fair value (PP1,000,000 × (0.0227 − 0.0222) = $500)				
When the forward rate changes, the fair value of the forward contract changes.	*March 1, Year 2*				
	Forward contract			200	
	Payable to bank (PP)	200			
	Exchange gain		200		200
	Revalue forward contract at fair value (PP1,000,000 × (0.0222 − 0.0220) = $200)				
	Payable to bank (PP)	22,000			
	Cash (PP)		22,000		
	Deliver PP1,000,000 to bank to pay off liability (PP1,000,000 × 0.0220 = $22,000)				
	Cash ($)	22,700			
	Receivable from bank ($)		22,700		
	Receive $22,700 from bank				
	Cash ($)			700	
	Forward contract				700
	Settle forward contract on net basis by receiving $700 (22,700 − 22,000)				

The $ symbol behind receivable from bank in the first entry indicates that the account receivable is denominated in Canadian dollars whereas the PP behind the payable to bank indicates that the accounts payable is denominated in Philippines pesos. In other words, Raven will receive Canadian dollars and will pay Philippines pesos to settle this forward contract.

The fair value of the forward contract on December 1, Year 1, is zero because the two parties have just entered into a contract at the market rate for forward contracts. Under the gross method, the receivable and payable are both recorded at the future rate. Since the receivable and payable are equal and offsetting, there is no entry under the net method.

Some accountants may object to recording the forward contract on December 1 because forward exchange contracts are "executory" in nature. An *executory contract* is one in which neither party has performed its obligation to the other. Most contracts trigger accounting recognition only when one of the parties fulfils the obligation as agreed. For example, when a company places an order with a manufacturer for the purchase of machinery, neither party makes an accounting entry. The delivery of the machinery, or a down payment prior to delivery, results in accounting recognition by both parties because of the performance by one.

Forward contracts must be recorded according to the CICA Handbook.

While forward exchange contracts are certainly executory, they are also firm commitments, and once entered cannot be cancelled. For this reason, the *CICA Handbook* requires that the forward contract be recorded.

On December 31, the forward contract is remeasured at fair value. We will use the market rate for forward contracts maturing on March 1 to determine the fair value of Raven's contract. On this date, the 60-day forward rate to sell Philippines pesos on March 1 is PP1 = $0.0222 whereas Raven's contract is locked in at PP1 = $0.0227. Raven's contract is going to generate $22,700 on March 1 whereas contracts executed on December 31 would only generate $22,200 on March 1 for 1 million Philippines pesos. Therefore, Raven's contract is worth an extra $500 as of March 1. Theoretically, we should discount this $500 for two months. Practically speaking, the amount would usually not be discounted because the difference between the nominal amount of $500 and the present value of $500 for two months is not material and is not worth the effort to calculate.

The forward contract is worth more when the PP declines in value, i.e., the Canadian dollar increases in value.

In the appendix to this chapter, we illustrate how this forward contract would be accounted for with discounting. Unless otherwise noted, all examples in the text will not use discounting. The forward contract will simply be valued at the forward rate for the term to maturity.

Notice that the gain of $500 is recorded under both the gross and net methods. When financial statements are prepared at December 31 under the gross method, the due from bank of $22,700 and due to bank of $22,200 will be offset against each other and only the net receivable of $500 will be presented and will likely be called forward contract. Therefore, the financial statement presentation will be the same under both the gross and net methods even though the underlying accounts have different balances.

On March 1, Year 2, the forward contract is once again revalued to fair value. Since the contract is being settled on this date, the market value of this forward contract is based on the spot rate for this date, i.e., PP1 = $0.0220. The contract is worth $700 because Raven is going to get $22,700 from the bank whereas PP1,000,000 is only worth $22,000 in the market on March 1. Therefore, Raven has gained $700 on this contract in total and $200 since December 31. The first entry on March 1 records this $200 gain. The other entries record the exchange of pesos for dollars.

If we combine all of the journal entries under both the gross and net methods, we end up with the following entry:

The gross and net methods produce the same overall result in the end.

Cash ($)	700	
Exchange gain — Year 1		500
Exchange gain — Year 2		200

In the end, Raven gained $700 by speculating on rate changes. If the exchange rates had changed in the other direction, i.e., if the Canadian dollar decreased in value rather than increased, Raven would have lost money on this speculative contract.

In the next few sections, we will illustrate how forward contracts can be used to hedge existing and anticipated exposure to foreign currency risk. Throughout the remainder of this chapter and in the end-of-chapter material, we will use the gross method of accounting for forward contracts. This makes it easier to see how the forward contract is effective in hedging against the currency risk under different situations.

Hedges

A hedge is a means of reducing or eliminating exchange losses on an overall basis by entering into a position to offset the risk exposure.

The previous examples illustrated the accounting for the foreign exchange gains and losses that result from holding a foreign currency denominated monetary position during a period of exchange rate changes. If an enterprise wishes to protect itself from the economic (and accounting) effects that result from such a position, there are many possible ways. This type of protection is generally referred to as "hedging," which can be defined as a means of transferring risk arising from foreign exchange (or interest rate, or price) fluctuations from those who wish to avoid it to those who are willing to assume it.[5] In order to hedge the risk of exchange rate fluctuations, a company takes a foreign currency position opposite to the position that it wishes to protect. The item with the risk exposure that the entity wishes to hedge and has taken steps to hedge is called the hedged item. The item used to offset the risk is called the hedging item. In the ideal case, the hedged item is perfectly hedged by the hedging item and there is no longer any overall exposure to currency fluctuations. The entity has eliminated the overall risk of further exchange losses but also loses any possibility of gains from currency fluctuations.

Section 3865 suggests that the following hedging items could be used to hedge against the risk of exchange fluctuations:

A hedging item is the item used to offset the risk exposure. The hedged item is the item with the risk exposure that the entity has taken steps to modify.

- A *derivative financial instrument.* For example, a forward exchange contract, a foreign currency option contract, or a foreign currency futures contract could be used to hedge a monetary asset or liability, commitment, or an anticipated future transaction;
- A *monetary item.* For example, an existing monetary asset or liability could be used to hedge a commitment or an anticipated future transaction.

Section 3865 also states that an anticipated future transaction can be a hedged item but it cannot be a hedging item. Therefore, it is not possible to designate a future revenue stream as a hedge of an existing monetary liability for accounting purposes. A derivative can be a hedging item but would not typically be a hedged item.

When accounting for the hedge, we want to properly reflect whether the hedge has been effective. If the hedge is truly effective, there should be no overall exchange gain or loss hitting the income statement other than the cost of establishing the hedge. The exchange gains or losses on the hedged item will be offset by exchange losses or gains on the hedging item. But what happens when the hedging item is

---

[5] See John E. Stewart. "The Challenges of Hedge Accounting." *Journal of Accountancy* (November 1989), pp. 48–56.

purchased in advance of the hedged item? For example, a forward contract may be purchased in Year 1 to hedge a transaction expected to occur in Year 2. How can the Year 1 gains or losses on the forward contract be offset against the Year 2 losses or gains on the anticipated transaction when the anticipated transaction has not yet occurred?

The solution is hedge accounting as defined and described in Section 3865 of the *CICA Handbook*. Under hedge accounting, the exchange gains or losses on the hedging item will be recognized in the income statement in the same period as the exchange gains or losses on the hedged item when they would otherwise be recognized in different periods. To qualify for hedge accounting, the following three conditions must be met:

Under hedge accounting, the exchange gains or losses on the hedging item will be reported in income in the same period as the exchange gains or losses on the hedged item.

1. At the inception of the hedging relationship, the entity has identified the risks being hedged and designated that hedge accounting will be applied;
2. At the inception of the hedging relationship, the entity has formal documentation of the hedging relationship, its purpose and method of assessing its effectiveness, and the method of accounting for the hedging relationship;
3. The entity has reasonable assurance that the hedge will be effective at the inception and throughout its term and the entity demonstrates at each measurement date that the hedge has indeed been effective.

First of all, notice that hedge accounting is optional. The entity can choose to apply hedge accounting and thereby ensure that gains and losses on the hedged item are reported in income in the same period as the gains and losses on the hedging item. Alternatively, it could choose to not apply hedge accounting and account for the hedged item and the hedging item in isolation of each other.

Secondly, hedges can be designated for accounting purposes as either fair value hedges, cash flow hedges, or hedges of a net investment in a self-sustaining foreign operation.[6] In a fair value hedge, the entity uses a hedging item to hedge against the fluctuation in the fair value of the hedged item. This method will be used when the hedged item (such as long-term debt) will be valued at fair value. The gain or loss in the fair values of the hedging item and hedged item are both recognized in net income in the period of the change in exchange rates.

The entity chooses whether to designate the hedge as a fair value hedge or a cash flow hedge.

In a cash flow hedge, the entity uses a hedging item (such as a derivative) to hedge against the fluctuation in the Canadian dollar value of future cash flows (such as future sales). The gain or loss on the hedging item is initially reported in other comprehensive income and subsequently reclassified to net income when the hedged item affects net income. Although there are many different types of hedging items, we will use forward exchange contracts as an example of a hedging item and to illustrate hedge accounting.

DISCUSSION QUESTION

Do We Have a Gain or What?

Interfast Corporation, a fastener manufacturer, recently has been expanding its sales through exports to foreign markets. Earlier this year, the company negotiated the sale

---

6 Accounting for self-sustaining subsidiaries will be discussed in Chapter 12.

of several thousand cases of fasteners to a wholesaler in the country of Loznia. The customer is unwilling to assume the risk of having to make payment in Canadian dollars. Desperate to enter the Loznian market, the vice-president for international sales agrees to denominate the sale in lrubles (LR), the national currency of Loznia. The current exchange rate for the lruble is $2.00. In addition, the customer indicates that he cannot make payment until all of the fasteners have been sold. Payment of LR100,000 is scheduled for six months from the date of sale.

Fearful that the lruble might depreciate in value over the next six months, the head of the risk management department at Interfast Corporation enters into a forward contract to sell lrubles in six months at a forward rate of $1.80. The forward contract is designated as a fair value hedge of the lruble receivable. Six months later, when payment is received from the Loznian customer, the exchange rate for the lruble is $1.70. The corporate treasurer calls the head of the risk management department into her office.

Treasurer: I see that your decision to hedge our foreign currency position on that sale to Loznia was a bad one.

Department Head: What do you mean? We have a gain on that forward contract. We're $10,000 better off from having entered into that hedge.

Treasurer: That's not what the books say. The accountants have recorded a net loss of $20,000 on that particular deal. I'm afraid I'm not going to be able to pay you a bonus this year. Another bad deal like this one and I'm going to have to demote you back to the interest rate swap department.

Department Head: Those bean counters have messed up again. I told those guys in international sales that selling to customers in Loznia was risky, but at least by hedging our exposure, we managed to receive a reasonable amount of cash on that deal. In fact, we ended up with a gain of $10,000 on the hedge. Tell the accountants to check their debits and credits again. I'm sure they just put a debit in the wrong place or some accounting thing like that.

Have the accountants made a mistake? Does the company have a loss, a gain, or both from this forward contract?

Hedging a Recognized Monetary Item

Vulcan Corporation of Toronto, Ontario, has a December 31 year-end. On November 1, Year 1, when the Swiss franc was worth $0.87, Vulcan sold merchandise to a Swiss customer for SF200,000. The terms of the sale required payment in full on February 15, Year 2. On November 15, Year 1, the spot rate was SF1 = $0.865 and the three-month forward rate was SF1 = $0.842. In order to protect the account receivable from further exchange losses, Vulcan entered into a contract with its bank on this date, to deliver SF200,000 in three months' time. At year-end, the spot rate was SF1 = $0.869 and the 45-day forward rate was $0.852. On February 15, Year 2, Vulcan received SF200,000 from the customer and settled the forward contract with the bank when the spot and forward rates were $0.860.

Before preparing the journal entries, try to understand the rationale for entering into the hedge and the expected results. From November 1 to November 14, the Canadian dollar value of the receivable declined in value from $174,000 (200,000 × 0.87) to $173,000 (200,000 × 0.865) because of the strengthening of the Canadian dollar relative to the Swiss franc. Vulcan is concerned about a further slide in the value of the franc and further erosion in the value of the receivable. To minimize the loss from a further decline, Vulcan entered into a forward exchange contract to fix the amount it will receive in Canadian dollars when the receivable is collected and that is $168,400 (200,000 × 0.842). In effect, Vulcan was prepared to pay $4,600 ($173,000 – $168,400) in order to avoid bigger losses. This differential of $4,600 is called a discount on the forward contract. It will be expensed as a foreign exchange loss over the term of the forward exchange contract.

The forward contract is used to offset the risk of decline in value of the accounts receivable from the customer.

Although the forward contract is a hedge of the accounts receivable, we will not have to use hedge accounting in this situation. Both the accounts receivable and the forward contract are valued at fair value at each reporting date with the exchange adjustments reported in net income. Since the exchange adjustments on both items are already being reported in net income in the same period, it is not necessary to use hedge accounting. We will account for each item separately as we did for the previous examples in this chapter. If the company wanted to use hedge accounting and designated the forward contract as a fair value hedge, the accounting would look exactly the same as accounting for each item separately. So, there is no point in using hedge accounting in this particular situation. Hedge accounting is only necessary when the exchange adjustments would otherwise be reported in income in different periods.

A time line for the transactions follows:

Nov 1	Nov 15	Dec 31	Feb 15
Sell goods on account	Hedge receivable	Year-end	Collect receivable and settle forward exchange contract

Vulcan will record the sale and the receivable at the spot rate on the transaction date with the following journal entry:

The SF indicates that the accounts receivable is denominated in Swiss francs. The $ indicates that the sale is being measured in dollars and will not be adjusted for exchange rate changes.

Nov. 1, Year 1		
Accounts receivable (SF)	174,000	
Sales ($)		174,000
SF200,000 × 0.87 = 174,000		

On November 15, the receivable is hedged when the spot rate is SF1 = $0.865. The exchange loss that occurred during the period when the account receivable was *not* hedged is recorded next, followed by the entry to record the forward contract.

Nov. 15, Year 1		
Exchange gains and losses	1,000	
Accounts receivable (SF)		1,000
Exchange loss prior to the date of hedge, SF200,000 × (0.87 – 0.865)		
Receivable from bank ($)	168,400	
Payable to bank (SF)		168,400
To record forward contract at forward rate — SF 200,000 × 0.842		

The receivable from the bank represents the amount of Canadian dollars that Vulcan will receive when it delivers SF200,000 to the bank in three months. As this is denominated in Canadian dollars, it will not be affected by subsequent changes in the spot rate. The payable to bank represents an obligation of Vulcan to deliver SF200,000 to the bank in three months' time and is denominated in Swiss francs. It should be reported at fair value throughout the term of the contract. The fair value is determined by multiplying SF200,000 by the forward rate for the remaining term of the contract. At year-end, the accounts receivable and payable to the bank are adjusted to fair value as follows:

The current rate is used when the item can be settled at any time whereas the forward rate is used when the item must be settled at a future date.

Dec. 31, Year 1

Accounts receivable (SF)	800	
Exchange gains and losses		800

To adjust the account receivable to the December 31 spot rate
— SF200,000 × (0.869 – 0.865)

Exchange gains and losses	2,000	
Payable to bank (SF)		2,000

To adjust the forward contract to the December 31 forward rate
— SF200,000 × (0.852 – 0.842)

The $2,000 adjustment can be broken down as follows:

- An $800 loss on forward contract, the hedging item, to offset the $800 gain on the accounts receivable, the hedged item;
- The other $1,200 is the portion of the $4,600 discount on the forward contract being expensed in this period.

Financial statements are prepared as at December 31. The following partial trial balance is presented to show only the accounts used to record these particular transactions.

PARTIAL TRIAL BALANCE
December 31, Year 1

	Dr.	Cr.
Accounts receivable	$173,800	
Exchange gains and losses	2,200	
Sales		$174,000
Receivable from bank ($)	168,400	
Payable to bank (SF)		170,400
	$344,400	$344,400

The accounts associated with the hedge have been segregated in the trial balance to emphasize their nature. These executory contract items should be shown at their net amount in the balance sheet because they will be settled simultaneously and on a net basis. The presentation of the items shown on the trial balance in the year-end financial statements is shown next.

VULCAN CORP.
PARTIAL BALANCE SHEET
December 31, Year 1

Assets

Accounts receivable	$173,800
Other items	XXX
	$ XXX

The receivable from and payable to the bank are offset against each other and only the net difference of a $2,000 liability is reported.

Liabilities and shareholders' equity

Forward contract	$ 2,000
Other items	XXX
	$ XXX

VULCAN CORP.
PARTIAL INCOME STATEMENT
for the Year Ended December 31, Year 1

Sales		$174,000
Expenses:		
Foreign exchange loss	2,200	
Other	XXX	XXX
Net income		$ XXX

The $2,200 foreign exchange loss consists of the $1,000 loss before the hedge was put in place and $1,200 expense pertaining to the $4,600 discount on the forward contract.

On the February 15 settlement date, the receivable from the Swiss customer and the payable to bank are adjusted to current value as follows:

Only the foreign denominated receivables and payables must be revalued. The receivable from the bank is denominated in Canadian dollars and is not affected by changes in exchange rates.

Feb. 15, Year 2

Exchange gains and losses	1,800	
Accounts receivable (SF)		1,800

To adjust the account receivable to the spot rate —
SF200,000 × (0.869 – 0.860)

Exchange gains and losses	1,600	
Payable to bank (SF)		1,600

To adjust the forward contract to the forward rate —
SF200,000 × (0.860 – 0.852)

The total of the exchange losses recognized in Year 2 is $3,400, which is the remaining amount of the discount on the forward contract. This brings the total exchange loss on the forward contract to $4,600 ($1,200 from Year 1 and $3,400 for Year 2), which is equal to the discount on the forward contract.

The Swiss customer sends SF200,000 to Vulcan, which is recorded in a Swiss franc cash account. Vulcan delivers the SF200,000 to the bank to discharge its forward contract obligation and receives C$168,400 as agreed. The following journal entries record these events:

Feb. 15, Year 2

Cash (SF)	172,000	
Accounts receivable (SF)		172,000
Collection from Swiss customer		

Payable to bank (SF)	172,000	
Cash (SF)		172,000
Delivery of francs to bank		

Cash	168,400	
Receivable from bank		168,400
Receipt of Canadian dollars from bank		

Accrual accounting is more complicated than cash accounting but, in total and over time, it presents the same overall effect on net income as cash accounting.

You may be overwhelmed with the number of entries above and may not appreciate the overall effect. To see the big picture, all of the above entries for Year 1 and Year 2 can be condensed into one entry as follows:

Cash ($)	168,400	
Foreign exchange loss before hedge	1,000	
Foreign exchange loss (= discount on forward contract)	4,600	
Sales		174,000

The net impact on income is equal to the amount of cash received. This is a typical result in accounting. Sales were recorded at the historical rate, which is consistent with our measurement model. The exchange losses occurred due to two reasons. First, the company lost $1,000 in the value of the accounts receivable due to the increase in value of the Canadian dollar relative to the Swiss franc before the hedge was put into place. Then, the company incurred a loss of $4,600 to put the hedge into place. In the end, the accounting for the hedge reflects the objective of the hedge in the first place.

Hedging an Unrecognized Firm Commitment

The forward contract is used to offset the risk of an increase in the cost of the inventory.

On June 2, Year 2, when the spot rate was US$1 = CDN$1.26, Manning Inc. of Vancouver ordered merchandise from an American supplier for US$350,000. Delivery was scheduled for August 1 with payment to be made in full on delivery. Upon placing the order, Manning immediately entered into a 60-day forward contract with its bank to purchase US$350,000 on August 1 at the forward rate of US$1 = CDN$1.28. Manning's year-end is June 30. On August 1, the merchandise was received, Manning purchased the U.S. dollars from the bank and paid its supplier.

In this example, the purpose of the forward contract is to fix the amount to be paid for the inventory. The hedged item is the commitment and the hedging item is the forward contract. The commitment to purchase the inventory is not recognized for accounting purposes because there is no asset or liability at the time of the commitment. The inventory and related accounts payable will only be recorded when the inventory is actually received. Since we must report the forward contract when the contract is signed, we will have a mismatch in the current year because the hedging item is recognized but the hedged item is not. Without hedge accounting, the exchange gains or losses on the forward contract would be reported in the current year whereas no exchange gain or losses would be reported on the accounts payable because it does not legally exist in the current year. Therefore, hedge accounting is necessary to report the exchange gains or losses on the hedged item and hedging item in the same period. We could designate the forward contract as a cash flow hedge and defer the recognition in net income of the exchange gains or losses on the forward contract. Alternatively, we could designate the forward contract as a fair value hedge and advance the recognition in net income of the exchange gains or losses on the commitment. As previously mentioned, in order to apply hedge accounting, very strict conditions must be met. These conditions are stated in paragraph 3865.08 of the *CICA Handbook*.

Cash flow hedge With a cash flow hedge, the gain or loss on the hedging item is initially reported in other comprehensive income. The exchanges gains/losses will be taken out of other comprehensive income and reported in net income when the hedged item affects net income. In our example, the hedged item is the commitment that will be included in income when the inventory is sold.

The premium on the forward contract is a cost of fixing the price of the inventory.

The premium on the forward contract is $7,000 [US$350,000 × (1.28 − 1.26)]. It is the amount that Manning is prepared to pay to fix the amount of the cash flows required to purchase the inventory. Since the forward contract was intended to fix the cost of the inventory, the $7,000 will be reported as a cost of the inventory and will be reflected in income when the inventory is sold.

The relevant exchange rates for this example are as follows:

Date	Spot Rate	Forward Rate
June 2	US$1 = CDN$1.260	US$1 = CDN$1.280
June 30	US$1 = CDN$1.268	US$1 = CDN$1.275
August 1	US$1 = CDN$1.272	US$1 = CDN$1.272

A time line for the transactions follows:

June 2	June 30	August 1
Order goods & hedge order	Year-end	Receive goods, settle forward contract and pay supplier

The order does not meet the definition of an asset or a liability.

Manning would not make a journal entry to record the merchandise ordered. However, the hedging of the commitment by entering into a forward contract to purchase U.S. dollars would be recorded with the following entry:

June 2, Year 2

Receivable from bank (US$)	448,000	
Payable to bank (CDN$)		448,000
To record forward contract at forward rate – 350,000 × 1.280		

"Payable to bank" represents the amount in Canadian dollars that Manning will pay the bank in August when it receives US$350,000. The amount recorded will not be affected by future exchange rate fluctuations. The receivable from bank is the hedge of the expected future liability. It is denominated in U.S. dollars and represents Manning's right to receive U.S. dollars from the bank in August. It should be reported at fair value and is accordingly translated at the forward exchange rate. Note that the net balance of this executory contract is zero, and if a balance sheet were prepared at this time the accounts would not be shown.

At the year-end, the receivable from the bank is adjusted to its fair value as follows:

The exchange gains or losses on the hedging item are reported in other comprehensive income for now and will be reported in income when the exchange gains or losses on the hedged items are reported in income.

June 30, Year 2

Other comprehensive income	1,750	
Receivable from bank (US$)		1,750
To adjust forward contract to June 30 forward rate — 350,000 × (1.280 – 1.275)		

Notice that the exchange adjustment is reported in other comprehensive income and not in regular income. On the June 30, Year 2 balance sheet, the $1,750 difference between the receivable from bank ($446,250) and the payable to bank ($448,000) would be reported as forward contract under current liabilities and cumulative other comprehensive income would be reported as a separate component of shareholders' equity. No foreign exchange gains or losses are reported on the income statement.

On August 1, the receivable from the bank is adjusted to its fair value, the forward contract is settled and the delivery of inventory is recorded as follows:

August 1, Year 2

Other comprehensive income	1,050	
Receivable from bank (US$)		1,050
To adjust forward contract to August 1 forward rate – 350,000 × (1.275 – 1.272)		

Payable to bank (CDN$)	448,000	
Cash		448,000
Payment to bank		

| Cash (US$) | 445,200 | |
| Receivable from bank (US$) | | 445,200 |

Receipt of US$350,000 from bank, translated at the
August 1 spot rate (350,000 × 1.272)

| Inventory | 445,200 | |
| Cash (US$) | | 445,200 |

To record the inventory purchase and payment at the
August 1 spot rate (350,000 × 1.272)

There are two options for removing the cumulative exchange adjustment of $2,800 from other comprehensive income. Option one is to remove the $2,800 when the inventory is delivered and report it as an adjustment of the inventory. In turn, this amount will affect the amount reported as cost of goods sold when the inventory is sold. The second option is to remove the $2,800 when the inventory is sold and show it as other income on the income statement. In both cases, the $2,800 will be reflected in the income statement when the inventory is sold. Since the objective of the hedge was to fix the price of the inventory, the first option will be used and is accounted for as follows:

August 1, Year 2

| Inventory | 2,800 | |
| Other comprehensive income | | 2,800 |

To remove exchange adjustments from other comprehensive income.

All of the above entries can be condensed into one entry as follows:

| Inventory | 448,000 | |
| Cash (CDN$) | | 448,000 |

The inventory will eventually become part of cost of goods sold. Therefore, the impact on income will once again be equal to the amount of cash paid. This is a typical result in accounting. At the beginning of this problem, we determined that the company was willing to pay a premium of $7,000 to fix the amount of the inventory. In the end, the inventory was recorded at $448,000, the amount fixed by the forward contract. Furthermore, no exchange gains or losses were reported in income because the commitment to purchase inventory was effectively hedged by the forward contract.

In the above example, the inventory was paid for on delivery. If Manning had purchased the inventory on credit, it would have been exposed to foreign currency risk on the accounts payable. It could have entered into a forward contract to hedge both the commitment to buy inventory and the amount required to settle the account payable. In this case, the $7,000 premium would have to be split between the two objectives. Part of the $7,000 would be reported as a cost of the inventory and reflected in income when the inventory is sold. The other part would be recognized in income over the period of time between the origination and settlement of the accounts payable.

Fair value hedge If Manning designated the forward contract as a fair value hedge, the gain or loss on the firm commitment would have to be reported in income in the current year to match the gain or loss on the forward contract. Although the inventory and cash payment are not recorded until the inventory is received, the accounting for the exchange gains or losses on the commitment resembles what would occur if the inventory was already purchased on account. If the inventory were recorded when it was ordered, the inventory and accounts payable would have been

---

Margin notes:

The exchange losses incurred on the hedging item to this point increase the cost of the inventory and will be reported in income when the inventory is sold.

The cash paid on the forward contract is allocated to the purchase of inventory consistent with the original intent of entering into the forward contract.

A premium on a forward contract designated as a fair value hedge is recognized in net income over the life of the forward contract.

recorded at $441,000 (US$350,000 × 1.260). The $7,000 premium on the forward contract will be expensed over the life of the forward contract as a cost of financing the purchase of the inventory.

When Manning entered into the forward contract on June 2, Year 2, the following journal entry would be recorded:

June 2, Year 2

Receivable from bank (US$)	448,000	
Payable to bank (CDN$)		448,000
To record forward contract at forward rate — 350,000 × 1.280		

At the year-end, the receivable from the bank is adjusted to its fair value and the change in the value of the cost of the commitment is recorded as follows:

June 30, Year 2

Exchange gains and losses	1,750	
Receivable from bank (US$)		1,750
To adjust forward contract to June 30 forward rate — 350,000 × (1.280 − 1.275)		
Exchange gains and losses	2,800	
Commitment liability		2,800
To adjust cost of commitment to June 30 spot rate — 350,000 × (1.268 − 1.260)		

The change in value of the accounts receivable is recognized in income to match the change in value of the commitment.

On the June 30, Year 2, balance sheet, the $1,750 difference between the receivable from bank ($446,250) and the payable to bank ($448,000) would be reported as forward contract under current liabilities. In addition, the commitment liability of $2,800 would be reported as a current liability. The exchange gains and losses of $4,550 ($1,750 + $2,800) would be reported in regular net income.

The receivable from bank and payable to bank are offset against each other and reported in the balance sheet on a net basis.

On August 1, the receivable from the bank and commitment liability are adjusted to their fair values as follows:

August 1, Year 2

Exchange gains and losses	1,050	
Receivable from bank (US$)		1,050
To adjust forward contract to August 1 forward rate — 350,000 × (1.275 − 1.272)		
Exchange gains and losses	1,400	
Commitment liability		1,400
To adjust cost of commitment to August 1 spot rate — 350,000 × (1.272 − 1.268)		

Manning settles the forward contract by paying CDN$448,000 to the bank and receiving US$350,000 and records the following journal entries:

Payable to bank (CDN$)	448,000	
Cash (CDN$)		448,000
Payment to bank		
Cash (US$)	445,200	
Receivable from bank (US$)		445,200
Receipt of US$350,000 from bank at August 31 spot rate — 350,000 × 1.272		

Manning then pays the supplier US$350,000 and records the following entry:

Part of the cash payment is for inventory and part is for the change in value of the commitment.

Inventory	441,000	
Commitment liability	4,200	
Cash (US$)		445,200
To record the inventory purchase and payment of commitment liability at the August 1 spot rate — 350,000 × 1.272		

All of the above entries can be condensed into one entry as follows:

Inventory	441,000	
Exchange gains and losses — old year	4,550	
Exchange gains and losses — new year	2,450	
Cash (CDN$)		448,000

The inventory will eventually become part of cost of goods sold. Therefore, the impact on income will once again be equal to the amount of cash paid. This is a typical result in accounting.

In the end, the hedge fixed the purchase price of inventory at the spot rate on the date of the hedge.

At the beginning of this problem, we determined that the company was willing to pay a premium of $7,000 as a cost of financing the purchase of the inventory. In the end, this $7,000 was charged to income as exchange gains and losses over the life of the forward contract. The final balance in the inventory account is $441,000, which is the amount it would have cost Manning to buy the inventory for cash on June 2, Year 1.

Hedging a Forecasted Transaction

The following example illustrates the accounting when long-term debt is used as a hedge of a future revenue stream and will be accounted for as a cash flow hedge.

The loan payable is the hedging item and the future revenue stream is the hedged item.

Alana Enterprises, a Canadian company that has carried out business activities in Switzerland for a number of years, has decided to protect itself against foreign currency fluctuations over the next three years, during which it expects a revenue stream of at least SF200,000 per year. On January 1, Year 1, the company borrows SF600,000, payable in full at the end of three years, and designates the loan as a hedge against the future three-year revenue stream. In order to simplify the illustration, we are going to omit the payment of yearly interest and assume that there is no difference between the exchange rate at the end of each year and the average exchange rate for that year.

Relevant exchange rates for the Swiss franc are as follows:

Jan. 1, Year 1	$0.852
Dec. 31, Year 1	$0.849
Dec. 31, Year 2	$0.835
Dec. 31, Year 3	$0.840

Applying the concepts of hedge accounting, Alana will make the following journal entries:

Jan. 1, Year 1

Cash	511,200	
Loan payable (SF)		511,200
(600,000 × 0.852)		

During Year 1, the revenue stream is recorded at the average exchange rate for the year. Thus, the following entry is recorded:

Cash	169,800	
Sales revenue		169,800
(200,000 × 0.849)		

On December 31, Year 1, the loan payable has to be reflected in the financial statements at fair value using the current rate. The entry to record the exchange gain on the loan payable resulting from a decrease in the exchange rate from $0.852 to $0.849 is as follows:

In Year 1, the entire loan is needed to hedge three years of forecasted revenues and the entire exchange gain on the loan should be reported in other comprehensive income to be eventually offset against the future revenue stream.

Dec. 31, Year 1
Loan payable (SF)	1,800	
Other comprehensive income, Year 1		1,800
(600,000 × 0.003)		

One-third of the hedged revenue stream has been received, and so the following adjusting entry is made to match one-third of the gain from the hedge against the revenue received:

Dec. 31, Year 1
Other comprehensive income, Year 1	600	
Sales revenue		600
(200/600 × 1,800)		

Since one-third of the revenue stream has been realized, one-third of the other comprehensive income should be brought into income.

Two-thirds of the exchange gain is deferred in other comprehensive income to be matched against the foreign currency revenues when they are received in the following two years. The company has *lost* because it has received less revenue in Canadian dollars than would be the case if the exchange rate had not changed, but it has also *gained* due to the fact that its liability (measured in Canadian dollars) has decreased. The liability hedges the revenue stream; consequently, the gain in one offsets the loss in the other. The total revenue for the year is $170,400, which is made up of the translated revenue of $169,800 plus the recognized exchange gain on the hedge of $600. Note that this is the same amount as would have been received in translated revenue if the exchange rates had not changed since January 1, Year 1 (200,000 × 0.852). If the exchange rates do not change over the next two years, the total translated revenue *plus* the recognized revenue from the hedge will be $170,400 each year.

Note also that while the loan is still SF600,000, one-third of the foreign revenue stream has been received; therefore, one-third of this loan balance no longer qualifies as a hedge and is exposed to foreign currency risk. Because of this, any future exchange gains and losses on this portion must be reflected immediately in income.

During Year 2, revenue in Swiss francs is received and translated at the average rate. This results in the following entry:

Cash	167,000	
Sales revenue		167,000
(200,000 × 0.835)		

On December 31, Year 2, the loan payable is reduced by $8,400 (600,000 × 0.014) to reflect its translation at the current rate; also, the gain on the one-third portion that no longer qualifies as a hedge is immediately reflected in income, and the balance of the gain from the hedge portion is initially deferred with the following entry:

In Year 2, only two-thirds of the loan is a hedging item. The other one-third of the loan is exposed to foreign currency risk; the related exchange gain is reported in income.

Dec. 31, Year 2
Loan payable (SF)	8,400	
Exchange gain (⅓ × 8,400)		2,800
Other comprehensive income, Year 2		5,600

The Year 2 other comprehensive income hedges the foreign currency revenues of Years 2 and 3. Year 2 revenue has been received and translated at the average exchange rate for the year. Therefore, the Year 2 portion (one-half) of the deferred gain is matched against this revenue with the following entry:

Dec. 31, Year 2

Other comprehensive income, Year 2	2,800	
Sales revenue (½ × 5,600)		2,800

In addition, the portion of the Year 1 exchange gain must be matched against Year 2 revenues with the following entry:

Dec. 31, Year 2

Other comprehensive income, Year 1	600	
Sales revenue		600

The final revenue figure of $170,400 is the equivalent Canadian dollar value of the anticipated sale when the hedge was first put into place.

Remember that the purpose of the hedge was to ensure that the foreign currency revenue in Year 2 was at least $170,400 (200,000 × 0.852). The actual foreign revenue adjusted for the hedge gains was equal to this amount, as the following calculation indicates:

Foreign currency revenue (200,000 × 0.835)	$167,000
Exchange gain on Year 1 hedge	600
Exchange gain on Year 2 hedge	2,800
	$170,400

In addition, the Year 2 income statement will reflect the additional exchange gain ($2,800) that came from the portion of the loan that no longer qualifies as a hedge.

The balance of the cumulative other comprehensive income (OCI) that will appear on the December 31, Year 2, balance sheet is:

OCI, Year 1		1,800	
Less reflected in income:			
Year 1	600		
Year 2	600	1,200	$ 600
OCI, Year 2		5,600	
Less reflected in income Year 2		2,800	2,800
Cumulative OCI,			
December 31, Year 2			$3,400

Because SF400,000 from the total revenue of SF600,000 has been received at the end of Year 2, the loan balance that still qualifies as a hedge is only SF200,000.

The Year 3 entries to record the foreign currency revenues and to adjust the loan to the current rate are as follows:

Cash	168,000	
Sales revenue		168,000
(200,000 × 0.840)		

In Year 3, only one-third of the loan is a hedging item. The other two-thirds of the loan is exposed to foreign currency risk; the related exchange gain is reported in income.

Dec. 31, Year 3

OCI, Year 3 (⅓ × 3,000)	1,000	
Exchange loss (⅔ × 3,000)	2,000	
Loan payable (SF)		3,000
(600,000 × 0.005)		

The foreign currency revenue has all been received, so none of the Year 3 loss pertaining to the hedge ($1,000) needs to be deferred. The remaining loss from the portion of the loan that is not a hedge ($2,000) is also expensed in the year.

By the end of Year 3, all of the OCI has been transferred to income to match the timing of the income recognition on the hedged item, being the revenue stream.

A final entry is made to match the balance of the other comprehensive income from prior years against the Year 3 foreign currency revenue:

OCI, Year 1	600	
OCI, Year 2	2,800	
OCI, Year 3		1,000
Sales revenue		2,400

An entry would also be made to pay off the loan that is due on this date. The following calculation summarizes the amount reflected in net income in Year 3 from the foreign currency revenue, the hedge gains and losses, and the exchange loss from the non-hedge portion of the loan:

The hedging item was used to fix the final revenue figure at $170,400, the equivalent Canadian dollar value of the anticipated sale when the hedge was first put into place.

Foreign currency revenue (200,000 × 0.840)		$168,000
Year 1 and 2 exchange gains on hedge	3,400	
Year 3 exchange loss on hedge	1,000	2,400
Hedged foreign currency revenue		170,400
Remainder of Year 3 loan exchange loss		2,000
Effect on Year 3 net income		$168,400

This simplified example has illustrated the possible use of hedge accounting. In a more realistic situation, differences would occur because the average rates used to translate the revenue stream are different from the year-end rates used to translate the foreign currency loan, and the actual revenues would probably turn out to be different from those expected when the hedge was designated. However, the broad concepts illustrated would still apply, and because an increasing portion of the foreign currency denominated debt ceases to be eligible for a hedge each year, the resultant income recognition pattern is similar to the defer-and-amortize pattern that used to occur for foreign currency debt.

Differential Reporting

Under Section 3865 on Hedges, a qualifying enterprise may elect to defer application of this section to interim and annual financial statements relating to fiscal years beginning on or after October 1, 2007.

An International Perspective

The *CICA Handbook* is substantially similar to the IASB's standards for foreign currency transactions and hedge accounting except that IAS 21 requires that nonmonetary items measured at fair value be translated at the date when the fair value was determined rather than the balance sheet date.

SUMMARY

Transactions denominated in foreign currency are recorded in Canadian dollars at the spot rate in effect on the date of the transaction. At the date of the balance sheet, foreign currency assets and liabilities are translated into Canadian dollars to preserve the normal measurement at either historical cost or current value. Any gains or losses arising from changes in exchange rates on the exposed items are reflected in income for the period.

The use of hedging instruments, such as forward exchange contracts, removes the risks associated with exchange rate changes. If all risks are removed, the hedge is "perfect." It also is possible to have a situation in which only a portion of a position is hedged and the balance is at risk, or in which, as was illustrated, a portion of the hedging instrument ceases to act as a hedge and becomes exposed to foreign currency risk.

> In a fair value hedge and in a speculative forward exchange contract, exchange gains and losses are recognized in net income in the period of the change in exchange rates. In a cash flow hedge, the exchange gains and losses on the hedging item are initially reported in other comprehensive income and subsequently reclassified to net income when the hedged item affects net income.

SELF-STUDY PROBLEM 1

Hedging an Existing Monetary Position

On November 15, Year 1, Domco Ltd. of Montreal bought merchandise from a supplier located in Switzerland for SF100,000. The Swiss franc was trading at $0.81 on that date, and the terms of the purchase required Domco to pay the account on January 30, Year 2. On December 1, when the spot rate was SF1 = $0.813, Domco entered into a forward contract with its bank to receive SF100,000 at the 60-day forward rate of SF1 = $0.82. On December 31, Year 1, Domco's year-end, the spot rate was SF1 = $0.825 and the 30-day forward rate was SF1 = $0.831. On January 30, Year 2, when the spot rate was SF1 = $0.838, Domco settled the forward contract with its bank and paid SF100,000 to the Swiss supplier.

Required:

(a) Prepare the journal entries required in Year 1 and Year 2 assuming that hedge accounting is not applied.

(b) Prepare a partial balance sheet as at December 31, Year 1 that shows the accounts payable and the presentation of the hedge accounts.

(c) Prepare one journal entry to summarize the combined effect of all entries in Part (a).

Solution to Self-study Problem 1

(a) *Nov. 15, Year 1*

Inventory ($)	81,000	
Accounts payable (SF) (SF100,000 × 0.81)		81,000

Dec. 1, Year 1

Exchange gains/losses	300	
Accounts payable (SF)		300

To adjust the accounts payable to the Dec. 1
  spot rate of SF1 = $0.813

Receivable from bank (SF)	82,000	
Payable to bank ($)		82,000

To record the forward contract at 82,000 (SF100,000 × 0.82)

Dec. 31, Year 1

Exchange gains/losses	1,200	
Accounts payable (SF)		1,200

To adjust the accounts payable to the Dec. 31
  spot rate of SF1 = $0.825

Receivable from bank (SF)	1,100	
Exchange gains/losses		1,100

To adjust the forward contract to the Dec. 31 forward
rate of SF1 = $0.831

Jan. 30, Year 2

Exchange gains/losses	1,300	
Accounts payable (SF)		1,300

To adjust the accounts payable to the Jan. 30
spot rate of SF1 = $0.838

Receivable from bank (SF)	700	
Exchange gains/losses		700

To adjust the forward contract to the Jan. 30
forward rate of SF1 = $0.838

Payable to bank ($)	82,000	
Cash ($)		82,000

Deliver Canadian dollars to bank

Cash (SF)	83,800	
Receivable from bank (SF)		83,800

Receive SF100,000 from bank

Accounts payable (SF)	83,800	
Cash (SF)		83,800

Pay SF100,000 to supplier

(b)

DOMCO LTD.
BALANCE SHEET
at December 31, Year 1

Assets		
Forward contract *	1,100	
Liabilities		
Accounts payable	82,500	
* Receivable from bank	83,100	
Payable to bank	82,000	
Net amount of forward contract	1,100	

(c)	Inventory	81,000	
	Exchange loss (before hedge)	300	
	Exchange loss (= premium on contract)	700	
	Cash		82,000

SELF-STUDY PROBLEM 2

Hedging an Unrecognized Firm Commitment

On October 15, Year 2, Sellcompany Ltd., located in Canada, signed a contract to
sell equipment to Buycompany, which is located in a country whose currency is the
foreign currency unit (FCU). The selling price of the equipment was FCU200,000

and the terms of the sale called for delivery to be made on January 30, Year 3, with payment in full due on delivery.

Having signed the sales order, Sellcompany immediately entered into a forward contract with its bank to sell FCU200,000 on January 30, Year 3, at the forward rate of FCU1 = $1.22. The spot rate on October 15 was FCU1 = $1.20. On December 31, the year-end of Sellcompany, the spot rate was FCU1 = $1.222 and the 30-day forward rate was FCU1 = $1.231. On January 30, Year 3, when the spot rate was FCU1 = $1.24, Sellcompany delivered the equipment, received FCU200,000 from Buycompany, and settled the forward contract with the bank.

Required:

(a) Prepare the journal entries required in Year 2 and Year 3 for Sellcompany assuming that the forward contract is designated as a cash flow hedge.

(b) Prepare a partial balance sheet as at December 31, Year 2, that shows the presentation of the hedge accounts.

(c) Prepare one journal entry to summarize the combined effect of all entries in Part (a).

Solution to Self-study Problem 2

(a)   *Oct. 15, Year 2*

Receivable from bank ($)	244,000	
Payable to bank (FCU)		244,000
To record the forward contract at 244,000		
(FCU200,000 × 1.22)		

Dec. 31, Year 2

Other comprehensive income	2,200	
Payable to bank (FCU)		2,200
To adjust the forward contract to the forward rate		
FCU200,000 × (1.231 − 1.220)		

Jan. 30, Year 3

Other comprehensive income	1,800	
Payable to bank (FCU)		1,800
To adjust the forward contract to the Jan. 30 forward		
rate FCU200,000 × (1.240 − 1.231)		

Cash (FCU)	248,000	
Sales		248,000
To record equipment sale at FCU200,000 × 1.24		

Payable to bank (FCU)	248,000	
Cash (FCU)		248,000
Deliver FCU to bank		

Cash ($)	244,000	
Receivable from bank ($)		244,000
Receive Canadian dollars from bank		

Sales	4,000	
Other comprehensive income		4,000
To reclassify other comprehensive income as an adjustment of sales		

(b)

SELLCOMPANY LTD.
BALANCE SHEET
at December 31, Year 2

Liabilities
Forward contract *   2,200

*Payable to bank   246,200
  Receivable from bank   244,000
    Net amount of forward contract   2,200

(c)   Cash   244,000
          Sales   244,000

In the end, the sales were recorded at $244,000, the amount fixed by the forward contract. Furthermore, no exchange gains or losses were reported in income because the commitment to sell the equipment was effectively hedged by the forward contract.

APPENDIX 11A

Determining the Fair Value of Forward Exchange Contracts

The fair value of a forward contract is based on its relative merits compared to other contracts in the market and the time value of money.

The fair value of a forward exchange contract is based on the relative merits of the contract compared to other contracts in the market and the time value of money. If the contract states that the company must sell foreign currency at a rate that is better than what is currently available in the market, the contract has a positive value. On the other hand, if the contract states that the company must sell foreign currency at a rate that is worse than what is currently offered in the market, the contract has a negative value. Therefore, the following factors are usually considered to determine the fair value of a forward contract at any point in time:

1. The forward rate when the forward contract was entered into.
2. The current forward rate for a contract that matures on the same date as the forward contract entered into.
3. A discount rate, typically the company's incremental borrowing rate.

On page 520, we considered the first two factors above when we valued the forward contract at $500 at December 31, Year 1. Since the $500 value will only be realized on March 1, Year 2, it should be discounted to derive its present value at December 31, Year 1. Assuming that Raven's incremental borrowing rate is 12 percent per annum or 1 percent per month, the fair value of the forward contract at December 31 is $490.15 ($500 × 0.9803).[1]

The journal entries to record the fair value of the forward contract for the example on page 520 under the gross and net methods when discounting is applied are shown in Exhibit 11A.1. Only the first three entries are shown here because the remaining entries would be the same as in Exhibit 11.2 on page 520.

---

[1] The present value factor for two months at 1 percent per month is calculated as $1/1.01^2$ or 0.9803.

Exhibit 11A.1

JOURNAL ENTRIES FOR SPECULATIVE FORWARD CONTRACT

	Gross Method		Net Method	
December 1, Year 1				
Receivable from bank ($)	22,700			
Payable to bank (PP)		22,700		
Record forward contract at forward rate				
(PP1,000,000 × 0.0227 = $22,700)				
December 31, Year 1				
Forward contract			490	
Payable to bank (PP)	490			
Exchange gain		490		490
Revalue forward contract at fair value				
(PP1,000,000 × (0.0227 – 0.0222) × 0.9803 = $490)				
March 1, Year 2				
Forward contract			210	
Payable to bank (PP)	210			
Exchange gain		210		210
Revalue forward contract at fair value				
([22,700 – 490] – PP1,000,000 × 0.0220) = $210)				

The value of a forward contract should be recorded in present value terms.

REVIEW QUESTIONS

1. Briefly summarize the accounting issues arising from foreign currency denominated transactions.

2. What is the difference between pegged and floating exchange rates?

3. You read in the newspaper: "One U.S. dollar can be exchanged for 1.15 Canadian dollars." Is this a direct or an indirect quotation? If your answer is "indirect," what is the direct quotation? If your answer is "direct," what is the indirect quotation?

4. Differentiate between a "spot" rate and a "forward" rate.

5. How are foreign currency denominated assets and liabilities measured on the transaction date? How are they measured on a subsequent balance sheet date?

6. Describe when to use the current rate and when to use the historical rate when translating assets and liabilities denominated in a foreign currency; explain whether or not this practice is consistent with the way we normally measure assets and liabilities under Canadian GAAP.

7. Differentiate between a "spot" rate and a "current" rate.

8. Differentiate between the accounting for a "fair value" hedge and a "cash flow" hedge.

9. List some ways that a Canadian company could hedge against foreign currency exchange rate fluctuations.

10. What are some typical reasons for acquiring a forward exchange contract?

11. If a foreign currency denominated payable has been hedged, why is it necessary to adjust the liability for balance sheet purposes?

12. Explain the application of lower of cost and market to inventory that was purchased from a foreign supplier.

13. How does the accounting for a fair value hedge differ from the accounting for a cash flow hedge of an unrecognized firm commitment?

14. What is the suggested financial statement presentation of hedge accounts recorded under the gross method? Why?

15. What is meant by "hedge accounting"?

16. Would hedge accounting be used in a situation where the hedged item and the hedging instrument were both monetary items on a company's balance sheet? Explain.

17. When long-term debt hedges a revenue stream, a portion of the long-term debt becomes exposed to the risk of changes in exchange rates. Why is this?

18. When will the premium paid on a forward contract to hedge a firm commitment to purchase inventory be reported in income under a cash flow hedge? Explain.

MULTIPLE-CHOICE QUESTIONS

Use the following data for Questions 1 to 3.

On April 15, Year 5, Bailey Inc. negotiated a large sale of their premium maple syrup to Sweet Co. for US$3,000,000. The contract required payment in three years from the date of delivery of the goods. Bailey delivered the goods on July 15, Year 5. The company has a December 31 year-end.

The exchange rates at various dates are given below.

	Spot rates	Forward rates
April 15, Year 5	US$1 = CDN$1.28	US$1 = CDN$1.22
July 15, Year 5	US$1 = CDN$1.30	US$1 = CDN$1.20
December 31, Year 5	US$1 = CDN$1.42	US$1 = CDN$1.25

1. Assuming the transaction is *not* hedged, which of the following is the amount that will be used to record the receivable in Bailey's books at July 15, Year 5?
   a. $3,000,000
   b. $3,840,000
   c. $3,900,000
   d. $4,260,000

2. Assuming the transaction is *not* hedged, which of the following is the amount that will be reported on Bailey's December 31, Year 5, income statement as an exchange gain from this transaction?
   a. $0
   b. $300,000
   c. $360,000
   d. $420,000

3. Assuming the transaction *is* hedged with a forward contract on April 15, Year 5 and hedge accounting is not applied, which of the following is the amount that will be used to report the receivable on Bailey's December 31, Year 5, balance sheet?

    a. $3,600,000
    b. $3,660,000
    c. $3,840,000
    d. $4,260,000

(CGA-Canada, from 2002 to 2007)

4. In November, Roy Incorporated purchased inventory for US$200,000 when the exchange rate was US$1 = CDN$1.25. At year-end, the inventory had a market value of US$210,000 and the exchange rate was US$1 = CDN$1.18. What will be the total gain (loss) on this inventory for the current year?
    a. zero.
    b. $2,200 loss.
    c. $14,000 loss.
    d. $12,500 gain.

(CICA adapted)

5. At December 31, Year 3, Post Inc. had a Swiss franc receivable resulting from export sales to Switzerland and a Mexican peso payable resulting from imports from Mexico. Post recorded foreign exchange gains related to both its franc receivable and peso payable. Did the foreign currencies increase or decrease in value from the date of the transaction to the year-end?

	Franc	*Peso*
a.	Increase	Increase
b.	Increase	Decrease
c.	Decrease	Increase
d.	Decrease	Decrease

6. A company purchases a piece of equipment from a Swiss supplier for SF100,000, payable 1 month later. On the date when the equipment is received, the company enters into a foreign-exchange forward contract whereby it agrees to purchase francs on the payment date of the equipment. Assuming that hedge accounting is not adopted and considering the following exchange rates, what will the carrying value of the equipment be after the equipment has been paid for?

Spot rate when the order was placed:	SF1 = CDN$0.83
Spot rate when the equipment was received:	SF1 = CDN$0.84
Spot rate when the payment was made:	SF1 = CDN$0.86
Foreign exchange forward contract rate:	SF1 = CDN$0.85

    a. $83,000
    b. $84,000
    c. $85,000
    d. $86,000

(CICA adapted)

7. On October 12, Year 5, Jiambalvo International, a clothing manufacturer, ordered bolts of fabric from an Asian supplier. The agreed upon price for the goods was FCU400,000. The fabric was received by Jiambalvo on December 1, Year 5. The invoice was paid on December 28, Year 5. All fabric from this order was in the company's inventory at their December 31 year-end. Exchanges rates during the period were as follows:

October 12	FCU1 = $0.36
December 1	FCU1 = $0.33
December 28	FCU1 = $0.32
December 31	FCU1 = $0.31

For inventory valuation purposes, what would be the cost of the purchased fabric?

    a. $124,000
    b. $128,000
    c. $132,000
    d. $144,000

8. If a company hedges an expected foreign currency denominated purchase of a capital asset for cash and accounts for the hedge as a cash flow hedge, how will the premium on the forward contract be treated?
    a. It will be charged to income when the capital asset is purchased.
    b. It will be charged to income over the life of the capital asset.
    c. It will be charged to other comprehensive income when the capital asset is purchased.
    d. It will be charged to other comprehensive income over the life of the capital asset.

Use the following data for Questions 9 to 11.

    PL Corporation has a December 31, Year 5, year-end. It submitted a purchase order for US$30,000 of equipment on July 1, Year 5, when the exchange rate was CDN$1 = US$0.6500. It received the equipment on September 30, Year 5, when the exchange rate was US$0.6667; it paid US$20,000 to the supplier on December 1, Year 5, when the exchange rate was US$0.6900. On December 31, Year 5, the exchange rate was US$0.7000. The company uses straight-line amortization commencing in the month following acquisition. The equipment is expected to last 5 years and has no residual value.

9. What would be the net book value of PL's equipment on its December 31, Year 5, balance sheet?
    a. $40,715
    b. $42,748
    c. $43,850
    d. $45,000

10. On PL's December 31, Year 5 financial statements, what amount would the accounts payable relating to the equipment purchase be recorded at?
    a. $6,500
    b. $7,000
    c. $14,286
    d. $15,385

11. Assume PL entered into a forward contract with the bank for the remaining $10,000 accounts payable on December 1, Year 5, to provide US$10,000 on January 31, Year 6 — the expected date of payment to the equipment manufacturer. Assume the forward rate on December 1, Year 5, was CDN$1 = US$0.6750 and CDN$1 = US$0.6755 on December 31, Year 5. Assuming that hedge accounting is not adopted, how much exchange gain/loss would PL record on the forward contract for the year ended December 31, Year 5?
    a. CDN$11
    b. CDN$161
    c. CDN$311
    d. CDN$322

(CGA-Canada, from 2002 to 2007)

Use the following data for Questions 12 and 13.

    On November 2, Year 5, a company purchased a machine for 200,000 Swiss francs with payment required on March 1, Year 6. To eliminate the risk of foreign exchange losses on this payable, the company entered into a forward exchange contract on December 1, Year 5, to receive SF200,000 at a forward rate of SF1 = $2 on March 1, Year 6. Hedge accounting is not applied. The spot rate was SF1 = $1.95 on November 2, Year 5, and SF1 = $1.97 on December 1, Year 5.

12. What is the amount of the premium or discount on the forward exchange contract?
   a. Discount of $6,000.
   b. Discount of $10,000.
   c. Premium of $6,000.
   d. Premium of $10,000.

(CICA adapted)

13. How should the premium or discount on the forward exchange contract be accounted for?
   a. It should be expensed on the inception date of the forward exchange contract.
   b. It should be expensed on the maturity date of the forward exchange contract.
   c. It should be expensed over the 3-month term of the forward exchange contract.
   d. It should be added to the cost of the machine.

(CGA-Canada, from 2002 to 2007)

14. On October 1, Year 1, CAR Ltd. issued a 6%, 10-year debenture denominated in Euros. What rate should be used to translate interest expense for this 10-year debenture for the year ended December 31, Year 1?
   a. The rate on October 1, Year 1.
   b. The average rate for the year ended December 31, Year 1.
   c. The average rate for the quarter ended December 31, Year 1.
   d. The rate on December 31, Year 1.

15. LET Inc. enters into a forward contract with the Scotia bank at a 3-month forward rate of FC1 = CDN$1.20. One month later, the rate for a 2-month forward contract is FC1 = CDN$1.22. Which of the following would result in a credit to other comprehensive income for the first month of the forward contract?
   a. The forward contract is designated as a cash flow hedge of an anticipated sale.
   b. The forward contract is designated as a cash flow hedge of an anticipated purchase.
   c. The forward contract is designated as a fair value hedge of an anticipated sale.
   d. The forward contract is designated as a fair value hedge of an anticipated purchase.

CASES

Case 1* Long Life Enterprises was a long-established, Toronto-based company engaged in the importation and wholesale marketing of specialty grocery items originating in various countries of the western Pacific rim. They had recently also entered the high-risk business of exportation, to several of these same countries, of fresh Atlantic lobster and crab.

Although Canada has extensive trading relationships with several countries in the Pacific rim, these transactions were not normally priced or settled in terms of the Canadian dollar. Both the U.S. dollar and the Japanese yen were somewhat more common in these transactions. Further, various local currencies were involved, especially for small transactions involving specialty items, and a wide variety of credit terms were in use for both imports and exports. The entire situation was complicated by the perishable nature of some of the imports and the high mortality risk for both lobster and crab. Both situations led to uncertainty as to the face amount of the associated receivable or payable, and hindered the ability of the firm to adopt the policy of specific hedging of each of the receivable or payable contracts.

Most recently, the Canadian dollar had risen against other major currencies, leading to major losses on the large receivables outstanding because of the seasonal lobster harvest. More generally, management was concerned about losses that might arise from both export and import transactions. For the most recent fiscal year, foreign currency losses had exceeded gains by some $40,000 — an amount more than the company could afford during the present stage of rapid growth.

Required:

What steps would you propose to the management of Long Life Enterprises to reduce the foreign exchange costs associated with their receivables and payables? As a part of this process, suggest a way of structuring transactions or affairs that would reduce the impact of fluctuations in the relative values of currencies.

(Case prepared by Peter Secord, St. Mary's University.)

Case 2 Canada Cola Inc. (CCI) is a public company engaged in the manufacture and distribution of soft drinks across Canada. Its primary product is Canada Cola ("Fresh as a Canadian stream"), which is a top seller in Canada and generates large export sales.

You met with Jim MacNamara, the partner in charge of the CCI audit engagement, to commence planning for the upcoming audit of CCI. During this meeting the partner informed you that early this year CCI entered into an agreement with the government of Russia and has commenced the manufacture and sale of Canada Cola in Russia. A short summary of this agreement is contained in Exhibit I. The partner would like you to prepare a detailed report that discusses the accounting implications of this new division of CCI for this engagement.

Required:

Prepare the report.

EXHIBIT I

SUMMARY OF AGREEMENT

1. The Russian government will provide the land and the building for the plant. It will make no further investment.
2. CCI will install bottling machinery costing $5 million in the Russian plant. Once installed, this machinery may not be removed from Russia.
3. CCI will be required to provide the funds for the initial working capital. CCI will sell US dollars to the Russian government in exchange for local currency (rubles).
4. CCI will be wholly responsible for the management and daily operations of the plant. Canadian managers will be transferred to Russia.
5. CCI will be permitted to export its cola syrup to Russia at CCI's Canadian cost.
6. CCI and the Russian government will share equally in the profits from the sale of Canada Cola in Russia.
7. Although foreign currency can be converted into rubles, rubles cannot be converted back into any foreign currency. Therefore, the Russian government will sell vodka to CCI (at the prevailing export market price in Russia) in exchange for the rubles CCI earns in profits. CCI will be permitted to export this vodka to Canada, where it may be sold in the Canadian domestic market only.

(CICA adapted)

PROBLEMS

Note: Some problems use direct exchange rate quotations, others use indirect quotations.

Problem 1   Manitoba Exporters Inc. (MEI) sells Inuit carvings to countries throughout the world. On December 1, Year 5, MEI sold 10,000 carvings to a wholesaler in a foreign country at a total cost of 600,000 foreign currency units (FCUs) when the spot rate was FCU1 = $0.741. The invoice required the foreign wholesaler to remit by April 1, Year 6. On December 3, Year 5, MEI entered into a forward contract with the Royal Bank at the 120-day forward rate of FCU1 = $0.781. Hedge accounting is not applied.

The fiscal year-end of MEI is December 31, and on this date the spot rate was FCU1 = $0.757 and the forward rate was FCU1 = $0.791. The payment from the foreign customer was received on April 1, Year 6, when the spot rate was FCU1 = $0.802.

Required:

(a) Prepare the journal entries to record:
    (i)   the sale and the forward contract.
    (ii) any adjustments required on December 31.
    (iii) the cash received in Year 6.
(b) Prepare a partial balance sheet of MEI on December 31, Year 5, that shows the presentation of the receivable and the accounts associated with the forward contract.

Problem 2   Moose Utilities Ltd. (MUL) borrowed $50,000,000 in U.S. funds on January 1, Year 1, at an annual interest rate of 12%. The loan is due on December 31, Year 4, and interest is paid annually on December 31. The Canadian exchange rates for U.S. dollars over the life of the loan were as follows:

January 1, Year 1	CDN$1.359
December 31, Year 1	CDN$1.368
December 31, Year 2	CDN$1.360
December 31, Year 3	CDN$1.352
December 31, Year 4	CDN$1.355

Exchange rates changed evenly throughout the year.

Required:

(a) Prepare journal entries for MUL for Year 1.
(b) Calculate the exchange gains or losses that would be reported in the net income of the company each year over the life of the loan.

Problem 3   Grammy Ltd., a Canadian company, is dealing with a supplier in a foreign country. On May 1, Year 4, the company made purchases totalling FF2,270,000; this amount is payable in six months. Grammy did not hedge the transaction in any way.

On the due date, Grammy found itself in financial difficulty. The supplier agreed to accept a non-interest-bearing note payable for FF2,000,000 and FF270,000 in cash. The note payable is due July 1, Year 6. Grammy did not hedge the note.

Grammy has a December 31 fiscal year-end.

May 1, Year 4	$1 = FF2
November 1, Year 4	$1 = FF2.6
December 31, Year 4	$1 = FF3.8

Required:

Prepare the journal entries for Year 4 for the accounts payable and the note payable.

(*CGA-Canada, from 2002 to 2007*)

Problem 4 On January 1, Year 5, Ornate Company Ltd. purchased $US1,000,000 of the bonds of the Gem Corporation. The bonds were trading at par on this date, pay interest at 9% each December 31, and mature on December 31, Year 7. The following Canadian exchange rates for U.S. dollars were quoted during Year 5:

January 1, Year 5	CDN$1.372
December 31, Year 5	CDN$1.321

Exchange rates changed evenly throughout the year. These bonds were trading at 102 at December 31, Year 5.

Required:

Prepare the journal entries for Year 5 assuming that the investment in bonds is:
(a) held-to-maturity
(b) held-for-trading
(c) available-for-sale

Problem 5 On October 1, Year 6, Versatile Company contracted to sell merchandise to a customer in Switzerland at a selling price of SF400,000. The contract called for the merchandise to be delivered to the customer on January 31, Year 7, with payment due on delivery. On October 1, Year 6, Versatile arranged a forward contract to deliver SF400,000 on January 31, Year 7, at a rate of SF1 = $1.20. Versatile's year-end is December 31.

The merchandise was delivered on January 31, Year 7 and SF400,000 were received and delivered to the bank.

Exchange rates were as follows:

	Spot Rates	Forward Rates
October 1, Year 6	SF1 = $1.18	SF1 = $1.20
December 31, Year 6	SF1 = $1.21	SF1 = $1.22
January 31, Year 7	SF1 = $1.19	SF1 = $1.19

Required:

(a) Prepare the journal entries that Versatile should make to record the events described assuming that the forward contract is designated as a cash flow hedge.
(b) Prepare a partial trial balance of the accounts used as at December 31, Year 6, and indicate how each would appear on the company's financial statements.
(c) Prepare the journal entries that Versatile should make to record the events described assuming that the forward contract is designated as a fair value hedge.
(d) Prepare a partial trial balance of the accounts used as at December 31, Year 6, and indicate how each would appear on the company's financial statements.

Problem 6 Hamilton Importing Corp. (HIC) imports goods from countries around the world for sale in Canada. On December 1, Year 3, HIC purchased 10,000 watches from a foreign wholesaler for DM600,000 when the spot rate was DM1 = $0.741. The invoice called for payment to be made on April 1, Year 4. On December 3, Year 3, HIC entered into a forward contract with the Royal Bank at the 120-day forward rate of DM1 = $0.781. Hedge accounting is not applied.

The fiscal year-end of HIC is December 31. On this date, the spot rate was DM1 = $0.757 and the 90-day forward rate was DM1 = $0.786. The payment to the foreign supplier was made on April 1, Year 4, when the spot rate was DM1 = $0.802.

Required:

(a) Prepare the journal entries to record:
   (i) the purchase and the forward contract.

(ii) any adjustments required on December 31.

(iii) the payment in Year 4.

(b) Prepare a partial balance sheet of HIC on December 31, Year 3, that presents the liability to the foreign supplier and the accounts associated with the forward contract.

Problem 7   On August 1, Year 3, Carleton Ltd. ordered machinery from a supplier in Hong Kong for HK$500,000. The machinery was delivered on October 1, Year 3, with terms requiring payment in full by December 31, Year 3. On August 2, Year 3, Carleton entered a forward contract as a cash flow hedge to purchase HK$500,000 on December 31, Year 3, at a rate of $0.165. On December 31, Year 3, Carleton settled the forward contract and paid the supplier.

Exchange rates were as follows:

	Spot Rates	Forward Rates
August 1 and 2, Year 3	HK$1 = C$0.160	HK$1 = C$0.165
October 1, Year 3	HK$1 = C$0.164	HK$1 = C$0.168
December 31, Year 3	HK$1 = C$0.169	HK$1 = C$0.169

Required:

(a) Assume that the entire balance in cumulative other comprehensive income on October 1, was transferred to the machinery account when the machinery was delivered. Calculate the following amounts for the financial statements for the year ended December 31, Year 3:

(i) machinery

(ii) exchange gains/losses

(iii) cash flows for the period

(b) Assume that 50% of the balance in cumulative other comprehensive income on October 1 was transferred to the machinery account when the machinery was delivered and the other 50% was reclassified into net income when the supplier was paid. Calculate the following amounts for the financial statements for the year ended December 31, Year 3:

(i) machinery

(ii) exchange gains/losses

(iii) cash flows for the period

(c) Explain the similarities and differences between the account balances under the two scenarios above.

Problem 8   EnDur Corp (EDC) is a Canadian company that exports computer software. On February 1, Year 2, EDC contracted to sell software to a customer in Denmark at a selling price of 600,000 Danish krona (DK) with payment due 60 days after installation was complete. On February 2, Year 2, EDC entered into a cash flow hedge with the Royal Bank at the 5-month forward rate of C$1 = DK5.20. The installation was completed on April 30, Year 2. On June 30, Year 2, the payment from the Danish customer was received and the forward contract was settled.

Exchange rates were as follows:

	Spot Rates	Forward Rates
February 2, Year 2	$1 = DK5.06	$1 = DK5.20
April 30, Year 2	$1 = DK5.09	$1 = DK5.18
June 30, Year 2	$1 = DK5.14	$1 = DK5.14

Required:

(a) Assume that the entire balance in cumulative other comprehensive income (COCI) on April 30 was transferred to sales when the installation was completed. Calculate the following amounts for the financial statements for the year ended June 30, Year 2:
   (i)   sales
   (ii) exchange gains/losses
   (iii) cash flows for the period

(b) Assume that the EDC could have entered into a 3-month forward contract on February 1, Year 2, to hedge the sale of equipment with a forward rate of $1 = DK5.15. If so, this forward contract would have fixed the sales price for the software. Also, assume that the amount transferred from COCI to the sales account on April 30 is the amount required to fix the sales price at the 3-month forward rate and the balance of the COCI is reclassified into net income when the EDC received payment from the customer. Calculate the following amounts for the financial statements for the year ended June 30, Year 2:
   (i)   sales
   (ii) exchange gains/losses
   (iii) cash flows for the period

(c) Explain the similarities and differences between the account balances under the two scenarios above.

Problem 9

Winn Ltd. conducted two foreign currency transactions on September 1, Year 4.

In the first transaction, it sold DM750,000 in merchandise to a foreign company. Since this sale was so special, Winn agreed to collect the note receivable on September 1, Year 8. There is no risk of default on the receivable, since the customer is a very large and prosperous company. The note has an interest rate of 10% per year, payable at the end of December each year. Both the interest and the note will be paid in DMs. This receivable was not hedged in any way.

In the second transaction, Winn purchased FF1,200,000 worth of inventory from a company in another foreign country. This amount will be payable on November 1, Year 5. There is no interest on this liability, and it is not hedged.

EXCHANGE RATES

September 1, Year 4	Spot rate	$1 = DM2.5	$1 = FF3.9
December 31, Year 4	Spot rate	$1 = DM2.8	$1 = FF3.4
Year 4 average rate		$1 = DM2.3	$1 = FF4.1
Sept.–Dec., Year 4 average rate		$1 = DM2.6	$1 = FF3.6
November 1, Year 5	Spot rate		$1 = FF3.1
December 31, Year 5	Spot rate	$1 = DM3.6	
Year 5 average rate		$1 = DM3.0	

Required:

Prepare all the journal entries for Year 4 and Year 5 for the two transactions. Assume a December 31 year-end.

(*CGA-Canada, from 2002 to 2007*)

Problem 10

On August 1, Year 1, Zip Ltd. purchased some merchandise from a foreign company for DM450,000. The liability was not due until March 1, Year 2. Zip was quite confident that the exchange rate fluctuations were not a problem and took no action to hedge the liability. On November 1, Year 1, Zip looked at the exchange rates and decided that they had better hedge the liability with a 120-day forward contract. Assume a December 31 year-end, that all months have 30 days, and hedge accounting is not adopted.

EXCHANGE RATES

August 1, Year 1	spot rate	$1 = DM2.5
November 1, Year 1	spot rate	$1 = DM2.1
November 1, Year 1	120-day forward rate	$1 = DM1.9
December 31, Year 1	spot rate	$1 = DM1.7
December 31, Year 1	60-day forward rate	$1 = DM1.8
March 1, Year 2	spot rate	$1 = DM2.7
December 31, Year 2	spot rate	$1 = DM2.9
March 1, Year 3	spot rate	$1 = DM2.4

Required:

(a) Prepare all the journal entries for Years 1 and 2 for Zip for these transactions.

(b) Assume that the liability was a note due on March 1, Year 3 (instead of Year 2, as given above), and that Zip does not hedge in any way. Prepare all the journal entries for Year 1.

(c) Explain why some of the financial statement items in this problem are translated at historical rates whereas other items are translated at current rates.

(CGA-Canada, from 2002 to 2007)

Problem 11   On February 1, Year 3, Harrier Ltd., a Canadian company, sold goods to a company in a foreign country and took a note receivable for FF6,200,000. The note was non-interest-bearing and would be paid on August 1, Year 5. There was no danger of default on the note, but Harrier decided to avoid all risk by hedging the fair value of the note with a forward contract. The contract was for one year and matured on February 1, Year 4. On that date, Harrier settled the forward contract and decided to leave the note in an unhedged position for the remainder of its life. Hedge accounting is not applied.

Harrier has a December 31 year-end.

	Spot Rates	Forward Rates
February 1, Year 3	$1 = FF3.9	$1 = FF3.3
December 31, Year 3	$1 = FF3.1	$1 = FF3.0
February 1, Year 4	$1 = FF4.2	$1 = FF4.2
December 31, Year 4	$1 = FF3.4	
August 1, Year 5	$1 = FF3.0	

Required:

Prepare all the journal entries related to the note receivable for Year 3 and Year 4.

(CGA-Canada, from 2002 to 2007)

Problem 12   On June 1, Year 3, Forever Young Corp. (FYC) ordered merchandise from a supplier in South Africa for R200,000. The goods were delivered on September 30 with terms requiring cash on delivery. On June 2, Year 3, FYC entered a forward contract as a cash flow hedge to purchase R200,000 on September 30, Year 3, at a rate of $0.73. FYC's year-end is June 30.

On September 30, Year 3, FYC paid the foreign supplier in full and settled the forward contract.

Exchange rates were as follows:

	Spot Rates	Forward Rates
June 1 and 2, Year 3	R1 = $0.70	R1 = $0.730
June 30, Year 3	R1 = $0.69	R1 = $0.725
September 30, Year 3	R1 = $0.74	R1 = $0.740

Required:

(a) (i) Prepare all journal entries required to record the transactions described above.
  (ii) Prepare a June 30, Year 3, partial trial balance of the accounts used in (i), and indicate how each account would appear in the year-end financial statements.

(b) Prepare all necessary journal entries under the assumption that no forward contract was entered.

(c) Prepare all necessary journal entries to record the transactions described above assuming that the forward contract is designated as a fair value hedge.

Problem 13   Hull Manufacturing Corp. (HMC), a Canadian company, manufactures instruments used to measure the moisture content of barley and wheat. The company sells primarily to the domestic market, but in Year 3 it developed a small market in East Huronia. In Year 4, HMC began purchasing semifinished components from a supplier in Mexico. The management of HMC is concerned about the possible adverse effects of foreign exchange fluctuations. To deal with this matter, all of HMC's foreign currency denominated receivables and payables are hedged with contracts with the company's bank. The year-end of HMC is December 31.

The following transactions occurred late in Year 4:

- On October 15, Year 4, HMC purchased components from its Mexican supplier for 800,000 pesos. On the same day, HMC entered into a forward contract for Ps800,000 at the 60-day forward rate of Ps1 = $0.408. The Mexican supplier was paid in full on December 15, Year 4.

- On December 1, Year 4, HMC made a shipment to a customer in East Huronia. The selling price was 2,500,000 Foreign Currency Units (FCU), with payment to be received on January 31, Year 5. HMC immediately entered into a forward contract for FCU 2,500,000 at the two-month forward rate of FCU1 = $0.226.

During this period, the exchange rates were as follows:

	Spot Rates	Forward Rates
October 15, Year 4	Ps1 = $0.395	
December 1, Year 4	FCU1 = $0.249	
December 15, Year 4	Ps1 = $0.387	
December 31, Year 4	FCU1 = $0.233	FCU1 = $0.222

Hedge accounting is not adopted.

Required:

(a) Prepare the Year 4 journal entries to record the transactions described above and any adjusting entries necessary.

(b) Prepare the December 31, Year 4, balance sheet presentation of the receivable from the East Huronian customer and the accounts associated with the forward contract.

Problem 14   As a result of its export sales to customers in Switzerland, the Lenox Company has had Swiss franc denominated revenues over the past number of years. In order to gain protection from future exchange rate fluctuations, the company decides to borrow its current financing requirements in Swiss francs. Accordingly, on January 1, Year 1, it borrows SF1,400,000 at 12% interest, to be repaid in full on December 31, Year 3. Interest is paid annually on December 31. The management designates this loan as a cash flow hedge of future SF revenues, which are expected to be received as follows:

Year 1	SF 560,000
Year 2	490,000
Year 3	350,000
	SF1,400,000

Actual revenues turned out to be exactly as expected each year and were received in cash. Exchange rates for the Swiss franc during the period were:

January 1, Year 1	$1.05
Average, Year 1	$1.10
December 31, Year 1	$1.15
Average, Year 2	$1.20
December 31, Year 2	$1.25
Average, Year 3	$1.27
December 31, Year 3	$1.30

Required:

Prepare the journal entries required each year.

Problem 15   On January 1, Year 4, a Canadian firm, Canuck Enterprises Ltd., borrowed 200,000 U.S. dollars from a bank in Seattle, Washington. Interest of 7% per annum is to be paid on December 31 of each year during the four-year term of the loan. Principal is to be repaid on the maturity date of December 31, Year 7. The foreign exchange rates for the first two years were as follows:

January 1, Year 4	US$1.00 = CDN$1.38
December 31, Year 4	US$1.00 = CDN$1.41
December 31, Year 5	US$1.00 = CDN$1.35

Exchange rates changed evenly throughout the year.

Required:

Determine the exchange gain (loss) on the loan to be disclosed in the financial statements of Canuck Enterprises for the years ended December 31, Year 4 and Year 5.

(*CGA-Canada, from 2002 to 2007*)

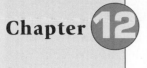

Chapter 12

Translation and Consolidation of the Financial Statements of Foreign Operations

LEARNING OBJECTIVES

After studying this chapter, you should be able to do the following:

- Contrast an enterprise's foreign currency accounting exposure with its economic exposure to exchange rate changes.
- Differentiate between an integrated and a self-sustaining foreign operation, and describe the translation method and unit of measure that is used in the translation of each type.
- Prepare translated financial statements for each type of foreign operation.
- Explain how the temporal method produces results consistent with the normal measurement and valuation of assets and liabilities for domestic transactions and operations.
- Explain why the reporting enterprise's exposure to exchange rate changes is limited to its net investment if the investment is in a self-sustaining foreign operation.
- Use translated financial statements to prepare consolidated financial statements, particularly in situations where there is a purchase discrepancy and a noncontrolling interest.

INTRODUCTION

Consolidated financial statements are required when one entity has control over another entity or when a venturer has joint control over a joint venture. With the ever-expanding global economy, it is now very common for a subsidiary to be in a foreign country as indicated by the following:

- * Magna International Inc., a leading global supplier of technologically advanced automotive systems, components, and complete modules, directly or indirectly owned 14 or more wholly owned foreign subsidiaries in 5 countries at December 31, 2006.
- * CHC Helicopter, a world leader in providing helicopter transportation services to both onshore and offshore petroleum markets around the world, directly or indirectly owned 28 or more foreign subsidiaries in 13 countries at April 30, 2006.
- * Potash Corporation of Saskatchewan, the world's largest producer of potash, directly or indirectly owned 46 or more foreign subsidiaries in 7 countries at December 31, 2006.

Companies establish operations in foreign countries for a variety of reasons including the development of new markets for their products, taking advantage of lower production costs, or gaining access to raw materials. Some multinational companies have reached a stage in their development in which domestic operations are no longer considered to be of higher priority than international operations.

Foreign currency denominated financial statements must be translated to the reporting currency of the reporting entity.

Prior to preparing consolidated financial statements or accounting for an investment under the equity method, the financial statements of the foreign subsidiary or investee company must be translated into the investor company's reporting currency, which is usually the Canadian dollar. This chapter deals with the issue of translating foreign currency financial statements into the parent's reporting currency.

Two major theoretical issues are related to the translation process: (1) which translation method should be used and (2) where should the resulting translation adjustment be reported in the consolidated financial statements. These two issues are examined first from a conceptual perspective and second by the manner in which these issues have been resolved by the CICA. We will start by discussing the difference between accounting exposure and economic exposure.

Accounting Exposure versus Economic Exposure

Exposure is the risk that something could go wrong. Foreign currency exposure is the risk that a loss could occur if foreign exchange rates were to change. Foreign currency risk can be viewed as having three components: translation exposure (accounting exposure), transaction exposure, and economic exposure.[1] Readers must keep these in mind as they interpret financial statements that contain foreign currency gains and losses.

Accounting exposure exists when financial statement items are translated at the current rate.

Translation (Accounting) Exposure   This exposure results from the translation of foreign currency denominated financial statements into dollars. Only those financial statement items translated at the current rate create an accounting exposure. If an item is translated at the historical rate, the Canadian dollar amount is fixed at historical cost and will not be affected by rate changes. However, if an item is translated at the current rate, the Canadian dollar amount will change every time the exchange rate changes. Each item translated at the current exchange rate is exposed to translation adjustment. A separate translation adjustment exists for each of the exposed items. Positive translation adjustments increase shareholders' equity whereas negative translation adjustments decrease shareholders' equity. Positive translation adjustments on assets can be offset by negative translation adjustments on liabilities. If total exposed assets are equal to total exposed liabilities throughout the year, the translation adjustments (although perhaps significant on an individual basis) net to a zero balance. The *net* translation adjustment needed to keep the consolidated balance sheet in balance is based solely on the *net asset* or *net liability* exposure.

---

[1] See "Foreign Currency Risk Management." Management Accounting Guideline #6. Hamilton: Society of Management Accountants of Canada, 1987.

Net asset exposure means that more assets than liabilities are exposed.

A foreign operation has a net asset exposure when assets translated at the current exchange rate are larger in amount than liabilities translated at the current exchange rate. A net liability exposure exists when liabilities translated at the current exchange rate are larger than assets translated at the current exchange rate. The relationship between exposure, exchange rate fluctuations, and effect on shareholders' equity (S/E) is summarized as follows:

	Foreign Currency	
Balance Sheet Exposure	Appreciates	Depreciates
Net asset	Increases S/E	Decreases S/E
Net liability	Decreases S/E	Increases S/E

The gains and losses that result from the translation usually are unrealized in the sense that they do not represent actual cash flows. Because these accounting gains and losses are reflected in the financial statements, they may have an impact on the enterprise's dividend policies, share prices, and so on. It is important to assess the extent to which they represent transaction and/or economic exposure.

Transaction exposure exists when there is a lapse in time between the origination of a receivable or payable and the settlement of the receivable or payable.

Transaction Exposure This exposure exists between the time of entering a transaction involving a receivable or payable and the time of settling the receivable or payable with cash. It affects the current cash flows of the enterprise. The resulting cash gains and losses are realized and affect the enterprise's working capital and earnings. The concept of transaction exposure was discussed in Chapter 11.

Economic exposure exists when the present value of future cash flows would change as a result of changes in exchange rates.

Economic Exposure Economic exposure takes a longer-term view of the situation than either of the others. It arises because of "the possible reduction, in terms of the domestic reporting currency, of the discounted future cash flows generated from foreign investments or operations due to real changes (inflation adjusted) in exchange rates."[2] It represents a long-term potential threat or benefit to a company carrying out business in foreign countries.

For example, a Canadian assembly plant that purchases components from a company in Japan will suffer economically if the dollar weakens in relation to the Japanese yen and the Canadian competition is such that the cost increase cannot be passed on to the company's customers. The situation is no different if the Japanese supplier is related to, or is a subsidiary of, the Canadian assembler, because it measures its results in yen and expects to be paid in that currency. Economically, there is a potential loss in this particular situation when the Canadian dollar weakens in relation to the yen. However, if the Canadian parent does *not* purchase the output of its Japanese subsidiary the economic exposure is quite different. If this was a stand-alone foreign operation with no intercompany transactions, the Canadian parent would benefit by receiving more dollars from its subsidiary's dividends. Therefore, the economic exposure is dependent on whether the foreign subsidiary is closely linked to the activities of the parent or operating independently of the parent. The *Handbook* section on Foreign Currency Translation tries to capture the economic effects by establishing a situational approach to determining the translation method to be used for certain foreign operations.

Economic exposure is not easy to measure.

---

[2] Ibid.

DISCUSSION QUESTION

How Do We Report This?

The Rider Corporation operates throughout Canada buying and selling widgets. In hopes of expanding into more profitable markets, the company recently decided to open a small subsidiary in California, USA. On October 1, Year 2, Rider invested C$928,000 in Riderville USA Ltd. Its investment was immediately converted into US$800,000. One-half of this money was used to purchase land to be held for the possible construction of a plant and one-half was invested in available-for-sale securities.

Nothing further happened at Riderville throughout the remainder of Year 2. However the U.S. dollar strengthened relative to the Canadian dollar and the exchange rate at December 31, Year 2, was US$1 = C$1.20. Fortunately, the value of the land purchased by Riderville increased to US$420,000 and the available-for-sale securities were worth US$425,000 at the end of the year.

The accountant for Rider realized that the investments of the U.S. subsidiary had increased in value but did not plan to report this unrealized gain in the consolidated financial statements. However, the CEO wants to report the true economic value of these investments.

What is the true economic value of the assets owned by Riderville USA at the end of Year 2? Can Rider report the economic value of these assets in the consolidated balance sheet under Canadian GAAP? If not, how should Rider report each of these assets on its consolidated balance sheet and how should the related gains be reported?

Translation Methods

The translated statements should reflect the reporting enterprise's exposure to exchange rate changes.

Two major methods for translating foreign operations are currently used under Canadian GAAP: (1) the temporal method and (2) the current rate method. The objective of translation is to express financial statements of the foreign operation in Canadian dollars in the manner that best reflects the reporting enterprise's exposure to exchange rate changes as determined by the economic facts and circumstances. We will discuss these methods from the perspective of a Canadian-based multinational company translating foreign currency financial statements into Canadian dollars.

The Temporal Method

The temporal method gives the same results as if the transactions had occurred in Canada.

The basic objective underlying the temporal method is to produce a set of translated financial statements as if the transactions had occurred in Canada in the first place. In other words, use the same process we used in Chapter 11 to translate individual transactions and account balances into Canadian dollars. Use the Canadian dollar as the unit of measure and value financial statement items according to the normal measurement practices for Canadian domestic transactions and operations.

Under normal measurement practices, certain financial statement items are reported at historical cost whereas other items are reported at current value. The temporal method is designed to maintain this reporting practice when translating the foreign currency statements into Canadian dollars.

If the financial statement item is supposed to be reported at current value, when translating the item into Canadian dollars we need to take the current value of the item in foreign currency and apply the current rate. This will produce the current

Use historical cost in foreign currency and historical rate to get historical cost in Canadian dollars.

value of this item in Canadian dollars. If a financial statement item is supposed to be reported at historical cost, we need to start with the historical cost of the item in foreign currency and apply the historical rate. This will produce the historical cost of this item in Canadian dollars. Therefore, to properly apply the temporal method, one needs to know which financial statement items are to be reported at historical cost and which items are to be reported at current value.

Monetary items are normally reported at current value. Nonmonetary items are usually reported at historical cost or historical cost less accumulated amortization but would be reported at fair value if there has been an impairment. Shareholders' equity is normally reported at historical values. Since income is a component of shareholders' equity, revenues, expenses, gains, and losses are reported at historical values.

Use historical exchange rates to translate revenues and expenses.

To obtain historical values, revenues and expenses should be translated in a manner that produces substantially the same reporting currency amounts that would have resulted had the underlying transactions been translated on the dates they occurred. To translate revenues of a foreign subsidiary, use the exchange rate on the date that the transaction giving rise to the revenue occurred. The following examples illustrate this concept. In all of these examples, assume the following exchange rates:

January 1	FC1 = $1.50
January 31	FC1 = $1.60
Average for January	FC1 = $1.56

Example A On January 1, Subco sold goods for cash of FC100. The revenue is earned and determined on this date. The revenue of FC100 would be translated into $150, its historical value.

Example B On January 1, Subco sold goods for FC100 with payment due within 30 days. On January 31, FC100 was received from the customer. The revenue is earned and determined on January 1. The revenue of FC100 would be translated into $150. Receiving the cash on January 31 does not change the historical value of the sale. It does result in an exchange gain on the accounts receivable of $10 [FC100 × ($1.60 – $1.50)].

Example C On January 1, Subco received FC100 as a prepayment for goods to be delivered within 30 days. On January 31, Subco delivered the goods and earned the sale. Although the revenue was earned on January 31, the amount of the revenue in Canadian dollars was determined on January 1 when the cash was received. The revenue of FC100 would be translated into $150.

Use average rates to approximate exchange rates throughout the period.

Example D On each day in January, Subco sold goods for cash of FC100. Rather than using 31 different exchange rates for the 31 days of the month, the average rate for the month, $1.56, can be applied to the total revenue for the month, FC100 × 31 × $1.56 = $4,836.

Use historical rates to measure expenses based on the historical cost of the related balance sheet items.

The same concept can be applied in translating expenses. Use the exchange rate on the date that the transaction giving rise to the expense occurred. Since depreciation expense is directly related to the purchase of a depreciable asset, depreciation expense should be translated using the exchange rate on the date that the depreciable asset was purchased. Similarly, cost of goods sold is based on the cost of the inventory. Therefore, use the exchange rate on the date when the inventory was purchased when translating the cost of goods sold.

The Current Rate Method

The current rate method preserves the relationship of balance sheet items.

Under the current rate method, all of the assets and liabilities of a foreign entity are translated at the current rate on the date of the balance sheet; this preserves the relationship in dollars between all balance sheet items that formerly existed in the foreign currency. Share capital is translated at historical rates. All revenues and expenses are translated using the exchange rate in effect on the dates on which such items are recognized in income during the period. If the revenues or expenses were recognized in income evenly throughout the period, the average rate for the period would be used to translate these items. Under the current rate method, the net assets of the foreign entity (and therefore the Canadian parent's investment) are exposed to foreign exchange fluctuations. A peculiarity resulting from this method is that a capital asset carried at historical cost in the foreign entity's statements will be translated into differing Canadian dollar values if exchange rates fluctuate over some time frame. This effect is particularly obvious with a capital asset not subject to amortization. The following example will illustrate this.

Using historical cost in foreign currency and the current rate does not provide historical cost or current value in Canadian dollars.

Example   A German entity has land in its balance sheet with a historical cost of 100,000 euros. On five successive balance sheets, denominated in euros, the land appears as €100,000. If the value of the euro changes with respect to the Canadian dollar each year during the five-year period and the current rate method of translation is used, the translated amount will be different each year. A reader of the German financial statements would observe the same amount reflected each year. A reader of the translated financial statements would see a different amount each year and may improperly conclude that land sales or purchases have taken place. Despite this particular shortcoming, this method is one of the two methods currently sanctioned under Canadian GAAP.

Both of the translation methods that have been discussed will produce different amounts for balance sheet and income statement items and different amounts for the translation gain or loss[3] because the total amount of the balance sheet items at risk to exchange rate changes is different under each.

Translation Under Section 1651

Section 1651 establishes accounting standards for the translation of the financial statements of a foreign operation (a subsidiary, joint venture, significant influence investee, etc.) for use by a reporting enterprise (a Canadian investor). A foreign operation is viewed as either *integrated* or *self-sustaining* for translation purposes.

The foreign financial statements should be adjusted to Canadian GAAP before they are included in the financial statements of the Canadian reporting entity.

Conformity with Canadian GAAP
Section 1651 also requires that the financial statements of foreign operations reflect Canadian accounting principles. In situations where the principles used are different from Canada's, the foreign operation financial statements must be adjusted to conform with Canadian GAAP and then translated into Canadian dollars.

Integrated Foreign Operations

An integrated foreign operation is one "that is financially or operationally interdependent with the reporting enterprise such that the exposure to exchange rate

---

[3] It is not inconceivable to have an exchange gain from the use of one method and an exchange loss from the use of the other method.

The temporal method should be used to translate an integrated foreign operation.

changes is similar to the exposure that would exist had the transactions and activities of the foreign operation been undertaken by the reporting enterprise" (*CICA Handbook*, paragraph 1651.03).

The *temporal method* of translation was chosen for this type of operation because it produces essentially the same results that would have occurred had the reporting enterprise itself undertaken all of the transactions that were incurred by the foreign operation.

If a foreign operation is considered to be integrated, the relationship between the two entities is such that the activities of the reporting enterprise are or will be directly affected by the cash flows of the foreign operation.

Self-sustaining Foreign Operations

The current rate method should be used to translate a self-sustaining foreign operation.

A self-sustaining foreign operation is one "that is financially and operationally independent of the reporting enterprise such that the exposure to exchange rate changes is limited to the reporting enterprise's net investment in the foreign operation." (*CICA Handbook*, paragraph 1651.03)

Because the foreign operation is assumed to be independent in all respects, exchange rate changes should not have a direct impact on the immediate or short-term future cash flows of the reporting enterprise. The current rate method was chosen to translate the foreign currency financial statements of a self-sustaining operation, with *one* exception, discussed next.

The temporal method should be used to translate a self-sustaining foreign operation operating in a highly inflationary environment.

Highly Inflationary Economies   While Canada has had fairly low rates of inflation in the past 20 years, this has not been the case in other parts of the world. Argentina, Brazil, Chile, Mexico, Turkey, and Israel have all had inflation rates higher than Canada's during this period. Between 1985 and 1993, Argentina experienced yearly rates of between 120 percent and 3,000 percent.

If the self-sustaining foreign operation operates in a highly inflationary environment relative to that of the reporting enterprise, translation using the current rate method could produce distorted and meaningless results. The CICA Accounting Standards Board has concluded that the temporal method should be used in such a situation. A definition of highly inflationary is not given, but both IASB and FASB standards suggest that a cumulative inflation rate of 100 percent over a three-year period would fit the description. The following example illustrates the kind of distortion that can occur when the current rate method is used during a period of very high inflation.

The temporal method should be used to translate a self-sustaining foreign operation operating in a highly inflationary environment.

Example   In Year 1, a Canadian company purchases a self-sustaining foreign subsidiary located in Chile. The exchange rate at this time is 1 peso = $1.00, and it remains constant during the year. The subsidiary has land carried at a historical cost of Ps1,000,000. On December 31, Year 1, the land is translated into dollars for consolidation purposes as follows:

$$Ps1,000,000 \times 1.00 = \$1,000,000$$

There is usually an inverse relationship between the strength of a country's currency and the level of inflation in that country.

During Year 2, Chile experiences an inflation rate of 500 percent. Because the inflation rate in Canada is minuscule during this period, this large inflation differential is fully reflected in the foreign exchange market. The result is a weakening of the peso relative to the Canadian dollar.

On December 31, Year 2, the exchange rate is Ps1 = $0.20. If the land were translated at the current rate on this date, the result would be as follows:

$$Ps1,000,000 \times 0.20 = \$200,000$$

While it is easy to see in this example that the $800,000 difference is due to the exchange rate change, large differences such as this are difficult to interpret without all the facts. When this self-sustaining operation is translated by the temporal method, the value of the land appears as $1,000,000 (which reflects the historical rate).

In passing, it should be noted that if the Chilean subsidiary prepared price-level-adjusted historical cost statements, the land would appear on the subsidiary's balance sheet at Ps5,000,000.

Translation using the current rate method on December 31, Year 2, would *not* produce distorted results, as the following illustrates:

$$Ps5,000,000 \times 0.20 = \$1,000,000$$

Price-level-adjusted financial statements are useful for countries experiencing high inflation but are not GAAP in Canada.

But price-level accounting is not GAAP in Canada, and therefore the subsidiary's financial statements must be adjusted back to nominal pesos before being translated using the temporal method.

Determining the Classification of Foreign Operations Section 1651 acknowledges that in the evaluation of the exchange rate exposure, the classification of a foreign operation as either integrated or self-sustaining requires professional judgment. It suggests that six factors should be considered in making the required evaluation. These are summarized in Exhibit 12.1. Note that the ability to control the foreign operation is not a factor in classifying the foreign operation. If the foreign operation is a subsidiary, the parent will control the subsidiary regardless of whether the subsidiary is integrated or self-sustaining.

Are the activities of the foreign operation closely linked with activities of Canadian companies?

Exhibit 12.1

FACTORS IN EVALUATING A FOREIGN OPERATION

Factor	Integrated	Self-sustaining
1. Cash flows of the reporting enterprise.	Directly affected by day-to-day activities of the foreign operation.	Insulated from day-to-day activities of the foreign operation.
2. Sales prices of the foreign operation.	Determined more by world-wide competition and international prices	Determined more by local competition and local government regulation.
	Responsive on a short-term basis to changes in exchange rates.	Immune on a short-term basis to changes in exchange rates.
3. Sales market of the foreign operation.	Primarily within the country of the reporting enterprise.	Primarily outside the country of the reporting enterprise.
4. Products and service costs of the foreign operation.	Obtained primarily from the country of reporting enterprise.	Obtained primarily from the foreign country.
5. Financing of day-to-day activities of the foreign operation.	Primarily from the reporting enterprise or borrowing from the country of the reporting enterprise.	Primarily from its own operations and local borrowings.
6. Day-to-day activity between the foreign operation and the reporting enterprise.	Strong interrelationship because of a high volume of intercompany transactions.	Weak interrelationship because of a low volume of intercompany transactions.

Accounting for Translation Gains and Losses

CICA came to the following conclusions regarding the presentation of the resulting exchange gains and losses from the two types of foreign operations.

Exchange gains and losses for an integrated foreign operation are reported in regular income.

Because of the interdependent relationship that exists between the reporting enterprise and the integrated foreign operation, the translation should reflect the same results "as if the underlying transactions had been undertaken by the reporting enterprise" (*CICA Handbook*, paragraph 1651.30). If the Canadian parent had undertaken the year's transactions of the foreign operation denominated in foreign currency, any exchange gains and losses from the translation of monetary items would be taken into income.

Because of the independent relationship that exists between the reporting enterprise and the self-sustaining foreign operation, the exposure of the reporting enterprise is limited to its net investment in the foreign operation. Since the resulting translation gain or loss has no direct effect on the activities of the reporting enterprise, the committee concluded that such gains and losses should not be reflected in the reporting enterprise's income statement.

Exchange gains and losses for a self-sustaining foreign operation are reported in other comprehensive income.

Prior to October 2006,[4] these unrealized exchange gains and losses were reported in a separate section of shareholders' equity called "cumulative translation adjustment." As of October 2006, these unrealized exchange gains and losses must, first of all, be reported in other comprehensive income for the year. In turn, cumulative other comprehensive income is reported as a separate component of shareholders' equity. When the parent sells all or part of its self-sustaining foreign operations, or receives a liquidating dividend, a proportionate portion of the cumulative exchange gains and losses on the foreign operation are taken out of the cumulative other comprehensive income section of shareholders' equity and the realized exchange gains or losses are reported in the regular income statement. We will illustrate the presentation of other comprehensive income and cumulative other comprehensive income later in this chapter. If the parent hedges its investment in a self-sustaining foreign operation with a forward exchange contract, the exchange gains or losses on the forward contract are reported in other comprehensive income to offset the unrealized losses or gains on the investment.

Unit of Measure

Section 1651 indicates that the two methods of translation actually use different currencies as the underlying unit of measure. The temporal method uses the Canadian dollar as the measuring unit, while the current rate method uses the foreign currency.

The temporal method uses the Canadian dollar as the underlying unit of measure.

Because it produces results that are identical to those that would have been produced had the Canadian parent itself entered into all of the transactions incurred by the foreign operation, the temporal method of translation essentially takes all of the transactions that have been measured in a foreign currency and remeasures them in Canadian dollars using the exchange rate in effect on the date of the transaction. Financial statement ratios computed using the foreign currency as the original measuring unit will change when the statements are remeasured using the Canadian dollar.

The current rate method uses the foreign currency as the underlying unit of measure.

Under the current rate method, the unit of measure is the foreign currency. Each transaction of the foreign operation is measured in foreign currency. In order that the consolidation can take place by adding dollars to dollars, the foreign currency financial statements are translated at the *current* rate for balance sheet items and at the *historical*

---

[4] *CICA Handbook* Section 1530, "Comprehensive Income," came into effect for public companies as of October 1, 2006, and for private companies as of October 1, 2007.

rate for income statement items. Balance sheet ratios (e.g., the current ratio) remain unchanged. Income statement ratios (e.g., net income to sales) will remain the same if revenues and expenses occurred evenly throughout the period and the average rate is used for all income statement items. Income statement ratios will change if revenues and expenses occurred at different times during the period and a number of different exchange rates were used in translating the revenues and expenses. Ratios of income statement items to balance sheet items (e.g., return on investment) will be different after the translation because the rates used to translate the balance sheet are different from the rates used for the income statement.

Illustration of Translation and Consolidation

The translation and preparation of consolidated financial statements will now be illustrated under the two translation methods required by Section 1651.

Example On December 31, Year 1, Starmont Inc., a Canadian company, acquired 100 percent of the common shares of Controlada S.A., located in Venezuela, at a cost of 2,000,000 bolivars. The exchange rate was B1 = $0.128 on this date. Starmont's journal entry (in Canadian dollars) to record the share acquisition is:

Dec. 31, Year 1
Investment in Controlada	256,000	
Cash		256,000

(B2,000,000 × 0.128)

When the parent acquires the subsidiary, the parent indirectly buys all of the net assets of the subsidiary.

This example assumes that the carrying values of the subsidiary's net assets were equal to fair values and that there is no goodwill on consolidation. Because this is an "acquisition" business combination, the exchange rate on the date of acquisition is used to translate all accounts of the subsidiary on acquisition date and becomes the historical rate to be used in subsequent years, where appropriate.

The translation of the balance sheet of Controlada from bolivars into Canadian dollars at December 31, Year 1, is shown in Exhibit 12.2. Note that the translation of a subsidiary on the date of acquisition is the same regardless of whether the entity is integrated or self-sustaining.

Exhibit 12.2

CONTROLADA S.A.
TRANSLATION OF BALANCE SHEET TO CANADIAN DOLLARS
at December 31, Year 1

For consolidation purposes, we never use an exchange rate older than the rate at the date of acquisition.

	Venezuelan bolivars	Exchange rate	Canadian dollars
Cash	B 40,000	0.128	$ 5,120
Accounts receivable	360,000	0.128	46,080
Inventories	1,200,000	0.128	153,600
Plant and equipment (net)	900,000	0.128	115,200
	B2,500,000		$320,000
Current liabilities	B 50,000	0.128	$ 6,400
Bonds payable	450,000	0.128	57,600
Common stock	1,500,000	0.128	192,000
Retained earnings	500,000	0.128	64,000
	B2,500,000		$320,000

With no purchase discrepancy and subsidiary wholly owned, investment account is equal to subsidiary's shareholders' equity.

The preparation of the acquisition date consolidated balance sheet appears in Exhibit 12.3. Note that the translated shareholders' equity of the subsidiary is equal to the parent's investment account, so the consolidating procedure is simply to eliminate one against the other.

Exhibit 12.3

Controlada has to be translated into dollars in order to consolidate with Starmont's Canadian dollar financial statements.

PREPARATION OF CONSOLIDATED BALANCE SHEET
at December 31, Year 1

	Starmont	Controlada	Starmont Consolidated
Cash	$ 70,000	$ 5,120	$ 75,120
Accounts receivable	90,000	46,080	136,080
Inventories	200,000	153,600	353,600
Plant and equipment	300,000	115,200	415,200
Investment in Controlada	256,000	—	—
	$916,000	$320,000	$980,000
Current liabilities	$ 80,000	$ 6,400	$ 86,400
Bonds payable	300,000	57,600	357,600
Common stock	200,000	192,000	200,000
Retained earnings	336,000	64,000	336,000
	$916,000	$320,000	$980,000

Translation and Consolidation Subsequent to Acquisition

On December 31, Year 2, Controlada forwarded the financial statements shown in Exhibit 12.4 to the Canadian parent. Sales, purchases, bond interest, and other expenses occurred evenly throughout the year.

The translation process will now be illustrated under these two assumptions: (a) the subsidiary is self-sustaining, and (b) the subsidiary is integrated.

The exchange rates for the year were as follows:

December 31, Year 1	B1 = $0.128
December 31, Year 2	B1 = $0.104
Average for year 2	B1 = $0.115
Date of purchase of inventory on hand	B1 = $0.110
Date dividends declared	B1 = $0.104

Exhibit 12.5 illustrates the rates to be used for self-sustaining operations (the current rate method) and integrated operations (the temporal method). Translation of the numerous revenues, expenses, gains, and losses at the historical rates is generally impractical. A weighted average exchange rate for the period would normally be used to translate such items.

Self-sustaining Foreign Operation If the subsidiary is considered self-sustaining, the translation of its Year 2 financial statements will be as shown in Exhibit 12.6 on page 566.

The procedure used in Exhibit 12.6 was to translate the income statement first, then the retained earnings statement, then the balance sheet. The following features of the current rate translation process are emphasized:

The average rate is used when the revenues and expenses occur evenly throughout the year.

- The average rate for Year 2 is used for all revenues and expenses in the income statement.

Exhibit 12.4

CONTROLADA S.A.
FINANCIAL STATEMENTS
December 31, Year 2
(in bolivars)

INCOME STATEMENT

The subsidiary uses its local currency, bolivar, in its own financial records and for reporting in its own country.

Sales	B9,000,000
Cost of goods sold	7,000,000
Depreciation expense	100,000
Bond interest expense	45,000
Other expenses	1,555,000
	8,700,000
Net income	B 300,000

STATEMENT OF RETAINED EARNINGS

Balance, beginning of year	B 500,000
Net income	300,000
	800,000
Dividends	100,000
Balance, end of year	B 700,000

BALANCE SHEET

Cash	B 100,000
Accounts receivable	400,000
Inventory	1,600,000
Plant and equipment (net)	800,000
	B2,900,000
Current liabilities	B 250,000
Bonds payable	450,000
Common stock	1,500,000
Retained earnings	700,000
	B2,900,000

All items within shareholders' equity are translated using the historical rate applicable for each item.

- All assets and liabilities are translated at the current rate.
- Common stock and beginning retained earnings are translated at the acquisition date historical rate, thus establishing the translated amount on that date. In future periods, the amount for the translated beginning retained earnings will have to be calculated. In practice, the accountant will look at last year's translated financial statements for this amount. Dividends are translated at the historical rate on the date of declaration. In situations where the dividends were not paid by year-end, the dividends payable will be translated at the current rate, and a hidden exchange gain or loss will result from the translation of these items. (In this example, the dividends were declared and paid on December 31.)
- The amount required to balance the balance sheet is the unrealized exchange loss from the translation of the subsidiary's financial statements using the current rate method. The unrealized exchanges losses must be presented as a part of other comprehensive income both on the balance sheet and on the income statement. The income statement presents the unrealized exchange loss for the year whereas the balance sheet presents the cumulative unrealized exchange

Exhibit 12.5

Exchange Rates

Financial statement items	Self-sustaining	Integrated
Monetary	current	current
Nonmonetary — at cost	current	historical
Nonmonetary — at current values	current	current
Deferred revenues	current	historical
Capital stock	historical	historical
Dividends	historical	historical
Revenues	historical *Avg*	historical *Avg*
Depreciation and amortization	historical	historical
Cost of sales	historical	—
Opening inventory	—	historical
Purchases	— *avg.*	historical
Ending inventory	—	historical

Differentiate between other comprehensive income for the year that is reported in comprehensive income and cumulative other comprehensive income that is reported in shareholders' equity.

losses for all years to date. Since Year 2 is the first year in which Controlada is reporting unrealized exchange losses, the cumulative losses on the balance sheet are equal to the loss reported in income for the year. In this example, comprehensive income is presented as a separate statement. It includes net income from the income statement and other comprehensive income. The components of cumulative other comprehensive income would typically be reported in notes to the financial statements.

In this illustration, the financial statements were translated sequentially, with the foreign exchange loss being the "plug" needed to complete the balance sheet. In reality, the gain or loss can be calculated before attempting the translation process. Exhibit 12.7 illustrates this process. In a self-sustaining operation such as this one, it is the net assets (assets less liabilities) that are at risk and are exposed to currency fluctuations. Net assets equal shareholders' equity, and if the capital stock remains unchanged, the only changes that usually occur are the net income and dividend changes to retained earnings. The process involves translating the opening position, using the historical rates at that time, and translating the changes at the rates at which they occurred. The result is a calculated position. The actual end-of-year net asset position is translated at current rates, with the difference between the two numbers representing the exchange gain or loss from translation. Notice that if the exchange rate had remained constant throughout Year 2, all items in Exhibit 12.7 would have been translated at $0.128 with no exchange gain or loss occurring.

Exchange gains and losses occur only on those items translated at the current rate and only if the rates change during the period.

Item of Interest Bombardier Inc. is a Canadian company with revenues of $14.7 billion in 2006. It is a world leader in the manufacturing and servicing of trains, regional aircraft, and business jets. It has subsidiaries in the United States, United Kingdom, and Germany. All of the significant subsidiaries are classified as self-sustaining operations for accounting purposes.

Prior to 2005, Bombardier's financial statements were presented in Canadian dollars. For the year ended January 31, 2004, the company reported a foreign exchange adjustment of $393 million as a result of the decline in the value of the American dollar and pound sterling. Effective, February 1, 2004, Bombardier adopted the U.S. dollar as its reporting currency. As a result, it will no longer be exposed to currency fluctuations and foreign exchange adjustments on transactions denominated in U.S. dollars and for subsidiaries reporting in U.S. dollars.

Exhibit 12.6

CONTROLADA S.A.
TRANSLATION OF FINANCIAL STATEMENTS TO CANADIAN DOLLARS
December 31, Year 2
(self-sustaining foreign operation)

INCOME STATEMENT

	Bolivars	Exchange rate	Dollars
Sales	B9,000,000	0.115	$1,035,000
Cost of goods sold	7,000,000	0.115	805,000
Depreciation expense	100,000	0.115	11,500
Bond interest expense	45,000	0.115	5,175
Other expenses	1,555,000	0.115	178,825
	8,700,000		1,000,500
Net income	B 300,000	0.115	$ 34,500

All revenues and expenses are assumed to have occurred evenly throughout the year.

STATEMENT OF COMPREHENSIVE INCOME

	Bolivars	Exchange rate	Dollars
Net income	B 300,000	0.115	$34,500
Other comprehensive income Unrealized exchange gains (losses) from self-sustaining foreign operations			(51,300)
Comprehensive income	B 300,000		$(16,800)

STATEMENT OF RETAINED EARNINGS

	Bolivars	Exchange rate	Dollars
Balance, beginning of year	B 500,000	0.128	$ 64,000
Net income	300,000	0.115	34,500
	800,000		98,500
Dividends	100,000	0.104	10,400
Balance, end of year	B 700,000		$ 88,100

Only the income from the regular income statement is carried forward to the statement of retained earnings.

BALANCE SHEET

	Bolivars	Exchange rate	Dollars
Cash	B 100,000	0.104	$ 10,400
Accounts receivable	400,000	0.104	41,600
Inventory	1,600,000	0.104	166,400
Plant and equipment (net)	800,000	0.104	83,200
	B2,900,000		$ 301,600
Current liabilities	B 250,000	0.104	$ 26,000
Bonds payable	450,000	0.104	46,800
Common stock	1,500,000	0.128	192,000
Retained earnings	700,000		88,100
Cumulative other comprehensive income Unrealized exchange gains (losses) from self-sustaining foreign operations			(51,300)
	B2,900,000		$ 301,600

All assets and liabilities are translated at the current rate.

Other comprehensive income is carried forward to cumulative other comprehensive income.

Exhibit 12.7

INDEPENDENT CALCULATION OF YEAR 2
TRANSLATION LOSS
(self-sustaining foreign operation)

Assets minus liabilities are called net assets and are equal in amount to shareholders' equity.

	Bolivars		Exchange rate	Dollars
Net assets, December 31, Year 1	B2,000,000	×	0.128	$256,000
Changes in net assets, Year 2				
Net income	300,000	×	0.115	34,500
Dividends	(100,000)	×	0.104	(10,400)
Calculated net assets				280,100
Actual net assets	B2,200,000	×	0.104	228,800
Exchange loss from translation				$ 51,300

Using the equity method of accounting, Starmont would make the following journal entries on December 31, Year 2:

Starmont's journal entries are recorded in Canadian dollars.

Investment in Controlada	34,500	
Equity earnings		34,500
100% of translated net income		

Cash	10,400	
Investment in Controlada		10,400
Dividend received		

Other comprehensive income	51,300	
Investment in Controlada		51,300

To record 100% of the change in the unrealized exchange loss
from translation for Year 2

Net equity earnings should be equal to the subsidiary's net income when there is no purchase discrepancy or noncontrolling interest.

Exhibit 12.8 illustrates the preparation of the consolidated financial statements. Notice that equity earnings are equal to the subsidiary's net income ($34,500), and are therefore eliminated and replaced with the subsidiary's revenue and expenses. The parent's investment account is eliminated against the shareholders' equity of the subsidiary in the following manner:

The investment account under the equity method should be equal to the subsidiary's shareholders' equity when there is no purchase discrepancy or noncontrolling interest.

Investment in Controlada		$228,800
Shareholders' equity — Controlada		
Common stock	192,000	
Retained earnings	88,100	
Cumulative other comprehensive income	(51,300)	228,800
Purchase discrepancy		–0–

With no purchase discrepancy or noncontrolling interest, the investment account is replaced with the assets and liabilities of the subsidiary. Notice that the parent's share (in this case 100 percent) of the subsidiary's cumulative other comprehensive income appears as a separate component of consolidated shareholders' equity. The parent's equity method journal entries made the consolidation process straightforward.

Exhibit 12.8

PREPARATION OF CONSOLIDATED FINANCIAL STATEMENTS
YEAR 2
(self-sustaining foreign operation)

STATEMENT OF NET INCOME AND COMPREHENSIVE INCOME

	Starmont	Controlada	Starmont Consolidated
Sales	$3,000,000	$1,035,000	$4,035,000
Equity earnings	34,500	—	—
	3,034,500	1,035,000	4,035,000
Cost of goods sold	2,500,000	805,000	3,305,000
Depreciation	20,000	11,500	31,500
Bond interest	30,000	5,175	35,175
Other expenses	200,000	178,825	378,825
	2,750,000	1,000,500	3,750,500
Net income	284,500	34,500	284,500

Other comprehensive income is reported separately from regular income.

	Starmont	Controlada	Starmont Consolidated
Other comprehensive income			
Unrealized exchange gains (losses) from self-sustaining foreign operations	(51,300)	(51,300)	(51,300)
Comprehensive income	$ 233,200	$ (16,800)	$ 233,200

RETAINED EARNINGS

Consolidated retained earnings are the same as the parent's retained earnings under the equity method.

	Starmont	Controlada	Starmont Consolidated
Balance — beginning	$ 336,000	$ 64,000	$ 336,000
Net income	284,500	34,500	284,500
	620,500	98,500	620,500
Dividends	50,000	10,400	50,000
Balance — end	$ 570,500	$ 88,100	$ 570,500

BALANCE SHEETS

	Starmont	Controlada	Starmont Consolidated
Cash	$ 100,000	$ 10,400	$ 110,400
Accounts receivable	290,400	41,600	332,000
Inventories	220,000	166,400	386,400
Plant and equipment (net)	280,000	83,200	363,200
Investment in Controlada (equity method)	228,800	—	—
	$1,119,200	$ 301,600	$1,192,000
Current liabilities	$ 100,000	$ 26,000	$ 126,000
Bonds payable	300,000	46,800	346,800
Common stock	200,000	192,000	200,000
Retained earnings	570,500	88,100	570,500

Cumulative other comprehensive income is reported separately from retained earnings.

	Starmont	Controlada	Starmont Consolidated
Cumulative other comprehensive income			
Unrealized exchange gains (losses) from self-sustaining foreign operations	(51,300)	(51,300)	(51,300)
	$1,119,200	$ 301,600	$1,192,000

Integrated Foreign Operation Assuming that Controlada is an integrated foreign operation, the statements would be translated using the temporal method. Exhibit 12.9 illustrates this process. The following discussion regarding the exchange rates used and the disposition of the translation gain should be noted:

- Monetary items are translated at the current rate, nonmonetary items at appropriate historical rates.
- Common stock and beginning-of-year retained earnings are translated at the

---

Exhibit 12.9

CONTROLADA S.A.
TRANSLATION OF FINANCIAL STATEMENTS TO CANADIAN DOLLARS
December 31, Year 2
(integrated foreign operation)

INCOME STATEMENT

Cost of goods sold and depreciation expense are translated using the historical rates of the related balance sheet accounts.

	Bolivars	Exchange rate	Dollars
Sales	B9,000,000	0.115	$1,035,000
Cost of goods sold	7,000,000	calculated	828,600
Depreciation expense	100,000	0.128	12,800
Bond interest expense	45,000	0.115	5,175
Other expenses	1,555,000	0.115	178,825
Total expenses	8,700,000		1,025,400
Net income (before translation loss — note 1)	B 300,000		$ 9,600

RETAINED EARNINGS

	Bolivars	Exchange rate	Dollars
Balance beginning	B 500,000	0.128	$ 64,000
Net income (note 1)	300,000		9,600
	800,000		73,600
Dividends	100,000	0.104	10,400
Balance — end	B 700,000		$ 63,200

BALANCE SHEET

Assets to be reported at current value are translated at the current rate and assets to be reported at cost are translated at the historical rate.

	Bolivars	Exchange rate	Dollars
Cash	B 100,000	0.104	$ 10,400
Accounts receivable	400,000	0.104	41,600
Inventory	1,600,000	0.110	176,000
Plant and equipment (net)	800,000	0.128	102,400
	B2,900,000		$ 330,400
Current liabilities	B 250,000	0.104	$ 26,000
Bonds payable	450,000	0.104	46,800
Common stock	1,500,000	0.128	192,000
Retained earnings (note 1)	700,000		63,200
			328,000
Balancing translation adjustment (note 1)	—		2,400
	B2,900,000		$ 330,400

Note 1: Because this translation adjustment is a preliminary balancing amount, the net income and retained earnings are not the final translated amounts.

Shareholders' equity accounts are translated at historical rates.

historical rate on the date of acquisition. In future years, the translated amount for retained earnings will have to be calculated.

- Revenue and expenses, with the exception of depreciation and cost of goods sold, are translated at the average rate for the year. Depreciation is translated at the historical rates used to translate the related assets.

- Because the components of cost of goods sold are translated using different rates, the translated amount for this item is calculated as follows:

The three components of cost of goods sold are each translated at the rate when these goods were purchased.

Beginning inventory	B1,200,000	×	0.128	=	$	153,600
Purchases	7,400,000	×	0.115	=		851,000
	8,600,000					1,004,600
Ending inventory	1,600,000	×	0.110	=		176,000
Cost of goods sold	B7,000,000				$	828,600

Purchases in bolivars were calculated as a balancing amount, and are translated at the average rate for the year. Inventories are translated at historical rates.

The exchange gain or loss is reported in regular income under the temporal method.

- The balance sheet item "Balancing translation adjustment" is the "plug" needed to balance the statements after translation. It represents the foreign exchange gain due to changes in the exposed position during the year. The *Handbook* requires that this amount be reflected in the Year 2 income statement. In Exhibit 12.11 on page 572, the financial statements of Controlada have been adjusted accordingly. The sequential translation illustrated in Exhibit 12.9 is cumbersome, because the translated net income does not contain the year's exchange gain or loss. A better method would be to first calculate the exchange gain or loss resulting from the monetary position, and then translate the financial statements and include the gain or loss in the income statement. Exhibit 12.10 shows how the gain or loss can be calculated before the actual financial statement translation takes place.

After the translation adjustment is reflected in Controlada's income statement (see Exhibit 12.11), the translated statements are ready for the consolidation process. They become the basis for the following equity method journal entries by Starmont on December 31, Year 2:

The translated income is quite different under the temporal method as compared to the current rate method.

Investment in Controlada	12,000	
Equity earnings		12,000
To record 100% of the Year 2 net income of Controlada Company		
Cash	10,400	
Investment in Controlada		10,400
Dividend received from Controlada Company		

Exhibit 12.11 shows the Year 2 financial statements of Starmont, the translated statements of Controlada using the temporal method, and the consolidated financial statements. Note that the investment account equals the shareholders' equity of the subsidiary, and that there is no noncontrolling interest or purchase discrepancy. The investment account is replaced with the assets and liabilities of Controlada, and equity earnings are replaced with revenues and expenses.

Exhibit 12.10

CALCULATION OF YEAR 2 TRANSLATION ADJUSTMENT
(integrated foreign operation)

	Bolivars		Exchange rates	Dollars
Net monetary position				
Dec. 31, Year 1*	B (100,000)	×	0.128	$ (12,800)
Changes during Year 2				
Sales	9,000,000	×	0.115	1,035,000
Purchases	(7,400,000)	×	0.115	(851,000)
Bond interest expense	(45,000)	×	0.115	(5,175)
Other expenses	(1,555,000)	×	0.115	(178,825)
Dividends	(100,000)	×	0.104	(10,400)
Net changes	(100,000)			(10,400)
Calculated net monetary position				
Dec. 31, Year 2				(23,200)
Actual net monetary position				
Dec. 31, Year 2*	B (200,000)	×	0.104	(20,800)
Exchange gain, Year 2				$ 2,400

This schedule reconciles the change in accounting exposure during the year and calculates the gains or losses due to the change in exchange rates.

Only monetary items are exposed to exchange rate changes in this illustration.

*NET MONETARY POSITION, BOLIVARS

	December 31	
	Year 2	Year 1
Cash	B 100,000	B 40,000
Accounts receivable	400,000	360,000
Current liabilities	(250,000)	(50,000)
Bonds payable	(450,000)	(450,000)
Net monetary position	B(200,000)	B(100,000)

The exchange gains or losses are based on the accounting exposure, which is based on the translation method.

In both illustrations (self-sustaining and integrated), the financial statements were translated first with the foreign exchange gain or loss determined as a plug to balance. Then, as a proof, the foreign exchange gain or loss was verified by translating the changes that had occurred in either the net asset position or the net monetary position. It should be obvious that in both situations the exchange gains and losses can be determined prior to the translation of the financial statements.

Comparative Observations of the Two Translation Methods

Integrated subsidiaries usually have a net liability exposure whereas self-sustaining subsidiaries usually have a net asset exposure.

Under the current rate method, the net assets position of the foreign entity is at risk from currency fluctuations, while under the temporal method it is the monetary position that is at risk. For most companies, monetary liabilities are greater than monetary assets, so they are usually in a net monetary liability position. This is the case with Controlada S.A. If the foreign currency weakens with respect to the Canadian dollar, a self-sustaining operation will show a foreign exchange loss while an integrated foreign operation will show a foreign exchange gain. This can be seen in Exhibit 12.7, where a self-sustaining operation produced a loss of $51,300, and Exhibit 12.10, where an integrated operation produced a gain of $2,400. If the Canadian dollar weakens with respect to the foreign currency (i.e., the foreign currency strengthens) a self-sustaining

Exhibit 12.11

PREPARATION OF CONSOLIDATED FINANCIAL STATEMENTS
YEAR 2
(integrated foreign operation)
INCOME STATEMENT

	Starmont	Controlada	Starmont Consolidated
Sales	$3,000,000	$1,035,000	$4,035,000
Equity earnings	12,000	—	—
	3,012,000	1,035,000	4,035,000
Cost of goods sold	2,500,000	828,600	3,328,600
Depreciation	20,000	12,800	32,800
Bond interest	30,000	5,175	35,175
Other expenses	200,000	178,825	378,825
Foreign exchange gain	—	(2,400)	(2,400)
	2,750,000	1,023,000	3,773,000
Net income	$ 262,000	$ 12,000	$ 262,000

The exchange gain is reported in regular income.

RETAINED EARNINGS

	Starmont	Controlada	Starmont Consolidated
Balance — beginning	$ 336,000	$ 64,000	$ 336,000
Net income	262,000	12,000	262,000
	598,000	76,000	598,000
Dividends	50,000	10,400	50,000
Balance — end	$ 548,000	$ 65,600	$ 548,000

The parent's income under the equity method is equal to consolidated net income.

BALANCE SHEETS

	Starmont	Controlada	Starmont Consolidated
Cash	$ 100,000	$ 10,400	$ 110,400
Accounts receivable	290,400	41,600	332,000
Inventories	220,000	176,000	396,000
Plant and equipment (net)	280,000	102,400	382,400
Investment in Controlada (equity)	257,600	—	—
	$1,148,000	$ 330,400	$1,220,800
Current liabilities	$ 100,000	$ 26,000	$ 126,000
Bonds payable	300,000	46,800	346,800
Common stock	200,000	192,000	200,000
Retained earnings	548,000	65,600	548,000
	$1,148,000	$ 330,400	$1,220,800

The subsidiary's assets and liabilities replace the investment account.

operation will reflect an exchange gain and an integrated operation will reflect an exchange loss. These observations are only true when monetary liabilities are greater than monetary assets.

Complications with a Purchase Discrepancy

The previous example assumed a 100 percent controlled subsidiary and no purchase discrepancy. The existence of a purchase discrepancy presents complications in the consolidation process when the current rate method is used and the subsidiary is less than 100 percent owned. We will change some of the facts from the previous example in order to illustrate this.

Example Assume that Starmont purchased 90 percent of Controlada on December 31, Year 1, at a cost of B2,250,000. The carrying values of Controlada's net assets were equal to fair values on this date, resulting in goodwill of B450,000. The same exchange rates are assumed; thus, the financial statements of Controlada and their translation will not change from the previous example. However, the change in the acquisition cost and the percentage purchased creates a purchase discrepancy and a noncontrolling interest. Starmont's journal entry to record the acquisition on December 31, Year 1, is as follows:

Investment in Controlada	288,000	
Cash		288,000

To record the acquisition of 90% of Controlada for $288,000
(2,250,000 × 0.128)

The following calculation of the purchase discrepancy in bolivars and dollars on December 31, Year 1, is made to prepare the acquisition date consolidated balance sheet:

<table>
<tr><td style="font-style:italic">The purchase discrepancy is translated at the exchange rate on the date of acquisition.</td><td>Cost of 90% investment</td><td>B2,250,000</td><td>×</td><td>.128</td><td>=</td><td>$288,000</td></tr>
<tr><td></td><td>Implied value of 100%</td><td>B2,500,000</td><td>×</td><td>.128</td><td>=</td><td>$320,000</td></tr>
<tr><td></td><td>Book value of subsidiary</td><td></td><td></td><td></td><td></td><td></td></tr>
<tr><td></td><td>Common stock</td><td>1,500,000</td><td>×</td><td>.128</td><td>=</td><td>192,000</td></tr>
<tr><td></td><td>Retained earnings</td><td>500,000</td><td>×</td><td>.128</td><td>=</td><td>64,000</td></tr>
<tr><td></td><td>Shareholders' equity</td><td>2,000,000</td><td></td><td></td><td></td><td>256,000</td></tr>
<tr><td></td><td>Purchase discrepancy</td><td>500,000</td><td>×</td><td>.128</td><td>=</td><td>64,000</td></tr>
<tr><td></td><td>Fair value differences × 90 percent</td><td>–0–</td><td></td><td></td><td></td><td>–0–</td></tr>
<tr><td></td><td>Balance — goodwill</td><td>B 500,000</td><td>×</td><td>.128</td><td>=</td><td>$ 64,000</td></tr>
</table>

Exhibit 12.12 shows the December 31, Year 1, balance sheets of the parent and subsidiary and the consolidated balance sheet.

Exhibit 12.12

PREPARATION OF CONSOLIDATED BALANCE SHEET
At December 31, Year 1

	Starmont	Controlada	Starmont Consolidated
Goodwill and noncontrolling interest appear on the consolidated balance sheet. Cash	$ 38,000	$ 5,120	$ 43,120
Accounts receivable	90,000	46,080	136,080
Inventories	200,000	153,600	353,600
Plant and equipment	300,000	115,200	415,200
Investment in Controlada	288,000	—	—
Goodwill	—	—	64,000
	$916,000	$320,000	$1,012,000
Current liabilities	$ 80,000	$ 6,400	$ 86,400
Bonds payable	300,000	57,600	357,600
Common stock	200,000	192,000	200,000
Retained earnings	336,000	64,000	336,000
Noncontrolling interest*	—	—	32,000
	$916,000	$320,000	$1,012,000

* 10% × $320,000

The subsidiary's separate entity financial statements are the same regardless of the parent's percentage ownership in the subsidiary.

Consolidation — Self-sustaining Assuming that Controlada is a self-sustaining operation, we will now illustrate the preparation of the Year 2 consolidated financial statements. The translated financial statements are the same as were shown in the previous example, and are reproduced again as part of Exhibit 12.13 on page 576. Included in the subsidiary's shareholders' equity is the cumulative unrealized loss of $51,300. The noncontrolling interest in the consolidated balance sheet includes 10 percent of the subsidiary's shareholders' equity and therefore includes 10 percent of this cumulative loss. Consolidated shareholders' equity will show the other 90 percent of this translation adjustment. A further exchange loss arises in the consolidation process because of the manner in which the purchase discrepancy amortization schedule is translated. Assume that after a goodwill impairment test was conducted at the end of Year 2, it was determined that a loss of B50,000 should be reflected. The changes between the opening and closing amounts must be calculated in the foreign currency and then translated into dollars as follows:

TRANSLATION OF PURCHASE DISCREPANCY AMORTIZATION SCHEDULE

Ending goodwill for a self-sustaining subsidiary is translated at the current rate.

Goodwill — December 31, Year 1	B500,000	×	.128	=	$64,000
Impairment loss — Year 2	50,000	×	.115	=	5,750
Calculated goodwill — December 31, Year 2					58,250
Actual goodwill — December 31, Year 2	B450,000	×	.104	=	46,800
Exchange loss — unrealized					$11,450

The following points should be noted:

- The purchase discrepancy (in this case goodwill) on December 31, Year 1, is translated at the historical rate on that date.

Goodwill impairment is translated at the rate when the impairment occurred.

- The Year 2 impairment loss is translated at the average rate for Year 2. In this case, the entire purchase discrepancy amortization was due to a goodwill impairment loss. A question arises as to which exchange rate to use to translate this loss. The logical answer is the average rate, because the impairment loss is assumed to have been incurred evenly throughout the year. If this subsidiary had used push-down accounting, the goodwill impairment loss would appear on its income statement and would be translated at the average rate. The fact that push-down accounting was not used should not result in a different translated amount for this loss.

- The unamortized balance on December 31, Year 2, is translated at the current rate.

An exchange adjustment occurs because the goodwill is restated when it is translated at the current rate at the end of the year.

When different exchange rates are used to translate the schedule, an exchange gain or loss will always result. In this case, there is a loss of $11,450, which appears as part of the cumulative other comprehensive income in the shareholders' equity of the parent company. The allocation of the two exchange losses resulting from the translation of the financial statements and the purchase discrepancy to controlling and noncontrolling interests is illustrated next.

DISPOSITION OF CUMULATIVE UNREALIZED LOSSES

	Total	90% control	10% noncontrol
Cumulative unrealized loss — subsidiary statements	$51,300	$46,170	$5,130
Cumulative unrealized loss — purchase discrepancy	11,450	10,305	1,145
	$62,750	$56,475	$6,275

Using the translated financial statements of Controlada (see Exhibit 12.13) and the translated purchase discrepancy amortization schedule, Starmont would make the following equity method journal entries on December 31, Year 2:

The equity method records the parent's share of the exchange adjustment reported by the subsidiary and relating to the purchase discrepancy.

Cash (90% × 10,400)	9,360	
Other comprehensive income (90% × 51,300)	46,170	
Equity earnings (90% × 34,500)		31,050
Investment in Controlada		24,480
To record the parent's share of dividends, net income, and loss on translation of statements		

Equity earnings (90% × 5,750)	5,175	
Other comprehensive income (90% × 11,450)	10,305	
Investment in Controlada		15,480
To record the amortization and exchange adjustment on the purchase discrepancy		

The preparation of the Year 2 consolidated financial statements is illustrated in Exhibit 12.13.

The following explanations regarding the preparation of the consolidated statements should be noted:

1. Consolidated statement of comprehensive income —

NCI on the income statement is based on the income recorded by the subsidiary plus the consolidation adjustments for goodwill impairment loss and exchange loss from restating goodwill.

    (a) Equity earnings are eliminated and replaced with the revenues and expenses of the subsidiary, the goodwill impairment loss, and the noncontrolling interest.

    (b) Noncontrolling interest in regular income is 10 percent of subsidiary net income less 10 percent of the goodwill impairment loss.

    (c) This statement takes the traditional net income and deducts the unrealized foreign exchange loss to determine comprehensive income.

    (d) Noncontrolling interest absorbs 10 percent of the unrealized exchange loss reported in other comprehensive income.

2. Consolidated retained earnings —

Because the parent has used the equity method, all items are identical to the parent's retained earnings.

3. Consolidated balance sheet —

    (a) The investment account is eliminated and replaced with the assets and liabilities of the subsidiary, the unamortized purchase discrepancy, and the noncontrolling interest.

NCI on the balance sheet is based on the subsidiary's shareholders' equity plus the consolidation adjustment for unimpaired goodwill at the end of the year.

    (b) The noncontrolling interest is calculated as follows:

Common stock	$192,000
Retained earnings	88,100
Cumulative other comprehensive income	(51,300)
Goodwill	46,800
	275,600
	10%
	$ 27,560

4. Consolidated cumulative other comprehensive income—

This account shows the parent's share of the cumulative unrealized foreign

Exhibit 12.13

PREPARATION OF CONSOLIDATED FINANCIAL STATEMENTS — YEAR 2
(self-sustaining)

STATEMENT OF NET INCOME AND COMPREHENSIVE INCOME

	Starmont	Controlada	Starmont Consolidated
Sales	$3,000,000	$1,035,000	$4,035,000
Equity earnings	25,875	—	—
	3,025,875	1,035,000	4,035,000
Cost of goods sold	2,500,000	805,000	3,305,000
Depreciation	20,000	11,500	31,500
Bond interest	30,000	5,175	35,175
Other	200,000	178,825	378,825
Goodwill impairment loss	—	—	5,750
	2,750,000	1,000,500	3,756,250
Individual net incomes	275,875	34,500	
Net income — entity			278,750
Noncontrolling interest			2,875
Net income	275,875	34,500	275,875
Other comprehensive income			
Unrealized exchange gains (losses) from self-sustaining foreign operations			
— entity	(56,475)	(51,300)	(62,750)
Less: noncontrolling interest			(6,275)
Other comprehensive income — Starmont's share	(56,475)	(51,300)	(56,475)
Comprehensive income	$ 219,400	$ (16,800)	$ 219,400

The goodwill impairment loss and noncontrolling interest appear only on the consolidated income statement.

Consolidated OCI includes $51,300 from translating the subsidiary's separate-entity statements plus $11,450 from translating the purchase discrepancy on consolidation.

RETAINED EARNINGS

	Starmont	Controlada	Starmont Consolidated
Balance — beginning	$ 336,000	$ 64,000	$ 336,000
Net income	275,875	34,500	275,875
	611,875	98,500	611,875
Dividends	50,000	10,400	50,000
Balance — end	$ 561,875	$ 88,100	$ 561,875

BALANCE SHEETS

	Starmont	Controlada	Starmont Consolidated
Cash	$ 66,960	$ 10,400	$ 77,360
Accounts receivable	290,400	41,600	332,000
Inventories	220,000	166,400	386,400
Plant and equipment	280,000	83,200	363,200
Investment in Controlada (equity)	248,040	—	—
Goodwill	—	—	46,800
	$1,105,400	$ 301,600	$1,205,760
Current liabilities	$ 100,000	$ 26,000	$ 126,000
Bonds payable	300,000	46,800	346,800
Common stock	200,000	192,000	200,000
Retained earnings	561,875	88,100	561,875
Cumulative other comprehensive income			
Unrealized exchange gains (losses) from self-sustaining foreign operations	(56,475)	(51,300)	(56,475)
Noncontrolling interest	—	—	27,560
	$1,105,400	$ 301,600	$1,205,760

Cumulative OCI is only the parent's share. The NCI's share of cumulative OCI is included in the $27,560 for NCI.

exchange losses at the end of the year. Since Year 2 is the first year after acquisition, the cumulative losses are equal to the losses reported in other comprehensive income for the year.

The unamortized purchase discrepancy can be verified by the following calculation:

Investment in Controlada		$248,040
Shareholders' equity of Controlada	228,800	
	90%	205,920
Unamortized purchase discrepancy (goodwill) — parent's share		42,120
— noncontrolling interest's share (10% × 46,800)		4,680
Total unamortized purchase discrepancy (goodwill)		$ 46,800

Consolidation — Integrated We will conclude this example by assuming that 90 percent owned Controlada is an integrated foreign operation. In this case, the existence of a purchase discrepancy and a noncontrolling interest poses no particular consolidation problems. The purchase discrepancy amortization schedule for Year 2 is shown below:

There is no exchange adjustment because goodwill is translated at the historical rate under the temporal method.

PURCHASE DISCREPANCY AMORTIZATION SCHEDULE

Goodwill — December 31, Year 1	B500,000	×	.128	=		$64,000
Impairment loss — Year 2	50,000	×	.128	=		6,400
Goodwill — December 31, Year 2	B450,000	×	.128	=		$57,600

Using the Year 2 purchase discrepancy amortization schedule and Controlada's translated financial statements (see Exhibit 12.14), Starmont would make the following equity-method journal entries on December 31, Year 2:

The parent accrues its share of the subsidiary's income after it has been translated into Canadian dollars.

Cash (90% × 10,400)	9,360	
Investment in Controlada	1,440	
Equity earnings (90% × 12,000)		10,800
To record parent's share of dividends and net income		
Equity earnings (90% × 6,400)	5,760	
Investment in Controlada		5,760
Amortization of purchase discrepancy		

The equity earnings are quite different under the temporal method as compared to the current rate method.

Note that Year 2 equity earnings are $5,040 in this example (integrated); in the previous example (self-sustaining), equity earnings were $25,875. The difference is due to (a) the use of different exchange rates in the translation, and (b) the fact that there is no exchange loss on the translation of the purchase discrepancy amortization schedule under the temporal method.

Exhibit 12.14 shows the preparation of the Year 2 consolidated financial statements.

The following points are worth noting in regard to the preparation of the consolidated statements:

1. Consolidated income statement —

   (a) Equity earnings are eliminated, and replaced with the revenues and expenses of the subsidiary, the goodwill impairment loss, and the noncontrolling interest, as follows:

Goodwill impairment loss and noncontrolling interest are consolidation adjustments.	Net income, Controlada	$12,000
	Goodwill impairment loss	(6,400)
	Noncontrolling interest	(560)
	Equity earnings	$(5,040)

Exhibit 12.14

PREPARATION OF CONSOLIDATED FINANCIAL STATEMENTS — YEAR 2
(integrated foreign operation)
INCOME STATEMENT

		Starmont	Controlada	Starmont Consolidated
	Sales	$3,000,000	$1,035,000	$4,035,000
	Equity earnings	5,040	—	—
		3,005,040	1,035,000	4,035,000
The goodwill impairment loss and noncontrolling interest appear only on the consolidated income statement.	Cost of goods sold	2,500,000	828,600	3,328,600
	Depreciation	20,000	12,800	32,800
	Bond interest	30,000	5,175	35,175
	Other expenses	200,000	178,825	378,825
	Goodwill impairment loss	—	—	6,400
	Foreign exchange gain	—	(2,400)	(2,400)
		2,750,000	1,023,000	3,779,400
	Individual net incomes	$ 255,040	$ 12,000	
	Net income — entity			255,600
	Less noncontrolling interest			560
	Net income			$ 255,040

RETAINED EARNINGS

		Starmont	Controlada	Starmont Consolidated
The parent's retained earnings under the equity method are equal to consolidated retained earnings.	Balance — beginning	$ 336,000	$ 64,000	$ 336,000
	Net income	255,040	12,000	255,040
		591,040	76,000	591,040
	Dividends	50,000	10,400	50,000
	Balance — end	$ 541,040	$ 65,600	$ 541,040

BALANCE SHEETS

		Starmont	Controlada	Starmont Consolidated
	Cash	$ 66,960	$ 10,400	$ 77,360
	Accounts receivable	290,400	41,600	332,000
	Inventories	220,000	176,000	396,000
	Plant and equipment (net)	280,000	102,400	382,400
	Investment in Controlada (equity)	283,680	—	—
	Goodwill	—	—	57,600
		$1,141,040	$ 330,400	$1,245,360
There is no cumulative other comprehensive income for exchange gains or losses under the temporal method.	Current liabilities	$ 100,000	$ 26,000	$ 126,000
	Bonds payable	300,000	46,800	346,800
	Noncontrolling interest	—	—	31,520
	Common stock	200,000	192,000	200,000
	Retained earnings	541,040	65,600	541,040
		$1,141,040	$ 330,400	$1,245,360

(b) Noncontrolling interest is 10 percent of subsidiary's net income less 10 percent of the goodwill impairment loss.

2. Consolidated retained earnings —

Because the parent has used the equity method, all items are identical to the parent's retained earnings.

3. Consolidated balance sheet —

(a) The investment account is eliminated and replaced with the assets and liabilities of the subsidiary, the unamortized purchase discrepancy, and the noncontrolling interest.

(b) The noncontrolling interest is calculated as follows:

NCI on the balance sheet is based on the subsidiary's shareholders' equity plus the unimpaired goodwill at the end of the year.

Common stock	$192,000
Retained earnings	65,600
Goodwill	57,600
	315,200
	10%
	$ 31,520

The unamortized purchase discrepancy can be verified by the following calculation:

Investment in Controlada		$283,680
Shareholders' equity of Controlada (192,000 + 65,600)	257,600	
	90%	231,840
Unamortized purchase discrepancy (goodwill) — parent's share		51,840
— noncontrolling interest's share (10% × 57,600)		5,760
Total unamortized purchase discrepancy (goodwill)		$ 57,600

Other Considerations

The previous examples have illustrated the translation of a foreign operation's financial statements and the consolidation of these statements with those of the reporting enterprise. We will now look at some other items that must be considered when a foreign subsidiary is being consolidated.

Inventory is translated at the current rate for a self-sustaining operation and the LCM principle need not be applied.

For an integrated operation, the LCM principle must be applied using historical cost in Canadian dollars and market value in Canadian dollars.

Lower of Cost and Market If the foreign operation applies Canadian accounting principles when preparing its financial statements, it will value certain items, such as inventory, at the lower of cost and market. If the subsidiary is self-sustaining, the method of valuation used is of no consequence in the translation because all of the assets are translated at the current rate regardless of whether they are carried at past prices (cost) or current prices (market).

If the foreign operation is integrated, assets carried at cost are translated at historical rates while assets carried at market are translated at the current rate. Remember that the temporal method remeasures, in Canadian dollars, transactions that have been incurred by the foreign operation. Therefore, the translated financial statements should reflect the lower of cost and market in Canadian dollars as if the parent itself had carried out the inventory acquisitions of its foreign subsidiary.

Section 1651 describes the proper treatment for assets of an integrated operation as follows:

When assets are valued at the lower of cost and market, a write-down to market may be required in the translated financial statements even though no write-down is required in the foreign currency financial statements. [1651.49]

For example, if the market price (denominated in foreign currency) is greater than historical cost (denominated in foreign currency), no write-down will have occurred in the foreign operation's statements. But if the foreign currency weakens, it is quite possible that the market price translated at the current rate will be less than historical cost translated at the historical rate. In this situation, translated market price will be used in the translated financial statements.

> On the other hand, it may be necessary to reverse a write-down in the foreign currency financial statements prior to translation if the market amount translated at the current rate exceeds historical cost translated at the historical rates. [1651.50]

For example, if the market price (denominated in foreign currency) is less than historical cost (denominated in foreign currency), a write-down would have taken place in the foreign operation's statements. If the foreign currency has strengthened so that the market price translated at the current rate is greater than historical cost translated at the historical rate, this write-down will have to be reversed prior to translation. The inventory (now carried at cost) will be translated at the historical rate.

Intercompany Profits   In the preparation of consolidated financial statements, intercompany profits in assets are eliminated. If the profits are contained in the assets of the Canadian parent, there is no particular problem eliminating them. The asset acquired was recorded by the parent at the foreign currency denominated price translated at the exchange rate on the date of the transaction. The profit rate can be applied for the items still on hand to determine the amount of profit to be eliminated. If the profits are contained in the assets of an integrated subsidiary, the amount of unrealized profit can still be determined in foreign currency. Because the asset itself is translated at the historical rate, using the historical rate to translate and eliminate the profit will result in a translated asset at historical cost to the consolidated entity.

The historical rate should be used in determining the intercompany profit to be eliminated. This eliminates the same profit that was recorded in the first place.

When the profit is contained in the assets of a translated self-sustaining subsidiary, the asset has been translated at the current rate. The question becomes this: What rate should be used to translate the profit before eliminating it in the consolidation process? The committee concluded that the historical exchange rate should be used to calculate the amount of the profit. This will *not* result in a translated asset recorded at historical cost to the entity.[5]

A cash flow statement is prepared by analyzing the change in a non-cash item on the balance sheet after it has been translated into Canadian dollars.

Cash Flow Statement   To prepare a cash flow statement for a foreign subsidiary, we would ignore the cash flow statement of the foreign subsidiary, i.e., we would not translate each item on the foreign-currency cash flow statement into Canadian dollars by applying a translation rate to each item. Rather, we would use the translated balance sheet and translated income statement to determine the cash flows during the year. We would analyze the changes in the translated balance sheet accounts from last year to this year using either a worksheet approach or T-account approach and then prepare the cash flow statement based on this analysis. This is a similar approach to what we used in Chapter 9 when we prepared a consolidated cash flow statement by analyzing the changes in the consolidated balance sheet from last year to this year.

---

[5] For a more detailed discussion of this, see Dr. Pierre Vezina, "Foreign Currency Translation," Toronto: CICA, 1985.

An International Perspective

Canadian accounting practices for foreign operations are substantially the same as the IASB standards.

The *CICA Handbook* is substantially similar to the IASB's standards for translation of foreign operations except for the following:

- IAS 39 requires unrealized foreign exchange gains and losses on available-for-sale financial assets to be recognized immediately in net income whereas these gains and losses would be reported in other comprehensive income under Canadian standards.

- IAS 21 takes a functional currency approach rather than classifying subsidiaries as integrated or self-sustaining. Functional currency is defined as the currency of the primary economic environment in which the entity operates. Each entity determines its functional currency and prepares its separate entity financial statements in its functional currency. Then, the separate entity financial statements are translated into the parent's reporting currency for inclusion in the consolidated financial statements.

- IAS 29 allows a company to adjust their financial statements for inflation prior to translation whereas financial statements cannot be adjusted for inflation according to Canadian standards.

These differences should be eliminated over the next few years when Canada adopts the IFRS or the IASB changes their standards by adopting the Canadian standards.

SUMMARY

Before the equity method or consolidation accounting can be used, the financial statements of foreign investees must be translated into Canadian dollars. If the investee is considered to be an integrated foreign operation, the temporal method of translation is used. It produces results that are consistent with the normal measurement and valuation of assets and liabilities for domestic transactions and operations. Exchange gains or losses are included in income.

The current rate method is used when the foreign operation is self-sustaining. It results in some assets and liabilities being reported in Canadian dollars at values other than historical cost or current value. Exchange gains and losses from the translation are not reflected in net income but rather are shown in other comprehensive income which ends up being reported on a cumulative basis as a separate component of shareholders' equity. The consolidation of the translated financial statements of a self-sustaining subsidiary creates additional exchange gains and losses from the translation of the purchase discrepancy.

SELF-STUDY PROBLEM

Jaap Corp., located in the Netherlands, is a 90%-owned subsidiary of a Canadian parent. The company was incorporated on January 1, Year 1, and issued its no-par common shares for 5.0 million guilders (G). The Canadian parent acquired 90% of these shares at this time for $2.25 million when the exchange rate was CDN$1 = G2. The financial statements for Jaap on December 31, Year 2, are shown on the next page.

Other Information
- On January 3, Year 1, Jaap issued bonds for G2.5 million.

- Jaap acquired the plant assets on February 1, Year 1, for G6.0 million. The plant assets are being depreciated on a straight-line basis over a 10-year life.
- Jaap uses the FIFO basis to value inventory. The December 31, Year 1, inventory was acquired on October 1, Year 1. The inventory on hand on December 31, Year 2, was acquired on December 15, Year 2.
- Jaap did not pay dividends in Year 1, and the Year 2 dividends were declared and paid on November 30, Year 2.
- Under the temporal method, Jaap's December 31, Year 1, retained earnings were translated as $561,169.
- Exchange rate information:

January 3, Year 1	CDN$1 = G1.98
February 1, Year 1	CDN$1 = G1.96
October 1, Year 1	CDN$1 = G1.94
Average, Year 1	CDN$1 = G1.95
December 31, Year 1	CDN$1 = G1.91
December 15, Year 2	CDN$1 = G1.80
Average, Year 2	CDN$1 = G1.86
December 31, Year 2	CDN$1 = G1.82

BALANCE SHEET
at December 31, Year 2

	Year 2	Year 1
Cash	G1,000,000	G 500,000
Accounts receivable	2,710,000	2,550,000
Inventory	1,050,000	1,155,000
Plant assets	6,000,000	6,000,000
Accumulated depreciation	(1,000,000)	(500,000)
	G9,760,000	G9,705,000
Accounts payable	G 50,000	G 850,000
Accrued liabilities	50,000	350,000
Bonds payable — due Jan. 3, Year 11	2,500,000	2,500,000
Common shares	5,000,000	5,000,000
Retained earnings	2,160,000	1,005,000
	G9,760,000	G9,705,000

INCOME STATEMENT
for the Year Ended December 31, Year 2

Sales	G35,000,000
Cost of sales	28,150,000
Depreciation	500,000
Interest	200,000
Selling	1,940,000
Miscellaneous expenses	800,000
Income tax	1,045,000
	32,635,000
Net income	G 2,365,000

STATEMENT OF RETAINED EARNINGS
for the Year Ended December 31, Year 2

Balance, January 1	G1,005,000
Net income	2,365,000
	3,370,000
Dividends	1,210,000
Balance, December 31	G2,160,000

Required:

(a) Translate Jaap's Year 2 financial statements into dollars, assuming that it is an integrated foreign operation.
(b) Assume that Jaap is a self-sustaining operation:
   (i) Translate the Year 2 financial statements.
   (ii) Prepare the Year 2 equity method journal entries that would be made by the Canadian parent.

Solution to Self-study Problem

(a) Integrated

	Guilders	Rate	Dollars
Year 2			
Inventory Jan. 1	1,155,000	/ 1.94	595,361
Purchases	28,045,000	/ 1.86	15,077,956
	29,200,000		15,673,317
Inventory Dec. 31	1,050,000	/ 1.80	583,333
Cost of sales	28,150,000		15,089,984
Net monetary position			
Dec. 31, Year 1*	(650,000)	/ 1.91	(340,314)
Changes Year 2			
Sales	35,000,000	/ 1.86	18,817,204
Purchases	(28,045,000)	/ 1.86	(15,077,956)
Interest	(200,000)	/ 1.86	(107,527)
Selling	(1,940,000)	/ 1.86	(1,043,011)
Miscellaneous expenses	(800,000)	/ 1.86	(430,108)
Income tax	(1,045,000)	/ 1.86	(561,828)
Dividends	(1,210,000)	/ 1.82	(664,835)
	1,760,000		931,939
Calculated Dec. 31, Year 2			591,625
Actual Dec. 31, Year 2**	1,110,000	/ 1.82	609,890
Exchange gain Year 2			18,265

* 500 + 2,550 – 850 – 350 – 2,500
** 1,000 + 2,710 – 50 – 50 – 2,500

	Guilders	Rate	Dollars
Translation of Year 2 income statement			
Sales	35,000,000	/ 1.86	18,817,204
Cost of sales	28,150,000	Calc.	15,089,984
Depreciation	500,000	/ 1.96	255,102
Interest	200,000	/ 1.86	107,527
Selling	1,940,000	/ 1.86	1,043,011
Miscellaneous expenses	800,000	/ 1.86	430,108
Income tax	1,045,000	/ 1.86	561,828
	32,635,000		17,487,560
Net income before exchange gain	2,365,000		1,329,644
Exchange gain	—		18,265
Net income	2,365,000		1,347,909
Translation of Year 2 retained earnings			
Balance Jan. 1	1,005,000	given	561,169
Net income	2,365,000	above	1,347,909
	3,370,000		1,909,078
Dividends	1,210,000	/ 1.82	664,835
Balance Dec. 31	2,160,000		1,244,243
Translation of Year 2 balance sheet			
Cash	1,000,000	/ 1.82	549,451
Accounts receivable	2,710,000	/ 1.82	1,489,011
Inventory	1,050,000	/ 1.80	583,333
Plant assets	6,000,000	/ 1.96	3,061,224
Accumulated depreciation	(1,000,000)	/ 1.96	(510,204)
	9,760,000		5,172,815
Accounts payable	50,000	/ 1.82	27,473
Accrued liabilities	50,000	/ 1.82	27,473
Bonds payable	2,500,000	/ 1.82	1,373,626
Common shares	5,000,000	/ 2.00	2,500,000
Retained earnings	2,160,000		1,244,243
	9,760,000		5,172,815

(b) Self-sustaining

(i)

	Guilders	Rate	Dollars
Year 1			
Net assets Jan. 1 Year 1	5,000,000	given	2,500,000
Net income — Year 1	1,005,000	/ 1.95	515,385
Calculated Dec. 31, Year 1			3,015,385
Net assets Dec. 31, Year 1	6,005,000	/ 1.91	3,143,979
Exchange gain Year 1 (to be reported in other comprehensive income)			128,594
Year 2			
Net assets Jan. 1, Year 2	6,005,000	/ 1.91	3,143,979
Net income — Year 2	2,365,000	/ 1.86	1,271,505
	8,370,000		4,415,484
Dividends	1,210,000	/ 1.82	664,835
Calculated Dec. 31, Year 2			3,750,649
Net assets Dec. 31, Year 2	7,160,000	/ 1.82	3,934,066
Exchange gain Year 2 (to be reported in other comprehensive income)			183,417

	Guilders	Rate	Dollars
Cumulative translation adjustment			
Balance Dec. 31, Year 1			128,594
Exchange gain — Year 2			183,417
Balance Dec. 31, Year 2			312,011
Translation of Year 2 income statement			
Sales	35,000,000	/ 1.86	18,817,204
Cost of sales	28,150,000	/ 1.86	15,134,409
Depreciation	500,000	/ 1.86	268,817
Interest	200,000	/ 1.86	107,527
Selling	1,940,000	/ 1.86	1,043,011
Miscellaneous expenses	800,000	/ 1.86	430,108
Income tax	1,045,000	/ 1.86	561,828
	32,635,000		17,545,700
Net income	2,365,000		1,271,504
Other comprehensive income —			
unrealized exchange gain			183,417
Comprehensive income			1,454,921
Translation of Year 2 retained earnings			
Balance Jan. 1	1,005,000	/ 1.95	515,385
Net income	2,365,000	/ 1.86	1,271,504
	3,370,000		1,786,889
Dividends	1,210,000	/ 1.82	664,835
Balance Dec. 31	2,160,000		1,122,054
Translation of Year 2 balance sheet			
Cash	1,000,000	/ 1.82	549,451
Accounts receivable	2,710,000	/ 1.82	1,489,011
Inventory	1,050,000	/ 1.82	576,923
Plant assets	6,000,000	/ 1.82	3,296,703
Accumulated depreciation	(1,000,000)	/ 1.82	(549,451)
	9,760,000		5,362,637
Accounts payable	50,000	/ 1.82	27,473
Accrued liabilities	50,000	/ 1.82	27,473
Bonds payable	2,500,000	/ 1.82	1,373,626
Common shares	5,000,000	/ 2.00	2,500,000
Retained earnings	2,160,000		1,122,054
Cumulative other comprehensive income			312,011
	9,760,000		5,362,637

(ii)   Equity method journal entries of Canadian parent — Year 2

Investment in Jaap Corp.	1,144,355	
Investment income		1,144,355

90% of Year 2 translated net income (90% × 1,271,505)

Cash	598,352	
Investment in Jaap Corp		598,352

90% of Year 2 dividends (90% × 664,835)

Investment in Jaap Corp	165,075	
Other comprehensive income		165,075

90% of Year 2 exchange gain (90% × 183,417)

REVIEW QUESTIONS

1. The temporal and current rate methods each produce different amounts for translation gains and losses due to the items at risk. Explain.

2. What are the two major issues related to the translation of foreign currency financial statements?

3. Why might a company want to hedge its balance sheet exposure? What is the paradox associated with hedging balance sheet exposure?

4. How are gains and losses on financial instruments used to hedge the net investment in a self-sustaining foreign operation reported in the consolidated financial statements?

5. What is the major objective to be achieved in the translation of foreign currency denominated financial statements?

6. What should happen if a foreign subsidiary's financial statements have been prepared using accounting principles different from those used in Canada?

7. What is the difference between a self-sustaining foreign operation and an integrated operation? What method of translation should be used for each?

8. What translation method should be used for a self-sustaining subsidiary that operates in a highly inflationary environment? Why?

9. How are translation exchange gains and losses reflected in financial statements if the foreign operation is integrated? Would the treatment be different if the foreign operation were self-sustaining? Explain.

10. Does the temporal method use the same unit of measure as the current rate method? Explain.

11. The amount of the cumulative unrealized exchange losses appearing in the translated financial statements of a subsidiary could be different from the amount appearing in the consolidated financial statements. Explain how.

12. The application of the lower of cost and market rule to the translated financial statements requires different treatment with regard to the two classifications of foreign operations described in the *CICA Handbook*. Explain fully.

13. If the translation of an integrated foreign operation produced a gain, the translation of the same company could produce a loss if the operation was instead considered to be self-sustaining. Do you agree with this statement? Explain.

14. Explain how the temporal method produces results that are consistent with the normal measurement and valuation of asset and liabilities for domestic transactions and operations.

15. When translating the financial statements of the subsidiary at the date of acquisition by the parent, the exchange rate on the date of acquisition is used to translate capital assets rather than the exchange rate on the date when the subsidiary acquired the capital assets. Explain the rationale for this practice.

16. If the sales of a foreign subsidiary all occurred on one day during the year, would the sales be translated at the average rate for the year or the rate on the date of the sales? Explain.

MULTIPLE-CHOICE QUESTIONS

1. What happens when the temporal method of foreign currency translation is used?
   a. Monetary assets and liabilities are translated at the historical rate.
   b. The lower of cost and market rule to determine the need for a write-down of inventory is applied after translation.
   c. Translation gains and losses are shown as a separate component of share-holders' equity.
   d. Deferred revenue is translated at the current rate.

2. The temporal and current rate methods are being compared. Which of the following statements is true?
   a. The amount reported for inventory is normally the same under both methods.
   b. The amount reported for equipment is normally the same under both methods.
   c. The amount reported for sales is normally the same under both methods.
   d. The amount reported for depreciation expense is normally the same under both methods.

3. What rates should be used to translate the following balance sheet accounts of a self-sustaining foreign operation?

Equipment	*Accumulated amortization — equipment*
a. current	current
b. historical	historical
c. average for the year	current
d. current	historical

4. An integrated subsidiary of a Canadian parent is located in Australia, whose currency is the dollar (A$). The subsidiary acquires inventory on October 31, Year 5, for A$300,000 which is sold on January 15, Year 6, for A$400,000. Collection of the money takes place on February 10, Year 6. Applicable exchange rates are as follows:

October 31, Year 5	A$1 = CDN$0.5075
December 31, Year 5	A$1 = CDN$0.5050
January 15, Year 6	A$1 = CDN$0.5000

   After translation, what amount should be reported for this inventory on December 31, Year 5?
   a. $150,000
   b. $151,500
   c. $152,250
   d. $200,000

5. At what point in the process should a Canadian parent company adjust its foreign subsidiary's accounts to bring them in accordance with Canadian GAAP?
   a. Prior to the beginning of the translation process.
   b. After translation, but prior to consolidation.
   c. After consolidation, but prior to reporting.
   d. No adjustments are necessary, since most foreign countries already use Canadian GAAP.

6. What rates should be used to translate the following balance sheet accounts of an integrated foreign operation?

Equipment	Accumulated amortization — equipment
a. current	current
b. current	average for the year
c. current	historical
d. historical	historical

Use the following data for Questions 7 and 8.

The following balance sheet accounts of a foreign entity have been translated into Canadian dollars at the following amounts:

	Current	Historical
Accounts receivable	$264,000	$240,000
Investment in held-to-maturity bonds	132,000	120,000
Land	66,000	60,000
Patents	102,000	96,000

7. The foreign entity is considered to be integrated. What total should appear on the balance sheet of this entity's Canadian parent for these items?
   a. $516,000
   b. $540,000
   c. $552,000
   d. $564,000

8. The foreign entity is considered to be self-sustaining. What total should appear on the balance sheet of its Canadian parent for these items?
   a. $516,000
   b. $540,000
   c. $552,000
   d. $564,000

9. A Canadian company owns a self-sustaining subsidiary in Argentina, where the currency is the peso (Ps). On January 1, Year 5, the subsidiary had Ps500,000 in cash and no other assets or liabilities. On February 15, the subsidiary used Ps100,000 to purchase equipment. On April 1, the subsidiary used cash to purchase merchandise inventory costing Ps80,000. This merchandise was sold on May 29 for Ps120,000 in cash. On November 29, the subsidiary paid cash dividends in the amount of Ps60,000, and on December 31 it recorded depreciation on the equipment for the year of Ps50,000. The appropriate exchange rates were as follows:

January 1, Year 5	Ps1 = $1.48
February 15, Year 5	Ps1 = $1.50
April 1, Year 5	Ps1 = $1.52
May 29, Year 5	Ps1 = $1.55
November 29, Year 5	Ps1 = $1.53
December 31, Year 5	Ps1 = $1.56
Average for Year 5	Ps1 = $1.50

What is the amount of the Year 5 translation adjustment to be included in cumulative other comprehensive income in the shareholders' equity section of the translated balance sheet?
   a. $31,000 debit.
   b. $31,000 credit.
   c. $37,600 debit.
   d. $37,600 credit.

Use the following data for Questions 10 and 11.

A subsidiary of a Canadian company purchased government bonds and inventory on March 1, Year 5, for 80,000 pesos each. Both of these items were paid for on May 1, Year 5, and were still on hand at year-end. The government bonds are classified as available-for-sale and are reported at their market value of Ps80,000. Inventory is carried at cost under the lower of cost and market rule. Currency exchange rates are as follows:

March 1, Year 5	Ps1 = $0.20
May 1, Year 5	Ps1 = $0.22
December 31, Year 5	Ps1 = $0.24

10. Assuming that the subsidiary is integrated, what balances are reported on the December 31, Year 5, consolidated balance sheet?
   a. Government bonds = $16,000, inventory = $16,000.
   b. Government bonds = $19,200, inventory = $16,000.
   c. Government bonds = $17,600, inventory = $17,600.
   d. Government bonds = $19,200, inventory = $19,200.

11. Assuming the subsidiary is self-sustaining, what balances are reported on the December 31, Year 4, consolidated balance sheet?
   a. Government bonds = $16,000, inventory = $16,000.
   b. Government bonds = $17,600, inventory = $17,600.
   c. Government bonds = $19,200, inventory = $16,000.
   d. Government bonds = $19,200, inventory = $19,200.

Use the following data for Questions 12 to 16.

On January 1, Year 4, Pizza purchased 100% of the outstanding common shares of Saza for 50,000 foreign currency units (FCUs). Saza is located in Zania, and on January 1, Year 4, had common shares of FCU30,000 and retained earnings of FCU10,000. At the date of acquisition, the purchase discrepancy was allocated entirely to buildings, with a remaining life of 20 years.

Saza's financial statements at December 31, Year 5, are shown below in the FCUs of its native country:

STATEMENT OF INCOME AND RETAINED EARNINGS
for the Year Ended December 31, Year 5

Sales	FCU130,000
Beginning inventory	12,000
Purchases	72,000
Ending inventory	(15,000)
Cost of goods sold	69,000
Gross profit	61,000
Operating expenses	32,000
Amortization expense	11,000
Net income	18,000
Retained earnings, Jan. 1, Year 5	12,000
	30,000
Dividends declared and paid	(15,000)
Retained earnings, Dec. 31, Year 5	FCU 15,000

BALANCE SHEET

Current monetary assets	ГCU43,000
Inventory	15,000
Plant and equipment (net)	34,000
	FCU92,000
Current monetary liabilities	FCU27,000
10% bonds payable	20,000
Common stock	30,000
Retained earnings	15,000
	FCU92,000

Sales, purchases, and operating expenses were made evenly throughout the year. Year-end inventory was purchased at the year-end rate. Equipment additions of FCU5,000 with a useful life of 5 years were purchased on January 1, Year 5. There were no other purchases or sales of capital assets in Year 4 or Year 5. In Year 4, Saza earned FCU20,000 and paid dividends of FCU18,000. Dividends were declared and paid on December 31 of each year. The bonds payable were issued on January 1, Year 4, and mature on January 1, Year 9.

> Saza's net current monetary position at December 31, Year 4, was FCU10,000. Exchange rates at various dates are given below.

January 1, Year 4	FCU1 = $2.10
Average, Year 4	FCU1 = $2.15
January 1, Year 5	FCU1 = $2.20
Average, Year 5	FCU1 = $2.25
December 31, Year 5	FCU1 = $2.30

12. Which of the following is the amount that would be reported as cost of goods sold on Saza's translated financial statements at December 31, Year 5, assuming it is an integrated subsidiary?
    a. $153,900
    b. $154,500
    c. $155,250
    d. $158,700

13. Which of the following is the amount that would be reported as amortization expense on Saza's translated financial statements at December 31, Year 5, assuming it is an integrated subsidiary?
    a. $23,100
    b. $23,200
    c. $24,200
    d. $24,750

14. Which of the following is the amount that would be reported in other comprehensive income as the unrealized foreign currency gain for the year ended December 31, Year 5, assuming Saza is a self-sustaining subsidiary?
    a. $2,100
    b. $4,100
    c. $5,100
    d. $10,100

15. Which of the following is the amount that would be reported as the cumulative translation gain in cumulative other comprehensive income on Saza's

translated financial statements at December 31, Year 5, assuming it is a self-sustaining subsidiary?
a. $5,000
b. $5,100
c. $6,000
d. $10,100

16. Which of the following is the translation gain that would arise from the translation of the purchase discrepancy on Pizza's consolidated financial statements at December 31, Year 4, and reported in other comprehensive income, assuming a self-sustaining operation?
a. $0
b. $900
c. $950
d. $975

(CGA-Canada, from 2002 to 2007)

17. Brass Ltd. has a wholly owned, self-sustaining subsidiary in Eastern Asia. For the past 6 years, the country in which the East Asian subsidiary is located experienced a very low level of inflation. Beginning in Year 5, the country has experienced a very high level of inflation. What method should be used to translate the financial statements of the East Asian subsidiary for the year ended December 31, Year 5?
a. The current-rate method should be adopted in place of the temporal method and the change should be accounted for retroactively.
b. The current-rate method should be adopted in place of the temporal method and the change should be accounted for prospectively.
c. The temporal method should be adopted in place of the current-rate method and the change should be accounted for retroactively.
d. The temporal method should be adopted in place of the current-rate method and the change should be accounted for prospectively.

(CGA-Canada, from 2002 to 2007)

18. On January 1, Year 2, CAN acquired a 70 percent interest in SEN, a Swiss company, for SF500,000. On that date, the exchange rate was SF1 = C$0.94. SEN is an integrated foreign operation. In translating the financial statements of SEN at December 31, Year 5, which of the following statements on accounting exposure is true?
a. SEN will recognize an exchange loss on translation pertaining to its investment in land if the exchange rate changes to SF = C$0.95.
b. SEN will recognize an exchange loss on translation pertaining to its investment in land if the exchange rate changes to SF = C$0.93.
c. SEN will recognize an exchange loss on translation pertaining to its accounts receivable if the exchange rate changes to SF = C$0.95.
d. SEN will recognize an exchange loss on translation pertaining to its accounts receivable if the exchange rate changes to SF = C$0.93.

(CGA-Canada, from 2002 to 2007)

19. Which of the following should be translated using the current rate for an integrated foreign operation?
a. Land held for speculation.
b. Land used in operations.
c. Inventory with a cost in excess of fair value.
d. Inventory with a fair value in excess of cost.

20. Which of the following will result in an exchange gain being reported in regular income for an integrated foreign operation?
   a. Translating notes receivable when the Canadian dollar has appreciated relative to the foreign currency.
   b. Translating notes receivable when the Canadian dollar has depreciated relative to the foreign currency.
   c. Translating land when the Canadian dollar has appreciated relative to the foreign currency.
   d. Translating land when the Canadian dollar has depreciated relative to the foreign currency.

CASES

Case 1   Summarized below are the balances in the cumulative unrealized exchange accounts in the consolidated balance sheets of four companies at the end of two successive years. Each company reported in footnote disclosures that its foreign subsidiaries were self-sustaining, and that the financial statements of the subsidiaries had been translated into Canadian dollars using the current rate method. Assume that the balance sheets of each of the companies' foreign subsidiaries have not changed significantly during Year 6.

	Cumulative unrealized exchange gains (losses) (millions of dollars)	
	Year 6	Year 5
A Company	201	30
B Company	52	(75)
C Company	(170)	(100)
D Company	(18)	(164)

Required:

For each company, give a logical explanation for the change that has occurred in the cumulative unrealized exchange accounts during the year. For each company, indicate whether the Canadian dollar is stronger or weaker in Year 6, compared with Year 5.

Case 2   The items shown as Exhibit 12.15 below are extracted from the summary of significant accounting policies of Altos Hornos de México (AHMSA), a steel producer. Your firm, a major Canadian steel producer, is contemplating a major equity investment in AHMSA; there is the potential for an eventual business combination between the firms.

Required:

In your capacity as financial analyst with the acquisitions department, prepare a briefing note for your chief financial officer on the financial reporting implications of the items outlined below.

What problems do you foresee in (a) the analytical process, and (b) the interface of the accounting systems of your firm and those of the proposed acquisition? (Note that you are primarily interested in raising questions at this stage, not in providing answers.)

Exhibit 12.15

SUMMARY OF SIGNIFICANT ACCOUNTING POLICIES [EXCERPTS]

The significant accounting policies followed by the Company, which are in accordance with generally accepted accounting principles (GAAP) in Mexico, are as follows:

a) *Application of new accounting principles*

Beginning January 1, 1997, the Fifth Amendment to Bulletin B-10 issued by the Mexican Institute of Public Accountants became effective. This amendment states that the only method to be used for the restatement of nonmonetary assets is the adjustment from changes in the NCPI (National Consumer Price Index). However, it permits the use of replacement costs for the recognition of the effects of inflation in the case of inventories and costs of sales and imported machinery and equipment, which is restated using the inflation rate of the country of origin and period-end exchange rate.

The Company, following the provisions of Bulletin A-8 issued by the Mexican Institute of Public Accountants ("Supplementary Application of International Accounting Standards") recorded the amortization of the excess of book value over the cost of certain shares ("negative goodwill") in other sales in the consolidated income statement.

b) *Recognition of the effects of inflation in the financial statements*

The Company restates its financial statements to reflect the purchasing power of the Mexican peso as of the most recent reporting date, thereby comprehensively recognizing the effects of inflation. The financial statements of prior periods have also been restated in terms of the purchasing power of the Mexican peso as of the most recent reporting date. Accordingly, prior period amounts differ from those previously reported. As a result, the amounts reported for the most current period are comparable with those of prior periods, being expressed in terms of the same purchasing power.

To recognize the effects of inflation in terms of Mexican pesos with purchasing power as of the most recent reporting date, the procedures used are as follows:

Balance Sheets

Inventories are restated to their most recent production or purchase cost, up to a maximum of their realizable value.

The laminating rollers are amortized based on units of production determined by the Company's technicians.

Inventory of scrap is valued at its recovery cost, in accordance with its market value, less the contribution margin and the cost incurred to process. Scrap is a by-product of AHMSA's production of molten pig iron that can be reused as a secondary raw material.

Property, plant, and equipment are initially recorded at cost of acquisition and/or construction and through 1996 were adjusted annually, to reflect their net replacement cost reported by independent appraisers. Beginning in 1997, domestic property, plant, and equipment are restated using NCPI factors, based on the restated value as of December 31, 1996, and imported equipment is restated using the inflation rate of the country of origin and the period-end exchange rate.

Depreciation of fixed assets is computed using the straight-line method, based on the estimated useful lives and appraisers' value of the assets and is restated to constant Mexican pesos using the NCPI.

Shareholders' equity and nonmonetary items other than inventory and property, plant, and equipment are restated using factors derived from the NCPI, cumulative from the date of contribution or generation.

Statements of Income

Revenues and expenses that are associated with a monetary item (trade receivables, cash, liabilities, etc.) are restated from the month in which they arise through the most recent reporting date, based on the NCPI.

Cost of sales is restated to estimated replacement cost at the time of the sale, through the use of standard costs that are periodically updated. Other costs and expenses associated with nonmonetary items are restated from the time incurred through period end, as a function of the restatement of the nonmonetary assets that are being consumed or sold.

The gain from monetary position in the income statement represents the effect of inflation on monetary items. This amount is computed on the net monetary position at the beginning of each month, adjusted by changes in the NCPI, and the monthly result is restated in terms of the purchasing power of the Mexican peso at period end.

Other Statements

The statement of changes in financial position presents the changes in financial resources measured in constant Mexican pesos, based on the financial position at the prior period end, restated to Mexican pesos as of the end of the most recent reporting period.

The cumulative restatement effect in shareholders' equity consists principally of the gain or loss from holding nonmonetary assets, which represents the change in the specific price level of those assets in relation to general inflation, as measured by the NCPI.

c) *Cash and cash equivalents*

Cash equivalents include short-term highly liquid investments with an original maturity of three months or less (including Mexican treasury bills) and bank deposits valued at market (cost plus accrued interest).

At December 31, 2007, there are Ps87,500 of security investments that guarantee the timely payment of the unsecured obligations of MINOSA, a subsidiary. For financial statements purposes this concept is recorded net of the related liability.

d) *Income tax and employee profit sharing*

The provisions for income tax and employee profit sharing are calculated based upon taxable income, which differs from income for financial reporting purposes due to certain permanent and timing differences which are expected to be replaced by items of a similar nature and amount.

e) *Financing and related costs*

Financing and related costs include interest income and expense, foreign exchange gains and losses, and gains or losses from monetary position.

Transactions denominated in foreign currencies are recorded at the exchange rate at the date on which they occur. The assets and liabilities denominated in foreign currencies are valued at the exchange rate in effect at the balance sheet date.

f) *Negative goodwill*

Negative goodwill represents the excess of the book value of shares acquired over the purchase price. Amortization is calculated on a straight-line basis during the period in which the new subsidiary will be integrated, the three-year period beginning January 1, 2007.

g) *Restatement of shareholders' equity*

Capital stock and accumulated earnings are restated by applying the NCPI from the date contributed or accrued. The restatement represents the amount necessary to maintain shareholders' equity in terms of purchasing power at year-end.

h) *Minority interest*

The minority interest principally represents the minority shareholders' proportionate share of the earnings and equity of 5% of Hullera Mexicana, S.A. de C.V.

(Case prepared by Peter Secord, St. Mary's University.)

Case 3 Nova Mine Engineering is a junior Canadian company with a variety of operating subsidiaries and other undertakings that provide mine engineering and management services in Canada and in several less developed countries. One of these subsidiaries is active in Zimbabwe, which is rich in mineral resources and has an active mining industry. This company, Zimbabwe Platinum Management (ZPM), is under review prior to year-end translation and consolidation. The staff of ZPM consists primarily of junior and intermediate Nova staff who have been seconded to the operation on one- to three-year terms. Between the companies there is information flow but no product movement. Capital investment in Zimbabwe is restricted to movable equipment and working capital with a value of about CDN$3,000,000.

Management of Nova has long been concerned about its inability to hedge against fluctuations in the Zimbabwean dollar. All payments to ZPM from the state Mineral Marketing Corporation have recently been made in this currency, rather than in U.S. dollars as specified in earlier contracts. It is this inability to hedge that has increased Nova's concern about the long-run fit of ZPM within the portfolio of Nova companies, and about current financial statement presentation. The currency has declined in value by 65 percent during the year. Other concerns include Zimbabwe's persistent high inflation, recently about 35 percent, which is expected to increase even further. Political uncertainty is also a concern, as a result of recent nationalizations in the agricultural sector and growing unrest among the poor.

Required:

In a briefing note, advise senior management of Nova how the investment in the subsidiary ZPM should be measured and reported, and what disclosures should be made with respect to this investment in the annual report of the parent company.

(Case prepared by Peter Secord, St. Mary's University.)

Case 4 Vulcan Manufacturing Limited (VML) is a Canadian-based multinational plastics firm, with subsidiaries in several foreign countries and worldwide-consolidated total assets of $500 million. VML's shares are listed on a Canadian stock exchange.

VML is attracted by the growing demand for its products in developing countries. In recognition of trade barriers designed to encourage domestic production in those countries and in order to service local demand, VML incorporated a foreign subsidiary in a South American country on September 1, Year 4. The subsidiary, South American Plastics Inc. (SAPI), manufactures patented sheet-plastic and sells virtually all of its output locally. Also, almost all labour and raw materials are provided locally. SAPI finances its day-to-day activities from its own operations and local borrowing.

During Year 4 and Year 5, the South American country suffered an inflation rate of more than 100 percent, accompanied by substantial devaluation of the local currency and a drastic increase in interest rates. The government is expected to impose wage and price controls in Year 6. The inflation rate is expected to stabilize at more moderate levels sometime in Year 6 or Year 7.

The chief financial officer (CFO) of VML has recently received SAPI's draft balance sheet as at August 31, Year 5 (Exhibit I), together with some comments prepared by SAPI's controller (Exhibit II). He is somewhat surprised by the return on investment of nearly 12 percent. This figure is well above the target rate agreed upon for bonus purposes, which was set at 3 percent in recognition of start-up costs associated with the first year of operations. The apparently favourable performance will result in large bonuses having to be paid to SAPI's management.

Increases in SAPI's domestic selling price have kept pace with the general rate of inflation and with increases in input prices and borrowing costs in the South American country. The CFO is satisfied that the inflation and devaluation the country has experienced has not seriously affected SAPI's cash flows from operations.

In the annual report to Canadian shareholders for the year ended August 31, Year 5, the CFO wants to communicate to shareholders the economic impact that inflation and devaluation in the South American country have had on VML's investment in SAPI. He is concerned that gains or losses arising from translation of the statements in accordance with Section 1651 of the *CICA Handbook* will mislead shareholders. The CFO believes that the exchange gains and losses will obscure the true impact of foreign inflation and devaluation on SAPI's economic value in Canadian dollar terms. He has called the audit partner and you, Senior, into his office. The following conversation ensues:

CFO: We have to issue our financial statements soon, and we have to apply Section 1651 to our South American subsidiary. I must confess that I don't know Section 1651 as well as you two do. My staff tells me that we must use the temporal method this year, due to the local hyperinflation, although I confess that I don't see why. Apparently we will have a choice between the temporal method and the current rate method once the inflation rate stabilizes, which I expect to happen in Year 6 or Year 7. I am very reluctant to use the temporal method on this year's statements. It forces me to include fictitious gains and losses in our consolidated income statement.

Partner: Your staff is correct in stating that the *Handbook* requires the use of the temporal method for the year just ended. However, shareholders should not be misled by exchange gains or losses in consolidated income provided that they are fully disclosed as such.

CFO: I guess I just do not understand Section 1651. For example, how might the adoption of the current rate method in Year 6 or Year 7 improve matters? It seems to me that an overall exchange loss will arise, if the rate keeps on going down. What does the loss mean? As long as our subsidiary's cash flows keep pace with local inflation, it will be able to maintain its expected rate of profitability and therefore its ability to pay dividends to us. Yet shareholders will see an exchange loss!

Partner: I will have Senior prepare a report that explains to you how the exchange gains or losses under either translation method tie in with the notion of risk underlying Section 1651. We will also explain how this notion alleviates your concern about communicating the true economic risk to shareholders. Senior will recommend ways to tell the whole story to shareholders.

CFO: Sounds great. I would also like Senior to provide advice on any other important issues related to SAPI. For starters, I have some concerns about the way our bonus plan for SAPI's management is working. One possibility I am considering is to evaluate SAPI's performance in Canadian dollar terms.

Required:

Prepare the report to the CFO.

(CICA adapted)

EXHIBIT I

SOUTH AMERICAN PLASTICS INC.
Extracts from draft balance sheet
as at August 31, Year 5
(in 000's)

Assets

Cash	FCU*	10,020
Available-for-sale securities (at cost)		3,120
Accounts receivable		93,000
Inventory (at cost)		67,200
Prepaid expenses		8,040
		181,380
Fixed assets		143,111
Less accumulated depreciation		14,311
		128,800
	FCU	310,180

Liabilities and Shareholders' Equity

Current monetary liabilities	FCU	65,140
Long-term debt		157,200
		222,340
Capital stock		51,000
Retained earnings		36,840
		87,840
	FCU	310,180

* An FCU is a unit of the currency used in the South American country in which SAPI is located.

EXHIBIT II

SOUTH AMERICAN PLASTICS INC.
Controller's comments on financial statements

1. Opening Balances
    SAPI's balance sheet on September 1, Year 4, consisted of cash of FCU 208,200,000, long-term debt of FCU 157,200,000 and common stock of FCU 51,000,000.
2. Available-for-sale Securities
    The available-for-sale securities, which are investments in a number of local companies, were purchased when one FCU = $0.30. The investments are considered temporary and can be sold easily on short notice. The aggregate market value for the securities at August 31, Year 5 was FCU 3,000,000.
3. Inventories
    Inventories were purchased when one FCU = $0.30. VML values inventory at the lower of cost and replacement cost. The aggregate replacement cost of the inventory was FCU 100,000,000 at August 31, Year 5.
4. Prepaid Expenses
    The amounts, representing prepaid rent and property taxes, were paid when one FCU = $0.25.
5. Fixed Assets
    Fixed assets were purchased shortly after the date of SAPI's formation at a time when one FCU = $0.40. The current replacement cost of the fixed assets (in their current condition) was FCU 200,000,000 at August 31, Year 5.
6. Current Liabilities
    All current liabilities were incurred at a time when one FCU = $0.25.

7. Long-term Debt
    The debt represents a floating interest rate loan, which will be repaid in foreign currency units on August 31, Year 8.
8. Retained Earnings
    No dividends were paid during the Year 5 fiscal year.
9. Exchange Rates

September 1, Year 4	1 FCU = $0.40
August 31, Year 5	1 FCU = $0.20
Average rate for year	1 FCU = $0.30

PROBLEMS

Note: Some problems use direct exchange rate quotations, while others use indirect quotations. For direct quotations, the foreign currency is multiplied by the exchange rate to arrive at Canadian dollars; for indirect quotations, division is used.

Problem 1   On December 31, Year 1, Precision Manufacturing Inc. (PMI) of Edmonton purchased 100% of the outstanding common shares of Sandora Corp. of Flint, Michigan.

Other Information

- Exchange rates

December 31, Year 1	US$1 = CDN$1.10
September 30, Year 2	US$1 = CDN$1.07
December 31, Year 2	US$1 = CDN$1.05
Average for Year 2	US$1 = CDN$1.08

- Sandora declared and paid dividends on September 30, Year 2.
- The inventories on hand on December 31, Year 2, were purchased when the exchange rate was US$1 = CDN$1.06.

Sandora's comparative balance sheets and Year 2 income statement are as follows:

BALANCE SHEET
at December 31

	Year 2	Year 1
Cash	US$ 780,000	US$ 900,000
Accounts receivable	6,100,000	4,800,000
Inventory	5,700,000	6,300,000
Plant and equipment (net)	6,600,000	7,200,000
	US$19,180,000	US$19,200,000
Current liabilities	US$ 1,900,000	US$ 2,400,000
Bonds payable —		
due Dec. 31, Year 6	4,800,000	4,800,000
Common stock	5,000,000	5,000,000
Retained earnings	7,480,000	7,000,000
	US$19,180,000	US$19,200,000

INCOME STATEMENT
for the Year Ended December 31, Year 2

Sales	US$30,000,000
Cost of sales	24,000,000
Depreciation expense	600,000
Other expenses	3,900,000
	28,500,000
Net income	US$ 1,500,000

Required:

PART A

Assume that Sandora is an integrated foreign subsidiary.

(a) Calculate the Year 2 exchange gain (loss) that would result from the translation of Sandora's financial statements.

(b) Translate the Year 2 financial statements into Canadian dollars.

PART B

Assume that Sandora is a self-sustaining foreign subsidiary.

(a) Calculate the Year 2 exchange gain (loss) that would result from the translation of Sandora's financial statements and would be reported in other comprehensive income.

(b) Translate the Year 2 financial statements into Canadian dollars.

Problem 2   On December 31, Year 1, Kelly Corporation of Toronto paid DM13 million for 100% of the outstanding common shares of Krugor Company of Germany. On this date, the fair values of Krugor's identifiable assets and liabilities were equal to their carrying values. Krugor's comparative balance sheets and Year 2 income statement are as follows:

BALANCE SHEET
at December 31

	Year 2	Year 1
Current monetary assets	DM10,780,000	DM 9,600,000
Inventory	1,800,000	2,400,000
Plant and equipment (net)	6,600,000	7,200,000
	DM19,180,000	DM19,200,000
Current monetary liabilities	DM 1,900,000	DM 2,400,000
Bonds payable, due Dec. 31, Year 6	4,800,000	4,800,000
Common stock	5,000,000	5,000,000
Retained earnings	7,480,000	7,000,000
	DM19,180,000	DM19,200,000

INCOME STATEMENT
for the Year Ended December 31, Year 2

Sales	DM 16,000,000
Inventory, January 1	2,400,000
Purchases	10,840,000
Inventory, December 31	(1,800,000)
Depreciation expense	600,000
Other expenses	2,360,000
	DM 14,400,000
Net income	DM 1,600,000

Other Information

• Exchange rates

December 31, Year 1	DM1 = $0.52
September 30, Year 2	DM1 = $0.62
December 31, Year 2	DM1 = $0.65
Average for Year 2	DM1 = $0.58

- Krugor Company declared and paid dividends on September 30, Year 2.
- The inventories on hand on December 31, Year 2, were purchased when the exchange rate was DM1 = $0.63.

Required:

PART A

Krugor is an integrated foreign subsidiary.
(a) Calculate the Year 2 exchange gain or loss that would result from the translation of Krugor's financial statements.
(b) Prepare translated financial statements for Year 2.

PART B

Krugor is a self-sustaining foreign subsidiary.
(a) Calculate the Year 2 exchange gain or loss that would result from the translation of Krugor's financial statements.
(b) Prepare translated financial statements for Year 2.
(c) Calculate the amount of goodwill that would appear on the December 31, Year 2, consolidated balance sheet, if there was an impairment loss of DM50,000 during the year.
(d) Calculate the amount, description, and location of the exchange gain or loss that would appear in Kelly's Year 2 consolidated financial statements.

Problem 3 On January 1, Year 3, Jets Ltd., a Winnipeg-based company, purchased 80% of the shares of Charmaine Inc. for FF1,900,000 — an amount which, at that date, translated to $655,172.

The Year 3 financial statements for Charmaine are:

BALANCE SHEET
at December 31, Year 3

Cash	FF 820,000
Accounts receivable	317,500
Inventory	730,000
Fixed assets, net	1,722,500
	FF3,590,000
Current monetary liabilities	FF 380,000
Notes payable	700,000
Common shares	900,000
Retained earnings	1,610,000
	FF3,590,000

INCOME STATEMENT
for the Year Ended December 31, Year 3

Sales	FF10,350,000
Cost of sales	6,400,000
Gross profit	3,950,000
Depreciation	122,500
Other expenses	3,367,500
Net income	FF 460,000

Additional Information

- The FIFO inventory method is used. The opening inventory, which was purchased before December 31, Year 2, cost FF600,000. The exchange rate at the time of inventory purchase was $1 = FF2.71.
  The purchases during the year were:

	FF	Exchange Rate
Purchase Number 1	2,000,000	$1 = FF3.0
Purchase Number 2	4,530,000	$1 = FF3.12

- The fixed assets were purchased when the company was formed (January 1, Year 1). The common shares were issued at the same time. The exchange rate at that date was $1 = FF1.5. The cost of the fixed assets is FF2,450,000, and the accumulated depreciation is FF727,500 at December 31, Year 3.
- The notes payable are due on January 1, Year 7, and were issued on December 31, Year 2. There is no interest on these notes.
- The "sales" and "other expenses" on the income statement were incurred evenly throughout the year. Also, the "other expenses" represent a monetary outflow.
- The dividends of FF200,000 were paid on December 31, Year 3.
- The balances in francs at December 31, Year 2:

Cash	FF 350,000
Accounts receivable	FF 405,000
Current monetary liabilities	FF(250,000)
Notes payable	FF(700,000)

- Exchange rates:

December 31, Year 2	$1 = FF2.9
January 1, Year 3	$1 = FF2.9
Year 3 average	$1 = FF3.25
December 31, Year 3	$1 = FF3.6

Required:

(a) There will be a foreign exchange gain or loss on the translated income statement prepared in part (b). Prepare a schedule to explain the calculation of the foreign exchange gain or loss under the temporal method.
(b) Prepare the Canadian dollar income statement for Charmaine for Year 3, using the temporal method and assuming that the income statement will be used to consolidate with Parent.

(CGA-Canada, from 2002 to 2007)

Problem 4   On January 1, Year 1, P Company (a Canadian company) purchased 90% of S Company (located in a foreign country) at a cost of 14,400 foreign currency units (FCUs).

The book values of S Company's net assets were equal to fair values on this date except for plant and equipment, which had a fair value of FCU22,000, with a remaining life of 10 years. A goodwill impairment loss of FCU100 occurred in Year 1.

The following exchange rates were in effect during Year 1:

January 1	1FCU = $1.10
Average for year	1FCU = $1.16
When ending inventory purchased	1FCU = $1.19
December 31	1FCU = $1.22

The balance sheet of S Company on January 1, Year 1, is as follows:

	S Company (FCUs)
Monetary assets (current)	10,000
Inventory	8,000
Plant and equipment (net)	20,000
	38,000
Current liabilities	9,000
Bonds payable (mature in 8 years)	16,000
Capital stock	10,000
Retained earnings	3,000
	38,000

The December 31, Year 1, financial statements of P Company (in $) and S Company (in FCUs) are shown below:

BALANCE SHEETS

	P Company $	S Company FCUs
Monetary assets (current)	31,552	17,000
Inventory	30,000	11,000
Plant and equipment (net)	60,000	18,000
Investment in S Company (at cost)	15,840	—
	137,392	46,000
Current monetary liabilities	26,000	12,000
Bonds payable	40,000	16,000
Capital stock	30,000	10,000
Retained earnings	41,392	8,000
	137,392	46,000

STATEMENTS OF INCOME AND RETAINED EARNINGS

	P Company $	S Company FCUs
Sales	360,000	100,000
Dividend income	4,392	—
Cost of sales	(180,000)	(59,000)
Depreciation	(11,000)	(2,000)
Other expenses	(144,000)	(30,000)
Net income	29,392	9,000
Retained earnings, beginning of year	22,000	3,000
Dividends (declared on Dec. 31)	(10,000)	(4,000)
Retained earnings, end of year	$ 41,392	$ 8,000

Required:

Prepare the December 31, Year 1, consolidated financial statements, assuming that S Company is:
(a) an integrated foreign subsidiary.
(b) a self-sustaining foreign subsidiary.

Problem 5 Mex Ltd. is an integrated foreign subsidiary. At the end of the current year, the inventory of the company was:

| Cost | 14,862,000 pesos |
| Market | 12,100,000 pesos |

Applying the lower of cost and market, the company wrote the inventory down by Ps2,762,000 for presentation in its financial statements. When these financial statements were received by the parent company in Canada for translation, it was determined that the year-end spot rate was $1 = Ps392. The closing inventory at cost is composed of the following:

Purchase	Amount in pesos	Historical exchange rate
1	3,200,000	$1 = Ps341
2	6,132,000	$1 = Ps360
3	5,530,000	$1 = Ps375

Required:

(a) At what amount would the inventory be shown on the translated balance sheet of Mex? And what is the amount of the loss from write-down that would appear on the translated income statement?

(b) If the year-end spot rate was $1 = Ps281, at what amount would the inventory be shown on the translated balance sheet? And what is the amount of the loss from write-down that would appear on the translated income statement?

(CGA-Canada, from 2002 to 2007)

Problem 6 Maple Limited (Maple) was incorporated on January 2, Year 1, and commenced active operations immediately in the southwestern United States. Common shares were issued on the date of incorporation and no more common shares have been issued since then.

On December 31, Year 4, the Oak Company (Oak) purchased 100% of the outstanding common shares of Maple.

The balance sheet for Maple at December 31, Year 10, was as follows:

Cash	US$ 100,000
Accounts receivable (Note 1)	200,000
Inventory (Note 2)	300,000
Equipment – net (Note 3)	1,100,000
	US$1,700,000
Accounts payable	US$ 250,000
Bonds payable (Note 4)	700,000
Common shares	100,000
Retained earnings	650,000
	US$1,700,000

Other Information

1. The accounts receivable relate to sales occurring evenly throughout the month of December, Year 10.

2. Maple uses the FIFO method to account for its inventory. The inventory available for sale during the year was purchased as follows:

Date of Purchase	Cost of Purchase	Exchange Rate
December 31, Year 9	US$100,000	US$1 = C$1.56
March 1, Year 10	1,000,000	US$1 = C$1.60
November 1, Year 10	180,000	US$1 = C$1.63

3. The equipment was purchased on May 26, Year 4.

4. The bonds were issued on May 26, Year 4, to finance the purchase of the equipment.

5. Maple reported net income of US$200,000, which was earned evenly throughout the year and paid dividends of US$160,000 on July 1, Year 10.
6. Foreign exchange rates were as follows:

January 2, Year 1	US$1 = C$1.30
May 26, Year 4	US$1 = C$1.40 —
December 31, Year 4	US$1 = C$1.42
December 31, Year 9	US$1 = C$1.56
July 1, Year 10	US$1 = C$1.61
Average for Year 10	US$1 = C$1.59
Average for December Year 10	US$1 = C$1.64
December 31, Year 10	US$1 = C$1.65

Required:

(a) Translate the balance sheet of Maple at December 31, Year 10, into Canadian dollars using the temporal method. Assume that the translated balance sheet will be consolidated with Oak's balance sheet. For retained earnings, simply use the amount required to balance your balance sheet.
(b) Calculate the foreign exchange gain or loss on the bonds payable for the year ended December 31, Year 10, and state how it would be reported on the year end financial statements.
(c) Prepare an independent calculation of the unrealized exchange gains or losses that would be reported in other comprehensive income for Year 10 assuming that Maple is a self-sustaining operation.
(d) Since the current-rate method uses the current rate to translate equipment, the translated amount should represent the current value of the equipment in Canadian dollars. Do you agree or disagree? Briefly explain.

(*CGA-Canada, from 2002 to 2007*)

Problem 7 In preparation for translating the financial statements of a foreign subsidiary that is integrated, you have the following information:

	Foreign francs
Inventory (FIFO cost, net realizable value, 1,300,000 Foreign francs)	1,150,000

An examination of the working papers of the foreign subsidiary's auditors shows the following information:

Opening inventory	FF 350,000
Purchases	
February 15, Year 3	205,000
April 15, Year 3	588,000
August 1, Year 3	410,000
October 12, Year 3	362,000
November 15, Year 3	547,000
Cost of goods sold for the year	1,312,000

Exchange rates:

January 1, Year 3 (opening inventory)	$1 = FF2.5
February 15, Year 3	$1 = FF3.1
April 15, Year 3	$1 = FF3.4
August 1, Year 3	$1 = FF4.3
October 12, Year 3	$1 = FF4.8
November 15, Year 3	$1 = FF5.5
December 31, Year 3	$1 = FF6.1
Year 3 average	$1 = FF4.0

Note: This is not considered excessive or high inflation in terms of the temporal method.

Required:

(a) Calculate the Canadian dollar amount of the inventory at the fiscal year-end (December 31), and the Canadian dollar amount of any item(s) that would appear on the income statement.

(b) If the foreign subsidiary were self-sustaining, what would your answer to part (a) be?

(c) Define accounting exposure and describe its impact on the translation of financial statement items in this problem.

(CGA-Canada, from 2002 to 2007)

Problem 8 On December 31, Year 2, PAT Inc. of Halifax, Nova Scotia acquired 90 percent of the voting shares of Spiele Limited of Bonn, Germany, for 690,000 Deutsche marks (DM). On the acquisition date, the fair values equalled the carrying values for all of Spiele's identifiable assets and liabilities.

Selected account balances from Spiele's general ledger on December 31, Year 2, were as follows:

Equipment	DM 250,000
Building	1,350,000
Accumulated amortization	195,000
Common shares	600,000
Retained earnings	96,000

Spiele purchased the building and equipment on January 1, Year 1.

The condensed trial balance of Spiele for the year ending December 31, Year 5, was as follows:

Accounts receivable	DM 197,000
Inventory	255,000
Building	1,350,000
Equipment	350,000
Cost of goods sold	1,200,000
Amortization expense	130,000
Other expenses	470,000
Dividends paid	300,000
Total debits	DM4,252,000
Current monetary liabilities	DM 682,000
Common shares	600,000
Retained earnings, beginning	300,000
Sales	2,250,000
Accumulated amortization	420,000
Total credits	DM4,252,000

Other Information

1. Spiele's sales, inventory purchases, and other expenses occurred uniformly over the year.

2. Spiele's inventory on hand at the end of each year was purchased uniformly over the last quarter of the year. On December 31, Year 4, the inventories totalled DM375,000, and on December 31, Year 5, they totalled DM255,000.

3. On January 1, Year 5, Spiele purchased equipment for DM100,000. The equipment has an estimated useful life of 8 years and a salvage value of DM5,000. Spiele uses the double-declining-balance method to calculate amortization expense. There were no other purchases of capital assets between Year 2 and Year 5.
4. The dividends were declared and paid on January 1, Year 5.
5. The exchange rates for the Deutsche mark and the Canadian dollar were as follows:

January 1, Year 1	C$1 = DM0.50
December 31, Year 2	C$1 = DM0.60
Average for the Year 4 fourth quarter	C$1 = DM0.68
December 31, Year 4/January 1, Year 5	C$1 = DM0.70
December 31, Year 5	C$1 = DM0.80
Average for Year 5	C$1 = DM0.76
Average for the Year 5 fourth quarter	C$1 = DM0.79

Required:

(a) Translate into Canadian dollars the following items on Spiele's financial statements for the year ended December 31, Year 5, assuming that Spiele is an integrated operation.
(i) Accounts receivable
(ii) Inventory
(iii) Equipment
(iv) Accumulated amortization
(v) Common shares

(b) Translate into Canadian dollars the following items on Spiele's financial statements for the year ended December 31, Year 5, assuming that Spiele is a self-sustaining operation.
(i) Cost of goods sold
(ii) Amortization expense
(iii) Inventory
(iv) Common shares

(c) Prepare an independent calculation of the unrealized exchange gains or losses to be included in other comprehensive income for Year 5, assuming that Spiele is a self-sustaining operation.

(d) For integrated foreign operations, the reporting enterprise's exposure to exchange rate changes is similar to the exposure that would exist had the transactions and activities of the foreign operation been undertaken by the reporting enterprise. Therefore, the financial statements of the foreign operation should be expressed in a manner which is consistent with the measurement of domestic transactions and operations.

Explain how the temporal method used in translating foreign operations is consistent with the measurement of assets and liabilities for domestic transactions and operations.

(CGA-Canada, from 2002 to 2007)

Problem 9 Dom Ltd. has a subsidiary, Tarzan Inc., in the country of Tarzania, which uses the tar (Tz) as its currency. Before this 100%-owned subsidiary can be consolidated, the financial statements must be translated from tars to Canadian dollars. However, the person responsible for the translation has quit suddenly and left you with a half-finished job. Certain information is available but the rest you must determine.

TARZAN INC.
FINANCIAL STATEMENTS (IN TZ)
December 31, Year 4

Cash	Tz 100,000
Accounts receivable	200,000
Inventory (1)	400,000
Land	500,000
Buildings (2)	800,000
Accumulated depreciation	(300,000)
	Tz1,700,000
Accounts payable	Tz 250,000
Note payable (3)	400,000
Common shares	300,000
Retained earnings	750,000
	Tz1,700,000
Sales	Tz5,200,000
Cost of goods sold	3,100,000
	2,100,000
Depreciation	(80,000)
Other expenses (5)	(1,870,000)
Net income	Tz 150,000

Other Information

1. The opening inventory was Tz500,000, and the purchases during the period were Tz3,000,000. Tarzan uses a periodic FIFO inventory system. The opening inventory had an exchange rate of $1 = Tz3.5, and the purchases were made 30% from the parent and 70% from the local area. The local area purchases were made evenly throughout the year; the purchases from the parent were recorded by the parent at $232,558. The ending inventory was purchased when the exchange rate was $1 = Tz4.0.

2. There were two buildings and one piece of land. The land and building #1 (Tz300,000) were acquired when Tarzan was formed by Dom. The exchange rate at that time was $1 = Tz2. Building #2 was acquired when the exchange rate was $1 = Tz3.2. The depreciation expense is proportional to the purchase prices. The accumulated depreciation relating to Building #2 is Tz200,000.

3. The note payable, which is due on January 1, Year 8, was created on July 1, Year 4.

4. The retained earnings at January 1, Year 4, translated into $181,818.

5. The other expenses were incurred evenly throughout the year.

6. No dividends were declared during the year:

7. Exchange rates:

January 1, Year 4	$1 = Tz3.7
2004 average, July 1, Year 4	$1 = Tz3.9
December 31, Year 4	$1 = Tz4.1

Required:

(a) Assume that Tarzan is integrated. Prepare the financial statements of Tarzan in Canadian dollars. Show your calculations *in good form*.

(b) If the fair value of the ending inventory was Tz350,000, what would the Canadian dollar value of the inventory be? Assume all the other information given in the question remains constant.

(*CGA-Canada, from 2002 to 2007*)

Problem 10   In Year 1, Victoria Textiles Limited decided that its European operations had expanded such that a European office should be established. The office would be involved in selling Victoria's current product lines; it was also expected to establish supplier contacts. In the European market, there were a number of small manufacturers of top-quality fabrics, particularly wool and lace, but from Victoria's home office in Ontario it was difficult to find and maintain these suppliers. To assist in doing so, a wholly owned company, Victoria Textiles (Luxembourg) Limited, was created, and a facility was established in Luxembourg in January Year 2. The new company, VTLL, was given the mandate from head office to buy and sell with other Victoria divisions and offices across Canada, as if it were an autonomous, independent unit. To establish the company, an investment of 10,000,000 Luxembourg francs (LF) was made on January 1, Year 2.

VTLL proved to be quite successful, as shown below in the financial statements at December 31, Year 4. After one year of operations, VTLL had borrowed funds and expanded facilities substantially, as the initial market estimates had turned out to be quite conservative. However, during this time the Luxembourg franc had fallen in value relative to the Canadian dollar. As a result, Victoria's management was somewhat confused about how to evaluate VTLL's success, given the changing currency values.

FINANCIAL STATEMENTS
(000s, Luxembourg francs)
BALANCE SHEETS

	Year 4	Year 3
Cash	4,100	3,900
Accounts receivable	2,900	2,100
Inventories	4,800	3,500
Prepaid expenses	1,900	1,700
Fixed assets (net)	7,900	8,900
	21,600	20,100
Current monetary liabilities	2,400	900
Unearned revenue	800	500
Long-term debt	6,000	6,000
	9,200	7,400
Common stock	10,000	10,000
Retained earnings	2,400	2,700
	21,600	20,100

INCOME AND RETAINED EARNINGS STATEMENTS

	Year 4	Year 3
Sales	20,200	12,000
Cost of sales	11,300	6,300
Gross profit	8,900	5,700
Operating expenses	3,400	2,100
Depreciation	1,000	700
Interest	700	400
Taxes	600	400
Net income	3,200	2,100
Opening retained earnings	2,700	1,100
	5,900	3,200
Dividends	3,500	500
Closing retained earnings	2,400	2,700

Additional Information

1. The exchange rate at January 1, Year 2, when VTLL was originally established, was $0.075 per Luxembourg franc.

2. Of the original investment of LF10 million, LF4 million was used to acquire plant and equipment, which is being depreciated on a straight-line basis over 10 years.

3. At June 30, Year 3, an expansion was completed at a cost of LF6 million, which was financed entirely by a 6-year note obtained from a Luxembourg bank. Interest is to be paid semiannually. The exchange rate at July 1, Year 3, was $0.062 per Luxembourg franc. The new expansion is also to be depreciated on a straight-line basis over 10 years. (A half-year's depreciation was recorded in Year 3.)

4. Inventory is accounted for on the FIFO basis. The inventory at the end of Year 3 and Year 4 was acquired when the exchange rates were $0.045 and $0.027 per Luxembourg franc respectively.

5. Sales, purchases, and operating expenses were incurred evenly throughout the year, and the average exchange rate for the year was $0.031.

6. The prepaid expenses and unearned revenue at December 31, Year 4, arose when the exchange rates were $0.03 and $0.028 per Luxembourg franc respectively.

7. Income taxes were paid in equal monthly instalments throughout the year.

8. Dividends are declared and paid each year on December 31.

9. The foreign exchange rates per Luxembourg franc at each of the following dates were as follows:

December 31, Year 3	$0.041
June 30, Year 4	$0.036
December 31, Year 4	$0.025

Required:

(a) Prepare a Canadian-dollar balance sheet at December 31, Year 4, and an income statement for the year then ended, assuming that VTLL is.
   (i)   an integrated foreign subsidiary.
   (ii) a self-sustaining foreign subsidiary.

(Note: There is insufficient information to translate retained earnings and cumulative other comprehensive income. Plug these two items with the amount required to balance the balance sheet.)

(b) Which method should Victoria Textiles Limited apply to its investment in this subsidiary? Explain.

(Adapted from a case prepared by Peter Secord, St. Mary's University.)

Problem 11   The financial statements of Voll, Inc., of Germany, as at December 31, Year 11 follow the Other Information section.

Other Information

- On January 1, Year 11, Crichton Corporation of Toronto acquired a controlling interest in Voll.

- Relevant exchange rates were:

January 1, Year 11	CDN$1 = DM2.05
December 31, Year 11	CDN$1 = DM2.20
Average for Year 11	CDN$1 = DM2.10

- The land and buildings were purchased in Year 5 when the exchange rate was DM1.50.

- During Year 11, equipment costing DM126,000 was purchased for cash. Depreciation totalling DM21,000 has been recorded on this equipment. The exchange rate on the date of the equipment purchase was DM2.18.

   The remaining equipment was purchased on the date the subsidiary was acquired, and no other changes have taken place since that date.
- The December 31, Year 11, inventory was acquired during the last quarter of the year, when the average exchange rate was DM2.04.
- On January 1, Year 11, the inventory was DM525,000, and was acquired when the average exchange rate was DM2.27.
- The bonds mature on December 31, Year 16.
- Other operating expenses were incurred equally throughout the year.
- Dividends were declared and paid on December 31, Year 11.
- On January 1, Year 11, liabilities were greater than monetary assets by the amount of DM1,082,000.
- The common shares were issued in Year 1 when the exchange rate was DM3.00.

FINANCIAL STATEMENTS
December 31, Year 11
BALANCE SHEET

Cash		DM 105,000
Accounts receivable		168,000
Inventories — at cost		357,000
Land		420,000
Buildings	1,470,000	
Accumulated depreciation	420,000	1,050,000
Equipment	483,000	
Accumulated depreciation	168,000	315,000
		DM2,415,000
Accounts payable		DM 210,000
Miscellaneous payables		105,000
Bonds payable		600,000
Capital stock		850,000
Retained earnings		650,000
		DM2,415,000

RETAINED EARNINGS STATEMENT

Balance, January 1	DM 420,000
Net income	630,000
	1,050,000
Dividends	400,000
Balance, December 31	DM 650,000

INCOME STATEMENT

Sales	DM3,150,000
Cost of sales	1,680,000
Depreciation — building	105,000
Depreciation — equipment	63,000
Other expenses	672,000
	2,520,000
Net Income	DM 630,000

Required:

PART A

Assume that Voll is an integrated foreign operation. Translate the financial statements into Canadian dollars.

PART B

Assume that Voll is a self-sustaining foreign operation. Translate the balance sheet only into Canadian dollars.

PART C

Explain whether the current rate method produces results that are consistent with the normal measurement and valuation of assets and liabilities for domestic transactions and operations.

Problem 12 SPEC Co. is a Canadian investment company. It acquires real estate properties in foreign countries for speculative purposes. On January 1, Year 5, SPEC incorporated a wholly owned subsidiary, CHIN Limited. CHIN immediately purchased a property in Shanghai, China, for 70 million Chinese yuan (Y). At that time, the land and building were valued at Y30 million and Y40 million, respectively. The previous owner had purchased the property in Year 1 for Y36 million when the exchange rate was $1 = Y5.13. The building had an estimated useful life of 20 years with no residual value on January 1, Year 5.

The draft financial statements for CHIN as at and for the year ended December 31, Year 5, follows:

CHIN LIMITED
Balance Sheet
at December 31, Year 5

Land	Y30,000,000
Building	40,000,000
Accumulated amortization	(2,000,000)
	Y68,000,000
Mortgage payable	Y50,000,000
Common shares	20,000,000
Retained earnings (deficit)	(2,000,000)
	Y68,000,000

CHIN LIMITED
Income Statement
for the year ended December 31, Year 5

Rent revenue	Y 6,000,000
Interest expense	(5,000,000)
Amortization expense	(2,000,000)
Other expenses	(1,000,000)
Net income (loss)	Y(2,000,000)

Additional Information

1. The purchase of the property was financed with Y20 million of equity provided by SPEC and a Y50 million mortgage from a Chinese investor. The mortgage payable has a term of 10 years and requires interest-only payments of Y5 million on December 31 each year and a final payment of Y50 million on December 31, Year 14. The market rate of interest on the mortgage was equal to the stated rate throughout Year 5.

2. The property is rented for Y0.5 million per month, which is consistent with rent being charged by other property owners in the area. The rent is due on the last day of each month. CHIN hires local workers and buys all of its materials and supplies from local suppliers. CHIN incurred the other expenses evenly throughout the year.

3. The exchange rates were as follows:

January 1, Year 5	$1 = Y6.92
Average for Year 5	$1 = Y7.20
Average for 12 days when rent payments were received	$1 = Y7.25
December 31, Year 5	$1 = Y7.50

Required:

(a) Should CHIN be classified as a self-sustaining or integrated subsidiary? Explain.

(b) Ignore your answer to part a. Calculate the foreign exchange adjustment under the current rate method for Year 5 and indicate how this adjustment will be reported in CHIN's Canadian dollar financial statements. Show supporting calculations.

(c) Ignore your answers to parts a and b. Translate CHIN's Year 5 income statement into Canadian dollars using the temporal method. Ignore foreign exchange gains and losses.

(d) Assume that SPEC does not own any shares of CHIN. Instead, SPEC acquired the property in Shanghai directly. SPEC financed the acquisition with Y20 million of its own funds and a Y50 million mortgage. If SPEC argued that the mortgage payable is a hedge of the anticipated sale of the land, what difference would it make for reporting purposes whether or not the mortgage payable is deemed to be an effective hedge of the anticipated sale of the land? Briefly explain.

(CGA-Canada, from 2002 to 2007)

Problem 13   White Company was incorporated on January 2, Year 1, and commenced active operations immediately. Common shares were issued on the date of incorporation and no new common shares have been issued since then. On December 31, Year 5, Black Company purchased 70% of the outstanding common shares of White for 1.4 million foreign pesos (FP). On this date, the fair values of White's identifiable net assets were equal to their book values except for a building, which had a fair value of FP100,000 in excess of book value. The remaining useful life of the building was 10 years at the date of acquisition.

The following information was extracted from the financial records of the two companies for the year ended December 31, Year 6:

	Black	White
Building — net	$3,000,000	FP2,700,000
Common stock	100,000	200,000
Retained earnings, beginning of year	800,000	900,000
Depreciation expense — buildings	200,000	300,000
Income before foreign exchange	150,000	160,000
Dividends paid	80,000	100,000

Additional Information

1. Black uses the cost method to account for its investment in White.
2. White purchased its building on December 31, Year 3.
3. The goodwill impairment loss for Year 6 was FP80,000.
4. Dividends were declared and paid on July 1.

5. Foreign exchange rates were as follows:

January 2, Year 1	FP1 = $0.30
December 31, Year 3	FP1 = $0.24
December 31, Year 5	FP1 = $0.20
Average for Year 6	FP1 = $0.18
July 1, Year 6	FP1 = $0.17
December 31, Year 6	FP1 = $0.15

Required:

(a) Compute the balances that would appear in the Year 6 consolidated financial statements for the following items assuming that White is an integrated subsidiary. White's income before foreign exchange is translated to $30,000 and the exchange gains from translating White's separate-entity financial statements is $50,000.

    (i)   Buildings — net

    (ii)   Goodwill

    (iii) Depreciation expense — buildings

    (iv) Net income (excluding other comprehensive income)

    (v)   Other comprehensive income

    (vi) Noncontrolling interest on the income statement

    (vii) Noncontrolling interest on the balance sheet

(b) Compute the balances that would appear in the Year 6 consolidated financial statements for the same accounts as in part (a) assuming that White is a self-sustaining subsidiary.

LEARNING OBJECTIVES

After studying this chapter, you should be able to do the following:

- Describe the not-for-profit accounting practices currently mandated in the *CICA Handbook*.
- Explain the purpose behind fund reporting.
- Explain the use and the workings of a budgetary control system that uses encumbrances.
- Prepare journal entries and financial statements using the deferred contribution method of recording contributions.
- Prepare journal entries and financial statements using the restricted fund method of recording contributions.
- Outline the basics of government financial reporting.

INTRODUCTION

Over 180,000 NFPOs in Canada receive more than $70 billion each year from government grants and private donations.

A substantial portion of Canada's economic activity is conducted by organizations whose purpose is to provide services (or products) on a non-profit basis. The size of the portion becomes clear when one considers that included in this *nonbusiness area* is the *government sector* encompassing the federal, provincial, and local governments, as well as the *not-for-profit sector*. This latter sector encompasses a wide variety of organizations such as charities, hospitals, universities, professional and fraternal organizations, and community clubs. While our major concern in this chapter is the accounting and financial reporting for Canadian not-for-profit organizations (NFPOs), the reporting requirements for governments are summarized in Appendix 13B. The not-for-profit organizations sector is a very large one in our economy and consists of over 80,000 registered charities and an additional 100,000 voluntary organizations. It has been estimated that the charity sector alone receives over $70 billion a year from governments, private individuals, and corporations.

Not-for-profit organizations are defined in the *CICA Handbook* as:

> … entities, normally without transferable ownership interests, organized and operated exclusively for social, educational, professional, religious, health, charitable or any other not-for-profit purpose. A not-for-profit organization's members, contributors and other resource providers do not, in such capacity, receive any financial return directly from the organization. [4400.02]

There are a number of ways in which NFPOs differ from profit-orientated organizations.

NFPOs differ from profit-oriented organizations in the following ways:

- They typically provide services or goods to identifiable segments of society without the expectation of profit. They accomplish this by raising resources and subsequently spending or distributing these resources in a manner that fulfils the organization's objectives.
- The resources are provided by contributors without the expectation of gain or repayment. Most of these resources consist of donations from the general public and grants from governments and other NFPOs. Often a portion of the resources received have restrictions attached that govern the manner in which they can be spent.
- As the definition cited above indicates, there is no readily defined ownership interest that can be sold, transferred, or redeemed in any way by the organization.
- While many NFPOs have paid employees, they are governed by volunteers who receive no remuneration or gain for the time and effort they provide. In some small organizations there are no paid employees and all effort is provided entirely by volunteers.

Well-defined GAAP for NFPOs has only existed in Canada since 1997.

While financial reporting for NFPOs in Canada is well defined today, this has only been the case since April 1997, when seven very detailed *Handbook* sections became operational. Prior to this date, accounting in this area was in a state of flux, moving from a situation where there were no real authoritative pronouncements at all, to one where there was only a single *Handbook* section that gave only broad guidance for some issues and left many other important ones unresolved. A few large organizations, such as hospitals and universities, published detailed manuals in an attempt to establish consistent reporting practices for all members of a given association. Unfortunately, the practices set out for hospitals were different from those recommended for universities, and in both situations members did not have to follow their organization's recommendations. Smaller NFPOs followed a wide range of diverse practices such as using the cash basis only, or a mixture of cash and accrual accounting. Many did not capitalize capital asset acquisitions, and of the few that did capitalize, many did not provide for subsequent periodic amortization. A wide range of practices was also followed for donated materials, services, and capital assets, ranging from no recording to a full recording of all items. A large number of NFPOs used fund accounting in their end-of-year financial statement presentations, and many organizations still do. Later in this chapter we fully explore the concepts involved in fund accounting and fund presentations in accordance with current *Handbook* requirements. First, though, it is useful to examine the basic idea behind fund accounting and to give a brief illustration as to how various funds were presented in an organization's financial statements.

The Basics of Fund Accounting

The resources that an NFPO receives can be broadly categorized as *unrestricted* or *restricted*. *Unrestricted resources* can be used for any purposes that are consistent with the goals and objectives of the organization. *Restricted resources* can be used only in accordance with the wishes of the contributor. For example, a donation may be

NFPOs often have unrestricted and restricted resources. A donor prescribes how a restricted resource can be spent. An endowment is a restricted resource that can never be spent.

Many NFPOs receive a major source of their revenues from endowment earnings.

Board created endowments and restrictions on future spending are not technically considered to be restricted resources in accordance with the *Handbook*. This is because future boards could reverse the restrictions.

Fund accounting is often used to convey information about restricted resources.

In the past, NFPOs typically presented statements that showed resources received, spent, and on hand and available for future spending.

received with the proviso that it be spent in some specified manner. In some situations the original donation must be maintained intact, and only the interest earned on the funds invested can be spent by the organization. A donation of this type is called an *endowment*.

There are many examples of endowments. University scholarships are often funded by the interest earned on endowment contributions made by donors in prior years. Some well-known private universities, such as Harvard and Stanford, have hundreds of millions of dollars in endowment funds, and use the earnings as their major source of revenue, since they do not receive government funding. The Toronto Symphony Orchestra has established an endowment fund as a device to help fund its daily operations. And finally, the Winnipeg Foundation, whose financial statements are reproduced in Appendix 13A, operates with substantial endowment funds.

Quite often, restrictions are also placed on how the endowment interest can be spent. In other words, interest revenue can be restricted or unrestricted. NFPOs sometimes conduct special campaigns to raise money for major acquisitions of buildings and equipment, and any moneys raised are restricted to this particular purpose. In some cases, the board of directors of an NFPO may pass a resolution designating a portion of unrestricted resources as restricted for a certain purpose, or to be held indefinitely, with only the interest earned to be spent. While such designations require disclosure, these resources are not technically considered as restricted, because future boards could reverse the designation. In accordance with the *Handbook*'s definition, true restricted resources are those that may only be spent in accordance with the wishes of the donor (or, in the case of endowments, may never be spent).

Fund accounting has been used very successfully to keep track of restricted resources and to convey information through the financial statements about the restrictions placed on the organization's resources. The concepts involved can be summarized as follows:

> Fund accounting comprises the collective accounting procedures resulting in a self-balancing set of accounts for each fund established by legal, contractual or voluntary actions of an organization. Elements of a fund can include assets, liabilities, net assets, revenues and expenses (and gains and losses where appropriate). Fund accounting involves an accounting segregation, although not necessarily a physical segregation, of resources. [4400.02]

Prior to 1997, it was typical to present a balance sheet and a statement of revenue and expenditure for each fund. Combined with the general practice of non-capitalization of land, buildings, and equipment, the results were a form of stewardship reporting, showing the resources received and spent during a period and the resources on hand at the end of the period that were available for future spending. The following simple example illustrates the use of fund accounting as a means of reporting this form of stewardship.

Example   The financial statements of the Helpful Society (HS) at the end of the current year are presented in Exhibit 13.1.

HS presents two funds in its year-end financial statements. The resources in the *general* fund can be used to carry out the normal activities of the organization, while the resources in the *building* fund, which was established during the current year, are restricted. Each year the organization raises money through donations and spends the funds raised on programs A, B, and C. During the current year, the general fund's revenues were $7,100 greater than its expenditures; as a result, its equity (described as fund balance) increased by this amount. Note that revenues and expenditures are measured under the accrual method, so the statement does not show cash inflows and outflows. During the year, the general fund acquired equipment at a cost of $25,000. Because this organization follows a policy of noncapitalization, the acquisition appears in the Program A expenditures on the revenue and expenditure statement. As a result, the assets on hand at the end of the year can be viewed as resources that are spendable. The liabilities at this date are a claim against these resources; therefore, the fund balance at the end of the current year represents net resources amounting to $32,200 that are available for spending next year.

Exhibit 13.1

This exhibit illustrates the fund basis financial reporting. When combined with a policy of noncapitalization of capital assets it becomes a resources in and out form of stewardship reporting.

HELPFUL SOCIETY
BALANCE SHEET
December 31, Current Year

	General Fund	Building Fund	Total
Assets			
Cash	$17,500	$ 6,000	$ 23,500
Pledges receivable	50,000		50,000
Investments	25,000	88,635	113,635
Total	$92,500	$94,635	$187,135
Liabilities and fund balance			
Accounts payable and accrued liabilities	$60,300		$ 60,300
Fund balance	32,200	$94,635	126,835
Total	$92,500	$94,635	$187,135

STATEMENT OF REVENUE AND EXPENDITURE
AND CHANGES IN FUND BALANCE
for the Year Ended December 31, Current Year

	General Fund	Building Fund	Total
Revenues			
Contributions	$923,000	$102,000	$1,025,000
Interest	2,700		2,700
Total	925,700	102,000	1,027,700
Expenditures			
Program A	$625,000		$ 625,000
Program B	190,000		190,000
Program C	100,000		100,000
Fundraising	3,600	6,410	10,010
Miscellaneous		955	955
Total	918,600	7,365	925,965
Excess of revenue over expenditure	7,100	94,635	101,735
Fund balance, January 1	25,100	0	25,100
Fund balance, December 31	$ 32,200	$ 94,635	$ 126,835

During the current year a special fundraising campaign was initiated to raise the money necessary to purchase and furnish a building. The building fund's resources on hand at the end of the year, amounting to $94,635, were the result of $102,000 that was collected during the year less the fundraising costs and miscellaneous expenses incurred, which amounted to $7,365. The campaign will continue until its goal is reached. At that time the purchase of the building and furnishings will be recorded as an expenditure of this fund. Once the liabilities have been settled, the building fund will cease to exist. Of course, if the organization raises more than the cost of the building, the fund will be continued until the surplus cash is spent in accordance with the conditions imposed.

> **NFPO accounting has shifted from reporting the cost of resources spent to provide services, to reporting the cost of services provided.**

This example was presented to illustrate the basic idea behind financial reporting on a fund basis. When capital asset purchases are shown as expenditures, the result is a reporting of resources received and spent and resources on hand that can be spent in the future. On April 1, 1997, the new *Handbook* sections became effective, and as a result many NFPOs must now capitalize and depreciate their long-lived assets. This has changed the reporting to one of cost of services provided, rather than one of reporting resources spent to provide services, which was the previous case. It should be noted that, in our example, the columnar approach was used to present the two funds. An alternative that gained some prior acceptance was the layered approach, which presented funds one after another, so that the first page would show the operating fund statements, the second page would show the building fund, and so on. Under the provisions of the new *Handbook* sections, this approach is cumbersome because of a requirement to show totals for each financial statement item for all funds presented.

Not-for-Profit Reporting Today

> **Many sections of the *Handbook* which previously applied only to profit-orientated organizations now apply to NFPOs as well.**

Prior to the issuance of the seven not-for-profit *Handbook* sections, the Accounting Standards Board amended the introduction to the *Handbook* so that it applied to both profit-orientated organizations and not-for-profit organizations. This made all sections of the *Handbook* potentially applicable to the financial reporting of NFPOs. Exposure drafts were then released on the proposed seven new sections. A very large number of replies were received, many of which were highly critical of some of the changes being proposed. The two most controversial areas related to the capitalization and amortization of long-lived assets and the consolidation of controlled entities. After considering the comments received, compromises were made and seven new *Handbook* sections were released. The introduction to the not-for-profit area contains a table that sets out the applicability of the various other *Handbook* sections to NFPOs. Each section is characterized as generally applicable (10 sections), applicable to an NFPO with relevant transactions (25 sections), or having limited or no applicability (27 sections). Exhibit 13.2 lists the sections that have limited or no applicability. Note that while Section 4100, "Pension Plans," is not applicable, Section 3461, "Employee Future Benefits," would be applicable for those organizations that provide pension benefits to their employees.

The new *Handbook* sections are as follows:

- Section 4400, "Financial Statement Presentation By Not-for-Profit Organizations"
- Section 4410, "Contributions — Revenue Recognition"
- Section 4420, "Contributions Receivable"

- Section 4430, "Capital Assets Held by Not-for-Profit Organizations"
- Section 4440, "Collections Held by Not-for-Profit Organizations"
- Section 4450, "Reporting Controlled and Related Entities by Not-for-Profit Organizations"
- Section 4460, "Disclosure of Related Party Transactions by Not-for-Profit Organizations"

Exhibit 13.2

CICA HANDBOOK SECTIONS
WITH LIMITED OR NO APPLICABILITY TO NFPOs

Section 1300, Differential Reporting
Section 1520, Income Statement
Section 1530, Comprehensive Income
Section 1540, Cash Flow Statements
Section 1581, Business Combinations
Section 1590, Subsidiaries
Section 1625, Comprehensive Revaluation of Assets & Liabilities
Section 1701, Segment Disclosures
Section 1751, Interim Financial Statements
Section 1800, Unincorporated Businesses
Section 3055, Interests in Joint Ventures
Section 3061, Property, Plant and Equipment
Section 3062, Goodwill and Other Intangible Assets
Section 3063, Impairment of Long Lived Assets
Section 3240, Share Capital
Section 3251, Equity
Section 3260, Reserves
Section 3465, Income Taxes
Section 3500, Earnings Per Share
Section 3610, Capital Transactions
Section 3800, Government Assistance
Section 3805, Investment Tax Credits
Section 3840, Related Party Transactions
Section 3841, Economic Dependence
Section 3870, Stock-based Compensation and Other Stock-based Payments
Section 4100, Pension Plans
Section 4211, Life Insurance Enterprises

The non-profit area of the *Handbook* contains seven sections which deal with issues that are unique to NFPOs.

These seven new sections deal with accounting issues that either are unique to not-for-profit organizations or are dealt with in the existing *Handbook* sections in a manner that is not appropriate for not-for-profit organizations. For example, Section 3061, "Property, Plant and Equipment," would apply to both not-for-profit and profit organizations if it were not for the existence of Section 4430, "Capital Assets Held by Not-for-Profit Organizations."

In the material that follows, the pronouncements of each section will be discussed and in some instances illustrated. Sections 4400 and 4410 will be discussed and illustrated last because they are closely related and involve fund reporting.

Section 4420, "Contributions Receivable" A contribution is a type of revenue that is unique to not-for-profit organizations. It is defined as "a non-reciprocal transfer to a not-for-profit organization of cash or other assets or a non-reciprocal settlement

Contribution revenue is a type of revenue which is unique to NFPOs, because it is non-reciprocal (the donor does not receive anything from the contribution).

In addition to contribution revenue, an NFPO may receive other types of revenue.

or cancellation of its liabilities" (paragraph 4410.02). Nonreciprocal means that the contributor does not directly receive anything for the contribution. Included here are donations of cash, property or services, government grants, pledges, and bequests. Besides receiving contribution revenue, not-for-profit organizations may also receive other types of revenue such as those from investments or from the sale of goods and services. These other types of revenue are accounted for in accordance with the regular *Handbook* Section 3400, "Revenue." Section 4420 provides guidance on how to apply accrual accounting concepts to contributions. It states the following:

> A contribution receivable should be recognized as an asset when it meets the following criteria:
> (a) the amount to be received can be reasonably estimated; and
> (b) ultimate collection is reasonably assured. [4420.03]

Restricted and endowment contributions require special treatment by an NFPO.

Normally a contribution receivable represents a future inflow of cash, but it could also represent the future receipt of other assets or services valued at fair value. The credit side of the journal entry could be to revenue, using the restricted fund method, or if the deferral method of recording is being used, to deferred revenue for a restricted contribution, or to increase net assets of endowments for an endowment contribution. (The restricted fund and deferral methods are discussed later in this chapter). The section provides additional guidelines for the recording of receivables associated with pledges and bequests.

Pledges are promises to donate cash or other assets to an NFPO, but they are legally unenforceable.

Because pledges cannot be legally enforced, collectibility is out of the control of the organization. If the organization has the ability to estimate the collectibility based on historical results, it should recognize the pledged amounts as a receivable offset with an allowance for estimated uncollectible amounts. Otherwise, the recognition of pledges should be delayed until the time cash is received. It should be noted that when an allowance is established, the debit is typically made to contribution revenue rather than to bad debt expense.

Bequests are normally not recorded until a will has been probated.

Bequests also pose a problem of uncertainty relating both to the timing of receipt and to the amount to be collected. Wills must be probated and at times are subject to legal challenges. Because of this extreme uncertainty, bequests generally are not accrued until probation has been completed and the time for appeal has passed.

Section 4450, "Reporting Controlled and Related Entities by Not-for-Profit Organizations"   This section outlines the financial statement presentation and disclosures required when an NFPO has a control, significant influence, joint venture, or economic interest type of relationship with both profit-oriented and not-for-profit organizations. The breakdown used is quite similar to that for profit-oriented organizations, but the required financial reporting has some differences.

A control investment is one that gives an NFPO control over both profit-orientated organizations and other not-for-profit organizations.

Control Investments   An NFPO can have an investment or relationship that gives it the continuing power to determine the strategic operating, investing, and financing policies of another entity without the cooperation of others. The other entity can be profit-oriented or a not-for-profit organization. Control of a profit-oriented organization would normally be evidenced by the right to appoint the majority of the board of directors because of ownership of voting shares. Because a not-for-profit entity does not issue shares, control of such an entity is normally evidenced by the right to appoint the majority of the board of directors as allowed by that entity's by-laws.

Control over Not-for-Profit Organizations An example of a not-for-profit control situation is a national organization with local chapters. A large portion of funds raised by the local chapters goes to the national body, and any projects carried out by the local bodies must be approved (and perhaps funded) by the national organization.

The *Handbook*'s reporting requirements are as follows:

An organization should report each controlled not-for-profit organization in one of the following ways:

Consolidation of a not-for-profit organization is one of three alternatives allowed.

(a) by consolidating the controlled organization in its financial statements;

(b) by providing the disclosure set out in Paragraph 4450.22; or

(c) if the controlled organization is one of a large number of individually immaterial organizations, by providing the disclosure set out in Paragraph 4450.26 [4450.14].

Because there is no investment account in one balance sheet and no shareholders' equity in the others, consolidation is achieved by simply combining the financial statements on a line-by-line basis and at the same time eliminating any transactions that occurred between the organizations.

The alternatives apply to each controlled NFPO.

Since three alternatives are allowed, the management of the organization has to determine the accounting policy to be used. Note that the alternatives listed above are for each controlled entity. This means that if an organization has control over three not-for-profit organizations, all of which are material, it could choose to consolidate only one, and provide the required disclosure for the other two, provided that it reports consistently on a year-to-year basis. Later paragraphs further clarify the overall meaning by suggesting that if an NFPO has control over a large number of NFPOs, the decision to consolidate or not should be applied on a group basis. For example, it could establish a policy to consolidate all organizations in Groups A and B and not consolidate the organizations in Group C.

Paragraph 22 requires the disclosure of the totals of all of the assets, liabilities, net assets, revenues, expenses, and cash flows of any controlled not-for-profit entities that are not consolidated.

Consolidation was a controversial topic when it was proposed in the earlier exposure drafts. The following arguments were presented in its favour:

- The statements present the economic substance of the situation.
- All controlled economic resources are reflected in a single set of financial statements.
- Users of the financial statements get a much better picture than would be the case if unconsolidated statements were presented.

Some arguments presented against consolidation were:

- Consolidation of entities that have different activities may be confusing to users.
- The consolidation of a research centre (with substantial endowments) with a hospital that struggles to break even on a yearly basis may present a misleading financial picture at first glance. Footnote disclosures should clarify the situation.
- The yearly cost of financial reporting will increase.

Control over Profit-Oriented Companies The *Handbook* states the following:

An organization should report each controlled profit-oriented enterprise in either of the following ways:

A controlled profit-orientated organization can either be consolidated or reported using the equity method. The alternatives are applicable to each controlled entity.

(a) by consolidating the controlled enterprise in its financial statements; or

(b) by accounting for its investment in the controlled enterprise using the equity method and providing the disclosure set out in paragraph 4450.32 [4450.30].

Control in this situation is defined in Section 1590 (discussed in Chapter 3). It should be noted that the requirements here are also applicable to each controlled entity, which could result in some subsidiaries being reported under the equity method and others being consolidated. Consolidation of profit-oriented enterprises was also controversial, with similar arguments for and against as those presented above. The final result was also a compromise.

A jointly controlled organization can either be proportionately consolidated or reported using the equity method. The alternatives are applicable to each jointly controlled entity.

Joint Control   This is the contractual right to jointly control an organization with at least one other entity. An interest in a joint venture would be reported either by:

- proportionately consolidating the joint venture, or
- reporting the interest using the equity method.

Consistent with the requirements for controlled entities, the alternatives here apply to each joint venture, so that some may be proportionately consolidated and others may not, depending on the accounting policy determined by management. The arguments for and against using the proportionate consolidation method are basically the same as those presented previously for controlled investments. The section also states that if the NFPO's proportionate interest in the joint venture cannot be determined, it should not be considered to be a joint venture in accordance with this section, but might be either a significant influence or control type of relationship. This would seem to indicate that the joint venture would have to be one that issued shares, and thus probably a profit-oriented organization. However, if two or three NFPOs created another NFPO as a joint venture to carry out certain activities, and agreed to the percentage owned by each of the non-profit venturers, then the reporting alternatives outlined here would apply.

A significant influence investment in a profit-orientated organization is reported using the equity method. A significant influence investment in another NFPO requires only full disclosure of the relationship.

Significant Influence   When control is not present, the NFPO may still be able to exercise significant influence over the strategic operating, investing, and financing activities of the other entity. Factors suggesting the presence of significant influence include the ability to place members on the board of directors, the ability to participate in policymaking, substantial transactions between the entities, and the sharing of senior personnel. If the significant influence investment is in a profit-oriented enterprise, it must be accounted for using the equity method. If the significant influence relationship is with another NFPO, the equity method is not used; instead, full disclosure of the relationship is required. This provision makes sense when one considers that the application of the equity method requires the use of a percentage based on the number of shares held. Because an NFPO does not issue shares, it would be virtually impossible to determine a percentage needed in order to apply the method.

Economic Interest   An economic interest in another NFPO exists if that organization holds resources for the reporting organization or if the reporting organization is responsible for the other organization's debts. There are varying degrees of economic interest, ranging from control or significant influence to neither of the two. The reporting requirement is stated in the following manner: "When an organization has an economic interest in another not-for-profit organization over which it does not have control or significant influence, the nature and extent of this interest should be disclosed" (paragraph 4450.45).

An investment in a profit-oriented organization that is neither control, nor significant influence, nor joint control, is accounted for using the cost method.

This concludes the discussion of Section 4450. A summary of the various types of investment that an NFPO can have and the reporting requirements for each follows:

Summary

Investment	*Required reporting*
Control of NFPO	Consolidate or disclose
Control of profit entity	Consolidate or equity method
Joint venture	Proportionately consolidate or equity method
Significant Influence	
NFPO	Full disclosure
Profit entity	Equity method
Economic interest	Full disclosure
Other investment	
Profit entity	Cost method

Section 4460, "Disclosure of Related Party Transactions by Not-for-Profit Organizations"

An NFPO must disclose all related party transactions with another NFPO or with a profit-orientated entity.

Related parties exist where one party is able to exercise control, joint control, or significant influence over another party. The other party may be either another NFPO or a profit-oriented enterprise. If one NFPO has an economic interest in another NFPO, the two parties are related. A related party transaction has occurred when there has been a transfer of economic resources or obligations or services between the parties. Unlike *Handbook* Section 3840, which prescribes both measurements and disclosures, this not-for-profit section prescribes only disclosures for related party transactions. The disclosures required here are virtually identical to those required in Section 3840.

Section 4430, "Capital Assets Held by Not-for-Profit Organizations"

There was strong opposition to the proposal that all NFPOs be required to capitalize and amortize acquisitions of capital assets.

Prior to the introduction of this section into the *Handbook*, NFPOs followed a variety of practices with regard to the financial reporting of their capital assets. Some organizations capitalized all acquisitions and amortized them over their estimated useful lives in the operating statement. Others capitalized them, but did not provide amortization. A fairly large number wrote them off in their operating statements in the year of acquisition in a manner similar to the equipment purchase illustrated in Exhibit 13.1, page 617. In this latter situation, the operating statement showed revenues and expenditures measured under the accrual method, and from a user perspective reflected the inflow and outflow of spendable resources.

When the Accounting Standards Board proposed the requirement of capitalization and amortization of all acquisitions, respondents to the exposure drafts voiced strong opposition. The arguments against capitalization were that:

- It would change the nature of the operating statement from one that reflects resources spent to one that reflects the cost of resources used.

- Users would not understand the new accounting, having become used to seeing capital asset acquisitions as expenditures.

- As most other assets appearing in a balance sheet represent spendable resources, the addition of non-spendable resources such as unamortized capital assets would confuse readers.
- Capitalization and amortization would be costly to apply, especially on a retroactive basis.
- Small NFPO financial statement users are only interested in seeing what money has been spent and what money is left over.

The counter-arguments in favour of capitalization were that:

- Readers of the financial statements of profit-oriented entities are quite used to seeing capital assets in the balance sheet and amortization in the operating statement. They are confused when they do not see it in the financial statements of an NFPO.
- The cash flow statement adequately shows resources spent. The operating statement should reflect resources used.

GAAP requires NFPOs to capitalize and amortize all of their capital assets.

Section 4430 requires an NFPO to capitalize all capital assets in the balance sheet and to amortize them as appropriate in the statement of operations. The cost of a purchased capital asset includes all costs incurred to make the asset ready for use. When a capital asset is donated, it is recorded at fair value (if known), and the resultant credit is to restricted contribution revenue. (The concept of restricted contributions is discussed later.) Capital assets of limited useful life are to be amortized on a rational basis over their estimated useful lives. No maximum period of amortization is specified. When an NFPO enters into a lease agreement that would be treated as a capital lease in accordance with *Handbook* Section 3065, the asset will be capitalized in accordance with the provisions of that section. When an asset no longer contributes to the organization's ability to provide services, it should be written down to estimated residual value, with the resulting loss reported as an expense in the statement of operations. Note that this section does not provide a quantitative impairment test in the same manner as prescribed by *Handbook* Section 3061.

When Section 4430 was first issued it required that yearly provisions be made for future asset removal and site restoration costs. In January 2003, Section 3110, "Asset Retirement Obligations" became operative and Section 4430 was revised to say that the new section's provisions should be used by all NFPOs where applicable. For example, if leasehold improvements must be removed at the end of a lease, provision for that future cost should be made each year by a charge to operations.

An exemption from the requirement to capitalize is granted to small NFPOs (those whose two-year average revenues are less than $500,000).

Small NFPOs Section 4430 contains a compromise provision applicable to NFPOs whose two-year average annual revenues are less than $500,000. Organizations such as these are encouraged to follow the section's recommendations, but are exempted from doing so if they disclose:

- their accounting policy for capital assets,
- information about capital assets not shown in the balance sheet, and
- the amount expensed in the current period if their policy is to expense capital assets when acquired.

This leaves a small NFPO the choice of:

- expensing when acquired,
- capitalizing but not amortizing, or

- capitalizing and amortizing.

If an NFPO has revenues above $500,000, it is required to capitalize and amortize. If its revenues subsequently fall below $500,000, it is not allowed to change its policy.

If an NFPO has revenues below $500,000, chooses not to capitalize and amortize and subsequently has revenues above $500,000, then it ceases to be a small NFPO, and must capitalize and amortize retroactively. This requirement should be recognized by all small NFPOs that decide to exempt themselves from the section's recommendations, because retroactive restatement can be costly.

Capitalization of capital assets was a contentious issue when the not-for-profit exposure drafts were being discussed. The small-organization exemption and the special provisions for collections (discussed next) were introduced to satisfy some of the objections that were raised.

Section 4440, "Collections Held by Not-for-Profit Organizations" Collections are works of art and historical treasures that have been excluded from the definition of capital assets because they meet all of the following criteria:

- they are held for public exhibition, education, and research;
- they are protected, cared for, and preserved;
- they are subject to organizational policies that require any proceeds from their sale to be used to acquire other items for the collection, or for the direct care of the existing collection.

Collections have been excluded from the definition of capital assets and NFPOs are allowed three alternative reporting requirements.

The requirements of Section 4440 allow an NFPO to choose an accounting policy from the following:

- Expense when acquired.
- Capitalize but do not amortize.
- Capitalize and amortize.

NFPOs that have collections are required to include in their disclosures a description of the accounting policies followed with regard to collections; a description of the collection; any significant changes made to the collection during the period; the amount spent on the collection during the period; and the proceeds from any sales of collection items, and a statement of how the proceeds were used.

Sections 4400 and 4410 Section 4400, "Financial Statement Presentation By Not-for-Profit Organizations," and Section 4410, "Contributions — Revenue Recognition," are so directly related to each other that we will discuss their requirements as a single topic. There are two very key points embodied in these two sections:

Under the matching concept for NFPOs, expenses are recognized first and then revenues are matched to expenses. This type of matching applies only to restricted revenues and only when the restricted fund method of accounting is not used.

- Restrictions on an organization's resources should be clearly stated in the financial statements;
- The matching concept as it applies to NFPOs must be applied in the measurement of yearly results.

For an NFPO that has restricted revenues, the concept of revenue and expense matching is the exact opposite to that for a profit-oriented enterprise. With the latter, revenues are recognized and then expenses are matched with those revenues. With an NFPO, restricted revenues are matched to expenses. This means that if contributions have been collected to fund certain expenses, and those expenses have yet to be incurred, the contributions are deferred until a later period, when they can be matched with the expenses. When the restricted fund method of accounting is used to account for restricted resources, this matching is not necessary; when this method is not used, this form of matching for restricted resources is imperative.

As outlined earlier, an NFPO can have two basic types of revenues:

- Contributions.
- Other types (from investments, or from the sale of goods and services).

Contributions are a type of revenue unique to NFPOs. They are specifically described in order to apply recognition and presentation principles. The *Handbook* defines three different types of contributions:

Handbook **Section 4410 describes three different types of contributions: restricted, endowment, and unrestricted.**

- Restricted contributions.
- Endowment contributions.
- Unrestricted contributions.

Restricted contributions are subject to *externally imposed* stipulations as to how the funds are to be spent or used. The organization must use the resources in the manner specified by the donor. There may be times when the directors of an organization decide to use certain contributions for certain purposes, but these are considered to be *internally imposed* restrictions, and do not fall within the definition of restricted contributions.

Endowment contributions are a special type of restricted contribution. The donor has specified that the contribution cannot be spent, but must be maintained permanently. Endowment contributions are often invested in high-grade securities.

Unrestricted contributions are those which are not restricted or endowment contributions.

As we shall see in the next section, financial statement presentations for NFPOs are based in part on these three types of contributions.

Financial Statements

An NFPO must present the following financial statements for external reporting purposes:

An NFPO must present four financial statements.

- A statement of financial position;
- A statement of operations;
- A statement of changes in net assets;
- A statement of cash flows.

The names provided here are for descriptive purposes only; an organization can choose the titles it wishes to use. The statement of operations can be combined with the statement of changes in net assets.

A fund basis can be used, but it is not necessary to prepare all statements using this method. For example, the operating statement could be presented on a fund basis while the rest of the statements could be presented on a nonfund basis.

The statement of financial position should show classifications for current assets, non-current assets, current liabilities, and non-current liabilities. Net assets (total assets less total liabilities) must be broken down into the following categories (if applicable):

The equity section of the balance sheet is called "net assets" and must be broken down into four categories (if applicable).

Equity:

- Net assets invested in capital assets.
- Net assets maintained permanently in endowments.
- Other restricted net assets.
- Unrestricted net assets.

The statement of operations will show the revenues and expenses for the period.

The statement of changes in net assets must show changes in each of the four categories required to be shown on the balance sheet. The statement of cash flows must report changes in cash under two classifications:

- Cash flows from operations.
- Cash flows from financing and investing activities.

Cash flows from operations can be presented using either the direct method or the indirect method.

The 2006 financial statements (excluding footnotes) of the Winnipeg Foundation are presented in Appendix 13B. A statement of cash flows is not included, and its absence is captured by Note 13 which states "a statement of cash flows has not been presented, as the required information is readily apparent from the other financial statements presented and the notes to the financial statements." This practice is in accord with paragraph 4400.55.

Accounting for Contributions

An NFPO is allowed to choose from two methods of accounting for contributions in order to satisfy the Handbook's matching concept. These methods are the deferral method and the restricted fund method.

To capture the matching concept that is unique to NFPOs, the *Handbook* has defined two methods of accounting for contributions: the *deferral* method and the *restricted fund* method.

An NFPO has to determine which method it is going to use. If it does not wish to report on a fund accounting basis, it will use the deferral method. If it does wish to report on a fund accounting basis, it will normally choose the restricted fund method, keeping in mind that some parts of the deferral method may also have to be used. This particular concept will be discussed later. However, it should be noted that an NFPO may chose to report on a fund basis without using the restricted fund method of accounting for contributions. For example, it may choose to draw attention to its programs by reporting each as a fund in its financial statements. If the program funds receive both restricted and unrestricted resources, the deferred contribution method of accounting for contributions must be used even though financial reporting is carried out on a fund basis.

The Deferral Method

The deferral method allows the required matching of restricted contributions with expenses. If the related expense has not occurred, the contribution revenue is deferred.

The deferral method matches revenues with related expenses. Unrestricted contributions are reported as revenue in the period received because there are no particular related expenses associated with them.

Endowment contributions are not shown in the operating statement; rather, they are reflected in the statement of changes in net assets. This is because endowment contributions, by definition, will never have related expenses.

Restricted contributions have to be matched against related expenses. This matching principle has different implications for different kinds of restricted contributions, as follows:

- Restricted contributions for expenses of future periods are deferred and recognized as revenue in the same periods as the related expenses are incurred.
- The handling of restricted contributions for the acquisition of capital assets depends on whether related expenses are associated with them. If the capital asset is subject to amortization, the related expense is the yearly amortization. The restricted contribution is deferred and recognized as revenue on the same basis as the asset is being amortized. If the capital asset is not subject to amortization (e.g., land), there will be no expenses to match against. In the same manner as for endowment contributions, the restricted capital asset contributions of this type are reflected in the statement of changes in net assets.
- Restricted contributions for expenses of the current period are recognized as revenue in the current period. Matching is achieved, and there is no need for deferral.

Investment income can be either unrestricted or restricted. Unrestricted investment income is recognized as revenue when it is earned. Restricted investment income has to be recognized in the same manner as restricted contributions. For example, if an endowment contribution states that the purchasing power of the contribution must be preserved, some portion of the interest earned must be used to increase the endowment. This portion would be treated in exactly the same manner as an endowment contribution, and would be reflected in the statement of changes in net assets. Other types of restricted investment income must be deferred and matched against expense in the manner previously discussed. If all investment income is restricted, it is quite possible that all investment income earned in a period will be deferred.

The Restricted Fund Method

Under the restricted fund method an NFPO must report a general fund, at least one restricted fund, and if it has received endowment contributions it must also report an endowment fund.

This method requires an NFPO to report a general fund, at least one restricted fund, and, if it has endowments or receives endowment contributions, an endowment fund. The restricted funds will be used to record externally restricted revenue. Specific requirements are outlined as follows:

- Endowment contributions will be reported as revenue in the endowment fund, and because there are no related expenses associated with endowment contributions, no expenses will appear in the statement of operations of the endowment fund.

Each restricted fund is used to record particular restricted revenue.

- The general fund records all unrestricted contributions and investment income, including unrestricted income from endowment fund investments.
- If some of the endowment fund income is restricted, it is reflected as revenue in the particular restricted fund involved.

The provisions of the deferral method might have to be applied when the restricted fund method is used. This would occur when an externally restricted contribution is received and there is no corresponding restricted fund to record it in.

- If some of the endowment fund income is permanently restricted, because the purchasing power of the endowment is required to be maintained, it is recorded as revenue of the endowment fund.
- If an externally restricted contribution or externally restricted investment income is received, for which there is no corresponding restricted fund, the amounts are recorded in the general fund in accordance with the deferral method. In other words they are recorded as deferred revenue in the general fund and matched with the related expenses in that fund when these expenses are incurred.

- If management decides to impose internal restrictions on general fund unrestricted contributions, these amounts are transferred to the relevant restricted or endowment fund, and such transfers are reported in the statement of operations and changes in net assets below the line "excess of revenue over expenses." Note disclosure should clearly indicate the amount of resources shown in restricted funds that have been designated as such by management, because these amounts do not satisfy the *Handbook*'s definition of a restricted resource.

The excess of revenues over expenses in the general fund represents the increase in unrestricted resources during the period. The fund balance in the general fund shows the unrestricted net assets at the end of the period.

A restricted fund shows no deferred revenue. The fund balance of a restricted fund represents the amount of net assets that are restricted for that particular fund's purpose.

The fund balance in the endowment fund represents the net assets that have permanent restrictions on them.

Under the restricted fund method, instead of presenting a statement of changes in net assets (as is required under the deferral method of recording contributions), a statement of changes in fund balances is prepared. Because of the requirement to capitalize long-lived assets, capital assets must appear on the balance sheet of either the general fund or one of the restricted funds (excluding the endowment fund). The fund balance section of that particular fund's balance sheet will have to show a corresponding investment in capital assets.

This has been a summary of the two methods of accounting for contributions. Before we illustrate these concepts in an extensive illustration, there are some additional topics that must be addressed.

A restricted fund shows no deferred revenue because the fund balance of a restricted fund's balance sheet represents the amount of restricted resources.

Net Assets Invested in Capital Assets

Under the restricted fund method, the amount presented for "net assets invested in capital assets" is equal to the unamortized portion of all capital assets shown on the balance sheet regardless as to whether they were purchased from restricted or unrestricted resources.

Under the deferral method the amount presented for "net assets invested in capital assets" represents the unamortized portion of the capital assets that were purchased with unrestricted resources.

The *Handbook* requires that the net asset (or fund balance) section of the balance sheet show a category called "net assets invested in capital assets." This amount represents resources spent on capital assets and therefore not available for future spending. The amount shown depends on the method used to account for contributions. If the restricted fund method is used, the amount represents the unamortized portion of *all* capital assets, regardless of whether they were purchased from restricted or unrestricted resources. If the deferral method is used, the amount presented represents the unamortized portion of capital assets that were purchased with *unrestricted* resources. The following example will illustrate the differences.

Example   At the beginning of the current period, NFPO purchases equipment costing $5,000 with a useful life of two years. We will assume first that the equipment is acquired from restricted resources, and then from unrestricted resources. We will focus on the equipment transaction only and the effect of the transaction on the financial statements of NFPO. In order to do this, we also assume that the organization was formed at the beginning of the period and that the equipment acquisition is the only transaction that has occurred.

The Restricted Fund Method
Purchase from Restricted Resources   Assume that the equipment is purchased from a restricted fund contribution of $5,100. The capital fund records contributions of this nature, as well as the acquisition of capital assets and their subsequent amorti-

The journal entries would be as follows:

Capital fund

Cash	5,100	
Contribution revenue		5,100
Equipment	5,000	
Cash		5,000
Amortization expense	2,500	
Accumulated amortization		2,500

Because the capital fund did not exist before the start of the period, the financial statements at the end of the period would appear as follows:

CAPITAL FUND
OPERATING STATEMENT AND CHANGES IN FUND BALANCE

Contribution revenue	$5,100
Amortization expense	2,500
Excess of revenue over expense	2,600
Fund balance — start of period	0
Fund balance — end of period	$2,600

BALANCE SHEET

Cash		$ 100
Equipment	$5,000	
Accumulated amortization	2,500	2,500
Total assets		$2,600
Fund balance		
Invested in capital assets		$2,500
Externally restricted funds		100
Total fund balance		$2,600

Under the restricted fund method, the unamortized balance of equipment purchased with restricted resources is reflected in the amount of fund balance invested in capital assets.

Note that the fund balance section shows two classifications:

- The $2,500 invested in capital assets represents the unamortized balance of spent resources that have not yet been reflected in the statement of operations as an expense.

- Externally restricted funds of $100 represent resources that can only be spent to acquire capital assets.

As the equipment is amortized on the operating statement, the fund balance itself is reduced, and it is the balance sheet category "invested in capital assets" that reflects the reduction.

Purchase from Unrestricted Resources   Now assume that the equipment is purchased from unrestricted resources. The general fund receives an unrestricted contribution of $5,000 and uses it to acquire equipment.

The journal entries in the general fund and the capital fund would be as follows:

General fund

Cash	5,000	
Contribution revenue		5,000

| Transfer to capital fund | 5,000 | |
| Cash | | 5,000 |

The general fund's operating statement after the transaction would show the following:

GENERAL FUND
STATEMENT OF OPERATIONS AND CHANGES IN FUND BALANCE

Revenues	$5,000
Expenses	0
Excess of revenue over expense	5,000
Transfer to capital fund	(5,000)
Fund balance — start of period	0
Fund balance — end of period	$ 0

It should be obvious that the general fund's balance sheet at the end of the period contains no elements.

The capital fund would record the acquisition of the equipment and its amortization with the following entries:

Capital fund

| Equipment | 5,000 | |
| Transfer from general fund | | 5,000 |

| Amortization expense | 2,500 | |
| Accumulated amortization | | 2,500 |

The end-of-period financial statements would show the following:

CAPITAL FUND
STATEMENT OF OPERATIONS AND CHANGES IN FUND BALANCE

Amortization expense	$2,500
Excess of revenue over expense	(2,500)
Transfer from general fund	5,000
	2,500
Fund balance — start of period	0
Fund balance — end of period	$2,500

BALANCE SHEET

Equipment	$5,000
Accumulated amortization	2,500
Total assets	$2,500
Fund balance	
Invested in capital assets	$2,500
Total fund balance	$2,500

In this example, where the restricted fund method has been used, the unamortized balance of equipment purchased with unrestricted resources is also reflected in the amount of fund balance invested in capital assets.

Note that regardless of the source of resources used to acquire the equipment (restricted or unrestricted), the unamortized balance appears as an asset on the balance sheet of the capital fund, and the fund balance shows a classification "invested in capital assets" in an amount equal to the asset balance. This is not the case when the deferred contribution method is used.

The Deferred Contribution Method

Purchase from Restricted Resources

Assume that the equipment is purchased from a restricted fund contribution of $5,100. The journal entries to record the contribution, the acquisition, and the first year's amortization are as follows:

Cash	5,100	
Deferred contributions — equipment purchases		5,100
Equipment	5,000	
Cash		5,000
Deferred contributions — equipment purchases	5,000	
Deferred contributions — capital assets		5,000
Amortization expense	2,500	
Accumulated amortization		2,500
Deferred contributions — capital assets	2,500	
Contribution revenue		2,500

Financial statements that reflect these transactions are as follows:

STATEMENT OF OPERATIONS AND CHANGES IN FUND BALANCE

Contribution revenue	$2,500
Amortization expense	2,500
Excess of revenue over expenses	0
Net assets start of period	0
Net assets end of period	$ 0

BALANCE SHEET

Cash		$ 100
Equipment	$5,000	
Accumulated amortization	2,500	2,500
Total assets		$2,600
Deferred contributions		
Equipment purchases		$ 100
Capital assets		2,500
Total deferred contribution		2,600
Net Assets		
Unrestricted		0
Total		$2,600

The account "deferred contributions — capital asset purchases" represents unspent resources restricted to purchase capital assets in the future. The account "deferred contributions — capital assets" represents restricted resources that have been spent to acquire capital assets, but which have not yet been matched to amortization expense.

You will notice that two deferred contribution accounts have been used. "Deferred contributions — equipment purchases" represents unspent resources restricted to future spending on capital assets. "Deferred contributions — capital assets" represents restricted resources that have been spent acquiring capital assets, but have not yet been reflected as revenue on the operating statement because there has yet to be an expense to match it against. When amortization occurs, an equal amount is recognized as revenue. Because there is no effect on the "excess of revenue over expense" amount, there is no effect on the equity section "net assets." As the equipment decreases on the asset side due to amortization, the amount "deferred contributions — capital assets" decreases by the same amount on the liability side.

Because this equipment was purchased from restricted resources, there can be no amount shown under "invested in capital assets" in the equity section "net assets."

Purchase from Unrestricted Resources Assume now that the equipment was purchased from an unrestricted contribution of $5,000. The journal entries to record the events are as follows:

Cash	5,000	
Contribution revenue		5,000
Equipment	5,000	
Cash		5,000
Amortization expense	2,500	
Accumulated amortization		2,500

The financial statements that reflect these transactions are as follows:

STATEMENT OF OPERATIONS

Contribution revenue	$5,000
Amortization expense	2,500
Excess of revenue over expenses	$2,500

BALANCE SHEET

Equipment	$5,000
Accumulated amortization	2,500
Total assets	$2,500
Net Assets	
Invested in capital assets	2,500
Unrestricted	0
Total	$2,500

In this example, using the deferral method, the amount of net assets invested in capital assets represents the unamortized balance of equipment purchased with unrestricted resources.

Note that the statement of operations does not include a reconciliation of opening and ending net assets. A separate statement is usually presented. Because "net assets" represents total equity, the changes in the classifications of this equity must be shown in the statement as follows:

STATEMENT OF CHANGES IN NET ASSETS

	Invested in capital assets	Unrestricted	Total
Balance start of period	$ 0	$ 0	$ 0
Excess of revenue over expenses	(2,500)	5,000	2,500
Investment in capital assets	5,000	(5,000)	0
Balance end of period	$2,500	$ 0	$2,500

Under the deferral method, a statement of changes in net assets is prepared.

The "unrestricted" column represents resources that can be spent for any purpose. The organization received an unrestricted contribution of $5,000 and spent it on equipment. At the end of the period it has no resources left to spend. The transfer of $5,000 to the category "invested in capital assets" depicts the acquisition of capital assets from unrestricted resources. The operating statement shows an excess of revenue over expenses of $2,500. A $2,500 deduction for the amortization of assets purchased with unrestricted resources was used to arrive at these operating results. Note that this does not represent resources spent, but rather the cost of services provided by the equipment. By transferring this deduction to "invested in capital assets," the amount of the operating results allocated to unrestricted resources becomes $5,000, which represents the actual inflow of spendable resources, and the amount shown for "invested in capital assets" is equal to the unamortized balance of the equipment purchased from unrestricted resources.

Donated Capital Assets, Materials, and Services

Donated capital assets must be recorded at fair value; or if fair value cannot be determined, at a nominal value.

Donated Capital Assets   An NFPO is required to record the donation of capital assets at fair value. If fair value cannot be determined, a nominal value will be used. A nominal value could be in the range of $1 to $100 for small NFPOs, and $1,000 and higher for large NFPOs. If an organization receives an unsolicited donation of a capital asset that it has no intention of using, it should be reflected in its financial statements as "other assets" instead of "capital assets," and a loss or gain should be reflected in the statement of operations when disposal of the asset occurs. The following illustrates the recording of donated capital assets.

Example   A capital asset with a fair value of $10,000 is donated to an NFPO. The initial treatment depends on which of the two methods of recording contributions is being used.

A donated capital asset is recorded as restricted contribution revenue.

If the deferral method is being used, and the capital asset is subject to amortization (e.g., equipment), the journal entry is:

Equipment	10,000	
Deferred contributions — capital assets		10,000

Assuming a five-year life, in each succeeding year the following entry will be made as the equipment is amortized:

Amortization expense	2,000	
Accumulated amortization		2,000
Deferred contributions — capital assets	2,000	
Contribution revenue		2,000

If the deferral method is being used and the asset is not subject to amortization (e.g., land), the following entry is made:

Land	10,000	
Net assets invested in capital assets		10,000

Because no future expense will be associated with the asset, deferral is not required and the donation of land is reflected in the statement of net assets.

If the restricted fund method is being used, the fair value of the donated capital asset is recorded as revenue in the capital fund as follows:

Capital fund

Equipment	10,000	
Contributions — donated equipment		10,000

Donated land will be treated in the same manner, except that the debit will be to land instead of equipment. Small NFPOs that have adopted a policy of non-capitalization of acquisitions of capital assets will still be required to record donated

noncapitalization small NFPOs

capital assets at fair value. For example, the donation of equipment with a fair value of $10,000 would be recorded in the following manner:

Equipment expense	10,000	
Contributions — donated equipment		10,000

Regardless of whether the organization uses the deferred contribution method or the restricted fund method, the entry is the same because the required matching automatically occurs with the entry.

Donated Materials and Services   The requirements for the reporting of donated materials and services are different from those for donated capital assets. An NFPO has the option of reporting or not reporting donated material and services; however, it should only do so if fair value can be determined, and if the materials and services would normally be used in the organization's operations and would have been purchased if they had not been donated.

The *Handbook* section also makes it clear that the fair value of the services of volunteers are normally not recognized due to the difficulty in determining such values. Furthermore, an organization would probably not record donated materials if it acts as an intermediary for immediate distribution. For example, due to the difficulty of determining fair values and the large number of transactions, a food bank would not normally record the donation of food that it distributes to its clients.

> An NFPO has the option of either reporting donated material and services at fair value, or not reporting them at all. They should not be reported if they were not needed by the organization.

Example   A radio station donated free air time to help a charity publicize its fundraising campaign. The fair value of the air time is $5,200, and the policy of the organization is to record the value of donated materials and services. The journal entry is:

Advertising expense	5,200	
Revenue — donated air time		5,200

If the restricted fund method was being used, this entry would be made in the general fund.

If the donation consisted of office supplies rather than air time, the entry to record the donation under the deferred contribution method would be:

Office supplies (asset)	5,200	
Deferred contribution		5,200

If half of the supplies were used, the entries would be:

Supplies expense	2,600	
Office supplies		2,600
Deferred contribution	2,600	
Contribution revenue		2,600

In order to achieve proper matching, the same entries would be used under the restricted fund method. Due to the nature of the items donated, the transaction would normally be recorded in the general fund.

Budgetary Control and Encumbrances

Governments and many NFPOs often use a *formal budget recording system* together with an *encumbrance system* as a device to help control spending. Prior to the commencement of a fiscal year, a formal budget is drawn up that shows the budgeted

The actual recording of the budget in the records, along with the use of an encumbrance system, are devices used by NFPOs, and governments to control spending.

revenues and expenses for the coming year. The usual starting point in the process is a preliminary expense budget based on how the managers of the organization would like to see spending take place. Then a revenue budget is prepared based on the expected results from the revenue-raising activities of the coming year. If this revenue budget is realistic, the next step is to scale down the controllable expenses so that the organization does not plan to have expenses greater than its expected revenues. NFPOs and local governments do not (and in the case of many local governments, are not allowed to) budget for a deficit in any one year unless they have a surplus from prior years. Because both types of organizations raise money each year and then spend it, any deficit spending in a particular year eventually must be offset by surplus spending in later years. Once the budget has been formally passed by the board of directors (or the local government legislative body), the spending for applicable budgeted expenses commences. Often an NFPO's actual expenses turn out to be equal to the amount budgeted, and problems arise when actual revenues are less than budget. Government grants are sometimes reduced, or do not increase as much as was budgeted for, or some fundraising activity is not as successful as was forecast. If this happens over a series of years, the accumulated deficit problem will have to be addressed and the NFPO will have to organize special deficit-reduction fundraising activities in addition to the normal, annual fundraising for operations.

Budgetary Control If deficits are to be avoided, the managers of NFPOs must have timely information regarding actual results compared with amounts budgeted. This can be accomplished by formally recording the budget into the accounting system.

Example The following is the summarized budget that was approved by the board of directors of an NFPO:

Budgeted revenues (in detail)	$900,000
Budgeted expenses (in detail)	890,000
Budgeted surplus	$ 10,000

If the organization records the budget in its accounting records, the following journal entry is made at the start of the fiscal year:

Estimated revenues (control account)	900,000	
Appropriations (control account)		890,000
Budgetary fund balance		10,000

Budget accounts are used as a control device, and the amounts are not reflected in an NFPO's external financial statements.

While it may appear strange to debit an account for budgeted revenues, and to credit an account for budgeted expenses, the logic becomes clearer when one considers that budgeted revenues represent *expected* resource inflows and that budgeted expenses (with the exception of amortization) represent *expected* resource outflows. The general ledger accounts used are control accounts to the very detailed subsidiary ledger accounts needed to keep track of actual versus budgeted amounts, particularly in relation to expenses. Spending is often a continuous process, while revenues are received at various times throughout the year. If during the year it appears that actual revenues will be less than budget, it is a difficult task to make reductions to the budgeted expenses remaining in order to avoid a deficit. It is, however, possible with a system such as this to ensure that actual expenses do not exceed budget. The overall concept of "spending" in this context is based on an accrual system of measurement, not on a cash basis. At the end of the fiscal year the budget accounts are reversed as part of the closing journal entries, and these amounts are not reflected in the organization's external financial statements.

Encumbrance accounting involves the actual recording of purchase orders at the time of issuance. From a control standpoint a budget item has been spent at this moment.

Encumbrance Accounting This involves making entries in the accounting records to record the issue of purchase orders for the acquisition of goods and services from outside suppliers. The amounts recorded are estimates of the actual costs. It is not the normal practice to use encumbrance accounting for employee wage costs because this particular type of expenditure can be controlled by other means; nor is it normal to use encumbrances for amortization. When the goods and services ordered are actually received, the original encumbrance entry is reversed and the invoiced cost of the goods or services acquired is recorded.

Example Purchase order #3056A is issued for the acquisition of office supplies expected to cost $950. The journal entry to record the purchase order is:

Encumbrances	950	
Estimated commitments[1]		950

When the supplies ordered under purchase order #3056A are received at an invoiced cost of $954, the journal entries required are:

Estimated commitments	950	
Encumbrances		950
Supplies expense	954	
Accounts payable		954

Control over expenditures is achieved by mandating that the spending of a budgeted amount has occurred when the purchase order is issued, not when the goods are received or paid for. In this example, if the budgeted amount for supplies is $3,000, there is an unspent budget amount of $2,050 after the purchase order is issued, and an unspent amount of $2,046 after the receipt of the actual supplies. The use of encumbrance accounting along with a system of budgetary control prevents the issuing of purchase orders when there are no uncommitted budgeted amounts.

Amounts for outstanding encumbrances are considered to be executory contracts, and therefore are not recorded in an NFPO's external financial statements.

The only accounting problem involved is the financial statement presentation of outstanding purchase orders at the end of a fiscal period. Should the encumbrances be reflected in the operations statement as similar to expenses, and the estimated commitments appear in the balance sheet as liabilities? In the past, NFPOs have presented these accounts in this manner. The *Handbook* sections do not mention the concept of encumbrances; however, a purchase order is an executory contract under which neither party has performed. It follows that outstanding encumbrances should not be reflected as elements of financial statements, but rather should be disclosed in the footnotes to the statements if the amounts are material.[2]

Illustration of the Restricted Fund Method

The following example will be used to illustrate the journal entries made for various funds, and the annual general-purpose financial statements prepared using the restricted fund method of accounting for contributions.

---

[1] An alternative term often used is "reserve for encumbrances."

[2] A similar conclusion was made in a CICA research study. See "Financial Reporting for Nonprofit Organizations," (Toronto: CICA, 1980), p. 52.

The Blue Shield Agency is a charitable organization located in a mid-sized Canadian city. The major goal of the organization is to provide food and shelter for the homeless. It operates out of its own premises, and while it has some permanent employees, it also relies heavily on volunteers.

The agency's funds have four sources:

- Government grants are received annually to fund the regular food and shelter operating activities. When the need arises, special government grants are solicited to fund capital asset additions and major renovations.
- Donations are received as a result of public campaigns held each March to raise funds for the current year's operating costs.
- A United Way grant is received each November to help fund the next year's operations.
- Interest is received from an endowment fund and other investments.

The agency maintains its records in accordance with the restricted fund method of accounting for contributions, and prepares its annual financial statements on this basis. The three funds being used are described below.

General Fund

This fund is used to record the agency's operating activities. Revenues consist of government operating grants, the proceeds from the annual fundraising campaign, the United Way grant, interest from the endowment fund, and term deposit interest. Each year the grant from the United Way is recorded as deferred revenue to be matched against the operating expenses of the year following. Expenses are for the food and shelter programs and for administration costs. An encumbrance system is used to ensure that costs do not exceed budgeted amounts, but the budget itself is not formally recorded in the accounting records. While some donated materials and services are received each year, no record of these donations is made in the ledger accounts. Small-equipment purchases made from this fund are capitalized in the capital fund.

Capital Fund

This fund is used to account for restricted funds raised for building and equipment acquisitions. The capital fund also records the capitalization of buildings and equipment and the amortization taken. Equipment acquisitions made from the general fund are also capitalized in this fund.

Because the agency's policy, prior to the issuance of the current *Handbook*, was non-capitalization of capital asset purchases, a retroactive catch-up entry was required.

Approximately 20 years ago the city donated a building to the agency. While the city retained title to the land on which the building is situated, the agency will not be required to move, and the building will not be torn down, as long as the agency continues with its programs. The value of the donated building was *not* recorded at the time of the donation because it was the organization's policy not to capitalize buildings and equipment. When the current *Handbook* sections became operative several years ago, the organization spent considerable time and money searching past records to determine the cost of capital assets purchased from both restricted and nonrestricted contributions and the fair values of capital assets donated. The new *Handbook* sections had to be applied retroactively, and the following journal entry was made at that time to accomplish this (000s omitted):

Equipment and furniture	1,100	
Buildings	2,000	
Accumulated amortization		1,200
Net assets (capital fund balance)		1,900

Endowment Fund   The $500,000 in this fund was bequeathed to the agency by its founder five years ago. Interest earned is to be used for operating purposes and is recorded in the general fund.

The balance sheets of the funds of Blue Shield as at January 1, Year 6 (the start of the next fiscal year), are presented in Exhibit 13.3.

This form of presentation of fund financial statements is called the *multicolumn approach* because each of the fund's financial statements is presented in its own separate column. If fund accounting is used, the *Handbook* requires that totals be shown for each item presented, so that the "big picture" for the entire organization can be seen. This approach can become very cumbersome if an organization has a large number of funds that need to be presented separately because of all of the restrictions involved. An alternative is to combine the funds into a single set of statements (the deferral method of accounting for contributions), with extensive footnote disclosure of resource restrictions.

Exhibit 13.3

BLUE SHIELD AGENCY
BALANCE SHEET
January 1, Year 6
(in thousands of dollars)

	General fund	Capital fund	Endowment fund	Total
Current assets				
Cash and term deposits	$417	$ 62		$ 479
Pledges receivable	490			490
	907	62		969
Investments			$500	500
Capital assets				
Equipment and furniture		1,482		1,482
Buildings		2,095		2,095
Accumulated amortization		(1,517)		(1,517)
		2,060		2,060
Total assets	$907	$2,122	$500	$3,529
Current liabilities				
Accounts payable	$613	$ 50		$ 663
Wages payable	70			70
Accrued liabilities	82			82
	765	50		815
Deferred revenue	40			40
Fund balances				
Investment in capital assets		2,060		2,060
Externally restricted		12	500	512
Unrestricted	102			102
	102	2,072	500	2,674
Total liabilities and fund balances	$907	$2,122	$500	$3,529

When reporting on a fund basis is used, the total for each financial statement item must be shown.

Year 6 Events   The year's events are summarized as follows (all dollar amounts are in thousands unless stated otherwise):

(a) The accounts and wages payable and the accrued liabilities at the beginning of the year were paid.

(b) The deferred revenue from Year 5 consisted of the grant from the United Way. An entry was made to recognize this as revenue in Year 6.

(c) The pledges receivable at the beginning of the year were collected in full.

(d) The Year 6 fundraising campaign was held in March. Cash of $1,187 was collected, and pledges expected to realize $800 were received. Total fundraising costs were $516, of which $453 was paid in cash, $50 is owed to suppliers, and $13 has been accrued.

(e) During Year 6, the agency announced a plan to construct an addition to its building at an estimated cost of $1.5 million. The budget includes equipment acquisitions. The addition will be built in two phases, with final completion expected in Year 8. At the end of Year 6 the first phase was out for tender, with construction to commence early in Year 7.

   The government announced a grant of $600 in Year 6 to cover the first phase and has remitted $450 of this, with the balance promised in Year 7. The agency spent $103 on equipment near the end of Year 6, of which $91 has been paid and $12 is still owing. At the beginning of the year the agency had $62 on hand from a previous building campaign and an unpaid liability of $50 for capital asset purchases. A public campaign will be conducted next year to raise the balance of the funds needed to complete the project.

(f) Government grants for operating purposes totalled $1,200 in Year 6, of which $910 was received during the year, with the balance expected in January, Year 7.

(g) The agency uses an encumbrance system as a means of controlling expenditures. (Note: Wages of agency employees are not subject to encumbrance because purchase orders are not issued for this type of expenditure.) During the year, orders estimated to total $1,964 were issued for the purchase of goods and services.

(h) Invoices totalling $1,866 were received on purchase orders originally recorded at an estimated cost of $1,870. Suppliers were paid $1,446 on account for these invoices, and the balance owing is still outstanding. The costs were allocated as follows:

Shelter program	$650
Food program	960
Administration	256

(i) The total wage costs were:

Shelter program	$ 90
Food program	150
Administration	300

of which $357 was paid and $183 is payable at year-end.

(j) The United Way grant amounting to $65 was received in December.

(k) Late in the year a prominent supporter donated $50 to be held in endowment, with the interest earned to be unrestricted.

(l) The investments in the endowment fund earned interest of $40; a further $14 in interest was received from the term deposits held in the general fund.

(m) Refrigeration equipment costing $3 was purchased with general fund cash.

(n) The Year 6 amortization charges amounted to $150.

(o) At the end of the year the balances in the encumbrance accounts were closed.

The journal entries required to record these events in each of the three funds are presented next in the order listed:

(a) *General fund*

Accounts payable	613	
Wages payable	70	
Accrued liabilities	82	
Cash		765

Capital fund

Accounts payable	50	
Cash		50

(b) *General fund*

Deferred revenue	40	
Revenue — United Way grant		40

(c) *General fund*

Cash	490	
Pledges receivable		490

(d) *General fund*

Cash	1,187	
Pledges receivable	800	
Revenue — donations		1,987

Expenses — fundraising	516	
Cash		453
Accounts payable		50
Accrued liabilities		13

(e) *Capital fund*

Cash	450	
Government grant receivable	150	
Revenue — government grant		600

Equipment	103	
Cash		91
Accounts payable		12

(f) *General fund*

Cash	910	
Government grant receivable	290	
Revenue — government grant		1,200

(g) *General fund*

Encumbrances	1,964	
Estimated commitments		1,964

(h) *General fund*

Estimated commitments	1,870	
Encumbrances		1,870
Expenses — shelter program	650	
Expenses — food program	960	
Expenses — administration	256	
Cash		1,446
Accounts payable		420

(i) *General fund*

Expenses — shelter program	90	
Expenses — food program	150	
Expenses — administration	300	
Cash		357
Wages payable		183

(j) *General fund*

Cash	65	
Deferred revenue — United Way		65

(k) *Endowment fund*

Cash	50	
Revenue — contribution		50

(l) *General fund*

Cash	54	
Revenue — investment income		54

(m) *General fund*

Transfer to capital fund	3	
Cash		3
Capital fund		
Equipment	3	
Transfer from general fund		3

(n) *Capital fund*

Expenses — amortization	150	
Accumulated amortization		150

(o) *General fund*

Estimated commitments	94	
Encumbrances		94

After these journal entries are posted, financial statements as at December 31, Year 6, can be prepared as shown in Exhibit 13.4.

Note that while a fund type of cash flow statement could be prepared, the one in this illustration has been prepared on a nonfund basis, which is in accordance with the *Handbook*'s pronouncements. Letters shown in parentheses represent the journal entries affecting the cash account.

Exhibit 13.4

BLUE SHIELD AGENCY
BALANCE SHEET
December 31, Year 6
(in thousands of dollars)

	General fund	Capital fund	Endowment fund	Total
Current assets				
Cash and term deposits	$ 99	$ 371	$ 50	$ 520
Pledges receivable	800			800
Government grants receivable	290	150		440
	1,189	521	50	1,760
Investments			500	500
Capital assets				
Equipment and furniture		1,588		1,588
Buildings		2,095		2,095
Accumulated depreciation		(1,667)		(1,667)
		2,016		2,016
Total assets	$1,189	$2,537	$550	$4,276
Current liabilities				
Accounts payable	$ 470	$ 12		$ 482
Wages payable	183			183
Accrued liabilities	13			13
	666	12		678
Deferred revenue	65			65
Fund balances				
Investment in capital assets		2,016		2,016
Externally restricted funds		509	550	1,059
Unrestricted funds	458			458
	458	2,525	550	3,533
Total liabilities and fund balances	$1,189	$2,537	$550	$4,276

continued

Exhibit 13.4　*continued*

BLUE SHIELD AGENCY
STATEMENT OF REVENUES, EXPENSES, AND
CHANGES IN FUND BALANCES
for the Year Ended December 31, Year 6
(in thousands of dollars)

	General fund	Capital fund	Endowment fund	Total
Revenues				
Government grants	$1,200	$ 600		$1,800
United Way grant	40			40
Contributions	1,987		$ 50	2,037
Investment income	54			54
	3,281	600	50	3,931
Expenses				
Shelter program	740			740
Food program	1,110			1,110
Administration	556			556
Fund raising	516			516
Amortization		150		150
	2,922	150		3,072
Excess of revenue over expenses	$ 359	$ 450	$ 50	$ 859
Interfund transfers	(3)	3		
Fund balances, January 1	102	2,072	500	2,674
Fund balances, December 31	$ 458	$2,525	$550	$3,533

BLUE SHIELD AGENCY
STATEMENT OF CASH FLOWS
for the Year Ended December 31, Year 6
(in thousands of dollars)

It is not required to present a cash flow statement on a fund basis.

Cash flows from operating activities	
Cash received from government operating grants **(f)**	$ 910
Cash received from United Way grant **(j)**	65
Cash received from general contributions **(c)**, **(d)**	1,677
Cash received from investment income **(l)**	54
Cash paid to suppliers **(a)**, **(h)**	(2,141)
Cash paid to employees **(a)**, **(i)**	(427)
Cash paid for fund raising **(d)**	(453)
Net cash used in operating activities	(315)
Cash flows from financing and investing activities	
Contributions of cash for endowment **(k)**	50
Cash received from government grant **(e)**	450
Cash paid for capital asset acquisitions **(a)**, **(e)**, **(m)**	(144)
Net cash generated through financing and investing activities	356
Net increase in cash and term deposits	41
Cash and term deposits — January 1	479
Cash and term deposits — December 31	$ 520

The closing entries for each fund would be prepared as follows:

General fund

Revenue — government grant	1,200	
Revenue — United Way grant	40	
Revenue — contributions	1,987	
Revenue — investment income	54	
Expenses — shelter program		740
Expenses — food program		1,110
Expenses — administration		556
Expenses — fundraising		516
Fund balance		359
Fund balance	3	
Transfer to capital fund		3

Capital fund

Revenue — government grant	600	
Expenses — amortization		150
Fund balance		450
Transfer from general fund	3	
Fund balance		3

Endowment fund

Revenue contributions	50	
Fund balance		50

This comprehensive example has illustrated the accounts used and the resulting financial statements under the restricted fund method. The extensive footnote disclosures required by the *Handbook* have not been illustrated.

Illustration of the Deferred Contribution Method

To illustrate the journal entries made and the annual general-purpose financial statements prepared using the deferral method of accounting for contributions, we will use the same basic information as was used in the previous example. A brief recap of the pertinent information is provided.

The Blue Shield Agency is a charitable organization located in a mid-sized Canadian city. The agency's funds come from four sources:

- Blue Shield receives annual government grants to fund its regular operating activities. As the need arises, it solicits special government grants to fund capital asset additions and major renovations.

- The agency receives donations through campaigns held each March to raise funds for the current year's operating expenses.

- The agency receives a United Way grant each November to help fund the next year's operations.

- Interest is accrued from endowments and other investments.

The agency maintains its records in accordance with the deferral method of accounting for contributions, and prepares its annual financial statements on this basis.

When the *Handbook's* current NFPO sections became operative several years ago, the organization spent considerable time and money searching past records to determine the cost of capital assets purchased from both restricted and nonrestricted contributions, as well as the fair values of capital assets donated. Because the new *Handbook* had to be applied retroactively, the following journal entries were made at that time to accomplish this (000s omitted):

Equipment and furniture	1,100	
Accumulated amortization		300
Net assets invested in capital assets		800

This entry recognized the cost of equipment acquired in past years using unrestricted contributions, and the accumulated amortization to date.

Buildings	2,000	
Accumulated amortization		900
Deferred contributions related to capital assets		1,100

This entry recorded the fair value of the building donated by the city and the accumulated amortization taken to date. A capital asset donation is treated in the same manner as a contribution restricted for the purchase of a capital asset. As the asset is amortized, a portion of the deferred contribution is recognized as a match against this expense.

The balance sheet of Blue Shield as at January 1, Year 6 (the start of the next fiscal year), is presented in Exhibit 13.5.

When this balance sheet is compared to the fund balance sheets from the previous example (see Exhibit 13.3), the amounts used on the asset side are fairly obvious. The liability side needs further clarification. The amount in *deferred contributions* is the United Way grant. The *deferred building campaign contributions* balance is the externally restricted fund balance from the capital fund, and represents restricted funds received but not spent on capital assets. When this money is spent, an amount will be transferred from this deferred contribution account to the *deferred contributions related to capital assets* account. The *deferred contributions related to capital assets* balance represents that portion of the unamortized balance of capital assets that were either donated or purchased from contributions restricted for capital asset purchases. This will be transferred to revenue in future periods as these assets are amortized. The balance of $550 was not shown in the capital fund balance sheet.

The differences in presentation are:

Restricted fund method:	
Investment in capital assets	$2,060
Deferred contribution method:	
Deferred contributions – capital assets	$ 550
Net assets invested in capital assets	1,510
	$2,060

The $500,000 *net assets restricted for endowment purposes* is the fund balance from the endowment fund and originated from the founder's bequest. Interest earned is not restricted.

The *unrestricted net asset balance* comes from the general fund balance.

Exhibit 13.5

BLUE SHIELD AGENCY
BALANCE SHEET
January 1, Year 6
(in thousands of dollars)

Current assets	
Cash and term deposits	$ 479
Pledges receivable	490
	969
Investments	500
Capital assets	
Equipment and furniture	1,482
Buildings	2,095
Accumulated amortization	(1,517)
	2,060
Total assets	$3,529
Current liabilities	
Accounts payable	$ 663
Wages payable	70
Accrued liabilities	82
	815

Deferred contributions related to capital assets represents the unamortized amount of capital assets either donated or purchased from restricted contributions.

Deferred revenue	
Deferred contributions	40
Deferred contributions related to capital assets	550
Deferred building campaign contributions	12
	602

Net assets invested in capital assets represents the unamortized amount of capital assets purchased from unrestricted contributions.

Net assets	
Net assets invested in capital assets	1,510
Net assets restricted for endowment purposes	500
Unrestricted net assets	102
	2,112
Total liabilities and net assets	$3,529

Year 6 Events The year's events are summarized as follows (all dollar amounts are in thousands unless stated otherwise):

(a) The accounts and wages payable and the accrued liabilities at the beginning of the year were paid.

(b) The deferred contribution revenue from Year 5, consisting of the grant from the United Way, was recognized as revenue in Year 6.

(c) The pledges receivable at the beginning of the year were collected in full.

(d) The Year 6 fundraising campaign was held in March. Cash of $1,187 was collected, and pledges expected to realize $800 were received. Total fundraising costs were $516, of which $453 was paid in cash, $50 is owed to suppliers, and $13 has been accrued.

(e) During Year 6 the agency announced a plan to construct an addition to its building at an estimated cost of $1.5 million. This figure included equipment purchases. The project will be built in two phases, with final completion expected in Year 8. At the end of Year 6 the first phase was out for tender, with construction to commence early in Year 7. The government announced a grant of $600 in Year 6 to cover the first phase and has remitted $450 of this, with the balance promised in Year 7. The agency spent $103 on equipment near the end of Year 6, of which $91 has been paid and $12 is still owing.

   At the beginning of the year, the agency had $62 on hand from a previous building campaign and an unpaid liability for capital asset purchases of $50. A public campaign will be conducted next year to raise the balance of the funds needed to complete the project.

(f) Government grants for operating purposes totalled $1,200 in Year 6, of which $910 was received during the year, with the balance expected in January Year 7.

(g) The agency uses an encumbrance system to control expenditures. (Note: Wages of agency employees are not subject to encumbrance because purchase orders are not issued for this type of expenditure.) During the year, orders estimated to total $1,964 were issued for the purchase of goods and services.

(h) Invoices totalling $1,866 were received on purchase orders originally recorded at an estimated cost of $1,870. Suppliers were paid $1,446 on account for these invoices, and the balance owing is still outstanding. The costs were allocated as follows:

Shelter program	$650
Food program	960
Administration	256

(i) Wage costs were:

Shelter program	$ 90
Food program	150
Administration	300

of which $357 was paid and $183 is payable at year-end.

(j) The United Way grant to finance Year 7 operations amounting to $65 was received in December.

(k) Late in the year a prominent supporter donated $50, to be held permanently in endowment, with the interest earned to be unrestricted.

(l) The endowment investments earned interest of $40, and the term deposits earned $14. All interest was collected.

(m) Refrigeration equipment costing $3 was purchased from cash received from unrestricted contributions.

(n) The Year 6 amortization charges were as follows:

On capital assets acquired from restricted resources	$ 90
On capital assets acquired from unrestricted resources	60
Total amortization	$150

(o) At the end of the year, the balances in the encumbrance accounts were closed.

The journal entries required to record these events are presented next in the order listed.

(a)	Accounts payable	663	
	Wages payable	70	
	Accrued liabilities	82	
	Cash		815
(b)	Deferred contributions	40	
	Revenue — United Way grant		40
(c)	Cash	490	
	Pledges receivable		490
(d)	Cash	1,187	
	Pledges receivable	800	
	Revenue — donations		1,987
	Expenses — fundraising	516	
	Cash		453
	Accounts payable		50
	Accrued liabilities		13
(e)	Cash	450	
	Government grant receivable	150	
	Deferred building campaign contributions		600
	Equipment	103	
	Cash		91
	Accounts payable		12
	Deferred building campaign contributions	103	
	Deferred contributions — capital assets		103
(f)	Cash	910	
	Government grant receivable	290	
	Revenue — government grant		1,200
(g)	Encumbrances	1,964	
	Estimated commitments		1,964
(h)	Estimated commitments	1,870	
	Encumbrances		1,870
	Expenses — shelter program	650	
	Expenses — food program	960	
	Expenses — administration	256	
	Cash		1,446
	Accounts payable		420
(i)	Expenses — shelter program	90	
	Expenses — food program	150	
	Expenses — administration	300	
	Cash		357
	Wages payable		183

| (j) Cash | 65 | |
| Deferred contributions — United Way | | 65 |

| (k) Cash | 50 | |
| Net assets — endowment | | 50 |

| (l) Cash | 54 | |
| Revenue — investment income | | 54 |

| (m) Equipment | 3 | |
| Cash | | 3 |

| (n) Expenses — amortization | 150 | |
| Accumulated amortization | | 150 |

| Deferred contributions — capital assets | 90 | |
| Amortization of deferred contributions | | 90 |

| (o) Estimated commitments | 94 | |
| Encumbrances | | 94 |

After these journal entries are posted, financial statements as at December 31, Year 6, can be prepared as shown in Exhibit 13.6.

The statement of revenue and expenses shows not only unrestricted revenues and expenses, but also the restricted revenues recognized during the year as a match to the expenses associated with them (amortization in this case). The $299 excess of revenues and expenses is transferred to the "total" column in the statement of changes in net assets.

The portion of the amortization expense from assets acquired with unrestricted resources is transferred so that it is deducted in the *invested in capital assets* column, leaving $359 as the amount of operating results allocated to unrestricted resources. Because a portion of amortization has been removed ($60), and the remainder ($90) has been offset with an equal amount of revenue, this amount represents the increase in resources that can be spent in future periods. The unrestricted resources that were spent on equipment during the period ($3) are shown as a transfer from the unrestricted column to the invested in capital assets column.

An examination of the balance sheet shows the following equality regarding capital assets purchased from restricted and unrestricted resources:

Deferred contributions — capital assets (restricted)	$ 563
Net assets — invested in capital assets (unrestricted)	1,453
Total capital assets (from both sources)	$2,016

The endowment contribution received during the year does not appear on the operating statement because no expenses will ever appear for the required matching process to occur. Instead, this special restricted resource is shown on the statement of changes in *net assets* as an increase in the column net assets restricted for endowment. Extensive footnote disclosure is required when statements are prepared using the deferred contribution method, in order to clearly define the amount and nature of restricted and unrestricted resources.

Exhibit 13.6

BLUE SHIELD AGENCY
BALANCE SHEET
December 31, Year 6
(in thousands of dollars)

Current assets	
Cash and term deposits	$ 520
Pledges receivable	800
Government grants receivable	440
	1,760
Investments	500
Capital assets	
Equipment and furniture	1,588
Buildings	2,095
Accumulated amortization	(1,667)
	2,016
Total assets	$4,276
Current liabilities	
Accounts payable	$ 482
Wages payable	183
Accrued liabilities	13
	678
Deferred revenue	
Deferred contributions	65
Deferred contributions related to capital assets	563
Deferred building campaign contributions	509
	1,137
Net assets	
Net assets — invested capital assets	1,453
Net assets restricted for endowment purposes	550
Unrestricted net assets	458
	2,461
Total liabilities and net assets	$4,276

BLUE SHIELD AGENCY
STATEMENT OF REVENUES AND EXPENSES
for the Year Ended December 31, Year 6
(in thousands of dollars)

Revenues	
Government grants	$1,200
United Way grant	40
Contributions	1,987
Investment income	54
Amortization of deferred contributions	90
	3,371

continued

Exhibit 13.6   *continued*

Expenses	
Shelter program	740
Food program	1,110
Administration	556
Fund raising	516
Amortization of capital assets	150
	3,072
Excess of revenue over expenses	$ 299

BLUE SHIELD AGENCY
STATEMENT OF CHANGES IN NET ASSETS
for the Year Ended December 31, Year 6
(in thousands of dollars)

The explanations for the transfers from (to) invested in capital assets to (from) unrestricted resources are shown on page 650.

	Invested in capital assets	Restricted for endowment purposes	Unrestricted	Total
Balance, Jan. 1	$1,510	$500	$102	$2,112
Excess of revenues over expenses	(60)		359	299
Endowment contributions		50		50
Investment in capital assets	3		(3)	
Balance, Dec. 31	$1,453	$550	$458	$2,461

BLUE SHIELD AGENCY
STATEMENT OF CASH FLOWS
for the Year Ended December 31, Year 6
(in thousands of dollars)

Cash flows from operating activities	
Cash received from government operating grants **(f)**	$ 910
Cash received from United Way grant **(j)**	65
Cash received from general contributions **(c)**, **(d)**	1,677
Cash received from investment income **(l)**	54
Cash paid to suppliers **(a)**, **(h)**	(2,141)
Cash paid to employees **(a)**, **(i)**	(427)
Cash paid for fund raising **(d)**	(453)
Net cash used in operating activities	(315)
Cash flows from financing and investing activities	
Contributions of cash for endowment **(k)**	50
Cash received from government grant **(e)**	450
Cash paid for capital asset acquisitions **(a)**, **(e)**, **(m)**	(144)
Net cash generated through financing and investing activities	356
Net increase in cash and term deposits	41
Cash and term deposits, Jan. 1	479
Cash and term deposits, Dec. 31	$ 520

Closing entries as at December 31, Year 6, are presented next.

Revenue — government grant	1,200	
Revenue — United Way grant	40	
Revenue — contributions	1,987	
Revenue — investment income	54	
Expenses — shelter program		740
Expenses — food program		1,110
Expenses — administration		556
Expenses — fund raising		516
Unrestricted net assets		359
To close the unrestricted revenues and expenses		
Unrestricted net assets	3	
Net assets invested in capital assets		3
To transfer the amount of capital assets acquired from unrestricted resources		
Net assets invested in capital assets	60	
Amortization of deferred contributions	90	
Expenses — amortization		150
To close restricted revenues and the expenses related to capital assets		

August 2007 Exposure Draft   This Exposure Draft recommends the following changes to the accounting for not-for-profit organizations:

- Consolidation will be required for all controlled profit-orientated and not-for-profit entities. Currently an NFPO is allowed the alternative of consolidating or not consolidating both types of entities. In addition, the concept of significant influence with another NFPO will be eliminated.

- The current requirement to show net assets invested in capital assets as a separate component of equity will be eliminated. Instead, this amount will be described as internally restricted under the category other restricted net assets.

- NFPOs will be required to present a cash flow statement showing the three categories of cash flows from operations, financing, and investing activities. Currently they are encouraged but not required to present such a statement, but if they do so, investing and financing can be presented as a single category.

- NFPOs that prepare interim financial statements will be required to follow Section 1751 in their preparation.

- It is proposed that when an NFPO acts as a principle in a transaction, revenues and expenses are to be reported at their gross amounts and are not to be reported at net amounts.

- Some NFPOs report expenses on a functional basis in their operating statements. A new section will be issued which will provide guidance on the allocation of fundraising and general support costs to other functions if such an allocation is chosen by an NFPO.

SUMMARY

The introduction of seven not-for-profit *Handbook* sections, together with amendments making thirty-five of the *CICA Handbook*'s other accounting recommendations applicable to this area, have dramatically changed the financial reporting of NFPOs. We have moved from a situation where virtually no authoritative standards existed to one where full and proportionate consolidation of controlled and jointly controlled entities are allowed, and asset capitalization and amortization is a requirement for all but "small" organizations. Rather than mandating a single reporting model, the new standard gives NFPOs the choice between the deferred contribution and restricted fund methods of financial statement presentation and allows them the flexibility to use a mix of both methods if they feel that it will result in a better presentation. While these changes have moved not-for-profit more towards a business approach of reporting and away from the stewardship-of-resources approach that was previously used, not-for-profit reporting is still very distinct, and certainly far more complex than it was before.

APPENDIX 13A

Sample Financial Statements

This appendix contains the 2006 balance sheet, statement of operations, and statement of changes in net assets of the Winnipeg Foundation. The Foundation was established in 1921 by a prominent Winnipeg citizen who made an initial contribution of $100,000. (The second contribution is described as "The Widow's Mite $15.") Since that date, endowment assets have grown to $351 million and encompass over 1,700 separate endowment funds. The board of directors has established an occupancy reserve fund to cover the costs of physical premises and an administration fund to fund the Foundation's day-to-day administration costs. The deferral method of accounting has been used for contributions, and expenses have been recorded using the accrual basis. The category "other assets" contains donated works of art, cash surrender value of life insurance, capital assets with a net book value of $1,237,262, and charitable remainder trusts amounting to $4,210,056. The Foundation is the owner and capital beneficiary of the charitable remainder trusts and will become entitled to the investment income from these funds upon the death of the income beneficiaries.

THE WINNIPEG FOUNDATION
BALANCE SHEET
September 30, 2006

	2006	2005
Assets		
Cash and short-term investments	$ 26,854,045	$ 19,102,631
Investment income receivable	2,241,656	2,205,377
Accounts receivable	38,484	287,259
Bonds and debentures, at market		
Government of Canada	56,474,999	56,555,162
Provincial Government	40,373,262	36,890,151
Municipal	415,901	—
Corporate	56,893,051	52,391,078
Pooled funds	20,110,344	19,303,965
Preferred and common shares, at market	205,831,528	191,221,303
Other (Note 3)	5,457,431	5,401,622
	$414,690,701	$383,358,548
Liabilities		
Accounts payable	$ 329,175	$ 320,904
Grant commitments (Note 5)	$ 14,848,307	13,714,847
	15,177,482	14,035,751
Capital held for investments		
Managed funds (Note 6)	44,969,979	40,940,915
Net assets		
Endowment funds (Note 7)		
Consolidated trust fund	256,531,428	231,832,135
Other trust fund	94,768,858	93,516,608
Invested in capital assets	133,337	172,266
Administration and occupancy reserve fund	2,532,490	2,231,293
Unrestricted	577,127	629,580
	$414,690,701	$383,358,548

Approved by the Board

_____ Director

_____ Director

STATEMENT OF OPERATIONS
September 30, 2006

	2006	2005
Income		
Investment income	$13,167,796	$13,364,798
Net realized capital gains apportioned		
to income (Note 2(b))	5,875,724	5,052,773
Gifts received for immediate granting	671,542	958,977
Grants from capital apportioned to income	180,444	120,613
Grants returned	5,586	21,557
	19,901,092	19,518,718
Less:		
Investment manager and trust company		
custodian fees (Note 11)	891,696	866,509
	19,009,396	18,652,209
Grants approved		
Community service	4,459,684	5,004,215
Education	3,341,401	3,439,030
Health	2,963,690	2,677,391
Environment	608,686	447,668
Heritage	1,083,983	1,147,243
Arts and culture	2,362,842	1,809,153
Recreation	962,289	699,960
Faith based designations	173,037	268,656
Special projects	729,374	714,626
	16,684,986	16,207,942
Administration and other expenses (Note 11)	2,106,480	1,940,896
Total expenditures	18,791,466	18,148,838
Increase in unrestricted net assets		
for the year from operations	$ 217,930	$ 503,371

STATEMENT OF CHANGES IN NET ASSETS
September 30, 2006

	2006						2005
	Administration & occupancy reserve fund	Other trust fund	Consolidated trust fund	Invested in capital assets	Unrestricted	Total	Total
Balance, beginning of Year	$2,231,293	$93,516,608	$231,832,135	$172,266	$629,580	$328,381,882	$298,030,818
Add							
New gifts	—	—	21,127,288	—	—	21,127,288	7,890,366
Increase in cash surrender value	—	—	11,536	—	—	11,536	30,255
Net realized capital gains (losses) (Note 2(b))	66,779	950,515	2,302,891	—	—	3,320,186	307,455
Net change in unrealized gain (loss)	11,288	301,734	1,242,186	—	—	1,555,208	21,507,202
Investment income (loss)	(6,090)	—	—	—	—	(6,090)	6,537
Income capitalized	17,402	—	97,158	—	—	114,560	236,674
Deduct							
Endowment funds returned	(97,494)	—	(81,766)	—	—	(179,260)	(123,050)
Transfer to managed fund	—	—	—	—	—	—	(7,746)
Increase in unrestricted net assets for the year from operations	—	—	—	—	217,930	217,930	503,371
Transfers							
Acquisitions of capital assets	—	—	—	16,681	(16,681)		—
Depreciation charge for the year	—	—	—	(55,610)	55,610		—
Other	309,312	—	—		(309,312)		—
Balance, end of year	$2,532,490	$94,768,858	$256,531,428	$133,337	$577,127	$354,543,240	$328,381,882

APPENDIX 13B

Accounting for Governments

Governments differ from business organizations in a number of ways.

Governments differ from business organizations in many ways, some of which can be summarized as follows:

- Governments do not exist to make a profit but rather to provide services.
- While the major source of business revenue comes from the sale of goods or services or both, most of a government's revenue comes from taxation.
- Businesses have to compete while governments operate in essentially a non-competitive environment.
- Often a major goal of government is the redistribution of wealth. A major goal of a business is the maximization of the wealth of its owners.
- The federal and provincial governments have virtually an unlimited capacity to borrow, constrained only by their ability to raise taxes in order to repay. A business's earning capacity is a major constraining factor in its ability to issue debt.
- While a business purchases capital assets in order to earn a return, a government's capital asset acquisitions are made to provide services.
- A government's budget plan, approved by a legislative process at the start of a fiscal period, attracts considerable attention in the press as does the eventual comparison of actual results with those budgeted for originally. Businesses do not normally report their budgets and their annual results are usually compared with results of prior periods with no mention of the year's budget.

With such differences it is not surprising that government reporting models have been quite different from those used by businesses. This was certainly the case ten or fifteen years ago, but lately, changes have been made that have brought government accounting rules much closer to those required for business, although many differences still exist. This will be more evident when government accounting standards are summarized later in this appendix.

The following paragraph outlines a brief history of government financial reporting.

Prior to the 1980s, a comprehensive body of accounting principles for governments did not exist. The CICA was involved only with setting the financial reporting standards for business organizations; no other body had established authoritative standards for governments. The desperate financial condition of some large American cities, which, it was argued, was not adequately reported in their financial statements, became the focus of attention of standard-setting bodies in the United States, soon followed by the CICA in Canada. Before plunging into this area the CICA created a committee with a mandate to determine what practices were being followed by the federal, provincial, and territorial governments[1] and to recommend changes that were needed. As a result of the findings and recommendations of this committee, the CICA established the Public Sector Accounting and Auditing Committee (PSAAC) in 1981 and charged it with the development of accounting principles for governments. Before proceeding, PSAAC created a second study group, with a similar mandate as that of the first one, to report on the financial reporting practices of cities, municipalities, towns, and villages.[2] This study group made reference to a previous research study commissioned by the Certified General

---

[1] "Financial Reporting By Governments," a research study, Toronto: CICA, 1980

[2] "Local Government Financial Reporting," a research study, Toronto: CICA, 1985

Accountants Association of Canada[3] and concluded that it would use the CGA study's findings and recommendations as a starting point for its own study. All three research studies came to similar conclusions about government financial reporting practices in general. These conclusions can be summarized by saying *that there was such a diversity of terminology, measurements, and reporting practices being used that comparability among similar government organizations[4] was virtually impossible and that this situation should not be allowed to continue.*

At first the standard-setting process proceeded slowly and only a few statements on accounting and auditing were issued by PSAAC. Then in 1998 the CICA formed the Public Sector Accounting Board (PSAB), and proceeded with the reorganization of the *CICA Handbook* by transferring the auditing recommendations to the Assurance section of the *Handbook*, and the creation of a new *Public Sector Accounting Handbook*. Previously issued accounting statements were revised and amended as *PS Handbook* sections.

> The CICA has created a new *Public Sector Accounting Handbook* which contains the generally accepted accounting principles applicable to federal, provincial, territorial, and local governments.

Compliance with PSAB Reporting Standards

If a business organization does not follow the *CICA Handbook* in its financial reporting it could suffer substantial penalties because legislation and security regulations require GAAP to be used. When a new accounting standard is issued, businesses (especially public companies) tend to adopt the new standard immediately. Not-for-profit organizations also tend to follow the *Handbook* in their financial reporting. Failure to do so could result in a reduction of support especially in the area of grants from governments and from other not-for-profit organizations. Governments, though, are different. They often exhibit tardiness in adopting new standards, and sometimes refuse to adopt certain standards. The reasons for this are as follows:

> Some governments in Canada have failed to adopt new government accounting standards for a number of reasons.

- The federal government and each of the provincial and territorial governments prepare their financial reports in accordance with the legislation enacted by each body. The adoption of a new reporting standard often requires an amendment to an Act.
- Local governments are created by an Act of the legislature of the province or territory in which they are located. Changes in local government reporting often require changes in legislation.
- Legislative changes necessary to adopt new accounting standards do not rank high in the priorities of many governments.
- When auditors report that a government is not following proper accounting practices in its financial statements (an event which often occurs), the press notes the outrage of the opposition parties and the government's denial of any impropriety, and then the matter is forgotten. The general public, which by and large does not understand accounting at all, does not seem to be particularly interested.
- The adoption of certain new standards may be perceived by a government as having the potential to make its financial condition look worse than the government is currently reporting. If so, a change in reporting would not be a high priority.

---

[3] A. Beedle, "Accounting for Local Government in Canada: The State of the Art," Vancouver: Canadian Certified General Accountants' Research Foundation, 1981.

[4] For example, the provinces of Manitoba and Nova Scotia, and the cities of Vancouver and Montreal.

GAAP for Governments

Prior to February, 2007, the *Public Sector Accounting Handbook* contained four sections that applied only to federal, provincial, and territorial governments, two sections that applied only to local governments, and a number of specific item sections that applied to all governments. In 2005, a new model for senior governments was introduced which involved some drastic changes from previous practices. While the old model focused mainly on government spending (the operating statement showed revenues and expenditures), the new model presents a government-cost approach although it still contains the reporting of government spending. One major change that took place was the requirement that senior governments capitalize their tangible asset acquisitions and amortize them in the statement of operations. In February 2007, an amendment withdrew both the local government sections and any references to federal, provincial, and territorial governments. Now the *Public Sector Accounting Handbook* contains thirty sections and seven accounting guidelines which apply to all governments in Canada. A transitional provision has been granted to local governments so that they are not required to commence the capitalization and amortization of tangible assets before January 1, 2009. The following briefly summarizes the reporting requirement of the PSAB standards.

Governments are required to present four financial statements.

Under the new model, four financial statements are required: a consolidated statement of financial position, a consolidated statement of operations, a consolidated statement of change in net debt, and a consolidated statement of cash flow.

The balance sheet must show financial assets, liabilities, net debt, non-financial assets, and accumulated surplus/deficit.

Consolidated statement of financial position This statement presents financial assets and then deducts liabilities, with the resultant difference presented as "net debt." Then non-financial assets are added or subtracted to arrive at a final line called "accumulated surplus/deficit."

Financial assets include cash and equivalents, receivables, inventories for resale, loans to other governments, available-for-sale investments, and investments in government enterprises.

Liabilities include accounts payable and accrued liabilities, pension and employee future-benefit liabilities, deferred revenue, borrowings, and loans from other governments.

The net debt position indicates the extent to which the government will have to raise revenues in the future to cover its past spending.

Non-financial assets are tangible capital assets, inventories held for consumption or use, and prepaid expenses. Tangible capital assets are assets used by the government to provide services and include land, buildings, equipment, roads, and so on. They *do not* include intangible assets, natural resources, and Crown lands.

The accumulated surplus/deficit represents the net recognized economic resources (net assets) of the government, and provides an indicator of the government's ability to provide future services at the end of a fiscal year.

Consolidated statement of operations This statement reports the government's revenues and expenses for the year with the difference described as the year's surplus or deficit. This result is added to the accumulated surplus/deficit at the beginning of the year to arrive at the last line, which is called the accumulated surplus/deficit at the end of the year.

Revenues include taxes, non-tax sources (including gains), and transfers from other governments. Revenue for the period should be accrued unless it is impractical to measure. If this is the case the cash bases should be used.

Expenses are to be reported by function or major program. Note disclosure should report the breakdown between the major types of expenses such as salaries, debt servicing costs, the amortization of the costs of tangible capital assets, and transfer payments to other governments. A comparison must be made between the actual results for the year and results of the prior year and also with expectations (the budget) at the beginning of the year.

Consolidated statement of change in net debt

This statement reconciles the net surplus/deficit for the year with the change in net debt for the year, by adding back amortization expense for the year (and other items) and deducting the cost of tangible capital assets and other non-financial assets acquired during the year. The change in net debt is then added to the net debt at the beginning of the year to arrive at the net debt at the end of the year.

This statement is designed to provide information about the extent to which expenditures for the year have been met by the year's revenues. An increase in net debt indicates that revenues of future periods will have to be raised to pay for this year's spending. This statement also has to be prepared in comparative form to the budget and prior years' results.

Consolidated statement of cash flow

This statement reconciles cash and equivalents at the beginning of the year with cash and equivalents at the end of the year by providing details of receipts and payments in the four categories of operating transactions, capital transactions, investing transactions, and financing transactions. Either the direct or indirect method can be used to arrive at cash from operations but the direct method is strongly encouraged because it provides details of cash receipts from a number of categories and therefore is much more informative than the indirect method. This statement is similar to the statement used by business organizations except that the latter would report capital asset acquisitions as an investing activity while this one reports such acquisitions as a separate category.

Section PS 1300 — The Financial Reporting Entity

Section PS 1300, issued in June 1996 and amended in January 2003, states the following:

- The government reporting entity comprises all organizations controlled by the government. An organization is controlled if the government has power over its financial and operating policies and benefits from or is exposed to the results of its operating activities.
- The government statements are prepared by consolidating the statements of the organizations comprising the government entity.
- An exception is that government business enterprises are not consolidated but rather reported using the modified equity method. This will reflect the business enterprise's profit or loss in the government's operating results but will not include its assets and liabilities on the government's balance sheet.
- The modified equity method is exactly the same as the equity method described in Chapter 2 except that the business enterprise's accounting principles are not adjusted to conform to the accounting principles used by the government.

The operating statement must show revenues, expenses, and the year's surplus or deficit. Comparative amounts for the previous year are required to be shown as well as the current year's budget.

A statement showing the year's changes in net debt is required in comparative form with both the budget and the previous year.

The cash flow statement shows operating, capital, investing, and financing transactions.

PS 1300 requires the consolidation of the financial statements of all organizations controlled by the government. Controlled business organizations are not consolidated but rather are reported using the modified equity method.

SUMMARY

The PSAB has exerted considerable effort on the establishment of a new financial reporting model covering federal, provincial, territorial, and local governments. The resultant standards exhibit significant differences from those required for businesses and not-for-profit organizations. Differences will always exist because the operations and user needs of governments, NFPOs, and business organizations are different. While separate standards previously existed for local governments, recent amendments have eliminated any differences so that now one set of standards applies to all government organizations.

REVIEW QUESTIONS

1. Briefly outline how NFPOs differ from profit-oriented organizations.

2. The *Handbook* describes revenue that is unique to not-for-profit organizations. What is this revenue called, and what characteristic does it have that makes it unique?

3. Distinguish between unrestricted and restricted resources of a charitable organization.

4. Briefly explain the concept of fund accounting.

5. Fund accounting is often used for external reporting purposes. Explain why.

6. It is common for an NFPO to receive donated supplies, equipment, and services. Do current accounting standards require the recording of donations of this kind? Explain.

7. Outline the *Handbook*'s requirements with regard to accounting for the capital assets of NFPOs.

8. What revenue recognition guidelines does the *Handbook* provide for pledges received by an NFPO?

9. The equity section of an NFPO's balance sheet should be divided into four main sections. List the sections, and explain the reasons for each.

10. How should transfers of resources between funds be presented in fund financial statements? How should they be presented in a single set of nonfund financial statements?

11. Is the layered approach to presenting fund financial statements allowed under current GAAP? Explain.

12. What is the major difference between the capital asset impairment tests used by profit-oriented and not-for-profit organizations?

13. Contrast the revenue recognition and matching concepts that apply to profit-oriented organizations with those that apply to NFPOs.

14. Outline the financial reporting requirements for an NFPO's investments in other organizations.

15. Explain the use of budgetary accounting and encumbrances by NFPOs.

16. Name the two methods of accounting for contributions, and explain how the methods differ from each other.

17. Is it possible that an organization would be required to use certain aspects of the deferral method even though it reports using the restricted fund method? Explain.

18. An organization raises funds for purchasing capital assets. Briefly outline how the accounting for such funds raised would differ under the two methods envisioned by the *Handbook*.

19. Distinguish between the ways in which the two methods of accounting for contributions report the amount "invested in capital assets."

20. Governments are different from business organizations and not-for-profit organizations in many respects and yet in some respect they are similar. Explain.

21. Explain why governments are so slow to adopt PSAB standards.

22. Distinguish between a government's financial assets and any other assets a government might have. Do governments have to report all assets on their balance sheets? Explain.

23. Are PSAB's reporting requirements the same for senior and local governments? Explain.

24. Briefly outline how the presentation of assets and liabilities on the balance sheet of a government differs from the presentation shown on the balance sheet of a typical business enterprise.

MULTIPLE-CHOICE QUESTIONS

1. NP is a not-for-profit organization that has held its annual fund raising drive every May for the past five years. Based on previous fund raising drives, it estimated that 95% of pledges received will be collected. During May, NP received $100,000 of pledges. NP recorded two journal entries for the pledges. The first was:

Contribution receivable	100,000	
Contribution revenue		100,000

Which of the following would be the second journal entry?

a. Bad debt expense   5,000
    Allowance for doubtful accounts   5,000
b. Bad debt expense   5,000
    Contributions receivable   5,000
c. Contributions revenue   5,000
    Contributions receivable   5,000
d. Contributions revenue   5,000
    Allowance for doubtful accounts   5,000

(*CGA-Canada, from 2002 to 2007*)

2. An individual contributed $100,000 of cash and pledged another $50,000 to a not-for-profit organization to cover the $50,000 salary of its executive director for the current year and the next two years. How should the contributions be reported, assuming that the organization uses the deferral method of accounting for contributions?
a. $50,000 should be reported as contribution revenue in the current year and $100,000 should be reported as deferred contribution revenue at the end of the current year, assuming that the pledge receivable is likely to be collected.
b. $100,000 should be reported as contribution revenue in the current year and $50,000 should be reported as contribution revenue when the individual remits the other $50,000.

c. $100,000 should be reported as contribution revenue in the current year and $50,000 should be reported as deferred contribution revenue at the end of the current year, assuming that the pledge receivable is likely to be collected.

d. $150,000 should be reported as contribution revenue in the current year.

3.   Which of the following treatments is *not* in accordance with GAAP for a not-for-profit organization (NFPO)?

a.   An NFPO with revenue of $480,000 in the current year and $450,000 in the preceding year recorded the purchase of capital assets as an expense in the current year.

b.   An NFPO with revenue in excess of $1 million recorded the donation of a collection of artwork at fair value but does not intend to amortize the artwork.

c.   An NFPO recorded at fair value the donation of the services of volunteer fund-raising canvassers.

d.   An NFPO received a collection of historical treasures but did not record the contribution because a fair value of the treasures could not be reasonably estimated.

(CGA-Canada, from 2002 to 2007)

4.   Mercy Hospital, a not-for-profit organization, has an investment in a joint venture. How should the hospital report its interest in the joint venture?

a.   It is required to use proportionate consolidation.

b.   It is required to use the equity method.

c.   It can choose between using the equity method or proportionate consolidation.

d.   Instead of using the equity method or proportionate consolidation, it can choose to disclose details of the joint venture in its notes to financial statements.

5.   Which of the following is an acceptable way for a not-for-profit organization to account for a donation of $50,000 that is restricted for the purchase of office equipment, assuming the restricted fund method of accounting for contributions is used?

a.   Revenues in the operating fund.

b.   Deferred revenues in the capital fund.

c.   Revenues in the capital fund.

d.   Direct increase in net assets in the capital fund.

(CGA-Canada, from 2002 to 2007)

6.   Under the deferral method, how should endowment contributions be recognized?

a.   As revenue in the year they are received.

b.   As revenue in the endowment fund.

c.   According to the terms of the endowment agreement.

d.   As direct increases in net assets in the period they are received.

(CGA-Canada, from 2002 to 2007)

The following scenario applies to Questions 7 and 8, although each question should be considered independently.

First Harvest (FH) collects food for distribution to people in need. During its first month of operations, the organization collected a substantial amount of food and also $26,000 in cash from a very wealthy donor. The donor specified that the money was to be used to pay down a loan that the organization had with the local bank. The loan had been taken out to buy land, on which the organization plans to build a warehouse facility. A warehouse is needed since, although the organization does not plan to keep a lot of food in stock, sorting and distribution facilities are crucial. FH has also received $100,000, which, according to the donor, is to be deposited, with any income earned to be used as FH sees fit.

7. In which of the following ways should the food donation and the $26,000 be reflected in the financial statements? Assume that fair market values are available and that FH uses the deferral method and does not maintain separate funds.

	Food donations	*$26,000 cash donation*
a.	Deferred revenues	Increase in net assets
b.	Revenues	Increase in net assets
c.	Revenues	Deferred revenues
d.	Not recorded	Deferred revenues

(CICA adapted)

8. In which of the following ways should the $100,000 contribution be accounted for under the following revenue recognition methods?

	Deferral method	*Restricted fund method*
a.	Direct increase in net assets	Revenue of the general fund
b.	Revenue	Revenue of the endowment fund
c.	Revenue	Revenue of the general fund
d.	Direct increase in net assets	Revenue of the endowment fund

(CICA adapted)

9. Wilson Centre, a not-for-profit organization, owns a collection of works of art estimated to be worth about $85,000. These were donated to the centre many years ago and have not been reflected in past financial statements. However, this year, the centre's new auditors wish to include them. If the *CICA Handbook*'s minimum requirements for collections is followed, how should the works of art be accounted for?
   a. Capitalization at fair market value.
   b. It should not be reported at all.
   c. Amortization over a maximum of 40 years.
   d. Disclosure of a description of the collection.

(CGA-Canada, from 2002 to 2007)

The following scenario applies to Questions 10, 11, and 12, although each question should be considered independently.

In the fall of Year 5, the city of Westra approved its budget of $10,000,000 for the construction of a new water treatment plant. Construction began in Year 6. The building was completed on November 30, Year 6, but none of the water treatment equipment had yet been installed. The city uses a fund accounting system and maintains separate funds for general operations and capital projects. It uses an encumbrance system to control operating and capital costs.

The following table summarizes the financial activities related to the water treatment plant for the year ended December 31, Year 6:

Nature of costs	Budget	Value of purchase orders issued	Value of purchase orders outstanding	Actual cost of work completed	Amount paid on work completed
Engineering	$ 2,000,000	$ 2,100,000	$ 200,000	$1,800,000	$1,500,000
Building	5,000,000	5,200,000	—	5,350,000	4,815,000
Equipment	3,000,000	2,860,000	2,860,000	—	—
Total	$10,000,000	$10,160,000	$3,060,000	$7,150,000	$6,315,000

Purchase orders have been issued to cover all work required to complete the facility. The work has not yet commenced on the activities for which purchase orders are currently outstanding but work has been completed on all of the other purchase orders. All of the engineering work completed to date relates to the building. The outstanding engineering work relates to the water treatment equipment. The building and equipment will be capitalized and amortized on a straight-line basis over 20 years for the building and 10 years for the equipment.

10. What amount should be used to report the water treatment building at the end of December Year 6?
    a. $4,815,000
    b. $5,350,000
    c. $6,315,000
    d. $7,150,000

    (CGA-Canada, from 2002 to 2007)

11. How should the outstanding purchase order of $2,860,000 for the equipment be presented on the financial statements for the year ended December 31, Year 6?
    a. Offset the $2,860,000 encumbrance against the $2,860,000 estimated commitment and show no impact on the financial statements.
    b. $2,860,000 should be added to the cost of equipment.
    c. $2,860,000 should be added as a current liability.
    d. $2,860,000 should be reported as an encumbrance expense on the income statement.

    (CGA-Canada, from 2002 to 2007)

12. Based on information available at the time, how much is the water treatment plant expected to cost once the equipment is installed and the plant is operational?
    a. $7,150,000
    b. $9,375,000
    c. $10,160,000
    d. $10,210,000

    (CGA-Canada, from 2002 to 2007)

13. John is an avid supporter of the Environmental Cleanup Organization (ECO), a not-for-profit organization. In Year 4, he donated land and buildings with a total fair market value of $150,000 to ECO. The land and buildings originally cost him $100,000. In Year 4, he also donated $10,000 of paper supplies that would not otherwise have been purchased by ECO. At what amount should John's donation be recorded on ECO's books in Year 4, under Canadian GAAP?
    a. $100,000
    b. $110,000
    c. $150,000
    d. $160,000

14. TK is a not-for-profit organization that runs camps for needy children. It recently received a donation of land with a fair value of $100,000. To record this donation, it used the deferral method and debited its land account. Which account should be credited, and for what amount?
    a. Credit contributions revenue for the nominal amount of $1.
    b. Credit net assets invested in capital assets for the nominal amount of $1.
    c. Credit deferred contribution revenue for $100,000.
    d. Credit net assets invested in capital assets for $100,000.

    (CGA-Canada, from 2002 to 2007)

15. How should a transfer of $50,000 from the operating fund to the capital fund be accounted for by a not-for-profit organization?
    a. As an expense of the operating fund and a revenue of the capital fund.
    b. As an expense of the capital fund and a revenue of the operating fund.
    c. As a decrease in the fund balance for the operating fund and an increase in the fund balance for the capital fund in the statement of changes in fund balances.
    d. As an increase in the fund balance for the operating fund and a decrease in the fund balance for the capital fund in the statement of changes in fund balances.

    (CGA-Canada, from 2002 to 2007)

16. FarmSafe is a not-for-profit organization involved in educating farmers how to cope with crop disease outbreaks. During the past year, it received $500,000 of unrestricted donations plus pledges of $100,000, of which 70% is expected to be collected. Which of the following should be reported on FarmSafe's financial statement for the year?
    a. $500,000 donation revenue.
    b. $570,000 donation revenue.
    c. $600,000 donation revenue.
    d. $600,000 donation revenue and $30,000 bad debt expense.

    (CGA-Canada, from 2002 to 2007)

17. The board of directors for the Ivory Rehabilitation Centre approved the following budget:

Revenues	$700,000
Expenses	680,000
Budgeted surplus	$ 20,000

    Which of the following would be the correct journal entry to record the budget?

a.	Estimated revenues	700,000	
	Appropriations		680,000
	Budgetary fund balance		20,000
b.	Encumbrances	700,000	
	Estimated commitments		680,000
	Budgetary fund balance		20,000
c.	Estimated expenses	680,000	
	Budgetary fund balance	20,000	
	Estimated revenues		700,000
d.	Encumbrances	680,000	
	Budgetary fund balance	20,000	
	Estimated commitments		700,000

CASES

Case 1   You have just completed an interview with the newly formed audit committee of the Andrews Street Youth Centre (ASYC). This organization was created to keep neighbourhood youth off the streets by providing recreational facilities where they can meet, exercise, play indoor sports, and hold dances. Since its inception, the organization has managed to survive on the basis of user fees charged to parents whose children use the program. This year the centre received support from a new provincial government program, in the form of an operating grant along with subsidy fees for those parents whose income is considered insufficient to pay the user fee. A local foundation, with a long history in the community and a reputation for honouring its commitments, has also come to the aid of the centre. This outside financial support came with the provision that the centre must now present audited financial statements annually.

Your firm is attempting to obtain the audit, as it is a November year-end, and the audit would be completed at a traditionally slow time of year. Many questions were posed during the interview and the ASYC audit committee has requested a written response to the issues raised. Excerpts from the interview follow:

- "We are looking for financial statements that are understandable to the board. For example, we have heard that we might have to capitalize and depreciate leasehold improvements. We have just completed $20,000 in expenditures to set up a weight room. We don't understand this amortization idea. Will it make us look like we exceeded our operating budget since this budget is based on all expenditures, capital and operating? The government might consider reducing our next operating grant because of this accounting. If you were selected as our auditor would you have any problem if we simply expensed fixed assets as incurred?"

- "The Parent Advisory Group has organized several fundraising events and the net receipts have been deposited in a separate 'Computer Fund' bank account to allow for the purchase of some PCs. Last year, our financial statements did not reflect this fund. Is that okay with you?"

- "The manager of Sports Supplies Ltd. is a good friend of the centre. This year his company gave us a variety of items such as exercise and body-building apparatus and some basketball equipment. This is pretty neat stuff and must be worth at least $12,000 to $15,000. The audit committee does not want to record this because they are concerned that if it ends up in revenue our operating grants might be reduced."

- "Certain of the parents have donated goods or their time, and would like to receive a tax receipt for the value of these donations. We are not certain whether we will have to reflect these in our financial statements this year. For example:
    1. Jane Barnes provided valuable advice on improved management efficiency. She is a professional consultant and although these consulting fees were not budgeted for, the centre made several changes that resulted in a reduction of administrative costs. Ms. Barnes estimates that her full-rate fee would have been $7,500.
    2. Rick James, who is a qualified Phys. Ed. instructor, has been substituting one day a week at no charge, which reduced our budgeted expenditures by $4,500 this year.
    3. Parents have donated an awful lot of their time to operate fundraising activities (in addition to those involved with the Computer Fund). This time must be worth thousands of dollars."

- "Some of the staff have not been able to take their vacation this year, due to scheduling problems. As a result, we will have to pay them vacation pay. These funds will be paid out after the year-end, and will likely be covered by next year's operating grant. To keep revenues and expenses matched, we want to record the vacation pay on a cash basis. Would that be okay? Otherwise, we'll record a portion of next year's grant as receivable, this year."

- "The local foundation has provided the centre with a $30,000 grant to cover the expenses of a volunteer coordinator for two years. We received an instalment of $12,000, but we haven't hired a coordinator yet. The coordinator will be paid on an hourly basis, and the number of hours each month will fluctuate over the next two years depending on the monthly activities."

Required:

Prepare a draft of the response that will be sent to the audit committee.

Case 2   You have been recently elected to the position of treasurer on the board of directors for Canoes Are Us, a community-based service and not-for-profit organization (NFPO) that provides canoeing lessons and canoe rentals to various community groups.

Canoes Are Us is a large NFPO with annual donations and grants in excess of $2 million. For the past several years, the canoe program has been funded through lesson fees, member contributions, and donations from the community. Canoes Are Us also relies on a large number of volunteers, including volunteers for the solicitation of donations and the performance of routine bookkeeping. Volunteer instructors are allowed to borrow canoes for their personal use for a nominal rental fee of $25 per month, as long as there are spare canoes available.

The board has recently set up a program in conjunction with the local community centre to provide lessons and rentals to various groups of children from low-income families. The municipal government and the lottery commission have announced that they will provide, in total, a one-time grant of $250,000 this year to Canoes Are Us for this initiative. The grant has a number of conditions:

1. $50,000 is to be used to purchase a new truck and trailer to transport the canoes.
2. $150,000 is to be used for the purchase of new canoes and safety equipment.
3. $50,000 is restricted to covering operating costs, such as salaries, advertising, and campaign costs.
4. An external audit by independent auditors must be conducted at the end of the year and the report must be submitted to the municipal government. The books and records of Canoes Are Us were not previously audited.

During a recent fundraising campaign, Canoes Are Us raised $45,000 in cash and received an additional $20,000 in pledges. The pledges are expected to be received by the middle of the next fiscal year. In addition, a local manufacturer has donated a new canoe valued at $2,500 to the program.

When you review the financial information for Canoes Are Us, you discover that the books and records have been kept on a modified accrual basis, whereby the cash basis is used for inflows but payables are accrued for outflows. Capital expenditures have been expensed in the year of purchase. There is no master list of existing canoes and, in fact, some of the canoes appear to be in the possession of volunteer instructors on a semi-permanent basis even though the organization has full storage facilities available. The secretary to the board of directors is one of the volunteer instructors who has a canoe in her possession. You have also been advised that several instructors have unpaid rental accounts ranging from $50 to $400 each, and it appears that no serious efforts have been made to collect these accounts.

In discussions with the previous treasurer about how the new grant and other funds are to be used and accounted for, you discover that she is very opposed to any changes in the way that the accounting records are kept and the financial statements are prepared. She says that changes would make it difficult to compare the programs and to understand how the funds are being used. She was very active in setting up the organization and was one of the driving forces behind obtaining the grant for the new program.

Required:

Prepare a memorandum to the board of directors recommending, with supporting explanations, what changes in accounting and reporting are required in order to comply with GAAP and to fulfill the stewardship reporting objective.

(*CGA-Canada, from 2002 to 2007*)

Case 3   The Sassawinni First Nation is located adjacent to a town in northern Saskatchewan. The Nation is under the jurisdiction of the federal government's Department of Indian Affairs and Northern Development, and for years has received substantial funding from that department. The money has been used mainly to fund housing construction on the reserve and to provide maintenance payments to families that do not have a source of income. The houses are the property of the Sassawinni First Nation, and the band council allocates them to families on the basis of need. In addition to the housing, the band has been able to build a recreational centre, which also contains the band's council chamber and administrative offices.

A few years ago some council members with an entrepreneurial flair persuaded the Nation's members to build a shopping centre containing a large grocery store and several small specialty stores. The shopping centre is located on reserve land, and the band provided approximately 20 percent of the financing with the balance coming from a provincially guaranteed bank loan. The shopping centre operates under the name Great Northern Centre, Inc., and the Sassawinni First Nation owns 100 percent of its outstanding common shares. The centre has been a financial success, drawing a large proportion of its business from the adjoining town and surrounding agricultural area. Not only has it been a source of employment for First Nation families, but it has also generated enough cash to keep its loan payments current, and recently has been able to declare and pay a dividend.

Flushed with its success, the Sassawinni First Nation has submitted to the provincial government a business plan to construct a gambling casino on band property. It will be an incorporated entity, and will be under the complete control of the Nation, subject only to provincial government gambling regulations.

Up to the present time, the band has provided stewardship reports to the Department of Indian Affairs and Northern Development that outline the funds received from the federal government and the manner in which they have been spent. Government auditors have verified these statements but no formal audit reports have been considered necessary. Now, with all of this new business activity taking place, proper audited financial statements will be required for the next fiscal year. You are employed by Fox, Fox, and Jameson, the public accounting firm that is the auditor of Great Northern Centre, Inc. Your firm has just been appointed auditor of Sassawinni First Nation and this will be the firm's first audit of an organization of this nature. Jane Fox, the managing partner in charge of this audit, has asked you to provide her with a written report outlining the specific accounting principles that will be applicable in this case. "I am going to have to catch up quickly," she said. "I am aware that there have been some changes in GAAP recently, but because our firm has not been involved with audits of this nature I have not paid much attention to what has been going on. One of the benefits of hiring new university grads like yourself is that you provide us with up-to-date technical knowledge."

You have just returned from interviewing the band chief, Joe Sullivan. "I am absolutely certain that we are going to get this casino," he said. "The announcement will be made by the premier within two weeks, and I have received information from a knowledgeable insider that we will be on the list of First Nations to be granted casino licenses. It will be a financial godsend to our people, employing well over 100 band members and providing us with substantial profits, a portion of which will have to be devoted entirely to accommodations in accordance with the licensing agreement. This will allow us to build more housing for our members, but with all the jobs that we now have, we will probably start charging rent for housing provided to those with jobs. Not only that, but we have three permanent employees who have been with us for a while, and council has instructed me to investigate the possibility of providing a pension plan for them as well as for the permanent employees in our business enterprises."

When asked about the band's accounting records, Sullivan responded, "We have a very good bookkeeper, and the government auditor has always complimented her on the accuracy of her records. She provides timely statements showing us how much we have to spend. Our records are all here and go back at least 20 years. I would just as soon carry on the way we have been doing things, but with this new casino we'll have to provide audited financial statements to the two governments — and, of course, to our members."

Required:

Prepare the report requested by your firm's managing partner.

Case 4 Confidence Private is a high school in the historic city of Jeanville. It engages students in a dynamic learning environment and inspires them to become intellectually vibrant, compassionate, and responsible citizens. The private school has been run as a not-for-profit organization since its inception 20 years ago.

In an effort to attract sports-minded students from a variety of economic backgrounds, Confidence initiated a fund-raising program in July, Year 8, to raise $5 million to build a new gymnasium, swimming pool, and fitness centre, and to create an endowment fund for scholarships. The fund-raising campaign was a huge success. By May 31, Year 9, the school had received the following contributions:

1. $2.0 million in cash contributions specifically designated for construction and maintenance of the facilities
2. $3.1 million in cash contributions specifically designated for the scholarship fund
3. Fitness equipment valued at $0.2 million

On June 15, Year 9, at the graduation ceremony, the headmaster thanked the parents, students, alumni, and staff for all their support, and officially closed the capital campaign. He provided the following details of the campaign:

- The construction of the facility was nearing completion and would be ready for classes in September, Year 9. The final cost for the facility would be approximately $1.9 million.
- The contribution of fitness equipment would more than adequately equip the fitness centre.
- $3.1 million in cash would be invested and managed by a professional investment adviser.

The income earned on the endowment fund would be used to provide scholarships to students. Five students would receive full or partial scholarships in the fall of Year 10. Each year thereafter, it was expected that 25 to 30 students would receive full or partial scholarships to offset the annual tuition fee of $15,000.

You are proud to be an alumnus of Confidence. You attended the graduation ceremony. At the garden reception after the ceremony, you accepted the headmaster's request to help out with the accounting for the capital campaign and related events. He was unsure of whether the school should use the restricted fund or deferral method of accounting for contributions. You agreed to provide a memo in which you would provide recommendations for accounting policies to be applied for the year ended June 30, Year 9, and for future years when the facilities are being used and when the scholarships are disbursed.

Required:

Prepare a memo for the headmaster. Explain the rationale for your recommendations and state your assumptions.

(CGA-Canada, from 2002 to 2007)

Case 5 Perth Housing Corporation (PHC) is a community-sponsored not-for-profit housing organization that was incorporated on September 1, Year 5. Its purpose is to provide residential accommodation for physically handicapped adults in the town of Perth. The nature of PHC's operations and its source of funding are described in Exhibit 1. The executive director of PHC has asked for your assistance in establishing accounting policies for PHC for its general-purpose year-end financial statements. The accounting policies should be consistent with generally accepted accounting principles.

Exhibit 1

NATURE OF OPERATIONS

- In October Year 5, PHC purchased a 15-unit apartment building in downtown Perth for $750,000. It then spent $250,000 in renovations to upgrade the building to make it accessible for physically handicapped adults.
- PHC offers 24-hour non-medical attendant care. Support care services are provided through a combination of staff members and volunteers. The staff members receive a monthly salary. As an inducement to recruit and retain qualified support care workers, each staff member is allowed 15 sick days per year. The employee can bank the sick days not used in any one year. Upon termination or retirement, the employee is paid for banked sick days at the wage rate in effect at that time.
- Rental payments are due the first day of each month and are geared to each tenant's income. Most of the tenants are very good about making their rent payments on time. Some rental payments are received late. On August 31, Year 6, there was $13,000 of unpaid rent.
- PHC plans to install central air conditioning in the building in April Year 7 at an expected cost of $50,000. This expenditure is being financed by a special fund-raising drive. By August 31, Year 6, this fund-raising drive had raised $20,000 in cash and $15,000 in pledges from citizens in the local community.

SOURCES OF FUNDING

- The cost of acquiring and renovating the apartment building was financed by a $1,000,000 cash donation received from the estate of Mr. Smith.
- The provincial government funds approximately 70 percent of non-medical care and support costs. Claims are made monthly for the previous month's eligible costs.
- PHC depends on outside fund-raising efforts, primarily door-to-door canvassing and sponsored bingos, to cover the remaining non-medical care and support costs.

Required:

Identify the major accounting issues, and provide recommendations on the accounting treatment of these issues in PHC's financial statements for the year ended August 31, Year 6. Assume that PHC would want to set up two funds for reporting purposes, a general fund and a capital fund, and that annual revenues exceed $700,000.

Case 6   You have recently become an employee of Warren and Associates, a small public accounting firm located in the town of Biscard, population 4,500. You were born and raised here, and since you really like the small-town life, when this job came up after your university graduation you jumped at the opportunity to come home. Approximately 35 percent of the firm's work is audit with the remainder consisting of financial statement preparation and tax returns.

The firm's senior partner, John Warren, has just called you into his office. "I had a golf game with Billy Richardson yesterday. You know him; he is the reeve of the village of Pense, just down the road from here. Well, he told me that they are going to be looking for a new audit firm, and asked if I would be interested. I said 'absolutely.' I never like to turn down the opportunity to get a new client no matter how small, because you never know where it will lead. Billy said that he had heard that maybe the audit of the municipality will be coming up next year as well. I have a problem, though. All our clients are businesses and individuals, and we have never had a government audit. I only keep up to date with new standards or tax act changes that affect our clients. About a month ago, I overheard a couple of my colleagues talking about some revolutionary new government accounting model and how it is going to take a big selling job to get it accepted. It was all Greek to me. A few minutes ago, I searched the CICA website and had a quick look at the public sector standards. Wow! There is a lot more there than I expected. I am probably going to have to meet with the village council in the next week or so and I have to get up to speed fast. I will take you to the meeting with me, but I need to have some knowledge of the area so that I can talk reasonably intelligently. To start out, I need a memo from you telling me what I need to read so that I know about this new model and also what I should be looking for and digesting as far as the *CICA Handbook* is concerned."

Required:

Prepare the memo to the partner.

PROBLEMS

Problem 1   The OPI Care Centre is a not-for-profit organization funded by government grants and private donations. It prepares its annual financial statements using the deferral method of accounting for contributions, and it uses only the operations fund to account for all activities. It uses an encumbrance system as a means of controlling expenditures.

The following summarizes some of the transactions that were made in Year 6.

1. The founding member of OPI contributed $100,000 on the conditions that the principal amount be invested in marketable securities and that only the income earned from the investment be spent on operations.
2. During the year, purchase orders were issued to cover the budgeted cost of $1,400,000 for goods and contracted services.
3. During the year, a public campaign was held to raise funds for daily operations for the current year. Cash of $800,000 was collected, and pledges for an additional $100,000 were received by the end of the year. It is estimated that approximately 95 percent of these pledges will be collected early in the new year.

4. The provincial government pledged $600,000 for the year to cover operating costs and an additional $1,000,000 to purchase equipment and furniture. All of the grant money was received by the end of the year, except for the last $50,000 to cover operating costs for December.

5. OPI used the $1,000,000 received from the provincial government to purchase equipment and furniture for the care facility. The amortization of these assets amounted to $100,000 for the year. A purchase order had not been issued for this purchase.

6. Invoices totalling $1,450,000 were received for goods and contracted services. Of these invoices, 90 percent were paid by the end of the fiscal year. Purchase orders in the amount of $1,375,000 had been issued for these services.

Required:

In accordance with the requirements of the *CICA Handbook*, prepare the journal entries necessary to reflect the transactions.

(*CGA-Canada, from 2002 to 2007*)

Problem 2   The Perch Falls Minor Hockey Association was established in Perch Falls in January Year 5. Its mandate is to promote recreational hockey in the small community of Perch Falls. With the support of the provincial government, local business people, and many individuals, the association raised sufficient funds to build an indoor hockey arena and it also established an endowment fund for paying travel costs to tournaments on an annual basis.

The following schedule summarizes the cash flows for the year ended December 31, Year 5.

PERCH FALLS MINOR HOCKEY ASSOCIATION
($000s)

	Operating fund	Capital fund	Endowment fund
Cash inflows			
Government grant for operating costs	$ 90		
Government grant for hockey arena		$500	
Corporate donations for hockey arena		460	
Registration fees	50		
Contribution for tournaments			$50
Rental of hockey arena	70		
Interest received			3
	210	960	53
Cash outflows			
Operating expenses	205		
Construction of hockey arena		960	
Purchase of marketable securities			50
Travel costs for tournament			3
	205	960	53
Cash, end of year	$ 5	$ 0	$ 0

Capitalized not expensed

Additional Information

1. The new hockey arena was completed in late August Year 5. The official opening was held on August 30 with a game between the Perch Falls Old-Timers and the local fire-fighters. The arena is expected to have a 40-year useful life and no residual value.

2. A long-time resident of Perch Falls donated the land on which the arena was built. The land was valued at $100,000. The association gave a donation receipt to the donor.

3. A former resident of Perch Falls donated ice-making and ice-cleaning equipment to the association. A receipt for $60,000 was issued for the donation. The equipment has a useful life of 10 years and no residual value.

4. The donation for tournaments was contributed on January 1, Year 5, with the condition that the principal amount of $50,000 be invested in 6% corporate bonds. The interest earned on the investment can be used only for travel costs for out-of-town tournaments. All investments in bonds will be held to their maturity date.

5. The provincial government pledged $100,000 a year for operating costs. 90% of the grant is advanced throughout the year. Upon receipt of the association's annual report, the government will issue the last 10% of the annual grant to the association.

6. Registration fees and rental fees for the hockey arena are received at the beginning of the hockey season and cover the entire season, from September 1, Year 5, to April 30, Year 6.

7. At the end of the year, the association owed $7,000 for services received in the month of December.

8. The assocation wants to use the restricted fund method of accounting for contributions and to use three separate funds — operating fund, capital fund, and endowment fund. All capital assets are to be capitalized and amortized, as applicable, over their estimated useful lives.

Required:

Prepare a statement of financial position and statement of revenue and expenses for each of the three funds as at and for the year ended December 31, Year 5.

(CGA-Canada, from 2002 to 2007)

Problem 3   Zak Organization is an NFPO set up for famine relief. It uses the restricted fund method of accounting and has three funds: a general fund, a capital fund (through which it is raising cash to support the purchase of a new administrative building), and an endowment fund. Zak has been operating for 25 years and has a December 31 year-end. Zak's policy with respect to capital assets is to capitalize and amortize the capital assets over their expected useful lives.

On June 30, Year 5, Zak received three donations from a former director:
- $30,000 cash for general famine relief efforts.
- $50,000 to be used solely for construction of the new administrative building. Of the $50,000, 70% was received in cash, with the remainder promised in February 2006. (Construction is expected to commence in October, Year 6.)
- $600,000 cash, which was invested on July 1, Year 5, in long-term Government of Canada bonds, with 10% interest to be paid semi-annually on December 31 and June 30. The $600,000 donation was given with the stipulation that it be invested in interest-bearing securities with the principal to be maintained by Zak, although interest earned on the securities is not restricted.

Required:

(a) Briefly explain how each of the three donations should be accounted for using the restricted fund method of accounting. In particular, should each of the donations be recognized as revenue for the year ended December 31, Year 5? If yes, in which fund(s) would the revenue be recognized (including interest earned in fiscal Year 5 on the bonds purchased with the $600,000 donation)? Note: Do not prepare journal entries.

(b) If Zak used the deferral method of accounting instead of the restricted fund method, how would this change the requirements for accounting for the $50,000 and $600,000 donations?

(c) Despite the recent donations from its former director, Zak is increasingly faced with severe budgetary constraints. Zak is considering implementing encumbrance accounting in the coming year.

   (i) Briefly describe the process of encumbrance accounting.

   (ii) Briefly describe how encumbrance accounting might serve as a device to help control spending when it is used in conjunction with a formal budgeting system.

(CGA-Canada, from 2002 to 2007)

Problem 4 You have been recruited to act as the treasurer on the board of directors of a not-for-profit organization that has had difficulty in recent years controlling its expenditures. The board of directors has very limited accounting experience. The organization, Protect Purple Plants (PPP), is considering implementing an encumbrance accounting system to assist in expenditure control. PPP receives an estimated $800,000 per year in regular contributions from the federal government.

Required:

(a) State *two* advantages and *two* disadvantages of implementing an encumbrance accounting system.

(b) PPP uses the deferral method of accounting for contributions and has no separate fund for restricted contributions. On January 1, Year 6, PPP received its first restricted cash contribution—$100,000 for the purchase and maintenance of land and a greenhouse building for its rare purple plant collection.

   On July 1, Year 6, PPP acquired land and a building for $22,000 and $60,000 cash, respectively. The building has an estimated useful life of 20 years and zero salvage value. On December 31, Year 6, the remaining $18,000 cash was paid to KJ Maintenance Ltd. for a three-year maintenance contract that requires KJ personnel to provide maintenance services four days per month until December 31, Year 9. Assuming that encumbrance accounting will *not* be implemented until Year 7, prepare the journal entries for the following dates:

   (i)   January 1, Year 6

   (ii) July 1, Year 6

   (iii) December 31, Year 6

(CGA-Canada, from 2002 to 2007)

Problem 5 The Fara Littlebear Society is a not-for-profit organization funded by government grants and private donations. It was established in Year 5 by the friends of Fara Littlebear to encourage and promote the work of Native Canadian artists. Fara achieved international recognition for her art depicting images of journey and exploration.

   The society leased a small building in January, Year 5. The building contains a small art gallery on the first floor and office space on the second floor. The society spent $84,000 for leasehold improvements. The art gallery opened for public viewing on May 1, Year 5.

   The unadjusted trial balance for the year ended Deember 31, Year 5 was as follows:

	Debit	Credit
Cash	$ 5,000	
Investment in bonds (Note 1)	80,000	
Artwork (Note 2)	300,000	
Leasehold improvements (Note 3)	84,000	
Government grant — operating costs (Note 6)		$90,000
Government grant — restricted for purchase of artwork		150,000
Corporate donations — restricted for purchase of artwork		150,000
Corporate donations — restricted for leasehold improvements		78,000
Individual donations restricted for scholarships Note 1)		80,000
Interest income		4,000
Revenue from admission fees to art gallery		67,000
Rent expense (Note 3)	26,000	
Salaries expense (Note 4)	66,000	
Other expenses	53,000	
Scholarship awarded	5,000	
	$619,000	$619,000

Additional Information

1. A wealthy individual donated $80,000 with the condition that the principal be invested in low-risk investments. The principal was invested in long-term bonds, which are expected to be held to maturity. The interest on the bonds is to be used to provide scholarships to aspiring Native artists who wish to study art at a Canadian university or college. The first scholarship of $5,000 was awarded in September, Year 5.

2. The artwork consists of 20 paintings from a number of Canadian artists. These paintings are expected to be held for at least 10 years. The paintings will likely appreciate in value over the time they are owned by the art gallery.

3. The society signed a five-year lease of the building with an option to renew for one further term of five years. The term of the lease commenced on January 1, Year 5. The total rent paid for the year included a deposit of $2,000 for the last month's rent. The leasehold improvements were completed on April 30, Year 5. The office space was occupied by the staff of the society and the art gallery was opened for business on May 1, Year 5.

4. Salaries earned but not yet paid amounted to $3,000 at December 31, Year 5.

5. The society received office equipment from a local business person on January 1, Year 5. A donation receipt for $10,000 was given for this contribution. The office equipment has a useful life of five years with no residual value.

6. The provincial government provided an operating grant of $100,000 for Year 5, of which $90,000 was received by the end of the year. The remaining $10,000 will be received once the society provides financial statements prepared in accordance with generally accepted accounting principles.

7. The society wishes to use the deferral method of accounting for contributions.

Required:

(a) Explain how the matching principle is applied when the deferral method is used to account for restricted contributions.

(b) Prepare a balance sheet for the society at December 31, Year 5. Show your supporting calculations and state your assumptions. (You can use an assumed number for excess of revenue over expenses to balance your balance sheet.)

(CGA-Canada, from 2002 to 2007)

Problem 6

The Brown Training Centre is a charitable organization dedicated to providing computer training to unemployed people. Individuals must apply to the centre and indicate why they would like to take the three-month training session. If their application is accepted, they must pay a $100 deposit. The deposit is refunded upon successful completion of the course or is forfeited as a processing fee if the individual does not complete the course.

During the first year of operations in Year 3, 90 individuals were accepted into the course. Of these 90 individuals, 50 completed the course, 10 dropped out, and 30 were still taking the course at the end of the fiscal year.

The centre receives most of its funding from the provincial government. During the year, the government advanced $500,000 to cover operating costs. Within two months of the year end, the centre must provide financial statements prepared in accordance with generally accepted accounting principles. The government will cover all operating costs. The excess of amounts advanced over the amount expended must be carried over and applied to operating costs of the next year. Operating costs to be reimbursed are defined to exclude purchases of capital assets and are to be reduced by the amount of application fees forfeited.

A private company donated computers and office equipment with a fair value of $160,000. The centre was fortunate to receive this donation. Otherwise, it would have had to raise money through other means to purchase these items. The capital assets were put into use as of April 1, Year 3, and have an estimated useful life of three years. The centre uses the straight-line method to amortize its capital assets.

The part-time bookkeeper for the centre prepared the following statement of cash flows for the year ended December 31, Year 3:

Cash receipts	
Government grant	$500,000
Deposits from course participants	9,000
Total cash receipts	509,000
Cash expenditures	
Salaries and benefits	310,000
Administration and supplies	110,000
Rent and utilities	80,000
Refund of deposits	5,000
Total cash disbursements	505,000
Cash balance at end of year	$ 4,000

At the end of the year the following costs had been incurred but not yet paid:

Accrued operating exp

Salaries and benefits	$ 4,000
Utilities	3,000

The executive director of the centre has asked you for assistance in preparing the financial statements for the centre for the first year of operations. The deferred method should be used in accounting for the contributions.

Required:

(a) Briefly explain how the accrual basis of accounting is applied when accounting for capital assets for a not-for-profit organization.

(b) Prepare the statement of revenues and expenses for the centre for the year ended December 31, Year 3.

(c) Compute the following liabilities on the balance sheet for the centre at December 31, Year 3:

(i) Accrued liabilities

(ii) Deposits from course participants

(iii) Deferred contributions

(CGA-Canada, from 2002 to 2007)

Problem 7 The Ford Historical Society is a not-for-profit organization funded by government grants and private donations. It uses both an operating fund and a capital fund. The capital fund accounts for moneys received and restricted for major capital asset acquisitions. The operating fund is used for all other activities.

The society uses the deferral method for the operating fund and the restricted fund method for the capital fund. An encumbrance system is used within the operating fund to ensure that expenditures made in any one year do not exceed the amounts budgeted. Donated materials and services are recorded if such items would have been purchased had they not been received as donations.

The following are some selected activities that took place during the current year:

- Purchase orders in the amount of $500,000 for goods and services were issued during the year.
- Pledges totalling $350,000 were made to the society, of which $150,000 applies to the operations of the following year. It is estimated that 3% of all pledges will be uncollectible.
- Pledges of $310,000 were collected, and pledges totalling $5,000 were written off.
- A government grant of $500,000 for acquisition and renovation of an office building for the society was approved by the government. All of the grant money was received except for the last 10%, which is expected to be received in the first month of the next fiscal year.
- Invoices for all of the goods and services ordered during the year were received. The total cost was $510,000, of which $480,000 was paid for by the end of the year.
- An old office building was acquired and renovated for a cost of $500,000. Amortization expense on the office building was $10,000.
- A local radio station donated free air time to the society. The society saved the $5,000 it would normally have paid for this air time.

Required:

Prepare the journal entries required to record these activities, and indicate which fund each journal entry will be recorded in.

(CGA-Canada, from 2002 to 2007)

Problem 8 Fairchild Centre is a not-for-profit organization funded by government grants and private donations. It was established on January 1, Year 5, to provide conselling services and a drop-in centre for single mothers.

On January 1, Year 5, the centre leased an old warehouse in the central part of Smallville for $2,000 per month. It carried out minor renovations in the warehouse to create a large open area for use as a play area for children and three offices for use by the executive director and counsellors. The lease runs from January 1, Year 5, to June 30, Year 7. By that time, the centre hopes to move into new quarters that are more suitable for the activities carried out by the centre.

The following schedule summarizes the cash flows for the year ended December 31, Year 5:

Cash inflows	
Government grant for operating costs (Note 1)	$ 50,000
Donations from individuals with no restrictions	63,000
Donations from individuals for rent of warehouse for 2.5 years	60,000
Donations from individuals for purchase of land (Note 3)	28,000
	201,000
Cash outflows	
Renovations of warehouse	25,000
Salary of executive director (Note 4)	33,000
Fees paid to counsellors (Note 4)	20,000
Rent paid for 2.5 years	60,000
Other operating expenses	34,000
	172,000
Cash, end of year	$ 29,000

Additional Information

1. The provincial government agreed to provide an operating grant of $50,000 per year. In addition, the government has pledged to match contributions collected by the centre for the purchase of land for constuction of a new complex for the centre. The maximum contribution by the government towards the purchase of land is $100,000.

2. The centre has signed an agreement to purchase a property in the downtown area of Smallville for $225,000. There is an old house on the property, which is presently used as a rooming house. The closing date is anytime between July 1, Year 6, and December 31, Year 6. The centre plans to demolish the existing house and build a new complex.

3. The centre has recently commenced a fundraising program to raise funds to purchase the land and constuct a new building. So far, $28,000 has been raised from individuals towards the purchase of the land. In the new year, the centre will focus its efforts to solicit donations from businesses in the area. The provincial government will advance the funds promised under its pledge on the closing date for the purchase of the property.

4. All the people working for the centre are volunteers except for the executive director and the counsellors. The executive director receives a salary of $36,000 a year while the counsellors bill the centre for professional services rendered based on the number of hours they work at the centre. The director has not yet received her salary for the month of December. One of the counsellors received an advance of $1,000 in December, Year 5, for work to be performed in January, Year 6.

5. The centre wishes to use the deferral method of accounting for contributions and to segregate its net assets between restricted and unstriced. It capitalizes the cost of capital assets and amortizes the capital assets over their useful lives.

Required:

(a) State the assumptions necessary to recognize the pledge contributions from the provincial government and prepare the journal entry to record the pledge, if applicable.

(b) Prepare a statement of revenues and expenses for the centre for the year ended December 31, Year 5. Show your supporting calculations and state your assumptions.

(c) Prepare a statement of changes in net assets for the centre for the year ended December 31, Year 5.

(CGA-Canada, from 2002 to 2007)

Problem 9 The Far North Centre is an antipoverty organization funded by contributions from governments and the general public. For a number of years it has been run by a small group of permanent employees with the help of part-timers and dedicated volunteers. It owns its premises, which are in the process of being renovated. The funds for this were obtained through a special capital-fund campaign carried out last year. Its main program is the daily provision of meals to the needy. It also distributes clothing, most of which is donated. Operating funds come from government grants, interest earned from endowment investments, and a public campaign held in the latter part of each year to raise funds for the needs of the next fiscal year. The organization maintains its records in accordance with the restricted fund method of accounting for contributions, and prepares its financial statements using an operating fund, a capital fund, and an endowment fund.

The following are the fund trial balances as at January 1, Year 6:

	Debit	Credit
Operating fund		
Cash	$ 570,500	
Pledges receivable	705,000	
Allowance for uncollectible pledges		$ 30,000
Grants receivable	217,500	
Accounts payable		427,500
Wages payable		137,250
Accrued liabilities		9,750
Deferred revenue		800,000
Fund balance		88,500
	$1,493,000	$1,493,000
Capital fund		
Cash	$ 287,500	
Grants receivable	112,500	
Furniture and equipment	491,000	
Land and building	810,250	
Accumulated amortization		648,200
Accounts payable		9,000
Investment in capital assets		653,050
Fund balance		391,000
	$1,701,250	$1,701,250
Endowment Fund		
Cash	$ 37,500	
Investments	375,000	
Fund balance		412,500
	$ 412,500	$ 412,500

The following transactions took place in Year 6.

1. The Year 6 budget, the totals of which are summarized below, was recorded.

Budgeted revenues	$2,200,000
Budgeted expenses	2,150,000
Budgeted surplus	$ 50,000

2. The agency uses an encumbrance system in the operating fund as a means of controlling expenditures. During the year, purchase orders for goods and services at an estimated amount of $1,450,000 were issued.
3. $35,000 from endowment fund cash was invested in marketable securities.
4. Office equipment costing $2,500 was purchased with operating fund cash.

5. Invoices totalling $1,375,000 were received on purchase orders originally recorded at an estimated cost of $1,392,000. These invoices were recorded as accounts payable and were allocated 55% to food program, 20% to clothing program, and 25% to administration.

6. The capital fund grants receivable were collected in full, and the $9,000 in accounts payable was paid. During Year 6, building renovations costing $300,000 and equipment purchases of $85,000 were made. Of this cost, 90% was paid, with the balance held back and still owing at year-end.

7. Operating fund accounts payable amounting to $1,560,000, and the wages payable and accrued liabilities at the beginning of the year, were all paid.

8. All of the operating fund pledges and grants receivable at the beginning of the year were collected in full.

9. The deferred revenue from the Year 5 fundraising campaign was made up of:

Contributions	$1,200,000
Less: campaign expense	400,000
	$ 800,000

An entry was made to recognize these items as Year 6 revenues and expenses.

10. Government grants for operating purposes totalled $900,000, of which $850,000 was received during the year, with the balance expected early in Year 7.

11. The total wage costs for the year amounted to $400,000, of which $325,000 was paid and $75,000 is payable at year-end. These costs are to be allocated 40% each to the food and clothing programs, with the balance to administration.

12. The campaign to raise funds for next year's operations was held in December. Cash of $500,000 was collected and pledges of $700,000 were received. It is expected that 5% of these pledges will be uncollectible. Total fundraising costs were $322,000, of which $75,000 is still owed to suppliers.

13. An endowment contribution of $8,000 cash was received. In addition, the investments in the endowment fund earned $31,200 in interest.

14. The annual depreciation on the buildings and equipment amounted to $92,000.

15. At the end of the year, the balances in the encumbrance accounts and the budget accounts were closed.

Required:

(a) Prepare the journal entries necessary to reflect the Year 6 events.
(b) For each fund, prepare a Year 6 balance sheet and statement of revenues and expenses and changes in fund balance.
(c) Prepare a statement of cash flows on a nonfund basis.
(d) Prepare closing entries.

Problem 10   All facts about this NFPO are identical to those described in Problem 9, except that the deferred contribution approach to recording contributions is used for accounting and for external financial reporting. Fund accounting is not used. The 2006 transactions are also identical to those described in Problem 9.

The organization's balance sheet on January 1, Year 6, is shown on the following page.

Required:

(a) Prepare the journal entries necessary to reflect the Year 6 events.
(b) Prepare a Year 6 balance sheet, a statement of revenues and expenses, and a statement of changes in net assets for the year.

(c) Prepare a statement of cash flows for the year.

(d) Prepare closing entries.

FAR EAST CENTRE
BALANCE SHEET
January 1, Year 6

Current assets

Cash	$ 895,500
Pledges receivable	705,000
Allowance for uncollectible pledges	(30,000)
Grants receivable	330,000
	$1,900,500
Investments	$ 375,000

Capital assets

Furniture and equipment	$ 491,000
Land and buildings	810,250
Accumulated depreciation	(648,200)
	653,050
	$2,928,550

Current liabilities

Accounts payable	$ 436,500
Wages payable	137,250
Accrued liabilities	9,750
	$ 583,500

Deferred revenue

Deferred contributions	$ 800,000
Deferred building campaign contributions	391,000
Deferred contributions related to capital assets	240,500
	$1,431,500

Net assets

Net assets invested in capital assets	$ 412,550
Net assets restricted for endowment purposes	412,500
Unrestricted net assets	88,500
	$ 913,550
	$2,928,550

Problem 11   The William Robertson Society is a charitable organization funded by government grants and private donations. It prepares its annual financial statements using the restricted fund method in accordance with the *CICA Handbook*, and uses both an operating fund and a capital fund.

The operating fund records the regular operating activities of the society. An encumbrance system is used within the fund to ensure that expenditures made in any one year do not exceed the amounts budgeted. It is the policy of the society to record donated materials and services received during the year, if such items would have been purchased had they not been received as donations.

The capital fund accounts for moneys received from special fundraising campaigns conducted when there is a need for major fixed assets acquisitions.

The following are *some* selected events that took place during the current year:

- Pledges amounting to $125,000 were received, of which $90,000 was collected in cash.

- Purchase orders were issued during the year as follows:

For office equipment	$ 15,000
For goods and services	100,000

- A grant of $70,000 for this year's operations was announced by the government, of which $55,000 had been received by the society at year-end.
- Employee wages totalled $60,000 for the year. Wages amounting to $2,000 were unpaid at year-end.
- Invoices for all of the goods and services ordered during the year were received. Of the invoiced amounts, 80% was paid. The invoiced amounts were equal to those on the purchase orders.
- The office equipment that was ordered arrived. The invoiced amount of $15,030 was paid in cash, using operating funds.
- A local radio station donated free air time to the society. The station would normally bill a customer $3,000 for this air time.
- A prominent citizen made a pledge of $35,000 to help fund the operating expenditures of the next fiscal year.

Required:

Prepare the journal entries required to record these events, and indicate which fund each journal entry will be recorded in.

Web-Based Problem 1

Go to the website of the Salvation Army (www.salvationarmy.ca). Download the most recent Canadian financial statements and answer the following questions.
  (a) Read the auditor's report. There is a paragraph there that is unique to not-for-profit organizations. Explain what message it is conveying.
  (b) Approximately how much of the organization's assets are restricted? What can they be spent on?
  (c) How many funds are reported?
  (d) Approximately what percentage of the year's revenues was spent on fundraising?
  (e) What is their largest single source of revenue?
  (f) Has the organization's cash increased or decreased over the past two years? What was a major factor in the change?
  (g) Outline what is included in the accounting entity.
  (h) Briefly explain the army's amortization policy. If you find part of it a bit strange, explain why they may have adopted it.
  (i) Which contribution method is being used?
  (j) What is their policy with respect to donated materials and services?

Web-Based Problem 2

Download the latest financial statements of the Canadian Cancer Society (www.cancer.ca) and answer as many of the questions from Web-Based Problem 1 as you can. (Not all questions are necessarily applicable.)

Credits

Index